D0153227

The Life of Benjamin Franklin VOLUME 1

June 2. 1725

174

347

344 174—175

Sir

      Having lately been
in the Nothern Parts of America, I
have brought from thence a Purse
made of the Stone Asbestus, a Piece
of the Stone; and a Piece of Wood,
the Pithy Part of which is of the
same Nature, and call'd by the Inhabitants Salamander Cotton.
As you are noted to be a Lover
of Curiosities, I have inform'd you
of these; and if you have any
Inclination to purchase them, or
see 'em, let me know your Pleasure by a Line directed for me at
the Golden Fan in Little Britain,
and I will wait upon you with
them.

      I am, Sir

    Your most humble Servant

      Benjamin Franklin

P.S. I expect to be
out of Town in 2 or 3
Days, and therefore
beg an immediate
Answer.

The Life of
Benjamin Franklin

VOLUME 1

～

Journalist
1706–1730

J. A. Leo Lemay

PENN

University of Pennsylvania Press
Philadelphia

Copyright © 2006 University of Pennsylvania Press
All rights reserved
Printed in the United States of America on acid-free paper

10 9 8 7 6 5 4 3 2

Published by
University of Pennsylvania Press
Philadelphia, Pennsylvania 19104–4112

Text design by Pat Callahan

Library of Congress Cataloging-in-Publication Data

Lemay, J. A. Leo (Joseph A. Leo), 1935–
    The life of Benjamin Franklin / J. A. Leo Lemay.
        p. cm.
    Includes bibliographical references and index.
    Contents: v. 1. Journalist, 1706–1730
    ISBN 0-8122-3854-0 (v. 1 : acid-free paper)
    1. Franklin, Benjamin, 1706–1790.   2. Statesmen—United States—Biography.
3. Scientists—United States—Biography.   4. Inventors—United States—Biography.
5. Printers—United States—Biography.   I. Title.

E302.6.F8L424   2005
973.3'092—dc22
[B]   2004063130

Front end papers: Franklin's Boston, drawn by Nian-Sheng Huang, based on John Bonner's map of Boston (1722).

Frontispiece: Franklin's first extant letter, written at age nineteen, to Sir Hans Sloane, founder of the British Museum, 2 June 1725. As Franklin remembered the event in 1771, Sloane (1660–1753) heard of Franklin's purse made of asbestos, "came to see me, and invited me to his House in Bloomsbury Square; where he show'd me all his Curiosities, and persuaded me to let him add that to the Number, for which he paid me handsomely" (A 44). Though Franklin recalled the event incorrectly, the meeting with the great naturalist Sloane was important enough for him to mention forty-six years later. The letter documents Franklin's early interest in natural philosophy. He later experimented with making paper from asbestos.

The ink's absorption into the paper reveals that Franklin wrote this letter on inexpensive stationery. In comparison to the promissory note of 5 May 1724, the handwriting is relatively graceful, though not so beautiful as Franklin's later holograph. Not only did Franklin evidently try to write a better hand in his letter to Sloane in 1725 than he had in his promissory note of the year before, but a comparison of the handwriting in this letter with the penmanship of the promissory note (Figure 20) and with handwriting in the epitaph (Figure 22, written much later) shows that as a young adult Franklin practiced and improved his handwriting. His early signature used the full name and often had a flourish underneath; the later ones generally used simply "B. Franklin," with a less ornate flourish or none.

Back end papers: Franklin's London, 1725–26. John Strype's map in John Stow, *A Survey of the Cities of London & Westminster* (1720). Courtesy, Huntington Library. Locations supplied by Marina Fedosik.

The biography as a whole is dedicated to
Ann C. Lemay, John C. Lemay, Lee C. Lemay, and Kate C. Lemay.

Volume 1 is dedicated to a number of Franklin scholars who are slightly
my senior, who are in most cases good friends, and from all of whom I have
learned greatly: A. Owen Aldridge, Whitfield J. Bell, Jr., I. Bernard Cohen,
Claude-Anne Lopez, C. William Miller, Robert H. Newcomb,
Edwin Wolf 2nd, and P. M. Zall.

❦

Contents

Illustrations

Preface

VOLUME 1 TAKES BENJAMIN FRANKLIN from his birth early in 1706 to his marriage in 1730. Much of the information in the early chapters is based on Franklin's *Autobiography* and on various anecdotes recorded in his letters or conversations. Beginning in 1721, when his brother James started the *New England Courant*, there is abundant material about Franklin's day-to-day activities. The *Courant* began as an anti-inoculation and anti-establishment paper, especially opposing Increase and Cotton Mather and their supporters. Franklin wrote the first essay series in America in 1722, fourteen letters supposedly by a middle-aged widow named "Silence Dogood," a pseudonym that mocked Cotton Mather. After writing the Silence Dogood essays, Franklin composed several hoaxes, satires, and essays for his brother's press, one a skit that used the first African American persona in American journalism and another a pamphlet (*Hoop-Petticoats Arraigned and Condemned by the Light of Nature, and Law of God*, 1722) travestying a recent sermon by the Reverend Solomon Stoddard, the grandfather of Jonathan Edwards.

In 1722 and again in 1723, James Franklin was jailed by the authorities, and Franklin took over the printing shop. Though James Franklin's friends helped, Benjamin Franklin ran the shop during James's two imprisonments.

The Franklin brothers often quarreled, and James Franklin sometimes beat his young apprentice, so Franklin quit and ran away at the age of seventeen. Finding no work in New York, he went on to Philadelphia where, in October 1723, he began employment with the eccentric Philadelphia printer Samuel Keimer. Franklin lodged next door to the printing shop with John and Sarah Read, whose daughter, Deborah, was to be his future wife. Pennsylvania Governor William Keith, impressed with Franklin's abilities, promised to make him the printer for the government if he could open his own shop. With a letter from Keith, Franklin returned to Boston to try to borrow money from his father, who had no funds to loan him, still being in debt for the money he had borrowed to set up James Franklin.

Back in Philadelphia, Governor Keith promised to set up Franklin in business but suggested he first go to London to buy the press and types and to arrange for exchanges with printers there. Franklin and Deborah Read became engaged, but her mother discouraged their courtship, asking them to wait until after Franklin returned from England. On 5 November 1724, Franklin sailed for London, arriving on Christmas Eve, when he discovered that Keith had sent no letters or bills of credit for him. Confused, he applied to a Philadelphia Quaker merchant, Thomas Denham, who had become his friend on shipboard. The Quaker told him that no one depended on Keith, who was liberal with promises but had no money. Denham advised him to find work as a printer. Franklin did and wrote Deborah Read of his predicament, saying that he could not soon return. On 5 August 1725, exactly nine months after Franklin left Philadelphia, Deborah married John Rogers, a potter.

While working for the London printer Samuel Palmer, Franklin set in type the third edition of William Wollaston's popular *Religion of Nature Delineated*. Franklin thought the book's theology foolish and wrote a burlesque of it, which Palmer allowed him to print at his press. Franklin's pamphlet, *A Dissertation on Liberty and Necessity, Pleasure and Pain* (1725), did not name its printer, author, or bookseller. A contribution to the clandestine, libertine literature of the day, it won Franklin the acquaintance of such figures as the freethinker Dr. William Lyons and the infamous genius Dr. Bernard Mandeville.

A year and a half later, Thomas Denham offered Franklin a position working as his clerk. Denham was returning to Philadelphia with a cargo of manufactured goods and suggested that if Franklin learned the mercantile business, he would send him with a cargo of Pennsylvania's produce to the West Indies and procure commissions from others for him. Franklin liked London but loved Philadelphia and America and agreed immediately.

During the voyage, Franklin kept a journal (22 July to 11 October 1726) and devised a "Plan of Conduct" for the future. Back in Philadelphia, he worked for Denham until the early spring of 1726, when he fell critically ill for two months. Denham too became severely ill and died the following year. When Franklin recovered, he returned to work for the printer Samuel Keimer. In the fall of 1727, Franklin formed the Junto, a mutual aid and self-improvement society of young men who met on Friday nights. In the spring of 1728 he and Hugh Meredith, a fellow printer, started their own business, with a loan from Meredith's father. That fall Franklin set down his religious beliefs and wrote out a worship service ("Articles of Belief and Acts of Religion"). About the same time, he projected a newspaper and indicated to George Webb, a journeyman printer, that he and Meredith would be able to hire him when the paper started. Webb, however, went to Keimer with the idea, and they started the *Pennsylvania Gazette*.

Angry with Webb, Franklin began an essay series titled the "Busy-Body," which he submitted to Andrew Bradford, an older, established Philadelphia printer, for publication in his newspaper, the *American Weekly Mercury*. Franklin intended to increase the circulation of Bradford's paper and ensure the failure of the Keimer-Webbe venture. As part of Busy-Body No. 8, he contributed a brief essay on the vexed political question of paper currency, but after a few copies were printed, the essay was suppressed. Two weeks later, Franklin published *A Modest Enquiry into the Nature and Necessity of a Paper Currency* (April 1729)—a daring political piece. In the early fall, he and Meredith bought the failing *Pennsylvania Gazette* from Keimer. Franklin's astute political analysis of the issues in a heated Massachusetts political controversy appeared in the second issue of the paper on 9 October 1729, signaling that a superior journalist had just appeared in America. Beginning in 1729 Franklin wrote essays, hoaxes, satires, jeux d'esprit, news reports, crime reports, obituaries, commercial statistics, editorials, and everything else that appeared in the first years of the *Pennsylvania Gazette*. It immediately became the most entertaining, wide-ranging, fact-filled, interesting, and daring newspaper of colonial America.

In January 1730 Andrew Hamilton, Speaker of the House of Representatives, had Franklin and Meredith appointed printers of the House journals and laws, thus ensuring a steady income for the partners. Meredith's father experienced financial difficulties and could not repay the merchant from whom he borrowed money to buy the press and types, and Meredith, who was often drinking, decided that he would do better if he were farming and away from the convenient attractions of Philadelphia's taverns. Meredith proposed that Franklin buy him out. Franklin arranged for security from two friends, borrowed the money, and paid off Meredith on 14 July 1730, thereby creating his own business.

Each volume concludes with a brief assessment of Franklin's life and character, often calling attention to his faults and to his (usually deliberate) metamorphoses.

The biography is mainly chronological, but Franklin did so many things that a straightforward chronological story, as inclusive as the one I am telling, would have all the disjointedness of life. I therefore treat some subjects topically while arranging the whole chronologically. (Anyone who wants a single chronological history of Franklin may find it on my Web site, a "Documentary History of Benjamin Franklin.") In Volume 1, the Junto (Chapter 14) and Franklin as a newspaperman (Chapter 18) are both treated topically. The Junto survived through Franklin's return to Philadelphia in 1762–64 and finally languished after he returned to England in 1764. It seemed preferable to treat the Junto in a single place rather than have occasional discussions of it scattered throughout the first four volumes of the biography. So too, although Franklin edited the *Pennsylvania Gazette* through 1747, he started it in 1729. His role as a journalist for the first few years deserves a coherent treatment, for he supplied all its local contents. One can tell when he hired others to set type a few years later: the number of news-note quips, ironic comments, and amusing brief hoaxes lessens as others took over printing the paper. Despite the topical appreciation of his early journalism, later writings in the *Gazette* appear only in the chronologically appropriate chapters.

Though William, Franklin's illegitimate son, was born about 1728, the mystery of his unknown mother is discussed in connection with Franklin's courtship and marriage to Deborah Read Rogers. That begins Volume 2.

One might wonder how this life of Franklin differs from previous ones. It is a literary biography, with more discussions of Franklin's writings than any previous life. Franklin was the most important writer of colonial America. The only ambition he ever mentioned was "to think I might possibly in time come to be a tolerable English Writer of which I was extreamly ambitious" (A 14).The biography also has far more detail about Franklin's life than any previous study. The major personal, literary and intellectual influences upon the young Franklin are a special subject of Volume 1. Thus, I attempt to show the influence the writers for James Franklin's *New England Courant* on Franklin and to prove that its major writer, Nathaniel Gardner, especially affected Franklin's subjects and prose style. I also suggest that the Reverend John Wise, a hero of the Popular Party of early eighteenth-century Massachusetts, and a dominant minister who opposed Increase and Cotton Mather, influenced the young Franklin. Neither Gardner nor Wise is mentioned in any previous biography. Further, except for the Silence Dogood essays, most of Franklin's early writings in the *New-England Courant* have been ignored by previous biographers, though a number of Franklin's writings, including the first African-American persona in American literature, deal with central issues in early American culture.

Part 2 of Volume 1 argues that the *Dissertation on Liberty and Necessity, Pleasure and Pain* (1725) is really a satire of its supposed premises, rather than, as all previous biographers have assumed, a philosophical exploration of the subject. Though many students of Franklin claim that he was primarily an impartial printer, the chapters on the "Busy-Body" and on *The Nature and Necessity of a Paper Currency* (1729) maintain that he was a bold political printer from his first publications in Philadelphia. A long penultimate chapter features a discussion of Franklin's early *Pennsylvania Gazette*. He wrote more news, editorials, obituaries, hoaxes, and satires than any previous newspaperman in America. He was the best journalist of colonial America and made the *Pennsylvania Gazette* the most entertaining, news-filled, and controversial paper of its day.

As I will suggest in subsequent prefaces, additional volumes in the biography will introduce other new facts, contexts, and theses.

If you wou'd not be forgotten
As soon as you are dead and rotten,
Either write things worth reading;
Or do things worth the writing.

—Poor Richard, May 1738

America has sent us many good things. . . . But you are the first Philosopher, and indeed the first Great Man of Letters for whom we are beholden to her.

—David Hume to Franklin, 10 May 1762

PART I

Boston: Youth
1706–1723

PROLOGUE

Quandary

IN AUGUST 1723 seventeen-year-old Franklin found himself jobless and ostracized. He had been working for his older brother, James Franklin, who was now twenty-six. Six months before, when James was forbidden by the authorities to continue printing his newspaper unless it were first supervised by the secretary of Massachusetts, he brought out the newspaper under the name of Benjamin Franklin. Since Franklin was apprenticed to James, the latter returned him the cancelled indenture so that he could, if challenged, show it to the Massachusetts authorities. At the same time, Franklin and James signed another, secret indenture, whereby Franklin agreed to continue his apprenticeship with James. But the brothers often argued, and when they next quarreled, James beat his young brother, and Franklin quit. He could do so, for he knew that James could not produce the new indenture to the authorities and force Franklin to come back to work. Later, in the *Autobiography*, Franklin ruminated: "It was not fair in me to take this Advantage, and this I therefore reckon one of the first Errata of my Life: But the Unfairness of it weigh'd little with me, when under the Impressions of Resentment, for the Blows his Passion too often urg'd him to bestow upon me. Tho' He was otherwise not an ill-natur'd man. Perhaps I was too saucy and provoking" (20).

Franklin knew that he was as fast and efficient a printer as his brother or any Boston journeyman, and he assumed that he could find work at one of the several other Boston printers. He probably first went to Thomas Fleet, a young printer whom he knew well, but Fleet refused to hire him. Since Fleet's business was expanding and since good journeymen printers were rare in Boston, Franklin was puzzled. But when the printers John Allen and Samuel Kneeland also refused to hire him, he began to suspect the truth. Old Bartholomew Green, his father's friend and fellow member of the Old South Church, a person whom Franklin had known all his life, also turned him down. Franklin realized that his brother had told every local printer that Franklin was really still apprenticed to him. No Boston printer would hire him. What was he to do? There were no printers in the surrounding towns, and he could not sail from Boston, for his father and his brother could force him back if he tried to book passage. Besides, he had little money, not enough to pay for a voyage.

Worse, he had become notorious in Boston as an infidel. He enjoyed arguing and practiced a Socratic method of asking questions and having his opponents

agree with statements that gradually led them to conclusions they had not foreseen. He confessed in the *Autobiography* that his "indiscrete Disputations about
Religion began to make me pointed at with Horror by good People, as an Infidel
or Atheist" (20). Moreover, he was infamous as a radical, whose newspaper
writings insulted the best-known ministers of Boston, Cotton and Increase
Mather, and who satirized the old, greatly respected chief justice, Samuel Sewall.
The sensitive adolescent found that his writing and his private Socratic arguments had ostracized him from many good people in Boston. Some parents told
their children to have nothing to do with him. How did he find himself in this
predicament, and how did he make such a mess of his life by age seventeen?
And what could he do?

ONE

Boston

It would certainly . . . be a very great Pleasure to me, if I could once again visit my Native Town, and walk over the Grounds I used to frequent when a Boy, and where I enjoyed many of the innocent Pleasures of Youth, which would be so brought to my Remembrance, and where I might find some of my old Acquaintance to converse with. . . . The Boston Manner, turn of phrase, and even tone of voice, and accent in pronunciation, all please, and seem to refresh and revive me.—Franklin to the Reverend John Lathrop, 31 May 1788

BOSTON WAS A SMALL TOWN of fewer than 8,000 persons at the edge of the wilderness, but it was the largest city in English North America in 1706 and had an excellent harbor. During the seventeenth and early eighteenth centuries, it dominated colonial American trade. Most of New England shipped via Boston to overseas ports, making shipping the key to the town's flourishing economy. Shipbuilding was the most important local industry. In 1698, Massachusetts Governor Lord Bellomont classed the ships belonging to Boston, listing twenty five of the largest category, one hundred to three hundred tons. He wrote: "I may venture to say there are more good vessels belonging to the town of Boston than to all Scotland and Ireland."[1] The three largest towns in the English colonies during Franklin's youth were Boston, New York, and Philadelphia. By 1720 Boston had a population of 11,000; New York, 6,000; and Philadelphia, 4,900.[2] Boston had numerous maritime communities surrounding it; although Philadelphia and New York also had nearby ports, they were few and minor in comparison to those near Boston.

Most people came to Boston by water. When Franklin was three, a sea captain visited, describing the port and town. Captain Nathaniel Uring mentioned the lighthouse on an island on the north side of the peninsula and the fort on another island "two Miles and an Half below the Town; the Channel for Ships lies very near it, so that no Ships can pass by it but what the Fort is able to command: It is a strong, regular, well built Fort, mounted with about 100 Pieces of Cannon, where they keep a Garrison, who are paid by the Country." Boston was built upon a peninsula connected to the mainland by an isthmus about forty yards broad, "so low, that the Spring Tides sometimes washes the Road. . . . The Town is near two Miles in length, and in some Places three Quarters of a Mile broad," with most of the houses "built with Brick."

Like other commentators, Uring was impressed by Boston's wealth and by its main wharf: "Some of the richest Merchants have very stately, well built, convenient Houses." The wharfs "jut into the Harbour for the Conveniency of Shipping; one of which goes by the Name of the *Long Wharf*, and may well be called so, it running about 800 Foot into the Harbour, where large Ships, with great Ease, may both lade and unlade: On one side of which are Warehouses, almost the whole Length of the Wharf . . . where more than 50 Sail of Vessels may lade or unlade at the same Time with great Conveniency." He took the public jakes on the wharves for granted, and concluded with appreciation, "The town altogether is most excellently situated for Trade and Navigation."[3]

Dr. Alexander Hamilton's 1744 description showed that the town remained essentially unchanged thirty-five years later. Hamilton presented a better overall view and noted the local divisions of North End and South End Boston. As we will see, during Franklin's youth these divisions were keys to the town's pageantries and rivalries. Hamilton said: "The town is built upon the south and southeast side of the peninsula and is about two miles in length, extending from the neck of the peninsula northward to that place called North End, as that extremity of the town next the neck is called South End."[4] From the town hall on Marlborough or Cornhill Street, King's (now State) Street led down to the harbor and continued into the bay as the Long Wharf.

Politics

The government of Massachusetts emerged from an early seventeenth-century trading company, with a governor, deputy governor, and eighteen assistants elected annually by the stockholders. The Massachusetts Bay colonists gradually transformed the trading company's 1628 charter into a semi-theocracy, with an executive, a judiciary, and a two-house legislature. The name for the whole government was the General Court. The system functioned fairly well but not for all constituents. Women could not vote (nor could they in England). The franchise was given only to church members, and the only church was Puritan New England Congregationalism. Even Anglicans were disenfranchised. Further, the Massachusetts authorities persecuted Quakers and other religious sects.

More upsetting to Great Britain, Massachusetts resisted or ignored the Acts of Trade and Navigation (a series of parliamentary economic acts that started in 1650 and favored England). British officials found the government of Massachusetts too independent and too intolerant. In 1684 England's Court of Chancery (to the disgust of most Massachusetts citizens) annulled the old Massachusetts charter. James II established the Dominion of New England, an administrative unit stretching from New Jersey to Maine. England's Glorious Revolution in 1688 overthrew the Catholic James II and installed the Protestant William and Mary on the throne. This provided New Englanders a chance to revolt against the former authorities. In 1689, Bostonians imprisoned the British-appointed governor, Edmund Andros, and the other Royal appointees, Joseph Dudley (a Massachusetts native) and Edward Randolph. The three were sent back to England. The Reverend Increase Mather returned with them, intending to have the old charter restored. Mather found that impossible, but he did secure a new one with two major changes. First, the new charter provided for a governor to be appointed by the crown (i.e., the English authorities) rather than elected by the Massachusetts General Court. Second, it made property rather than religion the basis of suffrage.

There were additional changes. The representatives were elected by popular vote from the towns and other organized units. Though the upper house, or council, was elected by the General Court (i.e., by vote of the former council members and the representatives), the choice of councilmen was subject to the governor's veto. The new charter also allowed appeals to the British authorities. After 1691, the General Court of Massachusetts consisted of the British-appointed governor, the council, and representatives. Under the new charter, Massachusetts lost much of its autonomy—or, to say it more directly, it was made more subservient to England.

The popular party in Massachusetts that grew up in opposition to the governor and other English appointees came to be called the Old Charter Party. Increase Mather was blamed by many for not securing the full benefits of the old charter. His fall from grace was symbolized by his removal from the presidency of Harvard ostensibly because the president was supposed to reside in Cambridge. But Elisha Cooke and Nathaniel Byfield, political leaders of the Old Charter Party, put in the Reverend Samuel Willard, who lived in Boston, as vice president of Harvard on 6 September 1701. The technicality that permitted Cooke and Byfield to oust President Mather and put in Vice President Willard was that though the president was required to live in Cambridge, the vice president was not.[5] Of course Willard served thereafter as the acting president.

Politics in Franklin's Boston followed the forms that had developed during the seventeenth century. The council and the House alternatively chose the minister who would preach the election sermon.[6] According to the new charter, Election Day would be the last Wednesday in May. Election Day itself was the third and last of three key annual elections. First came the election of the Boston selectmen in March. One could usually judge from that election what group was in power and would win in the following election of representatives. Next, representatives were elected in mid-May. Election Day came third, a major Massachusetts holiday. Though it was the ceremonial high point, it was in some ways the least significant of the three. Politics after the election of the Boston selectmen in March was relatively predictable.

As Nathaniel Hawthorne makes clear in *The Scarlet Letter*, the minister had an important role on Election Day. Not only was it an occasion with an invariably large audience, but the minister had an opportunity to declare what could be considered the coming year's political platform. On Wednesday, 29 May 1706, in the year Franklin was born, the General Court met and listened to the annual election sermon, which the Reverend John Rogers of Ipswich preached on 1 Kings 8:57–58: "The Lord Our God be with us, as he was with our Fathers: Let him not leave us, nor forsake us: that he may encline our hearts unto him, to walk in all his ways, and to keep his Commandments, and his Statutes, and his Judgments, which he commanded our Fathers."

After the sermon, the new assembly members elected the Speaker of the House. Then the assembly and former council met together and elected the new council members. If the governor did not approve of a council member, he could veto (in colonial usage, "negative") him. In that case, the General Court usually elected another. Sometimes, however, it reelected the same person. The governor could either negative him again or could dissolve the assembly—whereupon the towns customarily reelected the same representatives.

The governor usually opened the first session of the legislature for the year with a brief state-of-the-province speech, with a request for new legislation (in 1706, for defense from a powerful French fleet in the West Indies that was thought to be making its way up the coast), and with the usual invocations of loyalty to Britain: "Every Body will agree that it is our Duty . . . to do the just Honour we owe to the Crown of *England*, to Her Majesty the best of Princes" (*Boston News-Letter*, 3 June 1706).

The popular attitude toward Election Day is documented in an anecdote concerning the Reverend Mather Byles, Franklin's contemporary, who became eighteenth-century Boston's most famous wit: "*Mather Byles*, one Election day, in Boston, a day of frolic, being in the Mall, he saw two of his acquaintances (one a very corpulent, and the other a slender man) walking arm in arm. Byles thrust himself between, and having parted them, went on observing, 'it was always the fashion to go through *thick* and *thin* on Election day.'"[7]

RELIGION

Religion was the most important topic of conversation in eighteenth-century New England until the pre-Revolutionary period. In Franklin's boyhood, every latest piece of news concerning theology, ministers, and churches became the talk of the town. Franklin read the Bible at five years of age and before his teens made his way through his father's "Books in polemic Divinity." Though Franklin later rejected the doctrines of New England Puritanism, he retained an interest in theology all his life. He wrote more theological essays than any other American layman of the colonial period. We associate Benjamin Franklin with George Washington, John Adams, Thomas Jefferson, James Madison, and other American Revolutionary leaders, but he was a contemporary of Jonathan Edwards, New England's greatest theologian. Edwards was just three years older than Franklin; in comparison, all the Revolutionaries named above were one or two generations younger than Franklin. George Washington, Franklin's closest contemporary among the Revolutionaries, was not born until 1732, twenty-six years after Franklin.

Like Jonathan Edwards, Franklin grew up in a religiously oriented world. The question that ordinary people like Franklin's father and mother worried about first was their salvation. It was their primary goal. Are you saved? was the question that dominated their lives—just as the churches dominated the skyline of William Burgess's 1722 engraving of Boston. Even in 1740, a visitor commented that Boston inhabitants' "observation of the Sabbath (which they rather choose to call by the name of the Lord's Day, whensoever they have occasion to mention it) . . . is the strictest kept that ever I yet saw anywhere. On that day no man, woman, or child is permitted to go out of town on any pretence whatsoever; nor can any that are out of town come in on the Lord's Day. . . . But that which is most extraordinary is that they commence the Sabbath from the setting of the sun on the Saturday evening; and, in conformity to that, all trade and business ceases, and every shop in the town is shut up: even a barber is finable for shaving after that time. Nor are any of the taverns permitted to entertain company; for in that case not only the house, but every person found therein, is finable."[8]

To be admitted a full church member (one who could receive communion) in seventeenth-century New England congregations, one had to attest publicly in church to a conversion experience, a "new birth." Some persons, however, no matter how much they might desire the experience, never achieved it. They could not give a confession of faith, a short spiritual autobiography, that ended with a conversion experience. Since church membership in New England depended on one's being reborn, religion could create conflict between civil and spiritual matters. The New England folk song "New England's Annoyances" stated the problem as early as the 1640s:

> And we have a Cov'nant one with another,
> Which makes a division 'twixt brother and brother:
> For some are rejected, and others made Saints,
> Of those that are equal in virtues and wants.[9]

Each Boston church had its own characteristics and generally the newer churches began as more liberal than the existing ones. The original or First Church had been joined by the Second or North Church in 1649 because of the increase in population. By that time, the children of church members who could not give a testimony of their personal conversion experience were nevertheless admitted to church membership, though they could not receive the Lord's Supper. Then, in 1662, a synod of New England churches approved the "Half-Way Covenant" (so called by its enemies), extending the limited church membership to the grandchildren of church members. When the conservatives at the First Church refused to adopt the Half-Way Covenant, a group of parishioners formed the Third or South Church, where Franklin was baptized and which he attended as a boy.[10] The Third or South Church was the largest meeting house erected in New England in the seventeenth century, measuring seventy-five feet by fifty-seven feet, with three galleries.[11] In contrast, the Old North was forty feet square, with a south gallery added in 1660 and a north gallery in 1673.[12]

The Reverend Samuel Willard (1640–1707), who baptized Benjamin Franklin, became minister of the Old South in 1678. Before his official appointment, he recorded the church's decision (14 February 1677/8) to allow members in some cases to give their spiritual confession to the elders rather than before the entire congregation.[13] Increase Mather and his son Cotton Mather retained the public requirement. The Mathers had been the leading ministers in late seventeenth-century New England. They lost their dominant position among the clergy partly as a result of their lukewarm opposition to the 1692 Salem witchcraft trials, whereas Samuel Willard, who strongly opposed them, correspondingly won recognition.

The Reverend Robert Ratcliffe, an Anglican minister, came to Boston in 1686 with Edmund Andros and other authorities from England. He and the small Anglican community built King's Chapel in 1687. Called Queen's Chapel during Queen Anne's reign, it was the only Anglican church in Boston in 1706. A fourth Congregational church, the Brattle Street Church, was organized in 1699 by a group of fashionable Congregationalists who intended to do away with the narrow provincialism of the existing Boston churches and substitute for it a tolerant cosmopolitanism. At its formation, the Brattle Street Church issued a manifesto containing several departures from the standard New England doctrine. First, all professed Christians could have their children baptized by promising to bring them up as Christians. Second, though only "visible saints" could receive communion,[14] the pastor was responsible for ascertaining their sanctity. Third (a corollary to the second), church members did not have to detail their conversion experience publicly. And fourth, all baptized persons, women and men, who contributed to the maintenance of the church had a vote in electing the minister.

Despite these innovations, the Brattle Street Church retained New England Puritanism's basic Calvinistic theology, pledging loyalty to the Westminister Confession (1643), the definitive statement of Presbyterian doctrine widely adopted by the New England Congregationalists. The organizers—Thomas Brattle, John Mico, the Cambridge minister William Brattle (Thomas Brattle's brother), and John Leverett—asked Benjamin Colman (1673–1747) to be their minister and advised him to take holy orders in England before returning to America.[15] A descendant of the first New Englanders, Colman had graduated from Harvard in 1692 before going to England where he was a successful preacher. He followed the New Englanders' advice, took ordination from the London presbytery on 4 August 1699, and returned to Boston, where the Brattle Street Church was organized on 12 December. Even the building proclaimed its fashionableness. It followed the architectural styles of late seventeenth-century England, complete with a tower and spire. One authority believes that it was also the first New England Congregational structure to be called a *church*.[16]

Some conservatives satirized the Brattle Street Church's liberal and fashionable tendencies. Here are the third and fifth stanzas of a 1701 lampoon:

> Relations are Rattle with Brattle & Brattle;
> Lord Brother mayn't command:
> But Mather and Mather had rather & rather
> The good old way should stand.
>
> . . . .
>
> Our Merchants cum Mico do stand Sacro Vico;
> Our Churches turn genteel:
> Parsons grow trim and trigg with wealth wine & wigg
> And their crowns are covered with meal.[17]

As the satire suggests, the Mathers opposed the new church. They tried to establish a Presbyterian-style church polity in Massachusetts, where synods of clergy would decide on doctrines and new ministers, but a number of clergy opposed the Mather group. The Reverend John Wise (1652–1725) led the resistance to the Mathers and wrote against the innovation. He was also, as we shall see, the hero of the Old Charter Party. Unlike Wise, the Reverend Benjamin Colman gradually mended fences with the Mathers and the other conservative Boston-area ministers.

The last Boston Congregational church founded during Franklin's youth was organized by seventeen mechanics, who resented the fact that the only liberal church in the city was controlled by gentlemen. The New North Street Church was gathered on October 1714, "without the assistance of the more wealthy part of the community, excepting what they derived from their prayers and good wishes."[18]

WITCHCRAFT

Like slavery, prosecution for witchcraft was an unpleasant aspect of colonial America—and of the seventeenth- and eighteenth-century Western world. If you believed in the devil, then you certainly believed in God. If, on the other hand, you denied the powers of the underworld, then perhaps you doubted God's power. At first, many good Massachusetts Puritan ministers welcomed the 1692 witchcraft hysteria at Salem for it proved to a backsliding community that the devil was abroad. The ministers believed that witchcraft existed—and found various proofs, including some practitioners of what seventeenth-century persons (and, no doubt, some modern ones) considered witchcraft. Belief in the devil guaranteed that the ministers' religious occupations not only were important but were at the world's moral center. Of course, it was the judges, not the ministers, who condemned persons to death.

Because of his book describing individual cases in the Salem witchcraft trials, *Wonders of the Invisible World* (1693), Cotton Mather is associated with Salem witchcraft. He is not, however, to blame for the trials. The person most responsible was the chief justice, Lieutenant Governor William Stoughton (1631–1701), who never admitted and apparently never felt any guilt. A repentant justice involved in the trials was Samuel Sewall. The Old South Church's Samuel Willard opposed the executions at the time and later pressed for a fast day confessing public guilt for the trials. On 16 September 1696, Willard preached in front of the governor, council, and assembly, scorning the authorities for not making "public confession of the guilt incurred in the witch trials." His parishioner Sewall recorded that Willard "spoke smartly at last about the Salem Witchcrafts, and that no order had been suffer'd to come forth by Authority to ask Gods pardon." Cotton Mather drafted a proclamation for a fast day, but it was rejected on 11 December. A week later, Sewall prepared one, which, with some changes, was adopted on 17 December 1696.[19]

At the public fast day for the witchcraft trials held on 14 January 1696/7, Sewall stood up in the Old South Church, handed his confession of guilt to Willard, and stood while Willard read it:

> Samuel Sewall, sensible of the reiterated strokes of God upon himself and family; and being sensible that as to the Guilt contracted upon the opening of the late Commission of Oyer and Terminer at Salem (to which the order of the Day relates) he is, upon many accounts, more concerned than any that he knows of, Desires to take the Blame and shame of it, Asking pardon of men, And especially desiring prayers that God, who has an Unlimited Authority, would pardon that sin and all other sins; Personal and Relative: And according to his infinite Benignity, and Sovereignty, Not Visit the sin of him, or of any other, upon himself or any of his, nor upon the Land: But that he would powerfully defend him against all Temptations to Sin, for the future; and vouchsafe him the efficacious, saving Conduct of his Word and spirit.

No doubt Willard prayed that God would forgive Sewall—and because of his confession and apology, later commentators have tended to. But young Benjamin Franklin, as shown below, castigated Sewall for his role in the witchcraft trials.

The historian Thomas Hutchinson, Franklin's contemporary who became governor of Massachusetts in 1771, reported that Chief Justice Stoughton, "being informed of this action of one of his brethren, observed for himself that when he sat in judgment he had the fear of God before his eyes and gave his opinion according to the best of his understanding; and although it may appear afterwards, that he had been in an error, yet he saw no necessity of a public acknowledgment of it" (2:46).

Witchcraft was part of the religious world system of the seventeenth century and existed in Salem.[20] Bridget Bishop of Salem village believed herself to be a witch. She practiced witchcraft, complete with dolls in the images of her neighbors, which she punctured with pins. She was the first person to be tried (2 June) and executed (10 June 1692). Tituba, a servant from the West Indies, also practiced witchcraft. In seventeenth-century New England, no one publicly treated witchcraft lightly. When Benjamin Franklin mocked it in his hoax of 22 October 1730, "A Witch-Trial at Mt. Holly" (discussed below, Chapter 18), he helped usher colonial America into a new world order.

WAR

Throughout most of Franklin's life, Europe and America were engaged in various wars. Often the peace that officially resolved the European war did not address the underlying causes, and an unofficial war in the colonies continued. Franklin became used to war and being prepared for it, but he also knew its wastefulness, destruction, and futility. At Franklin's birth on 6 January 1705/6, England was at war with the French and the Spanish (Queen Anne's War, 1702–13), and Spanish and French navies as well as their privateers threatened Boston from the sea. The French and Abnaki Indians attacked along the frontier—with depredations occurring only fifteen miles outside town. Bostonians learned the international and local news by word of mouth, by English newspapers in the local coffeehouses, and by reading the only American newspaper, the *Boston News-Letter*, a small folio sheet printed on both sides and folded to make four pages. Postmaster John Campbell had begun the newspaper in 1704. The *Boston News-Letter* chiefly printed English and European news, though American triumphs and disasters sometimes appeared.

Most of the war news was brief and vague, but Captain Andrew Wilson's heroic maritime defense filled the *Boston News-Letter* the week after Franklin's birth. Wilson "in the ship *Sarah* Galley of Boston of 12 guns, 22 men, met a French privateer sloop, about 80 men." Realizing that he could not outrun the privateer, Wilson had his men haul up the sails and retire to their close quarters where they prepared to fight. The French boarded the *Sarah* and lashed the ships together, but Wilson and his men fired on them from behind locked gratings. Finding they could not withstand Wilson's fire and could not do him any damage, the French retired to their sloop, "and from thence ply'd small Arms on *Wilson*, and *Wilson* on them, till at last the Privateer was glad to cut his Lashings and get clear of him; and left 3 Fuzees, 3 Swords, and some Axes and Pistols behind them on *Wilson's* Deck and one of their men dead in his chains; and they saw several fall and throw down into their Hold, and the blood running very plentifully out of their Scuppers; Capt. *Wilson* had no men kill'd, only himself and Son received several Wounds; at parting Capt. *Wilson* discharged two Great Guns loaden with small Shot, which he supposes did great execution among the Privateers men." The 11 March *News-Letter* followed up the earlier account with the French privateer captain's statement that Andrew Wilson had killed "22 of his men."

As a boy Franklin no doubt heard stories about the heroic activities of sailors like Wilson. Such tales inspired him to want to "break away and get to Sea" (A 10). Franklin's father would have countered such stories with realistic descriptions of a sailor's hard life and with sadness for the unknown fate of Franklin's older half-brother Josiah, who had run off to be a sailor.

The major American item in the *News-Letter* during 1706 was the attempted French and Spanish invasion of Charleston, South Carolina, during August, filling three columns in the 14 October paper. The *News-Letter* also frequently featured stories about Indian raids. In the most important early New England battle of Queen Anne's War, French soldiers and Abnaki Indians under Captain Hertel de Rouville ravaged Deerfield, Massachusetts, on the night of 28 February 1703/4, killing 54 settlers and taking about 120 prisoners. Throughout 1706, news of raiding Indians was common. From Dover, New Hampshire, on 3 May came the report: "On the 27th last, Some Skulking Indians about 10 or 12, came on part of Oyster River, and suddenly Kill'd and Captivated 8 Persons, who had been Stragling abroad out of Garrison." In his *History of Massachusetts*, Franklin's contemporary Thomas Hutchinson added: "There was a garrison house near, where the women of the neighbourhood had retreated, their husbands being abroad at their labor, or absent upon other occasions. This house being attacked, the women put on their husbands hats and jackets, and let their hair loose, to make the appearance of men; and firing briskly from the flankarts, saved the house and caused the enemy to retreat" (2:121). Like Hutchinson and other contemporaries, Franklin would have heard anecdotes about various skirmishes.

On 10 June the *Boston News-Letter* reported that "6 or 8 of the Skulking Enemy Indians on *Tuesday* last came unawares upon 3 or 4 persons that were working in their field at *Cachethe*, [Maine,] and killed two of them being Young men, e'er they could escape to the Garrison, as the other did." From Piscataqua, New Hampshire, the 7 June newspaper reported that John Shaplie and his son "Riding on the Road near Kittery, their Horses were found all bloody without their Riders; a Party of the Garrison that went out in Quest of the Skulking Enemy, found Mr. *Shaplies* Body, and his head cut off, but cannot tell what is become of the Son." Every few weeks throughout 1706, the paper reported Indian attacks. In the Revolutionary period, Franklin wrote there never was a good war or a bad peace (31:437).

FOLKWAYS

Militia training days brought out crowds. Militia drills and parades were a subject for humor in seventeenth-century England and became a common subject of American humor.[21] The English satirist Edward Ward observed of Bostonians in *A Trip to New-England* (1699) that "*Election, Commencement,* and *Training-days,* are their only *Holy-days.*"[22] The Boston matron Sarah Kemble Knight (the oft-repeated claim that she taught Benjamin Franklin is false)[23] wrote in her 1704 *Journal*: "Their Diversions in this part of the country [Connecticut] are on Lecture days and Training days mostly." She noted that one entertainment on militia training day was "Shooting at the Target, as they call it, (but it very much resembles a pillory,) where hee that hitts neerest the white has some yards of Red Ribbin presented him which being tied to his hattband, the two ends streaming down his back, he is Led away in Triumph, with great applause, as the winners of the Olympiack Games."[24]

The New England folk song "Yankee Doodle" confirms other evidence that the annual training day was a time of revelry, with drinking, foot races, and shooting matches. The militia training verses of "Yankee Doodle" begin:

> Father and I went down to camp
> Along with Captain Goodwin
> And there we see the men and boys
> As thick as hasty pudding.[25]

The Boston artillery company was a semi-professional military organization. Its annual civic ceremony took place early in June. It began with a minister preaching the annual artillery election sermon. On 3 June 1706, the Reverend Rowland Cotton of Sandwich, chose as his text Matthew 11:12: "The Kingdom of Heaven suffereth Violence, and the Violent take it by Force." After the sermon, the militia company elected officers, appointed new noncommissioned officers, admitted new soldiers, and then went to the battery at Castle Island in Boston Bay and practiced firing cannons. The day-long spectacle always attracted a crowd. Franklin's favorite brother John became a member of the Boston Artillery Company, and Franklin attended the rituals with him in 1743.

The Massachusetts authorities often appointed fast and thanksgiving days, sometimes following the lead of official English proclamations but more frequently in celebration or lamentation of local conditions. Samuel Willard preached a thanksgiving sermon on 28 December 1705, "on the Return of a Gentleman from his Travels," celebrating Jonathan Belcher's homecoming from England. In response to an order from England to give thanks for victories in Europe, Massachusetts held a thanksgiving day on 24 January 1705/6. Governor Joseph Dudley proclaimed a fast day in Boston for 18 April 1706, praying that "Her Majesties Life and Government long continued, Her Counsels and Just Arms prospered; the Designs of the barbarous Salvages against Us, defeated; Our Exposed Plantations preserved; And the poor Christian Captives in their Hands, returned." As usual, "all Servile Labour upon the said Day is Inhibited."[26]

New Englanders gave thanks for the return of those held captive by Indians. The *Boston News-Letter* reported on 25 November 1706 the success of negotiations for exchanges: "On Thursday the 20th Current arrived here Capt. *Samuel Appleton* Esq. Commissioner sent by His Excellency our Governor a Flag of Truce to *Canada* for the Exchanging of Prisoners, who has brought with him in the Brigandine *Hope*, whereof *John Bonner* is Master, 57 of ours, of whom is the Reverend Mr. *John Williams*, Pastor of Deerfield and his Two Sons." Abnaki Indians had taken Williams, his wife, and five of his children captive at the

Deerfield attack on 28 February 1703/4. They killed his two youngest children in the assault. On the captivity trail, when his wife and about twenty other prisoners could not keep up, the Indians tomahawked them. Two of Williams's sons returned with him. A daughter, Esther, and another son were returned separately. But Williams' daughter Eunice was kept for years, became a Catholic, married an Indian, and remained in Canada.

At the Boston lecture day (held every Thursday) on 5 December 1706, Williams preached in the Second or North Church (the Mathers' church) a sermon on Luke 8:39: "Return to thine own house, and shew how great things God hath done unto thee." Cotton Mather recorded that "a great Auditory" attended. A few weeks later, when Williams returned to Deerfield, a notice appeared in the paper.

> Hatfield, January 9. The People of this Country are fill'd with Joy, for the Arrival of the captives; especially, for the Return of the Reverend and Pious Mr. *John Williams*, to *Deerfield* again, upon Saturday the 28th of *December* last: which is esteemed a general Blessing. All Thankfully acknowledge His Excellency's [the governor's] effectual Care of us therein. And a Design is formed for Rebuilding the Town more Commodiously, and regularly Fortifying of it. *Wednesday*, the 8th Current was a Day of Thanksgiving there, to Praise GOD for His great Goodness. The Reverend Mr. *Solomon Stoddard*, and Mr. *William Williams* assisted at the Solemnity, each Preaching a Thanksgiving Sermon, Besides the *Inhabitants of Deerfield*, Sundry Persons of Quality from other Towns were present, helping forward this Religious Exercise.

The following year, Williams published *The Redeemed Captive, Returning to Zion: A Faithful History of Remarkable Occurrences, in the Captivity and the Deliverance of Mr. John Williams*, appending to it the sermon he had preached in Boston. Reprinted without the sermon, it became a classic story of Indian captivity, second in importance only to Mary Rowlandson's 1682 narrative. Franklin recalled it among others when he imitated the genre and mocked the English celebrations of Indian oratory in "An Account of the Captivity of William Henry" (25 June 1768).

Franklin surely attended Harvard's commencement days, for they were a festive local pageant. Writing Samuel Danforth, a friend of half a century, on 25 July 1773, Franklin jokingly anticipated "the jolly Conversation we and twenty more of our Friends may have 100 Years hence over that well-replenish'd Bowl at Cambridge Commencement." Visiting notables turned out for the occasion. When Admiral Hovenden Walker was in Boston on 4 July 1711, he noted: "This was the Day of Commencement at the *New England* University of *Cambridge*, where there was a great Concourse of People of all Degrees, and both Sexes: We were all invited to see the Ceremony."[27] The night before, a graduating senior named John Wainwright became drunk and boisterous with Richard Waldron, a junior, resulting in "a Riot [i.e., a commotion], late in the Night, to the great disturbance of the Neighbourhood and Scandal of the College." The next morning, the Harvard Corporation voted to deny Wainwright the degree and to strike his name from the thesis sheet. His offense and punishment were the talk of the town. When the government authorities and the visiting military dignitaries heard of his dismissal, they discussed it and appealed to the corporation to forgive Wainwright. The plea of Governor Joseph Dudley, General Hill, and Admiral Walker prevailed. Wainwright graduated.[28]

Since commencement entertainments often featured drinking, the ministers deplored their "excesses." (Solomon Stoddard did so on 3 July 1707.) As the eighteenth century advanced, the wits' satires reinforced the ministers' criticisms. Mather Byles's poem "The Commencement" appeared in 1726 and was reprinted in *A Collection of Poems* (1744).[29] Matthew Adams, who loaned books to the young Franklin, wrote "The Sequel of Commencement," which appeared in the *New England Weekly Journal* on 3 July 1727. Byles's poetic nemesis, Joseph Green, added *A Satyrical Description of Commencement. Calculated to the Meridian of Cambridge in New-England.*[30] All three poems ridiculed the early eighteenth-century version of tailgating.

Few seventeenth-century Puritans celebrated Christmas. When the Anglican Governor Samuel Shute prorogued the meeting of the Massachusetts General Assembly over Christmas in 1722, it occasioned objections from the Boston justice and diarist Samuel Sewall (1652–1730) and other older New Englanders. James Franklin used the occasion to print two poems, one for and one against the celebration of Christmas in his 24 December 1722 *New-England Courant.*[31] Three years later he daringly listed it as a holiday in Nathan Bowen's *New England Diary, or Almanack for . . . 1725.* By the 1760s, its celebration was widespread in New England.

Thanksgiving as a fixed annual official holiday began only in 1864. New Englanders, however, had various local occasions for festivities, including harvesttime hustings. On 3 October 1687, Sewall recorded that he and his wife went to a friend's where they "Husk Corn and trace." The visiting English humorist Edward Ward wrote in 1699: "Husking of *Indian-Corn*, is as good sport for the Amorous *Wag-tailes* in *New England*, as *Maying* amongst us is for our forward Youths and Wenches."[32] Some "Yankee Doodle" verses dating from the early or mid-eighteenth century celebrate hustings:

> Husking time is coming on
> They all begin to laugh sir—
> Father is a coming home
> To kill the heifer calf sir.

> Now husking time is over
> They have a deuced frolic,
> There'l be some as drunk as sots
> The rest will have the cholic.[33]

New Englanders not only reveled in rustic plentitude and domestic plea-
sures, but from the beginning of the eighteenth century to the Stamp Act they
increasingly celebrated important anniversaries of the royal family. During
Franklin's childhood, Queen Anne's birthday and the anniversary of her acces-
sion to the throne both occasioned festivities—and proclamations of loyalty.[34]
(Good seventeenth-century Puritans had ignored such occasions.) When St.
George's Day fell on a Sunday, 23 April 1704, its celebration was so new in
Boston that it irritated the Puritan diarist Judge Samuel Sewall. He sarcastically recorded: "There is great firing at the town, ships, Castle, upon account of it
being the Coronation day, which gives offence to many. Down Sabbath, up St.
George!" Two years later Sewall commented that St. George's Day was only an
excuse for the new pernicious practice of toasting: "Because to drinking Healths,
now the Keeping of a Day to fictitious St. George, is plainly set on foot."

Public execution days remained popular holidays in the eighteenth century.
Ministers preached in the morning, accompanied the criminals to the gallows,
prayed one last time with them, heard their confessions, listened to their dying
words, and prayed over their dead bodies. Printers sometimes secured copies of
the sermons beforehand and even, on occasion, printed the criminals' supposed
dying words before they were uttered. The assembled crowds eagerly purchased
the sensational literature. Captain Kidd, the most famous pirate of the day, was
captured in Boston in 1701 but sent to England to be tried, thus depriving Bostonians of a great spectacle. A local pirate, however, Captain John Quelch, was
captured in 1704 and, along with five of his men, hanged in Boston on 30 June
1704. At the preceding Boston lecture, Thursday, 22 June, Cotton Mather
preached in the presence of the condemned pirates: *Faithful Warnings to prevent
Fearful Judgments, Uttered in a brief Discourse, Occasioned, by a Tragical Spectacle, in a Number of Miserables under a Sentence of Death for Piracy.*[35] The pirates'
presence made the sermon more dramatic, but the exhortation failed to affect
them.

Like numerous others, Sewall attended the execution:

Many were the people that saw [the execution] upon Broughton's Hill. But
when I came to see how the River was cover'd with People, I was amazed: Some
say there were 100 Boats. 150 Boats and Canoes, saith Cousin Moody of York.
. . . Mr. Cotton Mather came with Capt Quelch and six others for Execution
from the Prison to Scarlet's Wharf, and from thence in the Boat to the place of
Execution about the midway between Hudson's point and Broughton's Ware-
house. . . . When the scaffold was hoisted to a due height, the seven Malefactors
went up; Mr. Mather pray'd for them standing upon the Boat. Ropes were all
fasten'd to the Gallows (save King, who was Repriev'd). When the Scaffold was
let sink, there was such a Screech of the Women that my wife heard it sitting in
our Entry next the Orchard, and was much surprised at it; yet the wind was sou-
west. Our house is a full mile from the place.

An Account of the Behaviour and last Dying Speeches of the Six Pirates, that were Executed on Charles River appeared within the week, describing the procession of the pirates with forty musketeers, constables, two ministers, etc., to Scarlet's Wharf, then by boat to the gallows[36] Concluding its report of the execution, the *Boston News-Letter* said on 3 July 1704: "And notwithstanding all the great labour and pains taken by the Reverend Ministers of the Town of *Boston*, ever since they were first Seized and brought to Town, both before and since their Tryal and Condemnation, to instruct, admonish, preach and pray for them; yet as they led a wicked and vitious life, so to appearance they dyed very obdurately and impenitently, hardened in their Sin."

Unlike the religious thoughts provoked by the spectacle of trials and executions, the emotions aroused on Guy Fawkes' Day or Gunpowder Plot Day (called Pope's Day in New England), 5 November, were rowdy, provoking anti-Catholic demonstrations. In Boston, the North Enders and South Enders paraded toward the center of town, each group bearing effigies of the pope, the devil, and the Stuart Pretender on a platform. On the front of the platform stood a lantern inside transparent paper, with inscriptions for the occasion. The Pretender, on a gibbet, stood next, and in the center of the stage was the extraordinarily fat figure of the pope, grotesquely dressed. At the back was the devil, sporting a long tail, a trident in one hand, and a dark lantern in the other. Under the platform, boys with rods could manipulate the figures, causing them to face left or right or rise up to look into chamber windows.

The pope was anathema to the New England Puritans for political as well as religious reasons, for the hostile Indians on the frontier were supported by the French colonists against the Americans. The first "Pretender" to the throne was the Catholic James II (1633–1701), the former king of England who was overthrown in the Glorious Revolution but claimed the English throne to his death. James II's son James Francis Edward Stuart (1688–1766) and the latter's son "Bonny Prince Charlie" (Charles Edward Louis Philip Casimir, 1720–1788) were called the Old Pretender and the Young Pretender. Since the Stuarts had been kings of Scotland before James I became king of England, the Pretender had special support among the Scots. Supporters of the Pretender were called Jacobites (from Jacobus, Latin for James). Today, the best-known descendents of such pageants as Pope's Day occur at the Rose Bowl and similar contests, as well as in New Orleans during Mardi Gras. A pasquinade used on Pope's Day in Boston when Franklin was a boy survives:

> Three Strangers blaze amidst a bonfire's revel,
> The Pope, and the Pretender, and the Devil;
> Three Strangers hate our faith, and faith's defender,
> The Devil, and the Pope, and the Pretender;
> Three Strangers will be strangers long, we hope,
> The Devil, the Pretender, and the Pope;

Thus in three rhymes three Strangers dance the lay,
And he that chooses to dance after 'em may.[37]

After parading about and collecting money from the houses they passed, the
North Enders and South Enders met at Union Street with riots and fighting,
each struggling to win possession of the other's effigies. Franklin was generally
identified with the South End, though there is no record of his (or practically
anyone else's) participating in these early eighteenth-century annual riots. If the
North Enders won, they burnt the South Enders' mannequins on Copps Hill; if
the South Enders triumphed, they burned the North Enders' effigies on the
Boston Common. From the late seventeenth century to the pre-Revolutionary
period, the mob leaders tended to be the local rowdies, though popular politics
may have played some part in the demonstrations. But beginning with the anti–
Stamp Act demonstrations of 1765, Boston's political leaders harnessed the ener-
gies of the town mobs, so the 5 November rallies changed from local rivalries
into anti-English and pro-American demonstrations.[38]

AMERICANISM

Versions of Americanism, that is, of the inhabitants' pride in their colony, its
achievements, history, and culture, began to appear by the mid-seventeenth century. By the early eighteenth century, expressions of local pride were not uncommon. Obituaries in newspapers, diaries, and histories revealed both a pride
in the achievement of New England's first settlers and a reaction to the not
uncommon British and European belief in the degeneration of life in America.
Thomas Hutchinson recorded in his *History of Massachusetts Bay* the death of
Peregrine White on 20 July 1704, "aged 83 years and 8 months, the first born in
Plimouth colony" (2:111n). He also noted the deaths of the first persons born in
Massachusetts Bay and in Rhode Island, commenting, "The longevity of the
first born in each of the three colonies is worth noting" (2:162). In 1706, a few
"first comers" were still alive. The 24 June *News-Letter* recorded from Water-
town, Massachusetts: "On the 16th Currant, Dyed here, Mrs. *Elizabeth Beers*
(Widow of Capt. *John Beers* who was kill'd at *Deerfield* in the first *Indian* Wars)
in the 92 Year of her Age: whose Grand-Daughter is a Grandmother; She came
to *New-England*, in *June* 1630 Being then Sixteen Year Old, and lived in *New-
England* 76 Years." Memorializing the deaths of the first English persons born
in Philadelphia and New York, Franklin cited some of these same statistics in
an article contradicting prejudice against the American climate titled "American
Longevity," published on 16 December 1767.

After attending the funeral of Elder Samuel Clap on 18 October 1708, Samuel
Sewall recorded: "He was the first man born in Dorchester, 74 years old." And
on Wednesday, 9 February 1708/9, the judge logged: "Mrs. Hannah Glover dies
in the 76th year of her Age; was widow of Mr. Habakkuk Glover, daughter of
Mr. John Eliot, who married here, and this daughter was born at Roxbury in

the Fall 1633, just about the time Mrs. Rock was born. So that this Gentlewoman, though born in N.E. pass'd not only 60. but 70. years, and became a Great Grandmother in our Israel." Cotton Mather asserted in a funeral sermon for Mrs. Mary Rock that she was "One of the First-born, if not the very *First* of her Sex that was Born, in this famous *Metropolis* of the *English-America*.[39]

On 9 April 1707, Samuel Sewall learned the "amazing News of Mr. Willard's dangerous Sickness." An example of the deferential treatment that eighteenth-century decorum expected for its distinguished citizens appears in Sewall's diary for 16 May 1707. The Harvard overseers were concerned about Willard's health and his ability to carry out the duties as Harvard's acting president. Sewall indirectly brought up the matter, asking when Willard was going to Cambridge: "He said next week, without any hesitancy: so rekon'd we were not to enquire any further. We sent to Mr. Pemberton [Willard's assistant minister] first, and his opinion was, we should not express our desires, or the desires of any other, of Mr. Willard's immediat giving over College-work, except he himself inclin'd to it." The 15 September *Boston News-Letter* reported, "On Fryday the 12th Instant Dyed here in the 68 year of his Age, the very Worthy and Rev. Mr. SAMUEL WILLARD, Pastor of the South Church, and Vice President of *Harvard College* in *Cambridge*, unto the Just Grief, not only of the Church and Town, but of all *New-England*."

Josiah Franklin and his family no doubt attended the funeral, though perhaps the twenty-month-old Benjamin Franklin was left with someone at home. The Reverend Ebenezer Pemberton preached his funeral sermon, which the *News-Letter* of 27 October advertised. Willard's great work, the series of Tuesday afternoon lectures delivered once a month from 1688 to his death on the Westminister Assembly's *Shorter Catechism*, expounded the New England Puritan way. Not published until 1726, *A Compleat Body of Divinity* was a monument to a way of life and of religion that was passing. A folio of over a thousand pages, it was the largest production to that date of the colonial American press. Like Cotton Mather's *Magnalia Christi Americana* (1702), the *Compleat Body of Divinity* commemorated New England's distinctive religion and culture. Despite its size and high price, Josiah Franklin subscribed for two copies, not only because it summarized the faith he believed in but also because it was a testimonial to the person Josiah probably respected above all others. The memory of Samuel Willard was a commanding presence throughout Franklin's youth.

HIERARCHY

The major social news in the 1706 *Boston News-Letter* concerned Jonathan Belcher. Under the dateline "Piscataqua, January 11," the paper reported, with unstated appreciation, his eagerness (and his bride's, though hers would have been indecorous to mention) to wed: "On Fryday the 4th Currant several Gentlemen went from hence as far as Hampton to meet Mr. *Jonathan Belcher* Merchant of Boston, where he was met being accompanied by several Gentlemen, and arrived here the said night in order to his Marriage on Tuesday the 8th Instant, being his Birthday, unto Mrs. *Mary Partridge* Daughter to William Partridge Esq late Lieutenant Governor of this Province; But at the motion of the Gentlemen that accompanyed him, they were Marryed the same night as he came off his Journey in his Boots: The Wedding was Celebrated on the Tuesday following, where there was a Noble and Splendid Entertainment for the Guests, and honoured with a Discharge of the Great Guns of the Fort." Sewall recorded on 23 January 1705/6 that Belcher and his bride came to town about 6 o'clock: "About 20 Horsemen, Three Coaches and many Slays." The children of the wealthy merchants, like Jonathan Belcher, were at the top of colonial New England's social scale.

Though America lacked the aristocracy of England and Europe, it had abject poor and persons without basic legal rights. Slavery existed throughout most of the world in the seventeenth and early eighteenth centuries. Some individuals protested against it. Samuel Sewall objected to it in *The Selling of Joseph* (1700). The *Boston News-Letter* published an essay against slavery on 10 June 1706, the first such editorial in an American newspaper, but the editorial also voiced the early eighteenth-century's typical racism: "Negroes are generally Eye-Servants, great Thieves, much addicted to Stealing, Lying and Purloining." No English colony prohibited slavery (Georgia was the exception, and it did so only in the 1740s). England did not abolish the slave trade until 1807. Europeans were enslaved in the Middle East, Africa, and other areas but rarely in Europe. European, especially American, slavery was usually racist. Americans enslaved Afro-Americans and Indians but not Europeans. Indian slavery, however, was comparatively minor because, among other reasons, Indians could not be captured in large numbers, and they escaped into the wilderness. Advertisements for runaway slaves appeared frequently in the *Boston News-Letter*. The 5 April 1708 paper advertised slaves for sale: "To be sold at the sign of the blew Anchor in Boston five Carolina Indians, viz. a Man, a Boy, and 3 Women." Josiah Franklin was probably not wealthy enough to own slaves, but he evidently had no religious or moral scruples against slavery, perhaps because the Bible frequently mentioned it. The 3 August 1713 *Boston News-Letter* advertised: "Three Negro Men and two Women to be sold and seen at the House of Mr. *Josiah Franklin* at the Sign of the blue Ball in Union Street Boston." Slavery was an accepted part not only of Franklin's Boston but also of his own home.

Modern readers often find it surprising that white colonial Americans, who frequently used clichés about the liberty of the individual, did not object to slavery. But the theory of liberty popular in the eighteenth century was mainly based on the writings of John Locke (1632–1704), the philosopher who justified England's Glorious Revolution. In Lockean thought, liberty was based on property, and slaves were considered property. Later, the French savant Montesquieu, in his *Spirit of the Laws* (1748), claimed that slavery was evil in itself and that since all men were created equal, slavery was unnatural.[40] In the mid-eighteenth century, the rise of natural law theory, of sentimentalism, and of moral consciousness all contributed to the rise of the antislavery movement. The Boston political leader James Otis, in *The Rights of the British Colonies* (1764), said, "The Colonists are by the law of nature born free, as indeed all men are, white or black." In 1751, as we shall see, Franklin attacked slavery for economic reasons, but it was not until he was convinced by the moral arguments against slavery, especially in the writings of his friend Anthony Benezet, a Philadelphia Quaker, that he became an abolitionist. Even after the rise of the antislavery movement, late eighteenth-century thinkers such as John Adams and Alexander Hamilton believed in the Lockean notion that liberty and property were inseparable, a belief that tended to vindicate the existence of slavery.[41]

Indentured servitude was common throughout colonial America. Poor people sold themselves for four years of servitude in order to be shipped to the New World. At the end of that time, they were given a small sum of money, new clothes, and a character reference. The system was frequently abused, however, and "spirits" enticed and sometimes kidnaped youths onboard ship in order to sell their time in the New World. The word "kidnapper" was coined in the late seventeenth century to describe the practice. Like almost everyone else in his day, Josiah Franklin saw nothing wrong with indentured servitude. He advertised in the 22 December 1719 *Boston Gazette:* "A Servant Boy's time for 4 years (who is strong, laborious, and very fit for Country Work) to be disposed of; Enquire of Mr. Josiah Franklin at the Blue Ball in Union Street." The boy was probably little older than Benjamin Franklin at that time, who was thirteen and already apprenticed to his older brother James. Many indentured servants resented their position. Josiah Franklin evidently employed one such unhappy servant. The same paper that carried Franklin's Silence Dogood essay No. 8, the 9 July 1722 *New-England Courant*, advertised: "RAN away from his Master Mr. *Josiah Franklin* of *Boston*, Tallow-chandler, on the first of this Instant July, an Irish Man Servant, named *William Tinsley*, about 20 Years of Age. Whoever shall apprehend the said Runaway Servant, and him safely convey to his abovesaid Master, at the blue Ball in Union Street Boston, shall have *Forty Shillings* Reward, and all necessary Charges paid."

The other kind of indentured servitude in colonial America was apprenticeship. Craftsmen were often paid a sum (£10 was usual) to teach apprentices the "art and mystery" of their craft. The apprentice signed an indenture (to age twenty-one was common) to work for room, board, clothes, and a small sum plus clothing upon the completion of the indenture. Almost all craftsmen began as apprentices—which called for a legal document setting forth the rights and obligations of both parties. Run-away apprentices, like runaway indentured servants, were subject to seizure, and rewards were often offered for their return. When Franklin ran away from Boston in the early fall of 1723, he noted that at the Pines in New Jersey and at the Crooked Billet Inn in Water Street, Philadelphia, "several sly Questions were ask'd me, as it seem'd to be suspected from my youth and Appearance, that I might be some Runaway" (A 22, 25).

THE FRANKLINS

Franklin was the child of Abiah (Folger) Franklin and Josiah Franklin. She was descended from a Nantucket Puritan family, and he was a pious Puritan who had been born in Ecton, Northamptonshire, England, on 23 December 1657.[42] Franklin reported in *the Autobiography* from notes his Uncle Benjamin had made that he knew his father's family "had liv'd in the same Village, Ecton in Northamptonshire, for 300 Years, and how much longer he knew not . . . on a Freehold of about 30 Acres, aided by the Smith's Business which had continued in the Family till his Time, the eldest Son being always bred to that Business. A Custom which he and my Father both followed as to their eldest Sons."

Franklin performed that American rite of visiting the ancestral home across the sea in 1758. "When I search'd the Register at Ecton, I found an Account of their Births, Marriages, and Burials, from the Year 1555 only, there being no Register kept in that Parish at any time preceding. By that Register I perceiv'd that I was the youngest Son of the Youngest Son for 5 Generations back" (A 3). Just after visiting Ecton and examining the register he wrote, "Had there originally been any Estate in the Family none could have stood a worse Chance for it" (8:118). In a world where primogeniture was common, Franklin was rather proudly asserting that even if his family had possessed wealth, he would have had to make his own way.[43] Franklin continued, "My Grandfather Thomas, who was born in 1598, lived at Ecton till he grew too old to follow Business longer, when he went to live with his Son John, a Dyer at Banbury in Oxfordshire, with whom my Father serv'd an Apprenticeship. There my Grandfather died and lies buried. We saw his Gravestone in 1758."

At Ecton in July 1758 he had the good fortune to meet the wife of the parish minister, the Reverend Ezra Whalley. She was the repository of local gossip and knowledge. The "good natured chatty old lady" gave him his father's family history: "My Grandfather had 4 Sons that grew up, viz. Thomas, John, Benjamin and Josiah. . . . Thomas was bred a Smith under his Father, but being ingenious, and encourag'd in Learning (as all his Brothers like wise were,) by an Esquire Palmer then the principal Gentleman in that Parish, he qualify'd himself for the Business of Scrivener, became a considerable Man in the County Affairs, was a chief Mover of all Publick Spirited Undertakings, for the County, or Town of Northampton and his own Village, of which many Instances were told us at Ecton, and he was much taken Notice of and patroniz'd by the then Lord Halifax. He died in 1702, Jan. 6 old Stile, just 4 Years to a Day before I was born." Pretending that *the Autobiography* was actually a letter addressed to his son William, Franklin wrote: "The Account we receiv'd of his Life and Character from some old People at Ecton, I remember struck you as something extraordinary from its Similarity to what you knew of mine. Had he died on the Same

Day, you said one might have suppos'd a Transmigration" (A 3–4). Perhaps William had the thought, but it would be like Franklin to have it and to attribute it to another.

"John was bred a Dyer, I believe of Woollens. Benjamin, was bred a Silk Dyer, serving an Apprenticeship at London. He was an ingenious Man, I remember him well, for when I was a Boy he came over to my Father in Boston, and lived in the House with us some Years. He lived to a great Age. His Grandson Samuel Franklin now lives in Boston." As usual, Franklin paid special attention to the writing of others. Uncle Benjamin "left behind him two Quarto Volumes, Manuscript of his own Poetry, consisting of little occasional Pieces address'd to his Friends and Relations." Franklin said he was named after him, "there being a particular Affection between him and my Father. He was very pious, a great Attender of Sermons of the best Preachers, which he took down in his Shorthand and had with him many Volumes of them."

Like other eighteenth-century descendants of Protestants, Franklin revealed pride in his family's early break from Catholicism: "This obscure Family of ours was early in the Reformation, and continu'd Protestants thro' the Reign of Queen Mary, and when they were sometimes in Danger of Trouble on Account of their Zeal against Popery." Protestants read the Bible, and few laymen among the Roman Catholics did. It meant punishment and possibly death in Bloody Mary's reign to be caught doing so. Franklin told an anecdote about his family's Bible, which, "to conceal and secure it . . . was fastned open with Tapes under and within the Frame of a Joint Stool. When my Great Great Grandfather read in it to his Family, he turn'd up the Joint Stool upon his Knees, turning over the Leaves then under the Tapes. One of the Children stood at the Door to give Notice if he saw the Apparitor coming, who was an officer of the Spiritual Court. In that Case the Stool was turn'd down again upon its feet, when the Bible remain'd conceal'd under it as before." The family remained in the Church of England until "about the End of Charles the Second's Reign, when some of the Ministers that had been outed for Nonconformity, holding Conventicles in Northamptonshire, Benjamin and Josiah adher'd to them, and so continu'd all their Lives. The rest of the Family remain'd with the Episcopal Church" (A 4–5).

According to Franklin, his father emigrated for religious reasons. In New England, Josiah and his friends "expected to enjoy their Mode of Religion with Freedom" (A 5). Josiah and his Puritan friends were proud that their religious ideals prevailed in New England. According to Uncle Benjamin, however, the primary reason for Josiah's emigrating was economic: "Things not succeeding there [in Banbury] according to his [Josiah's] mind, with the leave of his friends and father he went to New England in the year 1683."[44] New England held the possibility of greater economic opportunity as well as political and religious sanctuary. New England also seemed a safe refuge from the turmoils of European wars. Uncle Benjamin Franklin recalled that his oldest brother, Thomas

(1637–1702), in one of his last letters wrote, "If I were 10 years younger and had a family I would be for going to New England for, said he, all the world about us is involved in war and 'tis well if the flame doos not reach us at last."[45] Evidently the English Franklins thought of Josiah and his family as safe and secure in America. Since Thomas Franklin was an Anglican, religion did not influence his wishful thinking about New England.

About 1680, Josiah moved to Banbury, Oxfordshire, where he learned the silk dyer's trade with his elder brother John. Josiah Franklin's first wife, Ann Child, was also from Ecton, probably a childhood sweetheart. They married before 1678. Though Restoration England outlawed private prayer meetings or conventicles in 1664, Josiah belonged to one in Banbury. Josiah must have chafed at the ridicule of the English seventeenth-century wits. The Royalist satirist Richard Brathwait characterized Banbury early in the seventeenth century:

> To *Banbury* came I, O prophane one!
> Where I saw a Puritane one,
> Hanging of his Cat on Monday,
> For killing of a Mouse on Sunday.[46]

Ann and Josiah had seven children, the first three born in England and four more in Boston after they emigrated in October 1683.[47] The first five children lived to adulthood, but the sixth, Joseph Franklin, died when he was five days old (6–11 February 1687/8). Ann Franklin died on 9 July 1689, probably from illness resulting from the birth of their seventh child, a second short-lived Joseph (30 June–15 July 1689). In Boston, Josiah abandoned dyeing and became a tallow-chandler and soapmaker. He probably changed trades because of better economic possibilities, but perhaps, in an age when society in general and Puritans in particular took sumptuary laws (laws against dressing above one's station) seriously, Josiah felt conscientiously uncomfortable making brightly colored cloths.[48]

Devout persons like Josiah joined together for private prayer meetings. He probably joined one shortly after moving to Boston. In 1708, his name turned up in the conventicle to which Judge Samuel Sewall belonged, and thereafter Sewall recorded several notices of Josiah's activities in the group.[49] Sewall reported on Thursday, 9 September 1708, "I was mov'd last night at Mr. Josiah Franklin's at our Meeting, where I read the Eleventh Sermon on the Barren Fig-Tree. 'Tis the first time of Meeting at his House since he join'd."

Josiah

Franklin recalled that his father "was ingenious, could draw prettily, was skill'd a little in Music and had a clear pleasing Voice, so that when he play'd Psalm Tunes on his Violin and sung withal as he some times did in an Evening after the Business of the Day was over, it was extreamly agreeable to hear" (A 8).[50] Samuel Sewall confirmed the quality of his voice. When meeting at the private prayer group at Brother (William) Manly's, Sewall remarked, "I was so hoarse with my Cold, that I got Brother Franklin to set the Tune, which he did very well" (874). When Sewall's voice began to fail, he suggested on Sunday, 23 February 1717/8, that Franklin should take his place as precentor for the congregation, but John White (a Harvard graduate of 1685) was chosen. Josiah's greatest compliment and disappointment, however, occurred on 17 April 1719, when he was nominated as a deacon of the Old South Church. He received a respectable ten votes for the position, but of the two deacons to be elected, he finished third. The thirteen-year-old Benjamin must have been disappointed for his father.

Josiah was a dutiful Boston citizen. In 1697 he was chosen a tithingman; in 1700/1, a clerk of the market; in 1702/3, a Boston constable; in 1714/5, a tithingman; in 1720, a scavenger; and in 1720/1, a tithingman yet again.[51] Since these positions paid little and could be onerous, many citizens refused them, but Josiah accepted the tasks and conscientiously carried them out. Less than five months after his first wife's death, Josiah remarried on 25 November 1689.

ABIAH

Abiah (Folger) Franklin became Josiah's second wife. Born in Nantucket on 15 August 1667, she was the last child of Peter Folger (d. 1690), a schoolmaster and Indian expert, and Mary (Morrill) Folger (d. 1704). Peter Folger had emigrated to Boston with his widowed father around 1635. He and his family moved to Martha's Vineyard in the 1640s and to Nantucket in 1663. Franklin recalled in *the Autobiography* that Cotton Mather mentioned Folger in the *Magnalia Christi Americana* and noted that Folger "wrote sundry small occasional Pieces." Franklin had seen one piece, *A Looking Glass for the Times*, written in 1676 and printed in 1725. In the "homespun Verse of that Time and People," the poem was "address'd to those then concern'd in the Government there. It was in favor of Liberty of Conscience, and in behalf of the Baptists, Quakers, and other Sectaries, that had been under Persecution; ascribing the Indian Wars and other Distresses that had befallen the Country to that Persecution, as so many Judgments of God, to punish so heinous an Offence; and exhorting a Repeal of those uncharitable Laws." Franklin thought that the work was "written with a good deal of Decent Plainness and manly Freedom" (A 6). His mother must have told him stories of his grandfather who was an expert translator of Algonquian and an indispensable citizen on Nantucket Island. Folger saved the Nantucket Indian John Gibbs when Metacomet ("King Philip") came to kill him. And Folger was a ringleader in the popular political revolt of the 1670s against the original proprietors of Nantucket, who abrogated to themselves governance of the island.[52]

In the stratified society of the seventeenth century, Folger's marriage to Mary Morrill, a former bond servant of the locally famous Reverend Hugh Peter (1598–1660, who returned to England in 1641, became a regicide, and was executed after the Restoration), may have caused some comment. Young Benjamin

Franklin must have known his grandparents' positions before their marriage. When he made his first persona, Silence Dogood, a bond servant who married her master, he presented her as someone like his grandmother Mary Morrill, who made an unusual advance in New England society.

Abiah Folger evidently moved to Boston and worked there for some time before she professed her faith and became a member of the Old South Church on 19 August 1688, just four days after her twenty-first birthday. The Reverend Samuel Willard married Abiah Folger and Josiah Franklin on 25 November 1689 in the Old South Church. She was twenty-two, and he was thirty-one. Four years later, the Old South admitted Abiah and Josiah to communion on 4 February 1693/4. Though Josiah had changed his trade from dyer to tallow-chandler, he continued to do home dyeing and taught his wife to do so. They may have supplemented the family income with the skill. Abiah was well-known for producing "Worsted of that beautiful Red" and taught several of her children dyeing (18:187).

Franklin recalled that his mother had "an excellent Constitution. She suckled all her 10 Children." At the same time, she was bringing up Josiah's five children, who ranged in age at her marriage from eleven (Elizabeth) to two (Anne). Franklin added, "I never knew either my Father or Mother to have any Sickness but that of which they died, he at 89 and she at 85 Years of age." When Franklin erected an obelisk over his parents' grave, he inscribed on it, "She was a discreet and virtuous woman." Franklin's appreciation of his mother and her family appeared in the name given his second son, Francis Folger Franklin.

According to Franklin's French friend Pierre Cabanis, Franklin praised his mother as an eminently reasonable person, full of common sense. She stressed practicality in daily living and taught the children to bear patiently with minor difficulties. Franklin said that his mother let him exercise and play various sports, knowing that it would be good for his physical health. She approved of his passing the days running around outdoors: in the winter, playing in the snow and ice; in the summer, on the beach and in the water. He would swim several hours at a time, sometimes twice a day. During the swimming season, he felt stronger and better. Though he ate prodigiously, he remained slender. Cabanis also recorded that Abiah found nothing wrong with Franklin's becoming a vegetarian. At first she said that it was a fad and would soon pass, but when he persevered and she was asked where he got the idea, she said it was from reading some mad philosopher. She nevertheless defended his vegetarianism, saying that it taught him self-discipline. She believed that with a strong will one could accomplish anything.[53] In effect, Franklin made his mother a precursor and inspirer of his belief in the American Dream and a world of possibilities for the common man. She was a loving mother and, as we will see, tried to reconcile James and Benjamin when the latter returned to Boston in 1724.

MILK STREET

Josiah probably began to rent the Milk Street house where Franklin was born within a few years of his 1683 emigration. The house occupied the corner of High (later called Marlborough and, after 1789, Washington) Street and Milk Street, on the southern side of Milk Street. Though the house burned in 1810, a gentleman made a pencil drawing of it shortly beforehand. A Philadelphia engraver, William Wood Thackara, copied the sketch in 1820 when visiting Boston.[54] Its last inhabitant described it years later. Its front upon High Street was clapboarded, and the sides and rear were covered with large rough shingles. The structure was about twenty feet wide and, including a later addition, thirty feet deep. It had two stories plus an attic, which presented a pointed gable toward the street. In front, the second story and attic projected perhaps a foot into the street over the first story.

The ground floor contained only one room. It was about twenty feet square, with two windows looking out on High Street. Another window opened onto the passageway, near enough to the corner to give the inhabitants a view of High Street. In addition to these windows there had been others in the days of its early proprietors that had opened upon the easterly side of the house, the seats of which were retained until the destruction of the building. In the center of the southerly side of the room was a large fireplace, situated in a capacious chimney; on its left was a closet, and on the right, a door opening to stairs leading to the rooms above and to the cellar. The cellar had another door, opening onto the street, situated partly in the sidewalk. On the ground floor, the kitchen was in a ten-foot addition to the rear part of the main building (perhaps this refers to the "eight foote square" addition—mentioned below— that Josiah built in 1692). The windows at the back looked out onto a vacant lot of land in the extreme rear of the lot, which served as a yard and a garden plot.

The second story originally contained one chamber. The windows, door, fireplace, and closet were similar in number and position to those in the room beneath it. Josiah, Abiah, and the infants, and probably the girls slept there. The attic was one room, not plastered, with a window in front and one on each side of the roof near the back. The older boys probably slept here. The southwesterly end of the lot contained a well, half of which belonged to the neighbor Jonathan Balston. In 1708, two years after Franklin's birth, Nathaniel Reynolds, the owner of the house, died, leaving his property to his three sons. The Franklins lived there until the beginning of 1712.

In 1689, Josiah Franklin rented a shop about half a block away at the site of 339–41 Washington Street. This was his place of business, where he boiled the fats for candles and soap and where he sold his products. When Josiah had a sign of a blue ball made in 1698, he probably put it over his shop on Cornhill Street rather than his house. The blue ball was a popular symbol with a variety

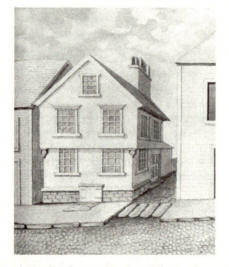

Figure 1. *William Wood Thackara's 1820 drawing of the small rented house at the corner of Milk and Marlborough Streets where Franklin was born, 6 January 1705/6. The same day, he was baptized across the street at the Old South Church. Thackara said he based the drawing upon an earlier pencil sketch made "by a gentleman a short time" before the house was destroyed. The Franklin family lived at the house, which was built in the 1640s, from 1685 to 1711/12. For its location, see #15 in the front end papers. When Franklin was six, the family moved to a house about five blocks north, at the corner of Union and Hanover Streets. For its location, see #5 in the front end papers. Courtesy, Mrs. Robert D. Crompton, Glenside, Pennsylvania. (P 1:4)*

Figure 2. *Nian-Sheng Huang's adaptation of the same drawing, with smaller windows, a style more typical of mid-seventeenth-century structures.*

of tradesmen and had no specific reference to a tallow-chandler. He kept this shop at least until 19 July 1707 and probably until he bought a house in 1712.

At 11 p.m. on 16 September 1690, a fire broke out at the house of John Allen, burning his apprentice to death, and spread to "the House of Lieut. Reynolds, Mr. Bligh, Langden, and a great part of Savil Simson's. The wind being Sou-west the South-Meeting House was preserv'd with very much difficulty, being in a flame in diverse places of it." "The house of Lieut. Reynolds" presumably refers to the Milk Street house that Josiah Franklin was renting. Josiah, Abiah, and their five children all escaped injury. Lieutenant Nicholas Reynolds took out a mortgage for £50 on the Milk Street house in 1691, probably for repairs. The Franklins may have stayed with friends for several months while portions of the house were being rebuilt, evidently again occupying it in 1691. On 27 April 1692, Josiah Franklin received permission "to erect a building of Eight foote square upon the Land belonging to Lt. Nathaniel Reynolds."[55] If, as a later re-port stated, there was a furnace in the room, the Franklins probably used it as their kitchen in the summer so that the main structure could remain relatively cool.

FRANKLIN AND HIS SIBLINGS

When Benjamin Franklin was born, he had eleven living brothers and sisters. Five were Josiah Franklin's children by Ann (Child) Franklin: Elizabeth (b. Ecton on 2 March 1677/8); Samuel (b. Banbury on 16 May 1681); Hannah (b. Banbury on 2 May 1683); Josiah (b. Boston on 23 August 1685); and Anne (b. Boston on 5 January 1686/7). Six were children by Josiah's second wife, Abiah, all born in Boston: John (7 December 1690); Peter (2 November 1692); Mary (26 September 1694); James (4 February 1696/7); Sarah (9 July 1699); and Thomas (7 December 1703). After Franklin's birth in 1706, two more sisters, Lydia (8 August 1708) and Jane (27 March 1712), followed. By the time Benjamin was born, all the children from Josiah's first marriage except perhaps the youngest, Anne, were off on their own. The eldest, Elizabeth, was twenty-eight, and the next year married her first husband. Samuel, twenty-five, had married Elizabeth Tyng on 16 May 1705. Hannah, twenty-three, the last child born in England, had married Joseph Eddy around 1699. Josiah, Jr., twenty-one, the first Boston child, had run away to be a sailor; this prodigal son reappeared in Boston once (about 1716) to be feted and then disappeared forevermore. Anne, eighteen, the young-est child of the first marriage, either still lived at Milk Street or worked and boarded elsewhere. She married William Harris at age twenty-five on 10 July 1712.

With six older siblings in the house (John worked as a tallow-chandler with his father, but Peter could have been living elsewhere), the Franklin home must have been bustling with activity. Alas, on one occasion, nearly four years before Benjamin was born, the activity was confusing, and sixteen-month-old Ebenezer Franklin was overlooked for a few minutes. Samuel Sewall recorded that on 5

February 1702/3, Benjamin's older brother Ebenezer "drown'd in a Tub of Suds." Two-year-old Thomas Franklin died on 17 August 1706, when Benjamin was just over seven months old.

Benjamin Franklin was born on Sunday, 6 January 1705/6, in his parents' rented home on Milk Street. The same day, the Reverend Samuel Willard baptized him in the Old South Church, which was just across the street. One anecdote, first reported in 1801, recorded that his mother went to church in the morning, had the child around noon, and had him baptized in the afternoon; "the Doctor used humorously to say that he attended meeting the whole of that day."[56] My guess would be that he was born in the early morning and that his father took him to church to be baptized in the afternoon after the usual Sunday services. Since there is no report to the contrary, he was probably a large, healthy baby, with brown hair and hazel eyes.

TWO

Child to Adolescent

From a Child I was fond of Reading, and all the little Money that came into my Hands was ever laid out in Books. Pleas'd with the Pilgrim's Progress, my first Collection was of John Bunyan's Works, in separate little Volumes. I afterwards sold them to enable me to buy R. Burton's Historical Collections; they were small Chapmen's Books and cheap, 40 or 50 in all.—A 10–11

HEARING FROM HIS BROTHER JOSIAH that his namesake, four-year-old Benjamin, wanted to become a soldier, Uncle Benjamin wrote to him, advising against the warrior's life:

> Sent to My Name upon a Report of his Inclination
> to Martial affaires 7 July 1710
> Beleeve me Ben. It is a Dangerous Trade—
> The Sword has Many Marr'd as well as Made.
> By it doe many fall, Not Many Rise;
> Makes Many poor, few Rich and fewer Wise;
> Fills Towns with Ruin, fields with blood beside;
> 'Tis Sloth's Maintainer, And the Shield of pride;
> Fair Citties Rich to Day, in plenty flow,
> War fills with want, Tomorrow, and with woe.
> Ruin'd Estates, The Nurse of Vice, broke limbs and scarts
> Are the Effects of Desolating Warrs. (1:4–5)

Although it is doubtful that Uncle Benjamin's verse changed Franklin's mind, we hear no more of his military ambitions. He may possibly have recalled the poem when he wrote in *Poor Richard* for 1745, "Wars bring scars."

FIRE

When Franklin organized the first private fire company in Philadelphia (1736), he began by writing a series of newspaper articles that revealed a knowledge of Boston's fire fighting. Boston's efforts had been galvanized by a great conflagration in 1711, but Josiah's home on Milk Street was spared (it had been damaged by a fire in 1690). News of the 1711 fire occasioned Uncle Benjamin's acrostic, where the first word of each stanza began with a letter that, in fourteen stanzas,

spelled JOSIAH FRANKLIN. The third, fourth, fifth, and sixth stanzas, beginning with "S," "I," "A," and "H" read:

> Sons, Daughters, Brothers, Sisters, all,
>> Joyne With us in this Great Address;
> And on one kind preserver call,
>> Who saved us when in Great Distress.
>
> In unrelenting Flames for sin,
>> God's much provoked Anger Rose,
> But Tender Mercy stept between
>> Us, and his Justice did oppose.
>
> Ah! hateful. Thy promis'd sweet,
>> To Colaquintida[1] is Turn'd;
> Thy sad Effects in every street,
>> We see to heaps of Rubbish Burn'd.
>
> Had not the Lord, Now may we say,
>> Had not the Lord Great pitty shown;
> Like Sodom on that Dreadful Day,
>> We'ed been Destroyed and overthrown.[2]

After the fire, Boston underwent a period of construction, building a new town
hall, a new church, and an even greater Long Wharf, which maintained Boston's
shipping superiority in the early eighteenth century.

UNION STREET

On 25 January 1711/2, shortly after Franklin turned six, the family left their
rented home on Milk Street and bought a property at the southwest corner of
Union and Hanover streets. The price was £320, and Josiah took out a mortgage
of £250 from Simeon Stoddard (1651–1730), a wealthy merchant and a fellow
member of the Old South Church. The property, with 38 feet on Union Street
and 93 feet on Hanover Street, was over 3,500 square feet, nearly six times as
large as the Milk Street lot of 600 square feet. Josiah Franklin gave up the shop
he was renting on High Street and moved his sign, the blue ball, to the corner
structure in Union Street. We know that on 22 June 1713, the blue ball distinguished the Union Street house.

The property had four structures on it, one facing Union Street and the
other three facing Hanover. The Franklins occupied the Union Street house and
rented out rooms in it. In his will, dated 20 October 1744, Josiah gave "to my
loving wife Abiah Franklin all the income or rents of my whole estate and goods,
and the use of the two rooms we now live in, allowing the lodgers to be in as it
is used, she allowing out of it the interest that will be due to my creditors while
she lives." In 1752 the total value of the four lots and structures was appraised
at £253.6.8.[3]

When Josiah's heirs decided to sell the property in 1752, they advertised an auction on Wednesday, 1 November, of "sundry sorts of household Furniture, consisting of Beds, Bedding, Chairs, Tables, Looking-Glasses, a Desk, Pewter and Brass, a *Philadelphia* Fire Place, some wearing Apparel, and sundry other Articles." On 6 November the *Boston Evening Post* advertised the property, but it did not sell. The following year, on 23 July 1753, while Franklin was visiting Boston, the *Boston Evening Post* advertised it as four separate properties: "Four Lots of Ground, with the Buildings thereon, fronting on Hanover and Union-Street, at the Blue Ball, viz. one Lot (No. 1) of Seventeen Feet four Inches Front on Hanover-Street, and twenty-five Feet deep. One ditto (No. 2) Twenty-one and an half Feet Front on said Street, and Twenty-five and an half Feet deep. (No. 3.) Twenty-seven Feet Front on said Street, and Thirty Feet deep. (No. 4.) a Corner Lot, Twenty-eight Feet Front on Hanover Street, and Thirty-eight Feet front on Union Street, very well situated for Tradesmen or Shopkeepers, being in the Heart of the Town, and the Buildings conveniently divided as above, having originally been different Tenements." Franklin's youngest sister, Jane (Franklin) Mecom, in a letter of 16 August 1787, recalled that though their house was "a Lowly Dwelling," they were happy there. She added, "Blessed be God that you & I by your means have the Addition of more Pleasing appearance in our Dwellings."

THE WHISTLE: A PARABLE

Late in his life, when replying to a letter from Madame Brillon, Franklin recalled a boyhood anecdote of approximately 1713. Franklin's 10 November 1779 letter said that he was pleased with her thought that "we should draw all the Good we can from this World. In my Opinion we might all draw more Good, from it than we do, & suffer less Evil, if we would but take care *not to give too much for our Whistles*." He explained:

> When I was a Child of seven Years old, my Friends on a Holiday fill'd my little Pocket with Halfpence. I went directly to a Shop where they sold Toys for Children; and being charm'd with the Sound of a Whistle that I met by the way, in the hands of another Boy, I voluntarily offer'd and gave all my Money for it. When I came home, whistling all over the House, much pleas'd with my Whistle, but disturbing all the Family, my Brothers, Sisters & Cousins, understanding the Bargain I had made, told me I had given four times as much for it as it was worth, put me in mind what good Things I might have bought with the rest of the Money, & laught at me so much for my Folly that I cry'd with Vexation; and the Reflection gave me more Chagrin than the Whistle gave me Pleasure.
> (31:73–74)

Franklin said that the lesson, *Do not give too much for the Whistle*, was "afterwards of use to me," and he gave a number of applications of his text. The first was to economize: "often when I was tempted to buy some unnecessary thing,

I said to my self, *Do not give too much for the Whistle*; and I sav'd my Money."
He applied the text successively to "Court Favour," to "Popularity" (and politics), to the accumulation of wealth, to hedonism or the pursuit of pleasure, to
vanity or the desire for the appearance of status and success, and to the gratification of sex. He drew the moral: "In short, I conceiv'd that great Part of the
Miseries of Mankind, were brought upon them by the false Estimates they had
made of the Value of Things, and by their *giving too much for the Whistle*."
The mature Franklin found the conclusion rather smug and, characteristically,
undercut himself. He added: "Yet I ought to have Charity for these unhappy
People, when I consider that with all this Wisdom of which I am boasting, there
are certain things in the World so tempting; for Example the Apples of King
John, which happily are not to be bought, for if they were put to sale by Auction,
I might very easily be led to ruin my self in the Purchase, and find that I had
once more *given too much for the Whistle*" (31:74–75). Franklin was thinking of
Apple-john, sometimes called the apples of King John, which mature relatively
late (about St. John's Day, 27 December) and supposedly come to perfection
about two years later "when shriveled and withered" (*OED*). They were reputed
to be a general curative for the ailments of old age—and an aphrodisiac. Thus,
Franklin concluded his letter to Madame Brillon by joking about his age and
his all-too-human-dissatisfaction with his health and physical condition—and
by flirting.

When Franklin told the same anecdote to Pierre Cabanis in the early 1780s,
he made his mother the bastion of good sense. She, rather than his older siblings, told him that he had paid extravagantly for the whistle and advised him
on the relative value of ambitions and desires. In that version, his mother drew
out the moral and made him aware that one should always consider in advance
the implications of the cost of anything. To show that neither his mother nor
he had merely the monetary value in mind, he told Cabanis that he had warned
his son William Franklin, when he solicited the governorship of a colony from
the Court of St. James, not to pay too much for the whistle. Franklin said he
advocated that William become an artisan because the man who lives by his
labor remains free, but William was infatuated with the title "Excellency" and
ashamed to imitate his father. The advice was apocryphal, at least as applied to
his son William. Franklin did give such advice to his son-in-law, Richard Bache
(29 January 1772), but Franklin raised William to be a lawyer, not an artisan,
and may have helped secure the position of governor of New Jersey for him. If
so, Franklin regretted it by the time that he told Cabanis the anecdote.[4]

Boyhood Recollections

At various times during his life, Franklin recorded scenes from his boyhood.
Three remembrances came while writing about natural history. When he mentioned that "water is specifically 850 Times heavier than Air," Franklin cited a
common childhood amusement—blowing bubbles: "Was ever a visible Bubble

seen to rise in Air? I have made many when a Boy with Soap Suds and a Tobacco Pipe; but they all descended when loose from the Pipe, tho' slowly, the Air impeding their Motion. They may indeed be forc'd up by a Wind from below, but do not rise of themselves, tho' filled with warm Breath" (4:473).

When suggesting that Philadelphia could use a second Anglican church, Franklin recalled another boyhood experience—keeping pigeons. "I had for several years nailed against the wall of my house a pigeon box that would hold six pair; and though they bred as fast as my neighbours' pigeons, I never had more than six pair, the old and strong driving out the young and weak, and obliging them to seek new habitations. At length I put up an additional box with apartments for entertaining twelve pair more; and it was soon filled with inhabitants, by the overflowing of my first box and of others in the neighbourhood" (4:42). Incidently, the anecdote is more proof that Josiah and Abiah indulged their children.

Discussing fossils with the Swedish naturalist Peter Kalm on 11 November 1748, Franklin recalled seeing two moose as a boy in Boston. He assured Kalm that the large bone fossils occasionally discovered in Ireland were not moose. Kalm recorded that Franklin told him, "they were not of such a size as they must have been, if the horns found in Ireland were to fit them. The two animals which he saw, were brought to Boston in order to be sent to England to Queen Anne. Anyone who wanted to see them had to pay two-pence. A merchant paid for a number of school-boys who wanted to see them, among whom was Franklin. The height of the animal up to the back was that of a pretty tall horse, but the head and its horns were still higher" (4:57). Since Queen Anne died in 1714, Franklin must have seen the moose before he was nine years old.

Several recollections had to do with his father and his home life. In a conversation with Dr. Benjamin Rush on 12 June 1789, Franklin praised the value "of learning Geography in early life, & said that he had taught himself it, when a boy, while his father was at prayers, by looking over four large maps which hung in his father's parlour."[5] The maps reveal Josiah Franklin's intellectual curiosity and striving, for maps were expensive, and comparatively few people at the time knew much geography. For example, Josiah's later minister, the Reverend Thomas Prince (who graduated from Harvard in 1707), recorded that he first saw a world globe as a sophomore: "Accidentally meeting with a Terrestrial Globe in the next chamber where a Classmate of mine lived with a Bachelor, my own Curiosity exalted me to take all opportunities when the Senior was gone out, to go in and view this entertaining and instructive Image of the Earth."[6]

Franklin's anecdote about his father's maps testifies to his own intellectual curiosity and his impatience with his father's prayers. Brissot de Warville, a Frenchman who visited America in 1788, recorded an anecdote of similar import that William Temple Franklin revised and included in his 1816 edition of Franklin's writings. Josiah preceded all his meals with long prayers and sometimes even said grace over each dish; Franklin was restless and bored during the prayers. At the beginning of a winter when he was about seven and his father was salting provisions, Franklin supposedly said, "You ought to ask a blessing, once for all, upon the whole cask of provisions, *as it would be a wonderful saving of time!*"[7] If Franklin had the thought, I doubt he told it to his father.

Franklin said of his father in the *Autobiography*: "At his Table he lik'd to have as often as he could, some sensible Friend or Neighbor, to converse with, and always took care to start some ingenious or useful Topic for Discourse, which might tend to improve the Minds of his Children." Franklin maintained that the conversation made him inattentive to the excellence of the meals: By focusing on "what was good, just, and prudent in the Conduct of Life; and by taking "little or no Notice . . . of what related to the Victuals on the Table, whether it was well or ill drest, in or out of season, of good or bad flavour, preferable or inferior to this or that other thing of the kind . . . I was bro't up in such a perfect Inattention to those Matters as to be quite Indifferent what kind of Food was set before me; and so unobservant of it, that to this Day, if I am ask'd I can scarce tell, a few Hours after Dinner, what I din'd upon" (A 8–9).

He added in the *Autobiography* that his ability to eat different foods "has been a Convenience to me in travelling, where my Companions have been sometimes very unhappy for want of a suitable Gratification of their more delicate because better instructed Tastes and Appetites" (A 9). I wonder. Could his companions sometimes have been unhappy because they could not have their beef and potatoes? Was he, perhaps, the real gourmet—happy with the native foods and regional cooking? Were his friends, like so many people, looking for the eighteenth-century equivalent of a McDonald's in France? Did they want only what the usual English pub offered? It would have been typical of Franklin's common-man postures in the *Autobiography* to pretend that he was not a gourmet—especially if he were.

Franklin probably exaggerated his supposed inattention to food. After he returned from London in 1762, where he had served for five years as Pennsylvania's agent, enemies accused him of padding the expenses. Though the accusation was false, it made Franklin want to appear frugal. He had been thrifty as a young man in Philadelphia, but his accounts and other evidence—including his portraits—from the middle of his life to the end testify that he enjoyed fine wine and food. He listed "Temperance" as the first of his thirteen "virtues" in the *Autobiography* because he recognized that overeating was among his faults. Nor can one believe that he was insensitive to his hosts and did not compliment them when they prepared fine meals. Further, he sometimes recalled, years later, details of what he ate. In 1771 he remembered that on his way to Philadelphia in 1723, an old lady in Burlington, New Jersey, gave him a "Dinner of Ox Cheek" (A 23).

Another childhood anecdote contradicts the above statements from the *Autobiography* and says that he overindulged. He told James Madison that as "a young man he was much subject to fits of indigestion brought on by indulgence at the table. On complaining of it to a friend, he recommended as a remedy a few drops of oil of wormwood, whenever that happened; and that he should carry a little viol of it about him. On trial he said he found the remedy to answer, and then said he, having my absolution in my pocket, I went on sinning more freely than ever." I suspect he made up the anecdote, for it illustrated his speculation that "the hope of impunity" was an encouragement to sin. Therefore he would be glad "to see an experiment made of a religion that admitted of no pardon for transgressions."[8]

The Wharf Prank

A major anecdote that Franklin recounted in the *Autobiography* probably occurred one summer around 1716. He said that he was "generally a Leader among the Boys, and sometimes led them into Scrapes, of which I will mention one Instance, as it shows an early projecting public Spirit, tho' not then justly conducted." Franklin's portrayal of himself as a public-spirited projector is a key persona in the *Autobiography*. He portrayed himself as a version of that eighteenth-century ideal, the friend of humankind, *amicus humani generis*, an ideal that he increasingly tried to emulate throughout in his life. Here, early in the *Autobiography*, he anticipated that characterization. The anticipatory technique was common in the spiritual autobiographies, where the "Saint" wished to prove that though he was an unworthy instrument, God predestined him for salvation from infancy and gave signs of his future saintly status. Franklin knew John Bunyan's *Grace Abounding to the Chief of Sinners* and similar spiritual autobiographies where the anticipatory technique was used. Like Franklin, his slightly older contemporary Jonathan Edwards used the anticipatory technique in his "Personal Narrative."

Just as most Calvinist spiritual autobiographies narrate the early sins of the reborn person, so Franklin's story contains an early error. Thus it is more similar to the religious tradition than to the life stories of most great men, which tended to be hagiographic. Nevertheless, the story tells of a child's attempt to undertake a public-spirited effort, a characteristic of the friend of humankind

> There was a Salt Marsh that bounded part of the Mill Pond, on the Edge of which at Highwater, we us'd to stand to fish for Minews. By much Trampling, we had made it a mere Quagmire. My Proposal was to build a Wharf there fit for us to stand upon, and I show'd my Comrades a large Heap of Stones which were intended for a new House near the Marsh, and which would very well suit our Purpose. Accordingly in the Evening when the Workmen were gone, I assembled a Number of my Playfellows, and working with them diligently like so many Emmets, sometimes two or three to a Stone, we brought them all away and built our little Wharf. The next Morning the Workmen were surpriz'd at Missing the Stones; which were found in our Wharff; Enquiry was made after

the Removers; we were discovered and complain'd of; several of us were corrected by our Fathers; and tho' I pleaded the Usefulness of the Work, mine
convinc'd me that nothing was useful which was not honest." (A 7–8)

If the fathers "corrected" the other boys, surely the ringleader's father corrected
him. Perhaps he was beaten before being lectured.

Nathaniel Hawthorne retold the anecdote in a biographical sketch of Franklin written for children. Hawthorne, an acute student of early New England
religion and culture, changed Franklin's story. Franklin wrote that his father
convinced him that "nothing was useful which was not honest." But is that
what a good New England Puritan like Josiah would have said? Franklin's moral
omits religion and the absolute. When Hawthorne retold the anecdote, he had
Josiah Franklin say: "No act . . . can possibly be for the benefit of the public
generally, which involves injustice to any individual. . . . Can we suppose that
our all-wise and just Creator would have so ordered the affairs of the world that
a wrong act should be the true method of attaining a right end? It is impious to
think so. . . . Remember, that, whenever we vary from the highest rule of right,
just so far we do an injury to the world. It may seem otherwise for the moment;
but, both in Time and in Eternity, it will be found so."[9] Franklin avoided such
religious language and appeals to an absolute. Hawthorne, like many nine-
teenth- and twentieth-century persons, lived in a theological world closer to the
seventeenth century than the mental world Franklin inhabited. Franklin left
God and absolutes out of the anecdote and out of his philosophy. His moral
was practical and pragmatic: "Nothing was useful which was not honest." Most
people who know both versions of the anecdote assume that Franklin's is correct
and that Hawthorne made his up. It seems to me more likely that Franklin
created his moral. Hawthorne's fiction was, I suspect, closer to what Franklin's
pious Puritan father would have said (appealing to God's order and to the measure of eternity) than Franklin's moral.

ADOLESCENT INVENTIONS

When Franklin told of his London swimming feats in the *Autobiography*, he
added: "I had from a Child been ever delighted with this Exercise, had studied
and practic'd all Thevenot's Motions and Positions, added some of my own,
aiming at the graceful and easy, as well as the Useful" (A 49). He probably read
Thevenot's *Art of Swimming* (1699) after he became an apprentice to his brother
James, when he knew the booksellers' apprentices well and could borrow books
from them. The studious young Franklin was also ingenious. After studying
Thevenot, he designed swim fins or flippers for both his hands and feet: "When
I was a boy, I made two oval palettes, each about ten inches long, and six broad,
with a hole for the thumb, in order to retain it fast in the palm of my hand.
They much resembled a painter's palettes. In swimming I pushed the edges of
these forward, and I struck the water with their flat surfaces as I drew them

back. I remember I swam faster by means of these pallets, but they fatigued my wrists." Unfortunately, no suitable material for fins existed in Franklin's day. If he had had access to modern supple materials like rubber or plastic, he might have been successful. "I also fitted to the soles of my feet a kind of sandals; but I was not satisfied with them, because I observed that the stroke is partly given by the inside of the feet and the ancles and not entirely with the soles of the feet."[10]

The creative youth made his first kite experiment when he was about twelve years old. Long before his famous and simple electrical experiment in 1752, he attempted kite floating: "I amused myself one day with flying a paper kite; and approaching the bank of a pond, which was near a mile broad, I tied the string to a stake, and the kite ascended to a very considerable height above the pond, while I was swimming. In a little time, being desirous of amusing myself with my kite, and enjoying at the same time the pleasure of swimming, I returned; and, loosing from the stake the string with the little stick which was fastened to it, went again into the water, where I found, that, lying on my back and holding the stick in my hands, I was drawn along the surface of the water in a very agreeable manner."

Had Franklin not brought up the practical matter, no one would have thought of leaving his clothes behind. In the eighteenth century, there were no swimming suits; one wore clothing until one went into the water, usually in underclothes or naked. "Having then engaged another boy to carry my clothes round the pond, to a place which I pointed out to him on the other side, I began to cross the pond with my kite, which carried me quite over without the least fatigue, and with the greatest pleasure imaginable. I was only obliged occasionally to halt a little in my course, and resist its progress, when it appeared that, by following too quick, I lowered the kite too much; by doing which occasionally I made it rise again. I have never since that time practiced this singular mode of swimming, though I think it not impossible to cross in this manner from Dover to Calais." Having finished the kite story with a flight of fancy, he wryly added, "The packet-boat, however, is still preferable."[11]

JOSIAH

Franklin's curious and ingenious traits partially mirrored those of his father, Josiah. The Swedish scientist Peter Kalm recorded an anecdote Franklin told about his father in 1748. Near Boston there were two rivers, "in one of which they caught great numbers of herring, and in the other not one." Yet the rivers flowed into the ocean close to one another. When the herring came in the spring, they always swam up one river but never the other. "This circumstance led Mr. Franklin's father, who had settled between the two rivers, to try whether it was not possible to make the herrings also live in the other river. For that purpose he put out his nets, as they were coming up for spawning, and he carried it across the land to the other river. It was hatched, and the consequence was that every year afterwards they caught more herring in that river, and this is still the case" (4:55–56).

An unnoticed version of this anecdote appeared in the Reverend Joseph Morgan's essay on fish ladders and other ways of making fish more plentiful in rivers and streams. Morgan was a Presbyterian minister whom Franklin knew as a child in Boston and who later moved to New Jersey. He corresponded with Franklin and sent him various essays for the *Pennsylvania Gazette*. Morgan's echo of Franklin's story appeared in the *Gazette* on 8 June 1732: "There is a Pond and Brook from it, nigh *Plymouth* in *N.E.* (as I am informed) where never *Herring* had been seen, while other Brooks were full; but a certain Man carried a Tub full of Water with a Number of them newly taken, and emptied 'em into that Pond; and ever after they went up that Brook." That the experiment was in character with Franklin's father may be deduced from two of his few extant letters. In 1705 Josiah asked his brother-in-law Peter Folger, Jr., to send him some rushes from Nantucket so that he could attempt to make rush candles.[12] Folger complied and Josiah experimented with them. In 1706 Josiah thanked him and in partial return gave him a book against atheism.

Uncle Benjamin

When Uncle Benjamin Franklin arrived in Boston on Sunday, 9 October 1715, Franklin was nine. Recalling his arrival in an autobiographical poem, Uncle Benjamin Franklin reported:

> And there a Kind, kind Brother found,
> Bless't with a Wife and Num'rous Race.
>
> Four years they did me kindly Treat
> But noe Imployment did present,
> Which was to me a burden great
> And could not be to their content.

Writing his sister Jane on 17 July 1771, Franklin remembered: "Our Father, who was a very wise man, us'd to say, nothing was more common than for those who lov'd one another at a distance, to find many Causes of Dislike when they came together; and therefore he did not approve of Visits to Relations in distant Places, which could not well be short enough for them to part good Friends. I saw a Proof of it, in the Disgusts between him and his Brother Benjamin; and tho' I was a Child still remember how affectionate their Correspondence was while they were separated, and the Disputes and Misunderstandings they had when they came to live some time together in the same House."

On one occasion, "an Entertainment was made in our House on Occasion of the Return of our Brother Josiah, who had been absent in the East Indies, and unheard of for nine Years" (9:18). Thirteen Franklin children gathered around the table. Pious Uncle Benjamin had composed an imitation of the

"Third part of the 107 psalm" for the reunion and sang it to welcome home his nephew. The first and last stanzas are:

> Those Who in Forreign Lands converse
> By Ships for Traffick and Commerce,
> Behold great Wonders in the Deep
> Which God's prescribed bounds doe keep.
>
> . . . .
>
> Adore this God who did us Save
> From the much feared Watery Grave
> And softly Set thee on thy Land
> O Bless his kind and pow'rfull Hand.

But Franklin's brother Josiah the sailor was, like his younger brothers James and Benjamin, an iconoclast in puritan Boston. The thirty-year-old sailor, "being unaffected with Gods Great Goodness in his many preservations and Deliverances," received the psalm "coldly."[13] Evidently the seldom-seen Josiah Franklin, Jr., was unlike his puritan parents and uncle. The sailor dropped from sight after appearing in Boston around 1715, presumably to perish at sea. In a list of his siblings made sometime after 1759, Franklin recorded that Josiah, Jr., "Went to Sea, never heard of" (8:454).

MINISTERS

As a group, the ministers, not the movie stars, news anchors, or sports figures, were the most famous persons in colonial Boston. Naturally Franklin knew and remembered them. Since he had to attend church while living at home, he must frequently have heard the regular ministers at the Old South Church: He would not have recalled Samuel Willard (1639/40–1707), who baptized him, but he no doubt remembered the others: Ebenezer Pemberton (1672–1718), who became an Old South minister on 28 August 1700 and died when Franklin was twelve; Joseph Sewall (1688–1769), who joined the Old South as a pastor on 16 September 1713; and Thomas Prince (1687–1758), who became an Old South minister on 1 August 1718, about the time Franklin was apprenticed to James Franklin. Of course, the best-known Boston ministers of Franklin's youth were Increase and Cotton Mather. Franklin recalled them on 7 July 1773: "The Father, Increase, I once when a Boy, heard preach at the Old South, for Mr. Pemberton; and remember his mentioning the Death of 'that wicked old Persecutor of God's People, Lewis XIV' of which News had just been received; but which proved premature." The historian Ralph Ketcham identified the date that Franklin heard Increase Mather as Sunday, 2 October 1715. Though I have not found evidence to corroborate it, the date makes good sense. Boston rumors at the time reported the death of the king of France, and Sewall recorded on 29 September that the Reverend Ebenezer Pemberton "was very sick of the Piles." Pemberton probably had some other minister replace him that Sunday.

Since Louis XIV was (after the devil, the pope, and the Stuart Pretender) the chief bogeyman of early eighteenth-century Puritan New England, it is not surprising that the nine-year-old Franklin would have remembered a sermon delivered on his death. The French king was infamous as a persecutor of Protestants, as the head of an enemy nation, and as the major supporter of the Pretender. (In 1715 and again in 1745, the Jacobites, i.e., supporters of James II and his descendants as the rightful king of Great Britain, attempted to invade England and seize the throne.) Louis XIV's death was regarded as a victory for Protestantism and the British Empire. The 3 October 1715 *Boston News-Letter* celebrated the French king's death. The occasion was among the most important in foreign affairs during Franklin's youth, and Increase Mather was the most famous New England minister. Franklin continued his reminiscence concerning Increase Mather, describing him as "apparently very old and feeble," sitting in an easy chair in his home. Cotton Mather, however, Franklin recalled "in the Vigour of his Preaching and Usefulness." Franklin knew his valuable role in the smallpox inoculation controversy and his diatribes against the *New-England Courant*, as we will see below. Since he was writing Cotton Mather's son Samuel when mentioning the two Mathers, he did not refer to the other famous New England ministers, most of whom opposed the Mathers. But Franklin certainly knew the Reverend John Wise, whom James Franklin published, and the Reverend Benjamin Colman, whose Brattle Street Church was close to the Union Street house.

LEARNING TO READ

In the *Autobiography* Franklin mentioned that he learned to read when he was very young: it "must have been very early, as I do not remember when I could not read" (A 6). His sister reported that Franklin read the Bible at five years of age. Franklin probably learned his ABCs from the *New England Primer*. It may have been an old, worn-out copy handed down from an older sibling, for the closest extant editions published before 1710 appeared in 1691.[14] Copies of the *New England Primer* that survive, however, are usually unique, so more editions must have been printed than we know. Next to the letter "A," the *New England Primer* read, "In Adam's Fall, We sinned all." If, on the other hand, Franklin learned from an English primer, it may have been one reprinted by the Old South Church's Bartholomew Green: *The Young Secretary's Guide* (1708). He evidently could read well by the time Green printed Nathaniel Strong, *England's Perfect Schoolmaster* (1711). The most popular catechism in New England was the Westminister *Shorter Catechism*, which had eight known reprintings in New England before 1714. James Noyes had the second most popular one, with four editions (1641, 1661, 1676, and 1694). And John Cotton's *Spiritual Milk for Babes* had three editions (1656, 1668, and 1690). But these last two books may have been difficult to obtain when Franklin was three and four (1709 and 1710).

Books

Franklin told of his early intellectual development in the *Autobiography*: "From a Child I was fond of Reading, and all the little Money that came into my Hands was ever laid out in Books. Pleas'd with the Pilgrim's Progress, my first Collection was of John Bunyan's Works, in separate little Volumes. I afterwards sold them to enable me to buy R. Burton's Historical Collections; they were small Chapmen's Books and cheap, 40 or 50 in all" (A 10–11).[15] *Burton's Books* constituted a kind of encyclopedia or *World Book* for adolescents, featuring popular entertainments and superstitions in addition to facts. Written by Nathaniel Crouch, the series contained titles such as *Admirable Curiosities, Rarities, and Wonders in England; The English Empire in America; England's Monarchs; The English Hero, or, Sir Francis Drake Revived; The General History of Earthquakes; The Kingdom of Darkness: or, The History of Daemons, Specters, Witches, Apparitions; The History of the Nine Worthies of the World;* and *The Surprising Miracles of Nature and Art.* These were among the most popular chapbooks of the times, praised as suitable reading for adolescents by contemporaries of Franklin as diverse as the gadfly John Dunton and the ponderous Dr. Samuel Johnson.[16]

Josiah Franklin's "little Library consisted chiefly of Books in polemic Divinity, most of which I read, and have since often regretted, that at a time when I had such a Thirst for Knowledge, more proper Books had not fallen in my Way, since it was now resolv'd I should not be a Clergyman." Josiah had, however, three books that Franklin valued: Plutarch's *Parallel Lives*, Daniel Defoe's *Essay Upon Projects*, and Cotton Mather's *Essays to Do Good*. He "read abundantly" in Plutarch, "and I still think that time spent to great Advantage" (A 11). According to Franklin's friend Pierre Cabanis, "Nothing had ever made on him a stronger impression than the simple and grand manner and the philosophy at the same time wise and generous" of Plutarch.[17] Plutarch's *Parallel Lives* was one of the many biographical studies that made the life of the protagonists seem representational of a type. Thus the great Greek orator Demosthenes was paralleled with the Roman master of orations, Cicero, and the separate biographies concluded by comparing the two. The characters in Plutarch's *Lives* were something like the popular "characters" of the seventeenth and eighteenth centuries.[18] Franklin's presenting himself as a representative "American" and *amicus humani generis* in the *Autobiography* probably owes something to Plutarch and to the characters he read about as a boy.

Franklin recalled: "There was also a Book of Defoe's called an Essay on Projects and another of Dr. Mather's call'd Essays to do Good, which perhaps gave me a Turn of Thinking that had an Influence on some of the principal future Events of my Life" (A 11). As we will see, Franklin twice quoted Defoe's *Essay Upon Projects* (1697) at length in his Silence Dogood essay series. In addition to *An Essay Upon Projects*, Franklin read and later alluded to a number of Defoe's works and cited *Robinson Crusoe* in the *Autobiography*. Defoe's belief

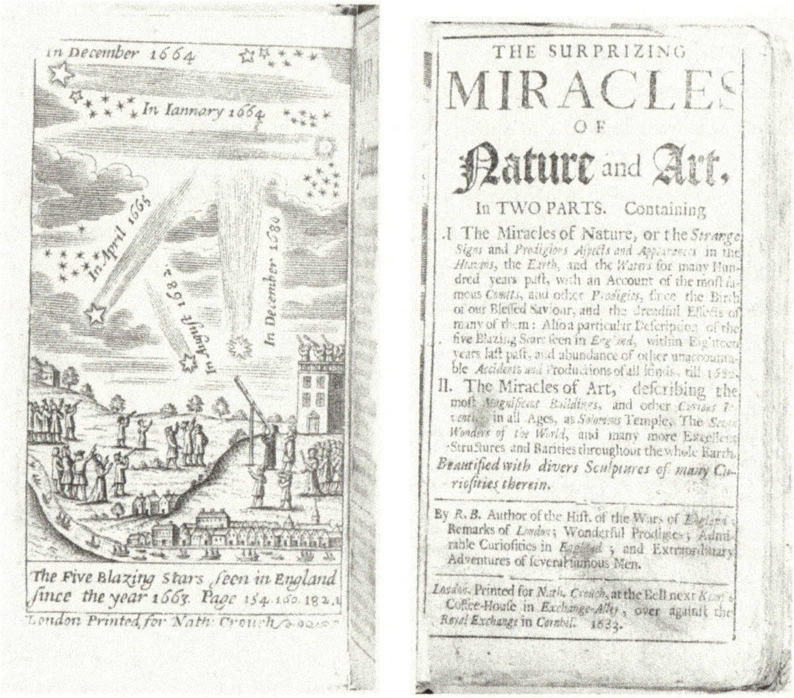

*Figure 3. About age eleven, Franklin bought a series of chapbooks by Nathaniel Crouch,
including* The Surprising Miracles of Nature and Art *(1683). When Franklin told of his
love of reading as a boy, he said, "all the little Money that came into my Hands was ever
laid out in Books. Pleas'd with the Pilgrim's Progress, my first Collection was of John
Bunyan's Works, in separate little Volumes. I afterwards sold them to enable me to buy
R. Burton's Historical Collections; they were small Chapmen's Books and cheap, 40 or 50
in all." The popular, cheap chapbooks contained knowledge, popular entertainments, and
superstitions. Writing an appreciation of Crouch's chapbooks in the* Annual Report of
the Library Company of Philadelphia *for 1966, Edwin Wolf 2nd thought that* The Surprising Miracles, *a miscellaneous collection of the strange and wonderful, like Ripley's*
Believe It or Not, *was the "most fascinating" of Crouch's chapbooks.*

*The illustration refers to four comets seen in England in the mid and late seventeenth
century. Though comets had always been regarded as signals of future important events
(usually catastrophes), the development of the telescope made the study of comets in the
late seventeenth century fashionable. The frontispiece dramatically illustrates the excitement and the scientific interest shown in the comets, while the text itself continues the old
tradition of suggesting portentous events being forecast by the comets. The two top dates
both refer to the same comet, which was visible in Europe from the fall of 1664 to the
spring of 1665. The last comet mentioned, 1682, was the one that caused Edmond Halley
to theorize that it was the same comet returning every seventy-six years. Samuel Pepys
recorded the intense interest generated by the 1664–65 comet on 15 December 1664 and
added on 17 December that the King and Queen had stayed up to see it. Courtesy, Library
Company of Philadelphia.*

that women were as intellectually able as men was among the many opinions that Franklin took from him—and from others. Franklin may have admired Defoe's prose style more than that of Addison and Steele or other English authors except Jonathan Swift, though I believe the writers for James Franklin's *New-England Courant* were more influential on him.

Like Defoe's *Essay Upon Projects*, Mather's *Bonifacius* (running title, "Essays to Do Good," 1710) may also have inspired a number of Franklin's lifelong attitudes, particularly his aspiration to be known as a doer of good. Mather wrote in *Bonifacius* that the "noblest question in the world" was, "What good may I do in the world?" Franklin echoed that belief numerous times. In *Poor Richard* for December 1737 he wrote: "The noblest question in the world is what good may I do in it?" Franklin seems to have been more willing to acknowledge Cotton Mather's influence as he himself grew older. Franklin introduced the reference to Mather and his *Essays to Do Good* not when he first wrote part 1 of the *Autobiography* in 1771 but when he revised it in 1788. In addition, the different countries in which Franklin wrote the parts of the *Autobiography* subtly influenced his ideas about audience. He wrote part 1 in England and seems especially conscious of an English audience (and of English influences on him) when he composed it. He wrote part 2 in France in 1784 and part 3 (and the brief part 4) in America in 1788 (and in 1790).

School

Franklin's formal education began in 1714: "My elder Brothers were all put Apprentices to different Trades. I was put to the Grammar School at Eight Years of Age, my Father intending to devote me as the Tithe of his Sons to the Service of the Church." When the lad entered the South Grammar School (now Boston Latin) in the fall of 1714, he studied with Nathaniel Williams, master, and Edward Wigglesworth, usher, both members of the Old South Church. Franklin explained his father's decision: "My early Readiness in learning to read . . . and the Opinion of all his Friends that I should certainly make a good Scholar, encourag'd him in this Purpose." Franklin added, "My Uncle Benjamin too approv'd of it, and propos'd to give me all his Shorthand Volumes of Sermons, I supposed as a Stock to set up with, if I would learn his Character" (A 6). Since Uncle Benjamin did not emigrate to Boston until the fall of 1715, his opinion must have been solicited by the post, which probably means that Josiah considered the decision for at least a year before sending Franklin to school. Shorthand was a common accomplishment in the seventeenth and eighteenth centuries. Numerous devout parishioners, like Uncle Benjamin, recorded in shorthand an outline, with headings and many details, of their ministers' sermons.[19]

In 1712, Franklin's schoolmaster, Nathaniel Williams, summarized elementary education in the South Grammar School. He mentioned six texts studied in the first years, most of which Franklin would have studied: "The first three years are spent first in Learning by heart & then acc[ording] to their capacities understanding the [1] Accidence and [2] Nomenclator, in construing & parsing acc[ording] to the English rules of Syntax [3] Sententiae Pueriles [4] Cato & [5] Corderius & [6] Aesops Fables."[20] The *Accidence* was Ezekiel Cheever's *Introduction to Latin* (1709), a book of grammar and readings. Cheever had been the most famous American schoolmaster of the previous two generations, teaching at the South Grammar School from 1670 to his death in 1708. The second book cited, the *Nomenclator* or *Nomenclatura*, was a small Latin-English dictionary. Bartholomew Green had reprinted the third text, Charles Hoole's *Sententiae Pueriles, or Sentences for Children*, in 1702.

The fourth text, Cato's *Distichs*, a collection of moral aphorisms, had many editions in English and Latin through the seventeenth and eighteenth centuries. In 1735 Franklin printed James Logan's translation, which he advertised as "Very proper to be put into the Hands of young Persons." Corderius was an edition of Charles Hoole's *Maturinus Corderius's School-Colloquies, English and Latin* (1652), which had numerous later editions. The last text Williams cited was Aesop's *Fables*, perhaps Charles Hoole's edition in Latin and English (1657 and many later printings) or perhaps an illustrated Latin edition. Of the six school texts, Aesop's *Fables* probably had the most influence on Franklin. He appreciated fables all his life, alluded to Aesop's and other fables often, wrote several original ones, and reprinted twelve fables of Aesop in his 1747 edition of Thomas Dilworth's *New Guide to the English Tongue*.

Franklin did well in school. "I continu'd however at the Grammar School not quite one Year, tho' in that time I had risen gradually from the Middle of the Class of that Year to be the Head of it, and farther was remov'd into the next Class above it, in order to go with that into the third at the End of the Year" (A 6–7).

CLASSMATES

Franklin's classmates were Boston's educated boys, and he had later contacts with several of them. We cannot be certain, however, who most of his classmates were.[21] One must have been Ebenezer Pemberton, Jr. (1704/5–1777), son of Franklin's minister. Pemberton was exactly eleven months older than Franklin. The authors of the nineteenth-century *Catalogue of the Masters and Scholars Who Have Belonged to the Boston Latin School* guess that Franklin matriculated at the grammar school in 1712.[22] If, however, Franklin accurately reported the date in the *Autobiobiography*, he started in 1714. I suspect that young Pemberton was among the boys whom Franklin outperformed at the South Grammar School. Though the Reverend Ebenezer Pemberton died early in 1717, his son attended Harvard on scholarships and graduated in 1721. Pemberton, Jr., served as minister of the First Presbyterian Church in New York from 1727 to 1753.[23] As I shall show below, Pemberton and Franklin later found themselves opposing one another, with Pemberton the victor. If Franklin had continued in the South

Grammar School and gone on to Harvard, would his career have been similar to Pemberton's? It seems unlikely.

The future merchant Edmund Quincy (1703–88) attended the South Grammar School with Franklin. Quincy, who graduated from Harvard in 1722 and corresponded with Franklin in 1761, called the Philadelphian his old schoolmate.[24] Because their parents attended the Old South Church and thus probably lived near the South Grammar School, Daniel Oliver (1704–27) and John Smith (1704–68), who both graduated from Harvard along with Quincy, surely knew Franklin and may have attended school with him.[25] Two 1723 Harvard graduates were also associated with the Old South Church: Samuel Hirst (1705–27), the grandson of Samuel Sewall, and Habijah Savage (1704–43).[26]

When Franklin received an honorary M.A. in 1753, his name was inserted in the catalog with the class of 1724, thus indicating that the college authorities believed he would have graduated with that class if he had gone to college.[27] But no Harvard graduates of 1724 appear to have attended the Old South Church. One Boston boy whom he surely knew was Nicholas Bowes (1706–55). Like Franklin, Bowes was baptized by Samuel Willard and lived on Union Street. Bowes graduated from Harvard in 1725 along with Jeremiah Gridley (1702–67), another Old South Church member.[28] Franklin probably knew the slightly younger Dr. William Clark (1709–60), who, like Quincy, later corresponded with Franklin. Clark was an Old South Church member who graduated from Harvard in 1726.[29] Franklin also must have known the unfortunate Simeon Stoddard (1707–76), who was baptized at the Old South on 23 November 1707 and declared *non compos* in 1751. His father, Anthony Stoddard, belonged to the same private prayer group as Josiah Franklin, and his grandfather, Simeon Stoddard, was the wealthy merchant who financed Josiah's mortgage on the Union Street property.[30]

The *Catalogue* says that Benjamin Gibson (1700–1723) definitely attended the school with Franklin. Gibson's dates, however, suggest that he should have been four to six years ahead of Franklin. Gibson went on to Harvard (class of 1719) and became a minister but died early. The compilers of the *Catalogue* speculate that three other boys entered the South Grammar School with Franklin: Mather Byles, Samuel Freeman, and Jeremiah Gridley. Byles and Freeman both graduated from Harvard in 1725, along with Bowes and Gridley.[31] Franklin knew Byles well and corresponded with both him and Samuel Mather (who presumably attended the North Grammar School) later in life. Both Mather Byles and Samuel Mather, grandsons of Increase Mather, were involved in 1721 and 1722 in the *New-England Courant*'s wars with the Mathers, though Samuel Mather had the more active role. The poet Joseph Green (born the same month, January 1705/6, as Franklin), probably also attended the same South Grammar School class with Byles, Freeman, and Gridley.[32] If any of the Boston boys influenced Franklin, it was probably not until the 1730s, when Franklin evidently read Joseph Green's poetic satires and travesties that were circulating in manuscript. I suspect that Green's writings affected both Franklin's "Speech of Miss Polly Baker" (1747) and "Verses on the Virginia Capitol Fire" (1747).

DISAPPOINTMENT

Despite Franklin's rapid progress in school, Josiah changed his mind and withdrew him. Franklin knew that most leaders of Boston and British America graduated from college and that education was the best route out of the comparative poverty, obscurity, and disagreeable work in which his father was mired. Evidently Josiah did not discuss the decision with him: "But my Father . . . from a View of the Expense of a College Education which, having so large a Family, he could not well afford, and the mean Living many so educated were afterwards able to obtain, Reasons that he gave to his Friends in my Hearing, altered his first Intention" (A 7). Josiah Franklin seemed to be content in his situation, and he evidently saw little reason why his son should not be. Josiah often quoted a proverb from Solomon, "*Seest thou a Man diligent in his Calling, he shall stand before Kings, he shall not stand before mean Men*" (A 75). Franklin may have wondered before what kings his father stood, but he dutifully obeyed. So Franklin was not to be educated, not to be a member of the elite. He was to be an artisan.

Franklin's frustration must have been overwhelming. His enormous self-discipline and ferocious private course of study may owe much to his father's decision to take him out of school. No doubt Josiah could hardly afford the school, and he was evidently too proud to ask for help. Had Josiah appealed to Samuel Sewall, the justice and other friends might well have helped Josiah with his brilliant son's education. The community later rallied to support young Ebenezer Pemberton. Franklin's 1722 satire of Harvard, his lifelong slighting references to the classics, and even his egalitarian attitudes may have resulted partly from his disappointment over his father's decision.

BROWNELL

When Josiah Franklin took Franklin out of the South Grammar School, he entered him in one that taught penmanship, composition, and mathematics.[33] George Brownell had advertised a catch-all of training for boys and girls several years earlier: "At the House of Mr. *George Brownell* in Wings-Lane Boston, is Taught, Writing, Cyphering, Dancing, Treble Violin, Flute, Spinnet &c. Also English and French Quilting, Imbroidery, Florishing, Plain Work, marking in several sorts of Stiches, and several other works, where Scholars may board."[34] Wings Lane was only two blocks west of the Franklin home on Hanover Street. Franklin explained in the *Autobiography* that his father "took me from the Grammar School, and sent me to a School for Writing and Arithmetic kept by a then famous Man, Mr. George Brownell, very successful in his Profession generally, and that by mild encouraging Methods. Under him I acquired fair Writing pretty soon, but I fail'd in the Arithmetic, and made no Progress in it"

(A 6). Were girls in school with Franklin? Does that partly explain Franklin's proto-feminism? Brownell later moved to Philadelphia where he continued to teach school and became Franklin's frequent customer for schoolbooks, stationery, and other supplies.

A TRADE

After the year at George Brownell's school in 1715–16, Franklin went to work with his father making candles and soap. He continued working for him "till I was 12 Years old; and my Brother John, who was bred to that Business having left my Father, married and set up for himself at Rhodeisland, there was all Appearance that I was destin'd to supply his Place and be a Tallow Chandler" (A 8–9). "Destin'd to . . . be a Tallow Chandler"! Franklin's dejection over his prospects, his feeling of helplessness, and his resentment of the economic situation all appear in his choice of the theological diction *destined*, with its strong Calvinistic connotation of *damned*. But even as the sixty-five-year-old Franklin wrote those words, he remembered that he meant to rebel against the trade and, if necessary, to run away and become a sailor. "I was employed in cutting Wick for the Candles, filling the Dipping Mold, and the Molds for cast Candles, attending the Shop, going of Errands, etc. I dislik'd the Trade and had a strong Inclination for the Sea; but my Father declar'd against it" (A 7).

Franklin must have heard adventure stories from numerous sailors, and he loved the water. He wrote: "living near the Water, I was much in and about it, learnt early to swim well, and to manage Boats, and when in a Boat or Canoe with other Boys I was commonly allow'd to govern, especially in any case of Difficulty" (A 7). We shall see a good example of Franklin's boyhood leadership in a later chapter when he tells of the crises on the English coast at the start of his 1726 sea voyage. "But my Dislike to the Trade continuing, my Father was under Apprehensions that if he did not find one for me more agreeable, I should break away and get to Sea, as his Son Josiah had done to his great Vexation." Therefore his father tried to find some trade that Franklin liked. He "sometimes took me to walk with him, and see Joiners, Bricklayers, Turners, Braziers, etc. at their Work, that he might observe my Inclination, and endeavour to fix it on some Trade or other on Land. It has ever since been a Pleasure to me to see good Workmen handle their Tools; and it has been useful to me, having learnt so much by it, as to be able to do little Jobs myself in my House, when a Workman could not readily be got; and to construct little Machines for my Experiments while the Intention of making the Experiment was fresh and warm in my Mind" (A 10). Franklin demonstrated this handicraft ability in his first inventions and in his work as a printer, as well as in his electrical experiments.

Josiah Franklin's efforts to find an acceptable trade for Franklin were more important for their mutual love than for the immediate purpose. "My Father at last fix'd upon the Cutler's Trade." Notice that Franklin does not say that he wanted to become a cutler or even that he was willing to. Franklin explained why his father chose the trade: "My Uncle Benjamin's Son Samuel who was bred to that Business in London being about that time establish'd in Boston, I was sent to be with him some time on liking." Evidently he lived with Samuel Franklin for a short time in 1717, at age eleven. In those days, when tradesmen kept the "secrets" of crafts from public knowledge, a premium, usually £10, was demanded from the apprentice (or his parents) to learn the craft.[35] Samuel wanted such a premium, but Josiah did not expect his nephew to charge him and so took young Franklin back home. It was ungenerous of Samuel to expect pay: not only was Josiah his uncle, but Josiah had been supporting Samuel Franklin's father, Uncle Benjamin Franklin, for over a year.

Franklin's recollection and description of the limited possibilities he had have something almost allegorical about them. They encapsulate the confining social structure of the early eighteenth century: the son of a tradesman was expected to become an apprentice to his father or to a relation. Franklin was to be a maker and dealer in candles and soap like his father, or a maker and dealer in knives and tableware like his older cousin. He only escaped the latter apprenticeship because of the demand for a fee. Josiah offered him alternative crafts: an apprentice to a carpenter or to someone else in the building trades or to a metal worker or to some other handicraftsman. All apprenticeships required a legal indenture of seven to eleven or more years—and at the end of that time, a youth had gained an expertise in a single handicraft which, in all but a few instances, doomed him to practice that trade all his life. Such were the eighteenth-century expectations for a tradesman's son (a laborer's son had less opportunity), even in England and America where the hierarchies were less strict than those in Europe. Franklin wanted to escape that destiny. Even though the life of a common sailor was obviously not desirable (impressment in the British navy in Boston and elsewhere proved that a common sailor's life was usually disagreeable), it offered an alternative to apprenticeship. Franklin preferred to reject the confining social order of his day even if it meant a life of harsh discipline and frequent danger. In the fictive world of Franklin's *Autobiography*, the story of his choosing a trade represents the old world that Franklin escaped.

In the late spring of 1718, however, Franklin's older brother James returned from England with a press and types, leading to a major change in Benjamin Franklin's life.

THREE

Printer's Devil

In a little time I made great Proficiency in the Business, and became a useful Hand to my Brother.—A 11

Puzzles Concerning James Franklin

The standard sources state that James Franklin served an apprenticeship to a printer in London and returned to Boston with a press and types in 1717.[1] Those assertions are probably incorrect, though they reflect Franklin's statement in the *Autobiography* that "in 1717 my Brother James return'd from England with a Press and Letters to set up his Business in Boston." The historian of American printing Isaiah Thomas repeated and added to Franklin's statement in the early nineteenth century: "I have been informed that James Franklin served an apprenticeship with a printer in England, where his father was born, and had connections. In March 1716/7, J. Franklin came from London with a press and types, and began business in Boston."[2]

Neither Franklin nor Thomas says definitely that James Franklin served an apprenticeship in London. Indeed, Benjamin Franklin does not say that James served an apprenticeship in England though Thomas does. His words could be interpreted as stating that James Franklin studied printing in Ecton, Northamptonshire ("where his father was born"), but Ecton was a tiny town, and no printers are known to have been established there.[3] Or Thomas might have meant simply that he served an apprenticeship somewhere in England.

James probably did not serve an apprenticeship in London, for he does not turn up in the London Stationers' Company records.[4] Moreover, most London apprentices were trained in large print shops and learned either typesetting or press-work, not both. James Franklin's multiple printing abilities suggest that he apprenticed in the English provinces or in America. The Philadelphia printer Samuel Keimer, who later employed Franklin, was typical of London-trained printers. Franklin said in the *Autobiography* that Keimer "was a mere Compositor, knowing nothing of Presswork" (27). In small printing shops, apprentices learned all aspects of printing. While an apprentice, James Franklin even mastered the art of making wood engravings—an unusual accomplishment even among provincial and colonial printers. He may have served his apprenticeship in Boston—or in rural England (perhaps in Northamptonshire or Oxfordshire, towns in which Josiah had lived and "had connections").[5]

It seems improbable that James Franklin returned to Boston in 1717 with a press and types. No James Franklin imprints exist for 1717. The earliest imprint that can be dated is during the summer of 1718. Two theories have been advanced to account for the lack of 1717 imprints. In 1946 Lawrence C. Wroth and Marion Adams speculated that James Franklin did not bring a press and types with him when he returned in 1717 but instead worked for a bookseller, Benjamin Eliot, to make relief cuts for various Boston printers for a year before purchasing the press and types from England. Wroth and Adams came up with the theory because several woodcuts appeared in Boston in 1717, some of which were signed "JF."[6] Bibliographers before 1946 had supposed that these were by the early American printer and printmaker John Foster (1648–81).[7] Another, undated cut of roughly the same period is signed "J. F. Sculp."[8]

But making woodcuts for a bookseller would hardly have supplied a living. If Wroth and Adams's theory (that James Franklin did not have his own press but was working in Boston in 1717) is correct, it seems likely that he worked as a journeyman printer there, probably for Bartholomew Green (1666–1732), Boston's most prolific printer. James Franklin had known Green all his life.

The bibliographer and historian Keith Arbour advanced another theory in 1999. He suggested that James Franklin did not return until 1718, that Benjamin Franklin merely had the date wrong, and that Isaiah Thomas followed his statement. He argued that the 1717 woodcuts signed "JF" were actually by John Foster and were reused long after Foster's death. He thought that James Franklin's known woodcuts were different in style from the ones attributed to him by Wroth and Adams, which were similar to those by John Foster. Wroth and Adams had also attributed to James Franklin a woodcut used in *Hodder's Arithmetick*, which he printed in 1719. But the rare book collector Michael Zinman noticed that it appeared earlier in an English edition of William Winstanley's *New Help to Discourse*, printed in 1716 in London by "B. H." Subsequently studying the typography in *New Help*, Keith Arbour found that the tailpiece in the same book turned up in James Franklin's printing of Samuel Gerrish, *Catalogue of Curious and Valuable Books*, which appeared about July 1718—the earliest dated Franklin imprint. Furthermore, Arbour determined that the main types used in Winstanley's *New Help to Discourse* were also used by James Franklin in 1718.

James Franklin must have purchased the used types and cuts owned by the printer of Winstanley's *New Help*. Arbour speculated that "B. H." was Benjamin Harris (fl. 1673–1716), the peripatetic English printer who lived in Boston from 1686 to 1695, when he became the first American journalist with the publication of *Public Occurrences Both Foreign and Domestick* (25 September 1690). Arbour conjectured that James Franklin served an apprenticeship with the printer Benjamin Harris in London.

Later, Arbour noticed that in his letterbook, Chief Justice Samuel Sewall addressed a letter of 27 January 1717/8 to "To Mr. Samuel Storke in London, per James Franklin."[9] Evidently James Franklin took a letter from Sewall in Boston and delivered it to Samuel Storke in London. If so, then James Franklin was in Boston in 1717 and evidently did not buy his press until early 1717/8 or return to Boston with it until the late spring or early summer of 1718. Other J. Franklins lived in Boston, though no other *James* Franklin is known.[10]

I suspect that James Franklin served a printing apprenticeship in Boston, that he and his father borrowed the money to buy printing equipment, that he went to London to do so at the beginning of 1717/8, and that he came back to Boston before the summer of 1718 with a press and types. (Under the English calendar in use at the time, 1718 did not begin until March 25, 1718, making Franklin's mistaken memory fifty nine years later slightly more probable.) My hypothesis dovetails with the evidence of his earliest known imprint (the summer of 1718) and with Samuel Sewall's note.

A hitherto unnoticed bit of evidence from James Franklin tends to confirm the supposition. After the General Court of Massachusetts ordered on 15 January 1722/3 that James Franklin must have everything he printed approved by the secretary of the province before its publication, he defied the order and went into hiding. After he surfaced, he was ordered to appear before the grand jury on 7 May 1723. The day before his grand jury presentation, James Franklin defended himself in the *New-England Courant*. Protesting against the order of the assembly; he argued that he, like "his Fellow-Tradesmen," served an apprenticeship and had a right to get "an honest Livelyhood by his Trade, to which he has serv'd his Time *in the Country*" (emphasis mine). He could have been referring to an apprenticeship in London or even in England as "his Time in the Country," but the words and context suggest that the country is Massachusetts. I suspect that he served his apprenticeship in Boston, sailed to England in late January 1717/8, and before mid-summer 1718 "return'd from England with a Press and Letters to set up his Business in Boston."

A further question concerning James Franklin bears importantly on Benjamin Franklin's biography. Where did James Franklin get the money to buy a printing press and types and to set up in business? Was Josiah Franklin wealthy enough to set up his son James in printing—but not, seven years later, his youngest son, Benjamin? No.

Josiah could not have loaned James sufficient money to go to England, buy a press and types, return to Boston, and set up in business. Josiah still owed Simeon Stoddard most of the £250 he had borrowed six years earlier (1712) to buy the Union Street property. When Josiah paid off Stoddard in 1723, he had to remortgage his property to Hannah Clark for £220. Josiah must have borrowed the money to loan to James in January 1717/8, but no note for a loan in 1717 or 1718 is known. However, on 7 June 1720, about two and a half years after Josiah somehow came up with the money to loan James, he and his son James signed a promissory note with James Bowdoin (1676–1747) for £346.11.8. The debt was in two bonds, one for £196.11.8, and the other for £150.[11]

Why two notes? Why such an exact sum as £196.11.8?

I hypothesize that the note for £196.11.8 paid off a former one that Josiah had borrowed for James before the young printer went to England in January 1717/8. Perhaps, since James's business was rapidly increasing by June 1720, the additional £150 was for buying a second press and additional types.[12] Since Massachusetts currency was worth about half as much as British sterling, the two bonds were worth approximately £175 sterling. (As we will see, a few years later Benjamin Franklin a few years later bought the materials for a single small printing press for approximately £75 sterling.) The two notes to James Bowdoin were paid off, with £20 interest, on 26 January 1731/2, but Josiah must have paid part of those notes from his own carefully nurtured funds, for in his will, dated 20 October 1744, Josiah forgave "all the Bonds and Obligations" that James's heirs still owed him.[13]

BOSTON PRINTERS

Competition in the printing business was keen. In 1718 Boston already had five printers, whereas the other colonies collectively had two: William Bradford in New York and his son Andrew Bradford in Philadelphia. The owner of Boston's largest printing establishment was Bartholomew Green, a son of Samuel Green (d. 1702), the second printer in Massachusetts. Bartholomew was a member of the Old South Church, the Franklins' church. He and Josiah Franklin knew one another well. John Allen (ca. 1650–ca. 1727) was the eldest Boston printer, semi-retired in 1718 and printing less every year. Thomas Fleet (1685–1758), who emigrated from London in 1712 to set up printing in Boston, was thirty-two. Beginning in January 1721/2, he contributed to James Franklin's *New-England Courant*. Thomas Crump (fl. 1714–18) had just broken off his partnership with Thomas Fleet. He printed for a few years on his own and then dropped out of sight. The last quite active Boston printer was Samuel Kneeland (1697–1769), a descendant of the Green dynasty of Boston printers (grandson of Samuel and nephew of Bartholomew). His shop was located near James Franklin, "over against the Prison in Queen Street."[14]

For a few years, James Franklin supplemented his printing income by dyeing clothing. Both Josiah and Uncle Benjamin Franklin had been dyers in England, and Uncle Benjamin Franklin had composed a "Treatise on Dyeing and Coloring."[15] Abiah Franklin no doubt learned dyeing from Josiah and taught it to her children. James Franklin promoted his clothes-dyeing business through his printing, advertising in the 25 April 1720 *Boston Gazette*: "The Printer hereof Prints Linens, Calicoes, Silks, &c in good Figures, very lively and durable Colours, and without the offensive Smell which commonly attends the Linens Printed here." Evidently he became recognized as a superior dyer. Advertising on 9 May 1720, James Franklin warned: "The Printer hereof [the *Boston Gazette*] having dispers'd Advertisements of his Printing Calicoes, &c., a certain Person in Charleston, to rob him of the Benefit of said Advertisements and impose upon Strangers, calls himself by the Name of Franklin, having agreed with one in Queen Street Boston to take in his Work. These are to desire him to be satisfyed with his proper Name, or he will be proceeded against according to Law." James Franklin evidently stopped dyeing clothes when he began the *New-England Courant* in 1721: printing the newspaper absorbed all his time. No subsequent Franklin advertisements for dyeing appeared.

APPRENTICE

After James Franklin started his printing business in 1718, he needed an apprentice. His brother Benjamin's "Bookish Inclination" suggested to their father to make Benjamin a printer, though the young Franklin "still had a Hankering for the Sea." To prevent Benjamin's running off, his father indentured him to the twenty-one-year-old James when he "was yet but 12 Years old." Franklin proved adept: "In a little time I made great Proficiency in the Business, and became a useful Hand to my Brother. I now had access to better Books. An Acquaintance with the Apprentices of Booksellers, enabled me sometimes to borrow a small one, which I was careful to return soon and clean. Often I sat up in my Room reading the greatest Part of the Night, when the Book was borrow'd in the Evening and to be return'd early in the Morning lest it should be miss'd or wanted" (A 11).

Boston had twelve active booksellers; the other colonies had none. The historian Carl Bridenbaugh noted: "The book trade of Boston was second only to that of London among English-speaking peoples."[16] The bibliographer Hugh Amory doubted that Boston was quite so dominant: Dublin probably printed more books than Boston, and Edinburgh about as many.[17] Boston, however, was certainly the center of the American book trade in the seventeenth and eighteenth centuries. Boston booksellers not only imported English and foreign books for litterateurs throughout the colonies, they also commissioned titles they believed would sell. Major Boston booksellers like Nicholas Boone (1679–1738), Joseph Edwards (1707–77), Samuel Gerrish (ca. 1680–1741), Benjamin Eliot (1665–1741), and Daniel Henchman (1689–1761) together commissioned scores of books every year during James Franklin's Boston printing career (1717–26). Booksellers were the printers' primary customers, followed by peddlers. Though some peddlers worked with the booksellers, others were independent. Carrying chapbooks among other items in their packs, they were a not uncommon sight throughout rural New England. The 16 April 1705 *Boston News-Letter* printed James Gray's obituary: he "used to go up and down the Country Selling of Books." Dying in Boston, the archetypal Yankee peddler left "a Considerable Estate," including £700 in coin.

FRANKLIN'S EARLY VERSE

Franklin said in the *Autobiography* that in 1718 he "took a Fancy to Poetry, and made some little Pieces." Actually, Franklin had been writing poetry since childhood. Franklin's verse was good enough when he was seven for his proud father to send Uncle Benjamin samples. Though Franklin's poems do not survive, Uncle Benjamin Franklin replied with the following:

> To my Name 1713
> Tis time for me to Throw Asside my pen
> When Hanging-sleeves Read, Write, and Rhime Like Men.
> This Forward Spring Foretells a plentious crop,
> For if the bud bear Graine what will the Top?
> If plenty in the verdant blade Appear,   5
> What may we not soon hope for in the Ear?
> When Flow'rs are Beautifull before they'r Blown,
> What Rarities will afterward be shown?
> If tree's Good fruit unoculated bear,
> You May be sure 'Twill afterward be Rare.   10
> If fruits are Sweet before th'ave time to Yellow,
> How Luscious will they be when they are Mellow!
> If first years Shoots such Noble clusters send,
> What Laden boughs, Engedi like, May We Expect I'th End?
> Goe on, My Name, and be progressive still,   15
> Till thou Excell Great Cocker with thy Quill;
> Soe Imitate and's Excellence Reherse
> Till thou Excell His cyphers, Writing, Verse.
> And show us here that your young Western clime
> Out Does all Down unto our present Time;   20
> With choycer Measures put his poesie Down,
> And I will vote for thee the Lawrell Crown.

Uncle Benjamin Franklin's little poem celebrates Franklin's verse with a series of appreciations of future prospects (ll. 3–14). The uncle modestly celebrated the child ("hanging-sleeves" was the name for a child's shirt with loose open sleeves[18]) as more talented than he. The last comparison, "Engedi like" (l. 14), refers to an oasis in the Bible (Cant. 1:4; Josh. 15:62), famous for its fruitfulness. Uncle Benjamin hoped his namesake would "Excell Great Cocker" (l. 16), referring to Edward Cocker, a schoolmaster of Northamptonshire and author of numerous school texts. The allusion to the western movement of arts and civilization (ll. 19–20; the *translatio* motif) may have introduced Franklin to an idea that was important for Americans. Its most famous seventeenth-century statement occurred in George Herbert's "Church Militant" (ll. 235–36): "Religion stands on tiptoe in our land, / Readie to passe to the *American* strand," which Cotton Mather echoed in the first line of the *Magnalia Christi Americana*: "I write the *Wonders* of the CHRISTIAN RELIGION, flying from the Deprivations of *Europe*, to the *American Strand*."[19]

As we will see, Franklin often used the *translatio* idea.

THE LIGHTHOUSE TRAGEDY

Franklin's first publication, a broadside ballad titled *The Lighthouse Tragedy*, depicted a calamity. The 10 November 1718 *Boston News-Letter* reported that the prior week, "an awful and Lamentable Providence fell out here, Mr. George Worthylake . . . Anne his Wife, Ruth their Daughter, George Cutler, a Servant, Shadwell their Negro Slave, and Mr. John Edge a Passenger; being on the Lord's Day here at Sermon, and going home in a Sloop, dropt Anchor near the Landing place, and all got into a little Boat or Cannoo, designing to go on Shoar, but by Accident it overwhelmed, so that they were Drowned, and all found and Interred except George Cutler." James Franklin, who knew his young brother wrote poetry, suggested he write a poem on the tragedy. Franklin recalled that it "sold wonderfully, the Event being recent, having made a great Noise" (A 12). No copy survives. The poem on the subject beginning "Oh! George, This wild November" is either a forgery or an imitation of what Franklin might have written. It contains numerous passages of typical nineteenth-century sentimentality.[20]

Like James Franklin, Cotton Mather appreciated the news opportunity offered by the drowning. On 10 November he recorded, "I entertained the Flock, with as pungent and useful a Discourse, as I can, on the Occasion given in the tragical Spectacle of a Number in our Neighbourhood, (among which were the Master of the Light-house, and his Wife) who were drowned the last Week, and carried all together to the Grave, with a very solemn Funeral." Though Mather's sermon, *Providence Asserted and Adored*, was a sizable pamphlet as opposed to Franklin's broadside, only one copy survives.[21] Mather's diary recorded that Robert Saunders (who succeeded Worthylake as lighthouse keeper) also drowned within two weeks. On Monday, 17 November, Mather noted: "Another Master of the *Light-house* [Saunders], is (with another Person) already drowned." So Mather resolved to preach on the occasion.[22] The second tragedy no doubt redoubled interest in the first one and helps explain why Franklin's ballad "sold wonderfully."

THE INTELLIGENCE OF WOMEN

In addition to poetry, the young apprentice wrote expository prose. Around 1718, when Franklin was twelve, he exchanged essays with John Collins, "another Bookish Lad in the Town" on "the Propriety of educating the Female Sex in Learning, and their Abilities for Study. He was of Opinion that it was improper; and that they were naturally unequal to it. I took the contrary Side, perhaps a little for Dispute sake" (A 12–13). The last phrase deliberately undercuts Franklin's avant-garde tendencies. He frequently downplayed his own advanced positions, partially to make himself seem less assertive. Throughout his life, however, Franklin advocated educating women and often argued that their mental abilities were equal to those of men (e.g., A 95). He was probably influenced both by his reading and his experience. His teacher George Brownell had girls as well as boys in some classes, though some subjects that he taught, like embroidery, would have been for girls only.[23] Perhaps the intelligence of Franklin's mother and sisters convinced him that girls should be educated. Or perhaps he was influenced by a knowledge of English history. The monarch on the throne when he was a child was Queen Anne, and it would have been traitorous for any Englishman or American to believe that she did not have as much ability as any man.

Anne Bradstreet wrote of Queen Elizabeth:

> Now say, have women worth? or have they none?
> Or had they some, but with our Queen is't gone?
> Nay masculines, you have thus taxed us long,
> But she, though dead, will vindicate our wrong.
> Let such as say our sex is void of reason,
> Know 'tis a slander now but once was treason.[24]

Though we have no evidence for Franklin's doing so, he surely read Anne Bradstreet, New England's most famous poet. Her *Several Poems* (Boston, 1678) would have been in numerous New England personal libraries. Though Michael Wigglesworth, author of *The Day of Doom* (Boston, 1666), was more popular (in England as well as in America), his reputation was not as great and his subject matter (New England Puritanism, aimed at least partly for an audience of children) would have been of less interest to Franklin. Franklin also read a long and impassioned plea for the education of women in Defoe's *Essay Upon Projects*, one of the books in his father's small library (A 11).

Josiah found the manuscripts that Franklin and Collins exchanged. "Without entring into the Discussion, he took occasion to talk to me about the Manner of my Writing, observ'd that tho' I had the Advantage of my Antagonist in correct Spelling and pointing [punctuation] (which I ow'd to the Printing House) I fell far short in elegance of Expression, in Method and in Perspicuity, of which he convinc'd me by several Instances. I saw the Justice of his Remarks, and thence grew more attentive to the *Manner* in Writing, and determin'd to endeavour at Improvement" (A 13). The technique he used to improve his writing and the source selected for comparison are both better remembered than the proto-feminism that occasioned the effort.

THE *SPECTATOR*

Franklin's exposure to excellent contemporary journalistic writing began when he found "an odd Volume of the Spectator. I had never before seen any of them." Since Franklin noted in the *New-England Courant* for 2 July 1722 that the *Courant*'s library contained a "large and valuable collection of Books," including Addison and Steele's *Spectator* in eight volumes, we can be certain that Franklin was describing a time at least two or three years before 1722, probably about 1718, when he was twelve. In a canceled passage, he identified the volume as the third. That volume contained *Spectator* No. 170 (originally published 14 September 1711) through No. 251 (18 December 1711). Franklin continued: "I bought it, read it over and over, and was much delighted with it. I thought the Writing excellent, and wish'd if possible to imitate it. With that View, I took some of the Papers, and making short Hints of the Sentiment in each Sentence, laid them by a few Days, and then without looking at the Book, try'd to complete the Papers again, by expressing each hinted Sentiment at length and as fully as it had been express'd before, in any suitable Words that should come to hand" (A 13).

Franklin applied determination and resourcefulness to learning to write. He found that compared to his rewriting of the *Spectator*, Addison and Steele had a more copious vocabulary, a greater range of specialized diction, a better sense of rhythm, and a more logical order. He failed to attain the excellence of the original *Spectators*, but he was young, bright, and determined. He tried again— and again: "I compar'd my Spectator with the Original, discover'd some of my Faults and corrected them. But I found I wanted a Stock of Words or a Readiness in recollecting and using them, which I thought I should have acquir'd before that time, if I had gone on making Verses, since the continual Occasion for Words of the same Import but of different Length, to suit the Measure, or of different Sound for the Rhyme, would have laid me under a constant Necessity of searching for Variety, and also have tended to fix that Variety in my Mind, and make me Master of it." Therefore he attempted the task of turning the essays into verse. No doubt the verse was execrable, but it enlarged his vocabulary and strengthened his sense of rhythm. Later, after forgetting the exact words used, he rewrote the essays in prose. To teach himself method, he "jumbled my Collections of Hints into Confusion, and after some Weeks, endeavour'd to reduce them into the best Order, before I began to form the full Sentences, and compleat the Paper." Then he compared his versions with the originals, finding "many faults," which he amended.

"But I sometimes had the Pleasure of Fancying that in certain Particulars of small Import, I had been lucky enough to improve the Method or the Language and this encourag'd me to think I might possibly in time come to be a tolerable English Writer, of which I was extreamly ambitious" (A 12). The style of that last long sentence, with its clear syntax and the delightful "p" consonance, testifies that Franklin did indeed become a "tolerable English Writer." Note how Franklin undercuts himself: he confesses that he was "extreamly ambitious," but the words occur as an added subordinate construction to what he thought he "might possibly in time come to be"—a "tolerable" English writer. Actually, by the time he wrote those words in 1771, he was widely regarded, in David Hume's phrase (10 May 1762), as a "Great Man of Letters." Franklin's 1751 "Idea of the English School" (4:107) advocated a scheme for teaching composition that was similar to his early self- education.

In the *Autobiography* Franklin only tells the reader once of any ambition, though the enormous drive and self-discipline that he brought to various tasks testify to his aspiration. "My Time for these Exercises and for Reading, was at Night after Work, or before Work began in the Morning; or on Sundays, when I contrived to be in the Printing-House alone, evading as much as I could the common Attendance on publick Worship, which my Father used to exact of me when I was under his Care: And which indeed I still thought a Duty; tho' I could not as it seemed to me, afford the Time to practice it" (A 14). In his private course of study, books were Franklin's teachers.

James Franklin's Increasing Business and Franklin's Reading

In 1719 James Franklin's business increased fourfold with his publication of at least eight pamphlets and books. These included the first separately published mathematical textbook printed in the colonies, *Hodder's Arithmetic*. We can add *Hodder's Arithmetic* to Seller's *Practical Navigation* and Samuel Sturmy's *Mariner's Magazine* (both mentioned in the *Autobiography*) as mathematical texts that Franklin read as a boy. Another James Franklin imprint that probably interested Benjamin Franklin was Thomas Robie's brief contribution to science, *A Letter to a Certain Gentleman Desiring a Particular Account May be Given of a Wonderful Meteor, That Appeared in New England, on Decemb. 11, 1719 in the Evening*. The Harvard tutor Thomas Robie was a talented mathematician. The 4 January 1719/20 *Boston Gazette* advertised that his pamphlet was to be published "Tomorrow." Robie proved that the supposed meteor was actually a display of the aurora borealis. He thus introduced Franklin to a subject that interested him all his life and upon which, early in December 1778, he wrote a paper giving his own hypothesis explaining the aurora borealis.

Blackbeard the Pirate

The second broadside poem Franklin mentioned in the *Autobiography* was a ballad on "Blackbeard the Pirate." Piracy flourished until the nineteenth century. The largely unpopulated and unpoliced American coast was a pirate's paradise. The notorious Captain William Kidd was captured in Boston in 1701 and sent to England for trial. In Franklin's adolescence the most infamous pirate was Edward Teach, "Blackbeard the pirate." On Monday, 23 February 1718/9, the *Boston News-Letter* briefly reported the news of his death. The report especially interested Boston citizens, for the sister of the heroic Lieutenant Maynard, who commanded the ship that took Blackbeard, was a Bostonian.

Franklin's "sailor Song on the Taking of *Teach* or Blackbeard the Pirate" was inspired by the *News-Letter* accounts. Recalling his two broadside ballads, Franklin wrote: "They were wretched Stuff, in the Grubstreet Ballad Stile, and when they were printed he [James Franklin] sent me about the Town to sell them." Their brisk sale "flatter'd my Vanity. But my Father discourag'd me, by ridiculing my Performances, and telling me Verse-makers were generally Beggars; so I escap'd being a Poet, most probably a very bad one" (A 12). Since street hawkers were of a lower class than tradesmen, Josiah may have been implying a class distinction. Of course the verse-maker that Josiah and Franklin knew best was Uncle Benjamin Franklin, the religious, impractical dependent who had then been living with Josiah for four years. Franklin certainly did not want to be like him. By the time Franklin reported the incident in the *Autobiography*, he had read and may have echoed John Locke's opinion of poetry in *Some Thoughts Concerning Education*: "it is very seldom seen, that any one discovers Mines of Gold or Silver in *Parnassus*. 'Tis a pleasant Air, but a barren Soil."[25]

Three different songs have been advanced as Benjamin Franklin's ballad. Mason Locke Weems, in his biography of Franklin, said that he recalled one stanza (the first) of the song:

> Come all you jolly sailors,
>   You all so stout and brave;
> Come hearken and I'll tell you
>   What happen'd on the wave.
> Oh! 'tis of that bloody Blackbeard
>   I'm going for to tell;
> And as how by gallant Maynard
>   He soon was sent to hell.
>   With a down, down, down, derry down.

James Parton thought that "even if the ingenious Weems borrowed from another author the stanza which he attributed to Franklin, it is a perfect specimen of the ancient ballad style."[26] In fact, it imitates two old ballad tunes. The "Come all you" opening is a standard identification for one series of song tunes, and the "derry down" refrain is standard for another.[27] But the inconsistent meter doesn't fit either well. In the above stanza, the odd-numbered lines usually have only seven syllables—one fewer than the meter calls for. It's like Weems's story of George Washington and the cherry tree—Weems made it up.

Justin Winsor recorded from oral tradition eight lines of another claimant:

> Then each man to his gun,
> For the work must be done,
> With cutlass, sword, or pistol:
> And when we no longer can strike a blow,
> Then fire the magazine, boys, and up we go.
> It is better to swim in the sea below
> Then to hang in the air, and to feed the crow.
> Said jolly Ned Teach of Bristol.[28]

But with its romantic suggestion of suicide and its "jolly" pirate, the poem is evidently a nineteenth-century creation. And it is not "in the Grubstreet Ballad Stile" (A 12).

Figure 4. The music for "The Downfall of Pyracy," or, as Franklin called it in the Auto-biography, "A sailor Song on the Taking of Teach or Blackbeard the Pirate" (A 12), the words of which Franklin wrote two months after turning thirteen. Reprinted with the permission of Ellen Cohn from "Benjamin Franklin and Traditional Music," in Reappraising Benjamin Franklin 298.

In 1898 Edward Everett Hale discovered an eighteenth-century ballad that he thought descended from Franklin's original. "The Downfall of Piracy" appeared in a popular small songbook, the *Worcestershire Garland* (ca. 1765).[29] Since it roughly follows the information published in the *Boston News-Letter* on 2 March 1719, it probably is Franklin's ballad. The compiler of the *Worcestershire Garland* had no idea that the song might be connected with Benjamin Franklin, who was by 1753 famous as a scientist. Neither did John Ashton, who reprinted it (evidently from the *Worcestershire Garland*) in 1891. Though the ballad includes some background on Teach and piracy not present in the *Boston News-Letter* account, such knowledge was common in 1719. The tune, according to the *Worcestershire Garland*, was "What Is Greater Joy and Pleasure." The musicologist Carleton Sprague Smith printed the tune, and the Franklin scholar Ellen Cohn added that the melody remained popular into the nineteenth century.[30]

Here are the ballad's next two stanzas:

> When the Act of Grace appeared, Captain *Teach* with all his Men,
> Unto *Carolina* steered, Where they kindly us'd him then;
> There he marry'd to a Lady, And gave her five hundred Pound,
> But to her he prov'd unsteady, For he soon march'd off the Ground.

> And returned, as I tell you, To his Robbery as before,
> Burning, sinking Ships of value, Filling them with Purple Gore;
> When he was at *Carolina*, There the Governor did send,
> To the Governor of *Virginia*, That he might assistance lend.

The *Boston News-Letter* account reported that Virginia Governor Alexander Spotswood "fitted out two Sloops" with "Fifty pickt Men of His Majesty's Man of War lying there." The ballad concurred:

> Then the Man of War's Commander, Two small Sloops he fitted out,
> Fifty Men he put on board, Sir, Who resolv'd to stand it out:
> The Lieutenant he commanded Both the Sloops, and you shall hear,
> How before he landed, He suppress'd them without fear.

The newspaper reported that Lieutenant Robert Maynard caught up with the pirate in North Carolina, hailed him, and said that he would take him dead or alive. "Teach called for a Glass of Wine, and swore Damnation to himself; if he either took or gave Quarters."

The ballad continued:

> Valiant *Maynard* as he sailed,[31] Soon the Pirate did espy,
> With his Trumpet he then hailed, And to him they did reply:
> Captain *Teach* is our Commander, *Maynard* said, he is the Man,
> Whom I am resolv'd to hang, Sir, Let him do the best he can.

> *Teach* replyed unto *Maynard*, You no Quarter here shall see,
> But be hang'd on the Mainyard, You and all your Company;
> *Maynard* said, I none desire, Of such Knaves as thee and thine,
> None I'll give, *Teach* then replyed, My Boys, give me a Glass of Wine.

> He took the Glass, and drank Damnation, Unto *Maynard* and his Crew;
> To himself and Generation, Then the Glass away he threw;
> Brave *Maynard* was resolv'd to have him, Tho' he had Cannons nine or ten;
> *Teach* a broadside quickly gave him, Killing sixteen valiant Men.

According to the *Boston News-Letter*, "Teach fired some small guns loaded with Swan shot, spick Nails and pieces of old Iron in upon Maynard; which killed six of his Men and wounded ten." Lieutenant Maynard then ordered all his men to go down in the hold, except Abraham Demelt of New York, a helmsman, and himself. Seeing so few on the deck, Teach said that they were all killed except two or three. Teach boarded the sloop and tied it to his ship. "Maynard and Teach themselves begun the Fight with their Swords." Maynard's men came out and joined the fray. One of Maynard's men, a "Highlander" with a broad sword, "gave Teach a cut on the Neck, Teach saying, well done Lad, the Highlander reply'd, if it not be well done, I'll do it better, with that he gave him a second stroke, which cut off his Head." The news article concluded that all Teach's men except two were killed. Teach's body was thrown overboard and "his Head put on the top of the Bowsprit." The ballad has Maynard, rather than a Scotsman, kill Blackbeard.

> *Maynard* boarded him, and to it They fell with Sword and Pistol too;
> They had Courage, and did show it, Killing of the Pirate's Crew.

Teach and *Maynard* on the Quarter, Fought it out most manfully,
Maynard's Sword did cut him shorter, Losing his head, he there did die.

Every Sailor fought while he, Sir, Power had to wield the Sword,
Not a Coward could you see, Sir, Fear was driven from aboard:
Wounded Men on both Sides fell, Sir, 'Twas a doleful Sight to see,
Nothing could their Courage quell, Sir, O, they fought courageously.

When the bloody Fight was over, We're inform'd by a Letter writ,
Teach's Head was made a Cover, To the Jack Staff of the Ship:
Thus they sailed to *Virginia*, And when they the Story told,
How they kill'd the Pirates many, They'd Applause from young and old.

The newspaper carried another story with a few more details on the back page, but Franklin took little material from it, except a celebration of the bravery of all concerned (his penultimate stanza). The second news account concluded: "Maynard's Men behaved like Hero's, and kill'd all Teach's Men that Entered without any of Maynards dropping, but most of them Cut and Mangled, in the whole he had Eight killed, and Eighteen wounded, Teach fell with Five Shot, and 20 dismal cuts, and 12 of his Men killed, and Nine made Prisoners, most of them Negro's, all wounded, Teach would never be taken had he not been in such a hole that he could not get away."

The ballad derives from the *Boston News-Letter* account. Though the newspaper report could have been reprinted in London where some balladeer might have composed the song, we know that Franklin wrote a ballad based on the newspaper account. In all likelihood, this is Franklin's ballad. If he wrote it, one can understand why his father ridiculed his verses. The ballad is wordy, inaccurate, and strains to make rhymes. Nevertheless, it is not much worse than the usual doggerel ballad. Not bad for a thirteen-year-old.

THE *BOSTON GAZETTE*

Dissatisfied with Postmaster John Campbell (publisher of the *Boston News-Letter*), John Hamilton, the deputy postmaster general of America, appointed William Brooker postmaster of Boston. Brooker began on 13 September 1719. The postmaster was in the best position to gather news and distribute a paper. Isaiah Thomas observed, "Postmasters established the first two newspapers published in Boston; and succeeding postmasters seemed to claim a right to such publication, or at least to think that a newspaper was an appendage to their office."[32] Newspapers were delivered free by the post (until Franklin, as postmaster general for North America, started charging for their delivery on 1 June 1758), but the postmaster could forbid the post riders to carry a rival's newspaper.[33] Brooker probably assumed that Campbell would give up the *Boston News-Letter* when Brooker became postmaster, but Campbell kept publishing the paper. So Brooker refused to allow the post riders to carry the *News-Letter* and started a second Boston newspaper, the *Boston Gazette*, on 21 December 1719. He hired James Franklin to print it. That ensured a steady employment for James Franklin's press. If he had not already hired a journeyman printer, he would have done so at this time.

The *Boston Gazette* opened by claiming that the public wanted a different newspaper and that persons living outside Boston "have been prevented from having the News Paper sent them by the Post, ever since Mr. Campbell was removed from being Post-Master." Of course Brooker did not say that he, as the new postmaster, had refused to allow the *Boston News-Letter* to be delivered. He promised to publish accounts "every other Week" of the price of merchandise, as well as the price of the local currency compared to sterling. He also promised the latest news, saying that the other postmasters in the colonies had promised to send on news notices by every post. Although Franklin was involved in setting the type, printing off the paper, delivering it to the subscribers, and hawking it in the streets, he did not mention the *Boston Gazette* in the *Autobiography*. Instead, he said that his brother started the second newspaper in America, the *New-England Courant* (A 17). In fact, if we count the single issue of Benjamin Harris's *Publick Occurrences* (1690), the *Boston Gazette* was America's third newspaper. But James Franklin only printed it, and that for only seven months; he did not own, edit, or publish it. Franklin forgot the *Gazette* because it was little different from the *Boston News-Letter*, founded in 1704, whereas the *Courant*, James Franklin's newspaper, was the most literary, audacious, and humorous newspaper of colonial America.

On 27 June 1718, England's postmaster general appointed Philip Musgrave postmaster of Boston. John Hamilton had not learned the news when he appointed Brooker postmaster. Musgrave finally came to Boston early in 1720, and his commission automatically superseded Brooker's.[34] The 14 March 1720 *Boston Gazette* mentioned that the post office was now at Philip Musgrave's in Cornhill. Since James Franklin's colophon continued to read "and may be had at the Post Office, where Advertisements are taken in," Musgrave evidently took over the *Boston Gazette* from William Brooker in March. The last extant *Gazette* printed by James Franklin was for 1 August 1720. Musgrave then replaced James Franklin with Samuel Kneeland as the *Boston Gazette*'s printer. Losing the job was a catastrophe for James Franklin—and no doubt resented by his apprentice.

Perhaps because he was printing the *Gazette* until August, James Franklin printed fewer imprints in 1720, five in comparison to eight in 1719. One of the five probably influenced the apprentice. James Franklin printed Edward Wigglesworth's anonymous *Letter from One in the Country . . . Containing Some Remarks upon a Late Pamphlet, Entitled, The Distressed State of . . . Boston.* Wigglesworth's pamphlet was advertised in the *Gazette* of 16 May as "Just Published."[35] If young Franklin had not previously focused on the paper currency issue (hotly debated in Boston during the period), the printing of Wigglesworth's pamphlet would have made him do so.

Since no gold or silver was mined in the English colonies, since the balance of trade was favorable to England, and since Parliament made it illegal either to allow the export of English coin to America or to allow the colonies to mint coins from foreign bullion, the colonies had a constant currency shortage. Wigglesworth opposed John Colman's plea for a paper currency in *The Distressed State of the Town of Boston*, which had been advertised in the 11 April 1720 *Boston News-Letter*. Wigglesworth advocated frugality as the answer. Franklin probably thought Colman and Wigglesworth were both partially right. He took up the question of paper currency in the Busy-Body essay on 27 March 1729 and thereafter wrote repeatedly on the subject.

Vegetarian

Franklin probably continued living at home for a year or two after beginning to work for his brother—otherwise his father would not have found the written exchanges with John Collins. When he was fourteen or fifteen, Franklin moved out of his parents' home and began living and boarding at the house where James Franklin lived. There, Franklin adopted vegetarianism. "When about 16 Years of Age, I happen'd to meet with a Book written by one Tryon, recommending a Vegetable Diet. I determined to go into it. . . . My refusing to eat Flesh occasioned an Inconveniency, and I was frequently chid for my singularity" (A 14). Later, when Franklin told his French friends such as the Abbé de la Roche and Pierre Cabanis of his early vegetarianism, he attributed it to reading Plutarch's *On the Eating of Flesh*[36] instead of Thomas Tryon's *Way to Health*. No doubt he read both. Plutarch, however, does not give menus. Those he learned from Tryon: "I made myself acquainted with Tryon's Manner of preparing some of his Dishes, such as Boiling Potatoes or Rice, making Hasty Pudding, and a few others, and then propos'd to my Brother, that if he would give me Weekly half the Money he paid for my Board, I would board myself. He instantly agreed to it, and I presently found that I could save half what he paid me. This was an additional Fund for buying Books" (A 14–15).

Franklin's vegetarianism also gave him more time for study: "But I had another Advantage in it [preparing his own meals]. My Brother and the rest going from the Printing-House to their Meals, I remain'd there alone, and dispatching presently my light Repast, (which often was no more than a Bisket or a Slice of Bread, a Handful of Raisins or a Tart from the Pastry Cook's, and a Glass of Water) had the rest of the Time till their Return, for Study, in which I made the greater Progress from that greater Clearness of Head and quicker Apprehension which usually attend Temperance in Eating and Drinking" (A 15).

Study

Franklin's favorite sister, Jane, told Ezra Stiles on 28 September 1779 that Franklin "studied incessantly a nights when a boy" and that he was "Addicted to all kinds of reading." Her testimony confirmed what we know from other sources. Franklin said in the *Autobiography* that he studied at night after work and on Sundays, when he spent the day at the printing house alone. At Brownell's school, Franklin had made no progress in arithmetic, and it was the first subject that he resolved to teach himself. He bought Edward Cocker's *Arithmetic* and "went thro' the whole by my self with great Ease." Franklin probably recalled that after reading his poetry, Uncle Benjamin Franklin had compared him to "great Cocker." Cocker's *Arithmetic* was a standard text from its publication in 1677 until the nineteenth century. Franklin sold hundreds of copies from his shop when he was a printer in Philadelphia (1729–48). Some knowledge of navigation was common in the seventeenth and eighteenth centuries. After studying Cocker, "I also read Seller's and Sturmy's Books of Navigation, and became acquainted with the little Geometry they contain, but never proceeded far in that Science" (A 15). Every good sailor knew the basics presented in the popular texts by John Seller *(Practical Navigation* [1669]) and Samuel Sturmy *(Mariner's Magazine* [also 1669]). Perhaps Franklin was still thinking of running away to sea. He had learned enough to be able to figure out the ship's longitude when he observed a lunar eclipse on 30 September 1726.

He also studied the greatest book of psychology, logic, and philosophy of the day—John Locke's *Essay Concerning Human Understanding*. Annotating the 1741 *Catalogue* of the Library Company of Philadelphia, Franklin wrote that Locke's *Essay* was "esteemed the best Book of Logick in the World."[37] Perhaps he first learned to distrust words and to question the value of syllogistic reasoning from Locke's *Essay*. If so, these tendencies were reinforced when he read Francis Bacon. He undoubtedly read all of Locke's writings that were conveniently available. At age twenty-five, Franklin started the Library Company, and shortly thereafter he donated to it Locke's *Two Treatises of Government* (London, 1698).[38] The book lover Franklin was unlikely to part with *Two Treatises* unless he had obtained a superior personal copy. He repeatedly revealed his knowledge of Locke's various writings. In *Poor Richard* for 1748, he celebrated the English philosopher: "On the 28th [of October], *Anno* 1704, died the famous *John Locke*, Esq; the *Newton* of the *Microcosm*: For, as *Thomson* says, '*He made the whole internal world his own.*' His book on the *Human Understanding*, shows it."

Many scholars have commented on Franklin's use of Locke, but another book that he mentioned in the same sentence (A 15) has been relatively ignored: Antoine Arnauld and Pierre Nicole, *Logic, or the Art of Thinking.*[39] Among the best critical histories and discussions of logic and philosophy before Locke, the Port Royal *Logic* (as it was generally called) often referred to previous writers. Though Locke built on his predecessors, he rarely named or cited them, but Arnauld and Nicole repeatedly paraphrased and praised St. Augustine, Descartes, and Pascal. They also repeatedly condemned Pyrrhonism and the author they considered its modern advocate, Montaigne. It may be that the Port Royalists introduced Franklin to Greek philosophers and to various concepts in Greek philosophy, including Pyrrhonism, that is, a thorough skepticism. Franklin's French friend the Marquis de Condorcet said in his eulogy of Franklin in 1790 that he was a Pyrrhonist.[40] The Port Royalists also censured Cicero and the "new Academics" for their skepticism.

Among numerous passages in the *Logic* that Franklin would have found fascinating was the following on skepticism: "some Philosophers . . . deny [clear and certain knowledge] and even have built upon this Foundation the whole Structure of their Philosophy: Among these, some have gone no further than to deny Certainty, admitting Probability, and these are the new Academics." If Franklin did not know it then, he later learned that the Port Royalists were referring to Carneades (214–129 B.C.), whom Franklin sometimes imitated. "The other sort, who are the Pyrrhonians, deny even Probability itself, and pretend that every thing is alike obscure and uncertain. . . . yet no Man could ever doubt, as St *Austin* affirms, whether he be, whether he think, or whether he live."[41]

The following passage struck Franklin as especially interesting, for he quoted part of it, evidently from memory, in 1732: "It is certain that there is nothing certain; and there is nothing but Obscurity and Uncertainty in every thing else. . . . So this Maxim of the Academicians, *That this is certain that there is nothing certain*, was contradicted differently by the Dogmatics and by the Pyrrhonists. For the Dogmatics opposed it, by maintaining that it was doubly false, because there were several Things that we know very certainly, and that therefore it was not true that it was certain we knew nothing: And the Pyrrhonists also said it was false for a contrary Reason, which was, that every thing was so uncertain, that it was even uncertain whether there was nothing certain."[42]

Besides logic, style was an important subject of the Port Royal *Logic*. The authors censured burlesque as a logical fault. Franklin, however, would have loved the ostensibly serious passage they quoted from Montaigne. They said:

> Who again could endure this other Argument of the same Author, upon the Subject of the Auguries, that the Pagans drew from the flight of Birds, and which the wisest among them ridiculed? *Of all the Predictions of times past*, says he, *the most ancient and most certain were those which were drawn from the flight of Birds: We have nothing now so admirable; that Rule, that Order of the shake of their Wing, by which they drew consequences of things to come, must certainly have been conducted by some excellent means to so noble an Operation; but to ascribe this great Effect to some natural disposition, without the Understanding, Consent, and Discourse of that which produces it, is an Opinion evidently false.* Is it not pleasant enough to hear a Man that holds nothing to be evidently true, or evidently false, in a Treatise wrote on purpose to establish Pyrrhonism, and to destroy Evidence and Certainty, vent these Follies for certain Truths, and call the contrary Opinion evidently false? But he laughs at us all the while he talks to us thus; and it is inexcusable in him, to play upon his Readers after this

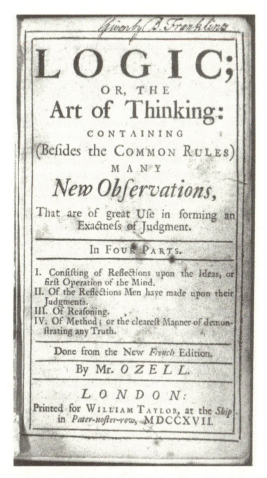

Given by B. Franklin

LOGIC;
OR, THE
Art of Thinking:
CONTAINING

(Befides the COMMON RULES)

MANY

New Obfervations,

That are of great Ufe in forming an
Exactnefs of Judgment.

In FOUR PARTS.

I. Confifting of Reflections upon the Ideas, or
firft Operation of the Mind.
II. Of the Reflections Men have made upon their
Judgments.
III. Of Reafoning.
IV. Of Method; or the cleareft Manner of demon-
ftrating any Truth.

Done from the New *French* Edition.

By Mr. *OZELL*.

LONDON:

Printed for WILLIAM TAYLOR, at the *Ship*
in *Pater-nofter-row*, MDCCXVII.

Figure 5. About age thirteen, Franklin bought the Port Royal Logic, *or* The Art of Thinking *(1717), which he donated to the Library Company in 1733. In the* Autobiography,
Franklin specified the Port Royal Logic *as a book he studied when a boy. It contains
judgments about writers and philosophers from the Greeks to the late seventeenth century.
When Franklin gave his copy to the Library Company, he added "Given by" before his
signature. The book-loving Franklin accumulated a large library in Boston, including this
volume.*

After being attacked by "Porcus" as a sceptic in the American Weekly Mercury, *he
recalled a passage in the Port Royal* Logic *and echoed it when replying in the* Pennsylvania Gazette, *30 March 1731/2. The Port Royalists quoted the Greek Academicians as saying
that "It is certain that there is nothing certain," whereas the Pyrrhonists said that "everything was so uncertain, that it was even uncertain whether there was nothing certain." In
his* Gazette *essay, Franklin adopted the persona of a confused, obtuse writer named
"Marcus" complaining of skepticism (burlesquing his attacker "Porcus") and replied:
"Scepticism infests almost every Conversation; and one continually meets with People,
otherwise seemingly of tolerable Sense, who openly declare, that they know not but as
much may be said against any Opinion as for it: Some profess they know only this, That
they know nothing; and there are others who assert, that even this cannot certainly be
known." Courtesy, Library Company of Philadelphia.*

manner, by telling them things that he does not believe, and which none in their right Senses can believe.[43]

The apprentice would shortly delight in such burlesques when James Franklin's collaborator Nathaniel Gardner used them against the Mathers and when the Reverend John Wise befuddled his opponents with them. Of course Franklin himself often later wrote travesties, as we shall see.

If Franklin had not previously read Cicero, Augustine, Montaigne, Descartes, and Pascal, he would have wanted to do so after reading the quotations, praises, and censures in the Port Royal *Logic*. Franklin adopted several techniques, beliefs, and themes that the Port Royalists emphasized, including the Cartesian method that one should go from the simple to the complex; the belief that syllogistic reasoning was useless in discovering new truths and in understanding reality; and the theme that humans are creatures of blind pride. His own copy survives; he gave it to the Library Company on 19 February 1732/3.[44] Echoes, and even partial quotations from it, turn up in his writings throughout his life. The Port Royal *Logic* importantly influenced the young Franklin.

Perhaps the most famous quarrel in moral philosophy of the early eighteenth century was between Anthony Ashley Cooper, the third earl of Shaftesbury, and Bernard Mandeville. In his *Characteristics of Men, Manners, Opinions, Times* (1711), Shaftesbury opposed the Hobbesian theory that humans are naturally selfish and claimed that humans had both natural affections for one another and an innate moral sense. Francis Hutcheson and others followed Shaftesbury. In reply, Mandeville, whom Franklin met in London in 1725, published *The Fable of the Bees* (1714), which reaffirmed that humans are selfish and claimed that public benefits often resulted from private vice. Allusions to their fundamental quarrel occur in the popular journalism of the day and in Franklin's writings, where he usually sided with Shaftesbury.[45]

While studying works on the English language, Franklin purchased the second edition of *A Grammar of the English Tongue* (1712), which contained as an appendix "The Arts of Poetry, Rhetoric, Logic, etc." He analyzed the appendix and was especially fascinated by "a Specimen of a Dispute in the Socratic Method."[46] When he saw Xenophon's *Memorable Things of Socrates*, translated by Edward Bysshe (1712), he purchased it, "wherein there are many Instances of the same Method" (A 15). He had the Library Company of Philadelphia later buy it.[47] Evidently his first deliberately adopted persona, the Socratic persona, had a lasting effect on him.

> I was charm'd with it, adopted it, dropt my abrupt Contradiction, and positive Argumentation, and put on the humble Enquirer and Doubter. And being then, from reading Shaftesbury and Collins, become a real Doubter in many Points of our Religious Doctrine, I found this Method safest for my self and very embarrassing to those against whom I used it, therefore I took a Delight in it, practis'd it continually and grew very artful and expert in drawing People even of superior

> Knowledge into Concessions the Consequences of which they did not foresee, entangling them in Difficulties out of which they could not extricate themselves, and so obtaining Victories that neither my self nor my Cause *always* [emphasis mine] deserved. (A 15–16)

Franklin here seems to concede that his religious opinions were wrong, but how sly that wonderful *always* is.

Franklin's many later writings using the dialogue form owe something to his early fascination with the Socratic method. Thomas Jefferson, perhaps in part echoing the above passage in the *Autobiography*, testified: "One of the rules which, above all others, made Doctor Franklin the most amiable of men in society was 'never to contradict anybody.' If he was urged to announce an opinion, he did it rather by asking questions, as if for information, or by suggesting doubts."[48]

Franklin's reading also changed his religious outlook. He recalled that his parents "had early given me religious Impressions, and brought me through my Childhood piously in the Dissenting Way. But I was scarce 15 when, after doubting by turns of several Points as I found them disputed in the different Books I read, I began to doubt of Revelation it self. Some Books against Deism fell into my Hands; they were said to be the Substance of Sermons preached at Boyle's Lectures. It happened that they wrought an Effect on me quite contrary to what was intended by them: For the Arguments of the Deists which were quoted to be refuted, appeared to me much stronger than the Refutations. In short I soon became a thorough Deist" (A 58). It seems likely that Franklin's father had purchased Samuel Clarke's *Demonstration of the Being and Attributes of God*, the Boyle lectures for 1704 and 1705. The English freethinkers Anthony Collins and David Hume had similar reactions to Clarke. Collins gibed that nobody doubted the existence of God until the Boyle lecturers tried to prove it, and Hume said that "he never had entertained any belief in Religion since he began to read Locke and Clarke."[49] After reading books against them, Franklin read the deists. A volume by Anthony Collins that he purchased about this time survives at the Library Company of Philadelphia, *A Philosophical Inquiry concerning Human Liberty* (London, 1717), which he echoed in *A Dissertation on Liberty and Necessity* (1725).[50]

When he told his young French friend Pierre Cabanis about his early study, Franklin mentioned these authors and added that a "bad translation" of Pascal's *Les provinciales* ravished him. He could probably imagine turning Pascal's ridicule of Jesuit casuistry against the New England Puritan tradition of cases of conscience. He reread Pascal several times. Even when Franklin had become an old man, *Les provinciales*, according to Cabanis, was one of the French books he most admired.[51] Franklin also did not mention in the *Autobiography* a linguistic work that he borrowed and from which he took long extracts: John Wilkins, *An Essay towards a Real Character and a Philosophical Language* (1668), which aroused his lifelong interest in a phonetic alphabet.[52] He wrote Ezra Stiles, president of Yale College, on 1 September 1755 enclosing long passages from it that he had copied at age sixteen. His study of linguistics (no doubt influenced by his egalitarianism) was responsible for his opinion, "I think the worst Spelling the best" (28:422).

Henry Care and John Wise

In 1721 James Franklin accomplished the extraordinary feat of publishing twenty-one books and pamphlets plus, beginning Monday, 7 August 1721, his own newspaper, the *New-England Courant*. As I suggested above, he must have purchased a second press about this time. In addition to his younger brother, before the end of 1721 James Franklin needed at least one journeyman and one other apprentice. (Franklin mentioned that James Franklin boarded himself and his "*Apprentices* in another family" [emphasis mine; A 14]; and when Franklin returned to Boston in the spring of 1724, James Franklin's "*Journey-men* were inquisitive where I had been, what sort of Country it was, and how I lik'd it" [emphasis mine; A 29]—thus it seems as if the journeymen knew him previously.) Franklin himself, however, at age fifteen, was no doubt an excellent printer, fast and efficient at all the normal printing tasks. Among the twenty-one imprints James Franklin produced in 1721, two are especially significant for Benjamin Franklin: a collection of documents by Henry Care and a pamphlet by John Wise. Care's *English Liberties, or the Free-born Subject's Inheritance; containing Magna Charta . . . the Habeas Corpus Act . . . A Declaration of the Liberties of the Subject . . . The Petition of Right.* The three-hundred—page book was the Whig Bible and contained the most important documents and statements in English history and law concerning liberty, property, and the rights of the individual (e.g., the Magna Carta). Care (1646–88) contributed nothing of significance to the compilation, but he made these essential materials widely available under one cover. Franklin knew its contents thoroughly. James Franklin cited it several times in defending himself against the Massachusetts authorities.

Franklin focused on the paper money controversy again when his brother printed, at his own risk, the Reverend John Wise's *Word of Comfort to a Melancholy Country*, a sixty-two-page book urging the printing of paper currency, which appeared in late January or early February 1720/1.[53] Though the pamphlet was published anonymously, the author, who used the pseudonym Amicus Patriae, was widely recognized. Perry Miller commented that everyone knew that "only one stylist in the land was capable of such wit."[54] Wise (1652–1725), redoubtable in physical strength, intellect, and courage, was the most popular minister in Massachusetts. He had opposed Governor Edward Andros's 1687 attempt to impose a tax with arguments from Magna Carta and with the argument that "no taxes Should be Levyed on the Subjects without Consent of an

Assembly Chosen by the free-holders."[55] Wise denied the right of the British to overturn the Old Charter by which Massachusetts had been governed since 1629.

For the young printer James Franklin, getting something by John Wise to print was a great coup. The other printers would have gladly printed it; any Boston bookseller would have paid for its publication. Though Wise had not been a best-selling author, he was increasingly famous in New England. In giving James Franklin his pamphlet to publish, the old minister was befriending and, indirectly, supporting him, perhaps because James Franklin often critiqued the Mathers.

When Wise offered the pamphlet to young James Franklin (or when the printer learned of it and asked to print it), he became, for the first time, his own publisher. He gambled his time, the use of his equipment, the investment in ink, and, most costly, a large quantity of paper. Most printers did only job printing (typically handbills and forms) and pamphlets paid for by the booksellers. If the printer had a large shop (journeymen were often guaranteed some work per week) and the press might otherwise be idle, a printer might venture, but some printers never did, and most published nothing more substantial than an almanac at their own risk. The books and pamphlets that James Franklin gambled on publishing were major financial investments and would have particularly concerned the printer and his apprentice.

Wise wrote extraordinary prose, sometimes with elaborate metaphorical language. When he claimed that Harvard College, like the economy in general, benefitted from the paper currency, he pointed to the increasing numbers of graduates:

> Sometimes we were wont to have One, and sometimes Two, or Three at a Birth, with abundance of groans to bring them forth; and in some Years nothing but Dead Embrio's, or Abortions; so poor and insufficient was the Seminal Matter and Flames of our State, *viz.* Our Medium. For indeed proportionally to our Number, we had more Corn and other Produce, than we have had in these late Years, but in those Times had no sufficient Medium at all. But of late our Dear Mother brings forth Thirty or Forty at a Birth; And escapes not a Season, but makes a great Addition Yearly to her Numbers; That if you crush our Medium, you will Abate her strength, and thereby suppress her fertile, and noble Conception; for Apparently this is the means that has awakened her Genial Powers. (11)

The possible influence of John Wise on young Benjamin Franklin has not previously been noted, but the printer's devil, like his older brother, must have known Wise and no doubt read his earlier works as well as these recent ones. Wise contributed to three of Franklin's characteristics. First, Wise's style was probably the most engaging among the American writers of Franklin's youth. Though Nathaniel Gardner, the most prolific writer for the *New-England Courant*, certainly influenced Franklin's style (as we shall see), Gardner was not famous among his American contemporaries as a writer. Wise was, and he took

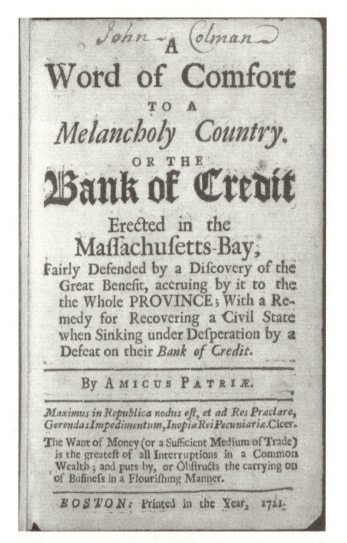

John ~ Colman

A
Word of Comfort
TO A
Melancholy Country.
OR THE
𝕭ank of 𝕮redit
Erected in the
Maſſachuſetts-Bay;
Fairly Defended by a Diſcovery of the
Great Benefit, accruing by it to the
the Whole PROVINCE; With a Remedy for Recovering a Civil State
when Sinking under Deſperation by a
Defeat on their *Bank of Credit.*

By AMICUS PATRIÆ.

Maximus in Republica nodus eſt, et ad Res Præclaro,
*Gerendas Impedimentum, Inopia Rei Pecuniariæ.*Cicer.

The Want of Money (or a Sufficient Medium of Trade)
is the greateſt of all Interruptions in a Common
Wealth; and puts by, or Obſtructs the carrying on
of Buſineſs in a Flouriſhing Manner.

BOSTON: Printed in the Year, 1721.

Figure 6. The Reverend John Wise (1652–1725), the old hero of Massachusetts resistance to British authority, allowed the rebellious young printer James Franklin to publish his Comfort to a Melancholy Country *(1720/1). James Franklin printed it at his own financial risk. Wise was perhaps the most respected minister of the day in colonial Massachusetts. He had opposed Governor Edward Andros's 1687 attempt to impose a tax with the argument that "no taxes Should be Levyed on the Subjects without Consent of an Assembly Chosen by the free-holders." Wise had been jailed for his stand.*

    Since any Boston bookseller or printer would have been honored to publish Wise, it is surprising that he turned to James Franklin. Perhaps he sympathized with James Franklin's opposition to the Matherian hegemony. Benjamin Franklin must have known him and certainly knew this pamphlet in favor of a paper currency. Franklin's later support of paper currency, his belief in egalitarianism, and his Americanism were all prefigured and perhaps partially created by the redoubtable six-foot-six-inch John Wise. Courtesy, Houghton Library, Harvard University, Cambridge, Massachusetts.

more stylistic chances than Gardner. Like Montaigne, Wise sometimes burlesqued opposite opinions, not only in logic but also in style. (Gardner also did.)
Franklin must have admired and remembered Wise's striking prose.

Second, Wise embodied proto-American ideals. He was an American patriot, famous as such among all his contemporaries. Numerous other citizens
of the day, including Samuel Sewall and Cotton Mather, revealed an incipient
Americanism, but New Englanders in general knew that Wise personified it.
Indeed, the pseudonym Amicus Patriae described Wise's reputation among his
Massachusetts countrymen. Third, Wise was an egalitarian.[56] In the dedication
of *A Word of Comfort*, Wise called the Massachusetts "Merchants & Farmers"
the "Grand Pillars of the Flourishing State of this Common Wealth." Franklin
later frequently celebrated and appealed to the tradesmen and farmers of Pennsylvania.

An anonymous pamphlet supporting Wise, titled *A Letter to an Eminent
Clergy-man*, was advertised in the 27 February 1720/1 *Boston Gazette*. The author
praised Wise as the writer of *A Word of Comfort*. Though no printer was indicated (James Franklin is a likely candidate), *A Letter* was published for the bookseller Benjamin Gray. The Massachusetts Council prosecuted Gray because of
the *Letter*'s portrait of the province's miserable economic condition. After the
grand jury declined to find a bill against Gray,[57] he hired James Franklin to
bring out a number of Daniel Defoe's *Review*, which he titled *News from the
Moon*, implicitly applying Defoe's defense of freedom of the press to Massachusetts.[58] The bookseller Daniel Henchman commissioned James Franklin to print
a reply to Wise: Thomas Paine's anonymous *Discourse Shewing, That the Real
First Cause of the Straits and Difficulties of This Province of the Massachusetts Bay,
Is Its Extravagancy & not Paper Money*.[59]

A correspondent in the *Boston Gazette* of 20 February 1720/1, who dated his
piece from "Castle-William" (the fort in Boston harbor), attacked Wise and *A
Word of Comfort*.[60] In reply, James Franklin, on his own venture, printed Wise's
*Friendly Check, from a kind Relation to the Chief Cannoneer, Founded on a Late
Information, Dated N.E. Castle William, 1720,21*.[61] Young Benjamin Franklin
must have been delighted by Wise's superb rhetorical strategy, which both lampooned and patronized his critic. In the deliberately befuddling first few sentences, Wise played on his opponent's dating the censure from Castle William.
Since it guarded the Boston harbor with cannon, Wise lampooned his opponent
with hyperbole in calling him the "Chief Cannoneer" and summoned up class
resentments against him, portraying his adversary as a wealthy gentleman who
hoarded money and oppressed the poor: "Kinsman, and Fellow-Soldier! The
Measures which I hear you Take are no ways proper for your high Station.
What, Sir! Only to flush, or Fire your Touchhole with the Dust, or sweepings of
the Powder-Room, in receiving that Capital Enemy, *Amicus Patriae*, who Boldly
with all his Canvas abroad, with his Jack, Ensign and Pendant proudly Flying,
has within the Reach of your Guns Entered our Chief Harbour; with a plain

Design of Mischief to many Principal Gentlemen, hoarders of our Bills in our Good Country; And plainly intends to break the Measures of such Eminent Benefactors to the Publick?"

A few weeks later, James Franklin printed for bookseller Benjamin Gray, Wise's *Freeholder's Address to the Honourable House of Representatives*, dated "March 15, 1720[/1]". In his last publication supporting paper currency, Wise pointed out how paper money had been useful in the past and suggested a series of projects that it might be used for in the future, including spinning schools for poor women and children, shipbuilding, paper mills, and an educational institution for poor boys. The last two became major projects of the adult Benjamin Franklin.

The first and in some ways the best historian of early American literature, Moses Coit Tyler, wrote in 1878 that "no other American author of the colonial time is the equal of John Wise in the union of great breadth and power of thought with great splendor of style; and he stands almost alone among our early writers for the blending of a racy and dainty humor with impassioned earnestness." Tyler thought Wise importantly influenced the writers of Revolutionary America.[62] Vernon L. Parrington rightly questioned the extent of his influence,[63] but neither literary historian connected Wise with the young apprentice who helped set Wise's last writings in print and sell them. Fifty years later, when Benjamin Franklin wrote his amazingly bold letter to Thomas Cushing on 24 December 1770 declaring that "the charter being a compact between the King and the people of the colony who were *out of the realm* of Great Britain, there existed nowhere on earth a power to alter it, while its terms were complied with, without the consent *of* BOTH *the contracting parties*" (17:308), he reflected the opinions of John Wise and the leaders of the Old Charter Party of his boyhood.

FOUR

Massachusetts Controversies
1716–1723

I remember his being dissuaded by some of his Friends from the Undertaking, as not likely to succeed.—On James Franklin's starting the New-England Courant (A 15)

WHEN GOVERNOR SAMUEL SHUTE arrived in Boston in 1716, Franklin was ten and probably cared little about Massachusetts politics. By the time Shute gave up the contest with the locals and clandestinely slipped away to England on 1 January 1722/3, the nearly seventeen-year-old Franklin knew the political scene intimately. Though no organized political parties existed in Massachusetts, most colonies had a group of assembly members who identified themselves with the "rights and liberties of the people" (especially with the assembly's right to control the taxes). On the other hand, the Royal (or Proprietary, in Maryland and Pennsylvania) Party was intent on maintaining the administration's prerogatives. In addition, Massachusetts and Virginia preferred the system of government that had existed before the crown imposed a degree of uniform organization on the colonial empire. Virginia's nostalgia appears often in Robert Beverley's *History and Present State of Virginia* (1705) with its praise for Virginia's "old Constitution."[1] In Massachusetts, the Old Charter Party testifies to its nostalgia. Thus "Elisha Trueman" (i.e., Thomas Lane, characterized below) in the 14 May 1722 *New-England Courant* identified one speaker in a skit as a "hearty Old Charter-man." Both colonies also revealed a pride in local identity and a resentment of favored newcomers: just as Massachusetts politicians resented "Strangers" (i.e., Englishmen) being promoted in their government while their own "*Countrymen* [were] neglected and despised," so, too, Virginians distinguished between natives and "Strangers" from England. Franklin used the same diction in 1755.[2]

POLITICAL PARTIES

Though not so defined as twenty-first-century American political parties, political alignments similar to political parties existed in the colonies. The background of late seventeenth-century politics is important for understanding early eighteenth-century Massachusetts politics. Though the Stuarts annulled the old charter of Massachusetts, the new regime under the Glorious Revolution gave Massachusetts a new one (1691). Beginning in 1691, the Lords Commissioners of Trade and Plantations (familiarly called the Board of Trade) oversaw colonial policies and sent its recommendation through the secretary of state to the Privy Council, which acted for the king. The Board of Trade reviewed colonial legislation and often disallowed it. (The favorite colonial method to get around this provision was to pass temporary laws, which would expire in a year; by the time the Board of Trade reviewed them, the laws would be about to expire.) Numerous Massachusetts citizens resented the review of the laws and other changes in the new charter of 1691, such as the British appointment of the governor. They called themselves Old Charter Men and their hero was the Reverend John Wise, who had opposed the Stuart representatives' tax assessments in 1687. He had claimed that there could be no taxation without representation.

The political leaders of the Old Charter group were Elisha Cooke, Sr. (1637–1715), and Elisha Cooke, Jr. (1678–1737). Though the Old Charter Men knew that the new charter was better than none, they remembered and preferred the greater privileges enjoyed under the old charter. They generally opposed royal authority over the colony and the governors' attempts to rule by prerogative. The belief in Old Charter privileges enjoyed a degree of mythic authority because it dovetailed so beautifully with the rhetoric of that favorite New England sermon genre, the jeremiad: the ministers constantly reminded New Englanders that the present age had degenerated in spirituality, and the politicians constantly reminded them that they had lost their original charter rights. Because the dominant theory of history held that humans had been degenerating since early biblical times,[3] both religion and politics reflected the popular belief in chronological primitivism.

Some practical New Englanders, however, embraced the new charter. The 5 February 1721/2 *Boston News-Letter* contained an advertisement stating the political position of New Charter Men who were identified with the governor and the Prerogative Party:

> Forasmuch as His Majesty's good People of this Government are Indissolubly United in the Common good of their Country and by the favour of GOD and the KING, continue very Thankful in the Enjoyment of the Privileges of the Royal CHARTER. Publick Notice is therefore hereby given to all Proud, Envious Persons, as well Jacobites, Nonjurors, as other Enemies to their happy Constitution, (who one would think are fitter Instruments to build up Bable, than to promote the Common Weal of Israel) That they do not to their utmost Peril, go on to Disturb or Interrupt the Inhabitants in their Quiet Possession of their inestimable Privileges; which were the Bequests and Gifts of their Ancestors; *who altho' they were born free, yet* with a great Sum obtain'd this freedom, *and which are justly Valued, and near the heart of all good Men.*

The New Charter group continually stressed the privileges that Massachusetts citizens held—and frequently reminded the Old Charter partisans that the royal government could take away these privileges. Increase and Cotton Mather pragmatically accepted the new charter, while most elected representatives to the General Court, especially the Bostonians, held Old Charter ideals. In addition to the two dominant parties, a small Royal Party existed, which included the governor; Joseph Dudley (1647–1720), who had been the first governor under the new charter; the jurist Paul Dudley (1675–1751), son of Joseph; and a few others.[4]

Reporting to the British authorities after his return to England in 1723, Governor Samuel Shute claimed that many country people but especially the Boston citizens were "too much dispos'd to a levelling spirit, too apt to be mutinous and disorderly, and to support the House of Representatives, in any steps they take towards encroaching on the Prerogative of the Crown." He reported, however, that "the whole Clergy of the Province, as well as the generality of the People, are zealously affected to your Majesty's person, and Government."[5] Cotton Mather was Shute's special partisan, much to the disgust of the Boston politicians. Once opposition to Shute began, Mather published the clergy's welcoming address to the governor, frequently visited him with bits of information, met with representatives from the House and tried to enlist their support for Shute, and wrote a pamphlet attacking Cooke and the Old Charter partisans, *News from Robinson Cruso's Island* (Boston, 1720). Mather also supported Shute in a sermon opposing paper currency, *Concio Ad Populum*, and in a Gunpowder Plot Day sermon, *Mirabilia Dei*.[6]

THE ISSUES

In addition to the general resentment of British authority, six political issues caused controversy. Because of the constant currency shortage in the colonies, paper currency was frequently debated as an option, usually with the Prerogative Party and the wealthy merchants opposing it. In Massachusetts during Governor Shute's administration, Elisha Cooke, Jr., led the paper currency party. Shute approved a paper currency issue (7 November 1716) but soon thereafter changed his mind and opposed it (10 April 1717). As we have seen, James Franklin printed John Wise's pamphlets supporting a paper currency. The Boston pamphlets argued whether there should be a paper currency—if so, how much could safely be printed without causing inflation, and what should be the basis of the paper money. Franklin wrote on these topics throughout his life.[7]

A second political problem, one that Franklin's contemporary Thomas Hutchinson believed to be "the beginning of the public controversy which continued until the end" of Governor Shute's administration, concerned the crown's rights to New England's large pine trees. England had imported trees from the Scandinavian countries to build its ships, but in the seventeenth century the mother country found that trees in the colonies could be used. The English authorities wanted to reserve the largest trees solely for the British Navy's ship masts. Parliament's White Pine Act, published in Massachusetts in

1711, forbade felling "any white or other sort of pine trees" not the property of private persons and over twenty-four inches diameter at twelve inches from the ground. Such trees were supposedly reserved for the crown.[8] Though shipbuilding became a major colonial industry (encouraged by the requirement that all shipping between England and the colonies must be in vessels built, manned, and owned in England or the colonies), the colonists often used the large white pines for their own shipbuilding, buildings, firewood, etc. After Elisha Cooke attacked John Bridger, royal surveyor of the woods, claiming that he accepted bribes to allow the inhabitants to cut the largest trees (14 February 1717/8), Bridger convinced Governor Shute to negative (i.e., to veto) Cooke as a council member (29 May 1718). Cooke then redoubled his efforts against the royal appointee, and the House censured Bridger (4 December 1718).

Surprisingly, historians have generally ignored the General Court's taxing of English goods shipped to Massachusetts.[9] In this amazing reversal of English mercantilism, the Massachusetts politicians revealed their resentment of the English Acts of Trade and Navigation and replied to them with their own tax. If the English were going to tax colonial goods, they would charge a duty on English goods. The impost bill (passed on 23 July 1715 and renewed annually through 1718) taxed English goods imported into Massachusetts. The Massachusetts General Court persisted in the face of direct instructions from Britain forbidding the colony to tax English goods (10 June 1718) and only failed to renew the impost bill when Governor Shute adamantly refused to pass it again (30 June 1719). In the following election, Governor Shute negatived the Bostonian Dr. John Clarke as councillor because he had been a chief supporter of the impost bill (28 May 1720). But, as Shute complained in his memorial to the king (ca. April 1723), a common maxim in Massachusetts said that "A Negatived Councillor makes A Good Representative." Clarke was elected a Boston representative on 12 May 1721 and elected Speaker of the House on 31 May. Shute dissolved the assembly on 20 July. At the new election on 2 August, Clarke was again elected a representative; at the meeting of the General Court, 23 August 1721, he was again elected Speaker; he continued to be elected Speaker for the next two years. The impost bill documented an incipient Americanism among Massachusetts citizens and a resentment of English authority, particularly the Acts of Trade and Navigation. Naturally, Old Charter adherents supported the impost bills.

A fourth political issue that developed during the administration of Governor Shute concerned his right to negative the Speaker of the House. Shute negatived Elisha Cooke, Jr., on 25 May 1720; when the House insisted that he could not do so, Shute dissolved the assembly on 30 May. In *A Just and Seasonable Vindication*, Cooke argued that the governor did not have the authority to negative the Speaker. After the Board of Trade disagreed, Cooke, in an amazingly bold speech on 1 September 1721, denied its authority. Thomas Hutchinson pointed out in his *History of Massachusetts* that Jeremiah Dummer, the Massachusetts agent to Great Britain, warned the Massachusetts representatives that the English feared they wanted independence. The issue was resolved after Franklin left Massachusetts, but he surely learned of it. The Explanatory Charter, asserting the governor's right to negative the Speaker of the House, was submitted to the House in December 1724 and passed on 15 January 1724/5. It marked the end, temporarily, of the Massachusetts politicians' denial of England's superior authority. It also avoided a parliamentary inquiry into the government of Massachusetts. Hutchinson observed that "it was feared the consequence of a parliamentary enquiry would be an act to vacate the charter of the province." The vote to accept the Explanatory Charter was 42 to 38. The names of the representatives and their votes were officially recorded, and James Franklin published them in the *New-England Courant* on 22 January 1725/6. For the Old Charter adherents, the publication documented the traitors to New England and its traditions. This was the first time in the English-speaking world that the names and the votes of elected representatives were officially recorded and published.[10]

A fifth issue was the governor's demand for a fixed salary. Since Shute was so busy with other matters, including an Indian war on the Massachusetts' frontier, he did not at first insist that the General Court pass this request from the Board of Trade, though it became more important throughout his administration. He was paid £800 for his brief time in office in 1716, and £1,200 for 1717, 1718, and 1719. Then, in the ever-depreciating Massachusetts currency, he was paid only £1,000 in 1720 and 1721, despite his and the council's complaints. In 1722, he was paid £500 and departed in December before the usual additional payment was made. In his memorial to the king (ca. April 1723), Shute complained bitterly about the low salary, "but even that they don't give me till I have passed the Bills in the Respective Sessions, thereby to Constrain me as far as they can to Consent to any Bills they lay before me." Unless the governor passed the acts the legislators wanted, they cut or entirely withheld his salary. As we will see, Pennsylvania's legislators did the same.

A sixth political issue concerned colonists settling along the Maine and New Hampshire frontiers. English policy, enforced by Governor Shute, discouraged the settlements. The English wanted to keep a large area of forest between the eastern Indians and the English colonists. But the Cookes, father and son, had immense estates in Maine and favored colonists settling there. The Massachusetts and New Hampshire representatives agreed with them. James Franklin's *New-England Courant* sided with Cooke, Jr. (the father had died in 1715), and the Popular Party. Warfare had been continuous on the northern frontier for decades. During King William's War (1689–97), the frontiers of New England were continually beset by Indian raids spurred on by the French. The inconclusive Treaty of Ryswick (30 September 1697) had not ended the fighting along the New England frontier. Queen Anne's War (1702–13) accelerated the Indian raids, and the Treaty of Utrecht (11 April 1713) again failed to resolve New England's frontier conflicts. Throughout Franklin's early life, Abnaki Indians raided the New England frontier, and the New Englanders frequently attacked the French and Indian strongholds.

Finally, a nonpolitical concern, inoculation for smallpox, was the most important controversy when James Franklin started the *Courant*. A smallpox epidemic began in Boston in May 1721, prompting Cotton Mather to circulate a letter among Boston's physicians, dated 6 June 1721, calling for a consultation among them concerning inoculation. Inoculation for smallpox was new to the Western world. Nearly all the physicians, led by Dr. William Douglass, feared that inoculation would spread smallpox. So did the general populace. The ministers supported Cotton Mather, who urged inoculation, while the Boston magistrates joined the majority of the physicians in opposing it. With life and death at stake, passions ran high. On 26 June 1721, Dr. Zabdiel Boylston (1674–1766) inoculated his son and two of his slaves. He gradually inoculated others. Boylston carried out the first large-scale (for the population of the day) inoculation in the Western world during the summer and fall of 1721.[11]

The two existing newspapers, the *Boston News-Letter* and the *Boston Gazette*, refused to publish anything opposing inoculation. When James Franklin started the *New-England Courant* in 1721, he gave the anti-inoculation forces a public voice. He knew that publishing material against inoculation would immediately win him some supporters. Though it has been assumed that he and his young brother Benjamin personally opposed inoculation, they may have privately supported it.[12] Like a good newspaperman, James Franklin welcomed "both Inoculators and Anti-inoculators" to write for the *Courant*. He proclaimed that "my own Sentiments" were of "no Consequence, nor any matter to any Body" (4 December 1721). The proponents of inoculation, however, had two other newspapers where they could publish and did not do so in the *Courant*. When the epidemic faded in February 1722, the controversy lost its immediacy in Boston, though smallpox inoculation continued to be controversial throughout the eighteenth century. In retrospect, one must admire and credit Cotton Mather and Dr. Zabdiel Boylston for their courageous actions.

Why Did James Franklin Start the *Courant*?

Isaiah Thomas suggested that James Franklin began the *New-England Courant* (1721–26) because he resented Philip Musgrave's taking away the printing of the *Boston Gazette* from him.[13] The early attacks on Musgrave's *Boston Gazette* (1719–), however, were by John Checkley and Dr. William Douglass, and they leveled the same charges at John Campbell's *Boston News-Letter* (1704–). Perhaps James Franklin's attacks on Musgrave as postmaster were partially motivated by revenge, but it hardly seems like a good reason for him to have begun the *Courant*.

James Franklin probably believed that he could produce a more interesting and entertaining paper than could either Campbell or Musgrave. He knew he had greater literary ability than the other newspaper editors, and he believed that his tastes were more akin to the best contemporary English literary journalism. Campbell and Musgrave rarely printed literary materials, copying instead English and European news and falling months, sometimes years, behind in their coverage. Amusing essays and poems, spoofs and satires, mock news notes and vibrant character sketches—all could and did enliven some of the best contemporary English newspapers. James hoped to gain writers and subscribers by publishing a more local, entertaining, and timely paper, one that featured more Boston and American news, more up-to-date English and European news, and more entertaining literature than appeared in either the *News-Letter* or the *Gazette*.

Second, he had a beautiful opportunity because the other two newspapers refused to publish anything against inoculation. The *Boston News-Letter* had even broken off the publication of a series of letters that Dr. William Douglass began writing against the supposedly dangerous practice. Since the public generally and the Boston magistrates in particular opposed inoculation, James thought many would buy his paper to see their own views expressed. He began by continuing the series of Douglass's letters that the *News-Letter* had refused to print.

Third, James Franklin no doubt hoped to attract such Massachusetts politicians as Elisha Cooke, Jr., and John Colman to write for the *Courant*. They were dissatisfied with the authorities, especially with Governor Shute. The two existing newspapers sided with the British and New Charter politicians and religious authorities against the Old Charter adherents. The printer probably believed a paper that would take up the quarrels of Cooke and the assembly against the placemen would find a popular audience. As Walter Isaacson commented, the *New-England Courant* became "America's first fiercely independent newspaper, a bold, antiestablishment journal that helped to create the nation's tradition of an irreverent press."[14]

Another group of writers and subscribers James Franklin believed he could attract were those who opposed the Mathers' religious position and the New England Puritan establishment, including the Anglicans (whether Old Charter or Royalist adherents), Baptists, skeptics, and liberal Congregationalist ministers and laymen such as the Reverend John Wise, the Reverend Benjamin Colman, and Nathaniel Gardner. The older newspapers supported the status quo—the old semi-theocratic attitudes, wherein an obedient and deferential people followed the leadership of ministers, especially the Mathers, and of magistrates like Judge Samuel Sewall. These attitudes, however, were anathema to James Franklin and the other Couranteers. They shared the eighteenth-century Whig ideology of John Trenchard and Thomas Gordon whose *Cato's Letters* (which were currently appearing in the London newspapers) were the *Courant*'s most frequently reprinted English essays. Ministers, religion, magistrates, and the authorities were all fair game for James Franklin and his friends.

These reasons—and James's friendship with several writers who could and would write for the *Courant*—made him fly in the face of his father's and his friends' best advice. His younger brother Benjamin remembered "his being dissuaded by some of his Friends from the Undertaking, as not likely to succeed" (A 17), but in the summer of 1721, James Franklin gambled and started the *New-England Courant*.

FIVE

Nathaniel Gardner
and the Couranteers

He [James Franklin] had some ingenious Men among his Friends who amus'd themselves by writing little Pieces for this Paper, which gain'd it Credit, and made it more in Demand; and these Gentlemen often visited us.—A 17.

THE STYLES, PERSONAE, AND EVEN JESTS of the *New-England Courant*'s first writers influenced young Benjamin Franklin. His personal file of the newspaper survives, containing issues from No. 1, which appeared on 7 August 1721, through no. 111, for 16 September 1723, the week before he ran away from Boston. Franklin annotated most of the first forty-three issues (7 August 1721 to 28 May 1722), giving the names of the local authors. Thirty-eight papers have annotations: the *Courant* of 7 August is lacking and those for 2, 23, and 30 October, and for 11 December 1721 have no local poems or essays and therefore no attributions.[1] Franklin did, however, name fourteen writers (not including himself) of ninety-four essays, letters to the editor, notes, and poems. Not all the writers took an interest in the paper at the same time, and seven wrote only one or two pieces, but eight Couranteers contributed repeatedly and some continued writing for the paper after Franklin ceased his annotations.

This chapter gives brief biographical sketches of the Couranteers, describes their anti-inoculation and belletristic writings, and assesses their influences on Franklin. Their political and religious writings are surveyed in the following two chapters. When James Franklin started the *New-England Courant* in August 1721, he gambled that he could assemble a group of amusing and controversial writers to contribute to it. After all, Bostonians eagerly purchased the local religious, political, and economic pamphlet literature, but the existing Boston newspapers avoided printing controversial material. Pamphlet writers such as John Colman, John Checkley, Elisha Cooke, Jr., and John Wise were the obvious persons for him to try to interest. He failed with Colman and Cooke, succeeded with Checkley and Wise, and cultivated others. Beginning with the fourth *Courant*, Nathaniel Gardner sometimes coedited the paper throughout the period that Franklin annotated it. Since eighteenth-century periodical essays and letters were almost always anonymous or pseudonymous, Benjamin Franklin's personal file of the *Courant* is extraordinary in itself and a revealing document for the literary and intellectual life of Boston. To give just one example: without it, we would never have known of any writings by Nathaniel Gardner.[2]

The *New-England Courant* was a major intellectual and financial gamble for James Franklin. Benjamin Franklin worked on every aspect of it: he set type, printed off the sheets, delivered the paper to the local customers, and heard their opinions—and later wrote for it. He also listened to the conversations of the Couranteers as they planned the paper and subsequently heard "their Accounts of the Approbation their Papers were receiv'd with" (A 17). Franklin must have known the writings in those early *Courants* almost by heart.

NATHANIEL GARDNER

Benjamin Franklin attributed thirty-two writings in various genres to the talented Nathaniel Gardner (1692–1770), and we know that he wrote others for the *Courant*, as well as an anonymous pamphlet that influenced the apprentice. Baptized at the First Church on 27 November 1692,[3] Gardner was admitted to membership on 30 January 1714/5. The Reverend Benjamin Wadsworth married him to Mary Green on 29 November 1716.[4] From 1717 to his death in 1770, he was an indispensable town official, serving in fifty-four minor posts. Throughout the colonial period, only nine Bostonians served longer than Gardner. A tanner and at this time a partner of Matthew Adams (who also contributed to the *Courant*), Gardner was the *Courant*'s most prolific and inventive writer, its best stylist, and often its coeditor. In a letter of 12 May 1801 on John Eliot's history of New England newspapers, Samuel Dexter commented that Gardner, "who for many years published the *bans of Matrimony* at the Thursday Lecture," contributed to the *Courant*.[5]

His first *Courant* piece, published on 4 September 1721 and written as "Zerubbabel Tindal" (the latter part of the pseudonym may have alluded to the infamous deist, Matthew Tindal), complained in a hyperbolic style that the *Courant*'s emphasis on inoculation bored the town. Zerubbabel Tindal said he belonged to a club of wits that could supply the *Courant* with constant entertainment: "Some of us are *Batchellors*, and well vers'd in the Theory of *Love*." The pose of a theoretical lover was charming. It applied Thomas Shadwell's 1676 burlesque of the virtuosi to the lover.[6] Other club members supposedly included poets, astronomers, philosophers, and politicians. Tindal/Gardner promised, in effect, to send in amusing pieces on all topics.

Either Gardner or James Franklin replied as "Timothy Turnstone" (a pseudonym for the editor), advising Tindal that "those among you who pretend to be *acute Astronomers* and *excellent Poets*, must be better acquainted with the Learned *N. Egyptiis Mesori Epagomenta* and *Tom L-w*,[7] before they set up for either." James Franklin continued the humor with lines about the best-known local balladeer, Tom Law:

> *Poor jingling* Tom, *wou'd he to rhiming keep,*
> *H'e* whirl *you*, roll *you*, soak *you in the Deep,*

> *At least his cutting Lines your Wings wou'd crop,*
> *Nor let you soar above* Parnassus *Top.*

These two brief pieces, unlike the materials in the previous several *Courants*, were fun.

A character sketch of a miser by Gardner on 11 September was dated from "Sagadahock, Aug. 25" and signed "JETHRO SHAM, *Advisor-General.*" Sham/ Gardner used the typical diction and tone of the periodical essay and began with the statement that "among the various Species of Creatures which the Omnipotent has formed (Devils only excepted) it is very observable that *Man* is the *most* capable of being his own Tormentor." After condemning the pursuit of money, the piece concluded with a sententia that Franklin later echoed: "he is not the Happy man, who has *abundance,* but he who is contented in the Enjoyment of what he has." (Cf. *Poor Richard* for July 1735: "Who is rich? He that is content.")

The 25 September paper contained two pieces by Gardner. The lead essay, dated from Cambridge (thus suggesting the author was a student or teacher at Harvard), derided those who prophesied the exact time of the world's end. Though ridiculing both millennialism (as did Franklin in later)[8] and religious charlatans, it ended with a traditional religious conclusion: "Let it suffice us then to know, that Christ will appear the second Time; that he comes quickly, and his Reward is with him, to remunerate to every man according to his Works. And seeing we look for such Things, let us be diligent and solicitous (not to know the precise time of his coming, but) that we may be found of our Judge in Peace, without Spot and blameless."

In the second piece, a mock advertisement, Gardner complained of women sitting down during public prayers and smiling and playing "with their Fans, an Indication of criminal Carelessness, and Unthoughtfulness of the awful Presence they are in." Gardner lampooned religious abuses frequently (as we will see in the following chapters) but without Franklin's savage irony. A church member, Gardner evidently believed in the essential tenets of Christianity, while chafing under the old assumptions of the minister's supposed superior authority and learning.

Gardner's sketch signed "S. B." in the 1 January 1721/2 *Courant* may have inspired aspects of Franklin's portrayal of Poor Richard's wife, Bridget. S. B. complained that he was "sadly fatigu'd with a Scolding Wife, and in short she is such a *Shrew,* as I believe cannot be match'd in all Christendom." In addition, "She is so close and stingy, that She locks up every thing from my Servants, and will not allow them necessary Food; nay she grudges them so much as Small Beer." S. B. did not know what to do: "I am such a quiet man, (as my Neigh-bours can all testifie) that I willingly part with any thing for peace (the Breeches not excepted) and am afraid to say my Soul is my own in her Presence." He hoped she would recognize her husband's complaint in the paper, "take the

Mr Gardner

To the Author of the New-England Courant.

SIR,   Cambridge, Sept. 22. 1721.

THAT the certain Knowledge of future Events is an undoubted Prerogative of the Almighty, and, to be found in the most sagacious & penetrating Creatures, no farther than he is pleas'd to reveal and discover it, is (I suppose) a Truth almost universally acknowledged.

I am, &c.

Monsieur Courante,

Reading in your last a Caution to the Fair Sex, I here send you one to Our Own, which if you will you may insert in your Courant, and if you won't you may let it alone, 'tis all the Case to

Your Humble Servant, LUCILIUS.

Mr James Franklin

A CAUTION to Batchellors.

BEware, fond Youths, of Nymphs deceitful Charms;
Nor take the fair Affliction in your Arms.

WOMAN! True to her Name, too strictly so;
For unto MAN she ever prove a WO.

ADVERTISEMENT.

Mr Gardner

Figure 7. Nathaniel Gardner's satire of millennialism, with Franklin's attribution of authorship, New-England Courant, 25 September 1721. Numerous writers of the Renaissance and of colonial America predicted the time of the end of the world. Occasionally they connected it with the supposed Hebrew origins of the American Indians. Colonial New England clergymen and laymen often argued that New England was to be the location of the Second Coming. One among the many examples of such reasoning that Nathaniel Gardner and, no doubt, Franklin knew was Samuel Sewall's Phadnomena Quaedam Apocalyptica (1697). Jonathan Edwards continued the tradition in his various Apocalyptic Writings, ed. Stephen J. Stein (New Haven: Yale University Press, 1977).

Gardner did not directly travesty the New England traditions, for that would have been too bold, but his criticism of European millenarians indirectly ridiculed New England writers like John Cotton, Thomas Shepard, Increase Mather, and Samuel Sewall. Gardner was probably the first New Englander to satirize millennialism. Franklin spoofed it later, in the preface to Poor Richard for 1751 and in his bagatelle, "The Ephemera," 20 September 1778. Courtesy, Burney Collection, British Library.

Hint, and use me better for the future." Gardner's little gem was the best social satire to appear thus far in an American newspaper.

Writing as "Hortensia" in the 29 January *Courant*, Gardner turned the tables and sketched an oppressed wife: "Seeing you are set up to reform the Age, I hope you will omit nothing that shall contribute to so good a Work. I suppose you will think it as reasonable to publish the complaints of our Sex as those of the other, unless you think that Women have no Souls." Franklin was probably delighted with Gardner's feminine personae and made his own earliest persona (Silence Dogood) a woman. In the first of Gardner's proto-feminist essays, Hortensia said: "Know then, that my Husband (who has had Liberal Education) is a cross ill-natur'd Fellow, who beats and abuses me at an intollerable Rate: And one Time in particular, after much ill Treatment, he threw me into a Pond. He is perpetually at the Taverns, sotting and drinking Flip, and setting People at Variance. I truly say, it is for the Good of his Soul and Body that I publish this Letter. He is a Man whom Nature has remarkably Stigmatiz'd and if he don't mend quickly, I shall give an Account of him which will not be at all pleasing to him." Franklin's Silence Dogood No. 3 and the "Reply to a Piece of Advice," 4 March 1734/5, both have similarities to Gardner's pieces. Franklin wrote in the latter: "There are in the World infinitely more He-Tyrants than She-Ones."

The editor (either Gardner or James Franklin) added a little prefatory joke, saying that if Hortensia "intends to make a Reformer of me, she will do well to write *Post paid* on her Letters for the future; for I don't intend to reform the Age at my own Charge." (Customarily the recipient paid the postage.) In the same paper, Gardner sent in a brief love poem by "Corydon," thus borrowing Virgil's rustic persona. In a sermonlike essay (26 February) concluding with "Amen," the anonymous Gardner called idleness "that *fertile Seminary* of most other Sins." In severely condemning idleness, Gardner parodied the excesses of a normal sermon. He condemned the "Fair Sex . . . in particular: . . . They can rise in the Morning, and spend the whole Forenoon between the Comb and the Glass, in dressing and prinking themselves; and then, perhaps they use the Afternoon . . . in impertinent Visits. Good God! What a stupid and senseless Prodigality is this?"

The following week, writing as "Fanny Mournful" (5 March), Gardner protested against a cruel stepmother who changed a formerly mild, indulgent father into a tyrant: "What barbarous Treatment I receiv'd from him one Night of late (by her Instigation) I shall particularly expose hereafter, if things go on as they do." As "Dulcimira," Gardner objected to the essay on idleness of 26 February because it singled out women for censure. Men, Dulcimira claimed, were at least as idle. This was Gardner's second proto-feminist piece. Then, as the author of the essay on idle women of the previous week, Gardner commented that as "an amorous Man" he was glad "to be thought worthy even of the Scorn of the fair Sex." In delightful dialogue, he claimed that he was recognized by a couple women as he walked along the street. "They broke out, . . . 'He's the ugliest

Fellow that ever I saw in my Life,—He's short Neck'd, stubbed Shank'd, rusty
Hair'd,—Lawful Heart! He's deform'd, and dull, and every thing.'"

Gardner also published a mock advertisement to the 5 March paper, announcing that "a full Meeting of the Couranteers, Gazeteers, etc.," unanimously
voted to thank the *Boston Gazette*'s Philip Musgrave for printing the exchanges
between the South Carolina legislature and their governor"— thereby implying
that the filler was so dull and uninteresting as to drive all readers to other papers.

Gardner again joined in the battle of the sexes with a short letter from "Sisyphus" in the 2 April 1722 *Courant*, complaining of his "*Virago* of a wife," who
dressed in fine clothes and spent her time drinking tea with her friends. On 9
April "Ben. Treackle" (Gardner) wrote a column anticipating the best features
of the "advice to the lovelorn" genre that has ever since been popular in American journalism. Gardner pretended to be a bashful young man captivated by the
"powerful Charms" of a "brisk young Widow." He asked if "it would be improper for the Lady to pop the Question first." Writing as the editor, Gardner
answered with a play on the word *pop*: "Improper! No, by no Means, Mr.
Treackle! Your *entire Affection for an Esteem of* the Widow, obliges her in Gratitude to *pop Questions* to you; especially since your Bashfulness renders you
incapable of giving her one single *Pop* for all the *good Manners and Pleasantness*
with which she treats you. And if the *brisk young Creature* deserves the Character
you give her, I doubt not but she can *pop* more Questions than you are able to
answer. Pray Mr. *Treackle*, read this to your Mistress at your next Meeting, and
if she does not *pop the Question first*, you may conclude (*in short*) that she *does
not love you*, and it will be your wisest way to *pop off.*" Franklin, who delighted
in verbal play, surely admired Gardner's fun.

Writing as "Will Coatless," Gardner sent in a piece (9 April) angrily address-
ing "You *Turnstone*," objecting to the paper's pointing at specific persons, particularly Poligrave's calling a certain fop in church *atheistical*. Coatless referred
to a piece of 26 March, signed "Poligrave," which Franklin left unattributed.
Gardner was probably also Poligrave. Replying to the complaint as editor Turnstone, Gardner said: "If the Person pointed at by Mr. *Poligrave* was not guilty
of an irreverent and atheistical Behaviour at Church, how came he to be *des-
crib'd and pointed at as it were with the Finger*, since his Name was not mention'd." In the same paper, Gardner contributed to the New England singing
controversy (the old-timers sang after a member of the congregation had "lined
out" the tune; now some congregations were singing from tune books). His
mock advertisement signed "John Harmony" complained of a few persons' irregular singing in church: "This is to advertise them, that for the future they
keep Time with the rest of the Congregation, so that Part of Worship may be
the more decently perform'd."

The 23 April *Courant* featured Gardner as "Philanthropos," writing on humans as social beings with conversation among their greatest delights: "Some
have maintained on the Principles of Reason, that if a Man were possess'd of

Celestial Happiness alone, and had it not in his Power to obtain Society there, he would repine at his own Felicity, and abandon Heaven it self, to seek Conversation on Earth." Though the opinion is not extraordinary, Franklin may have echoed Gardner in his 1726 journal (1:85).[9] Gardner especially praised conversation between friends: "the more open, free and ingenuous any Conversation is, the greater Pleasure and Satisfaction arises to the Persons engaged in it." Franklin wrote Lord Kames an appreciation of conversation on 3 January 1760: it "warms the Mind, enlivens the Imagination, and is continually starting fresh Game that is immediately pursu'd and taken and which would never have occur'd in the duller Intercourse of Epistolary Correspondence." Franklin put Gardner's theories concerning a formal method of conversation, "regulated by the Rules of Prudence and Virtue," into practice both in the twenty-four queries that started each meeting of Franklin's Junto and in the club's rules governing conversation (1:256–59).

On 30 April 1722, pretending to be a widower who had lost his wife to smallpox, Gardner told the story of his new courtship that abruptly concluded when, just before marriage, he had a lawyer "draw up an Instrument to secure all that she was worth to my self." The lady refused and broke off the marriage plans. The insensitive, avaricious widower therefore advertised for a woman who had "five or six hundred Pounds to secure to him by Deed of Gift." The widower appeared again on 7 May, said that he had seen the error of his ways, apologized, and announced the marriage banns for "the third Time." He therefore regretfully announced that he would not now be able to marry the wealthy young virgin or widow requested in the last paper. This lout is one of the more interesting personae created by Gardner. The unbelievably selfish widower anticipated such Franklinian personae as Count de Schaumbergh ("The Sale of the Hessians," 18 February 1777), but Gardner's underlying voice is without the ferocious disgust for human nature characteristic of Franklin's savage ironic personae.

I suspect Gardner also wrote the unattributed lead essay for the 3 September 1722 *Courant* on flattery. "Funeral Complements are for the most part bestow'd on the Rich & Honourable: not that *they* are the most deserving, for mean obscure Persons may be, and often are full as pious as they; but the misery is they are not able to bequeath such large Donations to the Orators, to Embalm their Memory, and fix an *Asterism* to their Names." The class-conscious essay anticipated the egalitarian sentiments of Benjamin Franklin (whose fine short obituary of James Merrewether, dated 22 April 1742, celebrated a "poor" and obscure person).

Though Gardner's talents appear in the above overview of his belletristic writings, especially in his advice to the lovelorn and in the creation of various personae, his literary ability is more apparent in his political and religious writings. He imitated and sometimes burlesqued the styles of others; responded in different personae to pieces that he himself wrote; mocked the opinions of hypocritical Puritan New Englanders; delighted in writing social, religious, and political satire; and used numerous literary techniques (like verbal play) that Franklin mastered shortly afterward. Gardner's favorite work of Mather's was *Bonifacius, an Essay upon the Good.* Though Franklin said he read it as a boy (A 9), he must have been impressed by Gardner's high opinion of the work. Gardner also identified with the common man against the presumed superiority of the authorities. And like his friend James Franklin, he was a radical Whig and a true Old Charter Man, believing steadfastly in the traditional rights of Americans. As Zerubbabel Tindal, Jethro Sham, Mr. Treackle, Hortensia, Philanthropos, and others, Gardner was Franklin's single most important teacher and model. Gardner's beliefs and values, which were similar to those of James Franklin, were ones the young genius adopted.

JAMES FRANKLIN

The second most prolific contributor to the *New-England Courant* was the obstreperous James Franklin himself.[10] Baptized in the Old South Church, he attended services but never became a full church member.[11] Though it has been asserted that he became an Anglican, the claim rests on the contribution of £10 in 1718 for "Building a Gallery, a New Pulpit, and adorning the Kings Chappel in Boston" by "J. Franklyn" (133).[12] Several other "J. Franklyns," however, lived in Boston besides Josiah (Franklin's father) and his sons Josiah, John, and James.[13] The printer could hardly have had the relatively large sum of £10 to spare for a church donation when he was twenty-one and starting his business. With his father, he owed money for the press, types, and other materials necessary to begin the shop. When James died in 1735, he still owed his father money. (In his will made out in 1744, Josiah Franklin forgave the debt due from James's estate.) Defending himself from Cotton Mather's attack published in the same paper, James Franklin mentioned on 4 December 1721 that the pastors of his church had not reproved him for anything in the *Courant* since issue No. 3 appeared on 21 August. When he married on 4 February 1723/4, the ceremony was performed by the Reverend John Webb at the New North Church, a Congregational church. Further, the printer subscribed for a copy of Samuel Willard's *Compleat Body of Divinity* (1726), the fundamental summary of New England Puritanism. So far as we know, James Franklin was a Congregationalist in 1721 and remained one, although, like many other Congregationalists, he evidently never became a full church member.[14]

   After setting up his printing shop in Boston in 1718, James Franklin increased his business dramatically through 1721, but it fell off thereafter. Perhaps, as the literary historian David S. Shields suggested, James Franklin gradually killed the *Courant*'s subscription base with the serial publication of Defoe's biography of Jonathan Wild.[15] In late 1726 or early 1727, Franklin gave up the *Courant* and moved to Rhode Island, where he was voted printer to the legislature. Though some scholars have suspected that he failed in Boston, it seems likely that the position of printer of the government business attracted him to Rhode Island.[16] Benjamin Franklin only attributed nineteen *Courant* pieces to James Franklin, and two of those he subsequently struck out (perhaps finding that the printer copied them),[17] but James probably wrote most of the local news (for which Franklin did not bother to ascribe authorship). The local news reflected James Franklin's Old Charter position. Only Nathaniel Gardner, the most prolific Couranteer, had more to teach young Franklin than his brother James. James masterfully stirred up controversy and kept his paper in the limelight. His writings will be discussed in subsequent chapters.

The Anglicans

The two newspapers that existed at the same time as the *Courant*, the *Boston News-Letter* and the *Boston Gazette*, both sided with the Mathers and the Matherian hegemony. They refused to publish materials critical of the Mathers, the royal authorities, or inoculation. James cultivated people who opposed the three groups. In addition to various New England Puritans, like the Reverend John Wise, James Franklin sought out Anglicans with a literary flair. Eight of the fourteen known Couranteers were Anglicans, and three of the eight were physicians who opposed inoculation. James Franklin asked the leading Anglican polemicist of Boston to write the opening *Courant* essay and the foremost opponent (another Anglican) of inoculation to contribute.

John Checkley

The indomitable John Checkley (1680–1754)[18] wrote the lead essay for the first *New-England Courant*, published on 7 August 1721. He kept a store at the sign of the "Crown and Blue-Gate," against the town house, which carried medicines, books, tobacco, and "notions" (miscellaneous items). Born in Boston, he attended the South Grammar School, studied at Oxford, traveled extensively on the Continent, and became an Anglican, serving as a vestryman of King's Chapel in 1719 and 1725–36.[19] To harass him, Boston authorities tendered him the oaths of allegiance to the crown and abjuration of the Stuarts on 9 February 1719/20, which he stubbornly refused to take.[20] The Boston authorities fined Checkley £6 on 5 April and forced him to post a bail of £100 for good behavior. John Gibbons, another Couranteer and Anglican, stood surety for half. Rumor had it that Checkley was a disaffected Jacobite. He finally took the oaths on 20 May 1724 to rid himself from the scandalous rumor—which had hindered his being ordained in the Church of England. That same day he was charged with libel for reprinting Charles Leslie's *Short and Easy Method with the Deists*, and another Couranteer, Dr. George Stewart, posted bond for him on 5 June 1724.[21] Reflecting public opinion, the Reverend John Bernard of Marblehead objected to Checkley's being ordained and wrote the Bishop of London, calling Checkley "a turbulent, vexatious and persecuting-spirited Non-juror."[22] Checkley finally took holy orders in 1738 from the bishop of Exeter and moved to Providence, Rhode Island, where he became rector of King's Church.[23]

In 1720, the Anglican Checkley censured the New England Puritan doctrines of election and predestination in a lively controversial pamphlet titled *Choice Dialogues between a Godly Minister & an Honest Countryman.* His former friend and Cotton Mather's nephew, the Reverend Thomas Walter (1696–1725),[24] answered with *A Choice Dialogue between John Faustus a Conjurer and Jack Tory His Friend.* In his *Choice Dialogues* and in his first *Courant* piece, Checkley used a country bumpkin persona who possessed considerable mother wit. This incipient American posture probably delighted young Franklin. The *Courant*'s opening essay complained that "a Man can't appear in Print now a days, unless he'll undergo the Mortification of Answering to ten thousand senseless and Impertinent Questions." As Franklin recognized, Checkley imitated the first issue of the *Spectator* (which began with a description of the supposed author) but transformed it with an American flavor. Checkley referred to the American bumpkin's habit of ceaselessly questioning a stranger—even when the stranger was himself asking a question. The motif was common in American humor and satire, parodied by Dr. Alexander Hamilton in 1746, called a "New England answer" by John Adams in 1816, and exemplified in the following popular apocryphal anecdote attributed to Franklin:

> He had observed, when he went into an ordinary, that every individual of the family had a question or two to propose to him, relative to his history; and that, till each was satisfied, and they had conferred and compared together their information, there was no possibility of procuring any refreshment. He, therefore, the moment he went into any of these places, inquired for the master, the mistress, the sons, the daughters, the men-servants and the maid-servants; and having assembled them all together, he began in this manner. "Worthy people, I am B. F. of Philadelphia, by trade a ————, and a bachelor; I have some relations at Boston, to whom I am going to make a visit; my stay will be short, and I shall then return and follow my business, as a prudent man ought to do. This is all I know of myself, and all I can possibly inform you of; I beg therefore that you will have pity upon me and my horse, and give us both some refreshment."[25]

Checkley's essay concluded with a promise to appear every two weeks (James Franklin at first intended to publish the paper biweekly) and with a triplet deriding the Mathers and the inoculation controversy:

> Who like faithful Shepherds take care of their Flocks
> By teaching and practicing what's Orthodox,
> Pray hard against *Sickness*, yet preach up the POX!

Checkley added: "N.B. This Paper will be published once a Fortnight, and out of meer kindness to my *Brother-Writers*, I intend now and then to be (like them) *very, very dull.*" The truth of the charge hurt all the more. Philip Musgrave of the *Boston Gazette* and John Campbell of the *Boston News-Letter* smarted.

Checkley's brief opening essay drew two pointed replies, ensuring the fledgling paper's immediate notoriety. John Campbell foolishly took upon himself and the *News-Letter* the charge of dullness—and proved the truth of the charge with his reply: "J[ohn] C[ampbell] to Jack Dullman" in the next *News-Letter* denigrated the *Courant* as by a "*Homo non unium Negotii*; Or, Jack of all Trades; and it would seem, Good at none: giving some very frothy fulsome Account of himself, but lest the continuance of that stile, should offend his readers: wherein with submission, (I speak for the Publisher of this Intelligence, whose endeavour has always been to give no offence, nor meddling with things out of his Province) the said Jack promises in pretense of Friendship to the other News-Publishers to amend, like soure Ale in Summer, Reflecting too much, that my performances are now and then, very, very Dull."

Learning that his old opponent Checkley had written the opening *Courant* essay, with its concluding triplet attacking the Mathers, Thomas Walter composed a vituperative response—which James Franklin happily printed as a broadside and evidently circulated with the *Courant*'s third issue.[26] *The Little-Compton Scourge: or, The Anti-Courant*, dated 10 August 1721, assaulted Checkley: "Go on Monsieur *Courant*, and prosper; Fear not to please your stupid Admirers, which will be an easy Task, if you will but consult your own heavy *Genius*, and write in your native Stile, of which you have been so sharp and discerning as to give us the apt and proper Character, VERY, VERY DULL!" Walter concluded with a couplet:

> Go on, dull Soul, labour in Spite
> Of Nature, and your Stars to write.

James Franklin's publication of Walter's attack showed that the printer had a shrewd understanding of news promotion. But Checkley contributed only one more piece to the paper before James Franklin dropped him. The third *Courant*, 21 August (the first four-page issue), outraged Boston. Two essays personally maligned the Mathers and the other ministers who advocated inoculation. Worse, the essays scurrilously assailed the talented young minister Thomas Walter, who wrote *The Anti-Courant*. With the third issue, the *Courant* lost several of its initial subscribers (Increase Mather, among others, canceled his subscription). Josiah Franklin must have recriminated with James, who later mentioned that his pastors also reproved him. Checkley's controversial reply began modestly: the "chief Design of" the *Courant* "was to oppose the *doubtful* and *dangerous* Practice of *inoculating* the *Small Pox*, and twas hop'd, that those Gentlemen of Piety and Learning who pleaded for the Practice, would have brought some other Arguments upon the Stage than the *naked Merits* of their *Characters*." Descending from this position, he vehemently attacked the supposed drunkenness of an "obscene and fuddling Merry Andrew," the "Little Compton

Scourge," calling Thomas Walter the "Tom-Bully" of the Mathers. He cited a letter Walter supposedly wrote him, promising Checkley "a Kick on the Arse, A Slap on the Chops." Checkley exceeded the bounds of propriety by writing these low words and by suggesting that Walter was lascivious: "The very same Night . . . that he wrote this Letter, he was with another Debauchee, at a Lodging with two Sisters, of not the best Reputation in the World, upon the Bed with them several Hours, and this Spark sent for Punch to treat them with, and would have had the Candle put out, but they not having a Conveniency to light it again, it was lock'd in a Closet, and . . . etc." Checkley's spiteful response to Walter signaled his last appearance in the *Courant*.

The fourth *Courant* (28 August) consisted of three pages, thus leaving a fourth page blank. Publishers rarely wasted a page. An extraordinary news item, like the outbreak of war, might cause a printer to publish less than a full paper, but the 28 August *Courant* featured no exceptional occasion. I suspect that James Franklin had set in type a four-page issue, but finding that his father, his ministers, and other friends thought the last *Courant* reprehensible, he suppressed a scandalous essay (probably by Checkley) from the fourth issue at the last moment, thus leaving a page blank. In the following *Courant* (4 September) the printer apologized for the coarse satire on Walter, saying that he had "chang'd his Author." Checkley wrote nothing more for the paper. Though an anonymous writer (Samuel Mather, as I will show) in the 15 January 1721/2 *Boston Gazette* thought that Checkley was the *Courant*'s dominant author, James Franklin replied on 22 January that Checkley had never written for the *Courant* (the printer lied) and that he did not even subscribe. Perhaps Checkley canceled his subscription when James Franklin dropped him as a contributor. Young Benjamin Franklin could hardly have learned much from Checkley's brief pieces, but Franklin's first Silence Dogood essay may owe to Checkley the slightly rustic persona, the challenging first paragraph, and a deliberate American variation on the *Spectator*'s opening.

Dr. William Douglass

Dr. William Douglass (1681–1752) led anti-inoculators. He believed that inoculation could be lethal and that it could spread the disease. Most early eighteenth-century physicians simply served an apprenticeship with an older "physician," but Douglass was Boston's only physician in 1721 with a formal medical degree. It was from Edinburgh, at the time the best medical school in Great Britain. He supplied the populace with a spokesperson of undoubted authority. An independent thinker, Douglass was a talented naturalist, physician, and historian. Though he took little part in Boston's official affairs, he did serve on Boston's fortifications committee, beginning 13 March 1732/3.[27] In 1736 he wrote the first clinical description of a scarlet fever epidemic, and later he wrote the first general history of colonial America by a resident, *A Summary, Historical and Political . . . of the British Settlements* (1749–51). He seems to have been a nominal

Anglican.[28] His *Summary* shows he was not a Presbyterian or a believer in predestination but a liberal Christian deist.[29] The historian Thomas Hutchinson,
who knew Douglass, characterized him as "assuming even to arrogance," a person who "in several fugitive pieces . . . treated all who differed from him with
contempt." Douglass offended strangers by being highly opinionated and self-
important. The talented Maryland litterateur Dr. Alexander Hamilton, who was
also an Edinburgh M.D., met him in 1744 and judged him "mischievously given
to criticism and the most compleat snarler ever I knew."[30]

Writing as "W. Philanthropos," Douglass had begun, in the 24 July 1721
Boston News-Letter, a series of essays on inoculation, attacking Dr. Zabdiel Boylston, who had begun inoculating at the suggestion of Cotton Mather. The following week, the ministers Increase and Cotton Mather, Benjamin Colman,
Thomas Prince, John Webb, and William Cooper replied with a letter, dated 27
July, printed in the 31 July *Boston Gazette*, arguing that inoculation could save
lives and that it no more interfered with God or nature to inoculate than to
bleed, blister, or use medicines in attempting to heal the sick. After the letter
appeared, the *Boston News-Letter* refused to print further pieces from Douglass,
who complained that the New England Congregational ministers "shut the Press
against" the anti-inoculators.[31]

In the first *Courant* (7 August 1721) Dr. Douglass continued the inoculation
history that he had begun in the *News-Letter* two weeks before: "At the Request
of several Gentlemen in Town: A Continuation of the History of Inoculation in
Boston, by a Society of the Practitioners in Physick." He began by slandering
Dr. Zabdiel Boylston, the foremost inoculator: "The bold undertaker of the
Practice of the Greek old Women, notwithstanding the Terror and Confusion
from his Son's Inoculation-Fever, proceeds to inoculate Persons from Seventy
Years of Age and downwards." Douglass pointed out that Boston's selectmen
had unanimously voted against the practice.[32] Referring to the clergy's *Boston
Gazette* letter, he said that "*Six Gentlemen of Piety and Learning, profoundly
ignorant of the Matter*" recommended "on the Merits of their Characters, and
for no other reason" that inoculation be allowed. They claimed that "the Operation it self is not much greater than Bleeding, Blistering, &c," but they failed to
consider "its dismal Consequences." According to Douglass, "*Old Mr. W——b
in a few Hours underwent the hot Service of Bleeding Vomiting, Blistering, Poul-
tices, &c. and narrowly escaped with his Life.*"[33] Douglass asked: "Is this no more
than Bleeding or Blistering? *Infatuation* I think is like to be as *Epidemick a Distemper of the Mind*, as at present the small Pox is of the natural Body."

Douglass also contributed to the second and third *Courant*s. His dream vi-
sion in the second *Courant* anticipated the genre young Franklin used to satirize
Harvard (Dogood No. 4), and Douglass replied to Walter's *Little Compton
Scourge* in the third paper. Then Douglass dropped out of the *Courant* for sev-
eral months. If James Franklin and Douglass fell out, they reconciled before
January 1721/2.

The Mathers gave James Franklin an article concerning inoculation from the *London Mercury* to reprint in the 1 January 1721/2 *Courant*. Douglass claimed in the 8 January *Courant* that it was not in the *London Mercury*. The Mathers, he said, made it up. Writing anonymously, young Samuel Mather replied in the 15 January *Gazette* that the article cited was present in the paper and attacked Douglass, Taylor, and the tobacconist John Williams. In the 22 January paper, Douglass identified the previous author as Samuel Mather and censured him. Douglass claimed, "The first Passage concerning *Inoculation* is no more to be found in the *London Mercury* here on the Table, than Cotton Mather D.D. is to be found in the List of the *Royal Society* affixed at the other end of the Room." (Douglass had left a copy of the *London Mercury* on the table in Robert Hall's coffee shop, where he had pasted on the wall a list of Royal Society members, which did not include Mather. Though Cotton Mather signed himself "D.D., F.R.S.," his name had been inadvertently omitted from a list of Royal Society members, thus causing Douglass and other enemies to believe he had not been elected.)[34] In his rambling essay, Douglass also defended his pamphlet *Inoculation of the Small Pox* (which James Franklin had printed and sold at his own risk) against an advertisement accusing him of "groundless and malicious" practices. The Mathers had said that Douglass continued to quarrel about inoculation after the epidemic was over. Douglass countered that the Mathers' advertisement testified to their "distinguishing Character of Inattention and rash Judgment," for he completed the *Inoculation* pamphlet on 20 December, when smallpox still survived in Boston.

In a second essay of 22 January, Douglass addressed a letter to "Old *Muss*," that is, Philip Musgrave, publisher of the *Gazette*: "I am not a little concern'd at the Loss you Weekly sustain of Customers, by your encouraging a certain Paper call'd the *Courant*." Douglass implied that any *Gazette* reference to the *Courant* was good for the latter. "It seems you gave the occasion of its first Appearance in this Town, by publishing a *Ministerial Inoculation Letter* [the 31 July *Gazette* letter] which has been a Fund of good Diversion for some Months past." As postmaster, Musgrave had "the best Opportunity to excel, and recommend your Paper by the freshest and best Intelligences, foreign and domestick." But Douglass advised Musgrave to fill his paper only "with *Speeches, Addresses, Proclamations*, and other *publick Notifications*." Stick to dull news, said Douglass, for it's what you do best. Franklin identified Douglass as the author in his personal file of the *Courant*, but the public would have recognized his authorship by the dateline, "Hall's Coffee-House," the rendezvous of Douglass's club of physicians.

Douglass's next two contributions appeared on 12 March. In the lead essay, Douglass discussed the recent inoculation literature: Zabdiel Boylston's article in the *Boston Gazette* (5 March); his own pamphlet titled *The Abuses and Scandals of Some Late Pamphlets Obviated* (printed by James Franklin), which came out "last Tuesday morning" (6 March); and a doggerel dialogue titled *A Second*

Part of the Vindication of Dr. C. M. (12 March).[35] Douglass attributed it to Samuel Mather: "It can be no other than the Performance of some Ill-bred School-Boy (a Chip of the old Block) with the Assistance of the Author perhaps of an *Essay to shake of[f] a Viper* [i.e., Cotton Mather's *The Right Way to Shake off a Viper*, 1711; reprinted in 1720] because several of the Ingredients are to be found no where but in his *Museum* or Shop." Douglass's second piece on 12 March was an extract from a *"Horse Doctor's* Harangue to the credulous Mob," a travesty of Dr. Boylston's reports.

In the 26 March 1722 *Courant,* writing anonymously but using his standard dateline, "Hall's Coffee-House," Douglass attacked a fable in the 19 March *Boston Gazette,* attributed it to Cotton Mather, and explained that Mather was angry because he had failed to get Boston politicians elected who were favorable to Governor Samuel Shute: "No doubt the Author was very angry to find himself disappointed, after the great Pains he had taken to get in Select Men that dance after his Pipe." On 12 March, Boston had elected as selectmen the Old Charter Party leaders: Elisha Cooke, Jr., Thomas Cushing, Captain Nathaniel Green, Ebenezer Clough, William Clark, John Marion, and Isaiah Toy. The 19 March *Courant* announced that Douglass's "Postscript to *Abuses &c. Obviated,* Being a Short and Modest Answer to Matters of Fact maliciously misrepresented in a late Doggerel Dialogue" would be published the following Wednesday. On 30 April and 21 May the *Courant* published his eighth and ninth contributions, both letters concerning inoculation and containing his ad hominem insults on Cotton Mather, as well as information about inoculation in London.

Though Douglass contributed nine pieces to the *Courant,* he wrote primarily on inoculation, and when the smallpox epidemic ended, the public lost interest in the subject. Though his dream essay in the second *Courant* may have influenced Franklin's satire on Harvard College, Franklin knew other dream essays from the *Spectator, Tatler, Guardian,* and elsewhere. Yet I suspect that Dr. William Douglass may have been an important negative influence. Franklin knew Douglass before he encountered the second edition of Charles Gildon's *Grammar of the English Tongue* (1712), which contained at the end "The Arts of Poetry, Rhetoric, Logic, etc.," including "a Specimen of a Dispute in the Socratic Method." Franklin delighted in the technique and practiced it among his friends for several years, particularly in discussing religion. The older Franklin reflected, "I wish well-meaning sensible Men would not lessen their Power of doing Good by a Positive assuming Manner that seldom fails to disgust, tends to create Opposition, and to defeat every one of those Purposes for which Speech was given us, to wit, giving or receiving Information, or Pleasure" (A 14). Franklin may have had the Scotsman and Edinburgh-trained snarler Dr. William Douglass in mind when he condemned persons of a disputatious turn: "Persons of good Sense, I have since observ'd, seldom fall into it, except Lawyers, University Men, and Men of all Sorts that have been bred at Edinborourgh" (A 12).

Thomas Fleet

The printer Thomas Fleet first appeared in the 15 January 1721/2 *Courant*. He contributed four pieces to Franklin's annotated file. Fleet (1685–1758), an Anglican and parishioner of King's Chapel, gradually became one of Boston's best printers and writers. Though a competitor in printing with James Franklin, Fleet was evidently a friend. He not only wrote for the *Courant*, but when James Franklin posted a £100 bond for his good behavior on 12 February 1722/3, Fleet stood surety for half the amount.[36] The early historian of American printing Isaiah Thomas celebrated Fleet's later newspaper, the *Weekly Rehearsal* (1731–35), for its writing and humor.[37] His literary techniques would have greatly interested young Franklin. The week before Fleet's first contribution, the Couranteers decided to attack Philip Musgrave for doing a miserable job as postmaster. Writing as "Lucilius," James Franklin led off by charging Musgrave with high-handed behavior, erratic business hours, keeping customers waiting interminably, opening letters to examine their contents, and even stealing from letters. "To mention all that have suffer'd by your Negligence and Ill-Nature (if not Dishonesty,) would be endless: However, I shall take the Liberty in my next Letter to *Couranto*, to mention enough to prove you unfit for a P[o]st M[aste]r." The blunt attack lacked the art that Fleet brought to bear the following week.

Writing as "Tom Tram," Fleet satirized Philip Musgrave with a mock travel allegory concerning Robinson Crusoe's island.[38] There the people "live by Trade and Merchandizing both by Sea and Land, . . . and consequently have occasion for Posts to carry our Letters." Though their town is the "Metropolis of the Island, yet we have such a poor careless, lazy, gump-headed (and being in a Passion, he had almost said knavish) Post-Master, as is not to be found in the whole *Lunar World*." Fleet's satire individualized and dramatized the charges that the postmaster of Crusoe's island stole money, lazily refused to see if letters were present, and possessed a "crabbed, surly, snappish Temper." Claiming to be in haste to return to his own distant regions, Tom Tram advised the islanders to "draw up a Memorial of their Grievances, and send it to the Post-Master General." Though Fleet repeated James Franklin's charges against Musgrave, his fictive setting and his list of individual complaints dramatized the charges, no doubt impressing Franklin with his improvement on his older brother's essay.

As "Ann Careful" in the *Courant* for 29 January, Fleet tried his hand at social satire. Ann Careful complained that her husband "of late is so taken up with Inoculation and State Affairs, that he spends most of his Time in going about from House to House, and from Shop to Shop, loitering and chattering." His neglect of business was reducing the family to "penury." No answer appeared to the cri de coeur of Ann Careful; perhaps the lack of an answer suggested that nothing could be done for her. As his political writings will reveal, Fleet had a radical social conscience. Along with James Franklin and Nathaniel Gardner, Fleet may well have inspired some of Franklin's social attitudes and literary techniques. Later, from Philadelphia, Franklin did business with Fleet, selling him *Poor Richard* almanacs and other publications.

Dr. George Steward

Like Checkley, Douglass, and Fleet, the physician George Steward (or "Stewart" [fl. 1713–41]) was an Anglican and a member of King's Chapel.[39] He, too, was harassed in 1719 by being tendered the oaths of allegiance and abjuration, implying that he was a disaffected Jacobite.[40] As noted above, when Checkley was charged with libel, Steward stood surety for him for half of his £100 bond.[41] Signing himself "C. A.," he sent in a letter to the second *Courant* (14 August 1721) against the "dangerous" practice of inoculation and enclosed a letter from a physician at Marseilles on the epidemic there. He later wrote the *Courant*'s lead essay, 18 December 1721, opposing inoculation, maintaining that only persons in excellent health were inoculated and that anyone who died shortly after inoculation died from the operation. Further, he claimed that inoculated persons could spread the plague and that fourteen persons had already died from inoculation. Surely, he argued, making a well man sick differed from making a sick man well. Though Franklin would have admired that antimetabole, the influence of Steward's two essays was negligible.

Dr. John Gibbins and the Reverend Henry Harris

Dr. John Gibbins (1688–1760) was the fourth physician to appear in the paper. He, too, had been reared a Puritan but had become an Anglican (another King's Chapel parishioner). Evidently a friend of Checkley, Gibbins posted half of Checkley's bond in 1724.[42] Like his fellow parishioners Steward and Checkley, he was tendered the oaths of allegiance and abjuration in 1719.[43] On 21 August 1721, Gibbins, like Checkley, replied to the Reverend Thomas Walter's *Little Compton Scourge* with an ad hominem attack accusing him of being a drunk and threatening to expose other scandals about him. The following week, the assistant minister of King's Chapel,[44] the Reverend Henry Harris (1689–1729), published a moderate, well-mannered essay against inoculation in the 28 August *Courant* titled "Little Compton" and signed "Frank Scammony."

John "Mundungus" Williams

"Mundungus" (a cant word for cheap, stinky tobacco), a.k.a. John Williams (fl. 1721–23), entered the contributors' ranks after Samuel Mather attacked him for his anti-inoculation pamphlet in the 18 January 1721/2 *Gazette*. Though Williams wrote only one piece in the annotated *Courants*, he was identified with James Franklin and the Couranteers by his contemporaries. A tobacconist and apothecary,[45] Williams wrote two pamphlets opposing inoculation, which James Franklin published and sold—successfully—at his own risk. The first one, *Several Arguments,* quickly sold out and Franklin reprinted it. Williams's opponent Cotton Mather thought it "incredible how much the mob about the country were enchanted by this poor smoky conjurer."[46] If the obscure Williams is the person of the same name who contributed to the King's Chapel building fund, he was an Anglican.[47]

In his pamphlets, Williams advocated positions that anticipated and may have inspired the Couranteers. Williams argued that ministers should stick to religious matters and stay out of political and economic affairs. Using the proverb that Shakespeare parodied ("the shoemaker should meddle with his yard, and the tailor with his last" [*Romeo and Juliet*, I.ii.40]), Williams wrote: "They daily see what Work Men make when they intermeddle with any thing they do not understand, or was not prentice to. Suppose a Taylor should go into a Cobler's Shop to work; his Tools are not fit, neither hath he skill to use the Cobler's tools, and so he makes but cobling work; and then his ware lies upon hand, and he derided and scoffed at, and that for his work" (*Several Arguments*, 14–15).[48] Williams portrayed an old saying dramatically and thereby made it new. Later Franklin employed that technique, among others, in revising Poor Richard's proverbs. In the dedication of *Several Arguments*, Williams wrote: "Say not who hath written, but consider what is written. . . . Say not that he is a Mechanick, and an illiterate Man; for there is good Mettal sometimes under a mean Soil." The democratic sentiments anticipate those of Franklin, who imitated Williams in the opening of Silence Dogood No. 1, where Silence satirized people who are afraid "either to commend or dispraise what they read" until they know the author.

The 12 March 1721/2 *Courant* included a letter by "J. W.," evidently John Williams. James Franklin said he printed it exactly as he received it, in the "*Mundungian Language.*" Williams addressed "the Author of a late Dialog" [Isaac Greenwood and Cotton Mather]: "Bot Sir, ould it not be of equll Benefet to the Poblecke, if while thay are theching the Arth of Lojeche, they could Infuese Onesti in to their Pupels to youse it onestly, that thaer may be no more fals erecketed *Hiphotices*, with a desine to delude the Peopole, wich they noes is a Lye before God, to dra Concluccnes ethar to gain the Point of Inockelacion or any other thing wich their secret Iehe shuld put them upon."

Was Williams really so terrible a speller? His contemporaries thought so. Cotton Mather wrote of him: "He forbad this *prates* [practice] because to *speake* [speak] for *hoomain invencions* [inventions] *in fisecke* [physick] is not *allowabel* (this is a specimen of the orthography in his manuscript)."[49] But the range of scholarly references in Williams's pamphlets makes it clear that he read widely in difficult theological literature. His pamphlets use standard spellings, but printers normally were responsible for spelling, punctuation, etc. If Williams really could not spell, James Franklin (who not only printed but also published his pamphlets) would have been insulting Williams by spelling his *Courant* letter just as he sent it in. Perhaps, though, one could argue that the printer indulged Williams's joke. After all, Williams deliberately cultivated a common-man persona. A mock illiterate dialect would have complemented his pose. On the other hand, a pamphlet by "Rusticus" that (as I show later) Nathaniel Gardner wrote and James Franklin published condescended to Williams. And the linguist G. L. Kittredge thought the incredible spellings were "doubtless" authentic.[50]

In general, the evidence suggests that Williams spelled miserably. Nevertheless, he undoubtedly influenced the young Franklin. Franklin echoed his reasoning in the presentation of the Silence Dogood persona and, as I shall argue below, Franklin wrote a mock illiterate letter in the *Courant*, which was inspired by "Mundungus" Williams. The mock illiterate persona became a major tradition in American humor—and, more generally, in American literature. Even if "Mundungus" was really a terrible speller, he made a contribution to American literature and to the use of the bumpkin persona;[51] if he was not, then he anticipated Franklin with America's first thorough mock illiterate persona.

Thomas Lane

The obscure "T. Lane" (fl. 1721–52) gave the hefty sum of £20 toward the building fund of King's Chapel in 1752.[52] He contributed two (though Franklin only identified one) letters concerning politics to the *Courant*. Silence Dogood's fourth essay (14 May 1722), was followed by a letter signed "Elisha Trueman," dated from Woodstock, which Franklin attributed to Lane. Just two weeks earlier, Elisha Trueman of Woodstock sent in a letter to the 30 April *Courant*, which Franklin left unattributed. The content, place, and pseudonym make it obvious that Lane also wrote the earlier letter. Lane called himself an Old Charter Man. Lane's writing is interesting because he used a countryman persona with a few mock illiterate spellings and because he editorialized against Prerogative Party leader Paul Dudley and the authorities. His second letter was no doubt intended to have some political influence, for it appeared the day before the 15 May 1722 town meeting that elected Boston's representatives to the General Court. Lane may have been a minor influence on Franklin.

OTHER MINOR COURANTEERS

Mrs. Staples

"Mrs. Staples" appeared only in the tenth *Courant* (9 October 1721), with a poem replying to a series of verse epistles on the war of sexes. It is the only known *Courant* contribution by a woman and the first known feminine writing in an American newspaper. No one has identified Mrs. Staples.[53] She may have been the Elizabeth Staples who, by her husband Thomas, had a son named Thomas on 5 July 1715.[54] If so, she was evidently the daughter of Daniel Morrison (ca. 1668–1736) and Hannah (Shatswell) Morrison (1671–1700) of Newberry, Massachusetts.[55] But another possibility is an older Mrs. Staples, the mother of Abraham and Ebenezer Staples.[56] The older Mrs. Staples was perhaps the former Mary Cox who married Benjamin "Stapils" at the First Church on 26 May 1699.[57]

The war-of-sexes verse epistles began with James Franklin's "Caution to Batchellors," signed "Lucilius," in the 25 September paper. "Amelia" replied in the 2 October issue. Since Franklin crossed out Amelia's poem in his copy of the *Courant*, I presume that he found it was (as he elsewhere noted on another piece he crossed out) "Stolen" (i.e., reprinted rather than original). Lucilius replied to Amelia on 9 October. Franklin attributed this also to James Franklin, then crossed out the attribution, perhaps after discovering that the printer borrowed the three-piece exchange. Mrs. Staples entered the fray with a twelve-line reply "to Lucilius, for his Caution to Batchellors," disdaining him as a cuckold and threatening him with syphilis.[58]

> The Fool by his Wit,
> Has shew'd he is bit:
> Sir Ass, braying betrays your long Ears;
> You need not have told
> Your wife was a scold,
> Nor, Alas, discover'd your Fears.
> Then prithee Man,
> Try if you can
> Put up your Horns in your Pocket,
> Lest sooner or later,
> (Without any Satyr,)
> Your Nose it be sunk in the Socket.

Though an insignificant literary influence on Franklin, Mrs. Staples may have helped confirm his belief in the equality of women.

Captain Christopher Taylor

Captain Christopher Taylor (ca. 1677–1734) was a hypocrite. He contributed seven pieces to the annotated *Courant* and at least one essay thereafter. Son of the treasurer of Massachusetts, Taylor had been brought up in the First Church,[59] though, unlike Gardner, he never became a member. The seaman lived with and had a child by his maid Anne Bell but often denounced immorality and licentiousness in the *Courant*. On one occasion he insulted Governor Shute in a "rude and insolent" manner.[60] In the 18 December 1721 *Courant*, he objected to an advertisement in the 11 December *Boston Gazette* and made an ad hominem attack on "the famous Mountebank who lives there [New Hampshire], [who] has lately lost his Watch, Diamond Ring, Peruke, &c." by gambling. On Christmas, Captain Taylor sent in a racist piece objecting to an elaborate wedding between two Africans, adding an attack on the lawyer who owned the black man for "cohabiting with a certain French Lady as his Wife." (Taylor presumably thought no one knew he wrote the piece.)

For the 5 March 1721/2 paper, Captain Taylor sent in an anonymous letter dated from "Gutteridge's Coffee House" complaining of a house of prostitution "not an Hundred Doors from the *old-South Church*." The piece may have partly inspired Silence Dogood No. 13, on nightwalkers. Writing again from "Gutteridge's Coffee House" in the 19 March 1721/2 paper, Taylor chastised those who did not attend the weekly Thursday lectures (i.e., sermons). Echoing his Christmas Day attack, Taylor on 16 April 1721/2 again satirized the lawyer who had supposedly been "cohabiting with a French Tayloress as his wife." His most interesting letters concerned politics and will be considered in the next chapter. Captain Taylor, though anticipating Franklin in an open concern with sexuality and lasciviousness, was an undistinguished writer, unimportant to Franklin.

John Eyre

A short letter by "Peter Hakins," whom Franklin identified as John Eyre (1700–1753),[61] marked his debut on, 6 November 1721. Eyre, who contributed four pieces to the *Courant*, graduated from Harvard in 1718 and took his master's in 1721. He no doubt knew James Franklin from the Old South Church, where his parents were members. He was not, however, a good New England Congregationalist, and after he moved to Portsmouth, New Hampshire, around 1733, he helped organize its Anglican church, Queen's Chapel.

In addition to three political pieces, Eyre wrote on 5 March 1721/2 as "Anthony De Potsherd." Dating the letter from "Cuckolds Point," the persona complained that his wife "continually" railed at and reviled him. She "won't allow me to stir abroad without her leave, and yet she leaves me sometimes Two or Three Hours together. . . . I once attempted to beat her into good Humour, but she came off Conqueror." He asked Couranto's advice about how to change her or get rid of her. The reply seemed flat and insipid. Couranto/ Eyre simply opined, *"What can't be cur'd, must be endur'd."* Perhaps Eyre remembered a sentiment from John Wise's *Word of Comfort*: "You must do by your Bills, as all Wise Men do by their Wives; Make the best of them."[62] Eyre had little effect on Franklin.

Matthew Adams

The 27 November *Courant* began with a poem by the tenth Couranteer, Matthew Adams (1694?–1753), who, like Eyre, contributed four pieces during the nine months that Franklin annotated the *Courant*. A member of Benjamin Colman's Brattle Street Church, a tanner, and at this time a partner of Nathaniel Gardner, Adams had earlier befriended Franklin by loaning him books. Thus he is the only Couranteer, other than James Franklin, to be mentioned in the *Autobiography* (A 10). Adams's brother, the Reverend Hugh Adams, graduated from Harvard in 1697; and his nephew, the Reverend John Adams, graduated in 1721. Matthew Adams later joined Mather Byles in producing an essay series for the *New England Weekly Journal*.[63] His conventionally religious short poem in the *Courant* was "occasioned by the melancholy Prospect which the Author had some time since of the present doleful Circumstances of the Place." His later contributions, which included an anecdote from Jonathan Swift's *Tale of a Tub*, lampooned Cotton Mather and the authorities and will be considered in a later chapter. Though Franklin remembered him for his kindness, the writings of Matthew Adams made slight impression upon young Franklin.

CONCLUSION: FRANKLIN'S STYLE

Though the influence of most Couranteers on Franklin was negligible, I believe that the influence of all fourteen combined (especially James Franklin and Nathaniel Gardner) was more important than any other single writer or writing—including the *Spectator*, *Cato's Letters*, Swift, or Defoe. Not only the literary techniques mentioned above but even Franklin's political attitudes, his Americanism, and his proto-feminism can be found in the Couranteers and the other local writers (especially John Wise) whom James Franklin published. Moreover, Franklin's informal, often colloquial style is that of the *Courant*, far different from the formal style of the typical English periodical essays of the early eighteenth century—and absolutely different from that of his major English contemporary, Dr. Samuel Johnson. Swift and Defoe used colloquial language in their fiction and poetry, but their essays are not as idiomatic as those of the Couranteers, John Wise, or Franklin.[64] Finally, however, Franklin's writings are sui generis. Even as a youth of sixteen and seventeen, his pieces have a greater range of feelings and voices than any other *Courant* writer or than the *Spectator* essays. Franklin is on occasion more earthy, bitter, vicious, savage, lascivious, ironic, and humorous than his immediate models. To make a recipe for the writings of Franklin, we may begin with the periodical essays of Addison and Steele in the *Spectator*, *Tatler*, and *Guardian*; mix well with the radical Whig beliefs of the Old Charter Party and *Cato's Letters*; dash in the Calvinistic depravity of humans according to the New England Puritans; add plentifully from the incipient American attitudes and country bumpkin personae of the Couranteers and John Wise; stir in constantly the most savage and bitter satires and ironies of Swift; spice generously with the cosmopolitanism and skepticism of Shaftesbury and Collins (and, later, of Montaigne and Pierre Bayle); flavor occasionally with the earthy and sexual humor of John Wise and oral anecdotes (and, later, of Rabelais); add copiously the comparatively plain style of the Puritan sermon and Defoe; and garnish with the idealism of Swift, Cotton Mather, and Defoe. Even then, however, we will still not quite account for Franklin's extraordinary range of voices, his passionate belief in the worth of the individual, or his pessimism concerning the human condition. The Couranteers exerted the most important early literary influence on Franklin, but his style, like the man, transcends explanation.

SIX

James Franklin:
America's First Newspaperman

The Courant . . . was hostile to the clergy, and to some of the most influential men in civil government; and it attacked some of the religious opinions of the day.—Isaiah Thomas 106–7

UNLIKE JAMES FRANKLIN, previous American newspaper editors did little more than reprint, copying the English and European news as the foreign newspapers came into port. In addition, they listed the ships entering and leaving the harbor, printed government announcements, and gave obituaries (usually written by ministers) of local notables. James Franklin changed American journalism. He featured local controversies, belletristic material, and news of New England events. He cut down drastically on the English and foreign news and relegated them to the second page. The historian Charles E. Clark shrewdly observed that in the *New-England Courant*, "News from Britain as well as from other places in Europe appeared under the heading 'Foreign Affairs,' an indication of a distinctly American self-consciousness" not found in previous American newspapers.[1] James Franklin wrote for the paper as well. He talked over the future contents of the paper with a group of friends, discussing its successes and failures. He was a genius in getting others to write for the paper. During the early years of the paper, he even allowed Nathaniel Gardner to write as the editor and to coedit it. James Franklin made the *New-England Courant* the first literary, lively, entertaining, humorous, and proto-nationalistic American newspaper.[2]

In format, the newspaper was identical to its rivals, the *Boston News-Letter* and the *Boston Gazette*. The *Courant* was usually half of a large folio sheet, approximately $6^{1}/_{2} \times 10$ inches, printed in two columns on each side; it expanded, whenever James Franklin had enough material, to an entire folio sheet, making a paper of four pages. Like its rivals, the *Courant* appeared on Monday, the day the mail arrived. James Franklin began by charging the standard price of ten shillings a year, raising it to twelve shillings in the late spring (13 May) of 1723. At the same time, he changed the price of a single issue from three to four pence. No circulation figures are known for the *Courant*, but John Campbell, publisher of the *Boston News-Letter*, wrote on 10 August 1719 that he could not sell three hundred copies of his paper. Once well established, the *Courant* probably sold about that amount, for James Franklin boasted on 11 February 1722/3 that it outsold the other Boston papers.

POLITICS

In the very first issue of the *New-England Courant*, James Franklin demonstrated that the *Courant* would feature Massachusetts politics. Governor Samuel Shute had dissolved the Massachusetts Assembly on 20 July 1721. A new election for Boston's representatives took place on 2 August, and Shute's opponents were reelected. Under the dateline "Boston, August 2," the first *New-England Courant* published the names of those who had won: "*John Clarke, Elisha Cook, William Hutchinson* Esqrs; and Mr. *William Clark* Merchant." Neither the *Boston Gazette* nor the *Boston News-Letter* carried the news. Indeed, it was the first time any American newspaper published election returns. Printing the returns trumpeted the governor's defeat and identified the *Courant* with the Old Charter Party, Shute's opposition. Perhaps Benjamin Franklin recalled James Franklin's ploy when he took over the *Pennsylvania Gazette*; he began the *Gazette* with a shrewd editorial on Massachusetts politics.

James Franklin subtly criticized the governor and council in reporting Indian warfare. The *Courant* related on 7 August 1721 that "sixty odd Soldiers" were sailing for Arowsick. Franklin added the editorial comment: "Nothing can be more grateful to the poor, affrighted *Strangers* in those Parts, than this well-timed Expedition, for it cannot be imagin'd with what Horrour and confusion those poor People were seized, when they received the cruel (but unexpected) Menaces of those treacherous *Barbarians*." The authorities must have chafed when they realized that the *Courant* had satirized them for not previously taking action. At the same time, the *Courant* sounded an American note by implying that those born in America were not (unlike recent English immigrants, or "*Strangers*") frightened by the Indian threat.

HELL-FIRE I

In an effort to blacken the *Courant*'s reputation, its enemies called the Couranteers the Hell-Fire Club—a name occasionally applied to London's impious clubs.[3] Americans knew of the infamous London clubs through occasional notes in the newspapers and through oral anecdotes. Knowledgeable colonists heard, for example, that the brother of New York Governor William Burnet was suspected of being the chief malefactor of the London Mohocks. On 6 July 1721, the *Boston News-Letter* reprinted the king's proclamation of 28 April against "certain scandalous Clubs or Societies of young Persons, who meet together, and in the most impious and blasphemous manner, insult the most sacred Principles of our Holy Religion, affront Almighty GOD Himself, and corrupt the Minds and morals of one another." Though the underlying reason for the king's proclamation may have been English politics,[4] the adverse publicity caused many clubs to become suspect.

After John Checkley and Dr. William Douglass criticized the Rev. Thomas Walter in the third *Courant* (21 August 1721), the *Boston News-Letter* (28 August) carried a reply defending Walter and blasting the *Courant*. The anonymous author (Douglass identified him as Cotton Mather, and I agree) began by recalling that several weeks earlier, the *News-Letter* "entertained your Readers with a sad account of an scandalous Club, set up in London; to Insult the most sacred Principles of the Christian Religion, tending to Corrupt the minds and Morals of the People." He charged that a similar club had appeared in Boston: "And for a Lamentation to our Amazement (notwithstanding of GOD's hand out against us, in His Visitation of the Small-Pox in Boston, and the threatening Aspect of the Wet-Weather,) we find a Notorious, Scandalous Paper, call'd the *Courant*, full freighted with Nonsense, Unmannerliness, Raillery, Profaneness, Immorality, Arrogancy, Calumnies, Lyes, Contradictions, and what not, all tending to Quarrels and Division, and to Debauch and Corrupt the Minds and Manners of New-England." Mather compared both the Couranteers and Dr. William Douglass's coffeehouse society of physicians in Boston to London's Hell Fire Club and predicted that worse than what befell several members of that club (were they prosecuted for blasphemy?) would overtake the Couranteers.

Douglass resented Mather's fulminations and replied in the 4 September *Boston Gazette* to the "heinous Charge" that Boston had a Hell-Fire Club. Douglass did not reply in the *Courant*, though he had written for each of its first three issues. Perhaps he had submitted it to James Franklin, who, after his bold *Courant* of 21 August, decided not to print it. Evidently Douglass, like Checkley, was angry with the printer, though the physician and the printer had reconciled by 22 January 1721/2, when the physician again appeared in the *Courant*. Douglass said in the *Boston Gazette* that if such a club existed, the authorities should seek it out and punish "such execrable wickedness," but if no such club existed, the authorities should seek out the authors of "such horrid aspersions" and brand them "as infamous Libelers." Nothing was done, and the charge that the Couranteers were a version of London's Hell-Fire Club recurred.

As we have seen, James Franklin apologized in the fifth *Courant*. Despite his apology of the previous week, James Franklin reprinted "Cato's" letter on calumny on 11 September (which first appeared in the 10 June 1721 *London Journal*). Had James Franklin composed something similar on calumny, it would have been considered too bold a reply to the "Hell-Fire" charge, but reprinting a good essay was acceptable. John Trenchard and Thomas Gordon's series of essays signed "Cato" became the greatest early eighteenth-century statement of Whig doctrines. The historian Bernard Bailyn pointed out that *Cato's Letters* "ranked with the treatises of Locke as the most authoritative statement of the nature of political liberty and above Locke as an exposition of the social sources of the threats it faced."[5]

GARDNER'S MOCK JEREMIAD

After Cotton Mather's "Faithful Account of what has occur'd under the late Experiments of the Small-Pox managed and governed in the way of Inoculation"[6] appeared anonymously in Musgrave's *Boston Gazette* for 30 October, the *Courant* attacked. The 6 November *Courant* was carefully orchestrated, perhaps by Nathaniel Gardner. It violated James Franklin's promise in the fifth *Courant* to avoid criticizing ministers or authorities. Douglass's dream vision in the second *Courant* (which referred to the three apocalyptic evils of "Sword, Famine and Pestilence") may have inspired Gardner's lead essay, dated "Westown, Octob. 20, 1721." Gardner travestied the ministers for spreading the pestilence (i.e., smallpox) in a mock jeremiad. The sins of the land, Gardner wrote, had called forth the smallpox. He intoned: "the *crying Abominations* that are found in the midst of us; the *Profaneness* and *Debauchery*; the *Pride, Idleness,* and *Luxury*; the *Injustice* and *Oppression*; and (to name no more) the *too general* Contempt of the Glorious Gospel."

A reader might wonder what "*Injustice* and *Oppression*" the writer had in mind, but the last charge revealed that the piece was a travesty—"the *irregular Conduct* of too many who make the loftiest Profession" of religion. For Gardner and many other contemporaries, the statement indicted the Mathers. Gardner's burlesque ended: "And to sum up all, Let us give Glory to God, by acknowledging, that he is righteous in all that he has brought upon us: Let us UNITE in our importunate and incessant Prayers to him, that he would sanctify and remove *this* Visitation; that he would save us from *greater Judgments*, which we both fear and deserve: And who knows, but he may hear from Heaven his dwelling Place, and forgive, and heal our Land."

Some readers were probably taken in and thought that a minister used the *Courant* to publish his sermon. The Mathers and other knowledgeable contemporaries, however, realized that the piece travestied the New England jeremiad tradition in general and especially Increase Mather's *Heavens Alarm to the World* (1681), a sermon occasioned by a comet. A few readers may also have connected the opening of the mock jeremiad with Douglass's dream vision. Some *Courant* readers must have laughed and others must have been shocked and amazed when they discerned that it satirized their ministers. Since the Mathers and some other ministers had alienated the populace by supporting both Governor Samuel Shute and inoculation, a number of readers must have been predisposed to admire the satire. Gardner's travesty of the archetypal New England sermon form testified to the declining role of ministers in New England.

A short letter in the same 6 November *Courant* by "Peter Hakins" (i.e., John Eyre) overtly attacked the ministers. He noted that in "last Monday's Gazette" (30 October), a piece concerning inoculation by a "Reverend Author" appeared.

To the Author of the New-England Courant.

SIR,   Weſtown, Octob. 20. 1721.

THAT the Sword, Famine and Peſtilence, are Three moſt amazing Rods, with which the Almighty has been wont to ſcourge a wicked World, is a Truth confirm'd by many tragical Inſtances, the Accounts whereof have been tranſmitted to us by the Hiſtorys of all Ages. The two former of theſe he inflicts more *mediately*, by the Inſtrumentality of Second Cauſes; as in *War* he ſometimes ſtirs up fierce and haſty Nations, making them the Staff in his Hand; and in *Famine*, by devouring Inſects, or noxious Blaſts, by exceſſive Rains, or ſcorching Droughts: But in the *latter*, his own immediate Hand is eminently to be ſeen and ador'd. Agreeable hereto, the Peſtilence is emphatically call'd, *HIS SWORD*, 1 Chron. 21. 12. and accordingly he threatned his rebellious People Iſrael, in ſuch awful Language as this Numb. 14. 14. *I will ſmite them with the Peſtilence.* And Verſe 15. where Moſes is expoſtulating with God on the Murmerers behalf, he ſays, If *THOU kill all this People*, &c. Hence it is, that *this* Judgment is moſt of all to be deprecated; and when it is ſent among a Nation or People, it beſpeaks the deepeſt Reſentments; for, as this ſeems to be the Almighty's ſtrange Work, ſo there are none can ſtand in his Sight, when once he is angry.

Figure 8. Nathaniel Gardner's mock jeremiad, with Franklin's attribution of authorship, New-England Courant, 6 November 1721. Scholars of New England Puritanism like Perry Miller, Larzer Ziff, and Sacvan Bercovitch have identified the jeremiad as the archetypal New England sermon genre of the second and later generations of New England ministers. According to the pastors, New Englanders had declined from the high religiousness of the early immigrants and were frequently warned of their degeneration. Dating the sermon "Westown, Octob. 20, 1721" probably suggested that it was delivered by the Reverend William Williams, Jr. (1688–1760), or by another minister visiting his parish. Williams's publication of two sermons entitled Divine Warnings *in 1728 shows that he, like Cotton Mather and almost all other New England ministers, occasionally used the jeremiad.*

    Some contemporary readers probably thought that it was an actual sermon written to recall the people from "the too general Contempt of the Glorious Gospel." Cotton Mather and others, however, would have realized that the piece travestied Increase Mather's Heavens Alarm to the World *(1681), a jeremiad occasioned by the appearance of the 1680 comet. Gardner satirized both the New England ministers who used the genre and the sermon form itself. Only the first paragraph (about one-fifth) of Gardner's mock jeremiad is printed here. Courtesy, Burney Collection, British Library.*

After saying that he would not dare to disagree with such an authority, Eyre undercut him by quoting from the *Life of General Monk* by Dr. Gumble: "Doubtless (says the Dr.) a Clergyman, while he keeps within the Sphere of his Duty to God and his People, is an Angel of Heaven; but when he shall degenerate from his own Calling, and fall into the Intrigues of State and Time-Serving, he becomes a Devil; and from a Star in the Firmament of Heaven, he becomes a sooty Coal in the blackest Hell, and receiveth the greatest Damnation."[7] Evidently Eyre, like the other Couranteers, believed Cotton Mather wrote the "Faithful Account."

A Chance Meeting

On Monday, 13 November 1721, Cotton Mather and James Franklin met on the street. Unable to restrain himself, Mather broke out:

> *Young Man*: You Entertain, and no doubt you think you Edify, the Publick, with a Weekly Paper, called *The Courant*. The Plain Design of your Paper, is to Banter and Abuse the Ministers of God, and if you can, to defeat all the good Effects of their Ministry on the Minds of the People. You may do well to Remember that Passage, in the Blessing on the Tribe of Levi, *Smite Thro' the Loins of them that rise against him, and of them that hate him.* I would have you to know, That the Faithful Ministers of Christ in this Place, are as honest, and useful Men as the Ancient *Levites* were, and are as Dear to their Glorious Lord as the Ancient *Levites* were: And if you Resolve to go on in serving their Great Adversary as you do, you must expect the Consequence.

James Franklin told his friends about the encounter. In the lead essay of the following week's *Courant* (20 November), Gardner, writing as "Hortensius," said the paper intended "to reform the present declining Age, and render it more polite and virtuous." After noting the difficulty of the task, Hortensius claimed the paper was impartial, treating all persons alike. The conclusion, however, made it apparent that the author believed that both civic and religious authorities, as well as those who normally were considered subjects for reformation, should be questioned: "*Briefly, promote Enquiries after Truth, quicken and rouze the Slothful, animate and inspire the Dull: And however the World has been impos'd on, it will soon appear, that Crimes are not lessen'd and sanctifi'd because committed by Men in High Station, or of Reverend Name; nor are they inhanced because they are perpetrated by the Obscure and Mean.*"

The second piece, also by Gardner, slyly alluded to the encounter with Cotton Mather. A brief letter "from an unknown Hand, in favour of Inoculation" opened: "*Tho' many, very many Useful and Excellent Arts, with which the World was bless'd in former Ages, are, they say, intirely lost; yet Our Age is happily favour'd with a wonderful and rare Discovery,* more Worth *than all of them: Shall I say,* More Worth than a World!" Franklin's annotation read: "Mr. Gardner in Imitation of Dr. Mather." Thus Gardner, as in the case of his mock jeremiad,

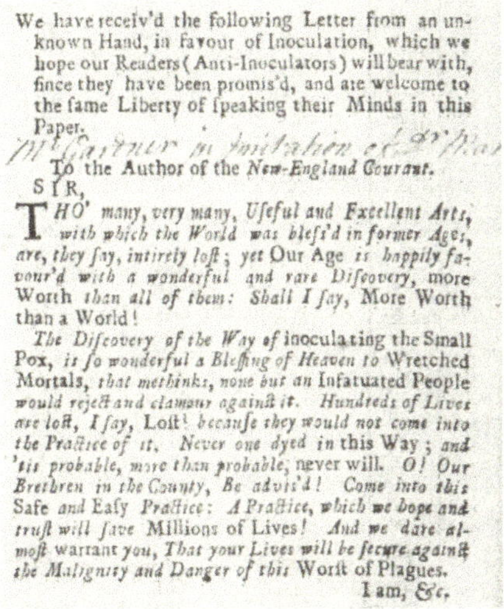

We have receiv'd the following Letter from an unknown Hand, in favour of Inoculation, which we
hope our Readers (Anti-Inoculators) will bear with,
since they have been promis'd, and are welcome to
the same Liberty of speaking their Minds in this
Paper.

To the Author of the *New-England Courant.*

SIR,

THO' many, very many, *Useful and Excellent Arts,*
with which the World was bless'd in former Ages,
are, they say, intirely lost; yet Our Age is happily favour'd with a wonderful and rare Discovery, more
Worth than all of them: Shall I say, More Worth
than a World!

The Discovery of the Way of inoculating the Small
Pox, is so wonderful a Blessing of Heaven to Wretched
Mortals, that methinks, none but an Infatuated People
would reject and clamour against it. Hundreds of Lives
are lost, I say, Lost! because they would not come into
the Practice of it. Never one dyed in this Way; and
'tis probable, more than probable, never will. O! Our
Brethren in the County, Be advis'd! Come into this
Safe and Easy Practice: A Practice, which we hope and
trust will save Millions of Lives! And we dare almost warrant you, That your Lives will be secure against
the Malignity and Danger of this Worst of Plagues.
I am, &c.

Figure 9. *Franklin noted that a brief piece favoring inoculation was by "Mr. Gardner in Imitation of Dr. Mather," New-England Courant, 20 November 1721. Gardner's imitation of Cotton Mather's baroque style must have been wonderful fun for Franklin. Among other sources, Franklin learned the possible effectiveness of imitations from Gardner. Franklin became a master of numerous prose styles (the Quaker style of "Queries on a Pennsylvania Militia," 1733/4; the Biblical style of "A Parable Against Persecution, 1753; the seventeenth-century style of "The Jesuit Campanella," 1761; and the Oriental style of "Sidi Mehemet Ibrahim on the Slave Trade," 1790).*

In addition to simply being a clever spoof, the piece had a serious purpose: James Franklin (and Nathaniel Gardner on his behalf) tried to appeal to readers who favored inoculation as well as those who opposed it. The Courant's editorial policy attempted to be neutral, but since the other two Boston newspapers would publish nothing against inoculation, all writers who opposed it had to publish in the Courant. Gardner's imitation of Mather was the only piece in the Courant favoring inoculation. Though it is usually assumed that James Franklin opposed it, he may have privately believed in inoculation. Courtesy, Burney Collection, British Library.

made it seem as if a religious person with Cotton Mather's style supported and contributed to the *Courant.* Mather recognized the ploy, and so he himself sent to the *Courant* (4 December) his verbal attack of 13 November on James Franklin quoted above.

The 20 November newspaper containing Gardner's two sly attacks on Mather also carried the best known of Cotton Mather's publications in the local newspapers. Mather reported the news of a grenade thrown into his house, by chance into the room where the Reverend Thomas Walter slept while recovering from inoculation:

At the House of Dr. Cotton Mather, there lodged his Kinsman, a worthy Minister, under the Small Pox, received and managed in the Successful Way of Inocu-

lation. Towards three of the Clock, in the Night, as it grew towards the Morning of Tuesday, the Fourteenth of this Instant November, some unknown Hand threw a fired Granado-Shell, into the Chamber of the Sick Gentleman, the Weight whereof alone, if it had fallen on the Head of the Patient, (which it seemed aimed at,) would have been enough to have done part of the Business designed. But the Granado was charged with such Materials, and in such Manner, that upon it's going off, it must probably have killed the Persons in the Room, and would have certainly fired the Chamber, and soon have laid the House in Ashes; which has appeared Incontestible to them that have since examined it. But the merciful Providence of God so order'd it, that the Granado passing thro' the Window, had by the Iron in the middle of the Casement, such a Turn given to it, that in falling on the Floor, the fired Wildfire in the Fuse, was violently shaken out unto some Distance from the Shell, and burnt out upon the Floor, without firing the Granado. When the Granado was taken-up, there was found a Paper so tied with a Thread about the Fuse, that it might outlive the breaking of the Shell; wherein were these Words,——"Cotton Mather, I was once one of your Meeting: But the cursed Lye you told of——you know who, made me leave you, you Dog. And Damn you, I'll inoculate you with this, with a Pox to you." This is the Sum of the Matter, without any Remarks upon it; which no doubt, will be various among the People, as they stand affected.

In his *History of Massachusetts Bay*, Thomas Hutchinson said that he had seen the grenade, "which was not filled with powder but a mixture of brimstone with bituminous matter." Mather published the account in all three Boston papers. In the *Courant*, James Franklin noted, "The above Account we receiv'd from the Doctor's own Hand." Though the government offered £50 reward "to any Person that shall discover the Authors of the abovesaid Villainy," no one was prosecuted for the crime, and no one knows who the culprit was. Though the *Courant* was well-known to be anti-Cotton Mather, it was shrewd of James Franklin to publish Cotton Mather's grenade story. It was important local news and sold papers, and it tended to support James Franklin's claim that he was an impartial editor. If the printer were suspected by some persons of the attack, publishing the piece would help divert the suspicion.

GARDNER TRAVESTIES THE MATHERS

Nathaniel Gardner's travesty of the syllogistic logic of Increase and Cotton Mather (27 November 1721) was the most outrageous piece published in the *Courant* to that date. Increase Mather had just published a broadside titled *Several Reasons Proving That Inoculation . . . is a Lawful Practice*, to which Cotton Mather added *Sentiments on the Small Pox Inoculated*.[8] The four reasons Increase Mather gave in its favor appealed to authority, used syllogisms, and were remarkably old-fashioned. The first claimed "a great regard is due to inoculation." The others were equally simple. The fourth "weighty consideration" stated "that some Wise and Judicious Persons among us, approve of Inocula-tion"—that is, himself and his son. On the other hand, Increase Mather claimed that "the known Children of the Wicked one are generally fierce enemies to Inoculation." Though some persons were "not clear in their Judgments for it," Increase Mather thought they would "change their minds, if they would advise with those who are best able to afford them Scripture Light in this as well as in other Cases of Conscience." (Gardner later burlesqued the Mathers' use of cases of conscience in an 8 January 1721/2 dialogue.)

Cotton Mather added to his father's broadside a series of syllogisms. His first proposition stated:

> *A most Successful, and Allowable Method of preventing* Death, *and many other grievous Miseries, by the* Small Pox, *is not only* Lawful *but a* Duty, *to be used by those who apprehend their Lives immediately endanger'd by the terrible Distemper. But the Method of managing and governing the* Small Pox *in the way of* Inocula-tion, *is a most successful and allowable Method of preventing* Death, *and many other grievous Miseries by this dreadful Distemper. Therefore, 'tis not only* Lawful, *but also a* Duty *to make use of it. None but very foolish, and very wicked People will deny the* Proposition *in this Argument; The* Assumption *is all that is disputed. But now, That this is a most Successful Method we have all the Evidence that Humane Reason can ask for.*

Rather than give a major premise that everyone would agree to, a minor premise that provided a subcategory, and a logical conclusion, Cotton Mather restated his major premise as his minor premise. Mather not only used the old-fashioned Aristotelian logic but used it poorly. Further, Mather's major premises were not statements of commonly accepted truths. Even as old-fashioned logic, Mather's reasoning invited refutation.

In the 27 November *Courant*, Nathaniel Gardner burlesqued the Mathers' logic, especially Cotton Mather's syllogisms. Indirectly, Gardner again lam-pooned the usual proofs of the New England sermon form, the authority of ministers, and the historiography formalized in the jeremiad tradition. The syl-logistic method and deductive logic had been attacked by numerous recent thinkers, including Francis Bacon, Descartes, the Port Royalists, and John Locke. Bacon destroyed the old logic when he wrote: "The syllogism consists of propo-sitions, propositions of words; and words are the signs of notions. Now if the very notions . . . (which are as the soul of words and the basis of the whole structure) be improperly and over-hastily abstracted from facts . . . the whole edifice tumbles."[9] The method of the new science, which was especially clear in Newton's *Optics*, seemed to confirm the irrelevance of Aristotelian logic and the deductive method and to confirm the triumph of experimentation and the inductive method.

Gardner created mock syllogisms that ridiculed the Mathers' logic and au-thoritarianism: "*Arg.* III. A method of preventing *Death*, which is approv'd by

Magistrates and *Ministers*, is not only lawful but a Duty. *But*, Magistrates and Ministers do approve of inoculating the Small Pox. *Therefore*, it is not only lawful, but a Duty." Gardner deliberately misstated the position of the Boston magistrates, who did not approve of inoculation,[10] but the irony underscored his point that appeals to authority had nothing to do with the success or failure of inoculation. The following silly syllogism ridiculed the Mathers' attacks on their enemies: "*Arg.* IV. A Method of preventing *Death*, which the known Children of the *Wicked One*, are fierce Enemies to, is not only lawful, but a Duty. *But*, The known Children of the *Wicked One*, do fiercely oppose Inoculation. *Therefore*, It is not only lawful, but a Duty." Gardner even named Increase and Cotton Mather: "*Arg.* VI. A Method of preventing *Death*, which Dr. I———e M———r and his Son, and several other Ministers say is the *right Way*, is not only lawful, but a Duty. *But*, Dr. I———e M———r and his Son, &c. do say, That Inoculation is the *right Way. Therefore*, Inoculation is not only lawful, but a Duty." After Cotton Mather read the parody, he confided to his diary on 9 December: "Warnings are to be given unto the wicked Printer, and his Accomplices, who every week publish a vile Paper to lessen and blacken the Ministers of the Town, and render their Ministry ineffectual. A Wickedness never parallel'd anywhere upon the Face of the Earth!"

The fifteen-year-old Franklin must have read and reread Gardner's travesty with relish. No one could have had a more appreciative audience than Gardner had in the apprentice printer. As we shall see, Franklin grew ever more suspicious of key words that called forth automatic responses, for cant terms appealed not to logic but only to emotional associations. Attention to logic became a hallmark of Franklin's later writings, and he delighted in exposing his opponents' logical fallacies.[11]

JAMES FRANKLIN'S DEFENSE

In the *Courant*'s 4 December 1721 lead article, James Franklin defended himself against Cotton Mather's onslaught: "The severe Treatment I have met with on account of some late Pieces inserted in this Paper, is known to all who know any thing of the present unhappy Divisions of the Town." He paraphrased Cotton Mather's verbal attack in their chance meeting and commented: "This heinous Charge and heavy Curse would have been more surprizing to me, if it had not come from one who is ever as groundless in his *Invectives* as in his *Panegyricks*." Readers knew the editor alluded to Mather's diatribes against him and to the minister's accolades for Governor Shute. Franklin repeated that he regretted printing the two pieces in the third *Courant*, though "my Printing [Thomas Walter's] the Anti-Courant, laid me under some Obligation to publish them." He wrote that Cotton Mather "has endeavour'd to make me an Object of *publick Odium*, for no other Reason than my publishing an Answer to a Piece in the *Gazette* of *October* 30. wherein the greatest Part of the Town are represented as

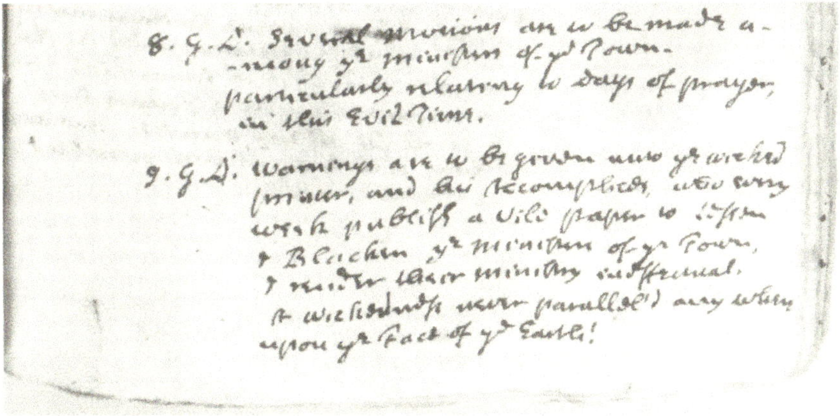
8. G.D. Several Motions are to be made a-
-mong ye Ministers of ye Town.
particularly relating to days of prayer,
in this Evil Time.
9. G.D. Warnings are to be given unto ye wicked
Printer, and his Accomplices, who every
week publish a vile Paper to lessen
& Blacken ye Ministers of ye Town,
& render their Ministry ineffectual.
A Wickedness never parallel'd any where
upon ye Face of ye Earth!

Figure 10. Cotton Mather, Diary, *entry attacking the* New-England Courant, *9 December 1721. On 13 November 1721, Cotton Mather verbally attacked James Franklin when he met him in the street. Three weeks later, in the* Courant *of 4 December, Cotton Mather defended his rebuking James Franklin: "The Reason of this faithful Admonition was, because the Practice of supporting, and publishing every Week, a Libel, on purpose to lessen and Blacken, and Burlesque the Virtuous, and Principal Ministers of Religion in a Country, and render all the Services of their Ministry Despicable, and even Detestable to the People,* is a Wickedness that was never known before, *in any Country, Christian, Turkish, or Pagan, on the face of the Earth, and some Good Men are afraid it may provoke Heaven, to deal with this Place, in some regards as ne'er any place has yet been dealt withal, and a Charity to this Young Man, and his Accomplices might render such a Warning proper for them."*

In reply, James Franklin, in the 4 December Courant, *quoted excerpts from previous aspersions on the Mathers in various English newspapers—attacks that proved the "never parallel'd" wickedness had actually occurred at least twice in Boston within the past five years. James Franklin's reply may have caused Mather to echo the remonstrance in his* Diary *for 9 December: "G. D. Warnings are to be given unto the wicked Printer, and his Accomplices, who every week publish a vile Paper to lessen and blacken the Ministers of the Town, and render their Ministry ineffectual. A Wickedness never parallel'd any where upon the Face of the Earth!" For a bit of context, I include the previous entry: "8. G.D. Several Motions are to be made among the Ministers of this Town. Particularly relating to Days of Prayer, in this evil Time."*

"G.D." was Mather's abbreviation for "Good Devised." From 1711 on, Mather typically began his diary entries with an admonition to himself on the good that he intended to do. Courtesy, Massachusetts Historical Society, Boston.

unaccountable Lyars and Self-Destroyers, for opposing the Practice of Inoculation."

Then James Franklin republished "Peter Hakins" (John Eyre) citing "Dr. Gumble's" opinion of a clergyman's proper sphere. (Since he reprinted the misspelling of "Monck" as "Monk," evidently he did not know the book.) Editor

Franklin falsely claimed that "the Authors of many of the Letters sent to me" were unknown. He added (no doubt truthfully) that several ministers both in the town and the country[12] subscribed to the *Courant*, "which I believe they wou'd not do, if they thought it publish'd on purpose to bring their Persons into Disesteem." He then made an argument that cast doubt upon his own religious convictions: "As, in Controversies of Religion, nothing is more frequent than for Divines themselves to press the *same Texts* from *opposite Tenets* [an opinion repeated by Benjamin Franklin in his spoof of titles on honor (18 February 1723)], they cannot fairly condemn a Man for dissenting from them in Matters of Religion; much less can any Man be thought to hinder the Success of the *Work of a Minister*, by opposing him in that which is not *properly a Minister's Work*."

James Franklin appealed to the freedom of the press: "to anathematize a Printer for publishing the different opinions of Men, is as injudicious as it is wicked." He called upon his favorite contemporary source, *Cato's Letters*: " 'To attempt to reduce all Men to the same Standard of thinking, is (as the British *Cato* observes) absurd in Philosophy, impious in Religion, and Faction in the State.' " His argument clearly had the high ground and made Cotton Mather seem an authoritarian tool of the governor. The printer concluded the 4 December essay by proclaiming "that both Inoculators and Anti-Inoculators are welcome" in the *Courant*: "I hereby invite all Men, who have Leisure, Inclination and Ability, to speak their Minds with Freedom, Sense and Moderation, and their Pieces shall be welcome to a Place in my Paper."

On page 2 of the 4 December paper, the printer added a prefatory note (giving it dramatic immediacy by dating it precisely) before a letter from Cotton Mather. "On Saturday in the Afternoon, soon after I had set my Types for the above Vindication, I received my Curse *at Large*, inclose'd in the following Letter." (If James Franklin had not already written his vindication, the letter from Cotton Mather would have caused him to do so.) Cotton Mather explained his 13 November attack on James Franklin: "The Reason of this faithful Admonition was, because the Practice of supporting, and publishing every Week, a Libel, on purpose to lessen and Blacken, and Burlesque the Virtuous, and Principal Ministers of Religion in a Country, and render all the Services of their Ministry Despicable, and even Detestable to the People, *is a Wickedness that was never known before*, in any Country, Christian, Turkish, or Pagan, on the face of the Earth, and some Good Men are afraid it may provoke Heaven, to deal with this Place, in some regards as ne'er any place has yet been dealt withal, and a Charity to this Young Man, and his Accomplices might render such a Warning proper for them."

Unfazed, James Franklin appended the following comment: "The Author of this *faithful Admonition*, is certainly under a Degree of Distraction, or he wou'd never desire a Thing to be made publick so much to his own Confusion: Nor could the best Friend I have in the World have done more to clear up my

Reputation." The printer then refuted Cotton Mather's charge that never before had the ministers of Boston been so attacked by quoting excerpts from an English news article on the expulsion from the House of Representatives of Gershon Woodel, a member from Tiverton, Massachusetts. The House had dismissed him on 15 July 1720, for expressing "himself with great Enmity to the Ministers of this Province." Significantly, the Boston periodical press (the *Courant* had not then started publication) did not mention the ouster. Printer Franklin also quoted extracts from a poetic satire against Boston's ministers that had appeared in the *St. James's Post* on the occasion.

Increasing Circulation

James Franklin tried to circulate his newspaper in the neighboring colonies. Indeed, his title, *New-England Courant*, suggested that its coverage would be more inclusive that that of the *Boston News-Letter* or the *Boston Gazette*. The *Courant*'s obituaries were not confined to Boston. It noted the death of John Rogers, "the famous Baptist Teacher at New London," on 30 October, and on 11 December printed a satiric notice about his death, supposedly written from New London, Connecticut. Rogers was the founder of a religious sect called the Rogerines, a compound primarily of Baptist and Quaker doctrines that survived into the twentieth century. James Franklin's obituaries were also more politically interesting than those of the rival papers. The 4 December *Courant* celebrated William Hutchinson, a Boston member of the House of Representatives, for defending "the just Rights and Liberties of this People." Neither the *Boston News-Letter* nor the *Boston Gazette* obituaries of Hutchinson used the Whiggish clichés to praise him. James Franklin also made his paper appealing by writing mock news items or reports to which he added an ironic comment, thus anticipating the filler that Benjamin Franklin later occasionally wrote. The 11 December *Courant* reported: "a certain Man at Stonington [Connecticut] . . . lately castrated himself; which has occasioned abundance of Waggish talk among the looser Sort of Female Tribe, who are so incensed against him, that some of them talk hotly of throwing Stones at him, if he lives to come abroad again." What a delight! No such ironic and amusing filler had ever previously appeared in the American periodical press. The items dated from Connecticut show that the editor was trying to sell newspapers in that colony.

*New-England Courant*s also circulated in New Hampshire. After a satirical advertisement in the 11 December *Boston Gazette* claimed that the *Courant*s were sent gratis to New Hampshire, the Couranteers on 18 December took up New Hampshire politics. That colony shared the same royal governor with Massachusetts but had its own legislature. Writing as editor "Timothy Turnstone," James Franklin replied with a personal attack on the anonymous author of the *Boston Gazette*'s advertisement as "your Worship," thus pointing to Samuel Penhallow (1665–1726), chief justice of New Hampshire's Superior Court and Cotton Mather's friend. In the same issue, Nathaniel Gardner rallied to the cause by writing as "Tom Penshallow." He complained of the slavery of New Hampshire's citizens as compared to the enjoyment of liberty and freedom in Massachusetts. Penshallow/Gardner wrote: *"Ever since the New Laws have been Enacted, there is not a private Man among us who dare open his Lips, unless it be to* flatter." The obnoxious "new law" was a bill to prevent riots by restricting the right of assembly. *"As for Freedom of Speech, it is utterly suppress'd among us, and I suppose quickly we shall be hang'd for our* Thoughts: *And that those Laws did not pass at B[osto]n, I hear is owing to the Conduct of some brave Men among you."* Penshallow remarked that rumor insinuated the *Courant* would be forbidden in New Hampshire because it "sometimes sets forth the Rights and Liberties of Mankind." Turning the knife in Cotton Mather by quoting him against himself, Penshallow/Gardner cited Mather's *Bonifacius* as saying that mischiefs have sometimes been established by laws.

On 25 December, still attempting to win circulation in New Hampshire, Gardner taught Franklin another gambit,—the fictitious reply. The older writer slyly replied anonymously to Tom Penshallow (i.e., himself), asking, "Have you any Laws that deprive you of Privileges, which belong to you as *Men*, and *Englishmen*, which you did not Consent to by your *Representatives*?" If they "enact Laws to enslave you and your Posterity, Cannot you *Ease your selves of such Adversaries*, and Elect better Men in their Room?" He again quoted Cotton Mather's *Bonifacius* as an authority against bad rulers. Gardner said that Massachusetts not only had juries, "but such as are of our own choosing and not such as are pick'd and cull'd by the high Sheriff at the Direction of his Superiors." The anonymous Gardner castigated New Hampshire's citizens for choosing New Charter and Royalist representatives: "If you are pleas'd with being Ass-rid, I know not who will pity you." At the end, he satirically questioned if a law against excessive *"Punch-Drinking"* should not accompany "the Law against Riots and Tumults."

James Franklin further tried to win circulation in New Hampshire. Though Franklin did not annotate it, the editor no doubt wrote the following clever bit of indirect self-advertising. A letter dated "Saybrook, Dec. 12, 1721" in the 25 December paper said: "The Political and humorous Letters of your Correspondents, with which you entertain us in these Parts, has sufficiently recommended your Paper to us; and as I find you begin to give a more full and particular Account of Domestick Affairs, than the other publick Prints, I shall venture to begin and carry on my Correspondence with you, by sending an Account of what occurs here worth your Notice." Two New Hampshire news items followed. Some New Hampshire residents probably started subscribing.

Gardner's Dialogue I

Continuing the debate over inoculation in the 8 January 1721/2 *Courant*, Gardner wrote the first dialogue to appear in an American periodical: "A Dialogue between a Clergyman and a Layman, concerning Inoculation. By an unknown

Hand." Franklin later used the genre numerous times—best known, perhaps, in his "Dialogue between the Gout and Mr. Franklin" (22 October 1780). Gardner's "Clergyman" opened: "The last Time I discours'd with you, you seem'd to discover a bitter Aversion to the new and safe Way of Inoculation; are you yet reconcil'd to that successful Practice?" The Layman made an understated point against inoculation: "I have but little reason to entertain a more favourable Opinion of that Practice than formerly, unless the Death of several Persons under the Operation of late, should induce me so to do. I confess, I am not yet convinc'd, that it is either a Lawful or useful Practice."

The Clergyman replied with the Mathers' typical appeal to authority: "The Ministers of the Gospel, who are our Spiritual Guides, approve and recommend this Practice, and they are great and good Men, who would not impose on the World; and surely, you ought to fall in with their Opinion." Gardner's Layman disagreed, cited the Bible, and made a homely comparison: "I think the Ministers who have drove on Inoculation so fiercely, have not only impos'd on others, but themselves also; so that we have reason to say in the Words of the Prophet, (Hos, 9. 7.) *The Days of Visitation are come;——the Prophet is a Fool, and the Spiritual Man is mad.* I have abundant Reason to think, that they and I are equally Ignorant of Inoculation, especially as to the Success of it; and if the Blind lead the Blind, both shall fall into the Ditch." The Layman's common sense and mother wit won that exchange.

Appealing to authority, the Clergyman referred to the cases of conscience written by Increase and Cotton Mather. "But why won't you believe the Ministers? They can explain the dark Passages of Scripture, and answer Cases of Conscience, better than illiterate Men." The democratic Layman, however, refused an automatic deference to anyone, including ministers. Only logic and proof would convince him. "I will believe no Man (tho' he be a Minister) because he is great and good; for such may err, and have sometimes deceived themselves and others: Nor have any of our Casuists as yet given satisfactory Answers to the Objections and Scruples which are rais'd against this upstart Way." To the clergyman's claim that the ministers were good men, the Layman replied that their goodness was irrelevant in assessing truth: "They are or should be good; but I remember a great Divine says, 'When we are about our Enquiry into Truth, let it be remembred, that neither the Great, nor the Learned, nor the *Good*, are absolutely to be confided in.'" Responding, the clergyman echoed the Mathers (especially *Several Reasons*, which Gardner had earlier parodied): "But I find, *all the Rakes in Town* are against Inoculation, and that induces me to believe it is a right Way."

The Matherian argument exasperated Gardner's Layman, and he ridiculed it, but, surprisingly for the generally cautious and ironic Gardner, he became almost sacrilegious in his reply: "Most of the Ministers are for it, and that induces me to think it is from the D——l; for he often makes use of good Men as Instruments to obtrude his Delusions on the World." Though the second independent clause in the compound sentence compliments the ministers, the first clause outraged them and the public at large. The Mathers and other anti-Couranteers seized upon it in later attacks.

Gardner continued: "*Cl[ergyman]*. You must not say it is from the D——l because of the Success of it, for the D——l was never the Author of any thing for the Good of Mankind." Gardner again cited his favorite book by Cotton Mather, *Bonifacius*, for authority: "*Laym[an]*. As to the Success of this Practice, the learned Dr. Edwards shall speak for me, and the rather, because Dr. C. Mather (*Bonif.* p. 180)[13] says, *More* Edward's *would be vast blessings.*' . . . It is a Maxim among the *Turks* generally, that whatever prospers hath God For its Author: And so from their Success in their Wars, they have been wont to conclude that their Religion is from God, and owned by him."

The amazingly bold Gardner charged that New England Puritans were like the Turks in associating God's blessings with success in wars, in commerce, and in life, and in allying God's displeasure with failure and sickness. Gardner ridiculed the common Puritan association between godliness and worldly success, which Cotton Mather had advocated at length in *A Christian and His Calling: Two Brief Discourses* (Boston, 1701).

Though inoculation had been learned from "the Heathen," Gardner's clergyman defended it: "Inoculation is not the worse because the Heathens first practis'd it: They make use of Food and Cloaths; and shall we reject those Gifts of Heaven, because they receive them: God forbid." The learned Layman replied: "The Use of Food and Cloaths, which you bring for an Instance; is no ways parallel; For the Sixth Commandment requires us to use such Things for the Support of our Lives. Are you willing to imitate the Heathen in other Things besides *Inoculation*? The King of *Calecus* in the *East Indies* lies not with his Queen the first Night, but one of the Priests doth, who hath a Gratuity bestow'd on him for that Service. I suppose it is not a worse Sin to break the Seventh Commandment than the Sixth." Naturally the clergyman condemned the "East Indian Practice because it is a *moral Evil*, which I think inoculation is not." The Layman replied: "You do but think it [inoculation] is not a moral Evil, for you cannot prove that it is not; none of you have done it as yet, and I presume you are all asham'd of your Craft, and will write no more in favour of the Practice." The clergyman concluded: "I see you are obstinate, and will not be convinc'd. I will adjourn the Discourse to our next Meeting."

Gardner's suggestions of anticlericism (in his last sentence, the Layman alluded to *priestcraft*—diction usually associated with anti-Catholic, especially anti-Jesuit propaganda, and deism[14]); his dissatisfaction with the role of the clergy; his suggestion that if the clergy were for a project, it was from the devil; and his charge that Puritans and Muhammadans alike viewed worldly success and failure as indications of God's judgments—all were shocking in 1720s New England. The Mathers rightly asserted that such expressions were unprecedented (at least in print) in New England.

Hell-Fire II

Philip Musgrave's 15 January *Boston Gazette* carried a letter dated from Cambridge, 11 January 1721/2, defending him from James Franklin's attack of 8 January. The Cambridge letter, signed "John Harvard," also supported the Mathers against Dr. William Douglass's charge that the 16 September *London Mercury* did not contain an article on inoculation saying that "Great Numbers in this City, and Suburbs are under the Inoculation of the Small Pox." The Cambridge author was Samuel Mather, Cotton Mather's son, and, much later, a correspondent to whom Franklin wrote his memories of Increase and Cotton Mather. Young Mather claimed: "Every one sees that the main intention of this Vile Courant, is to Vilify and Abuse the best Men we have, and especially the Principal Ministers of Religion in the Country. And tho' they have been so left of GOD, and of Sense, as to tell People in Print, that they live in a *Wickedness, which no Country besides*, whether Christian, Turkish, or Pagan, was ever known to be guilty of; yet they go on in it; and in this last Courant they taught the People *That if the Ministers do approve, & advise a thing, 'tis a Sign that it is of the Devil.*"

Samuel Mather continued his wide-ranging attack: "If such an horrid Paper, called, *The New-England Courant*, should be seen in other Countries, what would they think of *New-England!*" Then, overlooking what foreigners would think if they read his attack, and referring to the *News-Letter* of 6 July, Mather revived the former slur against the Couranteers: "If you call this Crew, the *Hell-Fire Club* of *Boston*, your Friend Campbell will stand God-father for it; having in one of his NewsPapers formerly assign'd this proper Name for them." Young Mather saw through the strategies of Nathaniel Gardner (though he evidently did not know the primary Couranteer's identity): "If there happen to be any thing that looks Religious in their Weekly Libel, 'tis really, and in effect, a Banter on Religion; as their Letter was in defense of *Inoculation*; which their great Hero & Champion, that Crackbrain'd *Mundungus Williams* foolishly pretends an Answer to."[15]

Mistakenly believing that John Checkley, whom James Franklin had terminated after the third *Courant*, still functioned as the chief Couranteer, young Mather wrote: "Every one knows that the Head of the Club is one who printed some *Choice Dialogues*, to prove, *That the GOD whom the Churches of New-England Pray to, is the Devil.*" He claimed that the *Courant*'s subscribers "will be justly looked upon, as the Supporters of a Weekly Libel written on purpose to destroy the Religion of the Country, and as Enemies to the faithful Ministers of it." He promised that if "this Hell-Fire Paper be still carried on," he would send in "a List of their Names, that all the Sober People at the Country may know who they are." He concluded, "I am not my self a Minister, nor have I advised with any such for this Letter; nor did I ever yet publish any thing. But there is a Number of us, who resolve, that if the wickedness be not stop'd, we will pluck up our Courage, and see what we can do in our way to stop it."

Making a flank attack upon young Samuel Mather, Gardner contributed to the twenty-fourth *Courant* (15 January 1721/2) a brief social satire from a father with "a very Wicked Disobedient Son, inclin'd to almost every Vice." The father has "sometimes endeavoured to allure him by Promises, and represented to him the unspeakable Pleasure and Satisfaction which Result from a Life of Vertue: And at other Times I have set before him the Fatal Consequences of a Dissolute Life, and told him, *that such Companions of Fools will be Destroy'd*: But I find *all will not do*." Practically every Bostonian knew that the description suited Cotton Mather and his dissolute son Increase, Samuel's older brother.

On 22 January 1721/2, James Franklin more openly replied to Samuel Mather. The printer began with an epigraph from Cotton Mather's *Magnalia* ("Bloody Fishing at Oyster-River, / And sad Work, at Groton") and with references to Mather's conversation: "That the *Courants* are carry'd on by a *Hell-Fire Club* with a *Nonjuror* at the Head of them, has been asserted by a certain Clergyman in his common Conversation, with as much Zeal as ever he discover'd in the Application of a Sermon on the most awakening Subject. This is one of the malicious Arts used by him, and his hot-headed Trumpeters, to spoil the Credit of the *Courant*, that he may reign Detractor General over the whole Province, and do all the Mischief his ill Nature prompts him to, without hearing of it." James Franklin then refuted Samuel Mather's charge that the Couranteers were Tories: "But, as this Report betrays the highest Pitch of Malice in themselves, so it discovers the greatest Ignorance in those that believe it; for if the few Gentlemen here, reputed Torys, are concern'd in writing the Paper, they are very much out in their Politicks in asserting the *Rights and Liberties of the Subject*, to prove the Doctrines of *Absolute Monarchy, Passive Obedience*, and *Non-resistance*."

Perhaps James Franklin believed that he should not reveal the identity of his authors. Instead of saying that John Checkley had not been involved in the paper since the third number, the newspaperman denied that he had ever been: "As to Mr. C[heckle]y's being concern'd in it, I affirm, I know not of one Piece in the *Courants* of his writing but am certain that he has been charg'd with being the Author of many (wherein the Ministers were touch'd upon) which I know he was not; nor is he so much of a *Courant Christian* as to promote the Paper by being a Subscriber for it."

James Franklin observed that nothing in the *Courant* had been against the law and that he had not "suffer'd the Disgrace of being call'd in by the Sheriff," unlike the author (Cotton Mather) of *News from Robinson Cruso's Island* (1720), "so justly censur'd by the Honourable House of Representatives."[16] He claimed that the hearty curses on the *Courant* by Cotton Mather had only given it good publicity and more subscribers. The printer then used a homely American comparison, a technique that his younger brother brought to perfection: "*as a Connecticut Trader once said of his Onions, 'The more they are curs'd, the more they grow.'*"

Benjamin Franklin echoed this anecdote (and perhaps other oral versions of it) in a letter of 19 May 1785. English rumors about the evils and troubles in America were false, he said, and America was flourishing. The English news reports reminded him of "a violent High Church Factor, resident some time in Boston, when I was a Boy. He had bought upon Speculation a Connecticut Cargo of Onions, which he flatter'd himself he might sell again to great Profit, but the Price fell, and they lay upon hand. He was heartily vex'd with his Bargain, especially when he observ'd they began to *grow* in the Store he had fill'd with them. He show'd them one Day to a Friend, 'Here they are,' says he, 'and they are *growing* too! I damn 'em every day; but I think they are like the Presbyterians; the more I curse 'em, the more they grow.'"[17]

Turning again to Samuel Mather's letter in the *Gazette*, James Franklin reversed young Mather's taunt concerning New England's reputation: "Poor Boy! When your Letter comes to be seen in other Countries, (under the Umbrage of Authority [the *Gazette* and the *News-Letter* both claimed to be "Printed by Authority"]) *what* indeed *will they think of* New England!" He then travestied the epigraph from the *Magnalia*: "They will certainly conclude, *There is bloody Fishing* for Nonsense *at* Cambridge, *and sad Work at the* Colledge." The printer complimented the New England clergy for being "as faithful to God and their Flocks, as any Clergy in the known World." Then he charged that "*some* of them of late, have been too industrious in reporting things, which tend to hurt the private Interest of *some* of their Hearers." He forthrightly said: "Their Endeavours of this Nature against my self, is too plain and too publick to be conceal'd; and as I freely forgive them, so I heartily ask Pardon for offending them." Had he ended the sentence there, he would have scored with all his audience, but he added "in following my proper Business." Many would have thought that "his proper business" hardly included attacking and satirizing ministers.

James Franklin called upon the rights of individuals to make their own private judgments, an argument Gardner had used in his 8 January dialogue: "For a Man to give up his Right and Title to his Senses, and allow his whimsical Minister (for some such there are in all Countries) to dispose of him Body and Soul, just as the Humour rakes him, is no Argument of Love, but on the contrary opens a Door for a dangerous Prejudice, if not an irreconcilable Hatred between them." Next, echoing John ("Mundungus") Williams, he used a sententious antimetabole that Gardner echoed on 19 February 1721/2 and young Franklin remembered and repeated in the *Courant* a year later (28 January 1722/ 3): "*The best of Men are but Men at the best*, and if of ambitious Tempers, are apt to receive all the Honour *given* them, without considering whether it is *due* to them *for their works sake*." The printer's argument challenged the hierarchical order of New England and may have partially inspired the egalitarianism of his young apprentice.

Defending himself against the persistent slur that the Couranteers were like the London Hell-Fire Club, James Franklin wrote: "It is a Pleasure to me, that I have never inserted any thing in the Courant, which charg'd any Man or Society of Men with being Guilty of the Crimes which were peculiar to the *Hell-Fire Club* in *London*, and which the Devils themselves are not capable of perpetrating." Then he echoed Dr. William Douglass: "And, whether Mr. M[usgrave] or his young Champion know it or no, 'tis look'd upon as a gross Reflection on the Government, that they should be told of a *Hell-Fire Club* in *Boston*, (in a Paper *publish'd by Authority*) and not use their Endeavours to discover who they are, in order to punish them."

GARDNER'S DIALOGUE II

Gardner contributed a third, major piece to the 22 January 1721/2 *Courant*, "*Another Dialogue between the* Clergyman *and* Layman," which developed the thesis that the clergy had and should have a diminishing role in New England. The Layman began: "In our last Discourse you were pleas'd to say that *all the rakes in Town are against Inoculation*: So that I plainly see, that Faith in the Doctrine of Inoculation, is by some Accounted a Discriminating Mark of the Godly." The Clergyman denied the consequence: "I did not mean that all who are against Inoculation are Rakes: and if any of those worthy Persons who favour that Practice, have made use of hasty Expressions in their Words or Writings, you ought to put the best Construction on them, and impute the same to their Pious Zeal for the Good of the People." The Layman granted that zeal is good when accompanied with discretion and cited the Reverend Mr. Thomas Foxcroft's ordination sermon against zeal that is "not according to Knowledge." Foxcroft (1697–1769), a Harvard graduate who was minister of Gardner's church, the First Church of Boston, said that "it becomes the Advocates of Truth always to offer unbroken Reason, that shall master and overmatch the Understanding."[18]

Gardner's Clergyman claimed that "the vulgar sort" cavil "at every thing the Ministers say or do," but "the Learned and Understanding Sort" are for inoculation. To the Clergyman's aristocratic posture, the Layman replied with a biblical quotation, identifying with ordinary persons. "So the Pharisees cry'd out, *John* 7.48. *Do any of the Rulers believe?* as if all others must make *their* Opinion and Belief, the Rule and Measure of their own; or if they do not, they are Accursed: for so it follows, v. 49. *This People who know not the Law*, (this Ignorant, Rascally Rabble, the Dregs of the Common-wealth and manners too,) *are cursed.*" The class opposition and Gardner's defense of ordinary persons anticipated Franklin's 1740 Obadiah Plainman series defending the "Meaner Sort." The Clergyman responded with praise of the old aristocratic order: "Why is it chiefly among the Vulgar Herd that this wicked Spirit of Party and Division prevails: It is they who oppose their Good Rulers and Ministers; and if any new Thing is propos'd they presently make it a Bone of Contention. For my Part I fear they will Sin away a Precious Ministry, & Pious Magistracy." The Layman defended the people and reminded the Clergyman that "some of your own Order have been broachers & fomenters" of differences and parties. "But there is a Sort of Men in the World who are Eagles abroad but Owls at Home; that is, they can see other Mens Faults, but not their own." The Clergyman sensibly replied that if the blame fell on the guilty, then it would not "all fall on the Clergy."

Gardner then unfairly connected Cotton Mather with the Salem witchcraft trials. He and the Boston public in general were currently recalling the trials because Robert Calef, Jr., son of the author of the attack on Mather, *More Wonders of the Invisible World* (1700), had recently died and the *Courant* currently carried an advertisement concerning his estate. The Layman said, "I pray Sir, who have been the Instruments of Mischief and Trouble both in Church and State, from the Witchcraft to Inoculation? who is it that takes the Liberty to Vilify a whole Town, in Words too black to be repeated? Who is it that in common Conversation makes no Bones of calling the Town a MOB? and whose Disciple is he who has lately done the same?" The references to Cotton Mather and his son Samuel were obvious. The Clergyman replied that "you must not Condemn all because some are Imprudent." The Layman, however, censured "them for their Imprudence and you for endeavouring to Justify the same."

Gardner's Clergyman returned to his aristocratic posture. The cause of our divisions was "too many Authors." He implied that only ministers should publish: "The Command of the Press is fallen into Laymen's Hands and is made an Engine to Detract from the Worth of Good Men." The Layman replied with the thesis of the dialogue: "I know you cannot endure that Laymen should write or Know any thing. You would have them know but just enough to get to Heaven."

One suspects that Gardner had read John Dryden's *Religio Laici* (1682), which defended an intelligent layman's ability and right to judge religious issues.[19] The most famous living English writer when Gardner was a young man, Dryden wrote in the preface to *Religio Laici*, "perhaps Laymen, with equal advantages of Parts and Knowledge, are not the most incompetent Judges of Sacred things." Gardner echoed Dryden's point. Gardner's Clergyman asserted, "we must needs Censure those who run from Place to Place hearing and telling News, & prating about Politics, and Promoting Jangles and Contention." The Layman responded that the clergy should "take Example by the Reverend Mr. S[ewal]l, and let Inoculation and State Affairs alone," referring to Judge Samuel Sewall's son, the Reverend Joseph Sewall, now the Old South Church minister. "Why must not Ministers," asked the Clergyman, "be suffered to speak their Minds as well as other Men?" The Layman replied: "They may do it in Private, but then they ought to be very Cautious and Circumspect." The Clergyman sarcastically rejoined: "You had best go into the Pulpit and teach us our Duty." But the outspoken Layman scored his point: "I should be in the Way of my Duty as much as you are, when you vend your private Opinions there, if I should."

The Clergyman complained about the changing role of the clergy: "Formerly there was nothing Transacted without the Clergy's Advice; but now they must be afraid to speak. A worthy friend of mine some Time since, did but touch on

Subjection to the higher Powers, and he was soon whipt up in Print." Gardner
here unfairly aligned the clergy with both the authorities and the tories, and
opposed them to both the Old Charter and New Charter parties. The Layman
commented on the changing times: "Formerly there were many Grave and Wise
Ministers; now there are but few." No doubt Gardner meant the pun on the
"Wise" ministers, alluding to the redoubtable old hero, the Reverend John Wise.
The Layman also commented that the people were changing: more were educated and did not need the advice of ministers. The Clergyman claimed, "Our
Business is, to lift up our Voice like a Trumpet, against growing Iniquity, and
to Exhort every Soul to be Subject to the higher Powers: and we must do our
Duty let Men say what they will." The Layman concluded, "The Clergy have no
Business with Inoculation, considered as a Practice in Physick." Reinforcing his
point, he quoted Mather's *Bonifacius* and Bishop Gilbert Burnet.

As artful writing, Gardner's dialogue was excellent. Though Gardner's Layman generally had a slightly better argument, the Clergyman was a sympathetic
figure. Though he seemed somewhat behind the times, he also scored good
points. The ideas contested were important, the characters fairly equal in ability,
and the exchanges lively.

CAPTAIN TAYLOR VS. SAMUEL MATHER

In the same 22 January 1721/2 *Courant*, Captain Christopher Taylor joined the
fray with a letter dated Ipswich, 19 January. Like James Franklin, Taylor assaulted Samuel Mather's Cambridge letter, claiming that it confused the issues
between Musgrave's "*Pride, Idleness, and Dishonesty*" and the ministers' support
of inoculation. "The Difference," he argued, "between *F[rankli]n* and *M[us-
grav]e*, is not about the *Gazette* but about the *P[o]st-M[aste]r*'s being defective
in his Office." Taylor also objected to the "Cambridge Letter's mentioning that
detestable Hell-Fire Club." To say that such a club existed in Boston brought
infamy upon the town. "And had Mr. Godfather *C[ampbel]l* been prosecuted
some Months ago, when he in his Weekly Paper [Cotton Mather in the 28 August 1721 *News-Letter*] insinuated to the World, that there was such a Club in
Boston, I am verily perswaded, it would not have now been brought on the Stage
to serve a Turn." He challenged the author of the Cambridge letter to make
good his promise "and give a *List of the Names* of the Persons that are pointed
at in that Letter, as a Hell Fire Club; that if any such there be, they may be
rooted up and banished: But on the other hand, if the Accusation appears to be
false and groundless, then set the Author of the *Cambridge* Letter, or the Publisher, to be branded with Infamy and suffer the utmost Rigour that the Law
can inflict."

Taylor concluded with a note on John Williams, who had attacked Cotton
Mather and inoculation in a pamphlet and whom Samuel Mather also criticized:
"I suppose he will answer for himself; he is a Man I don't know, nor do ever
remember to have seen in my whole Life time; if he be *crackbrain'd*, as the

Cambridge Letter avers, truly the poor Man is almost without a Remedy in the Law; but if he be a sober Man, and of sound Reason, 'tis highly probable that some of the Lawyers would tell him that he has a good Action against the Fictitious Cambridge Champion or Mr. [Samuel] *M[athe]r.*"

After this spate of recriminations, James Franklin tried to turn the Couranteers away from local quarrels. On Monday, 29 January 1721/2, writing as "Abigail Afterwit," James Franklin tried his hand at social satire: "It is my Misfortune to be wedded to a Stranger . . . whose Carriage persuades me he had no other Design in his Addresses than to make me miserable, if it were in his Power to do otherwise. He thinks himself under no Obligation to be agreeable in my Company, because he is already possess'd of my Love." Worse yet, her husband does not work but "goes abroad with the greatest Pleasure, and returns with the greatest Reluctance." What gives Abigail Afterwit the greatest uneasiness, however, is that he "has gain'd the Reputation of a good natur'd Man abroad, and among my Friends, who look upon him only as unfortunate." Since he enjoys the good opinion of others, she cannot complain though he "has already spent the little Money, and wore out the fine Cloaths by which he deceiv'd me." Yet he does not try to work. "This unhappy Temper of mind has brought him to the last Extremity." James Franklin concluded with an "Italian Proverb" that Addison had cited in *Spectator* No. 191: "The Man who lives by Hope, will die by Hunger." Later Franklin used the proverb, shortening it and making it mildly scurrilous: "He who lives upon Hope, dies Farting" (*Poor Richard*, February 1736). Benjamin Franklin evidently remembered Abigail Afterwit. Franklin used the persona "Abigail Twitterfield" the following year (8 July 1723) and "Anthony Afterwit" nine years later (10 July 1732).

INCREASE MATHER'S THREAT

James Franklin's attempt to avoid controversy was short-lived. Increase Mather had so far played comparatively little part in the newspaper wars. His son Cotton Mather and his grandson Samuel Mather had both failed to stop the *Courant*; now Increase tried. Both the *News-Letter* and the *Gazette* for 29 January carried "Advice to the Publick from DR. INCREASE MATHER": "Whereas a *Wicked Libel* called the *New-England Courant*, has represented me as one among the *Supporters* of it; I do hereby declare, that altho' I had paid the Printer for two or three of them, I then (before that last *Courant* was published) sent him word, that I was *extreamly offended* with it! In special, because in one of his *Vile Courants* he insinuates, that if *the Ministers of GOD approve of a thing, it is a Sign it is of the Devil*; which is a horrid thing to be related!"

Increase Mather charged that the *Courant* said that some "*Busy Inoculator*" imposed on the public a false statement from the 16 September 1721 *London Mercury* that a number of persons were being inoculated in London. Mather himself, however, read those words in the *London Mercury*. Mather then directly threatened James Franklin with the wrath of God: "And he doth frequently abuse the *Ministers* of Religion, and many other worthy Persons in a manner which is intolerable. For these and such like Reasons I signified to the Printer, that I would have no more of their *Wicked Courants*. I that have known what New-England was from the Beginning, cannot but be troubled to see the Degeneracy of this place. I can well remember when the Civil Government could have taken an effectual Course to suppress such a *Cursed Libel!* which if it be not done I am afraid that some *Awful Judgment* will come upon this Land, and that the *Wrath of GOD will arise, and there will be no Remedy.*" Mather said that he pitied "poor *Franklin,* who tho' but a *Young Man*, it may be *Speedily* he must appear before the Judgment Seat of GOD, and what answer will he give for printing things so vile and abominable?" He added that in reading such a wicked newspaper, the *Courant*'s subscribers were as guilty as the printer.

Increase Mather's references to the earlier times in New England and his threat suggesting he spoke for God were attitudes that had become outdated. With exceptions, most persons who found the *Courant* too outspoken and antireligious must have been uncomfortable if not embarrassed by his words.

Reply

James Franklin answered Increase Mather in the next *Courant* (5 February 1721/2), giving "an Account of the first Cause of the Difference between us." He explained that the week before the 1 January *Courant* appeared, Increase Mather's grandson (Mather Byles, as a later reference makes clear) brought the printer an extract from the *London Mercury* concerning smallpox with the request that he print it. The printer did so on 1 January. But Dr. William Douglass had a copy of the *London Mercury* and claimed that most of the quotation did not appear in the attributed source, so James Franklin printed Dr. Douglass's letter (22 January) denying that the quotation existed in the *Mercury.* Subsequently, James Franklin was presented with another, complete *London Mercury* and found the other part of the quotation in the paper's last sheet. The printer claimed, "I have been imposed on by both Sides, and shall take Care for the future, not to insert any thing in the *Courant* upon the Word of another."

James Franklin said that although Increase Mather only subscribed for the first three *Courant*s and then canceled his subscription, he nevertheless continued for the next several weeks to send "his Grandson Biles" every week to buy the paper and finally subscribed again, "and express'd no Dislike of the Paper till after Mr. *Musgrave* had publish'd his Grandson's Letter in the *Gazette* of Jan 15. So that he had and paid me for one Paper after that which he so much dislikes." The printer turned next to the statement from Gardner's dialogue that "if the Ministers of God do approve of a Thing, its a sign it is of the Devil." He quoted the entire sentence, which concluded: "for he often makes use of good Men as Instruments to obtrude his Delusions on the World." Concerning Increase Mather's threat that he may "speedily . . . appear before the Judgment seat of God," the printer replied, "there is no Man living which doeth good and sinneth not, and that I expect and Hope to appear before God with safety in the Righteousness of Christ."

Printer Franklin objected to the minister's saying that no one should buy the *Courant* and compared it to forbidding people to purchase goods of any "particular Merchant or Shopkeeper. . . . I desire him to consider how it would be taken, if upon a Misunderstanding, between any particular Minister and my self, I should publickly advise his People not to hear him, or contribute to his Support." (Though the word *boycott* was not coined until 1880, the practice had been applied to persons and politics for centuries.) Finally, the printer said that in the next *Courant* he would reply to a pamphlet attacking him that had just appeared, *A Vindication of the Ministers of Boston*.[20]

Nathaniel Gardner also came to James Franklin's defense. Writing as "Zechariah Hearwell" in the same 5 February *Courant*, he again quoted Thomas Foxcroft's *Practical Discourse Relating to the Gospel Ministry* saying that ministers should not force their own opinions from the pulpit: "Ministers should perswade Men, *by the meekness and gentleness of Christ*; but the reverse of this, tends to obstruct their Ministry, and prejudice Men against their Persons." Everyone recognized that Increase and Cotton Mather did not use meekness and gentleness to appeal.

In the lead essay in the *Courant* for 12 February, James Franklin replied to the *Vindication* by Cotton Mather and others: "Let Men once be condemn'd as irreligious, for opposing only the *Humours* of those who profess Religion, they will naturally be tempted to say, *That Religion is nothing but Humour*." In fact, claimed the printer, "Religion derives its Authority from GOD alone, and will not be kept up in the *Consciences* of Men by any Humane Power." James Franklin believed Cotton Mather wrote the pamphlet: "He has thrown Praise in his own Face till he is blind to his own Failings; and (to speak like himself) quarrels with his Neighbours because they do not *look* and *think* just as he would have them." The printer pointed out that Mather took words out of context in order to make his point: "I doubt not but it wou'd grieve him to hear, that his abusing his Neighbours under Colour of Religion, has been such a stumbling Block to some, that they were even tempted to think Religion to be nothing but a Cheat or Contrivance, impos'd on the World upon politick Grounds."

James Franklin's criticism was bold for 1722 Boston. He continued: "But this I assure him I have often heard of late; and this, if any thing, will perswade me to be silent to any other Pieces of this Nature publish'd against me, unless the Authors first endeavour to prove what they assert, before they pronounce Judgment against me as a *Castaway*." In the same *Courant*, James Franklin reprinted an account of London's Hell-Fire Club from *Applebee's Journal* (6 May 1721). The scandalous account must have immediately boosted the sale of the *Courant*. Like his printing of Thomas Walter's *Little-Compton Scourge: Or, The Anti-Courant*, the action revealed the talents of a good newspaperman.

Gardner blasted Cotton Mather in an anonymous letter to the *Courant* on

19 February: "When the *Faults* of some particular Men (for they are but *Men*) [echoing John Williams] have been expos'd; how has the same been *falsely* and *maliciously* (with an intent to *amuse* and *impose* on the Ignorant) deem'd, *a striking at the Foundation of Religion*." He said he wished that while "some of a certain Order are condemning cruel Invectives and railing Language in *others*, they would not become guilty of the same *themselves*; and while they are undertaking to reform what is amiss, that they would not do it in a Manner which tends into *Infidelity* and *Atheism*; and that they would take Care when they are exclaiming against *Contention*, that *they* are not the chief Promoters of it."

Gardner's partner, Matthew Adams, reinforced the charge against Cotton Mather with an anonymous letter in the 26 February *Courant*. Adams's misogynist speaker portrayed a group of women arraigning the *Courant* "at the Bar of Female Impudence." In this setting, "a certain Gentleman" exclaimed "bitterly against the Supporters of that Weekly Libel, which infects the sober Part of the Town, and tends to debauch the Minds of unthinking Youth, and set us all in a Flame: crying out, *Oh! the Divisions, the Quarrelings, the Backbitings of the Times.*" Then Adams borrowed from Swift's *Tale of a Tub* the story of the mountebank who primarily caused the complaint he himself made.[21] Adams made Mather the mountebank.

SOCIAL SATIRES

Though James Franklin knew that controversy sold newspapers, he also wanted—indeed, needed—the *New-England Courant* to be a respectable paper, even if frequently controversial; the alternative, in the small town of Boston, was failure. In mid-February 1721/2, he succeeded in temporarily separating himself from local skirmishes. The next few newspapers contained primarily belletristic material and social satires. James Franklin wrote the second *Courant* essay of 19 February addressed to "Mr. Turnstone" (the bachelor pseudonym for the editor) by "Betty Frugal." The printer's best social essay featured a forty-five-year-old virgin, pestered by a young merchant who (she believes, referring to Gardner's characterization of would-be lovers of rich women in the 29 January *Courant*) is really a "journeyman Gentleman." She lives happily and would not "think of changing my Condition, if it were not for Fashion sake, and to shake off the false Reproaches cast on us discreet Women by foolish Boys and Girls." Her suitor "calls my Eyes a couple of *Stars*, and says my Face is the *Sun*, nay better than the Sun, for he says the chief Benefit of the Sun is Light, and the greatest Advantage of Light to him is that it shews my Face: He commends my Lips too, and says my Teeth are Pearl. He often says he shall never be happy without me, and told me three Times in one Night, that he would *drown* himself if I would not smile upon him." Betty Frugal concluded: "He talks of *Flames* and *Darts*, and the like, which has a strange effect upon me, tho' I can't understand what he means."

In a comment on the piece, Turnstone ridiculed the proposal. "Your Face the *Sun!*" Preposterous! "If you marry him, 'tis ten to one but he'll find another Sun to pay his Respects to, when you have shone away all your Benefits on him. Prithee *Betty*, (if you must be advised by me,) turn him off; I had rather have you my self than see you ruined." The last clause, unexpectedly revealing Turnstone's supposed interest, ends the skit delightfully. Young Benjamin learned from his older brother how amusing such absurd postures were. Years later he had a Quaker lady be surprised when her would-be lover did not, contrary to his vow, kill himself; and in his conduct book, *Reflections on Courtship and Marriage* (1746), Franklin burlesqued high-flown, exaggerated sentiments.[22]

A shrewd printer-editor-publisher, James Franklin sometimes used the local news to cultivate relations with friends and possible authors. The Reverend Thomas Walter of Roxbury had not only given him *The Little-Compton Scourge, or The Anti-Courant* to publish, but he (and the bookseller Samuel Gerrish) had commissioned James Franklin to print Walter's *Grounds and Rules of Musick* (1721). The 5 March *Courant* noted that at the previous Thursday's lecture, Walter had preached "an excellent Sermon" at a meeting of "the Society for promoting Regular Singing." Walter (and Gerrish) subsequently—and perhaps consequently—replied by hiring him to print *A Sermon Preached at the Lecture Held in Boston, by the Society for Promoting Regular and Good Singing.*

Gardner Inspires Benjamin Franklin

Dr. William Douglass recorded in the 12 March *Courant* that Isaac Greenwood and Cotton Mather's anonymous *Friendly Debate; or, A Dialogue between Academicus; And Sawny & Mundungus*[23] had appeared on Tuesday afternoon, 6 March. A young Harvard graduate (1721), Greenwood shortly thereafter went to London where he studied science for several years (1723–26) and where he probably spent some time with Franklin in 1725 and 1726 before returning to Boston. Greenwood and Mather's dialogue portrays Sawny (Dr. Douglass) and Mundungus (John Williams) as stupid, hypocritical fools. "Academicus" (a version of Greenwood and Mather) takes up nine-tenths of the dialogue lambasting the straw men/opponents. It contains passages of Mather's typical self-adulation ("he has been above Forty Years a Celebrated Preacher, and has been so acknowledged by *Foreign Universities*, as no *American* ever was before him, and justly merited the Honour of being a *Member* of the ROYAL SOCIETY").

The significance of the inept *Friendly Debate* is that it provoked the best literary pamphlet by a Couranteer. The 12 March *Courant* advertised, "On Thursday next [15 March] will be publish'd *A Friendly Debate; Or, A Dialogue between Rusticus and Academicus, about the late Performance of Academicus.*" James Franklin advertised it as "Just publish'd, and sold by the Printer hereof" in the 19 March *Courant*. Whether or not Benjamin Franklin set the type for the pamphlet, he knew it well. George Lyman Kittredge and others have mentioned it, but no one has suggested an author.[24] The *Dialogue* has four parts: an advertisement; a satirical dedication to Cotton Mather signed by RUSTICUS and dated "From the South Side of my Hay-stack, March 9. 1721,2"; the dialogue itself; and an appendix. One clue to the authorship lies in the appendix, which consists of a brief introductory paragraph; a "Short Answer" to John Williams's *Several Arguments*, signed "TOBACCO PROOF" and dated "Cambridge, Dec. 19. 1721"; and a conclusion. Everything in the pamphlet except the "Short Answer" to John Williams is by the same author.

The brief introduction to the appendix says: "Whereas an *Academical Brother* (Son to a Fellow of the Royal Society) having sent the following Answer to *John Williams* unto the Publisher of the *Courant*, who has favour'd us with the MSS, we thought we could not fill up the vacant Pages more to the Satisfaction of the ingenious and learned Reader, than by annexing it to this *Dialogue*." The clue is not in the (mistaken) ascription of the "Short Answer" to Samuel Mather but Rusticus's ability to decide, first, not to publish the letter in the *Courant* and, second, to print it in the *Dialogue*. The author had to be James Franklin or Nathaniel Gardner—the only two Couranteers at this time who planned and decided the contents of the paper and the only two Couranteers who could later have exercised the editor's control of using a submission to the *Courant* in a pamphlet.

I believe Nathaniel Gardner wrote the *Dialogue*.

The advertisement credited "I[saac] G[reenwood]" with authorship of the earlier *Friendly Debate* and advised him that his "broad Panegyricks" inadvertently satirized Cotton Mather. Though Benjamin Franklin knew the sentiment from other sources, he used the technique of great praise as satire often, beginning with Dogood No. 7 (25 June 1722), where he extravagantly celebrated the New England funeral elegy. Later, in his second Busy-Body essay (11 February 1728–29) Franklin wrote: "There is no Satyr he Dreads half so much as an Attempt towards a Panegyrick." Still later, Poor Richard said, "Praise to the undeserving, is severe Satyr" (November 1752).

Rusticus also satirized Mather's learned jargon by promising to give "a short History of all the VITILITIGATING DICTAMENS that have lately appear'd from the North." (Gardner burlesqued Mathers' learned diction and opinionated strictures while alluding to their origin at the Mather's North Church.) In the dedication, he said that Cotton Mather's name "shall be mention'd with Dishonour, while those Clergymen and others, who have distinguish'd themselves by their Meekness and *Silence* [emphasis mine], shall be otherwise spoken of." Writing as "Zechariah Hearwell," Gardner had previously praised ministers who imitated the "meekness and gentleness of Christ" on 5 February, implicitly contrasting them with Cotton Mather. Gardner's use of "Silence," published just a month before the first Silence Dogood essay, perhaps partially inspired Franklin's pseudonym, Silence Dogood.

The dialogue itself (pp. 1–8) is well done, with the two characters, Rusticus and Academicus, having almost equal space, and with each character nicely individualized. Rusticus uses colloquial, even rather slangy language, whereas

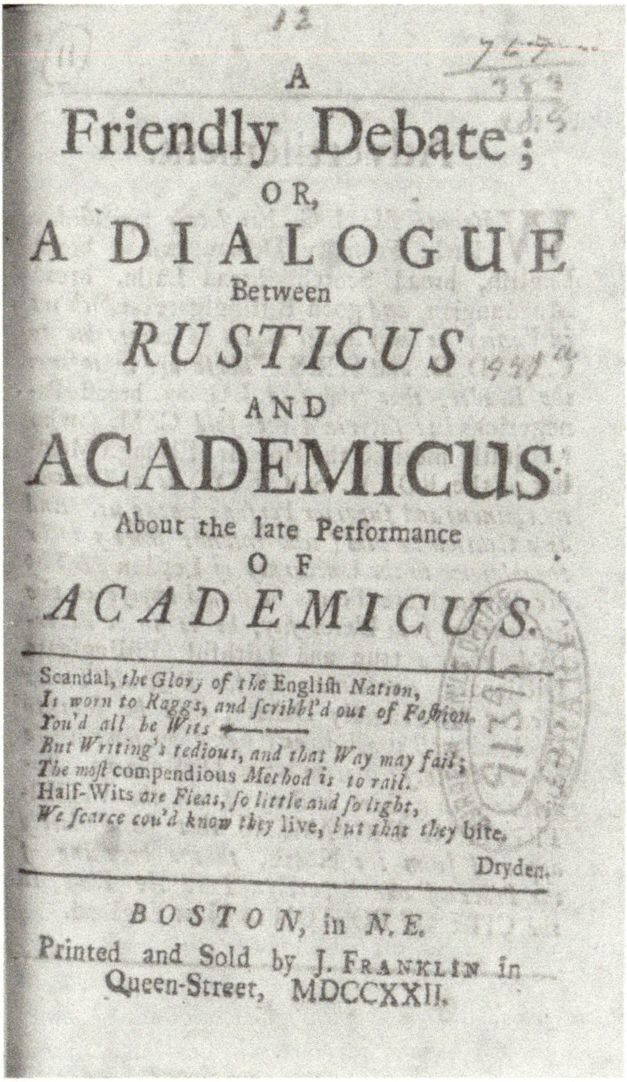

A
Friendly Debate;
OR,
A DIALOGUE
Between
RUSTICUS
AND
ACADEMICUS.
About the late Performance
OF
ACADEMICUS.

Scandal, *the Glory of the* English *Nation,*
Is worn to Raggs, and scribbl'd out of Fashion.
You'd all be Wits ——
But Writing's tedious, and that Way may fail;
The most compendious Method is to rail.
Half-Wits are Fleas, so little and so light,
We scarce cou'd know they live, but that they bite.

Dryden.

BOSTON, in N.E.
Printed and Sold by J. FRANKLIN in
Queen-Street, MDCCXXII.

Figure 11. *Nathaniel Gardner's* Friendly Debate; Or, A Dialogue *(1722), an immediate inspiration for Franklin's Silence Dogood essays. The pamphlet appeared on 19 March 1721/2 and directly influenced Franklin's Silence Dogood essay series, which began two weeks later (2 April 1722). In his reply to a similarly titled pamphlet by Isaac Greenwood (Cotton Mather's nephew), Gardner lampooned Greenwood and Mather. Gardner's speakers in this early version of a* roman á clef *are Rusticus, a common man who represents a typical* New-England Courant *writer; Academicus, who stands for Isaac Greenwood and Cotton Mather; Sawney, the Scotch physician Dr. William Douglass; and Mundungus, the tobacconist John Williams.*

Franklin's reference to a "Leather Apron Man" in the beginning of Silence Dogood No. 1 marks one influence of the diction in Gardner's Friendly Debate. *Gardner's dialogues in the* Courant *and in this pamphlet were the most interesting ones in American journalism to that date. Franklin later demonstrated mastery in the genre. Courtesy, Houghton Library, Harvard University, Cambridge, Massachusetts.*

Academicus uses formal diction and constantly condescends to Rusticus and, by implication, to the ordinary person. The opening gives an example of the interplay between the characters: "*Rust.* Hark ye, Mr. 'Demicus, a Word with you. *Ac.* With me, Sir; Good now, what Business can you have with me? Do you understand Latin?" Though the *Friendly Debate* does not obviously cast either character as a winner, the underlying satire of Academicus makes the ordinary reader sympathize with Rusticus.

The most obvious and direct influence on young Franklin occurs almost immediately. When Rusticus asks what Academicus intends by the late *Dialogue*, he condescendingly replies: "I intended to let you know that I am a Man of Letters, and that not only Sawny, but all the illiterate Scribblers of the Town (the Leather Apron Men) are proud and vain Fellows, and that 'tis not possible for them once in their Lives to speak a Word of Truth." Here is evidently Franklin's source for his unusual epithet "Leather Apron Man" in Silence Dogood No. 1.[25]

Echoing the solipsistic attitude of Cotton Mather, Academicus claims that Sawny, Mundungus, and "their Accomplices" designed "to ridicule the Principal Ministers of Religion in the Town, and render their Ministry odious to the People." Rusticus replies, "If declaring against the Opinion of Ministers in Things indifferent, will rob them of the People's Affection, and destroy the Religion of a Country, their own Order have done more this Way than the Laity." Academicus hotly denies it and accuses Rusticus of lying. In reply, Rusticus quotes two dissenting English ministers. His reasoning is identical to Gardner's on 22 January, which also quoted two Boston ministers for his evidence. When James Franklin responded on 4 December to a similar charge by Cotton Mather, he used criticism of the Boston ministers from the English periodical press. Evidently James Franklin rarely read religious controversy unless it directly affected him, but, like many later newspapermen, he devoured newspapers. Gardner, however, read and frequently quoted religious writers. Though there are other reasons for thinking that Gardner, not James Franklin, wrote this *Dialogue* (Gardner had already written two good dialogues in the *Courant*), the citation of religious controversial literature is among the key reasons for attributing the essay to Gardner rather than to James Franklin.

Rusticus/Gardner quotes Richard Baxter, *Against the Revolt to a Foreign Jurisdiction* (1691): "It's one of the saddest notices in the World, that studious Learned Pastors that are grown old in Studies, and profess all to be devoted to Truth and Love, are so far from having *Skill or Will to heal us*, that they are the Men that *cause the Wound*, and *keep it open*, and are greater hinderers of our Concord and Peace, than Princes, Lords, or any Seculars." Then Rusticus/Gardner cites from the Reverend Jean Daille's *Treatise Concerning the Right Use of the Fathers* (1651): "Who sees not, that, if we must have regard to the Capacity of men, there are sometimes found, even among the plain ordinary sort of Christians in a Church, those that are more considerable, both for their Learning and Piety, than the Pastors themselves?" The last quotation echoes the main thesis of Gardner's second *Courant* dialogue: "I know you cannot endure that Laymen should write or Know any thing: You would have them know but just enough to get to Heaven" (22 January).

When Academicus objects that the quoted authorities are English and French, not American, and that Boston "can Boast of almost an unparallel'd Happiness in their Ministers," Rusticus claims that "whether you will allow it or no, there are as famous Men for Piety and Learning, among the Dissenting Clergy in *England*, as any among our selves." (He probably had Isaac Watts, among other admired English dissenting ministers, in mind.) He then asks who the principal New England ministers are. "Ac.: *Who!* Dr. Increase Mather *and his Son.*" Rusticus questions how they excelled. Academicus replies with the Mathers' standard self-praise, including the words celebrating Cotton Mather in Greenwood and Mather's *Friendly Debate*: "*The young Gentleman* has been above Forty Years a celebrated Preacher, and has been so acknowledged by *Foreign Universities*, as no *American* ever was before him, and justly merited the Honour of being a Member of the ROYAL SOCIETY: He has a GREAT NAME in distant Lands; and *foreign Countries* have a great *Veneration* for him." Rusticus/Gardner ironically comments that "he has certainly a *great Name* abroad for *Something*" and then quotes John Oldmixon's attack on Mather's out-of-date prose style, his old-fashioned beliefs and attitudes, and his education. Naturally Oldmixon's *British Empire in America* (London, 1708)—the only recent history of all the American colonies—was well-known in America. As we will see, the *Courant*'s library had a copy. Gardner repeatedly objected to New England's provincial self-centeredness, and the last several points in his *Friendly Debate* echo his earlier protests.

Until late in the dialogue, Gardner gave Academicus the diction and opinions that we might expect of Isaac Greenwood or any other Mather devotee, but in the following sentence, Academicus himself expresses an attitude that undercuts Mather: "Ac. *Then you dont like his whining Preaching; you can't profit by his Canting Ministry, I'll warrant ye.*" Though Academicus generally remains in character as a Mather supporter, Gardner slyly satirizes him in Academicus's last speech: "I hope our Ministers will stir up all their Friends to get in better Select-Men next Monday: I am certain Dr. Mather has done his Duty in the Affair: His Pastoral Visits have (upon this Account) been more painfully and faithfully manag'd, of late than ever they were before, and I hope they will have the desir'd Effect." Gardner implied that Mather's pastoral visits were really electioneering attempts and that through his ministerial office he was trying to convince people to vote for the politicians who supported Governor Samuel Shute.

The authorship of the letter or "Short Answer" contained in the appendix is uncertain. Rusticus/Gardner seemed to attribute it to Samuel Mather, but young Mather advertised in the 19 March *Courant* that he did not write or compose "the said Answer."[26] Perhaps it is one of Gardner's mock letters. John Williams had not realized that Gardner imitated Mather in his essay of 21 November 1721 and therefore replied to him (ostensibly to Mather) in his pamphlet *Several Arguments* (11 December 1721). It may have amused Gardner to continue the subterfuge. The only passage in the letter that seems to echo another piece condemned Williams as an "*Omnium Horarum Homo*, i.e. Jack of all trades and Good at None." John Campbell (or the person who spoke for him) made a similar statement in the 14 August *Boston News-Letter*, replying to James Franklin. Campbell or his spokesman had called James Franklin "Homo non unium Negoti; or, Jack of All Trades; and it would seem, Good at none." But the sentiment is proverbial.

Benjamin Franklin evidently found another part of the pamphlet extremely interesting. The concluding comment by Rusticus/Gardner mocks the "*Sons* of Harvard" for their use of learned languages, recommending instead that they take up the *Mundungian*, "the very *Sound* of which is *rhetorical* and *perswasive*, and will add a peculiar Beauty to their Performances." Rusticus concludes by making fun of "our Academical *Elegiac* Poets, who in all their Funeral Elegies (or *Tears dropt at Funerals*) burlesque the Dead with *Double Rhimes*, and render the Use of all rhiming Monosyllables *altogether useless*." Gardner referred to hudibrastic rhymes, which are often humorous in themselves and would obviously clash with the prevailing tone of elegies. Not only does Rusticus's satire of Harvard throughout the pamphlet anticipate Franklin's in Silence Dogood No. 4, but his sneers at the New England funeral elegy probably inspired Franklin's satire in Silence Dogood No. 7, where his "RECEIPT to make a New-England Funeral ELEGY" echoes the pamphlet in calling for "A sufficient Quantity of double Rhimes."

Social Skits: Courtship and Marriage

Two weeks before Franklin's first Silence Dogood essay appeared, James Franklin wrote in the lead essay (19 March 1721/2) an amusing social satire as "Belinda." Belinda complained of a bashful, humble, awkward suitor afraid to declare himself. It may have inspired Nathaniel Gardner's "Ben Treackle" essay of 9 April 1722 about the young suitor who was afraid to "pop" the question. In the 26 March issue, writing as "Anthony Fallshort," James Franklin protested against Fallshort's wife. Though she claimed to be wealthy before their marriage, she had no money, did not keep house herself, and demanded servants, fine food, and sumptuous furnishings. Fallshort claimed he was no "Journeyman Gentleman" but a hardworking merchant who began with a reasonable estate. He itemized his wife's past expenses, calculating that after ten years of marriage she cost him £1,486.04.04. He ended with the reflection, "A Good Wife saves more than she brings, and a bad one spends more than she pretends to bring." The Anthony Fallshort essay thematically prefigures Franklin's Anthony Afterwit skit (10 July 1732).

Cotton Mather's Fable

Following the lead of the previous year's *Courant*, the 19 March 1721/2 *Boston Gazette* published the election results: Elisha Cooke, Jr., Thomas Cushing, Captain Nathaniel Green, Ebenezer Clough, William Clarke, John Marion, and Isaiah Toy were chosen Boston selectmen; and Governor Shute's supporters were defeated. Immediately after the election results, a fable appeared in the newspaper in an extraordinary position. Most belletristic materials were printed on page 1, but this short piece appeared immediately after the election results. Its position suggested it commented on the election. All Boston knew that the persons elected selectmen were the Old Charter leaders. The local election augured that the Old Charter adherents would be elected provincial representatives in mid-May. The fable, which alluded to William Dampier's *Voyage* (1697), read:

> It is related by *Dampier* in his *Travels*, that being to take a long Walk in a Road where the Trees were full of Monkeys, the wretches kept throwing *sticks* at him all the way as he went along. He could easily have kill'd some of the *Monkeys*; but he was of the Opinion that for him to *Answer* any of them, would be for one so Superiour to them to take too much Notice of such sorry Creatures; their *Impotent Sticks* also did him little Damage; But if he had by any returns brought the whole Body of the *Monkeys* upon him, he knew that in *their Way* they might out do him, so he let them *throw on*, without any Answer to them. And wise Men were of the Opinion, he did Wisely in doing so.

The author was offended by the election results and considered himself superior to the voters. After reading it, locals realized that the reason the *Boston Gazette* published the election return was to link it to the fable.

The Couranteers recognized the author. An anonymous letter in the 26 March 1722 *Courant* recalled that "about Thirty Years ago . . . a *Reverend Person* handed about a Paper of Fables, wherein he calls himself *Orpheus* his Father *Mercurius*, the Governour an *Elephant*, (a Beast of Burden) and the whole Country are compared to no better than *Beasts*." The correspondent alluded to Cotton Mather's four political fables, written in 1692 to justify Increase Mather's acceptance of a new charter against those "Old Charter" stalwarts who believed that he had sacrificed their rights.[27] The anonymous *Courant* correspondent said that author of those fables had sent in another fable between "A *Wiseman* and his *Monkeys*." Another Couranteer also identified the author. Writing anonymously from "Hall's Coffee-House," Dr. Douglass attacked the fable, saying that "it came out of the *North*" (i.e., the North Church). "No doubt the Author was very angry to find himself disappointed, after the great Pains he had taken to get in Select Men that dance after his Pipe." Douglass ironically added, "We think he is very modest in comparing them, and the whole Town, to a Parcel of *Monkeys*, seeing it is not long since (in his Letter to his Friends at Portsmouth) he was pleased to call them *Dogs*, and *worse than the Monsters of Africa*."[28]

Though young Franklin disagreed with Mather's politics, he must have been fascinated by Mather's technique and later wrote fables, partially inspired, I suspect, by Cotton Mather.

The following week's *Courant*, 2 April 1721/2, contained the first Silence Dogood essay, inaugurating Benjamin Franklin as a published writer.

JAMES AND BENJAMIN FRANKLIN

Assessing the political turmoil of these years, Thomas Hutchinson wrote: "The minds of the people were prepared for impressions from pamphlets, courants, and other newspapers, which were frequently published, in order to convince them, that their civil liberties and privileges were struck at."[29] Hutchinson evidently did not remember James Franklin's name or the title of his newspaper, but he described the point of view and the writings of James Franklin and the Couranteers. The first American newspaperman, James Franklin was also, with Nathaniel Gardner, the most important influence on young Franklin. But the siblings' relationship was strained. Franklin recalled in the *Autobiography*: "Tho' a Brother, he considered himself as my Master, and me as his Apprentice; and accordingly expected the same Services from me as he would from another; while I thought he demean'd me too much in some he requir'd of me, who from a Brother expected more Indulgence" (18). Their relationship grew worse as Franklin became more recognized and appreciated by his brother's friends and by others.

Nevertheless, Benjamin Franklin learned about the printing business, running a newspaper, drumming up interest in the paper, and literary techniques from his older brother. Just as he learned to set type and do presswork, he also learned that if a cut were needed and no one else could supply it, an ingenious printer could do so himself—as James Franklin did. Benjamin Franklin learned the arts of publicity and of controversy from his brother—how to start a newspaper, manage it, and make it interesting. He also learned a number of journalistic techniques from James, who sometimes wrote editorial comments on the news, who used racy, common sayings, who occasionally wrote splendid filler that altered local news items, and who created political, religious, and social satires, as well as poetry. As we will see, Franklin also imbibed his older brother's radical Whig ideology as well as his resentment of the assumption of superiority by ministers and the civil authorities. The talented James Franklin supplied his brother with an extraordinary training. The young genius surpassed his older brother as a writer at age sixteen in the Silence Dogood essays, but without the latter's training and influence, Franklin's life would have been entirely different.

SEVEN

Silence Dogood in Context

Women are the prime Cause of a great many Male Enormities.—Franklin, age sixteen, Silence Dogood No. 5

IN 1722, AT SIXTEEN YEARS OF AGE, Benjamin Franklin wrote the first American essay series and proved that he had become the peer of Boston's best authors. Though focusing on the essay series, this chapter also gives its contexts and briefly characterizes the other materials Franklin annotated that appeared in the same issues of the *New-England Courant*. In the *Autobiography*, Franklin told about his subterfuge in publishing the Silence Dogood essays.

> He [James Franklin] had some ingenious Men among his Friends who amus'd themselves by writing little Pieces for this Paper, which gain'd it Credit, and made it more in Demand; and these Gentlemen often visited us. Hearing their Conversations, and their Accounts of the Approbation their Papers were receiv'd with, I was excited to try my Hand among them. But being still a Boy, and suspecting that my Brother would object to printing any Thing of mine in his Paper if he knew it to be mine, I contriv'd to disguise my Hand, and writing an anonymous Paper I put it in at Night under the Door of the Printing-House. It was found in the Morning and communicated to his Writing Friends when they call'd in as Usual. They read it, commented on it in my Hearing, and I had the exquisite Pleasure, of finding it met with their Approbation, and that in their different Guesses at the Author none were named but Men of some Character among us for Learning and Ingenuity.
>
> I suppose now that I was rather lucky in my Judges: And that perhaps they were not really so very good ones as I then esteem'd them. Encourag'd however by this, I wrote and convey'd in the same Way to the Press several more Papers, which were equally approv'd. (17–18)

Franklin's Dogood essays grew out of the social satires pioneered by Nathaniel Gardner and James Franklin in the *Courant*. The readers must have thought at first that one of the known Couranteers had started the series, but Dogood gradually revealed qualities that none of the earlier writers possessed. When Franklin's first Silence Dogood essay appeared in the 2 April 1722 *Courant*, Nathaniel Gardner's essay on honor, signed "Philanthropos," had the lead position in the paper. Thereafter Silence Dogood was always given the front page, top left—an indication both that the first essay was well received and that James Franklin and Nathaniel Gardner did not know the identity of their new correspondent.

As someone using the pseudonym "John Harvard" pointed out on 28 May, Gardner adapted his essay on honor from Addison's *Guardian* No. 161. The critic did not note that Gardner transformed Addison's moral essay into an attack on the conservative magistrates of Massachusetts. The magistrates sought "Preferment," claimed Philanthropos/Gardner, "with this Design and View, that they may Squeeze and Oppress their Brethren; that they may Crush and trample them in the Dust!" Gardner's resentment of the upper social class and of the establishment appeared elsewhere in the *Courant*.[1] He cited Jeremiah Dummer's *Defense of the New England Charters* and Cotton Mather against such men. Contemporary readers would have recognized that Gardner especially satirized the sons of the recently deceased Governor, Joseph Dudley (1647–1720). Like their father, both Paul Dudley (1675–1751) and William Dudley (1686–1743) possessed superior abilities, but they were imperious and supported the royal government and prerogative rights.

From the *Guardian*, Gardner borrowed both the epigraph (which had been taken from Addison's popular play *Cato*) and the essay's most striking sentence: "The religious man fears, the Man of Honour scorns to do an ill Action."[2] But almost all of Gardner's essay is his own. His concluding definition of the man of honor no doubt strongly appealed to Franklin, for it contained many of the qualities of the *amicus humanis generis* (friend of humankind), which was Franklin's lifelong ideal: "Influenc'd and Acted by a Publick Spirit, and fir'd with a Generous Love to Mankind in the worst of Times; Who lays aside his private Views, and foregoes his own Interest, when it comes in competition with the Publick: Who dare adhere to the Cause of Truth, and Manfully Defend the Liberties of his Country when boldly Invaded, and Labour to retrieve them when they are Lost. Yea, the Man of Honour, (when contracted sordid Spirits desert the Cause of Vertue and the Publick) will stand himself alone, and (like *Atlas*) bear up the Massy Weight on his Shoulders: And this he will do, in Spite of Livid Envy, Snakey Malice, and vile Detraction." In addition to his man-of-honor essay, Gardner published a short letter from "Sisyphus" in the same *New England Courant*, which complained of his "*Virago* of a wife" who dressed in fine clothes and spent her time drinking tea.

THE PSEUDONYM

The pseudonym "Silence Dogood," who was supposedly a minister's widow, had several connotations. The surname mocked Cotton Mather, referring to Mather's most popular single book, *Bonifacius*, better known by its running title, "Essays to Do Good."[3] As we have seen, Gardner and James Franklin both quoted it—the only book by Mather to be approvingly cited in the *Courant*. The first name, "Silence," also alluded to Cotton Mather, who was a notorious busybody and never silent; in this, it echoed Gardner's "Rusticus" essay. The name probably also alluded to Mather's recent sermon, *Silentiarius*, published in the fall of 1721. The satire of Mather was immediately obvious to Franklin's contemporaries—and was reinforced by the travesty of Mather's *Magnalia Christi Americana* in the first essay. The second meaning of "Silence Dogood" only gradually emerged. It alluded to Franklin's altruistic purpose, for he hoped that the essays might do good for Boston and New England. The series contained schemes to improve society and censured bad habits like alcoholism. Thus the oxymoronic pseudonym was both a satire and an idealistic statement—an apt reflection of the mind of the adolescent Franklin.

Silence Dogood No. 1: Cotton Mather Burlesqued

Franklin's early Silence Dogood essays were ostensibly entertainment, though with satiric touches.[4] On an underlying level, however, Franklin mocked the *Spectator* and the old aristocratic world order. Though the second paragraph in Silence Dogood No. 1 imitated the *Spectator*'s opening, Franklin used better contrasts along with a franker and more humorous tone. He wrote: "the Generality of People now a days, are unwilling either to commend or dispraise what they read, until they are in some measure informed who or what the Author of it is, whether he be *poor* or *rich, old* or *young,* a *Schollar* or a *Leather Apron Man,* &c. and give their Opinion of the Performance, according to the Knowledge which they have of the Author's Circumstances." Compare the *Spectator*'s opening: "I have observed that a reader seldom peruses a book with pleasure until he knows whether the writer of it be a black or a fair man, of a mild or choleric disposition, married or a bachelor, with other particulars of the like nature, that conduce very much to the right understanding of an author." Franklin's three oppositions concerned important social distinctions; Richard Steele's *Spectator* opening did not. Instead, Steele's categories tended to be irrelevant (*black* refers not to someone of African descent but to a person with a dark complexion) or old-fashioned ("mild or choleric disposition" alluded to the four cardinal humors that corresponded to the four elements—earth, air, fire, and water—but no one believed in that cosmology any longer). Steele used a formal, even rather stilted diction: *peruse, conduce very much to the right understanding;* Franklin used informal, even colloquial expressions: *now a days, Leather Apron Man.* Steele's *Spectator* is wordy: "with other particulars of the like nature" in place of Franklin's "&c." Steele's tone is straightforward and serious. He seems to believe that such characteristics "conduce very much to the right understanding of an author." Franklin's tone is ironic, and his sentiments are egalitarian and subversive. Readers should care about the opinions, not the qualities of the person who expresses them. Franklin's viewpoint and tone are indebted to "Mundungus" Williams, to Checkley's opening of the first *Courant,* and to a number of Gardner's writings, but there is a greater ironic distance between the author and the persona than in any of these models.

After the long introductory clause, Dogood continued: "it may not be amiss to begin with a short Account of my past Life and present Condition, that the Reader may not be at a Loss to judge whether or no my Lucubrations are worth his reading." The unusual length of the sentence, the three negatives, and the self-mockingly learned word "Lucubrations" all contrast with the prevailing colloquial and humorous tone of the sentence. Though the opening sentiments alluded to the *Spectator*, the highfalutin diction parodied the *Tatler*, which called its essays "lucubrations" and titled its collected essays *The Lucubrations of Isaac Bicker Staff* (the *Courant* office held a set of the *Tatler* as well as the *Spectator*).

Even without recognizing that the pseudonym mocked Cotton Mather, one sees that Silence Dogood No. 1 ridiculed pious rhetoric and a somber worldview. Franklin had read Mather's *Magnalia Christi Americana* and found the account of "The Death of Mr. John Avery" almost a self-burlesque. Shipwrecked, Avery was clinging to a rock when he "lifted up his eyes to heaven, saying, 'We know not what the pleasure of God is; I fear we have been too unmindful of former deliverance: Lord, I cannot challenge a promise of the preservation of my life; but thou hast promised to deliver us from sin and condemnation, and to bring us safe to heaven, through the all-sufficient satisfaction of Jesus Christ; this therefore I do challenge of thee.'" A wave immediately carried him off, taking Avery "away to heaven indeed."[5]

Franklin's third paragraph, telling of Silence Dogood's birth, alluded to the fate of the religious Avery, spoofed the archetypally humorous situation of the father's predicament at the birth of his child, and ironically undercut Mather's religious clichés: "At the time of my Birth, my Parents were on Ship-board in their Way from *London to N. England*. My Entrance into this troublesome World was attended with the Death of my Father, a Misfortune, which tho' I was not then capable of knowing, I shall never be able to forget; for as he, poor Man, stood upon the Deck rejoycing at my Birth, a merciless Wave entred the Ship, and in one Moment carry'd him beyond Reprieve. Thus was the First Day which I saw, the Last that was seen by my Father; and thus was my disconsolate Mother at once made both a Parent and a Widow." The witty style, the clever tone, the humorous reversal (the father died at the birth of the child), and the comic situation all burlesque the ostensible tragedy with its sentimental diction ("a merciless wave") and religious clichés ("this troublesome World," "beyond Reprieve").

Silence Dogood/Franklin used religious clichés to say that she "past [her] Infancy and Childhood in Vanity and Idleness." She continued the sentence with a sentimental portrayal of her mother's hardships: "until I was bound out Apprentice, that I might no longer be a Charge to my Indigent Mother, who was put to hard Shifts for a Living." Franklin ironically undercut the religious rhetoric and the maudlin portrayal by concluding with a low diction that suggests the mother earned a living by taking off her underclothes. Besides meaning underclothing, *shifts* can mean "lying" or "stealing" (*OED* 10); thus the diction furnishes a series of inappropriately clashing suggestions. In the *Courant* and in American journalism, Franklin is the first author to play with frank sexual suggestions. Few New England authors did—with the exception of the master stylist John Wise. (Compare his references to paper currency cited above as the "Seminal Matter and Flames of our State" that has impregnated "Dear Mother" Harvard to bring forth "Thirty or Forty at a Birth.") Sexuality and a blunt animality often characterize Franklin's writings.

Silence Dogood described her education. She exceeded the usual "Knowledge and Learning which is necessary for our Sex" by her interest "in reading ingenious Books," thus becoming a suitable mate for her master, the country minister. Franklin introduced the perennial subject of the battle of the sexes in concluding the first essay: "Thus I past away the Time with a Mixture of Profit and Pleasure, having no affliction but what was imaginary, and created in my own Fancy; as nothing is more common with us Women, than to be grieving for nothing, when we have nothing else to grieve for." Franklin twice used a later version of this antimetabole (*Poor Richard*, July 1741 and October 1742).

Delighted to have a good essay from an unknown hand, James Franklin and the Couranteers published the following note at the end of the letter: "*As the Favour of Mrs.* Dogood's *Correspondence is acknowledged by the Publisher of this Paper, lest any of her Letters should miscarry, he desires they may for the future be deliver'd at his* Printing-House, *or at the Blue Ball in Union-Street, and no Questions shall be ask'd of the Bearer.*" The Blue Ball in Union Street was, of course, Josiah Franklin's home. Although Franklin wrote in the *Autobiography* that he slipped the manuscript "under the Door of the Printing House," he evidently sent in the first essay some other way. Perhaps later ones were slipped "under the Door."

SILENCE DOGOOD NO. 2: POLITICIAN

The Silence Dogood essay of 16 April contained advice on marital etiquette and summarized her politics. She said that her "Reverend Master who had hitherto remained a Batchelor, (after much Meditation of the Eighteenth verse of the Second Chapter of *Genesis*) took up a Resolution to marry; and having made several unsuccessful fruitless Attempts on the more topping Sort of our Sex, and being tir'd with making troublesome Journeys and Visits to no Purpose, he began unexpectedly to cast a loving Eye upon Me, whom he had brought up cleverly to his Hand." The punning Franklin implied that the cleric was first interested in women with the largest breasts ("the more topping"). Though she broke into laughter at his awkward proposal, Silence Dogood consented, perhaps from "Love, or Gratitude, or Pride."

The "unexpected Match was very astonishing to all the Country round about, and served to furnish them with Discourse for a long Time after; some approving it, others disliking it, as they were led by their various Fancies and Inclinations." Franklin probably alluded to the Reverend Michael Wigglesworth's second marriage: at age forty-seven, he scandalized New England by marrying Martha Mudge, age nineteen, his servant girl. She was approximately six years younger than his own daughter. Wigglesworth's son Edward (by Michael Wigglesworth's third wife, Sybil Sparhawk Avery) was Franklin's teacher at the Boston Latin School and a member of the Old South Church. Franklin must have known both the history of Michael Wigglesworth's life and his poem, *The Day of Doom* (1666). It was written for young persons, expounded New England's theology, and became a best-seller in England and early America. Like Michael Wigglesworth, Franklin's grandfather Peter Folger had married a bond servant, Mary Morrill, but neither their social difference nor their age was so great, and their union caused no known scandal.

Silence Dogood described her present situation and introduced her politics. After seven years of happy marriage, blessed with two daughters and a son, Silence Dogood lost her husband. Now, several years later, she lived in the same small town and provided lodging for the new minister. Since the political season was underway in Massachusetts (the election of Boston selectmen had taken place in March and the key election of representatives to the General Court would take place early in May, with the ceremonious Election Day taking place at the end of May), Silence Dogood declared her politics. She was "a mortal Enemy to arbitrary Government & Unlimited Power. I am naturally very jealous for the Rights and Liberties of my Country; and the least appearance of an Incroachment on those invaluable Priviledges, is apt to make my Blood boil exceedingly." Thus she proclaimed herself an Old Charter member, a devotee of Boston's Popular Party, an adherent to the positions of the Reverend John Wise, Elisha Cooke, Jr., and the country representatives, and an opponent of Governor Samuel Shute, the Dudleys, and the Mathers.

The young Franklin no doubt held these same popular, egalitarian positions, which were the politics of James Franklin, Nathaniel Gardner, and the *New-England Courant*. Silence Dogood concluded her self-characterization on a humorous note: "I have likewise a natural Inclination to observe and reprove the Faults of others, at which I have an excellent Faculty." This Puritan characteristic was especially true of Cotton Mather, as the Boston readers no doubt recognized.

The same *Courant* advertised an anonymous, patriotic political pamphlet, *English Advice to the Freeholders, &c. of the Province of the Massachusetts-Bay, Chiefly Relating to the New Choice of Representatives*, to be published "next Friday," 20 April. Printed and sold at his own risk by James Franklin, *English Advice* contained electioneering propaganda for the Old Charter Party. It opposed electing anyone who held a "publick Post in the Government; such as Sheriffs, Military Officers, and the like," as well as any person who "hath a Place of Profit deriving from the Government" (2). The author was a New Englander who objected to anyone other than a native holding public office: "You may already see . . . how Strangers are promoted, and your *Countrymen* neglected

Figure 12. Silence Dogood No. 2, with the sixteen-year-old Franklin's attribution of authorship, New-England Courant, 16 April 1722. Beginning with this second installment, Franklin's Silence Dogood essays were given the lead position in the Courant. *Franklin's persona as a chatty, opinionated, middle-aged minister's widow was an amazing achievement for a boy. The situation described in Dogood No. 2 of an older minister marrying his young servant girl recalled for many readers the example of the Reverend Michael Wigglesworth (1631–1705), author of* The Day of Doom *(1662), who at age forty-eight married his young housekeeper. Courtesy, Burney Collection, British Library.*

and despised: And 'tis said, that in a short Time you must be Vassals to Strangers; from which CURSE, *Conserva nos Domina*: And may we never have Cause to complain, as in Lam.5.2. *Our Inheritance is turned unto Strangers, our Houses to Aliens*" (6).

As pointed out in the beginning of Chapter 4, the same prejudice against English placemen as "strangers" existed in Virginia by 1701. When Franklin later (27 May 1731) satirized the sending of English officials to America, he echoed *English Advice*. Dated "April 18, 1722," *English Advice* was signed "Brutus and Cato" and contained as a postscript ten lines from *Cato's Letters*. Since the *Courant* advertised the pamphlet two days before it was completed and dated, since the pamphlet used the cliché that John Williams, James Franklin, and Nathaniel Gardner (twice) applied to the Mathers ("Altho' they may be good Men," yet they are but Men" [2]), and since it quoted the *Courant's* favorite contemporary source, *Cato's Letters*, I suspect a Couranteer wrote it, probably Nathaniel Gardner.

Also appearing in the 23 April *Courant* was a short piece that complained of a deceased husband's creditors who insisted on "prizing the Widow's Clouts and other Child-bed Linen." The author, Thomas Fleet, asked the "hungry Creditors to consider whether they act like Gentlemen or like Christians in their Proceedings against a distress'd Widow." Fleet was the first to criticize moneylenders in an American newspaper. His outrage against rapacious moneylenders may have influenced Franklin's censure in Busy-Body No. 8 and in *A Modest Enquiry into the Nature and Necessity of a Paper Currency* (1729).

Silence Dogood No. 3: Do Good

The third essay introduced Franklin's civic and altruistic concerns, prefiguring his numerous attempts to do good in the civic life of Philadelphia and Pennsylvania. Silence Dogood wrote in the 30 April *Courant* that all persons should serve the country they live in, confessed that she had not done so, and resolved "to do for the future all that *lies in my Way* for the Service of my Countrymen." She conceded that no one of her writings would please everyone, for "Various Persons have different Sentiments." But she intended to deal with a variety of different subjects from politics to love by employing a wide range of tones: "merry and diverting . . . solid and serious . . . sharp and satyrical . . . sober and religious. . . . Thus will every one, one Time or other find some thing agreeable to his own Fancy." (The paragraph echoes *Spectator*, No. 179.) "According to this Method I intend to proceed, bestowing now and then a few gentle Reproofs on those who deserve them, not forgetting at the same time to applaud those whose Actions merit Commendation." Franklin ended this Dogood essay with a light ironic note: "Having nothing more to write at present, I must make the usual excuse in such Cases, of *being in haste*."

In the same *Courant*, Matthew Adams, as "Harry Meanwell," told of a landlord who threatened to turn out his tenants unless they voted for the representative he chose. The landlord "commonly goes with one Eye half shut, and his Mouth screw'd up into a whistling Posture." The biographer Clifford K. Shipton thought that Adams pointed at Paul Dudley, though his brother William was the representative from Roxbury,[6] whereas Paul was a member of the council. With this and the next essay, class consciousness achieved new heights in the *Courant.* "Elisha Trueman" sent in a political letter advocating the Old Charter position. As I pointed out while discussing the Couranteers, the piece (left unattributed by Franklin) was evidently by Thomas Lane. The first name "Elisha" alluded to Elisha Cooke, Jr., and the colloquial style of the letter and its contents suggested that the persona was supposed to be a farmer who supported the Old Charter Party. "For besides, you must know, several of us has got the *Deplorable State of New-England,* and we hear the Story in the Votes concerns one of a great Family, mention'd in that Pamphlet." The allusion was meant to call attention to Cotton Mather's changed position and perhaps to label him a hypocrite. In the *Deplorable State* (1708; reprint, 1721), Mather had viciously attacked former Governor Joseph Dudley and had quoted (9–10) his son Paul saying, "This country will never be worth Living in, for Lawyers and Gentlemen, till the Charter is taken away." Now Mather was supporting the Dudleys, Governor Shute, and the Royal Party.

Nathaniel Gardner had the lead essay on 7 May 1722, with a piece against corrupt magistrates, quoting from *Cato's Letters* in the *London Journal.* The local audience would have recognized the attack on magistrates as a satire on Paul Dudley, formerly the attorney general of the colony and currently a judge of the Superior Court. The same *Courant* published several extracts from the votes of the House of Representatives (6 and 7 July 1721) concerning the election of a counselor for the territory lying between Sagadock and Nova Scotia, which Paul Dudley had filled for several years. The House, however, questioned whether he owned land in the area and judged him "not qualified for that Post according to the Direction of the Charter." He refused to produce evidence of his ownership and so the House voted his election "null and void."

Silence Dogood No. 4: Harvard

On 14 May 1722 Silence Dogood lampooned both the clergy and a college education in an allegorical dream vision, resembling, in genre, *Spectator* No. 3 and Dr. William Douglass's essay in the second *Courant.* Silence asked her boarder "Clericus" whether she should bring up her son at college. He argued that she should, despite the fact that many students "idle away" their time there. Thinking of the excesses that Clericus had described, Silence fell asleep and dreamed that she was traveling over "pleasant and delightful Fields and Meadows, and thro' many small Country Towns and Villages" where every peasant who had money "was preparing to send one of his Children at least" to the "Temple of Learning." But the peasants "consulted their own Purses instead of the Childrens Capacities: So that I observed, a great many, yea, the most part of those who were traveling thither, were little better than Dunces and Blockheads."

One cannot help but suspect that Franklin was recalling his own promising academic career, cut short by his father's financial woes and his father's belief that many persons educated at Harvard earned a poor living. Franklin now, years later, channeled his disappointment and resentment into a satire. In the dream vision, Silence advanced to the gate of the temple where "two sturdy Porters named *Riches* and *Poverty*" guarded the entrance, with "Poverty" refusing entrance to any that had not gained the favor of "Riches." Silence, however, as a spectator, was admitted. On a high throne, up two difficult steps, sat "Learning" writing pieces for the *New-England Courant*. On her right hand sat English and on her left, "with their Faces vail'd," reclined Latin, Greek, Hebrew, etc. The latter "were very much reserv'd, and seldom or never unvail'd their Faces here, and then to few or none, tho' most of those who have in this Place acquir'd so much Learning as to distinguish them from *English*, pretended to an intimate Acquaintance with them." Silence asked why they were veiled, "in this Place especially." And she was shown the figures of Idleness and Ignorance, "who first vail'd them, and still kept them so."

Lewis P. Simpson offered the most thoughtful analysis of the implications of Franklin's satire: "This is a symbolization (it may well be the first in American literature) of the expansion of the Third Realm—of the triumph of the vernacular languages and of the periodical press. We note that the satire does not present Learning as prostituted to the press. On the contrary, Learning has accepted her new role as printer-editor-publisher of a newspaper. If Idleness and Ignorance have veiled the learned languages, they have not veiled the goddess herself. She still reigns. The implication is that the center of the Republic of Letters has shifted from the university to the printing shop and the self made author like Silence Dogood. Franklin . . . offers a kind of celebration of the freeing of letters and learning from the authority of the university."[7]

Though a crowd of young men were trying to ascend the throne, "the Work proving troublesome and difficult to most of them, they withdrew their Hands from the Plow, and contented themselves to sit at the Foot, with Madame *Idleness* and her Maid *Ignorance*." Those, however, who nearly made it part way to the first step asked "the Assistance of those who had got up before them, and who, for the Reward perhaps of a *Pint of Milk*, or a *Piece of Plumb-Cake*, lent the Lubbers a helping Hand." Though plumb or plum cake (usually raisin cake) was a traditional minor delicacy, Franklin may be suggesting either that the older students could easily be bribed or that the attainments were not worth much. The same happened at the next step, and at the concluding usual ceremonies, "every Beetle-Scull seem'd well satisfy'd with his own Portion of Learning, tho' perhaps he was *e'en just* as ignorant as ever."

Silence followed the graduates' careers as they left the temple: "Some I perceiv'd took to Merchandizing, others to Traveling, some to one Thing, some to another, and some to Nothing; and many of them from henceforth, for want of Patrimony, liv'd as poor as Church Mice, being unable to dig, and asham'd to beg, and to live by their Wits it was impossible." Most graduates, however, "went along a large beaten Path, which led to a Temple at the further End of the Plain, call'd *The Temple of Theology*. The business of those who were employ'd in this Temple being laborious and painful, I wonder'd exceedingly to see so many go towards it; but while I was pondering this Matter in my Mind, I spy'd *Pecunia* behind a Curtain, beckoning to them, with her Hand, which Sight immediately satisfy'd me for whose Sake it was, that a great Part of them (I will not say all) travel'd that Road."

Franklin's satire was unfair. Though ministers earned a competitive living in colonial New England, few became wealthy. Silence further slandered them: in the temple of theology she found many of them following "the ambitious and fraudulent Contrivances of Plagius." The plagiarism charge anticipated Franklin's telling in the *Autobiography* that his uncle Benjamin promised to give him his voluminous notebooks of sermons if the boy would learn his shorthand, "I suppose as a Stock to set up with" (6). (As we will see, Franklin changed his mind: when he defended the Reverend Samuel Hemphill in 1735, he said that he preferred good plagiarized sermons to bad originals.) After Silence Dogood awakened, she related her dream to Clericus, who told her "*it was a lively Representation of* Harvard College." The dream vision essay is Franklin's first piece using a framework structure. He later used it beautifully, but in this apprentice work, the envelope structure did not strongly reinforce, contradict, or complement the enclosed dream. It merely provided a setting and occasion and was much less complex and less structurally interesting than his later frames.

In Musgrave's *Boston Gazette* for 28 May 1722, "John Harvard" replied to Franklin's satire on Harvard College. Harvard/Samuel Mather[8] charged that the entire paper on "Idleness" (*Courant* for 26 February 1721/2) was borrowed from Richard Allestree's *Gentleman's Calling*. Further, he alleged that the paper on the character of the "Man of Honour" (Gardner's 2 April 1722 essay) was taken from *Guardian* No. 161. He also attacked Franklin's mixed figure of speech in Silence Dogood No. 4: "P.S. Is not Couranto a fine Rhetorician, and a correct writer, when he says in his last but One, 'Now I observed that the whole Tribe, who entred into the Temple with me, began to climb the Throne, but the work proving troublesome and difficult to most of them *they withdraw their hands from the Plow*, &c.' Friend, who ever heard of entring a Temple and ascending the Magnificent Steps of a Throne with a *Plough in his Hand!* O rare Allegory! Well done Rustic Couranto!" Franklin must have smarted at this criticism of his inappropriate metaphor.

After Franklin's Silence Dogood essay, a letter signed "Elisha Trueman," dated from Woodstock, which Franklin attributed to "Mr. T. Lane," followed in the same 14 May *Courant*. As we have seen, the countryman Elisha Trueman had appeared earlier (30 April). Opening the essay, Trueman told his neighbors it would be a pity for base, covetous people to have positions in the government. Within the body of the piece, a "hearty Old Charter-man, (who had been at *College*)" told of "Roman ambassadors *Fabious Pictor* and his Colleague." The Old Charter Man related an attempt to buy his vote, obviously condemning Paul Dudley and his supporters. He concluded:

> Let us consider how it will be with us, if a haughty, covetous, revengeful Man should get in Power, he may wheedle us to choose his Relations and Tools into Places of Trust, by a specious Pretense of Piety, in giving a Piece of Plate to the Church [an accompanying note, cited below, makes clear that Lane referred to William Dudley], and making large Promises of doing Justice to all; but when his Sycophants are at hand to support him, if he should invert Justice by drawing up an Indictment against any one of us, and be a JUDGE of it himself; or if he or his Relations should think fit to assault us, and we for defending our selves shall be prosecuted for it, and thread by him. . . . If, I say, such an one should attempt to do any or all of these Things, what may we not expect he will do to gratify his Desires.

Using a country bumpkin (Alice Truman) as the narrator at the opening and closing of the piece and a learned persona ("who had been at *College*") within its framework became a standard structure in New England humor. James Russell Lowell's *Biglow Papers* is one major example. The typical Southern framework structure of the nineteenth century reversed the roles, using an educated persona in the opening and closing, and the countryman within the frame.[9]

Either Gardner or James Franklin coordinated the series of attacks on Dudley that appeared in the 14 May *Courant*. Besides the essay by Thomas Lane, the Couranteer John Eyre contributed an anonymous political piece warning against those who attempted to gain popularity by gifts. Though Clifford K. Shipton printed an excerpt from Eyre's piece in his biographical sketch of Paul Dudley, it pointed primarily at Paul's brother William. Eyre's essay contained a series of brief notes made to resemble news articles from Roxbury, 7 and 8 May; Portsmouth, 5 May; and Boston, 10 May. They all, however, were actually part of Eyre's attack on William Dudley and the Prerogative Party. The 7 May note from Roxbury commented on "a Present of a fine Piece of Plate, from a noted Family among us" and questioned the motive for the gift. The 8 May note from Roxbury announced that William Dudley had been chosen the town's representative. The Portsmouth report facetiously lamented that no butter could be procured for entertaining the governor.

Dated Boston, 10 May, the final news note in Eyre's contribution reminded the public that next Tuesday was the time appointed for the election of Boston's representatives. Eyre asked two rhetorical questions: first, "Whether those Gentlemen who held up their Hands in the House, for the Payment of Mr. B[ridge]r's Money, are fit for Representatives?" (As pointed out in Chapter 4, Bridger was the English placeman who inspected pine trees.) Second, Eyre asked: "Whether one who gives no Account of Money appropriated by Law to purchase Arms and Ammunition for the Town's Use, be fit to serve the Town in that Station?" The next week's *Boston Gazette* (21 May 1722) foolishly publicized Eyre's suggestion by denying that William Dudley's gift of plate to the Roxbury church was meant as a bribe.

Besides Thomas Lane and John Eyre, Captain Christopher Taylor sent in an Old Charter political essay. He protested against the late act "for supplying *Great Britain* with Naval Stores from the Plantations" and sent in an extract from Trenchard and Gordon's *Cato's Letters* in the *London Journal* discussing law. Echoing Locke's theories justifying revolution, Trenchard and Gordon wrote: "The Violation therefore of Law does not constitute a Crime where the Law is bad; but the Violation of what ought to be Law, is a Crime even where there is no Law. The Essence of Right and Wrong, does not depend upon Words and Clauses inserted in a Code, or a Statute Book, much less upon the Conclusions and Explications of Lawyers; but upon the Reason and Nature of Things, antecedent to all Laws."[10]

A news note in the *Courant* containing Silence Dogood No. 4 said: "We hear from the Eastward, that two Women have lately murder'd their Bastard Children, one at Salem, the other at Hampton." The note may be one of the incidents of unwed mothers murdering their infants that Franklin alluded to in "The Speech of Miss Polly Baker" in 1747.[11] Some additional weight is given to the possibility because the "Cato's Letter" quoted in this *Courant* exemplifies the proverb, "Where there is no law, there is no transgression"—a proverb Franklin used in an address to Judge Samuel Sewall nine months later (4 February 1722/3) and in "The Speech of Miss Polly Baker."

Finally, at the end of this 14 May *Courant*, the printer advertised an agrarian tract as just published, "Printed for the Author," *The Original Rights of Mankind Freely to Subdue and Improve This Earth, Asserted and Maintained. By J[oseph] M[organ].*[12] Morgan, a Presbyterian minister, later moved to New Jersey, and in Philadelphia, Benjamin Franklin printed two similar tracts for him: *The Nature of Riches* (1732) and *The Temporal Interest of North America* (1733).

The 21 May *Courant* opened with a letter from Dr. Douglass concerning inoculation, which contained his usual ad hominem attacks on Cotton Mather. Except for Franklin's annotation "B. F." on the next Silence Dogood essay (28 May) this was the last issue of the newspaper that Franklin annotated and the last one whose contents I will systematically chronicle, though I will continue to note a few pieces that concern Franklin.

Silence Dogood No. 5: Feminist

Though the selection of a feminine persona suggests a feminist point of view, Franklin made his first public feminist argument in this Dogood essay. As we have seen, he earlier argued for the natural equality of women in his written exchanges with his adolescent friend John Collins. He would return to this androgynous position numerous times in later life. He also first used a letter within an essay and a pseudonym within a pseudonym in the fifth Dogood essay. He used the same double framework structure on numerous subsequent occasions (e.g., "Captain Samuel Gerrish's" letter enclosing "James Craufurd's" letter in the fictitious *Supplement to the Boston Independent Chronicle* [April 1782]. Silence had supposedly received a letter from "Ephraim Censorious," blaming her for not trying to reform her own sex before reforming men. Introducing the letter, Silence wrote, "Men have not only as great a Share in those Vices ["pride, Idleness, &c."] as the Women, but are likewise in a great Measure the Cause of that which the Women are guilty of." The irreverent young Franklin may have thought the statement humorously reversed the Genesis story of the origin of evil—Adam fell because of Eve.

Ephraim Censorious claimed that "when you have once reformed the Women, you will find it a much easier Task to reform the Men, because Women are the prime Cause of a great many Male Enormities." (Franklin must have been delighted with the salacious pun on male enormities.) Silence defended women from the charge of idleness by citing the proverb "Woman's Work is never done." She then granted for argument's sake that men work harder—only to blame men for women's idleness: "Who is there that can be handsomely Supported in Affluence, Ease and Pleasure by another, that will chuse rather to earn his Bread by the Sweat of his own Brows?" The underlying theory of human nature, which supposes that people are naturally lazy and prone to follow a life of ease, also reflected a belief that surfaces often in Franklin's writings.[13] "And if a Man will be so fond and so foolish, as to labour hard himself for a Livelihood, and suffer his Wife in the mean Time to sit in Ease and Idleness, let him not blame her if she does so, for it is in a great Measure his own Fault."

Defending women from the charge of ignorance and folly, Dogood/Franklin cites Defoe's *Essay Upon Projects* on the need for women's education, and then satirizes the reasons for the usual claims that women are proud: "Why truly, if Women are proud, it is certainly owing to the Men still; for if they will be such *Simpletons* as to humble themselves at their Feet, and fill their credulous Ears with extravagant Praises of their Wit, Beauty, and other Accomplishments (perhaps where there are none too), and when Women are by this Means perswaded that they are Something more than humane, what Wonder is it, if they carry themselves haughtily, and live extravagantly." (Here Franklin echoes James Franklin's essay of 19 February 1721/2.) Silence Dogood nevertheless said that more extravagant pride is to be found among men than women.

SILENCE DOGOOD NO. 6: ON PRIDE

The sixth Silence Dogood essay continued Franklin's thoughts on pride. It appeared 11 June 1722 and anticipated later sentiments in *Poor Richard* and the *Autobiography*. "The proud Man aspires after Nothing less than unlimited Superiority over his Fellow-Creatures. He has made himself a King in *Soliloquy*; fancies himself conquering the World, and the Inhabitants thereof consulting on proper Methods to acknowledge his Merit." Silence Dogood confessed, "I speak it to my Shame. I my self was a Queen from the Fourteenth to the Eighteenth Year of my Age, and govern'd the World all the Time of my being govern'd by my Master." Silence Dogood is in some ways a version of Franklin. Here the young genius confessed his feelings of "unlimited Superiority over his Fellow-Creatures"—and satirized these feelings partly because they so dramatically contrasted with the reality of his boyhood and apprentice status. At age sixteen, he "govern'd the World" in his imagination, "all the Time of my being govern'd by my Master," James Franklin. No wonder he quarreled with his older brother.

Silence's primary subject was pride of apparel. Commenting on the foolishness of wearing expensive clothes, she said, "This Sort of Pride has been growing upon us ever since we parted with our Homespun Cloaths for *Fourteen Penny Stuffs*, &c." Franklin alluded to expensive (and mainly smuggled) French silk. Throughout his life, Franklin prided himself on homespun clothing and advocated home manufacturing: "I had once been cloth'd from Head to Foot in Woollen and Linnen of my Wife's Manufacture . . . I never was prouder of any Dress in my Life" (6 April 1766). In his 1722 sentiment, Franklin probably revealed the influence of the Boston currency controversy. Whether for or against a paper currency, the writers advocated frugality and homespun clothing as a partial remedy. Silence satirized new fashions and those who believed them important with a witty sententiae: "by striving to appear rich they become really poor."

Hoop-petticoats, one of the recent fashions, receive special condemnation. Though *Spectator* No. 127 and *Tatler* No. 116 had satirized them, Franklin took nothing from those essays, reflecting instead the military metaphors of an earlier American pamphlet, the anonymous *Origin of the Whale Bone-Petticoat* (Boston, 1714). Silence wrote: "These monstrous topsy-turvy *Mortar-Pieces*, are neither fit for the Church, the Hall, or the Kitchen; and if a Number of them were well mounted on *Noddles-Island*, they would look more like Engines of War for bombarding the Town, than Ornaments of the Fair Sex." Franklin elaborated the image almost into a tall tale: "An honest Neighbour of mine, happening to be in Town some time since on a Publick Day, inform'd me, that he saw four Gentlewomen with their Hoops half mounted in a Balcony, as they withdrew, to the Wall, to the great Terror of the Militia, who (he thinks) might attribute their irregular Volleys to the formidable Appearance of the Ladies Petticoats." Jokes on training days and the poorly prepared militia were a staple of American humor long before the classic treatment in "Yankee Doodle." Franklin's treatment of hoop-petticoats inspired a *Courant* essay of 20 August and anticipated a chapbook that appeared in November that I believe Franklin wrote, *Hoop-Petticoats Arraigned and Condemned by the Light of Nature, and Law of God* (1722).

JAMES FRANKLIN JAILED

An ironic news note in the 11 June *Courant* raised the ire of the Boston authorities against James Franklin. Following an account of the quick action by Rhode Islanders who set out after an enemy privateer, the *Courant* reported: "We are advis'd from Boston, that the Government of the Massachusetts are fitting out a Ship to go after the Pirates, to be commanded by Capt. Peter Papillion, and 'tis thought he will sail sometime this Month, if Wind and Weather permit." The article satirically implied that the Massachusetts authorities were not speedily trying to apprehend pirates. Moreover, some legislators thought the printer was suggesting that they were conspiring with the pirates.[14] The implication infuriated the General Court. The next day, 12 June, the council demanded the printer attend its meeting, examined him, and resolved that the paragraph "was a High affront to this Government." The House of Representatives concurred and ordered "the Sheriff of the County of Suffolk do forthwith Commit to the Goal in Boston the Body of James Franklyn Printer, for the Gross affront offered to this Government, in his Courant of Munday last, there to remain during this Session." The council agreed and the printer was jailed.[15]

Franklin had either this incident or one some six months later in mind when he wrote in the *Autobiography*: "One of the Pieces in our News-Paper, on some political Point which I have now forgotten, gave Offence to the Assembly. He [James Franklin] was taken up, censur'd and imprison'd for a Month by the Speaker's Warrant, I suppose because he would not discover his Author. I too was taken up and examin'd before the Council; but tho' I did not give them any Satisfaction, they contented themselves with admonishing me, and dismiss'd me; considering me perhaps as an Apprentice who was bound to keep his Master's Secrets" (19). Perhaps the legislators also thought the sixteen-year-old boy was too young or too insignificant to punish.

James Franklin was jailed from 12 June until 7 July. On 15 June, he petitioned the General Court that he was "Truely Sensible & Heartily Sorry for the offence," entreated "the Courts forgiveness," claimed he was "Indisposed, & Suffering in his health by the Said Confinement," and submitted a certificate from Dr. Zabdiel Boylston testifying to his illness. The choice of Boylston was clever, for everyone knew that the *New-England Courant* opposed Boylston and inoculation. Dr. William Douglass, who was evidently James Franklin's personal friend as well as his author, might well have been doubted by the authorities, but Boylston would hardly lie for James Franklin. The House put off its decision until the following Monday, 18 June, when the representatives could see what the next issue of the *Courant* said.[16]

Young Franklin took charge of the *Courant* for three weeks (18 June–2 July). He had to tread lightly, or James might well have had to languish inside a small, dark cell. The 18 June *Courant* gave no occasion for concern. It opened with a character of "*Proteus, or Old Janus,*" a new pseudonym for the editor. A piece by "Hypercarpus" criticized the reasoning in Silence Dogood's last letter. Silence had written, "*The Pride of Apparel has begot and nourish'd in us a Pride of Heart*, &c." The critic commented, "To make that the Effect, which is really the Cause, is an Absurdity so gross, that methinks it should not pass unobserved by the most ignorant of Readers. I have ever thought the Sins of Men are Originally in the Heart, and are from thence brought forth into Acts; according as I have learn'd from the Mouth of Infinite Truth, that out of the *Heart* of Man proceeds evil Thoughts, &c., even every Abomination." This criticism was the second Franklin sustained. He had not replied to the charge by "John Harvard" of an inappropriate trope in his fourth Dogood essay, but this argument, over whether the chicken or the egg came first, made him add a Latin postscript to his next Silence Dogood: "I shall make no other Answer to *Hypercarpus's* Criticism on my last Letter than this, *Mater me genuit, peperit mox filia matrem*" (My mother gave birth to me, and eventually the daughter will give birth to a mother). In effect, he said that no one could tell which came first, the chicken or the egg.

Later that same day the House voted that James Franklin could have the "liberty of the Prison House & Yard, upon his Giving Security for his faithful abiding there."[17] The council concurred, Governor Samuel Shute consented, the printer gave security, and the General Court granted him freedom of the yard on 20 June.[18] With "the Liberty of the Prison House and Yard," James Franklin might have had a hand in preparing the *Courant* for 25 June and 2 July.

Silence Dogood No. 7: The New England Elegy

The best-known Dogood essay, the seventh, appeared on 25 June 1722. It satirized the New England elegy and ridiculed an especially wretched one on Mrs. Mehitabel Kittle by Dr. John Herrick of Beverley (a former ship doctor who, in the third *Courant* [21 August 1721] supported Dr. William Douglass). Franklin had two major sources and one minor one: John Gay's burlesque of the pastoral elegy in "The Shepherd's Week" (1714); Alexander Pope's "Receipt to Make an Epic Poem," which had appeared in *Guardian* No. 78 (Franklin quoted *Guardian* No. 80 at length in Dogood essay No. 14); and Gardner's criticism of the New England funeral elegy in his pamphlet *Dialogue*.

Silence remarked that many travelers to New England have said that good poetry is not to be expected there. The reason, she claimed, is that "we do not afford that Praise and Encouragement which is merited, when any thing extraordinary of this Kind is produced among us." Therefore she had determined, "when I meet with a Good Piece of *New-England* Poetry, to give it a suitable Encomium, and thereby endeavour to discover to the World some of its Beautys, in order to encourage the Author to go on, and bless the World with more, and more Excellent Productions." The hyperbolic tone is one indication that Silence/Franklin is joking. As Franklin learned from Nathaniel Gardner, praise to the undeserving is severe satire. "There has lately appear'd among us a most Excellent Piece of Poetry, entituled, *An Elegy upon the much Lamented Death of Mrs.* Mehitable Kitel, *Wife of Mr.* John Kitel *of* Salem, &c. It may justly be said in its Praise, without Flattery to the Author, that it is the most *Extraordinary* Piece that ever was wrote in *New-England.* The Language is so soft and Easy, the Expression so moving and pathetick, but above all, the Verse and Numbers so Charming and Natural, that it is almost beyond Comparison."

Silence/Franklin then quoted Isaac Watts on the superiority of genius to the rules of criticism. The praise was extravagant, but perhaps some readers were not positive that the piece was a satire until reading the following:

> I find no English Author, Ancient or Modern, whose Elegies may be compar'd with this, in respect to the Elegance of Stile, or Smoothness of Rhime; and for the affecting Part, I will leave your Readers to judge, if ever they read any Lines, that would sooner make them *draw their Breath* and Sigh, if not shed Tears, than these following.

> >   *Come let us mourn, for we have lost a Wife, a Daughter, and a Sister,*
> >   *Who has lately taken Flight, and greatly we have mist her.*
> >   In another Place,
> >   Some little Time *before she yielded up her Breath,*
> >   *She said, I ne'er shall hear one Sermon more on Earth.*
> >   *She kist her Husband* some little Time *before she expir'd,*
> >   *Then lean'd her Head the Pillow on, just out of Breath and tir'd.*

Franklin implied that the verse was so bad that any critic would draw his "Breath and Sigh, if not shed Tears," at it. Not until Mark Twain had Huck Finn recite the simple-minded verse of Miss Emmeline Grangerford do we have a comparably humorous satire of dreadful poetry. Twain, however, created the deliberately execrable poetry; Franklin used an actual elegy. Twain's "Ode to Stephen Dowling Bots, Dec'd" outdoes even the lugubrious, sentimental, and awkward verse of Dr. Herrick. According to Huck Finn, Emmeline "could rattle off poetry like nothing. She didn't ever have to stop to think." If Herrick thought, it was in vain.

Silence observed: "BUT the Threefold Appellation in the first Line, '——— *a Wife, a Daughter, and a Sister,*' must not pass unobserved. That Line in the celebrated *Watts,* 'GUNSTON *the Just, the Generous, and the Young,*' is nothing Comparable to it. The latter only mentions three Qualifications of *one* Person who was deceased, which therefore could raise Grief and Compassion but for *One.* Whereas the former, (*our most excellent Poet*) gives his Reader a Sort of an Idea of the Death of *Three Persons,* viz. '——— *a Wife, a Daughter, and a Sister,*' which is *Three times* as great a Loss as the Death of *One,* and consequently must raise *Three Times* as much Grief and Compassion in the Reader." Franklin's satire of the confusing reference to the seeming death of three persons and his burlesque of the automatic sentimentality whereby the sorrow for three deaths would be greater than the sorrow for one, anticipate Twain's satire of Emmeline Grangerford's sentimental pictures:

> It was a picture of a young woman in a long white gown, standing on the rail of a bridge all ready to jump off, with her hair all down her back, and looking up to the moon, with the tears running down her face, and she had two arms folded across her breast, and two arms stretched out in front, and two more reaching up towards the moon—and the idea was, to see which pair would look best and then scratch out all the other arms; but, as I was saying, she died before she got her mind made up. . . . The young woman in the picture had a kind of a nice sweet face, but there was so many arms it made her look too spidery, seemed to me.

The confusing three deaths and the confusing three sets of arms are both splendid comic satires. Franklin did not bother to comment on the unintentionally humorous and awkward Hudibrastic rhyme, "sister" and "mist her."

Franklin claimed that Herrick's elegy was so different from any other poetry that it deserved a new name, and, "in Honour and Remembrance of the Dead," dubbed it *Kitelic*. He then dropped the irony and pronounced that most New England elegies are "wretchedly Dull and Ridiculous." Since poets would not be bad if they knew how to do better, he gave "A RECEIPT *to make a* New England *Funeral* ELEGY." He emphasized the clichés in the titles and subjects of elegies, then wrote:

> *Having chose the Person, take all his Virtues, Excellencies, &c. and if he have not enough, you may borrow some to make up a sufficient Quantity: To these add his last Words, dying Expressions, &c. if they are to be had; mix all these together, and be sure you strain them well. Then season all with a Handful or two of Melancholly Expressions, such as,* Dreadful, Deadly, cruel cold Death, unhappy Fate, weeping Eyes, &c. *Having mixed all these Ingredients well, put them into the empty Scull of some young* Harvard; . . . *there let them Ferment for the Space of a Fortnight, and by that Time they will be incorporated into a Body, which take out, and having prepared a sufficient Quantity of double Rhimes, such as,* Power, Flower; Quiver, Shiver; Grieve us, Leave us; tell you, excel you; Expeditions, Physicians; Fatigue him, Intrigue him; &c. *you must spread all upon Paper, and if you can procure a Scrap of Latin to put at the End, it will garnish it mightily; then having affixed your Name at the Bottom, with a* Moestus Composuit, *you will have an Excellent Elegy.*

Franklin added that the receipt "*will serve when a Female is the Subject of your Elegy, provided you borrow a greater Quantity of Virtues, Excellencies, &c.*" Franklin's essay remained well-known in New England for a decade, with references to poor elegies as "Kitelic" poetry turning up in the Boston papers long after the apprentice had run away to Philadelphia.[19]

Franklin composed an accompanying mock panegyric poem, signed "Philomusus," titled "*To the Sage and Immortal Doctor* H[erric]k, *on his Incomparable ELEGY, upon the Death of Mrs.* Mehitabell Kitel, &c. A PANEGYRICK." Opening the thirty-two lines of iambic pentameter, Franklin charged that the Kitelic elegy was written without any of the usual characteristics of poetry. Moreover, the "Mysterious Ode" by Dr. Herrick does not make sense:

> Thou hast, great Bard, in thy Mysterious Ode,
> Gone in a Path which ne'er before was trod,
> And freed the World from the vexatious Toil,
> Of Numbers, Metaphors, of Wit and Stile. (ll. 1–4)

Since the author was a physician, Franklin glances at the possible connection between a physician and an elegist:

> The healing Race thy Genius shall admire,
> And thee to imitate in vain aspire;
> For if by Chance a Patient you should kill,
> You can Embalm his Mem'ry with your Quill. (ll. 7–20)

The diction "Embalm" is both suitable and wonderfully grotesque, reminding me of T. S. Eliot's line in "The Love Song of J. Alfred Prufrock": "Like a patient etherized upon a table." Philomusus closed by saying that Dr. Herrick was so unique and wonderful a poet that no one else could do him justice. He must "Write your own Elegy against you're Dead."

THE *COURANT* LIBRARY

The 2 July *Courant*'s most interesting item listed books from the *Courant*'s library. It testifies to the young bookman's interest and pride in books. Those that Franklin mentioned in his *Autobiography* are sometimes discussed, but this list, which he compiled and published while James Franklin was in jail, is rarely noted. The books in the *Courant*'s library were "Pliny's *Natural Hist[ory]*; [Flavius] Josephus, *Ant[iquities of the Jews]*; Aristotle's *Politicks*; *History of France*; *Roman History*; Her[man] Moll's *Geography*; [John Dunton's] *Athenian Oracle*, Four Volumes; *British Apollo [or, Curious Amusements*, a periodical]; [Peter] Heylin's *Cosmography*; [Peter] Heylin's *Sum of Christian Theology*; Cot[ton] Mather's *History of New England* [i.e., *Magnalia Christi Americana*]; [John] Oldmixon's *History of the American Colonies* [i.e., *The British Empire in America*]; [George] Sandys' *Travels*; [Guillaume S.] Du Bartas [no doubt Joshua Sylvester's translation of *Divine Weeks*]; [Bishop Gilbert] Burnet's *History of the Reformation*; [Thomas] Burnet's *Theory of the Earth*; Virgil; [Samuel Butler's] *Hudibras*; Milton [probably *Paradise Lost*]; *The Spectator*, Eight Volumes; *The Guardian*, Two Volumes; [Giovanni Marana's] *The Turkish Spy*; [Port Royal] *Art of Thinking*; [Port Royal] *Art of Speaking*; [Richard Steele, ed.], *The Reader*; [R. Steele, ed.] *The Lover*; [Abraham] Cowl[e]y's *Works*; [Charles Gildon, *The Post Boy Rob'd of His Mail; or*] *The Ladies Pacquet broke open*; [Richard Allestree,] *The

Ladies Calling; *History of the Affairs of Europe*; [John] Oldham's *Works*; Shakespear's *Works*; [Jonathan Swift's] *The Tail of the Tub*; and St. Augustine's *Works*." At the end Franklin added a number of volumes of the popular ministers: "[John] Tillotson's, Dr. [William] Bates's, Dr. [Robert] South's, Mr. [John] Flavel's, & Mr. [Stephen] Charnock's Works" and mentioned "a great Number of Latin Authors, and a vast Quantity of Pamphlets."

For Franklin's intellectual development, the inventory is the most significant booklist between his discussion of his early reading in the *Autobiography* and the books ordered annually by the Library Company of Philadelphia (1731–57). To give just one example of his later references to books in the *Courant* library, Franklin mentioned in his 7 November 1773 letter concerning experiments with oil and water that he had, "when a Youth, read and smiled at Pliny's Account of a Practice among the Seamen of his Time, to still the Waves in a Storm by pouring Oil into the Sea; which he mentions as well as the use of Oil by the Divers." When he observed similar phenomena, he remembered his early reading.

James Franklin Freed

On 5 July, just before the end of the current session of the General Court when James Franklin was due to be released, the Massachusetts Council tried to impose censorship on the *New-England Courant*: "Many passages have been published boldly Reflecting upon his Majesties Government and on the administration of it in this Province, The Ministry Churches & Colledge, and it very often Contains Paragraphs that tend to fill the Readers Minds with Vanity to the dishonour of God & Disservice of Good men, Resolved, That no Such Weekly paper be hereafter printed or published, without the Same be first perused by the Secr[etar]y (as has been usual) and that the Said Franklyn Give Security before the Justices of the Superior Court, in the Sum of One hundred pounds, to be of the Good Behaviour to the End of the Next fall Sessions of this Court." The measure was too authoritarian for the House, however. Besides, the Old Charter members of the House had often been pleased with the *Courant*'s satires of the ministers and the authorities and with the Couranteers for supporting their positions. Therefore, on 6 July 1722, the House "Non Concurr[e]d."[20]

When the General Court session ended on Saturday afternoon, 7 July, James Franklin was automatically released. In the 16 July *Courant*, the unrepentant printer published the council's attempt to muzzle him and the House's vote defeating the council.

Silence Dogood No. 8: Freedom of the Press

Franklin had probably already set in type Dogood No. 8, since it appeared on Monday, 9 July, only two days after James Franklin was released. It defended the freedom of the press. In order not to make the defense actionable—and to give it more weight and authority—Franklin reprinted most of the essay from a recent but already classic article on freedom of speech *Cato's Letters*. This *Courant* contained an advertisement by Josiah Franklin for his indentured Irish servant William Tinsley, who had absconded.

In the 16 July paper, the recently freed James Franklin stated that he "never publish'd anything with a Design to affront the Government" and promised "to proceed with the like Caution as long as I have the Liberty granted me of following my Business." The printer found a parallel to his case in a speech by John Aislabie before the House of Lords (19 July 1721).[21] James Franklin concluded by asking whether colonists had the rights of Englishmen: "I know not the Power of a General Assembly in his Majesties Plantations, nor whether an *Englishman* may have Liberty to answer for himself before the Legislative Power." All Old Charter Party devotees recognized that the printer was being more modest than John Wise, who had asserted in 1687 that Massachusetts citizens had "the priviledges of Englishmen according to Magna Charta."[22]

In the same paper another Couranteer sent in an essay attacking Paul Dudley and the magistrates in general. Though he mainly quoted English essayists, he printed the first name of the person particularly attacked in capital letters (PAUL) in the following sentence: "Then, like the SheeP in our Fable, we mAy cry oUt aLoud for help, and oppose with all our might against the treacherous WATCHDOG." The author quoted *Cato's Letters*: "All Ministries who were *Oppressors*, or intended to be *Oppressors*, have been loud in their Complaints against Freedom of Speech, and the License of the Press, and always, restrained, or endeavoured to restrain, Both. In Consequence of this, they have browbeaten Writers, and punished them violently, and against Law, and burnt their Works; by all which they shew'd, how much Truth alarmed them, and how much they were at Enmity with Truth."

Silence Dogood No. 9: Sewall Attacked

The *Courant's* lead essay for 23 July, Silence Dogood No. 9, attacked religious hypocrites who became politicians: "But the most dangerous Hypocrite in a Common-Wealth, is one who *leaves the Gospel for the sake of the Law*: A Man compounded of Law and Gospel, is able to cheat a whole Country with his Religion, and then destroy them under *Colour of Law*." Though ostensibly a sketch of the detested Royalist Governor Joseph Dudley, it slyly pointed out the ministers' influence over politicians, hinting that James Franklin had been incarcerated because the ministers were angry with him. Though partially attacking the Mathers, the essay mainly satirized Chief Justice Samuel Sewall, an eminently religious man who had at one time considered becoming a minister. Not everyone would have realized its underlying purpose, but surely the Mathers and Sewall did. It was a bold and vicious personal satire.

In addition, Franklin satirized the ministers' praise in funeral sermons of wealthy persons, suggesting that they were religious hypocrites who oppressed the poor. The clergy were blind to the wealthy's oppression of the poor because the ministers "are honourable supported (as they ought to be) by their People, and see nor feel nothing of the Oppression which is obvious and burdensome to every one else." Thus the apprentice implies that the clergy, as well as the wealthy religious persons who became lawyers, were hypocrites, influenced by money. Franklin concluded the piece with an excerpt from *Cato's Letters*.

James Franklin took up his trial again in the 30 July *Courant*. He began by citing Chapter 29 of *Magna Charta*: "No Freeman shall be taken or imprisoned, or disseised of his Freehold, or Liberties, or free Customs, or be outlawed, or exiled, or any otherwise destroyed, nor will we pass upon him, nor condemn him, but by *lawful Judgment of his Peers*, or by *the Law of the Land*. We will sell to no Man, we will not deny or defer to any Man, either Justice or Right." The printer simply copied the series of comments on the passage by Lord Coke from Henry Care's *English Liberties*, which he had republished the previous year. He added a passage from the 1691 Massachusetts charter saying that only the judiciary could hear, try, and determine "ALL MANNER OF CRIMES, Offences, Pleas, Processes, Plaints, Actions, Matters, Causes and Things whatsoever arising or happening within Our said Province or Territory." According to the Magna Charta, Lord Coke, and the current charter of Massachusetts, the legislature had illegally imprisoned James Franklin. Only the courts could try and imprison persons.

James Franklin was still smarting from his imprisonment two months later. A Hudibrastic poem by "Dic. Burlesque" (James Franklin, I think) in the 17 September *Courant* gave a mock history of New England and parodied the proceedings of the General Court, ending with its treatment of the printer. Dic. Burlesque said that there lately has appeared among us

> *A Painter, who in factious Pieces,*
> *Does represent our sacred Faces:*
> *And tho' his vile seditious Practice,*
> *We own but too often Fact is,*
> *His Crime has on* Rebellion *border'd,*
> *And therefore by our selves 'tis ORDER'D,*
> *That Bumbo shall forthwith with him go,*
> *And put him close into the Limbo,*
> *There to remain for his Transgression,*
> *Until the ending of this* ———— [session].

"Insulanus" contributed a piece dated "Newport on Rhode Island" to the 6 August *Courant*, following Franklin's lead in satirizing "the *Kitelian* Tribe." Evidently James Franklin still did not know at this time that his young apprentice was writing the Dogood series. An editorial note stated: "*Mrs. Dogood's Letter coming to hand too late to be inserted this Week, will be publish'd in our next.*"

Silence Dogood No. 10: Relief for Poor Widows

The third Dogood essay had revealed Franklin's civic and humanitarian concerns, but the tenth proposed his first public do-good project. In this column (13 August) Franklin quoted for the second time from Defoe's *Essay Upon Projects* and advocated forming a society for the relief of poor widows. Dogood argued that "the Country is ripe for many such Friendly Societies, whereby every Man might help another, without any Disservice to himself." Widows should help one another, but, "above all, the Clergy have the most need of coming into some such Project as this." Franklin joked about the supposedly extraordinarily active sexuality of the clergy: "They as well as poor Men (according to the Proverb) generally abound in Children." He may have had in mind the saying, "The rich get rich and the poor. . . ." Though he joked in the essay, the project was serious.

Silence Dogood No. 11: Relief for Spinsters

Instead of proposing another serious project, Dogood No. 11 (20 August) spoofed virgin spinsters with a petition from "Margaret Aftercast," which asked for "Relief of all those penitent Mortals of the fair Sex, that are like to be punish'd with their Virginity until old Age, for the Pride and Insolence of their Youth." Supposedly replying to Margaret Aftercast, Silence Dogood devised a plan to ensure women against protracted virginity. The amusing conclusion testified how wonderful sex was to a formerly virgin older woman: "No Woman, who after claiming and receiving, has had the good Fortune to marry, shall entertain any Company with Encomiums on her Husband, above the Space of one Hour at a Time." The epigraph from Plautus, *Cistellaria*, lamented, "I was not allowed to come and see my darling during all that time."

Silence Dogood No. 12: On Drunkenness

Dogood No. 12, a moral essay on drunkenness, appeared on 10 September. Silence said, "A true and natural Representation of any Enormity, is often the best Argument against it and Means of removing it, when the most severe Reprehensions alone, are found ineffectual." What would "a true and natural Representation" of drunkenness be? In his later writings, Franklin sometimes gave portraits of drunkenness or its horrible effects (7 December 1732; 24 October 1734), but here he did not. Perhaps, as the literary critic Robert D. Arner suggested, Franklin intended to ridicule the "severe Reprehensions" that the ministers constantly made against drunkenness.[23] The next sentence uses the typical sermon diction when Silence promises to "improve the little Observation I have made on the Vice."

With a light, mocking tone, Franklin paradoxically claimed: "I doubt not but *moderate Drinking* has been improved for the Diffusion of Knowledge among the ingenious Part of Mankind, who want the Talent of a ready Utterance, in order to discover the Conceptions of their Minds in an entertaining and intelligible Manner." Here Franklin imitated *Tatler* No. 252, but whereas Steele's tone is entirely serious, Franklin mocked both Steele and the opinions of Silence Dogood. Franklin then quoted *Spectator* No. 247 on women who could "talk whole Hours together upon Nothing." But he appreciated the *Spectator's* belief that the learned categorization of various figures of speech could sometimes be found in the speech of ordinary persons when drunk or in anger. Franklin added, however, an extraordinary comparison between drinking and washing laundry, thereby undercutting the supposed positive powers of drink: "Some shrink in the Wetting, and others swell to such an unusual Bulk in their Imaginations, that they can in an Instant understand all Arts and Sciences, by the liberal Education of a little vivifying *Punch*, or a sufficient Quantity of other exhilarating Liquor" (1:40). As the literary critic Douglas Anderson noted, "The delightful analogy to laundry preserves a sense of domestic comedy."[24]

Franklin briefly discussed the nature of the pleasure derived from drinking and its different effects on different persons. He ended with a brief listing of the "Vocabulary of the Tiplers," which may have been suggested, as James Parton observed, by Rabelais. The word catalog anticipated Franklin's much longer list in "The Drinker's Dictionary" (13 January 1736/7). Though the essay satirized drunkenness, it was not savage, unlike a number of his later news notes or his essay "On Drunkenness" (1 February 1732/3). Nor was it so effective as the cautionary character sketch of his childhood friend John Collins in the *Autobiography*.

At the end of this *Courant*, James Franklin changed his imprint. Jacob Sheafe had left his Queen Street school to become writing master at the South Writing School,[25] so James Franklin changed his imprint from "at his Printing-House in Queen-street, over against Mr. Sheafe's School," to "at his Printing-House in Queen-street, near the Prison."

Silence Dogood No. 13: Boston Night Life

The penultimate Silence Dogood appeared on 24 September and lightly satirized Boston's night life, expertly using the naive persona of Silence Dogood, who supposedly did not recognize as prostitutes the group of women whom she described. At first, though, Franklin played with the identity of Silence—just as he would later do with the identity of Poor Richard: "I met indeed with the common fate of *Listeners*, (who *hear no good of themselves*,) but from a Consciousness of my Innocence, receiv'd it with a Satisfaction beyond what the Love of Flattery and the Daubings of a Parasite could produce." Franklin also employed the specialized vocabulary of sailors: "I met a Crowd of *Tarpolins* and their Doxies, link'd to each other by the Arms, who ran (by their own Account) after the Rate of *Six Knots an Hour*, and bent their Course towards the Common. Their eager and amorous Emotions of Body, occasion'd by taking their Mistresses *in Tow*, they call'd *wild Steerage*: And as a Pair of them happen'd to trip and come to the Ground, the Company were call'd upon to *bring to*, for that Jack and Betty were *founder'd*."

In the same issue, James Franklin scooped the rival newspapers by breaking the story of the Connecticut apostasy, which I will discuss in the next chapter.

SILENCE DOGOOD NO. 14: ON RELIGION

The fourteenth and last Silence Dogood (8 October 1722) again satirized the clergy but changed its target from the Mathers to Timothy Cutler, Samuel Johnson, and the other Connecticut Congregational ministers who had just proclaimed their Anglicanism. Silence (echoing Gardner's "Another Dialogue" [22 January 1721/2]) maintained that "an indiscreet Zeal for spreading an Opinion, hurts the Cause of the Zealot." And, with a possible reference to Cotton Mather's failure to reform his son Increase, "he that propagates the Gospel among *Rakes* and *Beaus* without reforming them in their Morals, is every whit as ridiculous and impolitick as a Statesman who makes Tools of Ideots and Tale-Bearers." The last jibe also lampooned Cotton Mather as both a tool of Governor Shute and a notorious talebearer.

The essay reflected Shaftesbury's *Letter Concerning Enthusiasm* (1708), thereby suggesting that Franklin was already a deist, though he cleverly quoted "two Ingenious Authors of the Church of England" to make his argument seem palatable. From Addison's *Spectator* No. 185, Franklin cited a passage concerning zeal and pride that anticipated several of his later writings on pride. Addison also quoted a passage from Ovid in order to condemn its thesis: *Video meliore proboque/Deteriora sequor* (I see and approve the better course; I follow the worse). As the historian of ideas Norman Fiering has noted, the passage espoused the voluntarist position (that the heart/will is separate from the intellect) as opposed to the intellectualist position (that the will is an aspect of the intellect).[26] Franklin agreed with Addison that the voluntarist position, which justified the Puritan belief in original sin, was absurd. Although doubly indirect (first, he was quoting the most famous English periodical of the day; second, the ostensible subject was excessive zeal in religion), the essay marked Franklin's first satire on the idea of original sin.

Alfred Owen Aldridge noted that in the essay Franklin suggested two "related themes, the absurdity of sectarian differences in Christianity and the importance of humanitarian ethics."[27] These motifs often recurred in Franklin's writings, as we shall see.

From *Guardian* No. 80, Franklin quoted Richard Steele's claim that "it is impossible to talk distinctly without defining the Words of which we make use." Steele pointed out that different people commonly meant different things by the word *church*.[28] Franklin had read similar statements in the Port Royal *Logic*, where the authors illustrated the point with interpretations of the words *true religion*. Franklin knew that language was shifty and deceptive. He later often expressed an epistemological skepticism, claiming that "Such is the Imperfection of our Language, and perhaps of all other Languages, that notwithstanding we are furnish'd with Dictionaries innumerable, we cannot precisely know the import of Words, unless we know of what Party the Man is that uses them" (11:277). In this skepticism, too, he echoed the Port Royal *Logic*. For its authors had said that it was necessary to know the religion of the speaker to be able to understand his language.[29] As I will show, Franklin took to heart Steele's statement that politicians used language "for managing the Loves and Hatreds of Mankind to the Purposes to which they would lead them."

Franklin's Style

Revealing his authorship of the Silence Dogood essays must have been one of the happiest moments of Benjamin Franklin's life—the epitome of his adolescence. Gardner and the other Couranteers must have been surprised, even amazed, and full of praise. James Franklin, however, may have been unhappy and chagrined at the disclosure. As usual, Franklin downplays his emotions in the *Autobiography*. He merely reports that when he ended the essay series, he revealed his authorship and consequently "began to be considered a little more by my Brothers' Acquaintance, and in a manner that did not quite please him, as he thought, probably with reason, that it tended to make me too vain" (A 17–18). In a fine appreciation, Walter Isaacson wrote that the Dogood essays are "historically notable" because "they were among the first examples of what would become a quintessential American genre of humor: the wry, homespun mix of folksy tales and pointed observations that was perfected by such Franklin descendants as Mark Twain and Will Rogers."[30]

Though Franklin wrote other essays for his brother's newspaper, the earliest ones especially reveal the young man's emerging thought. His subjects included education, feminism, a liberal Whiggish political philosophy, pride, civic projects (a topic not found elsewhere in the *Courant*), writing itself, and satires of the clergy and of religion. These subjects recur frequently in his later writings. The essays also demonstrate several techniques he used throughout his life, such as his reversal of an expected, commonplace opinion, as in his argument that men are responsible for the vices of women.[31] This habit of mind appeared in the *Autobiography* when he said that he became a religious doubter by reading books against deism wherein the arguments of the deists that were quoted to be refuted appeared to him stronger than the refutations (58).

Another Franklin characteristic is a fondness for rhetorical feats and for logic, including the burlesque of patently false logic. As we have seen, he studied logic and delighted in the Socratic method. Franklin's use of persona in the first four essays was masterful. Silence Dogood emerged as a sympathetic, wholesome, colloquial, humorous, and politically aware personality, concerned for the rights of her country. Since he had not previously demonstrated his literary ability, it is not surprising that his brother and daily companions, the *Courant* wits, did not guess he was the author of the Dogood series, but his exploitation of the persona's possibilities in his earliest essays is surprising. After the first four essays, however, he used the persona effectively only in Dogood No. 13 (on Boston's night life). For most of the other essays, a minister's widow was not the best possible speaker. I suspect that he dropped the essay series because he so often found it necessary to violate or ignore the supposed persona, perhaps offending his aesthetic sense. Just as he "put on" poses in life, so in his writings he repeatedly selected the most suitable speaker in order to achieve the desired effect.[32]

It was especially noteworthy that Franklin chose a female persona. She was a likable widow, probably in her thirties (she had a son whom she was thinking of sending to Harvard). She had spunk and opinions, like many of Franklin's later feminine personae, including Poor Richard's wife, Bridget Saunders. Franklin so often used feminine personae that the novelist John Updike labeled his imagination "androgynous."[33] How many male authors have the daring to try to see life through a woman's eyes? Few essayists of Franklin's day adopted female personae. Where, one might ask, are Dr. Samuel Johnson's feminine personae? One could suggest that Franklin's proto-feminism stems from his adoption of a feminine persona—or the reverse may be true: his use of a feminine persona may stem from his proto-feminism. At any rate, the Silence Dogood essay series is the first essay series in American literature, and it is also the first sustained use of a feminine persona.

The Dogood essays also demonstrate an extraordinary range of tone, from the bantering quality of the war-of-the-sexes essay to the subtle, though savage, assault on Sewall. An aspect of Franklin's style is revealed in his use of aphorisms, perhaps partly resulting from his hearing sermons in which biblical texts and occasionally proverbs were used as proofs, and perhaps partly showing a delight in rhetorical adroitness. The most characteristic technique may be his consciousness of the implications of style. He recognized and manipulated the pious and sentimental styles and undercut them with jarring realism and vivid colloquialisms. He had earlier recognized (see Figure 9) Nathaniel Gardner's imitation of Increase Mather's jeremiad style and appreciated how effectively Gardner ridiculed Mather by adopting his style. Franklin later delighted in and imitated Swift's parodies, and during his career he successfully imitated numerous styles of the past and present. No other author of his time used so many styles so well. Dr. Henry Stuber, who wrote a continuation of Franklin's autobiography in 1790 and 1791, said that his last public writing, the pretended speech of Sidi Mehemet Ibrahim against freeing Christian slaves, furnished "a no less convincing proof of his power of imitating the stile of other times and nations, than his celebrated parable against persecution. And as the latter led many persons to search the scriptures with a view to find it, so the former caused many persons to search the book stores and libraries, for the work from which it was said to be extracted."[34] An extraordinary grasp of the implications of syntax and diction characterize Franklin's best writings. In a satire on religious enthusiasm, he once wrote that diction and style are the only tests of truth: "It is therefore much the best, considering human Imperfection, that each Party describes itself as good, and as bad, as sincerely and as insincerely as they can and will, and leave it to such as are capable, to gather as much as is possible of what is true and solid, from Peoples Stile and Expressions" (24 February 1742/3).

On 3 December 1722, Franklin published "Hugo Grim," addressed to Silence Dogood, berating her for not writing more essays. "Is your Common-Place Wit all Exhausted, your stock of matter all spent?" He mocked himself with a pastiche of quotations from a number of the Dogood essays, emphasizing these echoes by printing them in italics. (In the following sentence, he quotes a phrase from the satire on the New England elegy.) "Has the Sleep of *inexorable unrelenting Death* procur'd your *Silence*?" And he appended an advertisement to the letter, asking for an account of Silence, "whether Dead or alive, Married or unmarried, in Town or Country." Typical of Franklin, he last mentioned the fleeting, local fame of the Silence Dogood essays in a self-satire. Years later, he ironically recalled the series and echoed his self-deprecation: "I kept my Secret till my small Fund of Sense for such Performances was pretty well exhausted, and then I discovered it" (A 18).

EIGHT

"Saucy and Provoking": Franklin Takes Charge

It was not fair in me to take this Advantage, and this I therefore reckon one of the first Errata of my Life: But the Unfairness of it weigh'd little with me, when under the Impressions of Resentment, for the Blows his Passion too often urg'd him bestow upon me. Tho' He was otherwise not an ill-natur'd man. Perhaps I was too saucy and provoking.—A 20

JAMES FRANKLIN'S CONTINUING ATTACKS on the religious and civil authorities of Massachusetts made his position risky. The governor and council, the Prerogative Party in general, the Mathers, and many conservative Congregationalists felt that he should be restrained, if not punished. When they took action against him, his younger brother took charge.

THE CONNECTICUT APOSTASY

The 24 September 1722 *New-England Courant* broke the Connecticut apostasy story and horrified New England's Congregationalists. The *Courant* declared that on 13 September, the day after Yale's commencement, the Reverend Dr. Timothy Cutler (Yale's president), together with "Four or Five other Dissenting Ministers, some of whom have been ordain'd to particular Congregations for Twenty Years past, publickly declared themselves to be of the Principles of the Church of England." The *Courant* could hardly do the news justice, for it was not horrifying to the secular and largely Anglican Couranteers. Confirming rumors on a related subject that had circulated in Boston for the past year,[1] the *Courant* added, "Some Gentlemen of the Church of England have lately purchas'd a Piece of Ground in the North Part of Boston, in order to erect a New Church there."

The 15 October *Boston News-Letter* reported the news with the genuine New England Puritan jeremiad tone:

> By Letters from Connecticut of the 25th past, we are informed that their College the Foundation and Nursery of Truth and Learning, set up there according to Scripture Rule, Free of Humane Traditions and Impositions (for which their and our Fathers left the Pleasant Land of our Fore-Fathers to enjoy the same,

came by a Voluntary exile into this rude Wilderness) is now become Corrupt.
. . . its lamentable that it should groan out *Ichabod* under it's second Rector Mr.
Timothy Cutler . . . who on the 13th of September, the Day after the Commencement at New-Haven, in the Library, before the Trustees and other Ministers *viva
voce*, with Mr. Brown, Tutor, and five others Ordained Ministers, viz. Mr. *Hart*
of East Guilford, Mr. *Whittlesey* of *Wallingford*, and Mr. *Johnson* of *West-Haven*,
Declared themselves Episcopal, and that their late Ordination received was of
no value . . . And Mr. *Cutler* also then Declared, *That it was his firm Perswasion,
that out of the Church of* England *ordinarily there was no Salvation.* . . . Among
those for Episcopacy then at New Haven, there were Mr. *Hart*, Mr. *Whittlesey*
and Mr. *Eliot* doubted of the Validity of their Ordination, and would be thankful
to GOD and Man in helping them if in an Error.

The *News-Letter* story paraphrased and partially quoted a letter reporting the
event that the Reverends John Davenport of Stamford, Connecticut, and Stephen Buckingham of Norwalk, Connecticut, sent Increase and Cotton Mather
on 25 September 1722.[2] I suspect that Cotton Mather revised it and sent it on to
the *News-Letter* for publication. Groaning "out *Ichabod*" alludes to the glory
departing from Israel (1 Samuel 4:21–22), and perhaps especially inspired the
burlesques of the Couranteers.

The Couranteers began satirizing the Connecticut apostasy with a heavy-
handed mock advertisement in the 1 October paper concerning a curiosity "TO
BE SEEN *gratis* at the *Grey-hound* in *Roxbury*" (the words were often used in
advertisements to attract customers to taverns featuring exotic animal shows of
camels, lions, etc.). The advertisement joked about "Mr. C[utle]r and the rest of
the Ministers at Connecticut, that have lately turned Churchmen." The letter's
conclusion adds to the American folk ancestry of such sham shows as the Duke
and Dauphin's "Royal Nonesuch" or "burning shame" in *Huckleberry Finn*:[3]
"For my own Part, I shall suspend my Judgment of him till I see him, which I
intend to do in my next Journey to *Boston*, provided he continues to be seen
gratis; for I have hated to part with my Money for a Show, ever since some
Fishermen in *Boston* made me pay *Two Pence* for the Sight of a *Tom-Cod* instead
of a *Maremaid*." The local news reported: "We hear the Reverend Dr. Cotton
Mather has been desir'd to take the Charge of the College at Newhaven, in the
room of the Reverend Mr. Timothy Cutler who has resign'd that Place." Mather
declined the informal approach.[4]

"JETHRO STANDFAST"

As we have seen, Benjamin Franklin's fourteenth and last Silence Dogood essay
in the 8 October *Courant* also satirized the apostasy. A mock illiterate letter by
"Jethro Standfast" in the same *Courant* attacked the ministers with arguments
similar to those advocated by Silence Dogood; I believe that Franklin wrote it.
Though an occasional mock illiterate spelling occurred in earlier *Courant* skits,

the only possible earlier mock illiterate letter was by "Mundungus" Williams in the 12 March 1721/2 *Courant*, but Williams probably simply did not spell correctly. Though an anti-inoculationist and an adversary of the Mathers, Williams was devout and relied on religious arguments to counter his opponents.[5] In contrast, Jethro Standfast mocked religion. The letter is dated from "Nuhauen" and signed, "Yors tel Deth, Jethro Standfast." Franklin's inspiration may well have come from Jonathan Swift's "Verses Wrote on a Lady's Ivory Table-Book."[6] Standfast/Franklin wrote: "Thare has bein a most grevous rout and hurle-burle amung us, ever sense the nine Ministurs are turn'd *Hi-Church-men*." Warned Standfast: "Fokes sa, they have draun up a riting and sind it, wharin tha declar, that all owr Churches are no Churches, and or Ministurs no Ministurs, and that tha haue no more Athorriti to adminstur the Ordenances thun so mani Porturs or Plow-Ioggurs: Sum of owr Pepel danse ater thare Pipe, and tel us that owr Ministurs formurli ware ordan'd by Midwiues and Coblurs; but others sa that this is folce Doktrin, and belongs to the Church of *Rume*." Referring to the mock advertisement in the last week's paper, Standfast says that a strange, fearsome freak has appeared among us. "Sum sa he is a Jeshuet, othurs sa he is Tore." He has converted the ministers by talking with them and lending them books.[7] "Now tis buzd abute, that in ordur to Saluashun, we must beleue the unentenrrupted Sukseshun of Bishups from the Upostels, and the Heredere Endefezabel Rite of Prenses, and that Parlementare Rite is a mere Noshun; that all the Churches in the Wurld that ant govern'd by Bishups, are no part of the Cathalike Church, but are out of the ordnare Rode of Saluashun."[8]

One might be uncertain at first of the underlying intent of Jethro Standfast. Though the voice is humorous and ironic, one might be tempted to argue that Standfast is only claiming that the issues are overblown, not that the whole matter is gibberish. But the coequal joining of the apostolic succession and "the Heredere Endefezabel Rite of Prenses" reduces the former to nonsense. (Franklin's techniques and attitudes anticipate Mark Twain's nonce word *preforeordestination* in chapter 18 of *Huckleberry Finn*.) Note that the author does not say the hereditary right of princes but the hereditary "Endefezabel" right of princes. Franklin makes a double joke here. Supposedly the simple-minded Standfast meant *indefensible* and is referring to the "hereditary right of princes." In fact, "Endefezabel" refers to the learned word *indefeasible* (not able to be made void). For the learned in the audience, Franklin is joking about the assumptions of the ordinary reader. At the same time, the underlying voice says that the doctrine of the hereditary right of princes is as absurd as the doctrine of the apostolic succession. In addition to Franklin, the only known *Courant* writer who might seem capable of the subtle mock illiterate techniques of Standfast is Nathaniel Gardner. He, however, attended the First Church.[9] Though he often satirized particular faults of religion or of ministers (especially the Mathers), he was a Christian and a Congregationalist. Standfast, however, treats the religious controversy with covert cynicism. Of the known Couranteers, only Franklin has the deeply ironic attitudes revealed in this mock illiterate letter.

The 15 and 22 October *Courants* contained several essays on the New Haven apostasy. Unlike the rival Boston papers, the *Courant* essays generally took a moderate position and allowed space for arguments from Anglicans. The most temperate essay was by "Harry Concord" on 15 October, which the Franklin biographer Arthur Bernon Tourtellot persuasively ascribed to a minor Couranteer, the Reverend Henry Harris, Anglican rector of Queen's Chapel, Boston.[10]

"Nausawlander"

Another sacrilegious paper in the controversy was also, I suspect, by young Franklin. "Nausawlander" (29 October 1722) mocked the whole argument. The pseudonym may have alluded to King William III, who was of the House of Nassau and championed religious freedom. (Princeton University's Nassau Hall is named for him.) Obviously a nonbeliever, the pseudonymous author thought the questions at stake were insignificant, unimportant, or meaningless. The essay has a poetic epigraph that might be original or might have been taken from some poem circulating at the time about the ministers' defection:

> Strange Aspects in Newhaven late were seen,
> Of Heavenly Bodies which 'twas thought had been
> Stars of the highest Orb, fix'd in their Sphere,
> But now at last but wandring Stars appear.

The persona facetiously claimed that if the ministers were not truly ordained, it "makes a great many think, that all they have been doing in that Office is void, and of none Effect; and then it is to be fear'd, that all those Husbands and Wives who have been married by them (who it seems as yet have no Right to officiate in holy Orders) will take the Liberty (except Love or Conscience oblige them to the contrary) to separate one from the other." The letter suggested that society will break down and chaos in social institutions will result from a disbelief in the validity of ordination. It travestied the *Boston News-Letter* account and the bewailing of the apostasy in various sermons by the Mathers and other New England Congregationalists.[11] The affair is treated as a reductio ad absurdum (a technique Franklin often employed).[12] The sexual subject matter is also typically Franklinian. The sly suggestion of a society of free love is beyond the reach of any other Couranteer: "Therefore it behoves all Men, as well in other Congregations as theirs, to love and cherish their Wives, and Wives to love and reverence their Husbands, for fear of the like Disaster."

Franklin also ridiculed the ordinance of baptism: "there is one thing . . . which lies very much upon the Minds of some judicious Men, and most old Women; and that is, what shall those Persons do who have been *christened*, alias *couzened*, in plain English, *cheated* by their Ministry, who had not Commission to baptize?" The phrase "old Women" suggests superstition, and the words *couzened,* and *cheated* have Franklin's savage note. The ending befuddles the reader, suggesting, in effect, that the whole issue of religious doctrine is a matter of mumbo jumbo. Franklin had learned the technique from the Reverend John Wise and from the authors of the Port Royal *Logic,* who criticized Montaigne for using it.[13] Nausawlander concluded, "And therefore I think it is well worthy of Enquiry, If the Administrators be wrong, the Mode or Manner of Baptising wrong, and the Subjects (to wit, Infants) wrong, whether they be not all wrong?" As Franklin wrote in the *Autobiography,* some of the dogmas of Presbyterianism and Congregationalism "such as the Eternal Decrees of God, Election, Reproba-tion, etc. appear'd to me unintelligible, others doubtful," so he "early absented myself from the Public Assemblies of the Sect" (76).

In his study of Franklin's youth in Boston, Arthur Bernon Tourtellot did not comment on the radicalism of Standfast's mock illiterate letter, but he did focus on Nausawlander's extraordinary impiousness. Tourtellot said the letter was "tantamount to dismissing all the doctrinal advocacy and insistencies of the Puritan teachers as just so much jargon and doctrinal straining at gnats. Never before had a publication, even though it was on the side of episcopacy or of adult baptism, suggested that *all* such dogma was perhaps in error. It was expli-cable, though not congenial and usually not tolerable, to the Puritan mind to have differences in doctrine; but to have no doctrine at all, or to question the validity of all, was totally beyond comprehension."[14] Though he appreciated the author's radical skepticism, Tourtellot did not ascribe it to Franklin.

The 5 November *Courant* contained a defense by three of the Connecticut ministers who had repudiated Congregationalism and declared for the Church of England. No other Boston paper would have printed it, though it was harm-less enough. James Wetmore, Samuel Johnson, and Daniel Brown defended Timothy Cutler from the "tragical Representation, given in Mr. *Campbell's* News-Letter [of 15 October], of the Declaration lately made at the College in *New Haven,* touching Episcopal Ordination." Cutler had not maintained that salvation did not exist outside the Church of England. Instead, he had only joined the church that "could best make out it's Claim to the Appellation of the true Church, with Relation to the Regularity of those Offices and Powers, which relate to its Constitution as a Society." The local news in the same paper an-nounced: "Last Week Mr. Cutler, Mr. Johnson, and Mr. Brown came to Town from Connecticut, in order to proceed on their Voyage to London." They left that day, 5 November. Evidently Wetmore, who was ordained in London on 25 July 1723, had sailed earlier.

Of the seven ministers involved in the Connecticut apostasy, three remained Congregational ministers: Jared Eliot (1685–1763) of Killingworth, Connecticut; John Hart (1682–1730/1) of East Guilford, Connecticut; and Samuel Whittelsey (1686–1752) of Wallingford, Connecticut. Four became Anglican ministers: Dan-iel Brown (1698–1723) died two weeks after being ordained in London; Timothy Cutler (1684–1765) became the first minister of Christ Church, Boston; Samuel

Strange Aspects in Newhaven late were seen,
Of Heavenly Bodies which 'twas thought had been
Stars of the highest Orb, fix'd in their Sphere,
But now at last but wandring Stars appear.

To the *Author of the* New-England Courant.

SIR,

HIS Instant *September* there was a compleat Number of Presbyterian Clergymen fac'd about, and declar'd for the Church; which has put the People into great Consternation. The reason of this Revolution may be easily guest at; the Effects Time will will bring forth: The present Pretence seems to be from a Scruple of Conscience, that they were not rightly ordain'd, *i. e.* they had no regular Commission; which in plain English is, they ran before they were sent. And it is thought, they intend by Adoption, to obtain a lineal Descent or Succession from St. *Peter,* to qualify them for their Office; which makes a great many think, that all they have been doing in that Office is void, and of none Effect; and then it is to be fear'd, that all those Husbands and Wives who have been married by them (who it seems as yet have no Right to officiate in holy Orders) will take the Liberty (except Love or Conscience oblige them to the contrary) to separate one from the other. Therefore it behoves all Men, as well in other Congregations as theirs, to love and cherish their Wives, and Wives to love and reverence their Husbands, for fear of the like Disaster.

But there is one thing more which lies very much upon the Minds of some judicious Men, and most old Women; and that is, what shall those Persons do who have been *christened,* alias *cozened,* in plain English, *cheated* by their Ministry, who had no Commission to baptize? It is thought many of them will turn *Anabaptists,* and be dipt; and indeed some think that is the right way of Baptising, as it is prescrib'd in the Churches Form of Publick Baptism.

And therefore I think it is well worthy of Enquiry, If the Administrators be wrong, the Mode or Manner of Baptising wrong, and the Subjects (to wit, Infants) wrong, whether they be not all wrong?

I am, SIR,
Your Humble Servant,
NAUSAWLANDER.

Figure 13. Viewed as an apostasy by New England Puritans, the defection of the president of Yale and several other Congregational ministers to Anglicanism occasioned a spoof by Franklin as "Nausawlander," New-England Courant, *29 October 1722. The New England Congregationalists were horrified when the Reverend Timothy Cutler, rector of Yale College, dramatically revealed his conversion to the Church of England at the Yale commencement on 12 September 1722. He and six other Congregational clergymen had been meeting at New Haven to discuss church polity and ordination. Four of the seven abandoned the New England Way and became Anglican ministers. Two of the seven, Samuel Johnson (who took orders as an Anglican minister) and Jared Eliot (who remained a Congregational minister), later became friends of Franklin.*

The other two Boston newspapers treated the event as a major tragedy, but the New-England Courant, *which broke the news the day after the Yale commencement, mocked the affair. With some sexual suggestiveness, Franklin burlesqued the possible implications of the apostasy. Courtesy, Burney Collection, British Library.*

Johnson (1696–1772) became the minister at Stratford Connecticut., and then the first President of King's College (now Columbia University); and James Wetmore (1695–1760) became the minister of Christ Church, in Rye, New York.[15] Franklin later corresponded with two, beginning in 1747 with Jared Eliot, who was interested in science and became a good friend, and beginning in 1750 with Samuel Johnson, whom he tried to interest in becoming the first president of the Academy of Philadelphia (now the University of Pennsylvania).

HOOP-PETTICOATS

With the defecting ministers off for London, the apostasy dropped out of the news, and the Couranteers returned to satirizing the local clergy. Solomon Stoddard wrote a sermon titled *An Answer to Some Cases of Conscience*, published in June 1722, which at the end, in large capital letters, condemned hoop-petticoats as "contrary to the law of nature," for they had "something of Nakedness" in them (15). On 26 November, James Franklin advertised *Hoop-Petticoats Arraigned and Condemned by the Light of Nature, and Law of God*, which burlesqued Stoddard's sermon. Though Nathaniel Gardner had the wit and ability to write the piece, and though he had earlier imitated and burlesqued the Mathers, he was essentially religious. This satire, as we will see, is irreligious and it contains the pre-Freudian sexual play that only Franklin, among the Couranteers, used. Later scholars have ignored the attribution, but John Bach McMaster suggested in 1887 that Franklin wrote it.[16] He had burlesqued hoop-petticoats in Dogood No. 6, and I agree with McMaster. As mentioned above, Franklin had been "ravished" by Pascal's *Les Provinciales*, which satirized casuistry, and perhaps Pascal inspired him to parody Stoddard's *Cases of Conscience*.

The eight-page pamphlet *Hoop-Petticoats* not only travestied Solomon Stoddard and the jeremiad tradition but also objected to the inferior status of women in the New England Puritan tradition and ridiculed the Bible (as Franklin later did in "The Speech of Miss Polly Baker"). These attitudes characterize the young freethinker Franklin and no other Couranteer. *Hoop-Petticoats* began like the typical New England jeremiad with a minister as the ostensible speaker: "It is just Matter of Lamentation, that Sin and Iniquity so much abounds amongst us, in this Land, notwithstanding our great Profession and Privileges, and the heavy Judgments of God upon us for our Sins." Despite numerous "humbling Judgements," the people of New England continue in their pride. "But what I would particularly insist upon is in our Apparel, in following vain and sinful Fashions, and particularly that vain, sinful, immodest one of *Hoop-Petticoats*, Now, that I may make good this Charge against them, I shall shew that they are condemned by the *Light of Nature*, and *Law of God*." The use of Stoddard's exact words must have made a few readers think at first that the pamphlet was actually a sermon by Stoddard.

In condemning hoop-petticoats, Franklin's foolishly literal minister persona used sexually suggesting diction. The speaker said that hoop-petticoats "answer not but contradict" the reasons for wearing clothing. "1. One End of Apparel is to *hide Nakedness*." Adam and Eve were naked and not ashamed, "but Sin brought Shame, and therefore after the Fall, they sewed Fig Leaves together to cover their Nakedness: But God provided better Covering for them, viz. Coats of Skins for this end." The minister persona declared that hoop-petticoats, "instead of covering our Nakedness they expose it; and upon some emergent Accidents, expose those Parts that *Adam* and *Eve* seem'd to take especial Care to cover, in the Aprons they provided; and those Parts which the Apostle stiles *less honourable*, yea; *uncomely Parts* which therefore have the more need of comely Covering. See 1 *Cor.* 12, 23, 24." Hoop-petticoats actually "make bare the Leg and uncover the thigh." Thus they "make those Parts liable to be exposed, which God and Nature required to be covered" (2–3). In his travesty of Stoddard, Franklin made the minister-persona neurotically lascivious.

The minister/speaker claimed that a second end of apparel "is to *defend the Body from the Injuries it is liable to*," for instance, "the Injuries of the Weather." Like Franklin, the persona delighted in proverbs. "I am apt to think, that our Hoop Gallants find not sufficient Warmth under the Skreen of their foolish Proverb (*Pride feels no Cold*) in some Seasons: But it may be some had rather part with their Health than their Hoops." Rambling on, he asserted that large hoop-petticoats are difficult to wear in narrow passages. Franklin wrote that women wearing such petticoats "can scarse enter in at the Doors of their Houses, or of the House of God: So that there seems a Necessity either of making our Doors bigger, or their Hoops less" (3). Though Joseph Addison's *Tatler* No. 116 has a humorous passage on the trial of a hoop-petticoat in a court of judicature,[17] it lacks Franklin's archetypally sexual suggestions concerning circular objects and narrow passages.

In a section recalling Franklin's bemusement at the London printers who thought they had to drink *strong* beer in order to be *strong* to work (A 36), the persona confuses metaphorical language with actuality: "Methinks they would do well to consider, that *Strait is the gate, & narrow the way that leads to Life*; and whether their extensive Hoops may not be some hinderance unto them in walking in this narrow way, and entering in at the Gates especially since it is necessary in order thereto we part with our right Hand or Eye when they offend us; Surely they ought to fear whether they shall have Entrance, who will not part with that which they have no more need of than they have of a Cough." The underlying author burlesqued the logic in this passage—and the reasoning used by some ministers who cited inappropriate passages of the Bible as "proofs" for their theses (3–4). At the same time, Franklin dwells on the possibly sexual symbolic possibilities of "*narrow the way that leads to Life*."

The third end of apparel is to adorn the body: "But how can that be an Ornament, which is contrary to the other Ends of Apparel, especially that of covering our nakedness? Can that be an Ornament which exposes whole Parts which God and Nature require to be covered, and which the most barbarous

Nations by the Light of Nature are taught to conceal? Is that an Ornament which is contrary to Modesty, Humility, Gravity, & Sobriety, which are required in Women professing Godliness?" The speaker complained that "Pride and Impudence" have usurped the former "Humility and Modesty, since Women are *almost naked*, and are *not at all ashamed*; for instead of being *ashamed of their Pride*, they are *proud of their Shame*." The last antimetabole must have pleased the young writer. "Thus we see, that *Hoop-Petticoats* answer not, but contradict all the Ends of Apparel, therefore are condemned by the Light of Nature and law of God" (4–5). Those two phrases again allude to—and by now burlesque—the title of Stoddard's sermon.

The speaker becomes more absurd:

> *Moreover the Lord saith, because the Daughters of Zion are haughty, and walk with stretched forth Necks, and wanton . . . walking and mincing as they go, and making a tinkling with their Feet.* A *tinkling with their Feet*: The Word from whence this has its Original signifies a *Fetter*, as most render it: They therefore render it, *going as if they were fetter'd*; and so understand it of such a nice kind of affected Pace as was in the former Term intimated, and there further described, by a Resemblance taken from Captives or Prisoners that have *Irons* on their Legs, and so cannot go freely and readily, but in a slow and stalking Manner, as their Irons give them leave: Or as others, from those *Cords* or *Fetters* that Horse-Breakers are wont to hamper young Colts withal, to bring to a Pace.

Here the persona travestied a common feature in Puritan sermons—the analyses of the derivations of biblical words. The persona quoted 1 Timothy 2:9: "*Women should adorn themselves in modest Apparel, with shamefacedness and sobriety; not to the braided Hair, but which become Women professing Godliness, with good Works*." Women should impress others, he claimed, not by their "outward Garb" but by the "inward Gravity of their Minds." The speaker then rhetorically asked, "Do they do it that wear the extensive Hoops?" (5–6).

The minister persona reverted to the jeremiad formula: "Is it not a Day of trouble, of Perplexity, and of treading down by the Lord of Hosts, in this Valley of Vision? Yea, a Day of Darkness and Gloominess, a Day of Clouds and thick Darkness, as the Morning spread upon the Mountains, in which the Inhabitants of the Land should tremble, by reason of the heavy Judgments of God upon us; a Day in which God is calling upon us." He claimed that hoop-petticoats revealed pride in clothing, and "Is not Pride of Apparel an Evidence of a proud Heart, and that our uncircumcised Hearts are not yet humbled? May we not therefore fear that the Lord will punish as yet seven Times for our Sins?" The phrase "uncircumcised Hearts," which Franklin may have thought absurd in itself, occurs literally in Leviticus 26:41, and figuratively several times in Jeremiah alone (including 4:4, 6:10, and 9:25–26), thus emphasizing the burlesque of the jeremiad tradition.

All authorities, said the speaker, should suppress "so great an Evil." He asked that civil magistrates make the "wearing of Hoop-Petticoats" a punish-ment "of such as have proved themselves to be Whores." The abrupt, savage diction "Whores" is unexpected. That savage note is rarely found in early Amer-ican literature—except in Franklin's writings. The persona claimed that the punishment "might probably suppress two great Sins at once: And what more significant Mark or Badge can be given?" Ministers should declaim against the practice. Husbands "*(unto whom the Wife should be in subjection)* should sup-press it in the Wife." The proto-feminist Franklin believed such thinking pre-posterous. Near the conclusion the minister/persona absurdly equated little girls playing with hoops to wearing hoop-petticoats: "*Parents (whom Children should obey)* instead of encouraging their Children as soon as they can go alone to go with a Hoop, (as many shamefully do) should exert their Parental Authority to prevent it." The foolish persona ended with a biblical passage that seemed to travesty not only the minister's message but also, in this context, the Bible itself: "Isa.32.9,11. *Rise up ye Women that are at ease, hear my voice ye careless Daugh-ters, give ear unto my speech. Tremble ye Women that are at Ease, be troubled ye careless ones; Strip ye and make ye bare, and gird sackcloth on your Loins.*"

In addition to satirizing Solomon Stoddard, the jeremiad tradition, and in-appropriate proofs from the Bible, *Hoop-Petticoats Arraigned and Condemned by the Light of Nature, and Law of God* travestied the misogyny of passages from the Bible and the sexism of New England's religious traditions. It also echoed Franklin's epistemological skepticism regarding such phrases as "the Law of Nature," or "natural law," "natural rights," and other increasingly popular key-words, which had little meaning in themselves and were usually twisted to what-ever purpose the writer asserted. Both subjects had been introduced in Silence Dogood—feminism in No. 4 and concerns about the meanings of words in No. 14. No single sexual suggestion in *Hoop-Petticoats* is as clever as the statement in Dogood No. 5 that "Women are the prime Causes of a great many Male Enormities," but an amusing sexual suggestiveness ran through the entire piece.

Politics

In addition to religion, the other major continuing subject of the *Courant* was local politics, which appeared in the paper far more often than in any preceding American newspaper. For the 10 December *Courant*, "Tom Freeman" sent in a piece attacking flatterers of princes and rulers. The author criticized the clergy openly, at one point drawing attention to Cotton Mather as a sycophant to Governor Shute: "NOR is the Matter much mended, when *Clergymen* turn Flat-terers, and take upon them to prescribe and dictate to a Prince, or the Conse-quence like to be less pernicious to a People. I would hope that Clergy *in general* are good Men; but it is notorious, that many of them are but *Tygers* and *Wolves* in Sheeps Cloathing . . . The late Conduct of a noted Clergyman in our Nation has sufficiently evinc'd the Truth of this; and therefore it must be suppos'd, that no prudent Prince will take the Measures of his Administration from them."

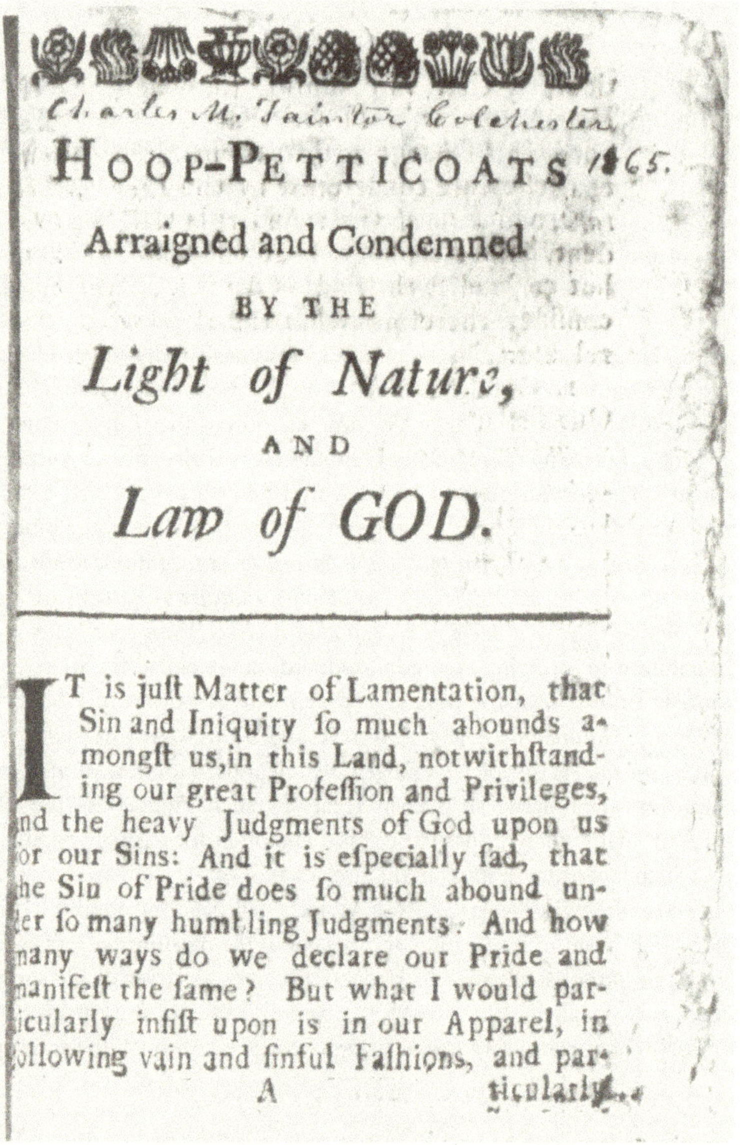

Charles M. Taintor Colchester

HOOP-PETTICOATS 1865.

Arraigned and Condemned

BY THE

Light of Nature,

AND

Law of GOD.

IT is juft Matter of Lamentation, that Sin and Iniquity fo much abounds a-mongft us, in this Land, notwithftanding our great Profeffion and Privileges, and the heavy Judgments of God upon us for our Sins: And it is efpecially fad, that the Sin of Pride does fo much abound under fo many humbling Judgments. And how many ways do we declare our Pride and manifeft the fame? But what I would particularly infift upon is in our Apparel, in following vain and finful Fafhions, and par-

A   ticularly,

Figure 14. *Franklin's* Hoop-Petticoats Arraigned and Condemned, by the Light of Nature, and Law of God *([Colophon:] Boston: J. Franklin, 1722) travestied a sermon by Jonathan Edwards's grandfather, the Reverend Solomon Stoddard, titled* An Answer to Some Cases of Conscience. *It was published in June 1722 and contained, at the end, in large capital letters, a condemnation of hoop petticoats as "CONTRARY TO THE LAW OF NATURE," for they had "SOMETHING OF NAKEDNESS" in them. Franklin had joked about hoop petticoats in Silence Dogood No. 6 (11 June 1722) and now, inspired by Stoddard, returned to the subject. In addition to satirizing Stoddard, the jeremiad tradition, and inappropriate biblical proofs,* Hoop-Petticoats Arraigned and Condemned *travestied the misogyny of biblical passages and the sexism of New England's religious traditions. Like a few passages in Silence Dogood, it is notable for its archetypal sexual suggestions. Courtesy, Library of Congress, Washington, D.C.*

Since Gardner had made the same point concerning Mather and Shute in his *Friendly Debate*, and since he often satirized ministers, I suspect he was Tom Freeman.

Another satire of the clergy appeared on 17 December and revealed a concern with class consciousness, a theme that appeared in the writings of John Wise, Nathaniel Gardner, and Thomas Lane. The essay, which began by noting that New England was famous for a strict observance of the Sabbath, objected to coaches being driven to and from church on Sunday. The seemingly religious essay turned into a sly satire on the hypocrisy of New England. In addition to causing a disturbing noise, the practice made coachmen work, thus profaning the Sabbath. In a series of objections and answers (suggesting the dialogues earlier used by Nathaniel Gardner), a mock naïf persona objected that since "great and rich Folks" follow the practice, it must be acceptable. The main persona answered that the offenders' estates are immaterial. But, the naïf replied, "if this be so great an Evil, why have we not been told of it from the Pulpit." The main persona said that if it had been done by the common people, "the Pulpits had rung with it long ago." Since Gardner's satire on eulogies of the wealthy (3 September 1722), his various burlesques of the Mathers and hackneyed sermon traditions, his use of the dialogue technique and his essays on the hypocrisy of seemingly religious New Englanders are all similar to this essay, I suspect he also wrote it.

"T. Freeman" (presumably the Tom Freeman of 10 December) said in the 24 December *Courant* that the New Hampshire legislature, due to the influence of Henry Care's book *English Liberties* (which James Franklin had just reprinted—a little indirect advertising pleasing to the booksellers who had commissioned it), insisted on examining the treasurer's accounts, thereby causing "the CHIEF" (i.e., the governor) to prorogue the convention "to some time in February next." The next *Courant* (31 December) announced Governor Shute's sudden decision to sail for England. The notice ironically declared that his abrupt departure has "depriv'd the Town of an Opportunity of showing those publick Marks of Respect, which are undoubtedly due to him for his WISE and JUST Administration." The printer emphasized the irony of Shute's furtive departure by printing it immediately following a dispatch from Williamsburg, Virginia, announcing the return of Colonel Alexander Spotswood, Virginia's former governor. About four miles prior to arriving in Williamsburg, "a Train of Nine Coaches and about 200 Gentlemen on Horseback" met him and conducted him to the governor's mansion, "where he was saluted with a Discharge of the Cannon; and at Night there were Bonfires, Illuminations, and other publick Marks of that Respect and Value which this Country has for a Gentleman, who had so long, and with so much Prudence and Justice, presided in the Administration." What a contrast!

Gardner's Seditious Essays

Franklin's sauciness was influenced by Nathaniel Gardner. The *Courant* went too far with Nathaniel Gardner's anonymous 14 January 1722/3 essay satirizing

New England's "Saints" as religious hypocrites, causing the gadfly Captain Christopher Taylor to break the bonds of secrecy concerning authorship. Gardner had demonstrated in his miser sketch (11 September 1721) that he could handle the "character" genre masterfully. Here, he outdid himself. The lead essay satirized the deceitful merchants who were always proclaiming their piety.[18] Such was the stereotypical hostile portrait of the Puritan (most brilliantly portrayed in Samuel Butler's *Hudibras*)—and of the Yankee. *Hudibras* was in the *Courant* office; Gardner no doubt also knew Edward Ward's *Trip to New England* (1699). Ward had written: "The Inhabitants seem very Religious, showing many outward and visible Signs of an inward and Spiritual Grace: But tho' they wear in their Faces the *innocence* of *Doves*, you will find them in their Dealings, as *Subtle* as *Serpents*."[19]

To find Yankee hypocrites delineated and attacked in a Boston newspaper amazed and confounded the authorities.[20] When the English Colonel Samuel Vetch wrote a piece a decade earlier satirizing New Englanders, he could not have it published in Boston.[21] Vetch's criticisms were by an outsider, not a native; Gardner's, written by one native and published by another, seemed to some New Englanders a betrayal. New Englanders resented his satire more than the lampoons by such English authors as Abraham Cowley, Samuel Butler, or Edward Ward. Franklin's satiric strokes, in Silence Dogood No. 9, were mild in comparison. Gardner wrote of New Englanders: "So if we observe them on the *Sabbath*, they are wonderful strict and zealous in the Sanctification of *that*; and it may be, are exact observers of the Evening before, and after it; or trace them to the solemn Assemblies, and who is there so devout and Attentive as they? Nay, sometimes they discover such distorted Faces, and awkward Gestures, as render them quite ridiculous. But yet, these very men are often found to be the grandest Cheats imaginable; they will *dissemble* and *lie*, *shuffle* and *whiffle*; and if it be possible they will overreach and defraud all who deal with them." Gardner accused New England Puritans of hypocrisy and suggested that any "man full of religious Cant and Palaver" was probably a knave. He called "religious knaves" the worst of all villains and said that "Publicans & Harlots will enter into the Kingdom of Heaven" before them.

Are there such religious knaves in New England? Yes, he answered. "A Few such Men, have given Cause to Strangers, (who have been bit by them) to complain of us Greatly; *Give me an honest Man* (say some) *for all a religious Man*." All New England, he said, "suffers for the Villainies of a few such Wolves in Sheeps Cloathing, and we are all represented as a pack of Knaves and Hypocrites, for their Sakes." Satires of New Englanders were abetted by the diction of Puritanism, in which the religiously "elect" or saved persons were called "visible saints." The phrase gave rise to the common derisive epithet, "New England Saints."[22]

Gardner also wrote the second 14 January essay, a mock jeremiad again burlesquing Cotton Mather's praise for Governor Shute and imagining that

Mather was now chastising New England for Shute's absconding: "And now, after all the *Mischief* that is come upon you, have you not very lately sinn'd *away* one of the most *Extensive Blessings* that ever you were possess'd of? Have you not compell'd a good spirited Governour, (you were told of it before*) to such an *inflexible Resolution,* as that (*when he returns*) he will make you *know he is your Governour*?" The asterisk referred to *News from Robinson Cruso's Island,* which Gardner attributed to Cotton Mather.[23] Following Gardner's second essay, a brief *Courant* piece commented on Shute's departure. The anonymous author (Captain Taylor, according to an advertisement in the 28 January *Courant*) recommended sending two political representatives to England to be present to contradict any falsehoods that Governor Shute might charge against the colony. Finally, a note asked whether the ministers' praying for Governor Shute was not in effect praying "for our Destruction?"

JAMES FRANKLIN CENSURED

The 14 January 1722/3 *Courant* angered the Massachusetts Council, which charged that the *Courant* "of this days date, Contains Many passages, in which the Holy Scriptures are perverted and the Civil Government, Ministers & people of this Province highly reflected on." The council appointed William Tailor, Samuel Sewall, and Penn Townsend to join with a committee from the House of Representatives "to Consider & Report, what is proper for this Court to do thereon." The House agreed and appointed Francis Fulham, Jonathan Remington, Ebenezer Stone, and Nathaniel Knowlton.[24] The following day, 15 January 1722/3, William Tailor presented the committee's recommendation to the council: "That the Tendency of the Said paper is to Mock Religion, & bring it into Contempt, That the Holy Scriptures are therein prophanely abused, that the Rev[e]r[en]d and faithful Ministers of the Gospell are Injuriously Reflected upon, his Majesties Government affronted, and the peace & Good Order of his Majesties Subjects of this Province disturbed by the Said Courant."

To prevent such an offense from occurring in the future, the committee proposed "that James Franklyn the Printer & publisher thereof be Strictly forbidden by this Court to print, or publish the New England Courant, or any Pamphlet or paper, of the like Nature, Except it be first Supervised, by the Secretary of this Province, and the Justices of his Majesties Sessions of the peace, for the County of Suffolk, at the Next adjournment be directed to take Sufficient Bond of the Said Franklyn for his Good Behaviour, for Twelve Months."[25] The council happily approved the order. The following day Edward Bromfield, a devout Old South Church member who must have known Josiah Franklin well, tendered the measure to the House. Divided, the House heatedly debated the report. Finally, the order passed by one vote.[26]

Frightened, Captain Taylor broke ranks with his fellow Couranteers. In the 21 January *News-Letter,* he advertised that he was not the author of the two first letters in the last *Courant,* that he "did never hear that those Letters were to be

Printed, or ever saw the Manuscripts; and that his first Knowledge of them, was, by his Reading the above said *Courant*, on Monday last." Unlike timorous Taylor, the Franklins and Nathaniel Gardner were fearless. On Monday, 21 January, they defied the order, and the *Courant* appeared as usual. The lead essay, by Nathaniel Gardner, expressed the surprise of "all Ingenious Foreigners who have traveled among us" (thus alluding to his essay on religious hypocrites the previous week) that New Englanders persisted in using the Bay Psalm Book when so many better versions were now available. As an example of the superiority of Isaac Watts's translation of the psalms, he printed two. Gardner selected ones that indirectly commented on the official actions against James Franklin. The fourth stanza of Psalm 56 follows:

> They wrest my Words to Mischief still,
>   Charge me with unknown Faults;
> Mischief doth all their Counsels fill,
>   And Malice all their Thoughts.

He also printed Psalm 58, which also could be read as an attack on Chief Justice Samuel Sewall. When the Reverend Ebenezer Pemberton was quarreling with Sewall in 1710, he had used the same psalm to blast Sewall.[27] Gardner no doubt knew of Pemberton's attack and relished echoing it.

The night before the *Courant* appeared, someone threw a libel into Samuel Sewall's doorway. The content of the libel is unknown, as is the author, but Sewall suspected it was someone who knew what the contents of the next day's *Courant* would be. He recorded in his diary on the twenty-seventh that "The Libel and the Courant look upon, and interpret, and sharpen each other." If Sewall was correct in supposing that the libel was connected with the *Courant*, it is more likely that Franklin rather than anyone else connected with the newspaper wrote it.

Sewall was surprised that James Franklin persisted in publishing the paper when he was sure to be jailed. Sewall noted in his diary on 21 January, the day the indirect satire on the judge appeared, "The Courant comes out very impudently." Under local news, the *Courant* printed the General Court's deliberations and the act forbidding James Franklin to print the *Courant*. The council seized the opportunity to silence James Franklin. On 24 January 1722/3, it ordered that a "Warrant for apprehending James Franklyn of Boston Printer" be issued and that he be bound over "to answer, at the next Assizes to be held for the Country of Suffolk, for his high contempt of the order of the General Assembly at the last Session." The court issued the warrant on 28 January. James Franklin, knowing he would be arrested, fled Boston. Later, defending himself in the 6 May 1723 *Courant*, he stated that he was in another government, more than sixty miles from Boston, when the order appeared and that he knew nothing about it until he "saw it in print." Undersheriff John Darrell searched in vain for him.[28]

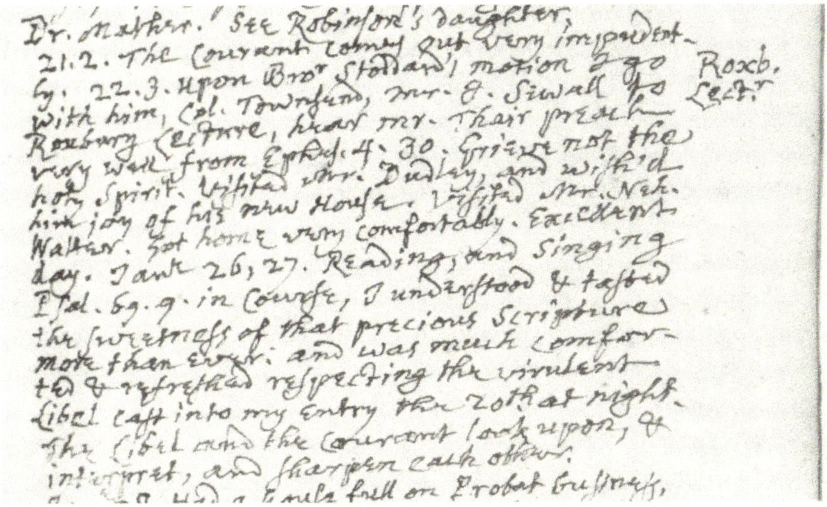
Dr. Mather.' See Robinson's daughter,
21.2. The Courant comes out very impudently. 22.3. Upon Bror Stoddard's motion I go Roxb.
with him, Col. Townsend, Mr. S. Sewall to Lectr
Roxbury Lecture, hear Mr. Thair preach
very well from Ephes. 4. 30. Grieve not the
holy Spirit. Visited Mr. Dudley, and wish'd
him joy of his new House. Visited Mr. Neh.
Walter. Got home very comfortably. Excellent
day. Janr 26, 27. Reading, and Singing
Psal. 69. 9. in Course, I understood & tasted
the sweetness of that precious Scripture
more than ever: and was much comfor-
ted & refreshed respecting the virulent
Libel cast into my Entry the 20th at night.
The Libel and the Courant look upon, &
interpret, and sharpen each other.

Figure 15. Samuel Sewall, the chief justice of Massachusetts, on Franklin and the New-England Courant, *Diary, 21 to 27 January 1722/3. After the 14 January* Courant *satirized religious hypocrites, the Massachusetts Council voted that the contents of James Franklin's paper had to be approved before the paper could be published. The assembly agreed by one vote. James Franklin, however, ignored the order, and Gardner published psalms in the* Courant *of 21 January which indirectly attacked Chief Justice Sewall, a leader of the council. Sewall noted in his diary: "21.2 [i.e., second day or Monday]. The Courant comes out very impudently." The night of the 20th, a calumny was thrown into Sewall's entrance. Sewall wrote in his diary for 26 and 27 January respecting "the virulent Libel cast into my Entry the 20th at night, the Libel and the Courant look upon, and interpret, and sharpen one another."*

Though the contents and the author of the libel are unknown, it seems more likely that the teenaged Franklin, rather than the older James Franklin or Nathaniel Gardner, would have written it. The following week a warrant was issued for the arrest of James Franklin, and Benjamin Franklin took over publishing the paper while his older brother hid from the authorities. Courtesy, Massachusetts Historical Society, Boston.

Franklin in Charge

With James Franklin away (and in hiding when he returned), young Franklin took charge of the *Courant* for the second time. Nathaniel Gardner had a living to make and a family to support; he could not take care of the day-to-day operation of the press. Besides, he was no printer. Franklin was now known by the Couranteers as the Silence Dogood author and as an excellent writer. Though James Franklin employed at least one journeyman printer and at least one other apprentice by this time, the well-coordinated and brilliant Franklin, just turned seventeen, had probably emerged as the best compositor and pressman in the shop. He now became the paper's primary editor and wrote the lead essay for 28 January 1722/3. In the *Autobiography*, Franklin said that while his brother was in hiding, "I had the Management of the Paper, and I made bold to give our Rulers some Rubs in it" (19). Previous biographers have assumed that Franklin referred to the four weeks in the summer of 1722 when James Franklin was in jail, rather than the several weeks from mid-January to mid-February 1722–23 while he was out of town and then in hiding.[29] The *Autobiography* confuses the two. Franklin began by talking about the earlier time, when James Franklin "was taken up, censur'd and imprison'd for a Month by the Speaker's Warrant," but concluded by recalling the later: "My Brother's Discharge was accompany'd with an Order of the House, (a very odd one) *that James Franklin should no longer print the Paper called the New England Courant*" (19). No wonder scholars have been misled.

The biographer Arthur Bernon Tourtellot said that no "Rubs" against the authorities appeared during the weeks in 1722 that James Franklin spent in jail. I agree. Franklin's only essay published during the four weeks from 12 June to 7 July was his literary satire on the New England funeral elegy, Silence Dogood No. 7. Though perhaps the best essay in the colonial American newspaper press to that date, it contains only indirect and minor "Rubs" against the authorities. The editors of the *Papers of Benjamin Franklin* (1:217) thought that Franklin referred to Silence Dogood Nos. 8 and 9. But they appeared after James Franklin was released from jail—and they were relatively tame. Though Dogood No. 8 (which came out two days after James Franklin was released) dealt with James Franklin's incarceration, it consisted almost entirely of an essay on liberty of speech reprinted from Trenchard and Gordon's *Cato's Letters*. Franklin could hardly have recalled the essay with pride. Dogood No. 9 (which came out two weeks later), on hypocrisy in religion and government, also contained mainly quotations from *Cato's Letters*. If the editors of the *Papers* are correct and the latter Dogood essay points only at the widely detested, recently deceased Governor Joseph Dudley, then it is pretty mild. But if I am correct in suggesting that its underlying butt is the powerful Chief Justice Samuel Sewall, it has considerable bite. In either case, however, the essay does not match Franklin's statement in the *Autobiography*, for it appeared on 23 July, not "During my Brother's Confinement" (A 19).[30]

Franklin's assertion that he "had the Management of the Paper" and "made bold to give our Rulers some Rubs in it" while his brother was confined matches perfectly with the 28 January "Rules" essay and the following one sent in by "Juba" on 4 February 1722/3 (both discussed below). Though James Franklin may have had some slight hand in the *Courant* even while in jail during the spring of 1721, Benjamin Franklin obviously edited the paper during late January and early February 1722/3. These two essays contain the most severe (and the latter contains the most open and direct) "Rubs" in the *Courant*. Unlike any earlier essays, these would have caused Franklin to be considered (as he recalled in the *Autobiography*) "in an unfavourable Light, as a young Genius that had a Turn for Libelling and Satyr" (A 19).

To be sure, even though James Franklin was hiding from the authorities, he could have found time to write essays and probably had the means to deliver them to Benjamin Franklin for publication; but the cool irony and the cutting satire of the 28 January *Courant* seem much more likely to have come from the young genius Franklin than his talented older brother.[31] Indeed, I believe that James Franklin is responsible for the rather graceless, outraged, and even somewhat confusing 4 February lead essay on King Alfred's hanging the judge who hung "Franckling."

"Rules" for Editing the *Courant*

The *Courant* for 28 January contained Franklin's essay on rules for editing the paper.[32] "Seeing your Courant is a Paper which (like the Primitive Christians) begins to be *every where spoken against*, it is our *humble Opinion* that it is high Time for you to think of some Method wherein to carry it on without ministering just Occasion of Offence to any, especially to the polite and *pious* People, of whom there are considerable numbers in this Land." The witty and highly original parenthetical comparison of the paper to the "Primitive Christians" admirably set the irreligious, mocking tone. The second paragraph began with a proverb: "It is a common saying; that it is a bad thing to have a Bad Name; when a Man has once got a bad Name, people are apt to misrepresent, and misconstrue whatever he says or does, tho' it be Innocent, nay, good and laudable in it self, and tho' it proceed from a good Intention, which is absolutely necessary to denominate any Action Good." Franklin pushes the logic beyond the expected conclusion, takes up underlying philosophical problems, and makes a nice discrimination.

In the third paragraph, Franklin (recalling Samuel Mather's attack on 15 January 1721/2) said that "many good people . . . say . . . there can be no good thing come out of that Paper." He claimed that discourses excellent in themselves "and strengthened by many Texts of Scripture, and quotations from the Works of the most Eminent Divines, who have great Names in all the Universities of Europe" are nevertheless condemned as "base and vile" when they appear in the *Courant*. Such discourses have been said to have a "wicked Tendency" and to be "written with a bad intention, with a design to mock and deride Religion, and the serious, conscientious professors of it." Franklin wanted to make the reader suspect that something was radically wrong with the "serious, conscientious professors" of religion who discover satire in works excellent in themselves and buttressed with Scripture and authoritative learning. Just as he did later (e.g., 27 April 1730), Franklin managed to lampoon religion and its "pious" professors at the very time he defended himself from the charge of satirizing them.

Franklin continued the persona's seeming reasonableness by saying he was "of Opinion that this matter has been strain'd a little too far, by persons whose Zeal is not sufficiently poized with Knowledge and Prudence." The tone is so reasonable ("of Opinion . . . a little too far") that one hardly realizes Franklin has said the *Courant*'s opposers are imprudent, stupid zealots. "Yet," he continued, "it may be very proper to lay before you some Rules, which if duly observ'd will render your Paper not only inoffensive, but pleasant and agreeable." Franklin had already used a variant of the "Rules" structure in his "Receipt to Make a New England Funeral Elegy" and later used it often, for example, in "Rules by Which a Great Empire May Be Reduced to a Small One" (11 September 1773).[33]

The first rule was to "be very tender of the Religion of the Country," for "The Honour of Religion ought ever to ly near our Hearts; nor should any thing grieve us so much as to see That reflected on, and brought into contempt." The underlying implication is that religion can easily be "reflected on, and brought into contempt." Franklin also implied that New England prided itself too greatly upon its religion (which he called "our strength and Glory"). Franklin had previously burlesqued New England provinciality in the Silence Dogood essays (especially No. 7, on the New England funeral elegy) and here reinforced Gardner's essay (the piece responsible for the order against the *Courant*) on New England Puritans as canting hypocrites. Rule two: "TAKE great care that you do not cast injurious Reflections on the Reverend and Faithful Ministers of the Gospel." The author claimed that "New-England may boast of almost an unparallel'd Happiness in its MINISTERS," for "take them in general, there is scarce a more Candid, Learned, Pious, and Laborious Set of Men under Heaven." Of course, the praise sounds not only a little too boastful but also dreadfully provincial. It burlesqued both the usual self-congratulatory praise of the Mathers by the Mathers and the third book of Cotton Mather's *Magnalia*, devoted to New England ministers' hagiography. Further, the rule particularly mocked Cotton Mather's diatribe to James Franklin, which had appeared in the 4 December 1721 *Courant*. Franklin continued by echoing an antimetabole that both James Franklin and Nathaniel Gardner had borrowed from John Williams: "But tho' they are the Best of Men, yet they are but Men at the best, and by consequence subject to like Frailties and Passions as other Men."

Franklin gradually allowed his underlying complaint about the ministers' excessive pride to become obvious: "And when we hear of the Imprudencies of any of them, we should cover them with the mantle of Love and Charity, and not profanely expose and Aggravate them." He indirectly charged that ministers and other "pious People" do just the opposite when speaking of the *New-England Courant* while, in fact, deliberately overlooking the ministers' "Imprudencies." He concluded the second rule: "Charity covers a multitude of Sins. Besides, when you abuse the Clergy you do not consult your own Interest, for you may be sure they will improve their influence to the uttermost, to suppress your Paper." Here the author not only said that the preachers' "multitude of sins" were overlooked but that the ministers were selfish and without charity. He even labeled them powerful instruments of prejudice.

Rule three stated, "BE very careful of the reputation of the People of this Land in general," for, the writer implied, these provincials are extraordinarily self-satisfied and proud. Then he burlesqued the usual message of the jeremiad (echoing Nathaniel Gardner in the 20 November 1721 *Courant*): "Indeed, it must be confess'd that there is a visible Declension and Apostasy among us, from the good ways of our Fore-Fathers." Franklin then reassured the audience that despite the declension, "a great number of serious Christians" dwell in New England. "Here it may be you will say, there has been more said and printed in some Sermons on this Head, than ever you published." Franklin joked and at the same time called the jeremiads boringly repetitive. "To this we Answer, that there are many things good and proper in the Pulpit, which would be vile and wicked in a Courant." The author implicitly called the situation absurd and indirectly argued that the paper should have a greater range of subjects than the pulpit. Most contemporaries would have agreed. Samuel Sewall, for example, thought it "inconvenient" for ministers to make science the subject of their discourse.[34] Franklin continued: "And what if all men are not molded according to your Humour? must you presently stigmatize them as Knaves and Hypocrites? Certainly on no Account whatsoever." But the Mathers had repeatedly called the Couranteers knaves and worse. The author not only complained against the double standard applied to the Couranteers but also lectured the ministers about how they should behave.

The fourth rule said, "By no means cast any Reflections on the Civil Government," for if you do, "we think you ought to smart for it." The author referred to James Franklin's former imprisonment and his present troubles: "And here we would caution you to avoid with care those Rocks, on which you have once and again almost suffered Shipwrack." Then Franklin burlesqued the old-fashioned interpretation of the biblical injunction to honor and obey one's parents as applying also to civil and religious authorities (the Geneva Bible glossed Exodus 20:12: "By the parents also is meant all that have authority over us"). "Furthermore, when you abuse and vilify Rulers, you do in some sense resist a Divine Ordinance, and he that resisteth shall receive to himself Damnation." The author followed this hyperbole with a satirical sentence revealing his egalitarian and Whiggish principles: "Princes, Magistrates, and Grandees, can by no means endure their Conduct should be scann'd by the meanest of their Subjects; and such may justly be offended when private Men, of as private parts, presume to intermeddle with their *Arcana*, and fault their Administration." Such sentiments were becoming outdated by the 1720s, especially in America, and the writer satirized the old-fashioned beliefs of Sewall and the Massachusetts General Court that prompted James Franklin's arrest. Franklin typically took the joke to another level, as he punned about investigating the "private parts" of the authorities, pruriently suggesting that the magistrates are as alarmed by anyone questioning their conduct as they would be by an investigation of their sexual parts.

The fifth rule advised the editor "to avoid Quotations from profane and scandalous Authors," especially Butler's *Hudibras*, for Butler lampooned "the Brethren" and "the Saints." The author referred to the locus classicus of anti-Puritan satire, reminding his readers that Puritans generally (and New Englanders) were regarded as laughingstocks by the majority in England. He also alluded to Gardner's essay on the New England character—the essay responsible for the printer's prosecution. The author asserted that it was "very unsuitable to bring in Texts of Sacred Scripture into your Paper." Next, "avoid the Form and Method of Sermons, for that is vile and impious in such a Paper as yours." Of course Gardner and Franklin had both travestied the usual jeremiad as well as the particular style of Increase and Cotton Mather. Franklin also alluded to Gardner's implied satires of judges by citing the psalms: "Nor is it suitable, as we conceive, to fill your Paper with Religious Exhortations of any kind; or to conclude your Letters with *the words of the Psalmist*, or any other sacred writer." The "words of the Psalmist" alluded to Gardner's satire of the magistrates and of Sewall. In effect, the *Courant* could print nothing either religious or secular, clearly an absurd position.

The last two rules ordained that specific persons should not be slandered and that the "worthy Society of *Gentlemen*, scoffingly call'd *The CANVAS CLUB*" should not have reflections cast upon them. For "some of them are Men of Power and Influence and (if you offend them) may contribute not a little to the crushing of your Paper." (The Canvas Club is otherwise unknown; could it have been a club of ship owners and ship captains?) Should the first six rules prove ineffectual, the last two, stressing the wealth and political power of those whom the *Courant* satirized, threatened the end of the saucy Couranteers. The "Rules" essay satirized the ministers, magistrates, religion, government, and provinciality of New England. For its length, perhaps no other satire on New England to that day was as wide-ranging or as severe.

FRANKLIN VS. SAMUEL SEWALL

The second 4 February essay contained the most direct attack on any magistrate in the *New-England Courant*. Everyone in New England would immediately have recognized that the person directly addressed—but not named—was seventy-year-old Chief Justice Samuel Sewall. The letter is prefaced by a brief paragraph signed "Juba" (Franklin used the name of the African prince of Numidia, which he knew from Addison's popular 1713 play *Cato*) claiming that the following "rough Draught of a Letter" has "lately been found in the Street." But the paragraph must have been written by a *Courant* editor, for it referred to the lead essay, saying that "this Case seems to be set in a true light" by the following letter. The letter opened: "Sir, I am inform'd that your Honour was a leading Man in the late Extraordinary procedure against *F[rankli]n* the Printer: And inasmuch as it cannot be long before you must appear at *Christ's* enlightned Tribunal, where every Man's work shall be tryed, I humbly beseech you, in the Fear of GOD, to consider and Examine, whether that Procedure be according to the *strict Rules of Justice and Equity?*"

This double-edged satire not only pointed out that Sewall would soon have to justify his actions before the ultimate judge, but it also echoed and mocked Increase Mather's condemnation of James Franklin: "I cannot but pity poor Franklin, who tho' but a Young Man, it may be Speedily he must appear before the Judgement Seat of God" (*Boston Gazette*, 29 January 1721/2). Juba/Franklin claimed: "It is manifest, that this Man had broke no *Law*; and you know, Sir, that where there is no Law, there can be no Transgression." The use of the apothegm is typical of Franklin, who cited the identical maxim in 1735 (2:119). The maxim contains a basic theme of "The Speech of Miss Polly Baker."[35] As pointed out above, Franklin may have been influenced by the essay on law in *Cato's Letters*, which Captain Taylor had cited in the *Courant* on 14 May 1722.

Franklin continued, "it is highly *unjust* to punish a Man by a Law, to which the Fact committed is *Antecedent*." And then he wrote an absolutely clear, well-balanced, and colloquial sententia: "The Law ever looks *forward*, but never *backward*." If the printer "had transgress'd any Law, he ought to have been presented by a Grand Jury, and a fair Tryal brought on." He told Sewall, "this Precedent *will not sleep*; and, Sir, can you bear to think that Posterity will have Reason to Curse you on the Account hereof!" In the last paragraph he recalled Sewall's role as a judge in the witchcraft trials and his confession of "Blame and Shame" at the Old South Church on 14 January 1696/7.[36] "I would also humbly remind your Honour, that you were formerly led into an Error, which you afterwards Publickly and Solemnly (and I doubt not, Sincerely) Confess'd and repented of."

Franklin's essays on "Rules" for editing the *Courant* and on Samuel Sewall's confession of repentance for his role in the Salem witchcraft trials, both written while James Franklin was in hiding, truly gave the Boston authorities some "Rubs."

THE SUBTERFUGE

Franklin reported in the *Autobiography*: "My Brother's Discharge was accompany'd with an Order of the House, (a very odd one) *that James Franklin should no longer print the Paper called the New England Courant*. There was a Consultation held in our Printing-House among his Friends what he should do in this Case. Some propos'd to evade the Order by changing the Name of the Paper; but my Brother seeing Inconveniences in that, it was finally concluded on as a better Way, to let it be printed for the future under the Name of *Benjamin Franklin*" (19). On Monday, 11 February, the *New-England Courant* appeared over Benjamin Franklin's name. A headnote explained: "The late Publisher of this Paper, finding so many Inconveniencies would arise by his carrying the

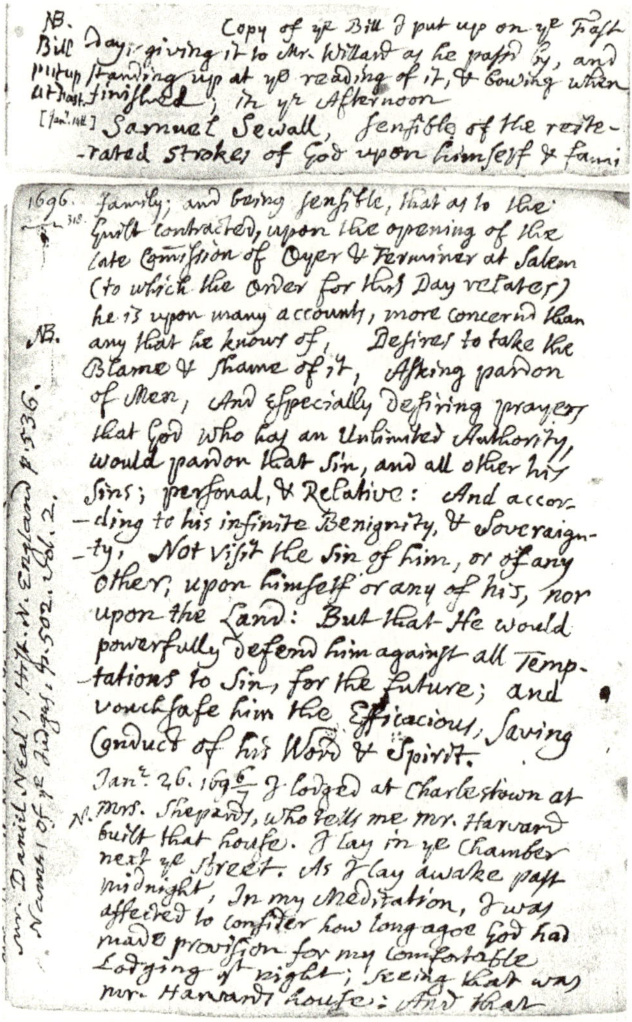

NB. Copy of ye Bill I put up on ye Fast
Bill day; giving it to Mr. Willard as he pass'd by, and
put up standing up at ye reading of it, & bowing when
at Fast finished; in ye Afternoon
[Jan. 14th] Samuel Sewall, sensible of the reite-
-rated strokes of God upon himself & fami
1696. family; and being sensible, that as to the
Guilt contracted, upon the opening of the
late Comission of Oyer & Terminer at Salem
(to which the order for this Day relates)
he is upon many accounts, more concern'd than
NB. any that he knows of, Desires to take the
Blame & shame of it, Asking pardon
of Men, And especially desiring prayers
that God who has an Unlimited Authority,
would pardon that Sin, and all other his
Sins; personal, & Relative: And accor-
-ding to his infinite Benignity, & Soveraign-
-ty, Not Visit the Sin of him, or of any
other, upon himself or any of his, nor
upon the Land: But that He would
powerfully defend him against all Temp-
-tations to Sin, for the future; and
vouchsafe him the Efficacious, Saving
Conduct of his Word & Spirit.
Jan. 26. 1696/7 I lodged at Charlestown at
N. Mrs. Shepard's, who tells me Mr. Harvard
built that house. I lay in ye Chamber
next ye Street. As I lay awake past
midnight, In my Meditation, I was
affected to consider how long agoe God had
made provision for my comfortable
Lodging yt night; seeing that was
Mr. Harvard's house: And that

Mr. Daniel Neal's Hist. N. England. p. 536.
Names of ye Judges; p. 502. Vol. 2.

Figure 16. Samuel Sewall's apology for his part in the Salem witchcraft trials, Diary, *14 January 1696/7. In the* New-England Courant *for 14 January 1722/3, James Franklin printed Nathaniel Gardner's satire on hypocritical New England Puritans. The satire so irritated the authorities that they decided to require that James Franklin's newspaper be approved before publication. James Franklin defied the order, printed another* Courant, *and fled before the sheriff could arrest him. In an essay of 4 February 1722/3, Benjamin Franklin writing as "Juba" attacked Chief Justice Samuel Sewall for being the main person behind the prosecution. Franklin reminded Sewall that he had been one of three persons most responsible for the Salem witchcraft trials in 1692 and that he had apologized for his mistake in the Old South Church on 14 January 1696/7. In effect, Franklin said that prosecuting James Franklin was another mistake for which the judge would be sorry.*

Sometime after 3 May 1720, when Sewall read Daniel Neale's History of New England, *2 v. (London, 1720), he jotted down in the margin a reference to the page where Neale gave the names of the judges in the witchcraft trials (v. 2., p. 502) and a reference to Neale's summary account of Sewall's public confession (v. 2, p. 536). Courtesy, Massachusetts Historical Society, Boston.*

Manuscripts and publick News to be supervis'd by the Secretary, as to render his carrying it on unprofitable, has intirely dropt the Undertaking. The present Publisher having receiv'd the following Piece, desires the Readers to accept of it as a Preface to what they may hereafter meet with in this Paper." Benjamin Franklin said that too many quarrelsome pieces had been published and that the *Courant* intended for the future to amuse and entertain the town. He claimed that "Pieces of Pleasantry and Mirth have a secret Charm in them to allay the Heats and Tumors of our Spirits, and to make a Man forget his restless Resentments. They have a strange Power to tune the harsh Disorders of the Soul, and reduce us to a serene and placid State of Mind." The persona of the editor would be "Janus," the common attribute/icon of printers, the god who looked two ways at once—a figure, that is, who could and did see both sides of a quarrel and one who would publish opposing views.[37]

With the *Courant* appearing under Benjamin Franklin's name, James Franklin was technically abiding by the order of the government. Benjamin Franklin explained in the *Autobiography*: "And to avoid the Censure of the Assembly that might fall on him, as still printing it by his Apprentice, the Contrivance was, that my old Indenture should be return'd to me with a full Discharge on the Back of it, to be shown on Occasion; but to secure to him the Benefit of my Service I was to sign new Indentures for the Remainder of the Term, which were to be kept private" (19). The strategy was flimsy, but since James Franklin had a number of supporters in the Massachusetts Assembly and since the assembly was loath to enforce censorship, the ruse succeeded.

James Franklin's Defense

The next day, 12 February 1722/3, James Franklin turned himself over to the Sussex County Court. The 6 May *Courant* supplied details. Though refused representation by the council, he was permitted to read a statement of five points, evidently prepared by his lawyer, which denied the right of the legislature and administration to find him guilty of any crime. According to James Franklin, only a trial by the courts could find him guilty of a crime. When the printer again asked if "his Lawyers might be allow'd to Plead," he was again denied and bound to his good behavior. He then posted a bond of £100: "on Condition that the s[ai]d James Franklyn shall be of Good Behaviour towards his Majesty and all his Liege People for the space of Twelve Months from this time." Two friends, "James Davenport of Boston Baker," who had married Franklin's sister Sarah on 3 May 1722, and "Thomas Fleet of S[ai]d Boston Printer" each put up a bond of £50 for his surety.[38]

A Couranteer sent an account of the proceedings to Andrew Bradford's *American Weekly Mercury*, the only newspaper outside Boston in the colonies. The Philadelphia *Mercury* of 26 February 1722/3 indicted the Massachusetts Assembly: "My Lord *Coke* observes, that to *punish first and then enquire*, the Law abhors, but here Mr. *Franklin* has a severe sentence pass'd upon him even to

the taking away Part of his Livelihood, without being called to make Answer."
The editorial then criticized the Massachusetts Assembly: "An Indifferent Person would judge by this vote against *Couranto*, that the Assembly of the Province of the *Massachusetts Bay* are made up of Oppressors and Bigots who make
Religion only the Engine of Destruction to the People; and the rather, because
the first Letter in the Courant of the 14th of January (which the Assembly Censures) so naturally represents and exposes the *Hypocritical Pretenders to Religion*." The *Mercury*'s editorial note concluded with a heavy-handed apocryphal
anecdote: "P. S. By private Letters from Boston we are informed, That the
Bakers there are under great Apprehension of being forbid baking any more
Bread, unless they will submit to the Secretary as Supervisor General and
Weigher of the Dough, before it is baked into Bread, and offered to Sale."

TITLES OF HONOR

The 18 February 1723 *Courant* featured Benjamin Franklin's anonymous spoof
on titles of honor and demonstrated his early egalitarianism. The essay repeated
two themes in the Port Royal *Logic*, the diversity of opinion among humans and
their dominant characteristic, pride. "Every Man sets himself above another in
his own Opinion." Franklin echoed that sentiment in his speech at the closing
of the Constitutional Convention on 17 September 1787. The other observation,
"there are not two Men in the World whose Sentiments are alike in every thing,"
also appeared in various guises throughout Franklin's life. The essay also echoed
his brother's words of 4 December 1721: "Hence it comes to pass, that the same
Passages in the Holy Scriptures or the Works of the Learned, are wrested to the
meaning of two opposite Parties, of contrary Opinions."

   In the essay, Franklin quoted William Penn's *No Cross, No Crown*, which
objected to what Penn called "hat honour." Franklin found Penn's opinions
whimsical and absurd. His first sentence, as quoted by Franklin, inanely argued:
"*Honour*, Friend, *says he*, properly ascends, & not descends; yet the Hat, when
the Head is uncover'd, *descends*, and therefore there can be no Honour in it."
Franklin perhaps remembered Penn's words when he wrote that honor ascends
rather than descends in his letter of 26 January 1784 satirizing the Order of the
Cincinnati. He concluded the *Courant* spoof of Penn by deriding all titles of
honor: "tho' Abraham was not styl'd *Right Honourable*, yet he had the Title of
Lord given him by his Wife Sarah," which made a member of the Old Janus
Club think she was entitled "to the Honour of *My Lady* Sarah; and Rachel being
married into the same Family, he concludes she may deserve the Title of *My
Lady* Rachel" (1:51–52). What nonsense! implied Franklin.

HIGH TIDE IN BOSTON

The most interesting 4 March piece was Franklin's news note on the extraordinary high tide at Boston. Filled with graphic details, the notice burlesqued the
Boston News-Letter's article of 28 February on the remarkably high tide. The

anonymous *Courant* author lampooned the logic used in the *News-Letter* account by piling one incredible explanation upon another in a manner that anticipated Franklin's satire of British news writers' nonsense about America (12:132–35). Meanwhile, revealing Franklin's rhetorical talent, the author buried the obvious explanation in a parenthetical remark: "(the Wind blowing hard at North-East)." At the same time, the enumeration of various superstitious possible causes and Franklin's use of Cotton Mather's unusual word *Hypothesimania* burlesqued Mather's credulity and his diction.[39] Evidently reflecting Dr. John Keill's *Examination of Dr. Burnet's Theory* (Oxford, 1698), the note mocked religious arguments by Thomas Burnet, Erasmus Warren, and William Whiston and revealed Franklin's early interest in the weather and his reading of scientific literature.[40]

Country Kitelic Verse

The 11 March 1723 *Courant* published an awful poem written the previous October by Major James Fitch of Canterbury, Connecticut, on the Connecticut apostasy. An introductory paragraph, which alluded to Silence Dogood's satire of the New England funeral elegy, set up the piece for ridicule. I suspect Franklin wrote the satire on Fitch. The other two persons who could have written it were James Franklin and Nathaniel Gardner. James Franklin, however, had come out of hiding less than a month earlier and was preparing for his libel trial (which took place on 7 May). It seems unlikely that he had either the time or inclination to write this humorous piece. Further, to judge by the competitive relationship between the siblings, James Franklin would not have complimented his younger brother by borrowing Silence Dogood's satire of Kitelic poetry as a referent and model. In addition, Fitch's poetry would have caught Franklin's attention, for it quoted the quartet that Nausawlander used as an epigraph.

Nathaniel Gardner could have written the prefatory letter to Fitch's poetry, but Gardner, I suspect, was "Hypercriticus," the poetic critic who first appeared in the 12 November 1722 *Courant*. (As I pointed out, Gardner's satire as "Rusticus" in *A Friendly Debate* had been one inspiration for Silence Dogood's criticism of the New England elegy.)[41] Though Hypercriticus/Gardner had, in turn, been influenced by Silence Dogood's satire and referred in the 12 November essay to Franklin's "Receipt to Make a New England Funeral Elegy," Hypercriticus did not reveal the thorough recollection of Silence Dogood No. 7 that this anonymous author possessed. Moreover, after being attacked in the 25 February paper by "J. R.," Hypercriticus replied in the 4 March 1722/3 *Courant*. If the author of the following week's satire on James Fitch were Hypercriticus/Gardner, he would probably have used that highly recognizable pseudonym.

In the introduction, the anonymous author/Franklin quoted John Dryden and John Norris on Pindaric verse, which "sometimes like an impetuous Stream" bears "down all before it." He found it also true of Kitelic poetry, "and a greater Honour is not due to *Pindar* than to the Immortal Dr. *H[erric]k*, the first Inventer of this sort of Verse, the Numbers of which are as boundless as those of the *Pindaric*." The author granted that Dr. Herrick's elegy on Mrs. Kitel was a wonderful example of the genre, yet Major James Fitch has "brought *Kitelic* Poetry to Perfection." In the future, Fitch's poem will be regarded as "a perfect Pattern for all *Kitelick* Poets." Then the satirist quoted the 148-line poem. Here are the first eighteen lines:

> Oh! how now alas, alas, what's come to pass
> In our Horizon?
> 'Tis strange for to tell, five Stars are now fell;
> And a very great one.
> The famous great Rector, a fine Director,   5
> To prevent Schisms and Heresy:
> However was devout, is now turned about
> To Episcopacy.
>   *Eliot, Johnson,* and *Hart,* did lately depart
> From the good old Way, in which their Fathers and they   10
> So long walked in:
> In which God did bless, Oh! with great Success!
> Was ever the like seen!
>   *Wetmore,* and *Whittelcie,* are turned to Episcopacy,
> And the Fellow *Brown,* wants he a fine Church Gown?   15
> And *Newhaven* is in Pain:
> But Oh! alas, it may soon come to pass,
> He is young and may return again.

Though truly dreadful, these lines illustrate the feelings of many elderly New Englanders concerning the Connecticut apostasy and their own Congregational beliefs. The old man's execrable verse spoke with the voice of old-time New England. The satiric preface concluded, I believe, Franklin's writings on the Connecticut apostasy.

The satire of Fitch, however, had an aftermath. The 21 June *Boston News-Letter* published a letter from Ebenezer Fitch complaining of the *Courant's* 11 March satire on the poetry of eighty-year-old James Fitch. In the next *Courant*, 24 March, Janus wrote an amusing reply. It seems unlikely that Benjamin Franklin wrote it. The condescending tone, satire of Ebenezer Fitch as a countryman, and emphasis on a printing error in the *News-Letter*, all seem uncharacteristic of the apprentice. Further, Janus speaks as the *Courant's* editor. Sometimes Franklin or Gardner adopted that persona (especially when James Franklin was away, in hiding, or busy preparing his legal defense), but James Franklin himself usually used it. In addition, the letter had a prefatory editorial comment, clearly by the same writer. James Franklin presumably was Janus. Ebenezer Fitch responded in the 27 June *News-Letter*, causing editor Janus to write another rejoinder in the 1 July *Courant*, in prose and verse (only James Franklin frequently wrote poems in the *Courant*), concluding: "*And had your* Dad *three Grains of Knowledge,* / *He ne'er had* bred you up at College."

Back in March the *Courant* advertised a poem on King George and the current ministry, *Gloria Britannorum*, published by James Franklin for N. Buttolph. Though still often mistakenly attributed to Francis Knapp, the poems were by some local youth not overburdened with poetic talent.[42] The following week (18 March) the *Courant* reported that two printed pamphlets were lately thrown about the streets, one titled *Truth and Day-light*, and the other *From the Town of Inquisition to the Great Don Pedro on Cruso's Island*. Neither is extant or recorded in the bibliographies, but both probably concerned the 11 March Boston elections. A second-rate jeremiad appeared as the lead piece in the 8 April *Courant*. The piece does not seem like a satire, though it is so bad that one might suppose it to be a mock jeremiad or a pastiche made up from various jeremiads.[43]

Timothy Wagstaff

Writing as "Timothy Wagstaff,"[44] Franklin appeared in the 15 April *Courant*: "The extravagant Notions which some Men entertain from the Influence of Education and Custom, may be thought worth Notice in your Paper, if we consider only, that the Sufferings of its late Publisher were owing in a great measure to his carrying it on in an *unusual Method*." The relativism is typical of Franklin. It had been a minor note in his satire on titles of honor. Later, in a letter to his parents (13 April 1738), he commented on "the unavoidable Influence of Education, Custom, Books, and Company upon our Ways of thinking." And in his speech at the close of the Constitutional Convention, he wrote, "when you assemble a number of men . . . you inevitably assemble with those men all their prejudices, their passions, their errors of opinion, their local interests, and their selfish views."

In the second sentence, Wagstaff revealed his class consciousness and his irritation with the social hierarchy by sarcastically referring to "some Gentlemen of the best Reputation in our Country." The body of the essay replied to the "Anti-Couranteer" criticism by showing how the Reverend Thomas Symmes (1677/8–1725), the respected author of *Utile Dulci, or A Joco-Serious Dialogue, Concerning Regular Singing* (1723), could be criticized on the same grounds. The excellent logic and humorous tone are Franklinesque. "Have you not often said, that the *Courant* offended GOD because it offended *good People*? And has not *he* (think you) offended many a weak Brother, almost as weak as your selves, by declaring against the *good old Way* of singing?" His comparisons between Symmes's techniques and those of the Couranteers are apt and convincing. The concluding lengthy quotation from the deistic essays of the notorious free-thinker Sir Thomas Pope Blount (1649–97) revealed Franklin's readings and beliefs. Timothy Wagstaff quoted Blount's opinion that some religionists "worship God just as the Indians do the Devil, not as they love him, but because they are afraid of him." A few years later, in Busy-Body No. 3, Franklin echoed the same passage from Blount: "(like the Worship paid by Indians to the Devil) rather thro' Fear of the Harm thou may'st do to them, than out of Gratitude for the Favours they have receiv'd" (1:121).

JAMES FRANKLIN'S FURTHER DEFENSE

On Tuesday, 7 May, the grand jury took up James Franklin's case. The previous day, the *Courant* outdid itself and mounted the most extraordinary press campaign for a public (though some contemporaries would have said *private*) cause to that date in American journalism. James Franklin no doubt drafted the long, three-page editorial, signed "Philo-Dicaios," on the printer's forthcoming trial, though it probably contained some revisions and contributions by the other Couranteers. It presented the printer's case. The first sentence asked if the proceedings against him were "consistent with *Justice* and the *Fundamental Laws* of our Nation." The charge against him "is *general*. It is said, that *the tendency of the said Paper is to mock Religion, and bring it into contempt*, &c., but no particular Passages are mention'd . . . so that we are at a Loss to know where the Offence lies, and Mr. *Franklin* must be innocent till his Offence is *known* and *prov'd*: And it has ever been accounted unfair to proceed against a Subject upon a *general Charge* of any Crime, without producing *particular Articles*." (Franklin echoed this reasoning in his "Half-hour's Conversation with a Friend" on 16 November 1733.) After citing two cases, the printer continued: "It is impossible for a Man to defend himself in such a Case, unless he knows what particular Words or Sentences are accounted *Treasonable, Seditious, tending to defame the Government*, &c. But in Mr. *Franklin*'s Case, the Gentlemen of the Council mention'd no particular Articles, nor did the House of Representatives desire any; and perhaps there may seem less need of it here, since he was not so much as call'd to answer for himself, or to discover the Authors of the several Letters in the Courant aforesaid, printed by him, as has always been usual in such Cases."

After citing Paul's trial (Acts 24–26) as a biblical parallel, Philo-Dicaios continued by ransacking Henry Care's *English Liberties* for ammunition, claiming that the Magna Charta itself, the "Bulwark of our Liberties," has sometimes been "but little minded by the Legislative Power." The author then claimed that the report of the committee left it "to the *Discretion* of Mr. Secretary, whether Mr. *Franklin* shall print (almost) *any thing* to get an honest Livelyhood by his Trade, to which he has serv'd his Time in the Country, and has an undoubted Right to live by, as well as the rest of his Fellow-Tradesmen." He then quoted the council's report and commented, "it is at the Secretary's Pleasure whether Mr. *Franklin* shall live or starve: He may disapprove of *every thing* he overlooks, and by Consequence Mr. *Franklin* can print *Nothing* with Safety, if the Secretary pleases to call it *of the like Nature* with the Courant. Mr. Secretary will not deny but that he has already refus'd to let him *Reprint* Part of a Letter from the *London Journal*; and if nothing must be reprinted here that is publish'd and allow'd of in *England* . . . it is not likely that the Secretary should allow of any thing of a political Nature wrote among our Selves."

Next, Philo-Dicaios gave an account of James Franklin's appearance before the court on 12 February, including his lawyer's written opinion. The author claimed that James Franklin was in another government when charged with contempt of court. He concluded with a quotation from John Hawles, *The Englishmans Right: A Dialogue between a Barrister at Law, and a Juryman*, emphasizing the necessity of trial by jury and denouncing condemnations without trials as illegal. In a postscript, Philo-Dicaios cited John Aislabie's speech to the House of Lords on 19 July 1721 (which James Franklin had used on 16 July 1722).[45]

Appearing before the grand jury James Franklin was charged with "high Contempt of an order of the Great and General Court or Assembly." After hearing the case, the grand jury returned the bill marked "Ignoramus," thus saying the evidence was insufficient to find the charge a true bill. The action against Franklin was necessarily dropped, and his friends Davenport and Fleet were released from their bond. The Couranteers and all their friends must have celebrated that night. The historian Clyde Duniway concluded, "The *Courant* case was of great importance in the development of freedom of the press, for it was the last instance of an attempt to revive and enforce censorship [by prior review] in Massachusetts."[46]

Abigail Twitterfield

Franklin's penultimate *Courant* essay appeared on 8 July. Samuel Sewall and other authorities of New England were the butt. The *Boston News-Letter* of 13 February 1731/2 had published Sewall's and John Winthrop IV's epitaphs on the Reverend Nathaniel Noyes. Sewall's poem was titled "On His Celebacy":

> Tho' Rome blasphem the Marriage Bed,
> And Vows of single life has bred;
> Chaste Parker, Stoughton, Brinsmead, Noyes,
> Shew us the odds 'twixt Force, and Choice:
> These Undefil'd, Contracted here,
> Are gon to Heav'n and Marri'd there.

As all Boston contemporaries knew, the references were to the Reverend Thomas Parker of Newberry, Lieutenant Governor William Stoughton, Reverend William Brinsmead of Marlborough, and Nicholas Noyes. Franklin's "Abigail Twitterfield" objected in the name of nine childless married women to a minister's sermon against barrenness. Abigail advised him to "deliver nothing but the plain substantial Truths of the Gospel." Twitterfield/Franklin also criticized the minister's logic: "for, by this manner of *Ratiocination*, one may as well argue thus: *Earthly Riches, the Confluence of outward good things, is a Blessing*; ergo, *Poverty is a Judgment and heavy Curse*." Abigail reminded the minister "that Four of our Reverend Pastors in this Town are deny'd the Blessing of Children." At the end, the persona self-mockingly claimed that "nineteen *Virgins . . .* are resolv'd to lead a Single Life, least they should incur the *Reproach and Curse of Barrenness.*"

Dingo

The 15 July *Courant* featured "Dingo," the first African American persona in the periodical press. Like Polly Baker later, Dingo was oppressed by the legal system. I believe Franklin was the author. Dingo cited the old proverb, "*Give a Dog an ill Name, and he is half hang'd.*" The sentiment is similar to the second paragraph of the "Rules" essay, which began, "It is a common saying; that it is a bad thing to have a Bad Name; when a Man has once got a bad Name, people are apt to misrepresent, and misconstrue whatever he says or does." Franklin was at the time increasingly alarmed by his growing infamy as a troublemaker and an atheist, and both the "Rules" essay and Dingo reveal that concern.

Dating the piece from "Susquehanah," Dingo said, "I am an aged Negro Man (and a Slave to a Gentleman in this Town) who took the Opportunity of a great Indian Dance which happened here lately, to sell a few Jills [variant of "gill"] of Rum of my own, in order to gain a little Money, since Age has render'd me almost incapable to do it by hard Labour." Dingo does not deny that he has broken the law; he merely claims that the law is severe in itself and particularly so in his case—Polly Baker said the same (15 April 1747). After Dingo refused to sell on credit to an Indian named Ben, Ben told his master Mr. Delator that Dingo was selling rum by the gill. Then, in a sentence of Faulknerian length, probably attempting to imitate the cadences of colloquial talk, Dingo said:

> Mr. *Delator* being a Man of a very tender Conscience, and not being able to bear that the Laws should be so notoriously abused, thought it his Duty to report this *evil Fame* of me to the Justice of the Peace for our Town; and he being under Oath to prosecute Law-breakers, issues out a Warrant to the Constable to take me up, and bring me before his Worship; who after hearing the Matter but cursorily, I having no Advantage of Council, my Master being also absent, order'd that I should pay the Cost of Court, and give 20 £ Bond with two Sureties, not to sell any more Rum by the *Jill* as long as I continu'd in this Town: Which Judgment I am not able to abide, as not having sufficient Estate to defray the Court Charges, and my Master (upon his Return) and other Friends upon whom I had a great Dependence, refused to be bound with me or for me; so that I am out of Goal only upon my *Parole*, which is a very *ticklish Condition*, and I can't expect that the Justices good Humour will last always: Therefore I publish this my *Manifesto*, in hopes some tender hearted Gentlemen will undertake to be bound with me, and relieve me from rigorous Justice. *Your aged Humble Servant, The Mark X of* Dingo.

That breathless sentence manages to conclude the appeal—and the skit fits perfectly in the lead column of the 15 July *Courant*, thus suggesting that a printer

Misteer JANUS,

YOU can't think how extraordinarily I was pleased at the hearing your Paper called the *Courant* (dated *April* the 15*th*) read, especially that part which tells of a famous Country Justice who sent a Warrant after poor *Jeremiah Levett*, because he *being of no good Name and Fame, did upon the* 19*th of* March *give out and utter reviling and blasphemous Words against a Justice of the Peace:* For here I took Notice in the first Place, that the old Proverb I had often heard, *Give a Dog an ill Name, and he is half hang'd*, was not made without reason: In the next Place, poor *Levett's* Case and mine are very much a-kin; and unless you had mentioned that particular Case, I doubt whether ever I should have found a Friend to represent my present pitiful plight to you; and I could never have done it my self, not having the Advantage of using a Pen.

In short, Sir, I am an aged Negro Man (and a Slave to a Gentleman in this Town)* who took the Opportunity of a great Indian Dance which happened here lately, to sell a few Jills of Rum of my own, in order to gain a little Money, since Age has render'd me almost incapable to do it by hard Labour; and an Indian Fellow named *Ben.* living with Mr. *Ephraim Delator*, applying to me for a Dram upon Trust, and I doubting his Credit, and refusing to let him have it, he was so highly exasperated, that truly he gave me an *ill Name* to his aforesaid Master *Delator*, and inform'd that I had sold Rum by the Jill. Mr. *Delator* being a Man of a very tender Conscience, and not being able to bear that the Laws should be so notoriously abused, thought it his Duty to report this *evil Fame* of me to the Justice of the Peace for our Town; and he being under Oath to prosecute Law-breakers, issues out a Warrant to the Constable to take me up, and bring me before his Worship; who after hearing the Matter but cursorily, I having no Advantage of Council, my Master being also absent, order'd that I should pay the Cost of Court, and give 20 *l.* Bond with two Sureties, not to sell any more Rum by the *Jill* as long as I continu'd in this Town: Which Judgment I am not able to abide, as not having sufficient Estate to defray the Court Charges, and my Master (upon his Return) and other Friends upon whom I had a great Dependance, refused to be bound with me or for me; so that I am out of Goal only upon my *Parole*, which is a very ticklesh Condition, and I can't expect that the Justices good Humour will last always: Therefore I publish this my *Manifesto*, in hopes some tender hearted Gentlemen will undertake to be bound with me, and relieve from rigorous Justice

Your aged Humble Servant,

The Mark × *of*

Dingo.

Figure 17. Dingo/Franklin, the first Afro-American persona in American journalism, New-England Courant, 15 July 1723. Earlier African American names in the newspapers, like Franklin's "Juba," did not present a recognizable African American persona but merely used a possible African name. Franklin portrayed the imagined plight of an older, illiterate slave who was being prosecuted by what, in his case, was a too-severe law.

Franklin frequently identified with the poor and with persons who were the victims of discrimination. Nevertheless, he owned slaves for many years and did not directly oppose slavery until he wrote "The Sommerset Case and the Slave Trade" (20 June 1772). For the second African American persona in American journalism, see Volume 2, Figure 7. Courtesy, Burney Collection, British Library.

wrote it. Dingo is a sympathetic character (similar to Franklin's persona "A. A." who was "old and lame of my Hands, and thereby uncapable of assisting my Fellow Citizens, when their Houses are on Fire" [4 February 1734/5]). Criticizing a double standard for rich and the poor before the law was a charge Franklin later made in "The Speech of Miss Polly Baker" (1747). Though Dingo is guilty, the law bears too hard upon him (another motif echoed in Polly Baker), for we know that unless someone is charitable (£20 was a considerable sum), Dingo could not possibly pay. The letter has thematic similarities, too, to Juba's 4 February 1722/3 attack on Samuel Sewall, another piece on the law's faults. (Though Juba, as pointed out above, refers to an African prince, the persona need not be an African American.) Furthermore, Franklin later used the pseudonym "Blackamore" (30 August 1733), the second time an African American persona appeared in the American periodical press. Dingo's piece is not up to the level of Franklin's later writing, for both the sarcasm aimed at the too-severe judge and the relatively high level of diction (e.g., *cursorily*) clash with the supposed speaker, a semi-literate person, but the themes are Franklinian and the persona is notable.[47]

Endings and Beginnings

A month before Benjamin Franklin ran away from Boston, Increase Mather died (Friday, 23 August 1723) at the age of eighty-five. All three Boston papers carried an obituary, though the *Courant*'s was the shortest. Two weeks later (9 September) the lead *Courant* essay, which I suspect Nathaniel Gardner wrote, questioned the ancient principles and practices of church order and discipline in New England, saying that Benjamin Colman first criticized them as narrow and defective and that others had done so since. That essay followed two earlier discussions of early New England religion: a 6 May *Boston Gazette* article claimed that New England Congregational churches were historically composed of separatists, to which a 30 May *Boston News-Letter* essay replied that the early New England ministers were not separatists but only wanted their own "purer worship."[48]

The literary historian Perry Miller dated the end of classic New England Puritanism in the 1720s, with the deaths of four ministers (Increase Mather [1723], Cotton Mather [1728], Solomon Stoddard [1729], and Edward Taylor [1729]), the apostasy of the Connecticut ministers (1722), and the advent of Benjamin Franklin and the *New-England Courant* (1721). Miller concluded: "Samuel Sewall, exercising to the last his sense of the symbolic, stretched his life into the hundredth year of Massachusetts Bay, and died on New Year's Day, 1730."[49] The poet Edward Taylor had something of the same insight regarding the end of New England Congregationalism. As a student at Harvard, he had elegized Richard Mather (d. 1669); now, about September 1723, he composed four drafts of an elegy on Increase Mather. Each mentioned the Reverend Timothy Cutler, and the first and last ones attributed Mather's death to the apostate:

> But Cutler's Cutlary gave th'killing Stob.
> Custler consider Sure Christs word stands true.
> Ev'n it, or else thyself shall Surely rue.
> And seeing Gods word is true, repent, & dread,
> Mans frothy brains can't Helmet thy proud head.
> Christs wounded Saints & Churches have their stings
> Which ere't be long will make Sinners within
> To Smart: repent then e'er it be too late
> Less thou eternally smart in the horrid Lake.[50]

I agree that the end of classic American Puritanism can also be dated from the start of James Franklin's *New-England Courant* in 1721, though it was foreshadowed by the appointment of the cosmopolitan Reverend Benjamin Colman to the Brattle Street Church in 1699. Colman brought the new fashions of the Augustan intellectual and literary world to Boston. Though James Franklin may have been considered an outsider to Boston's establishment, the *New-England Courant* was succeeded by the *New England Weekly Journal*, 1727–41, edited in its early years primarily by Mather Byles, grandson of Increase Mather and nephew of Cotton Mather. The *Weekly Journal*, like its predecessor, contained the urbane tones and neoclassic prose styles of eighteenth-century London that the *Courant* had introduced.

FRANKLIN ABSCONDS

Franklin tells in the *Autobiography* that a "fresh Difference arising between my Brother and me, I took upon me to assert my Freedom, presuming that he would not venture to produce the new Indentures" (19–20). James Franklin could not point out that the canceled indenture with his young brother was fraudulent or that the apprentice had signed another secret indenture, for that testimony would open James to court action as the actual printer of the *New-England Courant*. In his *Autobiography*, Franklin ruminated: "It was not fair in me to take this Advantage, and this I therefore reckon one of the first Errata of my Life: But the Unfairness of it weigh'd little with me, when under the Impressions of Resentment, for the Blows his Passion too often urg'd him to bestow upon me. Tho' He was otherwise not an ill-natur'd man. Perhaps I was too saucy and provoking" (20). In 1723 Franklin was seventeen and his brother was twenty-six. The nine-year difference in their ages was no longer so great as the difference between a twelve-year-old untrained boy and a twenty-one-year-old journeyman. No doubt the teenager treated his brother with less deference and more arrogance than he had five years earlier. Judging from the last *New-England Courant* in Franklin's personal file (Monday, 16 September 1723),[51] he left his brother sometime after 16 September but before 23 September, when the next *Courant* appeared.

James Franklin knew that his brother was now an expert printer and assumed that he would look for work as a journeyman in Boston, so James Franklin asked the other Boston printers not to hire him. John Allen, Thomas Fleet, Bartholomew Green, and Samuel Kneeland agreed. Finding Boston closed to him, Franklin resolved to go to New York, the nearest town with a printer. "I was the rather inclin'd to leave Boston, when I reflected that I had already made my self a little obnoxious to the governing Party; and from the arbitrary Proceedings of the Assembly in my Brother's Case it was likely I might if I stay'd soon bring my self into Scrapes; and farther that my indiscrete Disputations about Religion began to make me pointed at with Horror by good People, as an Infidel or Atheist" (A 20). The sensitive adolescent found that his publishing and his private Socratic arguments had ostracized him from the good people of the town.

Franklin had insufficient money for the fare to New York, but he had a large library, so he sold a number of books. Then further problems arose: "My father now siding with my Brother, I was sensible that if I attempted to go openly, Means would be used to prevent me. My friend [John] Collins therefore undertook to manage a little for me. He agreed with the Captain of a New York Sloop for my Passage, under the Notion of my being a young Acquaintance of his that had got a naughty Girl with Child, whose Friends would compel me to marry her, and therefore I could not appear or come away publickly" (A 20). Franklin was "taken on board privately," and off he sailed. The 30 September 1723 *Courant* advertised: "James Franklin, Printer in Queen-Street, wants a likely lad for an Apprentice."

†*† James Franklin, Printer in Queen-Street, wants a likely lad for an Apprentice.

BOSTON: Printed and ſold by BENJAMIN FRANKLIN in Queen-Street, where Advertiſements and Letters are taken in. Price 4 d. ſingle, or 12 s. a Year.

Figure 18. To replace Franklin, James Franklin advertised for "a likely lad for an apprentice," New-England Courant, *30 September 1723. Courtesy, Massachusetts Historical Society, Boston.*

NINE

Assessing Franklin as a Youth,
to Age Seventeen

But being still a Boy, and suspecting that my Brother would object to printing any Thing of mine in his Paper if he knew it to be mine, I contriv'd to disguise my Hand, and writing an anonymous Paper I put it in at Night under the Door of the Printing-House.—A18

FRANKLIN CONFESSED TO ONLY ONE AMBITION: when he told in the *Autobiography* how he taught himself to write by imitating the *Spectator*, he concluded: "By comparing my Work afterwards with the original, I discover'd many faults and amended them; but I sometimes had the pleasure of Fancying that in certain Particulars of small Import, I had been lucky enough to improve the Method or the Language and this encourag'd me to think I might possibly in time come to be a tolerable English Writer, of which I was extreamly ambitious" (14). By the time he ran away from home and Boston, Franklin had demonstrated a literary ability superior to any Couranteer and perhaps to anyone in America. It is extraordinary that he wrote the first essay series in America at age sixteen and surprising that he used a feminine persona, Silence Dogood. Where are the feminine personae of the great English essayists of the eighteenth century? Women make occasional appearances in Addison and Steele, though rarely as speakers, and feminine personae are absent from the works of Franklin's slightly younger contemporary, Dr. Samuel Johnson. It is also extraordinary that Franklin used an African American persona.

As a writer, Franklin was precocious and brilliant. The trouble was, he knew it. The *Autobiography* testifies that the adolescent was saucy, provoking, proud, and rebellious. He had an arrogant streak; the theft of the workmen's stones to build a fishing pier showed it (A 7–8). Disregarding the rights and property of others, he even tried to justify the theft when his father took him to task. The headstrong boy thought himself more important than the builders.

Since Franklin's father intended "to devote [Franklin] as the Tithe of his Sons to the Service of the Church," Franklin entered grammar school at age eight. He was taken out, however, at the end of the year, even though he had progressed through two classes and been placed with a third for the following year (A 6–7). Franklin was bitterly disappointed with his father's decision. His

ferocious private course of study attempted to substitute self-education for formal education. Several years later, satirizing Harvard (Silence Dogood No. 4),
he indirectly revealed his resentment. His 1788 comment on his honorary degrees, "Thus without studying in any College I came to partake of their Honours" (A 130) seems, even at age eighty-two, still to reveal some anxiety about
his unusual education. His frequent derogation of the classics—"the quackery
of literature"—he called them on 12 June 1789—derived from his being denied
a college education. Though he learned Latin in his thirties (after studying German, French, Italian, and Spanish), he compensated for his feelings of inferiority
and insecurity concerning the classics by scorning them.

Franklin's interest in science and his inventiveness also appeared when he
was a youth. Franklin read the available scientific books and pamphlets and,
when he could, applied that knowledge to his environment. He was curious
about numerous things. He minutely observed such natural objects as seaweeds
and tiny crustacea. He experimented with swimming strokes and mastered those
in the standard book on swimming. He designed swim flippers and played with
kite floating. An interest in natural philosophy, its underlying principles, and its
possible uses remained with him throughout his life.

His father's trade did not appeal to Franklin (boiling fats and making soap
and candles was a hot, stinking job). Like many boys, he dreamed of adventure
and wanted to be a soldier; later, he thought of running away to become a sailor;
but finally, as a twelve-year-old, he reluctantly attempted the trades his father
wanted him to try—a cutler first, then a printer. Apprenticed to his older
brother James, Franklin no doubt secretly thought that if he could not stand the
printing trade, he would run away to sea. Fortunately, being a printer had numerous satisfactions, though his relations with James degenerated as Franklin
moved through his teens. By 1723 the seventeen-year-old probably thought he
was a better writer than James. Perhaps, too, Franklin came to think that he was
the better printer. He had achieved the skills of a superior journeyman printer
before leaving Boston. (As we will see, he belittled the craftsmanship of the
Philadelphia printers Samuel Keimer and Andrew Bradford and was recognized
in London as an excellent pressman and compositor.)

When Franklin quit working for his brother, his father Josiah sided with
James. Franklin's rebellion against both his brother and father promised ill for
the future. On the other hand, who would want to put up with physical beatings? Though Franklin said that running away was among his first errata in his
life, he also justified the action, saying that James's "harsh and tyrannical Treatment of me might be a means of impressing me with that Aversion to arbitrary
Power that has stuck to me thro' my whole Life" (A 20, 18–19). Since Franklin
wrote this in 1771, he was implicitly comparing James Franklin's severity toward
him to the British government's actions in the Stamp Act of 1765, the Declara-
tory Act of 1766, and the Townshend Acts of 1767. Implicitly, Franklin personified America's resentment of British imperiousness.

Franklin manifested his adolescent arrogance in libeling and satirizing Boston's authorities, not only the ministers (especially Cotton Mather) but also the

magistrates (especially Samuel Sewall). He earned a reputation as an overbold troublemaker—someone outside the bounds of respectable society. The self-justifying Franklin conceded in the *Autobiography* that he "had already made myself a little obnoxious to the governing Party" (20). To the sensitive young Franklin, who was conscious of this infamous reputation, it was a good reason to leave Boston and start over. His lampooning was, according to Franklin, a trait that his father advised him against when he returned to Boston in 1724: "My Father . . . gave his Consent to my Returning again to Philadelphia, advis'd me to behave respectfully to the People there, endeavour to obtain the general Esteem, and avoid lampooning and libelling to which he thought I had too much Inclination" (A 31). It would be more than another decade, however, before Franklin could heed his father's advice.

Even as a boy, he wanted to do good, and that was one reason for his choice of the pseudonym "Silence Dogood." The Silence Dogood essay on the support of poor widows and the one on temperance testify to that ambition. Franklin also sympathized and identified with those persons subject to society's prejudice. The intellectual and legal bias against women was part of the reason for his adopting the first feminine persona in American journalism, and the prejudice against blacks was partially responsible for Franklin's creating the first African American persona, Dingo.

As a Boston youth, Franklin demonstrated facets of his genius and his desire to do good, but he also showed a number of traits that he had to overcome to have a happy and successful life. Though he had become a brilliant writer and an expert printer and though he had studied and learned a great deal, he had failed miserably in several key personal relations, especially with his brother and with the town's religious and sectarian authorities. He noted in the "Outline" for the *Autobiography*, "Costs me nothing to be civil to inferiors, a good deal to be submissive to superiors" (205); that was even truer when he was an adolescent and had few "inferiors" but numerous "superiors." He frequently manifested resentment about his situation. When he ran away in 1723, there was little reason to think that he would achieve more than his friend John Collins, who "was much respected for his Learning by several of the Clergy and other Gentlemen, and seem'd to promise making a good Figure in Life" (A 32). But young persons of great promise are common, and like so many others, Collins disappeared without a trace. If knowledgeable contemporaries in 1723 Boston had been asked who among the Boston adolescents had the greatest future, the replies might well have included Mather Byles, Samuel Mather, and Isaac Greenwood. No one would have named Franklin. When the ostracized and rebellious youth ran away at age seventeen, his personal problems outweighed his promise.

Franklin's worst fault concerned religion. The religious satires, especially the letters by "Jethro Standfast" and "Nausawlander" (8 and 29 October 1722), were too bold. In Puritan Boston, he acquired an abhorrent reputation. He recalled that he confounded his religious opponents with the Socratic method, which he found "safest for my self and very embarassing to those against whom I used it." He delighted in it and practiced it continually. He grew "artful and expert in drawing People even of superior Knowledge into Concessions the Consequences of which they did not forsee, entangling them in Difficulties out of which they could not extricate themselves, and so obtaining Victories that neither my self nor my Cause *always* deserved" (A 15–16; emphasis mine). Though Franklin recommended diffidence in conversation and argument no less than four times in the *Autobiography*, he could not practice it as an adolescent. The lesson came hard for him, for he wanted to win. He confessed in the *Autobiography* that he failed. To Franklin, who valued and respected ordinary people, the reaction of Boston's citizens to his reputation as a freethinker caused him acute discomfort. But he could not refrain from satirizing and burlesquing religion. Indeed, years later, when writing the above passage in the *Autobiography*, the penultimate word in the quotation, *always*, suggested that he still believed his early iconoclastic religious opinions were often right. By the time he wrote that in 1771, he had taken to heart Poor Richard's observation: "Singularity in the right, hath ruined many: Happy those who are Convinced of the general Opinion" (7:86).

As a boy and young man, Franklin was tall, muscular, well-coordinated, and athletic. Perhaps he was the best swimmer in Boston. He delighted in strenuous exercises like swimming and in leading his friends into "scrapes." Slightly later anecdotes, like his pitching John Collins "head-foremost into the River" (A 33) or carrying "up and down Stairs a large Form of Types in each hand, when others carried but one in both Hands" (A 45–6) show that he was muscular. He even boxed as a boy: he recalled on 7 March 1782, "when I was a boxing boy, it was allowed, even after an adversary said he had enough, to give him a rising blow." At age seventeen he was probably about five feet nine inches tall with brown hair and hazel eyes. The bumptious upstart still had some growing to do, physically and emotionally. He had especially to conquer his sense of superiority.

Franklin frequently revealed his debt to his New England background. The preceding chapters have connected various passages from his later life and writings with his youth in Boston. Further examples will appear throughout the biography. Let me here cite just two. As befitted a New England Puritan, Franklin learned the Bible as a child. Throughout his life, he cited appropriate passages from memory. Hundreds of biblical references occur in his writings. He was particularly fond of the Old Testament wisdom literature, especially proverbs. He also called on his knowledge of biblical tones, prose rhythms, settings, and names in his writings, for example in his two biblical imitations of 1755, "A Parable against Persecution" and "A Parable on Brotherly Love." Second, when he organized a voluntary militia association during King George's War, he remembered the fast days of his youth and "propos'd" to the government officials "the Proclaiming a Fast, to promote Reformation, and implore the Blessing of Heaven on our Undertaking. They embrac'd the Motion, but as it was the first

Fast ever thought of in the Province, the Secretary had no Precedent from which to draw the Proclamation. My Education in New England, where a Fast is proclaim'd every Year, was here of some Advantage. I drew it in the accustomed Style, it was translated into German, printed in both Languages and divulg'd thro' the Province. This gave the Clergy of the different Sects an Opportunity of Influencing their Congregations to join in the Association" (A 110–11).

Besides the religious, social, and cultural influences on the child and adolescent, numerous individuals Franklin knew in Boston affected him later, both directly and indirectly. The influence of his parents, his brother James, and Nathaniel Gardner will reappear in the following chapters. I suggested above that the Reverend John Wise was a continuing influence on Franklin's politics and writing. Wise, like Defoe in *An Essay Upon Projects*, was also a projector of economic good for his country. In the 1740s, when Franklin became the primary single backer of new paper mills in Pennsylvania and the surrounding area, he may have remembered John Wise's urging that a paper mill be established near Boston: "some thousands of Pounds [of paper] is Imported in a Year in this one Commodity, which would be prevented by the erecting a Mill our Selves, and the cost would be very small. Considerably less than a thousand Pounds will set it to work, and by this means thousands of Pounds would be raised out of the Streets, and out of the Dust: For now the Rags which would then be greedily and Industriously pickt up by the poor People, lay and rot."

Other influences, both positive and negative, will be mentioned throughout all volumes of the biography. I wonder, for example, if Franklin did not learn from the quarrels and sneers that Cotton Mather occasioned when he insisted on praising himself and signing himself "D. D. and F. R. S." Franklin knew the numerous jibes at Mather. On the other hand, Samuel Willard customarily signed himself "Teacher of a Church in Boston" and was frequently praised for his modesty. Did such early memories cause Franklin, even after receiving two honorary doctorates, to sign himself "Benjamin Franklin, Printer"?

Finally, Franklin's own attitude toward himself, even at sixteen, was partially amused and mocking. Silence Dogood was a version of Franklin. When Silence confessed to a feeling of "unlimited Superiority over her Fellow-Creatures," Franklin burlesqued himself. Silence Dogood fancied herself "a Queen from the Fourteenth to the Eighteenth Year of my Age, and govern'd the World all the Time of my being govern'd by my Master." King Franklin, the apprentice, did the same, recognized the absurdity of his daydream, and spoofed himself.

PART II

Adrift: Age Seventeen to Twenty-four
1723–1730

TEN

The Runaway

I have been the more particular in this Description of my Journey, and shall be so of my first Entry into that City, that you may in your Mind compare such unlikely Beginning with the Figure I have since made there.—A 20

FRANKLIN'S HAS BEEN THE MOST POPULAR autobiography in the world since its 1790 publication. Its account of his journey to Philadelphia and first impressions of the town are touchstones in American literature. Leaving Boston, "we had a fair Wind, in three Days I found my self in New York near 300 Miles from home, a Boy of but 17, without the least Recommendation to or Knowledge of any Person in the Place, and with very little Money in my Pocket" (A 20). To move the story quickly, Franklin temporarily omitted an interesting incident that called for an ironic reflection. Becalmed the second day off Block Island, Rhode Island, the sailors and passengers "set about catching Cod and haul'd up a great many." The vegetarian Franklin was tempted and succumbed: "Hitherto I had stuck to my Resolution of not eating animal Food; and on this Occasion, I consider'd with my Master Tryon, the taking every Fish as a kind of unprovok'd Murder, since none of them had or ever could do us any Injury that might justify the Slaughter. All this seem'd very reasonable. But I had formerly been a great Lover of Fish, and when this came hot out of the Frying Pan, it smelt admirably well. I balanc'd some time between Principle and Inclination: till I recollected, that when the Fish were opened, I saw smaller Fish taken out of their Stomachs: Then, thought I, if you eat one another, I don't see why we mayn't eat you."

A lover of proverbs, Franklin knew "Big fish eat little fish," a saying that reflected the Hobbesian view of life as warfare and anticipated the Darwinian survival of the fittest.[1] The adult writer of the *Autobiography* implicitly set up an opposition between the view of life as a struggle and the prophecy in Isaiah 2 of the lion lying down with the lamb. Idealism lost the struggle. "I din'd upon Cod very heartily and continu'd to eat with other People, returning only now and then occasionally to a vegetable Diet." He ironically observed that "Inclination" would invariably win out over "Principle" because people could always press that most treacherous and versatile of human resources, reason, into play. "So convenient a thing it is to be a *reasonable Creature*, since it enables one to find or make a Reason for every thing one has a mind to do" (A 35).

Like Jonathan Edwards,[2] Franklin believed that the reason followed the inclination of the passions. He had cited Ovid's locus classicus of the voluntarist
position, "Video meliore proboque Deteriora sequor" (I see and approve the
better course; I follow the worse), in Silence Dogood No. 14 (8 October 1722).
He surely knew the version in Romans 7:19: "The good that I would I do not:
but the evil which I would not, that I do." Since he was interested in everything
Mandeville wrote, Franklin no doubt read *An Enquiry into the Origin of Honour*
shortly after its appearance in 1732, which contained the statement, "all human
creatures are swayed and wholly governed by their passions, whatever fine notions we may flatter ourselves with." By the time he recounted eating the cod in
1771, Franklin had also read David Hume and may echo him: "Reason is, and
ought only to be the slave of the passions, and can never pretend to any other
office than to serve and obey them."[3] Mandeville and Hume, however, seem
brusque and pedantic.

Franklin's voice is amused at human frailty and at himself, tinged with sympathy for the human beings who lie to themselves in pursuit of their desires,
and ironic about his own complicity in continuing the round of life as struggle.
Adding to the self-satire, Franklin uses reason to burlesque reason. He knew
that the persons from whom he hoped to solicit opinions of the autobiography
in manuscript (Richard Price and Benjamin Vaughan in England; the duke de
La Rochefoucald and Louis Le Veillard in France) would recognize the anecdote
as a contribution to the long history of the debate on reason versus the passions.
They would recognize his anecdote as a statement of his position in the continuing debate and as a way of bringing the philosophical quarrel into ordinary life.
The limitations of reason was a continuing theme throughout Franklin's life.

The Journey to Philadelphia

Franklin wrote that he arrived in Philadelphia on a Sunday morning in October
1723, but when he described the trip in 1771, he had forgotten the exact date.
Nevertheless, there have long been good clues for deducing it. The last *Courant*
in Franklin's personal file of the *New-England Courant* was 16 September. Examining the Boston papers, we find that the only boats that left Boston for New
York between early September and late October were William Beckman's, clearing out on 14 September, and Arnout Schemerhoorn's *Speedwell*, clearing customs and sailing on 25 September. Since Franklin was still in Boston on the
sixteenth, he could not have sailed with Beckman. Since James Franklin knew
before 30 September when he advertised for a "likely lad" to replace Franklin
that the apprentice had left Boston, Franklin evidently sailed with Schemerhoorn.

In 1980, Claude-Anne Lopez, an editor of the *Papers of Benjamin Franklin*,
examined a series of jottings on the back of a 29 November 1783 letter from
Franklin's French banker, Ferdinand Grand, and she hypothesized that the jottings related to Franklin's 1723 journey to Philadelphia. In Passy, France, Frank-

lin had within the past year received letters from Abel James and Benjamin Vaughan urging him to continue his autobiography (he had written part 1 in 1771) and he took it up again sometime in 1784 (A 91, 182). Sometime after receiving Grand's letter, Franklin came across the day and date of Monday, 23 September 1723, and recalled that was about the time he ran away from Boston. With that date before him, he jotted down the dates and places of his journey to Philadelphia on the back of Grand's letter. Scribbling hurriedly, he noted the days and dates ("T[uesday]—24; W[ednesday] 25," . . .), until after "Sund—29" he wrote "Monday— 30," and "Tuesd—31," then remembered that September had only 30 days. Still writing hurriedly, he mistakenly wrote "1" over the "O" in "30" and added "Oct" after it; realizing his mistake, he cancelled the numbers and "Oct" and went on to cancel the "3" in in 31, leaving "1" and added "Oct."

Franklin continued with "Wedn—2 Water"; and "Thursd—3 Amb." Realizing that he had gotten ahead of his actual journey, he scribbled "Friday—4; Sat—5; Sund—6." Next, in reverse order, he noted before the days of the week where he was on that day: before "Sund—6," he wrote "Philad"; before "Sat—5," he wrote "River D"; before "Friday— 4," he wrote "Brown's"; before "Thursd—3 Amb," he wrote "Pines" (thus correcting his previous jotting "Amboy," which he did not bother to cancel); before "Wedns—2 Water," he wrote "Amboy"; and before "Tuesd—1 Oct," he wrote "Bay."

The jottings document the dates and places of his journey to Philadelphia. By 1785, when he had returned to Philadelphia and recovered part 1 of the *Autobiography*, he had misplaced the letter from Grand and had again forgotten the precise dates. He did not record them in revisions to the *Autobiography* made in 1787, 1788, and 1790. The notes, however, confirm the hypothesis that he sailed with Arnout Schemerhoorn from Boston on the *Speedwell* about 25 September.[4] He said in the *Autobiography* that the voyage took three days. If Schemerhoorn left on the twenty-fifth, Franklin arrived in New York on Friday, 27 September, probably late that afternoon.

When he was younger, Franklin had wanted to become a sailor. Now, however, "My Inclinations for the Sea, were by this time worne out, or I might now have gratify'd them. But having a Trade, and supposing my self a pretty good Workman, I offer'd my Service to the Printer of the Place, old Mr. William Bradford." Bradford (1663–1752), who had been a printer in Pennsylvania (1685–1693) before moving to New York, was sixty years old and a printer to the New York legislature. Since people worked six days a week in the eighteenth century, Franklin probably called on William Bradford on Saturday morning, 28 September. He would have shown Bradford the cancelled indenture and offered himself as a journeyman printer. He "could give me no Employment, having little to do, and Help enough already: But, says he, my Son at Philadelphia had lately lost his principal Hand, Aquila Rose, by Death. If you go thither I believe he may employ you" (A 21). Aquila Rose had been the clerk of the Pennsylvania

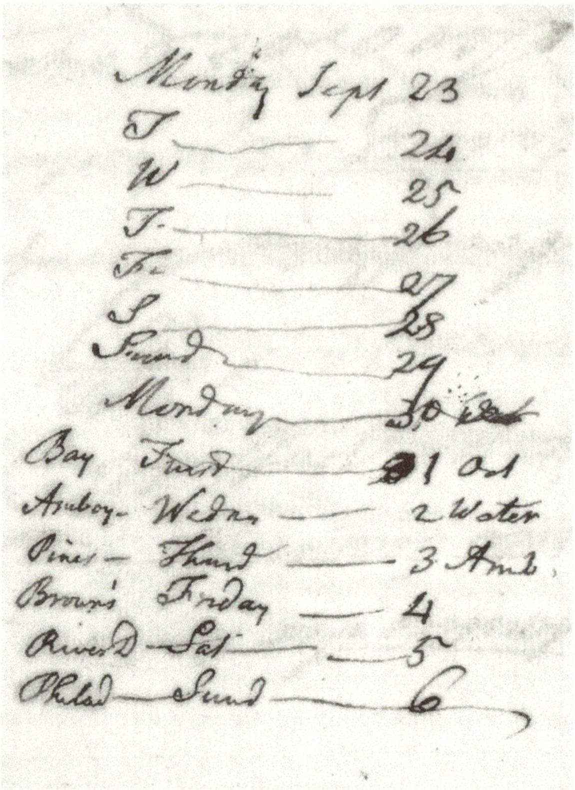

Monday Sept 23
T — 24
W — 25
T — 26
F — 27
S — 28
Sund — 29
Monday — 30
Bay Tuesd — 31 Oct
Amboy — Wedn — 2 Water
Pines — Thursd — 3 Amb
Brown's Friday — 4
River D — Sat — 5
Philad — Sund — 6

Figure 19. Franklin's notes on the dates of his journey to Philadelphia in the fall of 1723. On the back of a letter dated 29 November 1783, Franklin jotted down the dates of his journey from New York to Philadelphia in the early fall of 1723. He evidently came across the day and date of Monday, 23 September 1723, and recalled that it was about the time he ran away from Boston. In 1771, he had written in the Autobiography *that he arrived in Philadelphia on a Sunday morning in October 1723, but had not bothered to try to ascertain the exact date. Now, with that date of Monday, 23 September 1723, before him, he hurriedly scribbled (the penmanship is nothing like his usual attractive hand) the dates and places of his journey to Philadelphia on the back of Grand's letter.*

Quickly, he wrote the days and dates ("T—24; W— 25" . . .), until after "Sund—29," he wrote "Monday—30," and "Tuesd—31," then remembered that September had only 30 days. Still writing too quickly, he jotted "1" over the "0" in "30" and added "Oct" after it. Immediately realizing his mistake, he cancelled the numbers and "Oct." Next, he canceled the "3" in in 31, leaving "1" and adding "Oct."

Franklin continued with "Wedn—2 Water"; and "Thursd—3 Amb." Recognizing that he had gotten ahead of his actual journey, he scribbled "Friday—4; Sat—5; Sund—6." Next, in reverse order, he noted before the days of the week where he was on that day: before "Sund—6," he wrote "Philad"; before "Sat—5," he wrote "River D"; before "Friday— 4," he wrote "Brown's"; before "Thursd—3 Amb," he wrote "Pines" (thus correcting his previous jotting "Amboy," which he did not bother to cancel); before "Wedns—2 Water," he wrote "Amboy"; and before "Tuesd—<3>1 Oct," he wrote "Bay." Courtesy, American Philosophical Society, Philadelphia.

Assembly and Philadelphia's best-known poet as well as a journeyman printer. Franklin promptly decided to go on to Philadelphia.

According to his jottings years later, Franklin left New York on Tuesday, 1 October. He chronicled the journey in the *Autobiography*. He sailed in a small boat for Perth Amboy, East Jersey's capital. The voyage normally took about two hours, but a squall came up as the boat crossed Upper New York Harbor, "tore our rotten Sails to pieces," and prevented the ship from reaching the safety of the Kill van Kull, a channel separating the northern tip of Staten Island from New Jersey. The storm drove the boat east, across Upper New York Harbor, to Long Island, where a great surf on the rocky beach threatened to wreck the ship.

Franklin interrupted his narrative to tell an anecdote about a passenger, a drunken Dutchman, who "fell over board; when he was sinking I reach'd thro' the Water to his shock Pate and drew him up so that we got him in again. His Ducking sober'd him a little, and he went to sleep, taking first out of his Pocket a Book which he desir'd I would dry for him. It prov'd to be my old favorite Author Bunyan's Pilgrim's Progress in Dutch, finely printed on good Paper with copper Cuts, a Dress better than I had ever seen it wear in its own Language."

Franklin's appreciation of *Pilgrim's Progress* as a literary classic was prescient, for the Couranteers and even (when he wrote this part of the *Autobiography* in 1771) other litterateurs had not yet come to regard the book as an artistic triumph but rather a Christian one. Franklin ignored the religious message but celebrated Bunyan's technique. After commenting on the allegory's great popularity, he analyzed its causes: "I have since found that it has been translated into most of the Languages of Europe, and suppose it has been more generally read than any other Book except perhaps the Bible. Honest John was the first that I know of who mix'd Narration and Dialogue, a Method of Writing very engaging to the Reader, who in the most interesting Parts finds himself as it were brought into the Company, and present at the Discourse. De foe in his Cruso, his Moll Flanders, Religious Courtship, Family Instructor, and other Pieces has imitated it with Success. And Richardson has done the same in his Pamela, etc." (A 21). Franklin was a shrewd literary critic, as well as a writer who learned from Bunyan and others to combine narration and dialogue in his own writing. He united them effectively not only in belletristic writings like the *Autobiography* but also in political pieces and even in his letters.

After Franklin established the passengers' dangerous situation with the detail of the Dutchman falling overboard, he suspensefully put off resolving their plight with the above discussion of literary art—the delay demonstrated narrative artfulness. Then he returned to the travelers' predicament: "When we drew near the Island we found it was at a Place where there could be no Landing, there being a great Surff on the stony Beach. So we dropped Anchor and swung round towards the Shore. Some People came down to the Water Edge and hallow'd to us, as we did to them. But the Wind was so high and the Surff so loud, that we could not hear so as to understand each other. There were Canoes on

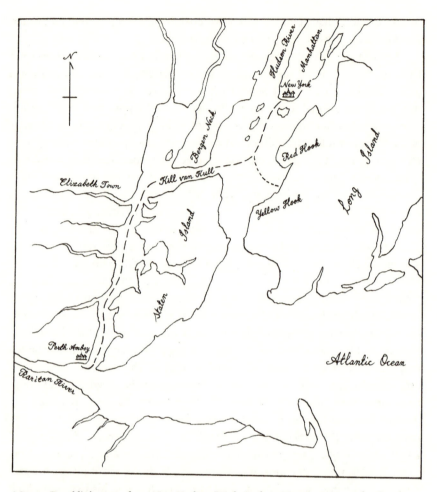

Map 1. Franklin's route from New York to Perth Amboy, New Jersey, 1 and 2 October
1723. After running away from Boston, Franklin sailed to New York, where the only
printer in the city, William Bradford, advised him to go on to Philadelphia. Franklin
sailed across the New York harbor to Perth Amboy, New Jersey, but encountered difficulties. A squall came up as the boat crossed Upper New York Harbor, "tore our rotten Sails
to pieces," and prevented the ship from reaching the safety of the Kill van Kull, a channel
separating the northern tip of Staten Island from New Jersey. The storm drove the boat
east, across Upper New York Harbor, to Long Island, where a great surf on the rocky
beach threatened to wreck the ship. Instead of taking two hours, the trip to Perth Amboy
took thirty hours, when Franklin, with a fever, reached Perth Amboy the next evening,
Wednesday, 2 October. Drawn by Nian-Sheng Huang, based upon two maps of the New
York Harbor in approximately 1730 (plates 27A and 29) in Isaac Newton Phelps Stokes,
Iconography of Manhattan Island, 1498–1909.

the Shore, and we made Signs and hallow'd that they should fetch us, but they either did not understand us, or thought it impracticable. So they went away" (A 21–22). The night left Franklin and his companions in a dangerous situation.

The scene portraying humans shouting and motioning and vainly trying to communicate but being overwhelmed by nature's powerful forces has archetypal suggestions. Stephen Crane read the *Autobiography* and described a similar situation in section IV of his story "The Open Boat" (1898). Several sailors, trapped in a boat and approaching an impossible surf, motion to the people on shore who return the gestures, and one individual waves his coat around and around over his head. At first the sailors hope that those on shore will come out with a life-saving boat or with "a fishing boat—one of those big yawls," but the sailors gradually lose hope and cannot figure out what the person waving his coat is trying to communicate. He gradually disappears in the dusk as night comes on. In Crane's story, the sailors in the lifeboat have no anchor and no alternative. They shipwreck. Though Crane's narrative is based on his own experience, no such scene occurred in the actual wreck.[5]

Franklin indirectly revealed ("the Boatman and I") that he had assumed the task of helping with the boat: "Night coming on, we had no Remedy but to wait till the Wind should abate, and in the mean time the Boatman and I concluded to sleep if we could." Franklin and his companions spent a miserable night off Long Island, "the Spray beating over the Head of our Boat leak'd thro' to us, so that we were soon almost as wet as" the drunken Dutchman. "In this Manner we lay all Night with very little Rest. But the Wind abating the next Day, we made a Shift to reach Amboy before Night, having been 30 Hours on the Water without Victuals, or any Drink but a Bottle of filthy Rum: The Water we sail'd on being salt" (A 22).

Wednesday night, 2 October, Franklin, sick with a fever, slept at an inn in Perth Amboy, New Jersey. "Having read somewhere that cold Water drank plentifully was good for a Fever, I follow'd the Prescription, sweat plentifully most of the Night, my Fever left me." Franklin had read the prescription just a few weeks before he left Boston. The 29 August *Boston News-Letter* featured an abbreviated version of Dr. John Hancock's recommendation concerning "A Short, a Safe, and a Sure, *Fever-Killer*." It was simple: drink plenty of cold water and sweat profusely.

On Thursday morning, 3 October, Franklin took Redford's Ferry across Raritan Bay to South Amboy, New Jersey, and set out to walk the fifty miles across New Jersey to Burlington, where he had been told "I should find Boats that would carry me the rest of the Way to Philadelphia." He walked along Governor Lowrie's (the Lower) Road across New Jersey, which went from South Amboy to Cranbury and Crosswicks, to Bordentown and to Burlington. (New Jersey state route 535 from South Amboy to Cranbury and then route 130 to Bordentown roughly follow Franklin's route.) But Franklin did not get far on Thursday: "It rain'd very hard all the Day, I was thoroughly soak'd and by Noon a good

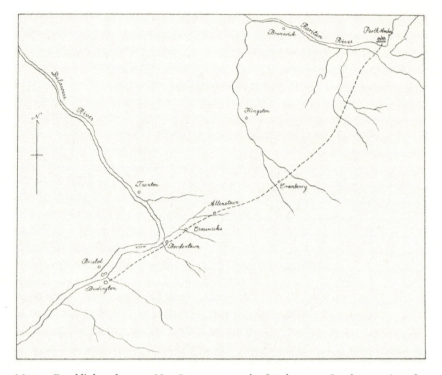

Map 2. Franklin's trek across New Jersey, 3, 4, and 5 October 1723. On the morning of 3 October, Franklin took Redford's Ferry across Raritan Bay to South Amboy, New Jersey, and set out to walk the fifty miles to Burlington. The route, sometimes called Governor Lowrie's (or the Lower) Road, went from South Amboy to Cranbury and Crosswicks, to Bordentown. But it poured rain, and by noon on Thursday, 3 October, the still feverish Franklin stopped at a poor inn. The next day, 4 October, feeling better, he walked on to Dr. John Browne's inn at Bordentown. Then, on Saturday, 5 October, he completed the journey to Burlington, New Jersey, where he expected to find a boat going to Philadelphia. Drawn by Nian-Sheng Huang, based on the map in Lewis Evans, Map of Pennsylvania, *1749.*

deal tir'd, so I stopt at a poor Inn, where I staid all night, beginning now to wish I had never left home" (A 22).

In his memorandum of the dates, penned sixty years later, Franklin wrote "Pines" by 3 October. Perhaps "Pines" was the name of the "poor Inn," but it is also a generic name for the area. Years later (23 April 1761) Franklin characterized the route as "chiefly" passing through "a heavy loose land, very fatiguing to the Horses [let alone to the foot traveler]: That being thro' a barren country, it was not well inhabited, nor the Inns well supply'd with Provisions." At the furthest, Franklin walked to Cranbury, New Jersey, in the rain before spending the night at the "poor Inn." He remembered his situation clearly: "I cut so miserable a Figure too, that I found by the Questions ask'd me I was suspected to be some runaway Servant, and in danger of being taken up on that Suspicion" (A 22). Franklin exaggerated his miserable condition. He must have had the cancelled indenture, signed by his brother and witnessed by two persons, handy in his satchel, but he does not mention it in the *Autobiography*. Nevertheless, in his working clothes, now thoroughly soaked, becoming dirtier and more disheveled every day, he probably did cut a sorry figure. The seventeen-year-old found that running away from home was turning into a nightmare.

On Friday, 4 October, Franklin walked from the "poor Inn" to Bordentown, New Jersey, where he spent the night at Dr. John Browne's inn (later known as Washington House), at the northwest intersection of Main (or Farnsworth) and Crosswick Streets.[6] Dr. Browne, then fifty-six years old, entered into conversation with Franklin "and finding I had read a little, became very sociable and friendly." Franklin appreciated his geographical knowledge and literary ability but recorded that Browne "was much of an Unbeliever, and wickedly undertook some Years after to travesty the Bible in doggerel Verse as [Charles] Cotton had done Virgil. By this means he set many of the Facts in a very ridiculous Light, and might have hurt weak minds if his Work had been publish'd; but it never was." One wonders if the youthful iconoclast did not enjoy a sacrilegious conversation with Dr. Browne. After Franklin became the major printer in the area during the 1730s, Browne may have asked him to publish the book; if so, Franklin refused. The authorities would have prosecuted the author and the printer. It is tempting to think that Franklin wrote a well-known letter giving reasons for not satirizing religion to Browne, but the letter was dated 13 December 1757, over twenty years after Dr. John Browne's death.

The next morning, Saturday, 5 October, Franklin walked from Bordentown to Burlington, the capital of West Jersey, about eighteen miles north of Philadelphia, on the east side of the Delaware River. When he reached Burlington about noon, he "had the Mortification to find that the regular Boats were gone, a little before my coming, and no other to go till Tuesday, this being Saturday. Wherefore I return'd to an old Woman in the Town of whom I had bought Gingerbread to eat on the Water, and ask'd her Advice; she invited me to lodge at her House till a Passage by Water should offer; and being tired with my foot Travelling, I accepted the Invitation. She understanding I was a Printer, would have had me stay at that Town and follow my Business, being ignorant of the Stock necessary to begin with." Franklin well knew that it was not just a press and types that a printer needed but authors, readers, booksellers, a distribution network, and a whole complex of elements that only a fair-size town could provide.[7] He did not, however, interrupt his story to say so. Instead, he commented, "She was very hospitable, gave me a Dinner of Ox Cheek with great Goodwill, accepting only of a Pot of Ale in return" (A 23). What wonderful detail! "A Dinner of Ox Cheek"! Did he actually remember the dinner? The cordiality of Dr. Browne and the old woman in Burlington reveals the friendliness and appeal of young Franklin. Dirty and tired, he was nevertheless engaging, attractive,

open, and pleasant. He liked them—and they enjoyed him. The characteriza-
tions also provide human interest and document Franklin's ability to spin a tale.

That evening a boat came by going toward Philadelphia; Franklin joined it.
As there was no wind, the people in the boat rowed all the way. By midnight,
some of the company were confident they must have passed the city, so they
decided to land, got into a creek, and endured a cold night in the open, huddled
around a fire. In the morning, one of the company recognized the place as
Cooper's Creek, just north of Philadelphia, site of present-day Camden, New
Jersey. As soon as they rowed out of the creek into the Delaware River, they saw
Philadelphia, where Franklin arrived on 6 October 1723, "about 8 or 9 o'clock,
on the Sunday morning, and landed at Market street Wharff" (A 24).

ARRIVAL, 6 OCTOBER 1723

Franklin's description of landing in Philadelphia and taking his first walk
around the city may be the most famous scene in American literature. He made
it graphic and specific because he wanted it to be memorable, and he may have
exaggerated his poverty and miserable appearance in order to heighten the contrast with the 1771 author. "I have been the more particular in this Description
of my Journey, and shall be so of my first Entry into that City, that you may in
your Mind compare such unlikely Beginning with the Figure I have since made
there" (A 24). Franklin deliberately never portrayed the "Figure I have since
made there," for that would have seemed like boasting. He only brought the
story of his life down to 1758, but when he wrote part 1 of the *Autobiography* he
may have had in mind the "Figure" he made when leaving Philadelphia for
London on 7 November 1764: three hundred people accompanied him to Chester, where he was greeted by a cannon salute and by a song adapted from "God
Save the King" (11:447–48).

He described the "unlikely Beginning":

> I was in my working Dress, my best Cloathes being to come round by Sea. I was
> dirty from my Journey; my Pockets were stuff'd out with Shirts and Stockings;
> I knew no Soul, nor where to look for Lodging. I was fatigu'd with Travelling,
> Rowing and Want of Rest. I was very hungry, and my whole Stock of Cash
> consisted of a Dutch Dollar and about a Shilling in Copper. The latter I gave the
> People of the Boat for my Passage, who at first refus'd it on Account of my
> Rowing; but I insisted on their taking it, a Man being sometimes more generous
> when he has but a little Money than when he has plenty, perhaps thro' Fear of
> being thought to have but little. Then I walk'd up the Street, gazing about, till
> near the Market House I met a Boy with Bread. I had made many a Meal on
> Bread, and inquiring where he got it, I went immediately to the Baker's he
> directed me to in Second Street; and ask'd for Bisket, intending such as we had
> in Boston, but they it seems were not made in Philadelphia, then I ask'd for a
> three penny Loaf, and was told they had none such: so not considering or know-

ing the Difference of Money and the greater Cheapness nor the Names of his Bread, I bad him give me three pennyworth of any sort. He gave me accordingly three great Puffy Rolls. (A 24)

The literary historian Perry Miller observed of Franklin, "There is in the record of American literature hardly a writer so fully aware of what he was about."[8] Franklin revised and rerevised the passage. It seems unlikely that Franklin remembered exactly what route he walked or what he ate. The graphic details, however, drive home the different situations and customs between Boston and Philadelphia, thus emphasizing Franklin's innocence and inexperience. He presented himself as a version of the country bumpkin come to the city. But actually he came from Boston, the largest town in the colonies.

"I was surpriz'd at the Quantity, but took it, and having no Room in my Pockets, walk'd off, with a Roll under each Arm, and eating the other." In the following sentence, the passage from "passing by the door" to the end, was added later. "Thus I went up Market Street as far as fourth Street, passing by the Door of Mr Read, my future Wife's Father, when she standing at the Door saw me, and thought I made as I certainly did a most awkward ridiculous Appearance" (A 24–25). The later addition allowed Franklin to escape his own point of view and to certify to the reader that he really did make "a most awkward ridiculous Appearance." Deborah was the one person who might possibly have seen him at the time and who might have recalled it afterward. Perhaps she actually saw him but probably not. He has proven from a supposedly impartial witness that he was a ridiculous bumpkin (the effect desired), and the reader is gratified by his superiority to Franklin.

Franklin omitted certain details of his first walk in Philadelphia. Later in the *Autobiography*, discussing his 1729 pamphlet titled *The Nature and Necessity of a Paper Currency*, Franklin remarked that "when I first walk'd about the Streets of Philadelphia, eating my Roll, I saw most of the Houses in Walnut street between Second and Front Streets with Bills on their Doors, to be let; and many likewise in Chestnut Street, and other Streets; which made me then think the Inhabitants of the City were one after another deserting it" (A 67). Philadelphia suffered a depression in 1723, but mentioning the depressed condition of Philadelphia would have detracted from the focus on the innocent youth and called for an explanation of Philadelphia's economy. He suppressed another detail that he later recalled to Benjamin Rush: Philadelphians then went to market with cut silver for money. (Silver was among the securities on which the Pennsylvania paper currency of 23 March 1721/2 could be borrowed.) Those who had neither ready money nor silver were forced to barter: "those who had it [silver] not, procured provisions by taking the country people to two Stalls in the market, & giving them goods for them, which goods were charged to their accounts and paid for once or twice a year."[9]

The *Autobiography* continued the description of his entry into Philadelphia:

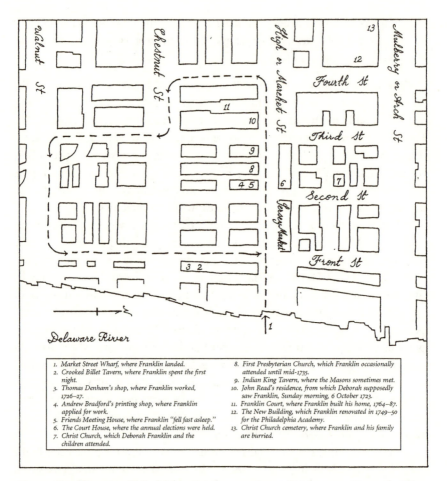

1. *Market Street Wharf, where Franklin landed.*
2. *Crooked Billet Tavern, where Franklin spent the first night.*
3. *Thomas Denham's shop, where Franklin worked, 1726–27.*
4. *Andrew Bradford's printing shop, where Franklin applied for work.*
5. *Friends Meeting House, where Franklin "fell fast asleep."*
6. *The Court House, where the annual elections were held.*
7. *Christ Church, which Deborah Franklin and the children attended.*
8. *First Presbyterian Church, which Franklin occasionally attended until mid-1735.*
9. *Indian King Tavern, where the Masons sometimes met.*
10. *John Read's residence, from which Deborah supposedly saw Franklin, Sunday morning, 6 October 1723.*
11. *Franklin Court, where Franklin built his home, 1764–87.*
12. *The New Building, which Franklin renovated in 1749–50 for the Philadelphia Academy.*
13. *Christ Church cemetery, where Franklin and his family are buried.*

Map 3. Franklin enters Philadelphia, Sunday morning, 6 October 1723. Drawn by Nian-Sheng Huang.

"Then I turn'd and went down Chestnut Street and part of Walnut Street, eating my Roll all the Way, and coming round found my self again at Market street Wharff, near the Boat I came in, to which I went for a Draught of the River Water, and being fill'd with one of my Rolls, gave the other two to a Woman and her Child that came down the River in the Boat with us and were waiting to go farther. Thus refresh'd I walk'd again up the Street, which by this time had many clean dress'd People in it who were all walking the same Way; I join'd them, and thereby was led into the great Meeting House of the Quakers near the Market." The great Quaker Meeting House was at the southwest corner of Second and Market Streets. "I sat down among them, and after looking round a while and hearing nothing said, being very drowsy thro' Labour and want of Rest the preceding Night, I fell fast asleep, and continu'd so till the Meeting broke up, when one was kind enough to rouse me. This was therefore the first

House I was in or slept in, in Philadelphia" (A 25). Franklin slyly joked about the tradition concerning the houses where great men have slept, while commenting on the Quaker "inner spirit." The inner spirit, he implied, stood little chance against an exhausted body.

"Walking again down towards the River, and looking in the Faces of People, I met a young Quaker Man whose Countenance I lik'd, and accosting him requested he would tell me where a Stranger could get Lodging. We were then near the Sign of the Three Mariners. Here, says he, is one Place that entertains Strangers, but it is not a reputable House; if thee wilt walk with me, I'll show thee a better. He brought me to the Crooked Billet in Water Street." At the time, innkeeper George Forrington kept the Crooked Billet Tavern at the site of the present 35 South Front Street.[10] "Here I got a Dinner. And while I was eating it, several sly Questions were ask'd me, as it seem'd to be suspected from my youth and Appearance, that I might be some Runaway." For the second time he suggested that he might fall into serious trouble with the authorities—thus making the story more suspenseful. He again omitted mentioning that the cancelled indenture secured him from that possibility. "After Dinner my Sleepiness return'd: and being shown to a Bed, I lay down without undressing, and slept till Six in the Evening; was call'd to Supper; went to Bed again very early and slept soundly till the next Morning" (A 25). Twelve days had passed since he left Boston.

THE AMERICAN DREAM

When the sixty-five-year-old Franklin described his journey to Philadelphia, he was the most famous American in the world.[11] As a scientist, an intellectual, a writer, and a politician, he was the consummate representative of the Third Realm, the Republic of Letters. The story of his running away from Boston and arrival at Philadelphia at age seventeen was a parable of possibility. It starkly contrasted with his situation only five years before, when he was twelve and condemned to a seven-year apprenticeship as a chandler or a cutler. Now the seventeen-year-old was starting over, in a different place and with a trade. Life had become an adventure and the future was possibility.

Franklin gave us the best formulation of the American Dream. What is the American Dream? The simplest possible answer, as well as the most common general impression, is expressed by the standard cliché, the rise from rags to riches. This theme was not new to Franklin's *Autobiography* or to American literature, though Franklin is often supposed to be the progenitor of the Horatio Alger success stories of nineteenth-century American popular literature.[12] Such tales are actually versions of popular Renaissance and seventeenth-century ballads and chapbooks like *The Honour of a London Prentice* and *Sir Richard Whittington's Advancement*. These tales portray the rise of the hero by a sudden stroke of good fortune or by knightly feats of heroic courage.[13] Franklin's version differs markedly, for his rise comes from hard work. That had been the message of numerous American promotion tracts for more than a century. Captain John Smith knew that only the promise of wealth would draw people from England. He emphasized the availability of land in America and stressed that hard work was the way to wealth: "I am not so simple, to thinke, that ever any other motive than wealth, will ever erect there a Commonweale; or draw companie from their ease and humours at home, to stay in New England to effect my purposes." Following Smith, writers like John Hammond in *Leah and Rachal* (1656) said the common man could gain land and wealth in America by industry and frugality.[14]

Franklin's *Autobiography* combines the kinds of popular appeal present in the old ballads with the realism of the best promotion tracts. To popular appeal and realism, the promotion tracts added an undercurrent of idealism, of life in America as possibility, thereby echoing the archetypal ideas of the West as both the terrestrial paradise and the culmination of the westward progress of civilization.[15]

The *Autobiography* is not primarily about Franklin's economic rise. At best, it is a minor subject. Nevertheless, Franklin knew that to spend one's time in science, literature, or other nonmaterial pursuits, it was necessary to have a sound economic basis. Matthew Arnold judged him "a man who was the very incarnation of sanity and clear sense."[16] Amid all of Franklin's complexities and his radical skepticism, no one ever doubts his uncommon possession in the highest degree of common sense.[17] That he retired from his most gainful pursuit upon reaching age forty-two is only one of many proofs that he did not blindly pursue wealth. Readers who believe that the *Autobiography* is excessively concerned with money themselves emphasize the demeaning message they decry.

A second and more important aspect of the American Dream, which is the fundamental reason for the *Autobiography*'s power and popularity, is the archetypal appeal of the individual's rise from impotence to importance, from dependence to independence, from helplessness to power. Franklin carefully paralleled this motif with the rags-to-riches motif in the opening of the *Autobiography*: "Having emerg'd from the Poverty and Obscurity in which I was born and bred, to a State of Affluence and some Degree of Reputation in the World" (A 1). In that normal development every human being experiences from nebulousness to identity, from infancy to maturity, we all recapitulate the experience of the American Dream.[18] That is why the American Dream has been and is so important to so many people, as well as to American literature. The archetypal experience of every individual's transformation from infant to adult explains the appeal of the myth of the log-cabin birth of our American presidents and the popularity of the role of the self-made man. The American Dream, on this level, embodies a universal experience.

But what is the identity, the strength, the power, or the independence that we adults enjoy? There's the rub. To an infant, the adult's power seems unlimited. To a child or adolescent, it seems a goal that cannot be too quickly achieved. But the achieved status is no great shakes, as every suicide bears ample witness. And we all recognize the lamentable truth of what Poor Richard said:

"9 Men in 10 are suicides."[19] Who could not feel disenchanted with life? It is not only every person who ever reads a newspaper or who constantly deals with the public; it is every person who goes through infancy and childhood anticipating that glorious state of adult freedom and independence and who achieves it—as, of course, we all do. How many qualifications there are, how little real independence, how constraining nearly all occupations, how confining the roles we must act, and how unpleasant all the innumerable forces that are so glumly summed up under the forbidding heading of the realities of life. Who could not feel disenchanted with the American Dream?

The first two meanings of the American Dream are common and found frequently in promotion tracts, biographies, and autobiographies. A third is almost unique to Franklin. An allegorical reading of the *Autobiography* gives the book much of its appeal. Readers have observed that the story of Franklin's rise has its counterpart in the rise of the United States. As Franklin was changing, so, too, were the American colonies: from dependence to independence, from poverty to wealth, from helplessness to power. Urging Franklin to go on with his autobiography, his friend Benjamin Vaughan wrote him: "All that has happened to you is also connected with the detail of the manners and situation of a *rising* people" (A 185–86). Franklin knew that his autobiography would be read as an allegory of the rise to independence of the United States.[20] Further, it would be read as a definition of what an American was. John Adams testified that Franklin's reputation "was more universal than that of Leibniz or Newton, Frederick or Voltaire, and his character more beloved and esteemed than any or all of them." All ordinary people, Adams continued, "seemed to think he was to restore the golden age."[21] Franklin was famous as an American. He frequently wrote about America, was familiar with all the eighteenth-century ideas about America, and knew that his *Autobiography* would be read by many persons as a book about America, about possibility. Further, it would define the American as a person not condemned by parentage to the same role in society as his family but as a person who, by hard work, could create himself, could become almost whatever he wanted to be.[22]

There are three more facets to the American Dream, all metaphysical interrelated underpinnings of the world of possibility. The American Dream is a philosophy of individualism: it holds that the world can be affected and changed by individuals. It is a dream of possibility—not just of wealth, or prestige, or power but of the manifold possibilities that human existence can hold for the incredible variety of people of the most assorted talents and drives. Generalized, the American Dream is the hope for a better world, a new world, free of the ills of the old, existing world. And for the individual, it is the hope for a new beginning for any of the numerous things that the disparate human beings may want to do.[23]

Although these desires can be as varied as the different people who exist, they have one thing in common. Before anyone can achieve any measure of competence, much less extraordinary success, in any field it is necessary to believe in the possibility of accomplishment. Franklin graphically expressed his attitude in a woodcut (America's first political cartoon), which portrays a Conestoga wagon stuck in the mud, with the wagoner beside it praying to Hercules.[24] Under it, Franklin printed the opening of Cato's well-known speech in Sallust. In effect, Hercules tells the wagoner to get up, whip up the horses, put his shoulder to the wheel, and push. Nothing will happen if you do not try.

The fourth definition of the American Dream, which holds that the world can be affected by individuals, goes much beyond the common sense enshrined in Franklin's wagoner cartoon and in such sayings as "God helps those who help themselves."[25] For there is something most uncommon implied in the American Dream. It posits the achievement of extraordinary goals, a distinction in some endeavor, whether football or physics, politics or scholarship, a distinction not to be achieved by ordinary application or ordinary ability. And common sense, though hardly so common as the phrase would have it, is still nothing extraordinary. When Franklin tells of his early grand scheme to promulgate the Art of Virtue (which, in his own mind, amounted to a new and better ethics), he succinctly expresses a philosophy of belief in the individual, a philosophy that allows for the extraordinary accomplishments of mankind: "And I was not discourag'd by the seeming Magnitude of the Undertaking, as I have always thought that one Man of tolerable Abilities may work great Changes, and accomplish great Affairs among Mankind, if he first forms a good Plan, and, cutting off all Amusements or other Employments that would divert his Attention, makes the Execution of that same Plan his sole Study and Business" (A 93).

A fifth definition of the American Dream that may be gathered from the *Autobiography* is, like the fourth, an underlying precondition of the first two themes. Philosophically, it subsumes the earlier four motifs I have mentioned. The fifth theme takes a position on the age-old dialectic of free will versus determinism; or, to put this opposition in its degenerate present guise, between those people who think that what they do (whether voting in an election, building a house, raising crops, or working in an office) might make a difference and those who think it does not. Obviously Franklin is to be placed with those who believe in the possible efficacy of action. But Franklin is nothing if not a complex man and a complex thinker. Several long passages in his writings—as well as his only philosophical treatise—argue just the opposite.[26] Even in that consummate and full statement of the American Dream, the *Autobiography*, he sounds discordant notes.

At one point, he says that his early mistakes had "something of *Necessity* in them." That is, the world is not governed solely by free will: experience, knowledge, and background—or the lack of them—may determine, indeed predestine, the actions of an individual. Franklin speaks of his conviction as a youth that "*Truth, Sincerity and Integrity* in Dealings between Man and Man, were of the utmost Importance to the Felicity of Life." He goes on: "And this Persuasion, with the kind hand of Providence, or some guardian Angel, or accidental favourable Circumstances and Situations, or all together, preserved me . . . without any *wilful* gross Immorality or Injustice that might have been expected from my Want of Religion. I say *wilful*, because the Instances I have mentioned, had something of *Necessity* in them, from my Youth, Inexperience, and the Knavery of others" (A 59).

A sixth and final definition of the American Dream is also a concomitant of the last two, as well as a precondition of their existence. It is a philosophy of hope, even optimism. Belief in individualism and free will, like the prospect of a rise from rags to riches or from impotence to importance, demands that the individual have hope. And so the *Autobiography* is deliberately optimistic about mankind and about the future. Nor is Franklin content with the implication. He gives a practical example of the result of an opposite point of view in his character sketch of the croaker, Samuel Mickle. It opens: "There are Croakers in every Country always boding its Ruin." Franklin tells of Samuel Mickle's prediction of bankruptcy for Franklin and for Philadelphia. Franklin testifies that Mickle's speech "left me half-melancholy. Had I known him before I engag'd in this Business, probably I never should have done it." And he concludes the sketch by telling that Mickle refused "for many Years to buy a House . . . because all was going to Destruction, and at last I had the Pleasure of seeing him give five times as much for one as he might have bought it for when he first began his Croaking" (A 61).[27]

Franklin falsifies the conclusion for the sake of the moral. No one knows anything about the personality of Samuel Mickle, who may well have been a pessimist. We do know that he was a real estate operator who owned numerous properties.[28] Franklin certainly knew it, although for the sake of showing the impractical results of a philosophy of pessimism, he falsifies the facts. And we all know that though the facts may be false, Franklin is right. It is better to be optimistic than pessimistic, more useful to be hopeful than hopeless. But we may not be able to be. Franklin knew, too, that men are at the mercy of their personalities and their worldviews, as well as their ability, background, finances, health, and age. To his Loyalist son, Franklin wrote after the Revolution: "Our Opinions are not in our own Power; they are form'd and govern'd much by Circumstances, that are often as inexplicable as they are irresistible."[29]

Franklin himself seems to have been blessed with a happy constitution, but it is better never to be too certain of Franklin. Poor Richard advised hosts: "If you wou'd have Guests merry with your cheer,/Be so your self, or so at least appear" (1:358). Since a dominant theme of the *Autobiography* is the American Dream, and since this theme holds that it is desirable and beneficial to have hope, even optimism, Franklin's *Autobiography* is an optimistic work. But that is too partial a view of life to satisfy Franklin. He tells us in the *Autobiography* that at age twenty-one, when he began to recover from a severe illness, he regretted that he had not died: "I suffered a good deal, gave up the Point in my own mind, and was rather disappointed when I found my Self recovering; regretting in some degree that I must now some time or other have all that disagreable

Work to do over again" (A 52). This pessimism surprises no Franklinist, for his writings contain numerous similar passages.[30] In his only straightforward philosophical treatise, he defined life as suffering and death as the absence of pain: "We are first mov'd by *Pain*, and the whole succeeding Course of our Lives is but one continu'd Series of Action with a View to be freed from it" (1:64).

Most sentences in Franklin's *Autobiography* are unrevised, but the one presenting the American Dream motif caused him trouble, and he carefully reworked it. The finished sentence coordinated two dependent clauses, one concerning Franklin's rise both from rags to riches and from obscurity to fame, the other telling that Franklin generally had a happy life; but the main clause says that Franklin will inform us *how* he was able to accomplish these: "Having emerg'd from the Poverty and Obscurity in which I was born and bred, to a State of Affluence and some Degree of Reputation in the World, and having gone so far thro' Life with a considerable Share of Felicity, the conducing Means I made use of, which, with the Blessing of God, so well succeeded, my Posterity may like to know, as they may find some of them suitable to their own Situations, and therefore fit to be imitated" (A 1). Franklin sees the means that a person can use in order to create himself, to shape his life into whatever form that he may choose, as the primary subject of his book—insofar as it is a book about the American Dream. He fulfilled that purpose in presenting his "Art of Virtue," which will be discussed in Volume 2.

The fictive world of Franklin's *Autobiography* portrays a more modern world than any previous one I know in Western literature: a nonfeudal, nonaristocratic, and nonreligious society. One has only to compare it with the fictive world of Jonathan Edwards's autobiography or Henry Fielding's *Tom Jones* to realize that Franklin's world, like Edwards's or Fielding's, was indeed a world of his imagination, although that imaginative world, as portrayed in the *Autobiography*, suspiciously corresponded to an ideal democratic world as imagined by European philosophers and men of letters. Franklin's persona—that runaway apprentice whose appetite for work and study is nearly boundless, that trusting youth flattered and gulled by Governor Keith, that impecunious young adult who spent his money supporting his friend Ralph and his friend's mistress—that youth is the first citizen in literature who lives in a democratic, secular, mobile (in place and in social order) society.[31] The persona has the opportunity of choosing (or, to put it negatively, faces the problem of choosing) what he is going to do and be in life. The apprenticeship choices—presented in poignant terms early in the *Autobiography* and presented against the background of his father's not being able to afford to keep even Benjamin, "the Tithe of his Sons" (A 6), in school so that he could become a minister or a member of another learned profession—function as a paradigm for the underlying question of the role of man in society. The scene describing Franklin's entrance into Philadelphia answers that question: it asserts that man does have choice in the New

World, that man can create himself. This is the primary message of Franklin's American Dream.

PHILADELPHIA

When Franklin arrived in Philadelphia on 6 October 1723, the town was smaller than Boston or New York. Philadelphia had about 6,000 inhabitants, New York had about 7,500, and Boston had about 12,000. William Penn had founded Philadelphia on the Delaware River, several miles north of its junction with the Schuylkill River. He designed the city as a rectangle two miles long and one mile wide, with wide streets running straight back from the Delaware River. The streets were intersected by cross streets at right angles. When Franklin first walked down the streets of Philadelphia, he delighted in the streets fifty feet wide, with Market Street nearly one hundred. Coming from Boston, where the streets were comparatively narrow and crooked (though the major ones were large by London standards), he must have been surprised by the regularity and spaciousness of Philadelphia. As he walked by the Jersey Market on the first two blocks of Market Street, he passed by rows of two- and three-story houses, mainly of brick, though many were wood.

BREINTNALL'S "DESCRIPTION"

As part of the Busy-Body essay series that Franklin started, Joseph Breintnall, Franklin's close friend, wrote "A plain Description of one single Street in this City" in the *American Weekly Mercury* (19 June 1729). The poem described a walk down Market Street, from the Delaware River to the Schuylkill. Market Street was the site of Franklin's Philadelphia home for all but two years (1748–50) from 1728 to 1765. Thereafter, his Philadelphia home was in Franklin Court, which one entered from Market Street. Breintnall's poem commences with a description of the area where Franklin first came into Philadelphia in 1723, beginning at the Market Street dock and merchants' houses on the Delaware:

> At *Delaware*'s broad Stream, the View begin,
> Where jutting Wharfs, Food-freighted Boats take in.
> Then, with th'advancing Sun, direct your Eye;
> Wide opes the Street, with firm Brick Buildings high:
> Step, gently rising, o'er the Pebbly Way,   5
> And see the Shops their tempting Wares display;
> (Chief on the Right, screen'd from rude Winds and blest,
> In Frost with Sunshine) Here, if Ails molest,
> Plain surfac'd Flags, and smooth laid Bricks invite
> Your tender Feet to Travel with Delight.   10

An especially large commercial building on the right or north side of Market Street had an area in front of it paved with flagstone and brick. Perhaps it was the store of William Allen, a wealthy young merchant.

> And Yew-Bow, Distance, from the Key built Strand,
> Our Court-house fronts Caesarea's Pine tree Land.

(Bows were often made of yew; and a yew-bow distance, or as far as one could shoot an arrow, was about a block.)

The courthouse (completed before the end of 1710) was a typical English town hall on pillars, crowned with a cupola. In the front, outside stairs led up from the ground to the second floor, across a balcony where the main entrance was located, and stairs continued on down to the ground on the other side. On Pennsylvania's annual Election Days (1 October for Philadelphia County, 2 October for Philadelphia City), Philadelphia's voters cast their ballots at the courthouse's main entrance on the second floor. In rowdy elections, "the fight for the stairs" sometimes determined political victory. The courthouse was at Market and Second, on the north side, with the market on the south side, between Second and Front Streets. Both the courthouse and the market were located in the middle of Market Street. From the second floor of the courthouse, one looked over the market down to the Delaware and beyond to "Caesarea," an early name for New Jersey.

> Thro' the arched Dome, and on each Side, the Street
> Divided runs, remote again to meet:

The street was divided by the market between Front and Second streets and then by the courthouse in the middle of Market Street, just north of Second Street. Next came the stocks.

> Here Eastward stand the Traps to Obloquy,   15
> And Petty Crimes, Stocks, Post and Pillory:
> And (twice a Week) beyond, light Stalls are set
> Loaded with Fruits and Fowls and *Jersey's* Meat.

Market days were Wednesdays and Saturdays. West of the court house were the "Shambles," or slaughterhouses.

> Westward, conjoin, the Shambles grace the Court;
> Brick Piles their long extended Roof support.   20
> Oft, West from these, the Country Wains are seen
> To crowd each Hand, and leave a Breadth between:
> Yet wider still (such is the City's Care)
> To Right and Left, strong Bars a Passage spare,

The Friends' Meeting House, where Franklin fell asleep on his first day in Philadelphia, was built in 1695–96. Fifty feet square, it occupied the southwest corner of Second and Market. It was replaced in 1755 by the Greater Meeting House.

> South of the Mart a Meeting-house is rear'd,   25
> Where by the Friends (so call'd) is Christ rever'd;

> With Stone and Brick, the lasting Walls are made
> High-rais'd the Roof, and Wide the Rafters spread.

Before the erection of Independence Hall, the Friends' meeting house was Philadelphia's largest structure and consequently the scene of its largest gatherings. Franklin reported in the *Pennsylvania Gazette* on 7 October 1736: "Last Week a Number of Indian Chiefs belonging to the Five Nations, arrived here, and on Saturday a Treaty was held between this Government and them in the Great Meeting House, in order to *brighten the Chain of Friendship, clean the Road of Communication, &c.*"

Breintnall's poem continued with the Presbyterian Church (1704), on the south side of Market Street between Second and Third Streets. Franklin sometimes attended it until the controversy over the Reverend Samuel Hemphill in 1735.

> Within a Voice of this, the Presbyters
> Of like Materials, have erected theirs, 30
> Thence, half a Furlong West, declining pace.
> And see the Rock-built Prison's dreadful Face.

The prison (erected in 1723) was on the southeast corner of Third and Market Streets. Continuing down Market Street, Breintnall cataloged various tradesmen's shops (blacksmiths, wheelwrights), then the public inns, and a few spacious homes (ll. 33–44). He described the other side of the street beyond the prison (ll. 44–55), and concluded (ll. 56–59) with some spacious houses with gardens:

> Beyond, the Street is thinly wall'd, but fair,
> With Gardens pal'd, and Orchards here and there
> On either Side, those beauteous Prospects lie;
> And some inclos'd with Hedges please the Eye.

The poem captures the scale of 1729 Philadelphia, a small urban center closely linked on the east to the Delaware River, which connected it to the ocean, and on the west to the Schuylkill River and roads leading west of it for fifty miles ending before a vast unknown land.

PHILADELPHIA'S ECONOMY

When Franklin entered Philadelphia in 1723, he was struck by its economic depression. Great Britain suffered a recession in the early 1720s brought on by the failure of the South Sea Company. Under its scheme, private investors bought up the national debt in return for trading monopolies with South America and the Pacific Islands. Its stock soared from 1711 to late 1720—and then crashed, wreaking economic havoc throughout England and the colonies. Philadelphia was a port city with an active coastal trade from New England and the southern colonies and with limited but ever-increasing trade to the West Indies, England, and Europe. Its port reflected the city's and the colony's economy. The number of vessels that entered the Philadelphia port dropped from 130 in 1721 to 97 in 1722 and to 79 in 1723, and then made a gradual recovery to 104 in 1724, 106 in 1725, and 132 in 1726.[32] The city was growing. And it experienced an accelerated rate of growth from 1730 to the Revolution. Until the rise of Baltimore during and after the Revolution, Philadelphia was the primary route from the Atlantic into the back country. The increasing population of Pennsylvania, New Jersey, and the surrounding areas throughout the eighteenth century caused a corresponding increase in Philadelphia's growth. Jacob Taylor celebrated Philadelphia in his 1723 almanac, the year Franklin arrived. Taylor wrote:

> Full Forty Years have now their Changes made,
> Since the Foundation of this Town was laid,
> . . . Swift was the Progress of the rising Town.
> . . . A City built with such propitious Rays
> Will stand to see old Walls and happy Days.[33]

In the eighteenth century, Philadelphia's market was generally considered the finest in British North America. The markets opened with bells ringing: from April through August, the bells rang between six and seven in the morning; for the remaining seven months, between eight and nine o'clock. No haggling over prices was permitted until two hours after the market's opening.[34] A Virginia visitor, William Black, wrote of the market in 1744, "you may be Supply'd with every Necessary for the Support of Life throughout the whole year, both Extraordinary Good and reasonably Cheap, it is allow'd by Foreigners to be the best of its bigness in the known World, and undoubtedly the largest in America."[35] Dr. Alexander Hamilton of Maryland, also visiting in 1744, concurred that the market was "perhaps the largest in North America."[36]

Philadelphia exported food, especially wheat, flour, and Indian corn, but it also sent abroad a great variety of other products. A list of Pennsylvania's shipping from 1731 featured food and drink: wheat, flour, biscuit, barrels of beef and port, bacon, hams, butter, cheese, cider, and apples. When Jacob Taylor returned to celebrating Pennsylvania's fertility in his 1738 almanac, he specified:

> A fruitful Soil, with gifts of nature blest,
> Improv'd by culture swifter than the rest.
> Like Palestine, a land of good repute
> For wheat and barley, honey, milk and fruit.

The Pennsylvania soil produced "ev'ry sort of grain."[37] After the produce of Pennsylvania's farmers, the 1731 list enumerated products from the forests: various kinds of lumber, sawed boards and timber for building houses, cyprus wood shingles, cask staves and headings, masts, and other ship timbers. Jacob Taylor also included varieties of native oaks and numerous other trees:

> The cedar, spruce and cypress here are seen,
> The pine and laurel, these are ever green.
> The ash, the beech and maple chiefly grow
> By streams of water and in vallies low
> The sable walnut, and the locust strong
> Grow here in groves.

Finally, the 1731 list mentioned the older American exports: deerskins, furs, and tobacco.[38]

Shipbuilding was an important industry. The historian Simeon John Crowther traced the number of vessels and the total tonnage of the ships built in Pennsylvania from 1722 to 1775. Here are excerpts from his findings.

Date	Number of Ships	Tonnage
1730	18	684
1740	16	1,028
1750	39	2,580
1760	30	2,192
1770	18	1,880

By mid-century Pennsylvanians were building annually an average of more than twenty ships.[39] The Maryland poet Richard Lewis celebrated shipbuilding in a poem in the *Maryland Gazette* on 30 December 1729, reprinted in the *Pennsylvania Gazette* on 13 January 1730, and in the *American Weekly Mercury* on 14 January1730. Iron was another important product. Jacob Taylor may have recalled Lewis's celebration of shipbuilding when he poetically described the local iron furnaces in his 1738 almanac:

> The well known metal of a gen'ral use,
> In copious stores the bounteous hills produce:
> In neighb'ring groves the trees as plenty grow,
> To melt the ore and make the metal flow. . . .
> So when a hundred kilns and forges glow,
> A thousand streams of melted metal flow,
> Not the possessors of the Mines alone
> Will hoard the gain, and make it all their own.
> The trade and profit, circling like the blood,
> Will then become a universal good.

Until after 1760, the major eighteenth-century route over the Appalachian mountains and into the backcountry began at Philadelphia, and Indian trade was of great importance to its economy. William Penn's policy of purchasing land from the Indians and attempting to deal with them honorably meant that Pennsylvania had the best Indian relations of any colony with a long frontier.

Unfortunately, Penn's son Thomas, who became the chief proprietor in the 1730s, changed that policy.

PENNSYLVANIA POLITICS

Pennsylvania's annual elections, "the most turbulent days in the whole year,"[40] were held on 1 and 2 October. The unicameral legislature met two weeks later on 14 October (a day later, 2 and 15 October, when 1 and 14 October fell on Sundays). Franklin was not elected a representative until 1751, but he was much involved in Pennsylvania politics from the time of his acquaintance with Governor William Keith in 1725. In Pennsylvania, as in other American colonies, the Popular Party opposed the Prerogative Party. The latter almost always consisted of the governor, council, and the salaried political appointees. They favored high, fixed salaries for those positions and wanted to control the taxes. In Pennsylvania, the council was appointed, not elected. The Popular Party, however, generally managed the funds. In Pennsylvania, the Popular Party was also called the Quaker Party. Not all members of the Quaker Party were Quakers. Indeed, Andrew Hamilton, Speaker of the House and leader of the Quaker Party in the 1730s, was a deist. The Quaker Party dominated the political life of Pennsylvania until the Revolutionary period. Quakers were the major religious group in the colony before the great German immigration in the 1730s and 1740s.

Extraordinary political leaders who were not Quakers, like the deist lawyer Andrew Hamilton (1676?–1741), could and did become Speaker of the House and thus leaders of the Quaker Party. (Franklin did on 26 May 1764.) The Speaker of the House was the primary political leader in almost every colony and was even more powerful in Pennsylvania. The Quaker Philadelphia Monthly Meeting, which was primarily concerned with matters of doctrine and with humanitarian help, sometimes decided Pennsylvania politics. The alliance between the Quaker Party and religion is especially evident in the case of John Kinsey (ca. 1693–1750), the clerk (i.e., the executive) of the Philadelphia Monthly Meeting (1739–50) who was also, during those same years, Speaker of the Assembly.

Friends ensured political control of the assembly during the first half of the eighteenth century by limiting the number of assembly members allowed to represent the newer counties, which were generally settled by Germans and Scotch-Irish. The three earliest counties, Philadelphia, Bucks, and Chester, each had eight representatives, and Philadelphia City had two. Lancaster County (created 1729) was allotted four members; York (created 1749) and Cumberland (1750), two each; and Northampton (1752) and Berks (1752), one each. Though the newer counties had the greater population by 1752, they had altogether only ten representatives, whereas the older counties and Philadelphia City together had twenty-six members.

About the mid-eighteenth century, the number of Scotch-Irish equaled the number of English and Welsh persons, while the Germans easily outnumbered them. But Quakers remained in power not only by granting the new counties fewer delegates than the older ones but also by keeping taxes low. The Quaker Party's common refusal to pay for defense meant that Pennsylvania had the lowest taxes of any American colony. Only when wars ravaged the frontier and enemy privateers roamed the Delaware Bay did the Quaker Party's position lose popularity. Until 1764, the Germans (who had been the dominant ethnic population for over twenty years) and the Scotch-Irish generally supported the Quaker Party.

Philadelphia City's local governing body was the Philadelphia City Corporation, which elected Franklin a member in 1748. It consisted of twelve councilmen, eight aldermen, a clerk, a recorder, and the mayor. William Penn appointed the first members, and membership was for life. The corporation was self-perpetuating, that is, the new councilmen were elected by the existing members of the Philadelphia City Corporation. Since the mayor was elected annually, the recorder was the highest semi-permanent official. During Franklin's years in Philadelphia, most members of the corporation were Proprietary supporters, and the recorders, like William Allen (recorder from 1741 to 1750), were usually key members of the Proprietary Party. The Mayor's Court consisted of the mayor, recorder, and aldermen. Within the city, the Mayor's Court had the same powers as the justices of the peace and of oyer and terminer as in the counties. But the latter were appointed by the governor, whereas the Mayor's Court consisted of persons elected within the corporation. The Philadelphia City Corporation held its elections the first Tuesday in October, which sometimes coincided with the colony's election.

Because of the generally good economy of Pennsylvania and because of the much greater equality of persons in Pennsylvania than in Europe, a German observer in the mid-eighteenth century recorded or created a saying concerning the colony: "Pennsylvania is heaven for farmers, paradise for artisans, and hell for officials and preachers." A German minister also noted an effect of the egalitarianism on the role of the preacher: "It is easier to be a cowherd or a shepherd in many places in Germany than to be a preacher here, where every peasant wants to act the part of a patron of the parish, for which he has neither the intelligence nor the skill."[41]

Social Life, Holidays, and Folkways

In addition to politics, organized social life was an important aspect of Philadelphia's culture. Several clubs existed in early Philadelphia, which usually met in taverns. When Franklin came to Philadelphia in 1723, Governor Sir William Keith (1680–1749) had formed two political clubs to support him and to further his programs—the Gentlemen's Club and the Tiff Club. According to the wealthy Quaker Isaac Norris, Sr., Philadelphia's politics in the late 1720s were controlled by Keith's clubs. Though Franklin did not mention it, he must have joined the Tiff Club after Keith befriended him early in 1724. Norris described its members as the "new, vile people . . . [who] may truly be called a mob."[42] Another club, more typical in its purpose, was the Bachelor's Club, formed for fellowship and pleasure before 1728. Franklin's friend Robert Grace was a member, along with Griffin Owen, Lloyd Zachary, Isaac Norris, Jr., and Charles Norris.[43] George Webb, whom Franklin trained as a printer, became a member, and celebrated it in a poem that Franklin printed titled *Bachelor's-Hall* (1731). Franklin mentioned another club, the Merchants Every-Night-Club, in his *Autobiography*. In 1727, Franklin founded the Junto. The Freemasons organized in Philadelphia in 1730, and Franklin joined in 1731. His friends Enoch Flower, Luke Morris, William Plumsted, Hugh Roberts, Philip Syng, and Joseph Wharton helped found the Schuylkill Fishing Company, a social club, in 1732.[44] When Dr. Alexander Hamilton visited Philadelphia in 1744, he attended the Governor's Club, which met at the Old Tun Tavern, and the Music Club, "where I heard a tollerable concerto performed by a harpsicord and three violins."[45] A dancing club was formed in 1739. By the mid-eighteenth century, Philadelphia had about a dozen clubs.

During the second quarter of the eighteenth century, holidays and celebrations became frequent. On New Year's Day the newsboy distributed a carrier's address along with the newspaper to the customers, receiving a tip in return. The first of March was St. David's Day, which also happened to be Queen Caroline's birthday. (She was the wife of George II and queen from 1727 to her death in 1737.) Philadelphia's Welsh Society observed the day at least as early as 1 March 1729, when Franklin printed tickets for the annual feast. On 5 March 1734, the *American Weekly Mercury* announced: "The first instant being the Anniversary of the Birth of Her Majesty, a great Number of the principle Gentlemen and Inhabitants of this Place waited on our Governour at his House about Noon, where all the Royal Healths, with that of our Honourable Proprietaries, were drank under the Discharge of several Pieces of Canon on Society-Hill. Our Proprietor, Governor and a very large Company were afterwards entertained at Dinner by the Society of *Ancient Britons*, established here in Honour of Her Majesty's Birth Day and the Principality of *Wales*; where the Royal Healths were repeated with all suitable Demonstrations of Loyalty."

Though the Irish began to outnumber the Welsh by the mid-eighteenth century, the only evidence for the observance for St. Patrick's Day (17 March) before the Revolutionary period was a poem that Franklin reprinted on 25 March 1731 from the *Maryland Gazette* of 17 March 1729/30, "Verses on St. Patrick's Day." In Boston the newly established Charitable Irish Society did not celebrate the day until 1737. St. George's Day, 23 April, was little observed in Philadelphia, though Samuel Sewall objected to it in Boston in 1706. Beginning in 1730, the Freemasons met on 24 June, St. John the Baptist Day, and paraded in public. Philadelphians first celebrated Scotland's St. Andrew's Day on 30 November 1749 with the formation of the St. Andrew's Society. Of course Christmas and New Year's Eve were popular holidays, as witnessed by the objections of good Puritans and strict Quakers to the celebrations on these days.[46] Franklin evidently celebrated them, for his first recorded purchase of an alcoholic beverage was on New Year's Eve 1739.

Rowdy, boisterous fairs, lasting three days, were held twice a year in Philadelphia, starting 16 May and 16 November. Many persons, including Franklin, disapproved of them, but he, like other printers, tried to have his annual almanacs ready for sale by the November fair. The mayor's feast occurred in late September, not long before his term expired on the first Tuesday in October. The wealthy merchant William Allen outdid all predecessors. On 23 September 1736, he used the almost completed State House (now called Independence Hall) for the mayor's feast. Franklin, who was surely invited and attended, reported in the *Pennsylvania Gazette*: "Thursday last [23 September] William Allen, Esq., Mayor of this City for the Year past, made a Feast for his Citizens at the State House, to which all the Strangers in Town of Note were also invited. Those who are Judges of such Things say that considering the Delicacy of the Viands, the Variety and Excellency of the Wines, the great Number of Guests, and yet the Easiness and Order with which the Whole was conducted, it was the most grand, the most elegant Entertainment that has been made in these parts of *America*." John Adams and others during the Revolutionary period made similar judgments concerning Philadelphia's opulence.

Though the queen's birthday coincided with St. David's Day and had an especially Welsh observation, the king's birthday called for an official celebration. The *Pennsylvania Gazette* reported on 1 November 1733: "Tuesday last [30 October], being the Anniversary of His Majesty's [George II's] Birth-Day, the Mayor and Alderman of this City, with several other Gentlemen of Distinction were invited to the House of our honourable Proprietor, and at Noon His Majesty's Health, the Queen's, his Royal Highness the Prince of Wales's and the rest of the Royal Family's were drank, the Guns firing; after which the Company was plentifully entertain'd at Dinner: Towards Evening Bonfires and Illuminations were made in several Parts of this City, and a splendid Entertainment was provided at the Governor's House, and a Ball given for the Entertainment of the Ladies."

In addition to the fixed days of celebration, Pennsylvanians enjoyed a series of movable feasts. Farming rituals were part of the American folkways. In the fall, corn "huskings" were a universal time for parties: on 21 October 1736, the *Pennsylvania Gazette* mentioned a party assembled "to assist in Husking Indian Corn." After the crops were harvested, animals that the farmer could hardly afford to feed through the winter were slaughtered, providing the occasion for an unofficial thanksgiving (our present official Thanksgiving Day dates only from 1864). Winter brought its own holiday festivity—horse sledding. Visiting in 1750–51, the Englishman James Birket described the sleighs brought out on cold winter days. Two long flat pieces of wood with the fore part turned up were covered with thin, smooth iron plates. These were mounted under a carriage, which was boarded up about eighteen inches high in the middle and about four feet in the front and three behind, with two seats, one behind another, each holding two persons. Two horses were harnessed as in a wheel carriage, with a pole from the front between them. "The driver Stands right up in the forepart of the Slay and goes at a prodigeous Speed. All Ranks of people Covet this kind of Traveling or diversion for whilst the Snow lyes upon the ground all the Carters or dray men lay all other business aside And Stand as regularly at proper places to be hired (as the Hackney Coaches do in London) to go to the Neighbouring villages there to Eat, drink & return in the Evening."[47]

Colonial cities were rowdy. Whenever an important citizen arrived or departed, he was accompanied by a crowd of citizens. On the occasion of news of victories, bonfires were lit and candles were put in windows as signs of support. The mob would break windows without candles.[48]

Franklin's Celebration of Philadelphia

On 18 May 1749, Franklin described the growth and present state of Philadelphia.

> The Dwelling Houses of this City, being lately numbered, from a Motive of Curiosity, by twelve careful persons, who each undertook a Part, there were found as follows, viz.

In the South Suburbs	150
In Dock Ward	245
In Walnut Ward	104
In South Ward	117
In Chestnut Ward	110
In Middle Ward	238
In High-Street Ward	147
In North Ward	196
In Mulberry Ward	488
In Upper Delaware Ward	109
In Lower Delaware Ward	110
In the North Suburbs	62
Total	2076

> Places of Worship and other Public Buildings, Warehouses, Workshops, and other Out-houses, not reckon'd.
>
> It is but a few Years, even within the Memory of Man, since this Country was a Wilderness,
>
> *Inhabited by Beasts of Prey,*
> *Or Men as fierce and wild as they:*

And the Ground-plat of this flourishing City had not a House on it:—What an Alteration! What a vast Improvement have our old Men seen!

Franklin praised William Penn for providing the location and the basic structure of government. Multitudes have abandoned their "native Soil (belov'd by all)" and suffered "infinite fatigues and Hazards by Land and Sea, to get hither." Like the "Inhabitants of the *Elysian Fields*," they hope never to return. "*Orpheus* is said, in old Poetic Fables, to have built a City by the Force of his Musick, the Sound of his Harp charming even the Trees and Stones to collect themselves together: But the sweetest of all Sounds is LIBERTY; and wholesome Laws with good Government makes the most enchanting HARMONY; Musick, which, like the last Trumpet, will be heard in the remotest Regions, and collect Mankind from the most distant Parts of the Globe."

One wonders who the "twelve careful Persons" could have been who undertook the population study out of "a Motive of Curiosity." The Junto had twelve members. Perhaps Franklin suggested the study as a Junto project.

Journeyman Printer

The day after arriving in Philadelphia, Franklin made himself as tidy as he could and applied for a job with Andrew Bradford. Franklin still wore his traveling clothes, as his trunk was coming from New York by ship. But he himself was no doubt presentable, even if his clothes looked rumpled and worn. The son of New York's William Bradford, Andrew, then age thirty-seven, was a prosperous printer whose *American Weekly Mercury* had supported James Franklin's stand against the Massachusetts Assembly only seven months earlier (26 February 1723).[49] Andrew Bradford knew Benjamin Franklin's name (listed as editor of the *Courant*, which he no doubt received in exchange for the *Mercury*) and would have greeted him with appreciation. Bradford's shop and home were at the sign of the Bible, on the site of the present 12, 14, 16, and 18 South Second Street.[50] As the printer for the province of Pennsylvania and the postmaster of Philadelphia, he was well established. His respected position in Philadelphia was confirmed in 1727 by his election to the Philadelphia City Corporation.

In Andrew Bradford's shop Franklin found his father, William Bradford, whom he had seen in New York, and who had advised him to apply to his son in Philadelphia for a job. William Bradford, traveling on horseback, had reached Philadelphia before Franklin. The older Bradford introduced Franklin to his son, who received him civilly and gave him breakfast but told Franklin that he had recently hired another journeyman. Andrew Bradford informed Franklin, however, that another printer, Samuel Keimer, had just set up in Philadelphia and might employ him. If not, Franklin could lodge with Bradford, who would give him a little work to do while the young man looked for employment. The elder Bradford volunteered to go with Franklin to the new printer. Samuel Keimer (1688?–1742) had served an apprenticeship in England from 6 December 1703 to 4 February 1711/2.[51] After a checkered career sometimes spent in debtor's prison, he had just arrived in Philadelphia. About thirty-three years old, Keimer was renting a house from John Read (whose daughter, Deborah, became Frank-

lin's wife) at the site of the present 318 Market Street, less than a block and a
half from Bradford's house and office.[52] Keimer was a strange-looking character
with a bushy, full head of hair and a great untrimmed beard.

William Bradford said to Keimer: "Neighbor . . . I have brought to see you
a young Man of your Business, perhaps you may want such a One." Keimer

> ask'd me a few Questions, put a Composing Stick in my Hand to see how I
> work'd, and then said he would employ me soon, tho' he had just then nothing
> for me to do. And taking old Bradford whom he had never seen before, to be
> one of the Townspeople that had a Good Will for him, enter'd into a Conversa-
> tion on his present Undertaking and Prospects; while Bradford not discovering
> that he was the other Printer's Father; on Keimer's Saying he expected soon to
> get the greatest Part of the Business into his own Hands, drew him on by artful
> Questions and startling little Doubts, to explain all his Views, what Interest he
> rely'd on, and in what manner he intended to proceed. I who stood by and
> heard all, saw immediately that one of them was a crafty old Sophister, and the
> other a mere Novice. Bradford left me with Keimer, who was greatly surpriz'd
> when I told him who the old Man was. (A 26)

Keimer's shop appalled Franklin. His printing house consisted of an old
shattered press and one small worn-out font of type, "which he was then using
himself, composing in it an Elegy on Aquila Rose, . . . an ingenious young Man
of excellent Character much respected in the Town, Clerk of the Assembly, and
a pretty Poet. Keimer made Verses, too, but very indifferently. He could not be
said to write them, for his Manner was to compose them in the Types directly
out of his Head; so there being no Copy, but one Pair of Cases, and the Elegy
likely to require all the Letter, no one could help him." Cases, which held small
boxes containing the letters of the alphabet, came in pairs, one for capitals and
a large one for the more numerous lowercase letters. "I endeavour'd to put his
Press (which he had not yet us'd, and of which he understood nothing) into
Order fit to be work'd with; and promising to come and print off his Elegy as
soon as he should have got it ready, I return'd to Bradford's who gave me a
little Job to do for the present, and there I lodged and dieted" (A 26–27).

Franklin began lodging with Bradford on Monday, 7 October 1723, doing
the occasional job printing to earn his keep—and probably making himself as
useful as possible. A few days later, "Keimer sent for me to print off the Elegy.
And now he had got another Pair of Cases, and a Pamphlet to reprint, on which
he set me to work." By chance, both the early printing jobs from Keimer's press
survive: Keimer's *Elegy on . . . Aquila Rose* and the pamphlet, Thomas Chalkley's
Letter to a Friend in Ireland. The young printer Franklin judged both Andrew
Bradford and Samuel Keimer to be "poorly qualified for their Business. Bradford had not been bred to it, and was very illiterate; and Keimer tho' something
of a Scholar, was a mere Compositor, knowing nothing of Presswork" (A 27).
Andrew Bradford was not illiterate; he could read and write. Since eighteenth-

century printers commonly corrected the spelling and punctuation of the original materials they printed, the charge that Bradford was "illiterate" probably meant that Franklin judged him to be a poor copyeditor. Franklin also intended to impugn his literary ability, though not all good printers were good writers.

Keimer had evidently learned only to set type during his London apprenticeship, but American printing shops were too small to specialize. American apprentices mastered all normal aspects of printing, presswork, and typesetting. The compositor's job was to set up the type attractively in forms (to do so fast and without errors took practice, good coordination, dexterity, and a sense of aesthetics). The pressman printed off the forms on exactly placed paper, applying just the right amount of pressure and then quickly but carefully removing the paper with its wet ink and hanging it up to dry. An apprentice often began by taking the just-printed sheet from the pressman and hanging it up. Presswork, like composition, was an art that had to be learned and practiced. If you pressed a little too hard, the ink would show through the paper so that when you printed the other side the printing was difficult to read. Paper also varied in thickness, in sizing (which determined how much ink the paper would absorb), and in quality—all of which affected the amount of pressure that should be applied. Presswork seemed simple, but like typesetting, it required expertise.

Keimer had been one of the French Prophets, or Camisards, a group that preached the imminence of doomsday, spoke in tongues, swooned, and had fits. Eighteenth-century writers generally regarded them with contempt. In the 1740s, descriptions of the fanatic excesses of the Camisards appeared in the newspapers as propaganda against the Great Awakening. When Franklin wrote about Keimer in the *Autobiography*, he no doubt knew *The Wonderful Narrative: or, A Faithful Account of the French Prophets, Their Agitations, Extasies, and Inspirations*, which had been reprinted in Boston in 1742. Franklin wrote that Keimer "could act their enthusiastic Agitations. At this time he did not profess any particular Religion, but something of all on occasion; was very ignorant of the World, and had, as I afterwards found, a good deal of the Knave in his Composition. He did not like my Lodging at Bradford's while I work'd with him. He had a House indeed, but without Furniture, so he could not lodge me: But he got me a Lodging at Mr. Read's before-mentioned, who was the Owner of his House" (A 27).

Settling In

By early November 1723, the seventeen-year-old Franklin began lodging with the Reads, next door to Keimer's shop. John Read (d. 1724), a forty-five-year-old carpenter and contractor, was married to Sarah White, forty-three (d. 1761). They had three living children: John Read, Jr., Deborah, and Frances. Both the Read home and the building Read rented to Keimer were located at the site of the present 318 Market Street.[53] "And my Chest and Clothes being come by this time, I made rather a more respectable Appearance in the Eyes of Miss Read,

than I had done when she first happen'd to see me eating my Roll in the Street"
(A 27). As weeks passed, Franklin found friends among his Philadelphia peers,
young men who loved reading. Industrious and frugal, Franklin saved money
and "lived very agreably, forgetting Boston as much as I could, and not desiring
that any there should know where I resided except my Friend Collins who was
in my Secret, and kept it when I wrote to him" (A 27).

Despite enjoying many aspects of life in Philadelphia, Franklin must often
have been disgusted with his employer. The scalawag Keimer thought it advantageous to pass himself off as a Quaker and did so in various pamphlets. The
Philadelphia Quaker Monthly Meeting on 20 December 1723 drew up an advertisement, published in Bradford's 24 December *American Weekly Mercury*,
charging Keimer with printing and publishing several "Papers, particularly one
Entituled, *A Parable*" which, by their style and language, suggested that he was
a Quaker: "This may therefore Certifie, That the Said *Samuel Keimer* is not of
the said People, nor Countenanced by them in the aforesaid Practices." Keimer
specialized in religious controversy, often reprinting popular religious tracts—
just the sort of publication that bored Franklin. Keimer also, however, reprinted
some English works that would have interested Franklin, particularly Trenchard
and Gordon's *Independent Whig*, published piecemeal in a sheet every Wednesday for nearly four months during the early part of 1724 before the remainder
was added and the whole volume sold. Later (both while Franklin was in England and after Franklin stopped working for him) Keimer printed several English translations of the classics.

In the winter of 1723–24, Franklin heard from a member of his family.
Franklin's older half-sister Mary (1694–1731) had married Captain Robert
Homes (d. 1744), whose sloop *Mary* plied the American coastal trade from
Maine to South Carolina. During the winter of 1723/4, Homes (often spelled
"Holmes") stopped at New Castle (now Delaware), about forty miles southeast
of Philadelphia on the Delaware Bay. He chanced to hear that Franklin was in
Philadelphia and wrote him, telling of "the Concern" of Franklin's "Friends in
Boston at my abrupt Departure, assuring me of their Goodwill" and saying
"that every thing would be accommodated to my Mind if I would return, to
which he exhorted me very earnestly" (A 28). Franklin replied immediately with
a letter, thanking Homes for his concern and setting forth his reasons for leaving
Boston and assuring Homes of his happiness in Philadelphia.

Keith's Proposal

Sir William Keith, lieutenant governor of Pennsylvania and Delaware (1717–26),
chanced to be with Homes when Franklin's reply arrived. Keith was an able
writer, who later gathered together his papers on colonial America in *A Collection of Papers and Other Tracts* (1740). Captain Homes spoke to Keith of Franklin and showed him the letter. "The Governor read it, and seem'd surpriz'd
when he was told my Age. He said I appear'd a young Man of promising Parts,

and therefore should be encouraged: The Printers at Philadelphia were wretched ones, and if I would set up there, he made no doubt I should succeed; for his Part, he would procure me the publick Business, and do me every other Service in his Power" (A 28). Homes later repeated the conversation to Franklin. Franklin knew nothing of Keith's interest in him until one day, Keimer and he, "being at Work together near the Window," saw Governor Keith and another finely dressed gentleman (Colonel John French [d. 1728], of New Castle, Speaker of the Delaware Assembly in 1721 and 1725) "come directly across the Street to our House, and heard them at the Door." Keimer ran down immediately, "thinking it a Visit to him. But the Governor enquir'd for me, came up, and with a Condescension and Politeness I had been quite unus'd to, made me many Compliments, desired to be acquainted with me, blam'd me kindly for not having made my self known to him when I first came to the Place, and would have me away with him to the Tavern where he was going with Colonel French to taste as he said some excellent Madeira. I was not a little surpriz'd, and Keimer star'd like a Pig poison'd" (A 28).

Off went Franklin, just turned eighteen, with two of the most important and influential men of Pennsylvania and Delaware. Over the Madeira Governor Keith "propos'd my Setting up my Business, laid before me the Probabilities of Success, and both he and Colonel French assur'd me I should have their Interest and Influence in procuring the Publick Business of both Governments." Franklin replied that he had no capital and that he doubted that his father would help. Governor Keith rejoined that "he would give me a Letter to him, in which he would state the Advantages, and he did not doubt of prevailing with him" (A 28–29). Amazed and delighted, Franklin agreed that he would return to Boston when an opportunity offered. Meanwhile, the three conspired to keep their intrigue a secret so that Franklin could continue working for Keimer until ready to set up for himself.

Such patronage might seem strange today; in the eighteenth century it was not uncommon. In addition, the secrecy was also essential to Keith, for had Keith's promises been generally known, someone would have told Franklin that Keith had no money and that his word was worthless. During the following weeks, Keith acted like Franklin's patron, often inviting him to dine and to talk with the leading men of the province. During this period, Keith no doubt invited Franklin to join his Tiff Club.

Return to Boston, 1724

In the spring of 1724, Franklin took leave of Keimer, explaining that he was going to visit Boston to see his family and friends and would return shortly. He received the governor's flattering letter and set out. He wrote in the *Autobiography* that he sailed from Philadelphia for Boston "about the End of April 1724." He evidently left Philadelphia slightly before then, for on 5 May 1724 he signed a promissory note to the Boston bookseller John Phillips for £3.3. (The book-

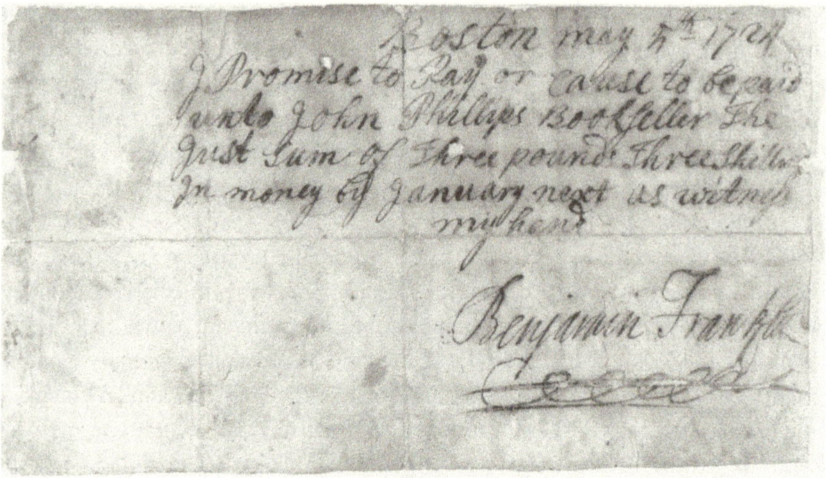

Boston may 5th 1724
I Promise to Pay or cause to be paid
unto John Phillips Bookseller The
Just Sum of Three pounds Three Shillings
In money by January next as witness
my hand
Benjamin Franklin

Figure 20. Franklin's promissory note to the Boston bookseller John Phillips, 5 May 1724. When Franklin returned to Boston in 1724 to try to borrow money from his father to start his own printing shop in Philadelphia, the youth visited the Boston bookstores and (probably after spending all the money he could afford) bought more books, giving this promissory note. Excepting for simply his signature, it is the earliest surviving example of Franklin's handwriting. Notice that the letters are comparatively awkwardly formed, that the appearance of the whole is not attractive, that he signed his full name, and that he added an elaborate flourish. (Cf. the frontispiece.)

When Franklin wanted an analogy in the Autobiography *(87) for his attempts to try to amend his faults and attain virtue, he wrote: "As those who aim at perfect Writing by imitating the engraved Copies, tho' they never reach the wish'd for Excellence of those Copies, their Hand is mended by the Endeavour, and is tolerable while it continues fair & legible." Perhaps Franklin improved his penmanship as a young adult by imitating "engraved Copies." Courtesy, Historical Society of Pennsylvania, Philadelphia.*

loving Franklin evidently could not resist the opportunity offered by Boston's booksellers.)

According to the *American Weekly Mercury*, the only ship to set out from Philadelphia for a northern colonial port in April or May was the sloop *Endeavour*, Captain Richard Robinson for Boston. It "Cleared for Departure" on 16 April. Franklin probably sailed on the *Endeavour*, though neither the *Mercury* nor any other colonial paper recorded every small vessel that sailed from the local port. The journey was difficult: "We struck on a Shoal in going down the Bay and sprung a Leak, we had a blustring time at Sea, and were oblig'd to pump almost continually, at which I took my Turn. We arriv'd safe however at Boston in about a Fortnight." The 27 April 1724 *New-England Courant* recorded that Robinson from Philadelphia had "Entered Inwards." Describing his visit

Franklin said, "I had been absent Seven Months and my Friends had heard nothing of me, for my Brother [Captain Robert] Homes was not yet return'd; and had not written about me. My unexpected Appearance surpriz'd the Family; all were however very glad to see me and made me Welcome, except my Brother" (A 29). Franklin misremembered. Captain Robert Homes was in Boston when Franklin arrived. The 13 April *New-England Courant* reported that Homes was "outward bound" for "North Carolina," but he evidently did not leave until shortly before 4 May when the *Courant* reported that "Holmes for South Carolina" had "cleared out."

In his relations with his brother James, Franklin was at his worst. Writing the *Autobiography* in 1771, Franklin could appreciate both his older brother's feelings and his own youthful behavior. At age eighteen, puffed-up with himself and his minor success, young Franklin was a show-off dandy: "I went to see him at his Printing-House; I was better dress'd than ever while in his Service, having a genteel new Suit from Head to foot, a Watch, and my Pockets lin'd with near Five Pounds Sterling in Silver." A watch in the early eighteenth century was a comparatively ostentatious display of wealth, and silver was not common in Boston or Philadelphia. Looking back, Franklin must have been amused and a little chagrined at his strutting as a young man—displaying his watch and his cash—though he also condemned his older brother's attitude: "He receiv'd me not very frankly, look'd me all over, and turn'd to his Work again. The Journeymen were inquisitive where I had been, what sort of a Country it was, and how I lik'd it? I prais'd it much, and the happy Life I led in it; expressing strongly my Intention of returning to it; and one of them asking what kind of Money we had there, I produc'd a handful of Silver and spread it before them, which was a kind of Raree-Show they had not been us'd to, Paper being the Money of Boston. Then I took an Opportunity of letting them see my Watch: and lastly, (my Brother still grum and sullen) I gave them a Piece of Eight to drink and took my Leave" (A 30).

Franklin offended his older brother, who felt that he had been humiliated before his workmen. "When my Mother some time after spoke to him of a Reconciliation, and of her Wishes to see us on good Terms together, and that we might live for the Future as Brothers, he said, I had insulted him in such a Manner before his People that he could never forget or forgive it" (A 30). During Franklin's absence, his older brother had married Ann Smith on 4 February 1723/4, whom Franklin probably met on this visit.[54] Despite his new marital state, James Franklin was not doing as well in 1724 as he had been when Franklin ran away nine months before. His paper was slightly less lively than it had been, and he now printed little else. Indeed, James Franklin's most productive year had been 1722, the year that Franklin wrote the Silence Dogood essay series. In addition to the *New-England Courant*, in 1721 he printed eleven titles, in 1722 fifteen, but in 1723 only two broadsides, and in 1724 only an almanac and a broadside. Nathaniel Gardner was writing less and less for the newspaper, probably because he had been taking too much time away from the tanning business with his partner Matthew Adams. Further, the most controversial issue, inoculation for the smallpox, had tapered off with the end of the epidemic in 1722. In 1726, James Franklin gave up printing in Boston and moved to Newport, Rhode Island, where he secured the contract for the government printing.

Visitors from afar often called on the important persons in town, and while in Boston, Franklin visited Cotton Mather. If the minister held young Franklin responsible for some of the contents of the *New-England Courant*, he was ready to forgive the former apprentice. It is just as surprising that the proud young Franklin was ready to socialize with the minister. Perhaps his father Josiah told him to call on Mather. Franklin related in a letter to Cotton's son Samuel written 12 May 1784 that the minister "received me in his library, and on my taking leave showed me a shorter way out of the house through a narrow passage, which was crossed by a beam over head. We were still talking as I withdrew, he accompanying me behind, and I turning partly towards him, when he said hastily, '*Stoop! Stoop!*' I did not understand him, till I felt my head hit against the beam. He was a man that never missed any occasion of giving instruction, and upon this he said to me, '*You are young, and have the world before you; STOOP as you go through it, and you will miss many hard thumps.*' This advice, thus beat into my head, has frequently been of use to me; and I often think of it, when I see pride mortified, and misfortunes brought upon people by their carrying their heads too high." Franklin omitted the fact that the hardworking and prodigiously publishing Mather had the sign "BE BRIEF" above the entrance to his study.

Franklin's boyhood friend John Collins, now a dissatisfied post-office clerk, resolved to go to Philadelphia with him. While Franklin waited for his father's decision, Collins "set out before me by Land to Rhodeisland, leaving his Books which were a pretty Collection of Mathematics and Natural Philosophy, to come with mine and me to New York where he propos'd to wait for me" (A 30). Franklin had taken comparatively little with him before, evidently leaving most of his books with his parents (he had also sold some to raise money for the passage). Franklin must have had misgivings about appealing to his father, for the very idea of a comparative stranger's writing a letter of recommendation, full of flattering statements about him, to his own father must have seemed ironic and perhaps slightly absurd. After some time, Josiah Franklin refused to finance him.

Josiah Franklin had disappointed his son before, but Franklin hardly hinted in the *Autobiography* that he was discouraged. The young man, however, must have been keenly disappointed. "My Father receiv'd the Governor's Letter with some apparent Surprize; but said little of it to me for some Days; when Captain Homes returning, he show'd it to him, ask'd if he knew Keith, and what kind of a Man he was: Adding his Opinion that he must be of small Discretion, to think of setting a Boy up in Business who wanted yet 3 Years of being at Man's

Estate. Homes said what he could in favor of the Project; but my Father was clear in the Impropriety of it; and at last gave a flat Denial to it" (A 30). Though Franklin misremembered when he said that Josiah waited for Homes to return, his father may well have waited to see Homes for a day or two and then delayed for some time before refusing. Perhaps Josiah did not reject Franklin outright out of consideration for the youth's feelings. In a cancelled passage, Franklin wrote that his father said "he had advanc'd too much already to my Brother James" (A 30). As we have seen above (Chapter 3), Josiah and his son James had borrowed £346.11.8 in Massachusetts currency from James Bowdoin in 1720. Josiah was still in debt to Bowdoin, and James was never able entirely to repay his father. Further, Josiah had refinanced his Union Street property just two years before (in 1722/3) for £220, seemingly only £30 less than he had originally borrowed when he bought it in 1712. Given the inflation of Massachusetts paper currency, however, those figures are deceiving. In 1712, £100 sterling was equal to £150 in Massachusetts currency; in 1722, £100 sterling equaled £229 in Massachusetts currency. Therefore, he had financed the house in 1712 for about £175 sterling; and he refinanced it in 1722 for approximately £99 sterling.[55]

In addition, on 1 May 1723 Josiah Franklin had signed a note with James Davenport (husband of his daughter Sarah) to borrow £100 from Josiah Hobbs for a year. They were unable to pay off the loan then, and renewed it on 1 May 1724, around the time Franklin showed up in Boston to borrow money. Josiah probably wanted to help Franklin, but he evidently had no money to spare.[56] Franklin recalled that Josiah "wrote a civil Letter to Sir William thanking him for the Patronage he had so kindly offered me, but declining to assist me as yet in Setting up, I being in his Opinion too young to be trusted with the Management of a Business so important; and for which the Preparation must be so expensive" (A 30).

Josiah Franklin had good reason to be suspicious of Governor Keith, for the proposal to fund an eighteen-year-old printer was extraordinary. Further, though Josiah had gone into debt for James Franklin and his son-in-law, what about the other siblings? The father had probably been able to give Franklin's older sisters only a slight dowry, and the two younger sisters Lydia and Jane were fast approaching the time when a dowry might be needed. And there were the two other brothers, John, a tallow-chandler like his father; and Peter, a sailor. If Josiah was going to help his youngest son, shouldn't he first give something to them? Or was he only expected to help the sons who became printers? In 1725 James Franklin was not doing as well financially as he had previously. Even if Josiah could have loaned Franklin the money, he must have thought that the printer's business was risky. Josiah probably had all these considerations in mind when he refused his youngest son. He

was yet pleas'd that I had been able to obtain so advantageous a Character from a Person of such Note where I had resided, and that I had been so industrious and careful as to equip myself so handsomely in so short a time: therefore seeing no Prospect of an Accommodation between my Brother and me, he gave his Consent to my Returning again to Philadelphia, advis'd me to behave respectfully to the People there, endeavour to obtain the general Esteem, and avoid lampooning and libelling to which he thought I had too much Inclination; telling me, that by steady Industry and a prudent Parsimony, I might save enough by the time I was One and Twenty to set me up, and that if I came near the Matter he would help me out with the Rest.—This was all I could obtain, except some small Gifts as Tokens of his and my Mother's Love, when I embark'd again for New York, now with their Approbation and their Blessing. (A 30–31)

Since most coastal ships going from Boston to Philadelphia went by way of New York, Collins had sailed there to await Franklin. In mid or late May 1724, Franklin sailed for New York via Newport, Rhode Island, where he renewed acquaintance with his favorite and eldest brother John, who, like his father, made soap and candles. "He received me very affectionately, for he always lov'd me." Though John had left Boston in 1715 when Franklin was nine, he had worked with Josiah as a tallow-chandler until then, and was thus the older brother whom Franklin knew best after James. John was an excellent craftsman who made a superfine, clear green soap that Franklin later sold in the shop he ran with his printing business. A friend of John Franklin, Samuel Vernon, "having some Money due to him in Pennsylvania, about 35 Pounds Currency, desired I would receive it for him, and keep it till I had his Directions what to remit it in." As Franklin noted, the money afterward occasioned him a good deal of uneasiness, for Franklin spent it, first on his boyhood friend John Collins and later on his London companion James Ralph, so that when Samuel Vernon finally asked for the money, Franklin at first did not have it (A 31).

At Newport, the sloop took on a number of passengers including "two young Women, Companions, and a grave, sensible Matron-like Quaker-Woman with her Attendants." The friendly young Franklin made himself useful to the older woman, who consequently took it upon herself to warn Franklin about his growing familiarity with the two young women. "Young Man, I am concern'd for thee, as thou has no Friend with thee, and seems not to know much of the World, or of the Snares Youth is expos'd to; depend upon it those are very bad Women, I can see it in all their Actions, and if thee art not upon thy Guard, they will draw thee into some Danger: they are Strangers to thee,—and I advise thee in a friendly Concern for thy Welfare, to have no Acquaintance with them." Franklin was dubious. Sensing his reaction, "she mention'd some Things she had observ'd and heard that had escap'd my Notice; but now convinc'd me she was right. I thank'd her for her kind Advice, and promis'd to follow it." When the ship docked in New York, the girls gave him their address and invited him to visit. Because of the matron's advice, he refrained. The next day, the ship captain discovered that some silver and other valuables were missing from his cabin, "and knowing that these were a Couple of Strumpets, he got a Warrant to search their Lodgings, found the stolen Goods, and had the Thieves punish'd." Franklin rounded off the anecdote by playing on the word *escape*: "So tho' we had escap'd a sunken Rock which we scrap'd upon in the Passage, I thought this Escape of rather more Importance to me" (A 32).

JOHN COLLINS

Collins awaited him in New York. He had, however, acquired drinking and gambling habits and had spent all his money. If Franklin had been older or cynical, he might have promptly given up the wastrel, but the talented Collins had been his best childhood friend, so Franklin paid his bill for lodging and his passage to Philadelphia. William Burnet, governor of New York, "hearing from the Captain that a young Man, one of his Passengers, had a great many Books, desired he would bring me to see him. I waited upon him accordingly, and should have taken Collins with me but that he was not sober. The Governor treated me with great Civility, show'd me his Library, which was a very large one, and we had a good deal of Conversation about Books and Authors." Burnet, then thirty-six years old, was the son of Bishop Gilbert Burnet, a well-known author. The governor had moved in literary circles since he was a boy and could tell anecdotes about the most famous authors of the late seventeenth and early eighteenth centuries. Franklin remembered, "This was the second Governor who had done me the Honor to take Notice of me, which to a poor Boy like me was very pleasing" (A 32–33). The eighteen-year-old boy was no doubt pleased, but the sixty-five-year-old writer regarded his earlier self with wry detachment.

Back in Philadelphia before mid-June 1724, Franklin returned to work for Keimer and secured lodging with the eccentric printer for himself and Collins (A 33). When Franklin gave Governor Keith the letter from his father refusing to help at this time, Keith judged that his father was too prudent. "There was great Difference in Persons, and Discretion did not always accompany Years, nor was Youth always without it" (A 34). Franklin no doubt gave that quotation ironically, for Franklin well knew that Keith himself never acquired discretion. Keith resolved to set up Franklin, promising to send to England for the equipment needed. Franklin was to repay Keith when he was able. Franklin had no reason to suspect that the governor was not a man of his word, and he believed him absolutely. Franklin kept his plan to set up printing in Philadelphia a secret, which allowed Franklin to be deceived. "Had it been known I depended on the Governor, probably some Friend that knew him better would have advis'd me not to rely on him, as I afterwards heard it as his known Character to be liberal of Promises which he never meant to keep. Yet unsolicited as he was by me, how could I think his generous Offers insincere? I believ'd him one of the best Men in the World" (A 34). An anonymous manuscript satire of about 1727 characterized Keith: "If you would learn the Art of Dissimulation, to impose upon the Ignorant, make fine Speeches & promise without any meaning, borrow of every Body without any Intention to pay, cheat all you deal with, & nevertheless be a fine Gentleman—follow the Example of Sir W[illia]m [Keith]."[57]

When Franklin presented Keith with an inventory for a small printing house, costing about £100 sterling, Keith seemed to think it reasonable but "ask'd me if my being on the Spot in England to chuse the Types and see that every thing was good of the kind, might not be of some Advantage. Then, says he, when there, you may make Acquaintances and establish Correspondencies in the Bookselling, and Stationary Way" (A 34). Franklin agreed, and Keith told him to be ready to go with Captain Thomas Annis on the annual mail packet, the *London Hope*. Since Annis would not sail until the fall, Franklin continued to work for Keimer, keeping the secret.

Collins became more and more of a burden; he drank when he had a little money and consequently was unable to find work. He lodged and boarded at Franklin's expense, continually borrowing from him, "promising Repayment as soon as he should be in Business." Vernon's money gradually diminished, and Franklin began worrying about "what I should do, in case of being call'd on to remit it." Franklin and Collins quarreled about his drinking, for when "a little intoxicated he was very fractious." Franklin told an anecdote describing their deteriorating relationship:

> Once in a Boat on the Delaware with some other young Men, he refused to row in his Turn: I will be row'd home, says he. We will not row you, says I. You must, says he, or stay all Night on the Water, just as you please. The others said, Let us row; What signifies it? But my Mind being soured with his other Conduct, I continu'd to refuse. So he swore he would make me row, or throw me overboard; and coming along stepping on the Thwarts towards me, when he came up and struck at me, I clapped my Hand under his Crutch, and rising, pitch'd him head-foremost into the River. I knew he was a good Swimmer, and so was under little Concern about him; but before he could get round to lay hold of the Boat, we had with a few Strokes pull'd her out of his Reach. And ever when he drew near the Boat, we ask'd if he would row, striking a few Strokes to slide her away from him. He was ready to die with Vexation, and obstinately would not promise to row; however seeing him at last beginning to tire, we lifted him in; and brought him home dripping wet in the Evening. (A 33)

That finished the friendship: "We hardly exchang'd a civil Word afterwards." Collins left Philadelphia in the early fall for Barbados, where he was going as a private tutor. He promised to send Franklin the first money he received. "But I never heard of him after" (A 34). So ended the career of Franklin's best childhood friend, a boy of verbal talent with a wonderful facility in mathematics, seemingly brighter and more promising than Franklin—but he became a drunk. Collins disappeared from Franklin's life and from history. Franklin did not draw the moral against drunkenness; it was obvious.

Keimer's Religious Plan

Throughout the summer and fall, Franklin worked for Keimer. They "liv'd on a pretty good familiar Footing and agreed tolerably well: for he suspected nothing of my Setting up. He retain'd a great deal of his old Enthusiasms, and lov'd an Argumentation. We therefore had many Disputations. I us'd to work him so with my Socratic Method, and had trapann'd him so often by Questions apparently so distant from any Point we had in hand, and yet by degrees led to the Point, and brought him into Difficulties and Contradictions, that at last he grew ridiculously cautious, and would hardly answer me the most common Question, without asking first, *What do you intend to infer from that?*" (A 35).

Like many another crackbrained zealot, Keimer intended to create his own religious sect. After all, as a Camisard he had been a true believer, expecting the prophet Thomas Emes to rise from his grave on 25 May 1708.[58] Since the clever Franklin could offer convincing arguments for almost any position, Keimer proposed that Franklin become his collaborator. "He was to preach the Doctrines, and I was to confound all Opponents." Taking Leviticus 19:28 literally, "Ye shall not round the corners of your heads, neither shal thou mar the corners of thy beard," Keimer wore a full head of hair and a full beard. Franklin presumably adopted both. Keimer also kept Saturday as his Sabbath. Franklin was glad to have the day off for study. In exchange for adopting Keimer's essential points, Franklin insisted that Keimer give up animal food: "I doubt, says he, my Constitution will not bear that. I assur'd him it would, and that he would be the better for it" (A 36).

Franklin enjoyed tormenting Keimer: "He was usually a great Glutton, and I promis'd my self some Diversion in half-starving him. He agreed to try the Practice if I would keep him Company. I did so and we held it for three Months. We had our Victuals dress'd and brought to us regularly by a Woman in the Neighbourhood, who had from me a List of 40 Dishes to be prepar'd for us at different times, in all which there was neither Fish Flesh nor Fowl, and the Whim suited me the better at this time from the Cheapness of it, not costing us above 18 Pence Sterling each, per Week. . . . I went on pleasantly, but Poor Keimer suffer'd grievously, tir'd of the Project, long'd for the Flesh Pots of Egypt, and order'd a roast Pig; He invited me and two Women Friends to dine with him, but it being brought too soon upon table, he could not resist the Temptation, and ate it all up before we came" (A 36). It must have been a small pig.

Philadelphia Friends

Franklin's three best friends in 1724 were young men about his age: Charles Osborne, Joseph Watson, and James Ralph. All were, he said, "Lovers of Reading." Osborne and Watson served as clerks to scrivener Charles Brockden (1683–1769, grandfather of the early American novelist Charles Brockden Brown), and

Ralph was a merchant's clerk. Watson, a Quaker, "was a pious sensible young Man, of Great Integrity." But Osborne and Ralph, like Collins earlier, had been "unsettled" by Franklin and became religious skeptics. Osborne was sensible, candid, and affectionate to his friends, "but in literary Matters too fond of Criticising." Ralph was ingenious and extremely eloquent. They all fancied themselves writers. "Many pleasant Walks we four had together, on Sundays into the Woods near Skuylkill, where we read to one another and conferr'd on what we read." Ralph was convinced that he could become a famous poet, "alledging that the best Poets must when they first began to write, make as many Faults as he did." Osborne assured him he had no genius for poetry, and should remain in the mercantile business. Recalling his father's advice concerning his broadside ballads and Uncle Benjamin's failure in practical matters, Franklin said, "I approv'd the amusing one's Self with Poetry now and then, so far as to improve one's Language, but no farther" (A 37).

One of the four, perhaps Ralph, proposed a poetry contest "in order to improve by our mutual Observations, Criticisms and Corrections." All agreed. "As Language and Expression was what we had in View, we excluded all Considerations of Invention, by agreeing that the Task should be a Version of the 18th Psalm, which describes the Descent of a Deity." Before they met the following Sunday, Ralph called on Franklin, who told him that he had been busy and had not written the poem. Ralph "then show'd me his Piece for my Opinion." Franklin thought it good and praised it. Ralph said, "Osborne never will allow the least Merit in any thing of mine, but makes 1000 Criticisms out of mere Envy. He is not so jealous of you. I wish therefore you would take this Piece, and produce it as yours. I will pretend not to have had time, and so produce nothing." Franklin agreed. Next Sunday, when they met, "Watson's version was read but the others all found fault with it. Osborne's was judged much better." Ralph said he had "nothing to produce" (A 38).

Franklin told the story beautifully, building up the suspense. Was he really the last to read? "I was backward, seem'd desirous of being excus'd, had not had sufficient Time to correct; etc. but no Excuse could be admitted, produce I must. It was read and repeated; Watson and Osborne gave up the Contest; and join'd in applauding it immoderately. Ralph only made some Criticisms and propos'd some Amendments, but I defended my Text. Osborne was against Ralph, and told him he was no better a Critic than Poet; so he dropped the Argument." As Osborne and Ralph went home together, "Osborne express'd himself still more strongly in favor of what he thought my Production, having restrain'd himself before as he said, lest I should think it Flattery. But who would have imagin'd, says he, that Franklin had been capable of such a Performance; such Painting, such Force! such Fire! He has even improv'd the Original! In his common Conversation, he seems to have no Choice of Words; he hesitates and blunders; and yet, good God, how he writes!" As the 1771 Franklin knew, the description was true of his writing—for he, not Ralph, was internationally celebrated as a writer, whereas Ralph, though a well-known London political hack before the mid-century, had died in 1762 and was already, by 1771, comparatively forgotten. In the *Autobiography* Franklin noted that at their next meeting, Ralph revealed the trick and Osborne was laughed at, and the "Transaction fix'd Ralph in his Resolution of becoming a Poet" (A 39).

OFF TO LONDON

Franklin courted Deborah Read in the summer and fall of 1724. Her father, John Read, a carpenter and contractor, died on 2 September and was buried in Philadelphia's Anglican Christ Church. Franklin proposed marriage to Deborah probably in September or October. Since Franklin reported the reaction of Deborah's mother but not her father to their prospective marriage, he evidently proposed after her father's death. "As I was about to take a long Voyage, and we were both very young, only a little above 18, it was thought most prudent by her Mother to prevent our going too far at present, as a Marriage if it was to take place would be more convenient after my Return, when I should be as I expected set up in my Business" (A 37). Franklin later directly mentioned that Deborah's mother prevented their marriage (A 71). Though Franklin here wrote that he and Deborah were the same age, authorities have differed concerning how old she was. She was probably a few months older than Franklin.[59]

Governor Keith continued to cultivate Franklin. Keith "had me frequently to his House, and his Setting me up was always mention'd as a fix'd thing. I was to take with me Letters recommendatory to a Number of his Friends, besides the Letter of Credit, to furnish me with the necessary Money for purchasing the Press and Types, Paper, etc. For these Letters I was appointed to call at different times, when they were to be ready, but a future time was still named.—Thus we went on till the Ship whose Departure too had been several times postponed was on the Point of sailing, Then when I call'd to take my Leave and receive the Letters, his Secretary, Dr. Bard, came out to me and said the Governor was extreamly busy, in writing, but would be down at New-castle before the Ship, and there the Letters would be delivered to me" (A 39). James Ralph decided to go with Franklin, ostensibly to establish business relations and to "obtain Goods to sell on Commission." Though Ralph had a wife and child in Philadelphia, he secretly intended never to return. Franklin took leave of his friends, "interchang'd some Promises with Miss Read," and left for New Castle, where the ship was anchored. Keith was there, but when Franklin went to him, "the Secretary came to me from him with the civillest Message in the World, that he could not then see me being engag'd in Business of the utmost Importance, but should send the Letters to me on board, wish'd me heartily a good Voyage and a speedy Return, etc. I return'd on board, a little puzzled, but still not doubting" (A 40).

The 5 November 1724 *American Weekly Mercury* reported: "On Monday the 2d of this instant *Andrew Hamilton*, Esq. our late Attorney General for this Province, set out from this Town, in order to Embark on board Capt. *Annis* for

London, and was accompanied so far as the Ferry, with some of the Chief of our Town, with about 70 Horse." James Logan, among others, accompanied lawyer Hamilton to New Castle, where, as Logan wrote, at the last minute Hamilton was called back to plead a case for the enormous fee of £300—a stroke of luck for Franklin and Ralph. Together with Thomas Denham, a Philadelphia Quaker merchant, and two Maryland ironmongers, Hamilton and his son James had engaged the ship's large cabin. Franklin and Ralph had been put in steerage— the miserable crowded area below deck. After Hamilton and his son left the packet, Colonel John French of New Castle came onboard with Governor Keith's dispatches and showed Franklin "great Respect." Consequently, Denham and the ironmongers invited Franklin and Ralph to share the cabin.

Franklin asked Captain Annis if he could have the letters from Governor Keith, but Annis said that "all were put into the Bag together; and he could not then come at them; but before we landed in England, I should have an Opportunity of picking them out." Reassured, Franklin sailed with Captain Annis on Thursday, 5 November. "We had a sociable Company in the Cabin, and lived uncommonly well, having the Addition of all Mr. Hamilton's Stores, who had laid in plentifully." Franklin learned to like and respect the Quaker merchant Thomas Denham. Though the voyage across the North Atlantic in November and December was a miserable one, with storms and bad weather (A 40), it took about the usual time, just over six weeks. When the *London Hope* reached the English Channel, Captain Annis gave Franklin the mail bag to pick out Governor Keith's letters.

ELEVEN

The Water American:
London Escapades

It is as if an ingenious Artificer, having fram'd a curious Machine or Clock, and put its many intricate Wheels and Powers in such a Dependance on one another, that the whole might move in the most exact Order and Regularity, had nevertheless plac'd in it several other Wheels endu'd with an independent Self-Motion, but ignorant of the general Interest of the Clock; and these would every now and then be moving wrong, disordering the true Movement, and making continual Work for the Mender—1:63

AFTER THE *LONDON HOPE* entered the English Channel, Captain Thomas Annis kept his word and gave Franklin "an Opportunity of examining the Bag for the Governor's Letters." With sinking heart, Franklin found no letters addressed to him and none that he was asked to deliver. He selected "6 or 7 that by the Handwriting I thought might be the promis'd Letters, especially as one of them was directed to Basket the King's Printer, and another to some Stationer." Franklin promised to deliver them, still hoping that Governor Keith had recommended him and given him a letter of credit. As soon as he arrived in London on 24 December 1724, he "waited upon the Stationer who came first in my Way, delivering the Letter as from Governor Keith. I don't know such a Person, says he: but opening the Letter, O, this is from Riddlesden; I have lately found him to be a compleat Rascal, and I will have nothing to do with him, nor receive any Letters from him" (A 41). With that, the stationer put the letter in Franklin's hand and turned to wait on customers. (William Riddlesden was a transported felon and confidence man who had defrauded Deborah Read's father.) Franklin gave no more examples; he must have delivered the "6 or 7" other letters in despair. After reading the letter that the stationer refused, he saved it, realizing that it might be useful in exacting a degree of revenge upon Governor Keith.

Franklin faced the truth—Governor Keith, for what reason Franklin could not fathom, had lied to him and sent him off to London on a fool's errand. The adolescent had paid his own way but had relied on Governor Keith for credit to buy a press and types and for funds to stay in London until the next ship for Philadelphia. What was he to do? He consulted Thomas Denham, with whom he had become friends on the voyage, told him the story, and asked for advice.

Denham confirmed his worst fears. The merchant "let me into Keith's Character, told me there was not the least Probability that he had written any Letters for me, that no one who knew him had the smallest Dependance on him, and he laught at the Notion of the Governor's giving me a Letter of Credit, having as he said no Credit to give." Franklin presents the story dispassionately in the *Autobiography*, but he must have been heartbroken and distraught. "On my expressing some Concern about what I should do: He advis'd me to endeavour getting some Employment in the Way of my Business. Among the Printers here, says he, you will improve yourself; and when you return to America, you will set up to greater Advantage" (A 41).

PALMER'S

Franklin "immediately" found employment at Samuel Palmer's printing office at Bartholomew Close, London. Just off Little Britain, Bartholomew Close was named for the remains of an ancient monastery attached to the church of St. Bartholomew the Great. Palmer's shop occupied the top floor at 54 Bartholomew Close. Later publisher of *Grub Street Journal* (1730–38) and author of parts of a *General History of Printing*, Palmer had, by London standards, a medium-large printing shop.[1] He was at the peak of his career in 1725. The Stationers' Company had elected him Renter Warden on 26 March 1724 and he served until 26 March 1725.[2]

London printing shops had specialized workforces, with printers working as either pressmen or compositors. Since an accurate, fast typesetter made more money, Franklin began as a compositor (S 9:531). Franklin and Ralph found lodging in nearby Little Britain, an alley in midtown London (A 43), next door to the sign of the Green Dragon, John Wilcox's bookstore. The "inseparable Companions" Franklin and Ralph lodged "in Little Britain at 3 shilling 6 pence per Week, as much as we could then afford." Ralph tried his relations, but "they were poor and unable to assist him." He revealed to Franklin that he meant to abandon his wife and child and to remain in England. He had exhausted his money "in paying his Passage." Franklin had fifteen pistoles. Just as Franklin had previously financed Collins, he worked and financed Ralph, whose goals were impractical. He "first endeavoured to get into the Playhouse, believing himself qualify'd for an Actor." Having no experience, the aspirant applied to Robert Wilks, Drury Lane Theater's actor-manager, who "advis'd him candidly not to think of that Employment, as it was impossible he should succeed in it." Then Ralph proposed to James Roberts, "a Publisher in Paternoster Row, to write for him a Weekly Paper like the Spectator." Since he had no more reputation as a writer than as an actor, Roberts, master of the Stationers' Company from 1729 to 1732,[3] rejected him. Finally, Ralph "endeavour'd to get Employment as a Hackney Writer to copy for the Stationers and Lawyers about the Temple: but could find no Vacancy." Franklin and Ralph "had together consum'd all my Pistoles, and now just rubb'd on from hand to mouth" (A 42–43).

London Events

Economically, London was still suffering from the collapse of the South Sea Bubble, and the *London Gazette* (29 December 1724) repeated the notice that had first appeared two weeks earlier: "The Trustees appointed by Act of Parliament for Raising Money out of the Estates of the late Directors of the South-Sea Company and others give Notice, That they intend to expose to Sale to the best Bidder, in the Hall of the South Sea House, on Wednesday the 20th Day of January next the several Estates following." After the preamble, long lists of bankrupt estates filled the paper for the next several months. Despite the aftereffects of the economic depression, London in 1725, like London today, delighted most Americans. The rituals, music, theater, and, in that age, the public sermons were all celebrated by colonial visitors. Franklin was no exception. He reported that though he was "pretty diligent," he nevertheless "spent with Ralph a good deal of my Earnings in going to Plays and other Places of Amusement" (A 43). In the "Outline" of the *Autobiography*, Franklin listed "Wilkes. Cibber. Plays." Robert Wilks and Colley Cibber were at the time managing and acting in the Drury Lane Theater. Franklin and Ralph no doubt often attended its productions, especially in the early months of their London stay. They probably saw the famous actor Barton Booth (1679?–1733) appear as Cato in Addison's play and perhaps saw him in his only slightly less famous roles as Hotspur, Brutus, Othello, and Lear. In December 1724, the artist William Hogarth featured Wilks, Cibber, and Barton in his engraving titled "A Just View of the English Stage." Since Franklin later twice bought all Hogarth's works for the Library Company, he no doubt enjoyed remembering his early London days when he looked on the Hogarth print.

Franklin and Ralph surely saw plays at Drury Lane on Saturday nights during their first months in London: Shakespeare's *Julius Caesar* (2 January); John Banks's *Virtue Betray'd; or, Anna Bullen* (9 January); Thomas Otway's *Venice Preserv'd* (16 January); George Etheridge's *Man of Mode* (23 January); Shakespeare's *King Richard the Third* (6 February); Otway's *Orphan* (13 February); Ambrose Philips's *Distressed Mother* (20 February); Beaumont and Fletcher's *Rule a Wife and Have a Wife* (27 February); Addison's *Cato* (6 March); Colley Cibber's *Double Gallant* (13 March); and John Crown's *Sir Courtly Nice* (20 March). No performances appeared during passion week (22 to 27 March). Of the above plays, Addison's *Cato* was one Franklin knew well, for he quoted from it in his "Articles of Belief" (20 November 1728) and in the *Autobiography* (82). He also knew Addison's comedy *The Drummer*, which he alluded to five years later (23 April and 7 May 1730). It played at Lincoln's Inn Fields on Saturday night, 23 January, and Friday night, 2 April 1725. After Ralph left London sometime in the spring of 1725, Franklin, surely concerned about his debt to Samuel Vernon, probably attended the theater less frequently.

Franklin mentioned the "Preachers I heard" as a topic in the "Outline" of the *Autobiography*. In the eighteenth century, preachers were famous figures. No extant evidence reveals which preachers he heard. Some likely probabilities, however, exist. He would have been especially interested in hearing the best-known ministers. He had evidently read the Reverend Samuel Clarke's Boyle lectures, *On the Being and Attributes of God*, and no doubt wanted to see and hear him. A good opportunity came on Sunday, 18 April, when Clarke preached on erecting a charity school; both the subject and the preacher interested Franklin. The Reverend Edmund Calamy was another famous minister, and Franklin would have been tempted to hear his sermon preached to a society of young men on Friday evening, 28 May. Since the young printer had met New York's Governor William Burnet on his return from Boston in 1724, knew the father's literary reputation, and probably had read Gilbert Burnet's *History of His Own Time* (first volume published in 1723), he would have been interested in hearing the Reverend Gilbert Burnet (brother of the New York governor and son of the famous bishop) when the latter preached on Sunday, 1 August, at St. Paul's. Franklin perhaps attended a sermon or two by the increasingly famous "Orator [John] Henley." The bishop of London, who was responsible for overseeing all American Anglican ministers, was Edmund Gibson, and Franklin no doubt wanted to hear him. The Reverend Edmund Massey was a well-known preacher whose *Sermon Preached before the Right Honourable the Lord-Mayor* Franklin may have heard on 1 August 1725. Another famous minister, the Reverend Thomas Wheatland, delivered *The Perpetual Security of the Christian Church . . . in a Sermon preach'd before . . . the Lord-Mayor . . . at the Cathedral of St. Paul . . . November 5, 1725.*

In addition to the better-known ministers, Franklin would have been interested in those who preached on subjects or occasions that especially interested him. In January 1724/5, he may have heard the Reverend Richard Mayo preach at Lambeth Chapel (Sunday, 3 January) at the consecration of Robert, Lord Bishop of Landaff. The next evening he may have gone to hear the Reverend Edward Chandler preach to the Societies for the Reformation of Manners at St. Mary-le-bow. On Friday evening, 19 February, he would have been interested in hearing the Reverend John Wynne, who preached before the Society for the Propagation of the Gospel in Foreign Parts, an organization that supported a number of American ministers. The Reverend William Wishart's sermon preached to a society of young men on Sunday, 7 March, might have attracted him.

The deist controversy was going strong in London. Franklin had read Anthony Collins as a boy in Boston. In London he no doubt pored over Collins's *Discourse on the Grounds and Reasons of the Christian Religion*, just published in 1724 and the subject of vehement controversy in 1725, provoking more than thirty-five replies. Among others, the Reverend John Rogers (1679–1729) preached against Collins. Franklin may have heard Rogers and others who lambasted him. Though Franklin's attendance at both plays and sermons probably dropped off in 1726, he would have been interested in the Reverend Carew Rey-nell's sermon against the deist Thomas Woolston (Sunday, 10 April 1726). Later, Franklin reported Woolston's imprisonment and death in the *Pennsylvania Gazette.*

Franklin followed the London news and must have tried to see the royal family. The 2 January 1724/5 *London Gazette* reported the court news: "On New-Year's-Day the King received the Compliments of the Nobility, foreign Ministers, and other Persons of Distinction; after which, His Majesty, with his Royal Highness the Prince of Wales, and the young Princesses, heard an Ode performed to Musick, as usual." The 8 February 1724/5 *Parker's Penny Post* noted that the previous Saturday, "being the Late Queen's Birth-Day, the same was observ'd with great Solemnity, the Shops were shut, and Her Wellwishers carousing to her Memory, as they regretted her Death." On Monday, 1 March, the Society of Ancient Britons celebrated St. David's Day, waited on "their Royal Highnesses," and from thence "proceeded with great Pomp and Magnificence, with Trumpets and Kettle-Drums playing before them, to Draper's-Hall to Dinner where a very sumptuous Entertainment was provided." As the St. David's Day festivities testify, London, with a population of more than 600,000 in 1725[4] (nearly one hundred times the population of Boston, the largest town in the colonies), celebrated the range of patriotic holidays earlier and more splendidly than did American towns. Friday, 28 May, "being his Majesty's Birth-Day, there was a very numerous and splendid Appearance at Court of the Nobility and other Persons of Distinction; and at Night there were Illuminations, Bonfires, and other publick Demonstrations of Joy throughout London and Westminster" (*London Gazette,* 29 May). On the Prince of Wales's birthday (30 October) "His Royal Highness received the Compliments of the Nobility and other Persons of Distinction who made a very numerous and splendid Appearance: And at Night there were Illuminations and other Publick Demonstrations of Joy" (*London Gazette,* 2 November). The Scottish gentlemen strutted and feasted on St. Andrew's Day (30 November).

A new international organization, one not yet with branches in Boston or Philadelphia, appeared in the news. "The Annual Feast of the most ancient Society of the Free and Accepted Masons" took place at Merchant Taylor's Hall on 27 December 1725. "The appearance was very splendid and composed of a very great Number of Persons." The Masons elected "The Right Honorable the Lord Paisley, Grand Master; Reverend J. T. Desaguliers, Deputy Master" (*Parker's Penny Post,* 29 December 1725). Franklin later cited works by Desaguliers, the Royal Society's official experimenter, who invented the planetarium and published widely on natural philosophy. Since Franklin's Boston acquaintance Isaac Greenwood was now living at the home of Desaguliers and assisting him in performing experiments for the Royal Society,[5] Franklin may have met Desaguliers through Greenwood.

Franklin no doubt joined the crowds on the major public occasions. Multitudes gathered on Sunday evening, 9 January 1725/6, when "His Majesty came through the City of London, and arrived at His Palace of St. James's." Two months later, on the evening of 1 March, the birthday of Her Royal Highness the Princess of Wales, "there were Illuminations, and other Publick Demonstrations of Joy" (*London Gazette*, 5 March). "Saturday last being His Majesty's Birth-Day, the Celebration of it at Court was deferred till to Day; when there was a very numerous and splendid Appearance here of the Nobility and other Persons of Distinction, and at Night a Ball. The usual publick Demonstrations of Joy were shewn on this Occasion throughout London and Westminster" (*London Gazette*, 31 May). Another day of pageantry was Lord Mayor's Day (29 October) the "great anniversary." Franklin referred to London's Lord Mayor's Day in "A Witch Trial at Mount Holly" and no doubt witnessed the ceremonies. Even a century later, Washington Irving, who knew from the *Autobiography* that Franklin had lived in Little Britain, wrote that its inhabitants regarded the Lord Mayor's "gilt coach with six horses as the summit of human splendour; and his procession, with all the Sheriffs and Aldermen in his train, as the grandest of earthly pageants. How they exult in the idea, that the King himself dare not enter the city, without first knocking at the gate of Temple Bar, and asking permission of the Lord Mayor."[6]

Advertisements for new literary works filled the London papers. Proposals for printing by subscription Pope's translation of Homer's *Odyssey* appeared in the *Gazette* through January 1724/5. The era's greatest thief-catcher (unofficial policeman) was revealed as its greatest criminal while Franklin stayed in London. The judge committed "Jonathan Wild the Thief Taker" to Newgate on Monday, 15 February 1724/5. On 24 March appeared *An Authentic Narrative of the Life and Actions of Jonathan Wild, (Citizen and Thief-Taker of London) with the Crimes He Stands Charged with, upon a Commitment Signed by Twelve of His Majesty's Justices of the Peace.* Wild had masterminded London's underworld. Hanged on 24 May, he attracted a crowd "greater than ever was known on such an occasion" (*Parker's Penny Post*, 29 May). On 29 May, *Mist's Weekly Journal* advertised, "This day is published" Daniel Defoe's *Life of Jonathan Wild.*

News of the writer Jonathan Swift appeared when he came to London from Dublin in the spring of 1726. He was Franklin's favorite contemporary author, so Franklin may have tried to see him. *Parker's Penny Post* noted that he had "arrived here last Saturday from Ireland" (23 March). The *London Journal* advertised Swift's poem *Cadenus and Vanessa* (21 May). On the publication of the third edition, "this day" (4 June), the paper announced, "The other Edition (which is not printed for N. Blandford) has more gross Errors, which entirely pervert the Sense, than there are Pages in the Poem." The 25 June *London Journal* printed the additions made in the poem since the first editions were published. An interesting critical commentary on the poem appeared in the 2 July issue, which announced that the fourth edition came out "this Day." And the

London Journal advertised the fifth edition on 9 July. Franklin would have read every edition with appreciation.

Franklin surely followed the American news in the London papers. The Indian fight at Pigwacket, Maine, telling of Captain Lovewell's death (he was Boston's most famous Indian fighter), appeared on 9 and 12 July 1725 (*Parker's Penny Post*). Franklin probably knew Lovewell and some of his soldiers. A speech by Governor Keith together with a reply by Speaker David Lloyd appeared in the 8 January 1725/6 *British Journal*. The captivity narrative of Philip Ashton occupied several columns of the 5 March 1725/6 *Weekly Journal*.[7] And the 7 March announcement of the new minister at Philadelphia's Christ Church would have interested Franklin: "Dr. Walton, the famous Nonjuror, being order'd home by the Government from the English Church in Philadelphia, We hear, the Revd. Mr. Archibald Cummings, lately arrived from Gibraltar, where he officiated as Chaplain to that Garrison for above 3 Years, is appointed by the Lord Bishop of London to be minister of the said church of Philadelphia" (*Parker's Penny Post*).

THE ENGAGEMENT WITH DEBORAH

Franklin wrote that he gradually forgot "my Engagements with Miss Read, to whom I never wrote more than one Letter, and that was to let her know I was not likely soon to return. This was another of the great Errata of my Life, which I should wish to correct if I were to live it over again. In fact, by our Expences, I was constantly kept unable to pay my Passage" (A 43). Though he reported that he mistreated a loving Deborah, it might well be closer to the truth to say that she abandoned him. Following Franklin's lead, all previous biographers have censured him. James Parton wrote: "Unfaithful as Franklin had been to Miss Read, he had not forgotten her . . . for he wrote, long after, that it was 'the cords of love' that had 'drawn him back from England to Philadelphia' [11 September 1755]. He returned to find the lady married and miserable; and both through his fault. Despairing of his return, her mother and her other relations had persuaded her to marry 'one Rogers, a potter,' to use Franklin's own language."[8] But long before he returned, he knew that Deborah had married, and the love that brought him back to Philadelphia was for the place and his fond memories of friends in general, not an undying love for the married Deborah.

Carl Van Doren's condemnation of Franklin is briefer: "Soon after" he and Ralph arrived in London, "Ralph had said he did not intend to go back to his wife and child in Philadelphia, and Franklin, either in imitation or out of a similar urge to freedom, had written To Deborah Read—his one letter to her while he was abroad—that he was not likely to return soon." A. Owen Aldridge refers to the "moral cynicism he had manifested in his desertion of Deborah." Claude-Anne Lopez and Eugenia W. Herbert mention that he wrote her only once and proceeded to forget her.[9]

Was Franklin really culpable in his relations with Deborah Read? Did he ignore his engagement? Sailing from Philadelphia to London usually took approximately six weeks, sometimes a bit less but often more. Opportunities to send letters between Philadelphia and London were uncommon during the winter. Franklin and Deborah both knew that ships normally did not sail across the North Atlantic in January or February, partly because the crossing was more difficult, partly because the cargo for the return voyage was less plentiful, and partly because the Delaware River might be frozen.[10] When Franklin sailed on 5 November 1724, Deborah could not reasonably have expected to hear from or see Franklin (if he could immediately conduct his business and return by the first possible ship) until April or May 1725. But she married a potter named John Rogers at Philadelphia's Christ Church on 5 August 1725, exactly nine months after Franklin sailed.[11]

How long before her marriage did Deborah receive Franklin's letter? As soon as he could, Franklin no doubt wrote her the news that Governor Keith had duped him and that he would have to work to save money to return. If Franklin was lucky enough to get a letter aboard the first possible ship, he would have sent it by the *Hanover*, Captain Branden Wallis. The 18 March 1725 *American Weekly Mercury* reported the *Hanover*'s arrival in Philadelphia and the news it brought of the safe landing of Captains Henry Wells and Thomas Annis in England. Unfortunately, there is no record of him at Deal, the harbor in the English Channel three days' journey from London.[12] The *Hanover* was in Dartmouth, outward bound, on 19 January, but he could have left London before January. It took Franklin two weeks and six days in 1726 to sail from Deal to "below Portland," which is closer to London than Dartmouth, but that was a much longer time than usual for the voyage. If it took Wallis as long, he would have sailed from London on 28 December. Franklin may not have had an opportunity to write by Wallis. Even if Franklin did, Wallis arrived in Philadelphia less than five months before Deborah married.

The next two ships docking in Philadelphia from London were the *Peace*, Captain Henry Nilers (22 April), and the *Thomas*, Captain Henry Wells (6 May). Franklin's letter reporting Keith's betrayal and the necessity for him to work in London must have come by Wallis, Nilers (less than four months before Deborah married), or Wells (three months before). The annual packet on which he had sailed to London, the *London Hope*, Captain Thomas Annis, did not return to Philadelphia until 1 July.

When did Deborah Read or a Philadelphia friend write Franklin? The first possible opportunity would have been by the ship *Richmond*, which advertised in the 13 May *Mercury* "for London directly." The next possibility would have been the ship *Thomas* which "Cleared for departure" in the 3 June paper. Deborah or another Philadelphia friend surely wrote by one of these two ships. Thomas Annis's *London Hope* advertised in the 19 August *Mercury* that it intended to "Sail for London the latter End of *September* next at farthest." If Deborah Read and John Rogers courted for merely three months before marrying on 5 August, they had to be courting before either the *Richmond* or the *Thomas* left Philadelphia. Someone no doubt wrote Franklin about Deborah's courtship with Rogers in May or June.

Franklin does not mention the Rogers-Read courtship in the *Autobiography*. He concealed his disappointment on receiving the news from Philadelphia that Deborah was seeing Rogers and the subsequent news that she was married. Was he shocked by her quick courtship and marriage? One would think from the *Autobiography* (and from all earlier biographers) that Deborah pined away for him, but she shortly married someone else. In fact, Franklin's supposed "errata" regarding Deborah is a chivalrous sham, written to preserve Deborah's image. (Or, one might argue that Franklin was concealing that he had been abandoned.) Franklin even compared his gradual forgetting of Deborah Read (the only healthy thing to do after he heard she was married) to Governor Keith's deliberate lies and false dealing. When Franklin mentioned Deborah's marriage in the *Autobiography*, it was after he related his return to Philadelphia and after he saw her again. He said that he would have been "as much asham'd at seeing Miss Read" as Governor Keith was at seeing him, "had not her Friends despairing with Reason of my Return, after the Receipt of my Letter, persuaded her to marry another, one Rogers, a Potter, which was done in my Absence." Franklin thus absolved Deborah of any guilt and even of the principal action in the affair. It is as if "her Friends," rather than Deborah, decided to marry. Franklin further commented that Rogers "was a worthless Fellow tho' an excellent Workman which was the Temptation to her Friends." Thus Franklin excused even the friends for supposedly urging marriage. After all, Rogers was an excellent potter. What strange reasoning! Franklin exonerates Deborah, her mother, and even her friends from Deborah's foolish choice. He added and cancelled that Rogers "soon spent what he receiv'd with her, got into Debt, and left her the Year after my Return. It was said he had another Wife" (A 52). Perhaps he cancelled the passage because any more words spent on Rogers would simply make the reader focus longer on Deborah's action.

LONDON ACQUAINTANCES

Nineteen-year-old Franklin made a number of friends and acquaintances in London. Just after finding lodging in London's Little Britain, the book-loving Franklin began to frequent John Wilcox's bookstore next door, buying what he could afford. Wilcox "had an immense Collection of second-hand Books." He was also, like many booksellers, a publisher—and, like all great booksellers, an open-minded negotiator. Franklin could not afford to buy all the books he wanted to read, so he proposed an ingenious expedient to Wilcox: "Circulating Libraries were not then in Use; but we agreed that on certain reasonable Terms which I have now forgotten, I might take, read and return any of his Books. This I esteem'd a great Advantage, and I made as much Use of it as I could" (A 43). Franklin probably encountered at Wilcox's Green Dragon a very rare book on witchcraft that he alluded to years later, Jacobus Rick's *Tractatus due singulares de examine sagarum*, published by T. H. Grentzii in 1685.[13]

In London Franklin called on the famous Philadelphia lawyer Andrew Hamilton, whose food and wine Franklin and others in the great cabin happily consumed on the voyage to London. Having settled the case that caused him to cancel his earlier voyage, Hamilton sailed from New York on the *Beaver*, Captain Thomas Smith, on 16 November 1724, arrived at Deal on 9 December, and no doubt reached London three days later (his quick voyage took just twenty-seven days; Franklin's took forty-nine). Franklin knew from William Riddlesden's letter to the stationer that he and Governor Keith had a "secret Scheme on foot to the Prejudice of Hamilton." Franklin waited on Hamilton "and gave him the Letter" concerning the "secret Scheme" (I have no idea it was). Hamilton "thank'd me cordially, the Information being of Importance to him. And from that time he became my Friend, greatly to my Advantage afterwards on many Occasions" (A 42). Though Franklin must have hoped the letter might provide some revenge for Keith's betrayal, the letter proved much more valuable. Andrew Hamilton not only became his friend but later, as Speaker of the House of Representatives of Pennsylvania, he secured for Franklin the job of printing for the colony—the very position that Keith had promised him. Hamilton became Franklin's most important patron.

Through his work at Palmer's printing house, Franklin met several persons who were later of importance to him. Charles Ackers, who was about three years older than the American, was completing his apprenticeship with Palmer. Franklin may have attended his marriage on 23 May and celebrated with him when Ackers completed his apprenticeship six weeks later, on 6 July 1725. Ackers continued to work for Palmer until 1727. Five years later, when the *London Magazine* started, Ackers was one of its owners and editors. Franklin probably introduced Ackers to James Ralph. After Ackers set up his own printing shop in 1727, he published Ralph's *Night: A Poem* in January 1727/8.[14] In the 1730s, Franklin sent Ackers colonial news for the *London Magazine*.[15] While Franklin worked for him, Palmer was printing Arabic editions of the Psalter and New Testament for the Society for Promoting Christian Knowledge (SPCK). William Caslon (1692–1766), the early eighteenth-century's premier type founder, designed the Arabic type that Ackers and possibly Franklin set in 1725. Franklin evidently met Caslon at the time and later became the first American printer to use Caslon's type.[16] Franklin also met Thomas James, whose type foundry was downstairs from Palmer's, and talked with James (as we will see in Volume 2) about lead poisoning.

Franklin surely looked up Isaac Greenwood, the Harvard graduate and Cotton Mather supporter whom he had known in Boston. He probably also met the Boston native Jeremiah Dummer, who had graduated from Harvard in 1699, had become the Massachusetts agent in England, and had written *A Defense of the New England Charters*, which Franklin must have read when it was published in Boston in 1721. In London, Franklin probably learned of Dummer's reputation as a rake and freethinker.

When Dr. Zabdiel Boylston, famous for his inoculations in Boston, visited London in 1725 at the Royal Society's invitation, Franklin saw him. Boylston had been James Franklin's physician and was well-known to Franklin. A Boylston family descendent in the late nineteenth century said that Franklin, "without money, friends or counsel," applied in "extreme distress" to Boylston, who supplied Franklin with twenty guineas. Franklin supposedly came to rely on Boylston's advice and "visited him as opportunities offered." By Boylston's "faithful counsels and encouragements," Franklin was saved from "the abyss of destruction." Franklin's "future fortune was based on" Boylston's "timely assistance." The story is obviously family folklore. Franklin was gainfully employed immediately after his arrival and worked until just before leaving London. The exaggerated diction of the account ("extreme distress," "the abyss of destruction," Franklin's "future fortune") is typical of nineteenth-century sentimentality and completely unlike Franklin. No doubt Franklin looked up Boylston, but the rest of the account is apocryphal.[17]

In the house where Franklin and Ralph lodged in Little Britain, a young milliner lived who had a shop in the Cloisters. "She had been genteelly bred, was sensible and lively, and of most pleasing Conversation. Ralph read Plays to her in the Evenings, they grew intimate, she took another Lodging, and he follow'd her." Franklin must have been glad—at least financially—to see Ralph go. Ralph and the milliner "liv'd together some time, but he being still out of Business, and her Income not sufficient to maintain them with her Child, he took a Resolution of going from London, to try for a Country School, which he thought himself well qualify'd to undertake, as he wrote an excellent Hand, and was a Master of Arithmetic and Accounts." Since Ralph deemed teaching beneath him and was certain "of future better Fortune when he should be unwilling to have it known that he once was so meanly employ'd, he chang'd his Name, and did me the Honour to assume mine" (A 44). Obviously Franklin wrote tongue in cheek.

Confirmed in the belief that he had the makings of a great poet by Osborne's praise of his version of the eighteenth psalm, Ralph sent Franklin long drafts of an epic poem by post, asking for Franklin's criticism and corrections. Since the recipient paid the postage, and since eighteenth-century postage was expensive, Franklin found the poem a financial burden, as well as boring. Edward Young's *Universal Passion* was appearing in parts during 1725, so Franklin copied and sent Ralph "a great Part of it, which set in a strong Light the Folly of pursuing the Muses without any Hope of Advancement by them." At least Ralph had to pay one hefty postal charge. But "All was in vain." The impractical Ralph did not care what his interminable poem cost Franklin, and "Sheets of the Poem continu'd to come by every Post" (A 45). The unwelcome correspondence terminated unexpectedly.

Franklin told an anecdote that sounds absolutely honest and reflects only discredit upon himself. Few autobiographers (none of his aspiring younger contemporaries who attempted autobiographies—John Adams, Thomas Jefferson, or Dr. Benjamin Rush) ever revealed that they behaved badly. The milliner, having on Ralph's account, "lost her Friends and Business, was often in Distresses, and us'd to send for me, and borrow what I could spare to help her out of them. I grew fond of her Company, and being at this time under no Religious Restraints, and presuming on my Importance to her, I attempted Familiarities, (another Erratum) which she repuls'd with a proper Resentment, and acquainted him with my Behaviour. This made a Breach between us, and when he return'd again to London, he let me know he thought I had cancel'd all the Obligations he had been under to me.—So I found I was never to expect his Repaying me what I lent to him or advanc'd for him. This was however not then of much Consequence, as he was totally unable. And in the Loss of his Friendship I found my self reliev'd from a Burthen" (A 45).

A DISSERTATION ON LIBERTY AND NECESSITY

In February 1724/5, the nineteen-year-old Franklin set in type the third edition of William Wollaston's *Religion of Nature Delineated*.[18] "Some of his Reasonings not appearing to me well-founded, I wrote a little metaphysical Piece, in which I made Remarks on them" (A 43). With Samuel Palmer's permission, Franklin worked after hours and printed one hundred copies on Palmer's press. He must have paid Palmer (perhaps in additional labor) for the paper and ink, plus a small fee. *A Dissertation on Liberty and Necessity, Pleasure and Pain* appeared about June 1725.[19] If ever a pamphlet came from an underground press, it was Franklin's *Dissertation*. The title page contained no author, publisher, or bookseller. The dedication to "J. R." (Franklin's friend James Ralph) revealed nothing. Who could trace the pamphlet to "J. R." or to the unknown young printer? In a 9 November 1779 letter to Benjamin Vaughan, Franklin wrote that he gave a few copies to friends, but that "afterwards disliking the piece, as conceiving it might have an ill tendency, I burnt the rest, except one copy, the margin of which was filled with manuscript notes by Lyons, author of the *Infallibility of Human Judgment*, who was at that time another of my acquaintance in London." Since at least seven copies of the *Dissertation* survive (none, unfortunately, with Lyons's manuscript notes), I doubt he really burned it. Indeed, for seven copies to have survived from one hundred is surprisingly good: it shows that the book was hardly read at the time. Primers and almanacs of the period, though printed in the thousands, survive mainly in unique copies. Moreover, a Dublin reprint (1733) of the pamphlet, which Franklin probably did not know about, is scarcer than the London original.[20]

Sources and Methods

Franklin noted in the *Autobiography* that Samuel Palmer "expostulated with me upon the Principles of my Pamphlet which to him appear'd abominable" (A

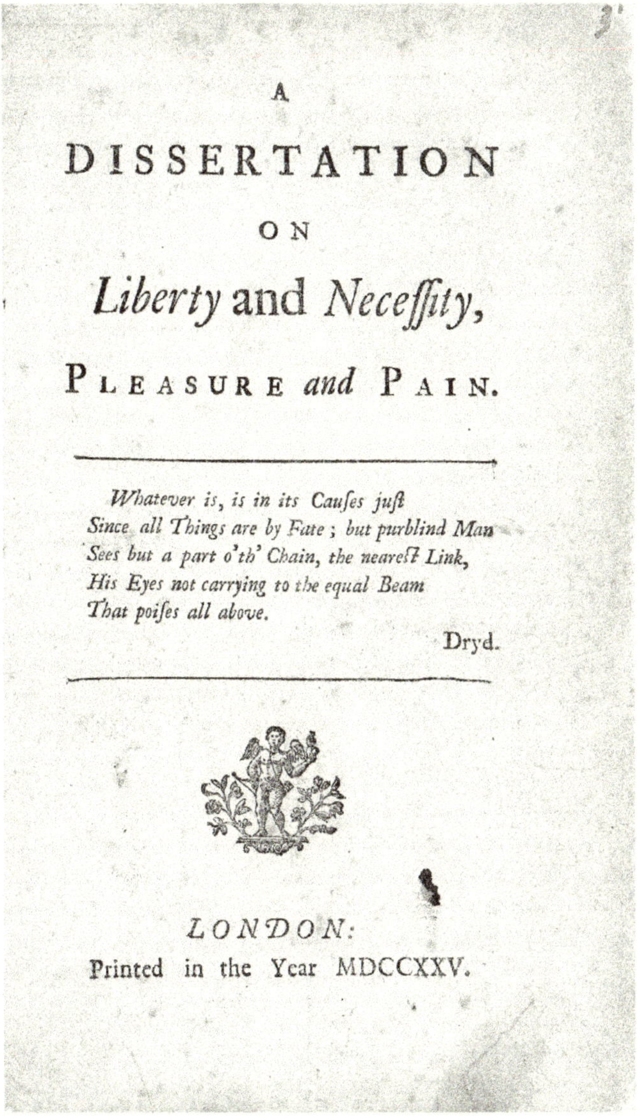

A

DISSERTATION

O N

Liberty and *Neceſſity,*

P L E A S U R E *and* P A I N.

Whatever is, is in its Cauſes juſt
Since all Things are by Fate ; but purblind Man
Sees but a part o'th' Chain, the neareſt Link,
His Eyes not carrying to the equal Beam
That poiſes all above.

Dryd.

LONDON:
Printed in the Year MDCCXXV.

Figure 21. Clandestine literature: the title page of A Dissertation on Liberty and Necessity, Pleasure and Pain *(London, 1725). With no author, publisher, or bookseller, the pamphlet was surreptitious literature. If it came to the attention of the authorities, they would not easily have been able to find its author or publisher. Franklin's Dissertation travestied the popular justifications of the ways of God to man, including John Dryden's lines on the title page. Franklin was inspired to write it when he set in type William Wollaston,* Religion of Nature Delineated *(London: S. Palmer, 1725), a book he especially ridiculed. Dr. William Lyons, who befriended Franklin in London, had been jailed for publishing* The Infallibility, Dignity, and Excellence of Humane Judgment *(1719), which is much less sacrilegious than Franklin's Dissertation. Though Franklin wrote that he destroyed all copies of the pamphlet, save one with Dr. Lyons's annotations, seven copies survive, none with the annotations. Courtesy, John Carter Brown Library, Providence, Rhode Island.*

43). The dedication emphasized that the argument was hypothetical, thereby suggesting that the arguments should not influence one's conduct. Scholars have viewed the document as a straightforward philosophical essay. It is not; it is a satire. In Boston the Couranteers, and then Franklin, satirized the ministers by imitating their style and message. In some ways, Franklin's *Dissertation* similarly burlesques the arguments of Wollaston and others by imitating them. Franklin cited on the title page a passage from John Dryden and Nathaniel Lee's *Oedipus* (III. I. 244–48):

> Whatever is, is in its Causes just
> Since all Things are by Fate; but purblind Man
> Sees but a part o'th'Chain, the nearest Link,
> His Eyes not carrying to the equal Beam
> That poises all above.

Gerald Stourzh, a historian of American foreign policy, cited the epigraph as evidence of Franklin's belief in the Great Chain of Being, but A. Owen Aldridge, reviewing Stourzh's work, claimed that the citation concerned only the doctrine of philosophical necessity.[21] The quotation was among the best-known examples in English literature of the cosmic optimism inspired partly by Gottfried Wilhelm Leibniz. (Pope's "Whatever is, is right" would supplant it when *The Essay on Man* appeared in 1732–34.) In part, the *Dissertation* spoofs Leibniz's theodicy and Shaftesbury's optimism. In so doing, Franklin anticipates Voltaire's *Candide* (1759). Voltaire, however, couched his satire as a fable from a somewhat bemused persona, whereas the young Franklin put his into a sometimes strident, humorless argument.

Religion, especially theodicy, is the major subject of the *Dissertation*. Writers on theodicy usually try to reconcile the existence of evil and suffering in the world with their religious beliefs. Franklin, however, like many of the deistic writers, shifted the focus from an attempt to account for the existence of evil and suffering to a burlesque of such attempts. His underlying models in the *Dissertation* were the deist writers Charles Blount, Anthony Collins, Matthew Tindal, and John Toland, all of whom have been considered covert atheists who practiced "the art of theological lying."[22] In addition to theodicy, Franklin took up free will versus determinism. His argument used the appeal to the *consensus gentium*, that is, the argument that the beliefs generally common to mankind are true.[23] He also touched briefly on immortality, reincarnation, heaven, hell, and identity. These topics, which often turn up in his writings, especially reflect his reading of John Locke and Lucretius. And, of course, the immediate occasion for writing the *Dissertation* was his scorn for William Wollaston's *Religion of Nature Delineated*.

Another subject of the *Dissertation* was human nature, with Franklin stressing pride as its major characteristic and self-interest as the usual basis for human actions. Here he was influenced by the Port Royal *Logic*; by the English moral writers, especially Addison and Steele, Shaftesbury and Mandeville; as well as by the major English philosophers of the past century, Bacon, Hobbes, and Locke. Such ideas as skepticism (including the frequent divergence of appearance and reality) and the moral complexity of the world (influenced by the tantalizing "Cases of Conscience" genre of popular religious literature, even though the tradition had been burlesqued by Nathaniel Gardner and Franklin) are present in the *Dissertation* and recur in his writings.

In method, Franklin was indebted to Nathaniel Gardner, particularly Gardner's 27 November 1721 burlesque of the syllogistic reasoning of Cotton and Increase Mather. Indeed, reasoning by the syllogistic method is one subject of Franklin's satire. Franklin believed in the inductive method of Bacon, Descartes, and the Port Royalists. As Franklin wrote, Bacon "is justly esteem'd the father of the modern experimental philosophy" (3:339). Gardner was also a source for the satiric method, along with John Wise, Montaigne, and especially Jonathan Swift. Franklin had not yet achieved the aesthetic distance of any of these three authors, but he had read works by and about all of them before leaving Boston in 1723.

Liberty and Necessity

Franklin began his *Dissertation* with two premises, both stated as hypotheses: "I. *There is said to be a* First Mover, *who is called God, Maker of the universe.* II. *He is said to be all-wise, all-good, all powerful.*" Despite immediately undercutting the two propositions ("said to be"), Franklin commented that they were "allow'd and asserted by People of almost every Sect and Opinion; I have here suppos'd them granted, and laid them down as the Foundation of my Argument; What follows from them, will stand or fall as they are true or false" (1:59). In the letter to Vaughan, written over fifty years later, he still called them the "supposed attributes" of God. He had learned from Descartes and the Port Royalists, among others, that most faulty reasoning followed from faulty initial premises. If he had already become, as he avers in the *Autobiography*, a doubter in religion, then he thought the premises were faulty.

The young logician's arguments in the *Dissertation* gradually burlesque, satirize, and then travesty the two premises. By the conclusion, Franklin has denied not only the normal feelings but also the pleasures and even the pains that everyone experiences. The conclusion is nonsense, a reductio ad absurdum. The real argument of the *Dissertation* maintains that only a denial of our common-sense experiences of life (and of pleasure and pain among other sensations) would be consistent with the absurd beliefs set out in the initial two propositions defining God. Propositions III and IV are straightforward: "III. If He is all good, whatsoever He doth must be good. IV. If He is all-wise, whatsoever He doth must be wise."

Then Franklin introduced the obvious difficulties—evil and suffering. Given the goodness and wisdom of God, from whence comes evil? "V. *If He is all-*

powerful, there can be nothing either existing or acting in the Universe against *or* without *his Consent; and what He consents to must be good, because He is good; therefore Evil doth not exist.*" Franklin conceded that he did not deny that "both Things and Actions" exist "to which we give the Name of *Evil* . . . as *Pain, Sickness, Want, Theft, Murder,* &c." But he claimed they could not be "in reality *Evils, Ills,* or *Defects* in the Order of the Universe." Such apparent evils were actually all for the best. Thereby Franklin ostensibly affirmed, but actually ridiculed, the eighteenth century's cosmic optimism. As he wryly wrote his wife Deborah on 10 June 1758 about an acquaintance who lost both his ship and mistress at the same time, "let him think, if he can, that whatever is, is best."

"VI. *If a Creature is made by God, it must depend upon God, and receive all its Power from Him; with which Power the Creature can do nothing contrary to His Will, must be agreeable to it; what is agreeable to it must be good, because He is Good; therefore a Creature can do nothing but what is good*" (1:59–60). The fifth proposition, if true (and the logic is without fault) makes nonsense of all systems of morality—including, of course, the Ten Commandments. Franklin's proposition argued that the greatest villains (from individual sadistic murderers to such mass butchers as [to be anachronistic] Stalin and Hitler) in the history of the world did nothing but good. Common sense tells us we can choose to steal, rape, torture, or murder, and these actions are not good. The *Dissertation* has become a satire on the usual idea of God, and it implied that if God exists, He must have an entirely different nature from that generally ascribed to him.

Then the young iconoclast quoted and satirized Wollaston: "Every Action which is done according to *Truth,* is good; and every Action contrary to Truth, is evil." Wollaston's simple-minded, circular assertions surely reminded him of Cotton and Increase Mather's syllogistic reasoning in *Sentiments on the Small Pox Inoculated* (1721) and of Nathaniel Gardner's 27 November 1721 *Courant* travesty of their method (Chapter 6, above). After burlesquing Wollaston's argument, Franklin, knowing that the theoretical position advanced in the *Dissertation* did not forbid crime, commented, "I would not be understood by this to encourage or defend Theft; 'tis only for the sake of the Argument, and will certainly have no *ill Effect.* The Order and Course of Things will not be affected by Reasoning of this Kind; and 'tis as just and necessary, and as much according to Truth, for *B* to dislike and punish the Theft of his Horse, as it is for *A* to steal him" (1:61). Here Franklin incidently explains why he chose the forbiddingly learned title, *A Dissertation on Liberty and Necessity, Pleasure and Pain.* He did not want the pamphlet to convince anyone that theft, immorality, or cynicism was good; the pamphlet was written only for learned persons, like the free-thinker and surgeon Dr. William Lyons and the intellectual Bernard Mandeville, who would enjoy its satire and not be morally affected by it.

The seventh proposition denied free will: "*If the Creature is thus limited in his Actions, being able to do only such Things as God would have him to do, and not being able to refuse doing what God would have done; then he can have no such Thing as Liberty, Free-will or Power to do or refuse an Action.*" Franklin defined *liberty* as "Absence of Opposition," but he derided the definition by observing that in this sense "all our Actions may be said to be the Effects of Our Liberty." Glancing at Newton's law of gravitation, he claimed that if liberty meant an absence of opposition, it is a "Liberty of the same Nature with the Fall of a heavy Body to the Ground; it has Liberty to fall, that is, it meets with nothing to hinder its Fall, but at the same Time it is necessitated to fall, and has no Power or Liberty to remain suspended" (1:61–62).

The young philosopher then considered the argument that we are "free Agents," basing his argument against freedom of the will on scientific deism or physico-theology. "As Man is a Part of this great Machine, the Universe, his regular Acting is requisite to the regular moving of the whole." Calling the universe the "great Machine" again alluded to Newton's laws, which had explained the behavior of the solar system. The machine metaphor also foreshadowed Franklin's use of the clockmaker analogy. Up to this point in the *Dissertation*, the tone had been dry and abstract, but a note of exasperation now entered the argument: "Among the many Things which lie before him to be done, he may, as he is at Liberty and his Choice influenc'd by nothing, (for so it must be, or he is not at Liberty) chuse any one, and refuse the rest. Now there is every Moment something *best* to be done, which is alone then *good*, and with respect to which, every Thing else is at that Time *evil*. In order to know which is best to be done, and which not, it is requisite that we should have at one View all the intricate Consequences of every Action with respect to the general Order and Scheme of the Universe, both present and future; but they are innumerable and incomprehensible by any Thing but Omniscience" (1:62).

Franklin was serious: a complete knowledge of all possible consequences of every action is impossible. The world is too complex. His statement of the moral complexity of the world is his earliest expression of a version of the heterogeneity of ends. He had probably already read *The Memoirs of Cardinal de Retz*, which quoted Oliver Cromwell's saying that a person never goes higher than when he does not know where he is going. Franklin later applied the law of unintended consequences, or the heterogeneity of ends, to society and ecology.[24] One undercurrent in his statement would lead one to a belief in God: the reason or mind of human beings is so limited that we cannot know what is really good. That position, in some persons (Pascal among others) and in some moods of Franklin, leads to fideism.

Franklin's tone grew increasingly brusque and impatient: "As we cannot know these, we have but as one Chance to ten thousand, to hit on the right Action; we should then be perpetually blundering about in the Dark, and putting the Scheme in Disorder; for every wrong Action of a Part, is a Defect or Blemish in the Order of the Whole." He posed the conclusion as a question. "Is it not necessary then, that our Actions should be over-rul'd and govern'd by an all-wise Providence?" Again he cited the design argument, the standard "proof" of scientific deism. "How exact and regular is every Thing in the *natural* World! How wisely in every Part contriv'd! We cannot here find the least Defect! Those who have study'd the mere animal and vegetable Creation, demonstrate that nothing can be more harmonious and beautiful! All the heavenly Bodies, the Stars and Planets, are regulated with the utmost Wisdom!" (1:62).

Turning from the design argument in science, Franklin maintained that the moral world was analogous. Herein, he used the clockmaker analogy. Franklin knew it from numerous sources,[25] including John Ray's *Wisdom of God Manifested in the Works of the Creation* (1691), which Franklin cited in his 1728 "Articles of Belief," and the Leibniz-Clarke correspondence (1717). Samuel Clarke had argued that God, like a clockmaker who periodically had to clean and reset a watch, must intervene occasionally in the cosmos to set things right. In reply, Leibniz maintained that God's cosmos was perfect. Clarke's theories, Leibniz said, implied that God was less than perfect, having to tinker with and set right the cosmos. Clarke responded that Leibniz restricted God's liberty and made him subservient to nature's laws. Except for God's constant care and intervention, Clarke claimed, the cosmos would turn into chaos.[26] Franklin wrote:

> And can we suppose less Care to be taken in the Order of the *moral* than in the *natural* System? It is as if an ingenious Artificer, having fram'd a curious Machine or Clock, and put its many intricate Wheels and Powers in such a Dependance on one another, that the whole might move in the most exact Order and Regularity, had nevertheless plac'd in it several other Wheels endu'd with an independent *Self-Motion*, but ignorant of the general Interest of the Clock; and these would every now and then be moving wrong, disordering the true Movement, and making continual Work for the Mender; which might better be prevented, by depriving them of that Power of Self-Motion, and placing them in a Dependance on the regular Part of the Clock. (1:63)

Ostensibly, Franklin agreed with Leibniz; actually, he covertly satirized Leibniz, Clarke, and the design argument. Franklin insinuated that everyone with common sense could see that everything in the world was not constantly good. Later, in an essay on the death of infants, Franklin returned to the clockmaker analogy, characterizing God as a crazy craftsman whose "intense Application had disturb'd his Brain and impair'd his Reason" (20 June 1734).

Having abolished free will, Franklin advanced two more propositions: "VIII. *If there is no such Thing as Free-Will in Creatures, there can be neither Merit nor Demerit in Creatures*" and "IX. *And therefore every Creature must be equally esteem'd by the Creator.*" After claiming that the most bloodthirsty, bestial murderer must be as saintly and deserving as Jesus Christ, Franklin proceeded to claim that all persons were "equally esteem'd" by God and that God used them equally (1:63). The starving, begging orphan, who grew up in disease and filth and died in misery, was really, Franklin argued in the travesty, as well off as the happiest, beloved child of a wealthy, loving family.

The first section of the *Dissertation* proved that if the first two propositions concerning the nature of God are true, there can be no free will and thus no evil—further, that there can be no immorality and thus no possible reason for the existence of hell. All people are equally good, and therefore all equally deserve heaven. Since theologians and philosophers commonly defined God by the first two propositions, Franklin was ridiculing the definition. Not content with attacking Christianity and the idea of God, Franklin also burlesqued the underlying ideas of physico-theology or scientific deism. Fundamental thinkers like Robert Boyle, John Locke, Newton, and Leibniz[27] and their popularizers like François Fénelon, John Ray, William Derham, Cotton Mather, and William Wollaston[28] all championed the notion that nature's order and regularity proved the existence of a supernatural intelligence responsible for nature. They generally supposed with Leibniz that God, having created the world, did not thereafter concern himself with the everyday actions of humans. Further, they usually believed in mankind's free will. (Calvinists like Cotton Mather, of course, were exceptions to these two corollaries.) Franklin found their position inconsistent and illogical. If a Grand Design and a Grand Designer existed, free will did not. He believed in free will; he was ridiculing the logical consequences of the first two premises. He restated the argument in *Observations on the Proceedings against Mr. Hemphill* (1735), again using a reductio ad absurdum: "to say that God regards Men for any thing else besides Goodness and Virtue, is such a Notion as makes all Men both virtuous and vicious capable of being equally regarded by him, and consequently there is no Difference between Virtue and Vice" (2:59). Franklin thought the absurdity of such opinions obvious.

Pleasure and Pain

Section 2 of the *Dissertation* was "Of Pleasure and Pain." Though section 1 began with commonly accepted propositions, section 2 began with seemingly unusual and personal propositions. The first premise was: "*When a Creature is form'd and endu'd with Life, 'tis suppos'd to receive a Capacity of the Sensation of* Uneasiness *or* Pain." Franklin used John Locke's synonym for pain, *uneasiness*.[29] Franklin argued, "This distinguishes Life and Consciousness from unactive unconscious Matter. To know or be sensible of Suffering or being acted upon is *to live*; and whatsoever is not so, among created Things, is properly and truly *dead*." Locke stated, "The chief if not only spur to humane Industry and Action is uneasiness." He claimed that nothing sets "us upon the change of State, or upon any new Action but some *uneasiness*."[30]

In making pain the primary agent of causation, Franklin reflected Locke and probably also the Greek atomists, particularly Lucretius, who based all actions on pain. In the proem opening book 2 of *De rerum natura*, Lucretius wrote, "Ah! miserable minds of men, blind hearts! in what darkness of life, in what great dangers ye spend this little span of years! to think that ye should not see that nature cries aloud for nothing else but that pain may be kept far sundered from the body, and that, withdrawn from care and fear, she may enjoy in mind the sense of pleasure!"[31] B. Cyril Bailey noted: "The ultimate goal of the Epicurean moral theory was 'pleasure,' but that did not mean the 'kinetic' pleasures of bodily and mental excitement, such as were recommended by Aristippus and the Cyrenaies, but the 'castastematic' pleasure of freedom from pain and care; the 'kinetic' pleasures were to be avoided, because they often produced pain as their consequence."[32] Since Lucretius was among the more popular classical authors in the eighteenth century, Franklin had likely already read one of the commonly available English translations. His interest continued. In 1749, Franklin borrowed Alessandro Marchetti's 1717 Italian translation of Lucretius from James Logan (2:185). Before 1757, Franklin was more responsible for the purchase of the Library Company of Philadelphia's books than any other person. He may well have ordered the 1699 edition of Lucretius that appeared in the Library Company's 1757 *Catalogue*. Franklin must also have been influenced by Hobbes's pessimistic views, since he held them more truthful than Locke's comparatively optimistic view of life. To be sure, Locke considered *pain* or *uneasiness* only one principle of causation, though Franklin called it the sole agent.

Franklin posited a mechanistic view of humans. "All *Pain* and *Uneasiness* proceeds at first from and is caus'd by Somewhat without and distinct from the Mind itself. The Soul must first be acted upon before it can re-act. In the Beginning of Infancy it is as if it were not; it is not conscious of its own Existence, till it has receiv'd the first Sensation of *Pain*; then, and not before, it begins to feel itself, is rous'd, and put into Action; then it discovers its Powers and Faculties, and exerts them to expel the Uneasiness." Franklin next gives an absolutely pessimistic view of the human condition: "Thus is the Machine set on work; this is Life. We are first mov'd by *Pain*, and the whole succeeding Course of our Lives is but one continu'd Series of Action with a View to be freed from it." Franklin's reference to man as a machine again recalls the Greek atomists and the Epicurean tradition, particularly Lucretius. But as with his doctrine of *uneasiness*, the classical ideas of man as machine had been reinforced by modern ones. In addition to Hobbes, Franklin was indebted to Descartes's notion of animals as automatons.[33] Franklin later defined man as "a tool-making animal" (Boswell, *Life of Johnson*, 7 April 1778), but here in 1725 he defined man as a machine moved by pain. "As fast as we have excluded one Uneasiness another appears, otherwise the Motion would cease. If a continual Weight is not apply'd the Clock will stop. And as soon as the Avenues of Uneasiness to the Soul are choak'd up or cut off, we are dead, we think and act no more" (1:64). In the first part of his dissertation, he had called the universe the "great Machine" and used the clockmaker analogy for the moral system. Here he again used the machine comparison, but now if there is a God, He made humans solely to experience pain. When the pain ceases, "the Clock will stop."

The second proposition was: "*This Uneasiness, whenever felt, produces* Desire *to be freed from it, great in exact proportion to the Uneasiness.*" In the popular eighteenth-century English history of classical philosophy, Thomas Stanley translated Sextus Empiricus's summary of skepticism, which stated, "The final Cause (*End* or *Aim*) of *Scepticism*" as the "Hope of *Indisturbance*: for Man's Mind being troubled at the unsetledness in things, and doubting what to assent unto, enquireth what is true and what false, that by determination thereof it may be quiet." Like the traditional skeptics, Franklin found "*that to every Reason there is an opposite Reason equivalent.*"[34] The Greek philosopher Carneades was especially famous for arguing one position—and then the opposite. Franklin knew this characteristic of the Greek skeptics from the Port Royal *Logic*, Stanley, and probably from Pierre Bayle; he employed it in writing about the supposed equivalence of pleasure and pain in every person's life; and he later often wrote on opposite sides of the same question.

Franklin said uneasiness was "the first Spring and Cause of all Action; for till we are uneasy in Rest, we can have no Desire to move, and without Desire of moving there can be no voluntary Motion." With great irony, he then echoed the cosmic optimism of Dryden, Leibniz, and the scientific deists: "I might here observe, how necessary a Thing in the Order and Design of the Universe this *Pain* or *Uneasiness* is, and how beautiful in its Place!" He was satirizing not only the epigraph for the *Dissertation* (and the optimistic thinking it so brilliantly encapsulated) but also the fundamental nature of a God who has created man as a machine moved by pain. "Let us but suppose it just now banish'd the World entirely, and consider the Consequence of it: All the Animal Creation would immediately stand stock still, exactly in the Posture they were in the Moment Uneasiness departed; not a Limb, nor a Finger would henceforth move; we should all be reduc'd to the Condition of Statues, dull and unactive" (1:64).

While echoing Locke, Franklin also alluded to Descartes. Franklin at first specified "All the Animal Creation" and subsequently referred to the "Animal Creation" as "they" and "we," thus making it clear that he included humans within the category (1:64). Franklin made mankind like Descartes's automaton-animals. Conversely, Locke stressed the pleasure that "our Wise Creator" endows us with—pleasure as causation. Further, Locke argued that man's aim is happiness[35] (in Jefferson's brilliant version, "the pursuit of happiness"). Franklin, however, claimed that man's only aim is to escape from pain. As shown above, Locke said that humans were pushed by pain and pulled by pleasure. Franklin omitted the latter in his travesty of Wollaston.

Franklin completed the comparison of humans to machines by portraying himself as the animal-automaton: "Here I should continue to sit motionless with the Pen in my Hand thus—and neither leave my Seat nor write one Letter more. This may appear odd at first View, but a little Consideration will make it evident; for 'tis impossible to assign any other Cause for the voluntary Motion of an Animal than its *uneasiness* in Rest." Note Franklin's diction: he is the "Animal." Franklin's irony increases: "What a different Appearance then would the Face of Nature make, without it! How necessary is it! And how unlikely that the Inhabitants of the World ever were, or that the Creator ever design'd they should be, exempt from it!" (1:64–65). God the Sadist created humans in order to torture them.

From a vicious, though indirect, condemnation of God's nature, the young freethinker turned to mankind: "I would likewise observe here, that the VIIIth Proposition in the preceding Section, viz. *That there is neither Merit nor Demerit,* &c. is here again demonstrated, as infallibly, tho' in another manner: For since *Freedom from Uneasiness* is the End of all our Actions, how is it possible for us to do any Thing disinterested? How can any Action be meritorious of Praise or Dispraise, Reward or Punishment, when the natural Principle of *Self-Love* is the only and the irresistible Motive to it?" (1:65). All human actions result from selfishness, strangely defined here by Franklin as the desire to be free from uneasiness.

The third proposition was "*This* Desire *is always fulfill'd or satisfy'd.*" Franklin explained: "In the *Design* or *End* of it, tho' not in the *Manner:* The first is requisite, the latter not." As an illustration, Franklin supposed that a person was "in a House which appears to be in imminent Danger of Falling, this, as soon as perceiv'd, creates a violent *Uneasiness,* and that instantly produces an equal strong *Desire,* the *End* of which is *freedom from the Uneasiness,* and the *Manner* or Way propos'd to gain this *End,* is *to get out of the House.* Now if he is convinc'd by any Means, that he is mistaken, and the House is not likely to fall, he is immediately freed from his *Uneasiness,* and the *End* of his Desire is attain'd as well as if it had been in the *Manner* desir'd, viz. *leaving the House.*" Franklin then enlarged what we normally think of as pain or uneasiness: "All our different Desires and Passions proceed from and are reducible to this one Point, *Uneasiness,* tho' the Means we propose to ourselves for expelling of it are infinite. One proposes *Fame,* another *Wealth,* a third *Power,* &c. as the Means to gain this *End;* but tho' these are never attain'd, if the Uneasiness be remov'd by some other Means, the *Desire* is satisfy'd. Now during the Course of Life we are ourselves continually removing successive Uneasinesses as they arise, and the *last* we suffer is remov'd by the *sweet Sleep* of Death" (1:65). In this bleak view, life is a series of unsatisfied desires: fame, wealth, and power were never completely satisfying to those who gained even the greatest share of them, so that all ostensible satisfactions are mirages. The only surcease from uneasiness/pain is death.

The fourth proposition dealt with Locke's primary causation, pleasure: "*The fulfulling or Satisfaction of this* Desire *produces the Sensation of* Pleasure, *great or small in exact proportion to the* Desire." But Franklin defined pleasure out of existence: "*Pleasure* is that Satisfaction which arises in the Mind upon, and is caus'd by, the accomplishment of our *Desires.*" Since desire had been shown "to be caus'd by our *Pains* or *Uneasinesses,* it follows that *Pleasure* is wholly caus'd by *Pain,* and by no other Thing at all." (Are there no unexpected pleasures in life?) Franklin concluded with his fifth proposition, "*Therefore the Sensation of* Pleasure *is equal, or in exact proportion to the Sensation of* Pain." He commented:

> As the *Desire* of being freed from Uneasiness is equal to the *Uneasiness*, and the *Pleasure* of satisfying that Desire equal to the *Desire*, the *Pleasure* thereby produc'd must necessarily be equal to the *Uneasiness* or *Pain* which produces it. . . . And as our *Uneasinesses* are always remov'd by some Means or other [death being the last way pain or uneasiness is removed], it follows that *Pleasure* and *Pain* are in their Nature inseparable: So many Degrees as one Scale of the Balance descends, so many exactly the other ascends; and one cannot rise or fall without the Fall or Rise of the other: 'Tis impossible to taste of *Pleasure*, without feeling its preceding proportionate *Pain*; or to be sensible of *Pain*, without having its necessary Consequent *Pleasure*: The *highest Pleasure* is only Consciousness of Freedom from the *deepest Pain*, and Pain is not Pain to us unless we ourselves are sensible of it. They go Hand in Hand; they cannot be divided. (1:66)

Franklin then gave a series of proofs. The last one argued that "the *Pain* of Absence from Friends, produces the *Pleasure* of Meeting in exact proportion. &c." He generalized: "This is the *fixt Nature* of Pleasure and Pain, and will always be found to be so by those who examine it" (1:66).

Afterlife

The young logician directly contradicted Wollaston's argument for an afterlife. Franklin wrote: "One of the most common Arguments for the future Existence of the Soul, is taken from the generally suppos'd Inequality of Pain and Pleasure in the present; and this, notwithstanding the Difficulty by outward Appearances to make a Judgment of another's Happiness, has been look'd upon as almost unanswerable:[36] but since *Pain* naturally and infallibly produces a *Pleasure* in proportion to it, every individual Creature must, in any State of *Life*, have an equal Quantity of each, so that there is not, on that Account, any Occasion for a future Adjustment." Franklin's observation of "the Difficulty by outward Appearances to make a Judgment of another's Happiness" reflects both Newton and Locke. Newton (especially on color) and Locke (especially on ideas) confirmed for eighteenth-century thinkers the illusoriness of appearance. Franklin had probably also read Montaigne, who earlier said that no judicatory instrument existed whereby we could judge appearances.[37] Though Franklin frequently commented on the deceptiveness of appearances, he repeatedly added that appearances are all we can know. In doing so, he anticipated David Hume's radical empiricism: "The mind has never anything present to it but the perceptions, and cannot possibly reach any experience of their connexion with objects."[38]

From the supposed equality of pleasure and pain, Franklin argued the obviously absurd position (to anyone with enough common sense not to lose sight of reality while arguing metaphysics) that all persons are equally used by the Creator and that

> no Condition of Life or Being is in itself better or preferable to another: The Monarch is not more happy than the Slave, nor the Beggar more miserable than Croesus. Suppose *A, B,* and *C,* three distinct Beings; *A* and *B,* animate, capable of *Pleasure* and *Pain, C* an inanimate Piece of Matter, insensible of either. *A* receives ten Degrees of *Pain*, which are necessarily succeeded by ten Degrees of *Pleasure: B* receives fifteen of *Pain*, and the consequent equal Number of *Pleasure: C* all the while lies unconcern'd, and as he has not suffer'd the former, has no right to the latter. What can be more equal and just than this? When the Accounts come to be adjusted, *A* has no Reason to complain that his Portion of *Pleasure* was five Degrees less than that of *B*, for his Portion of *Pain* was five Degrees less likewise: Nor has *B* any Reason to boast that his *Pleasure* was five Degrees greater than that of *A*, for his *Pain* was proportionate: They are then both on the same Foot with *C*, that is, they are neither Gainers nor Losers. (1:67)

Franklin's underlying satire of such reasoning made insensibility equal to life.

Franklin posed a commonsense objection: "even common Experience shews us, there is not in Fact this Equality: 'Some we see hearty, brisk and chearful perpetually, while others are constantly burden'd with a heavy Load of Maladies and Misfortunes, remaining for Years perhaps in Poverty, Disgrace, or Pain, and die at last without any Appearance of Recompence.'" Franklin knew that most people were doomed to poverty and despair. He said, "Now tho' 'tis not necessary, when a Proposition is demonstrated to be a general Truth, to shew in what manner it agrees with the particular Circumstances of Persons, and indeed ought not to be requir'd; yet, as this is a common Objection, some Notice may be taken of it." Franklin said that "we cannot be proper Judges of the good or bad Fortune of Others." Why not? We know only the appearance and are apt to interpret the appearance according to our own situation: "we are apt to imagine, that what would give us a great Uneasiness or a great Satisfaction, has the same Effect upon others: we think, for Instance, those unhappy, who must depend upon Charity for a mean Subsistence, who go in Rags, fare hardly, and are despis'd and scorn'd by all; not considering that Custom renders all these Things easy, familiar, and even pleasant. When we see Riches, Grandeur and a chearful Countenance, we easily imagine Happiness accompanies them, when oftentimes 'tis quite otherwise: Nor is a constantly sorrowful Look, attended with continual Complaints, an infallible Indication of Unhappiness" (1:67). Franklin concluded, "In short, we can judge by nothing but Appearances, and they are very apt to deceive us."

He then gives a series of examples:

> Some put on a gay chearful Outside, and appear to the World perfectly at Ease, tho' even then, some inward Sting, some secret Pain imbitters all their Joys, and

makes the Balance even: Others appear continually dejected and full of Sorrow; but even Grief itself is sometimes *pleasant*, and Tears are not always without their Sweetness: Besides, Some take a Satisfaction in being thought unhappy, (as others take a Pride in being thought humble,) these will paint their Misfortunes to others in the strongest Colours, and leave no Means unus'd to make you think them thoroughly miserable; so great a *Pleasure* it is to them *to be pitied.* ... These, with many others that might be given, are Reasons why we cannot make a true Estimate of the *Equality* of the Happiness and Unhappiness of others; and unless we could, Matter of Fact cannot be opposed to this Hypothesis. (1:67–68)

Franklin maintained that one could not even be certain of one's own pleasure and pain: "Indeed, we are sometimes apt to think, that the Uneasinesses we ourselves have had, outweigh our Pleasures; but the Reason is this, the Mind takes no Account of the latter, they slip away unremark'd, when the former leave more lasting Impressions on the Memory. But suppose we pass the greatest part of Life in Pain and Sorrow, suppose we die by Torments and *think no more,* 'tis no Diminution to the Truth of what is here advanc'd; for the *Pain,* tho' exquisite, is not so to the *last* Moments of Life, the Senses are soon benumb'd, and render'd incapable of transmitting it so sharply to the Soul as at first; She perceives it cannot hold long, and 'tis an *exquisite Pleasure* to behold the immediate Approaches of Rest. This makes an Equivalent tho' Annihilation should follow" (1:68). Note Franklin's diction: not *death,* which might suggest the possibility of an afterlife, but *annihilation,* which connotes an absolute end, gave the pleasure.

The satirist took up the Lockean notion of *duration:*[39] "For the Quantity of *Pleasure* and *Pain* is not to be measur'd by its Duration, any more than the Quantity of Matter by its Extension." Locke had used a number of analogies in discussing duration, or time, and Franklin gave an original scientific analogy: "And as one cubic Inch may be made to contain, by Condensation, as much Matter as would fill ten thousand cubic Feet, being more expanded, so one single Moment of *Pleasure* may outweigh and compensate an Age of *Pain.*" In discussing duration, Locke also considered the eternal, and Franklin, too, turned to that idea.[40] Franklin lampooned the notion of heaven, calling it an ancient heathen fable: "It was owing to their Ignorance of the Nature of Pleasure and Pain that the Antient Heathens believ'd the idle Fable of their Elizium, that State of uninterrupted Ease and Happiness! The Thing is intirely impossible in Nature! Are not the Pleasures of the Spring made such by the Disagreeableness of the Winter? Is not the Pleasure of fair Weather owing to the Unpleasantness of foul? Certainly. Were it then always Spring, were the Fields always green and flourishing, and the Weather constantly serene and fair, the Pleasure would pall and die upon our Hands" (1:69). He made a criticism of the idea of heaven that has frequently been made, for example by Wallace Stevens in stanza 6 of "Sunday Morning."

Franklin claimed that unchanging paradise "would cease to be Pleasure to us, when it is not usher'd in by Uneasiness." Still implicitly attacking the idea of heaven, Franklin turned to the old-fashioned location of heaven and to eighteenth-century ideas of a multiplicity of solar systems: "Could the Philosopher visit, in reality, every Star and Planet with as much Ease and Swiftness as he can now visit their Ideas, and pass from one to another of them in the Imagination; it would be a *Pleasure* I grant; but it would be only in proportion to the *Desire* of accomplishing it, and that would be no greater than the *Uneasiness* suffer'd in the Want of it. The Accomplishment of a long and difficult Journey yields a great *Pleasure*; but if we could take a Trip to the Moon and back again, as frequently and with as much Ease as we can go and come from Market, the Satisfaction would be just the same" (1:69).

The Soul and Identity

Franklin returned to the idea of the soul. "The *Immateriality* of the Soul has been frequently made use of as an Argument for its *Immortality*; but let us consider, that tho' it should be allow'd to be immaterial, and consequently its Parts incapable of Separation or Destruction by any Thing material, yet by Experience we find, that it is not incapable of Cessation of *Thought*, which is its Action. When the Body is but a little indispos'd it has an evident Effect upon the Mind; and a right Disposition of the Organs is requisite to a right Manner of Thinking. In a sound Sleep sometimes, or in a Swoon, we cease to think at all; tho' the Soul is not therefore then annihilated, but *exists* all the while tho' it does not *act*; and may not this probably be the Case after Death?" (1:69).

The iconoclast based his reasoning on Lockean epistemology, but he used the tabula rasa comparison to demolish if not the existence, then any significance of the soul:

All our Ideas are first admitted by the Senses and imprinted on the Brain, increasing in Number by Observation and Experience; there they become the Subjects of the Soul's Action. The Soul is a mere Power or Faculty of *contemplating* on, and *comparing* those Ideas when it has them; hence springs Reason: But as it can *think* on nothing but Ideas, it must have them before it can *think* at all. Therefore as it may exist before it has receiv'd any Ideas, it may exist before it *thinks*. To remember a Thing, is to have the Idea of it still plainly imprinted on the Brain, which the Soul can turn to and contemplate on Occasion. To forget a Thing, is to have the Idea of it defac'd and destroy'd by some Accident, or the crouding in and imprinting of great variety of other Ideas upon it, so that the Soul cannot find out its Traces and distinguish it. (1:69–70)

Franklin progressed from Locke's epistemology and psychology to his reasoning on identity. Locke said that at no moment of our lives do "we have the whole train of all our past Actions before our Eyes in one view." Even the best memories lose "the sight of one part whilst they are viewing another." Moreover,

Locke continued, for the "greatest part of our Lives," we do not spend our time "reflecting on our past selves, being intent on our present Thoughts." And persons "in sound sleep" have "no Thoughts at all."[41]

The young philosopher applied Locke's thoughts on memory and identity to the soul:

> When we have thus lost the Idea of any one Thing, we can *think* no more, or *cease to think*, on that Thing; and as we can lose the Idea of one Thing, so we may of ten, twenty, a hundred, &c. and even of all Things, because they are not in their Nature permanent; and often during Life we see that some Men, (by an Accident or Distemper affecting the Brain,) lose the greatest Part of their Ideas, and remember very little of their past Actions and Circumstances. Now upon *Death*, and the Destruction of the Body, the Ideas contain'd in the Brain, (which are alone the Subjects of the Soul's Action) being then likewise necessarily destroy'd, the Soul, tho' incapable of Destruction itself, must then necessarily *cease to think* or *act*, having nothing left to think or act upon. It is reduc'd to its first inconscious State before it receiv'd any Ideas. (1:70)

In effect, Franklin asked what difference does it make, even if souls exist eternally, if they are not conscious and aware? He applied Locke's arguments concerning identity to the soul. "And to cease to *think* is but little different from *ceasing to be*." Here, he alluded to Descartes's dictum, "I think, therefore I am," thus possibly attempting to ridicule Cartesian fideism along with Lockean Christianity.

Then Franklin introduced one of those amazing somersaults in his thinking. So far, he had been attacking and satirizing the traditional ideas of Christianity. He now introduced one of the competing systems, reincarnation or the transmigration of souls. (When he suggested in the *Autobiography* that his uncle Thomas Franklin's soul may have transmigrated to him [A 4], he attributed the thought to William Franklin, though it was likely his own.) "Nevertheless, 'tis not impossible that this same *Faculty* of contemplating Ideas may be hereafter united to a new Body, and receive a new Set of Ideas; but that will no way concern us who are now living; for the *Identity* [emphasis mine] will be lost, it is no longer that same *Self* but a new Being" (1:70). Not only is it irrelevant if souls exist, it also does not matter if they transmigrate from one person to another. Franklin's thought seems closer to Lucretius than to Locke. In *De rerum natura*, Lucretius supports the idea of reincarnation while at the same time saying that reincarnation is insignificant, since it does not carry memory with it.[42] The last section of part 2 of the *Dissertation* abandoned ridiculing the standard definition of God and instead straightforwardly attacked the immortality of the soul, maintaining that even if souls existed, they did not have identity attached to them (or even perhaps had different identities at different times), so it would be irrelevant if they did exist.

Conclusion

Franklin finished with "a short Recapitulation of the Whole, that it may with all its Parts be comprehended at one View." He listed the five propositions concerning liberty and necessity (1:70). He stated the relation of the two halves of his pamphlet in the conclusion: "Now our common Notions of Justice will tell us, that if all created Things are equally esteem'd by the Creator, they ought to be equally us'd by Him; and that they are therefore equally us'd, we might embrace for Truth upon the Credit, and as the True Consequence of the forego-ing Argument" (1:70–71). Since he realized that most people would deny that everyone was "equally used," he had attempted to prove it in the second half of his pamphlet, dealing with pleasure and pain. He recapitulated its five proposi-tions and finished: "Thus both Parts of this Argument agree with and confirm one another, and the Demonstration is reciprocal."

Then he added an ironic postscript. "I am sensible that the Doctrine here advanc'd, if it were to be publish'd, would meet with but an indifferent Recep-tion. Mankind naturally and generally love to be flatter'd: Whatever soothes our Pride, and tends to exalt our Species above the rest of the Creation, we are pleas'd with and easily believe, when ungrateful Truths shall be with the utmost Indignation rejected. 'What! bring ourselves down to an Equality with the Beasts of the Field! with the *meanest* part of the Creation! 'Tis insufferable!' But, (to use a Piece of *common* Sense) our *Geese* are but *Geese* tho' we may think 'em *Swans*; and Truth will be Truth tho' it sometimes prove mortifying and distaste-ful" (1:71). Humans were animals, Franklin implied, only slightly more intelli-gent than the other animals—and they used that intelligence to fool themselves. Franklin's postscript probably echoed Mandeville, who wrote: "We are all so desperately in Love with Flattery, that we can never relish a Truth that is morti-fying, and I don't believe that the Immortality of the Soul, a Truth broach'd long before Christianity, would have ever found such a general Reception in human Capacities as it has, had it not been a pleasing one, that extoll'd and was a Compliment to the whole Species."[43]

Reception

Franklin wrote that "by some means" a copy of the *Dissertation* fell into the hands of Dr. William Lyons, a surgeon, who admired it and looked up Franklin (A 43). The "means" was almost certainly John Wilcox, the bookseller who lived next door to Franklin. Wilcox had published the first two editions of Lyons's *Infallibility, Dignity, and Excellence of Humane Judgment* "Printed for J. Wilcox at the *Green Dragon* in *Little Britain*" (1719 and 1721). The fourth edition (1724) of Lyons's work even appended another work by Lyons called *A Dissertation on Liberty and Necessity*. Franklin's copy of Lyons's fourth edition is extant.[44] Though it was nothing like Franklin's *Dissertation*, the similar titles were strik-ing. Franklin may have given Wilcox some copies of his *Dissertation* to sell. Even if Franklin only gave Wilcox a personal copy, the bookseller and publisher would have recognized its similarity to Lyons's *Infallibility*. If Wilcox had not already introduced the two book-loving freethinkers, he would now have called Lyons's attention to Franklin's work and informed him that the young author lived next door. Like Franklin's *Dissertation*, Lyons's *Infallibility* proceeded by syllogisms, though his reasoning was looser. Lyons perhaps had no idea that Franklin mocked as well as used the old logic. Like Franklin, Lyons also concluded by recapitulating the whole as a series of propositions.

Lyons's 1719 pamphlet (increasing in size through each edition) was a success: a second edition appeared in 1721, a third in 1723, and a fourth in 1724.[45] In the last, he revealed in an appendix that he had been "barbarously us'd" by the courts for publishing the tract. He was "produc'd in Three successive Terms [but] neither Adversary, Objection, or Complaint appear'd." He thanked Dr. Richard Mead, a famous London physician and author of a standard book on poisons, who had heard "of my Confinement on this account, with an indefatigable Industry undertook and perfected my Deliverance" (249). Lyons's major thesis was simply that "*Reason* is the distinguishing Excellency, Dignity, and Beauty of Mankind" (1). His attacks on transubstantiation, predestination, and the trinity were not atypical among liberal Anglicans. In contrast, Franklin's *Dissertation* was radical, even atheistic. Franklin recorded that Lyons "took great Notice of me, call'd on me often, to converse on these Subjects, carried me to the Horns a pale Ale-House in [Gutter] Lane, Cheapside, and introduc'd me to Dr. [Bernard] Mandeville, Author of the Fable of the Bees who had a Club there, of which he was the Soul, being a most facetious entertaining Companion" (A 43–44).

Franklin had no doubt read Shaftesbury's *Characteristics* and Mandeville's *Fable of the Bees* before coming to London. It was a heady experience for the provincial young Franklin to spend time with the brilliant and iconoclastic Dr. Mandeville. Like Lyons, Mandeville had been charged in court. The Middlesex grand jury presented *The Fable of the Bees* as a nuisance in July 1723, and "Theophilus Philo-Britannus" censured it in the *London Journal* five months before Franklin arrived in London.[46] In March 1725, just before Franklin met Mandeville, Francis Hutcheson defended Shaftesbury's ideas on an innate moral sense in human beings. Everyone in Mandeville's circle would have read Hutcheson's *Inquiry into the Original of Our Ideas of Beauty and Virtue . . . In which the Principles of the Late Earl of Shaftesbury Are Explain'd and Defended, against the Author of the Fable of the Bees . . . With an Attempt to Introduce Mathematical Calculation, in Subjects of Morality.*[47] Shortly after Franklin left England, Edmund Gibson, bishop of London, wrote a pastoral letter attacking Mandeville and urging magistrates to suppress works that satirized revealed religion.[48] Had Franklin's *Dissertation* come to any magistrate's attention, the young libertine would have been tried if he could have been identified. But the author, printer, and bookseller were all concealed.

Writing his sister Jane on 30 December 1770, Franklin recalled that he had known another freethinker in London. "Her name was *Ilive*, a Printer's Widow. She dy'd soon after I left England, and by her Will oblig'd her son to deliver publickly in Salter's Hall a Solemn Discourse, the purport of which was to prove, that this World is the true Hell or Place of Punishment for the Spirits who had transgress'd in a better State, and were sent here to suffer for their sins in Animals of all Sorts." He explained that Mrs. Ilive thought "that tho' we now remember'd nothing of such pre-existent State; yet after Death we might recollect it, and remember the Punishments we had suffer'd, so as to be the better for them; and others who had not yet offended, might now behold and be warn'd by our Sufferings." Franklin added his own reasons for finding the doctrine not unreasonable: "In fact we see here that every lower Animal has its Enemy with proper Inclinations, Faculties and Weapons, to terrify, wound and destroy it; and that Men who are uppermost, are Devils to one another; So that on the establish'd Doctrine of the Goodness and Justice of the great Creator, this apparent State of general and systematical Mischief, seem'd to demand some such Supposition as Mrs. Ilives, to account for it consistent with the Honour of the Deity."

Though the opinions were similar to those Franklin held as a young man, he added a cautionary note concerning the limitations of reason: "But our reasoning Powers when employ'd about what may have been before our Existence here, or shall be after it, cannot go far for want of History and Facts: Revelation only can give us the necessary Information, and that (in the first of these Points especially) has been very sparingly afforded us." It might seem from this letter that the older Franklin had some belief in Revelation, yet one must take into account that he was writing his sister Jane, whom he would not have wanted to upset. We can be fairly certain that Franklin had indeed met Mrs. Elizabeth James Ilive, for she was the daughter of the type founder Thomas James, whose shop was downstairs from Palmer's printing house.[49] Ten years after his London acquaintance with James and Mrs. Ilive, Franklin reprinted (21 February 1733/4) an advertisement from Samuel Keimer's *Barbados-Gazette*: "This Day is publish'd (Price One Shilling) Dedicated to the Right Hon. John Barber, esq; Lord Mayor of London) An ORATION spoke at Joyner's Hall in *Thames street*, on Monday, Sept. 24. 1733, pursuant to the Will of Mrs. *Januarye Ilive*, who departed this Life Aug. 29. Aetat. 63. Proving I. The Plurality of Worlds. II. That this Earth is Hell. III. That the Souls of Men are the Apostate Angels. And, IV. That the Fire which will punish those who shall be confined to this Globe after the Day of Judgment, will be immaterial. With large Notes confirming the Hypothesis and refuting Dr. *Lupton's* Opinion of the Eternity of Hell-Torments." In his notes about Mrs. Ilive, Keimer showed that he, too, had known her personally.[50]

While associating in London with people like Dr. Lyons and Bernard Mandeville, Franklin must have heard discussions of the most recent thoroughgoing skeptical, yet fideist, work: Bishop Pierre Daniel Huet's *Traité de la foiblesse de l'esprit*, which was first translated into English in 1725 and had three editions that year. One, translated by Edward Combe, was titled *The Weakness of Human Understanding* and had two editions; the other translation was titled *A Philosophical Treatise Concerning the Weakness of Human Understanding*. Huet was the most Pyrrhonistic thinker between Bayle (and possibly Berkeley) and Hume. Franklin probably read Huet in 1725.[51]

In addition to introducing Franklin to a circle of radicals, Dr. Lyons also took him to Batson's Coffee House, a rendezvous for physicians at No. 17, Cornhill, "against the Royal Exchange." Here Franklin met Dr. Henry Pemberton, a physician and member of the Royal Society who was then superintending publication of the third edition of Newton's *Principia* (1726). Since Dr. Richard Mead occasionally received mail at Batson's Coffee House,[52] he must have patronized it, so Franklin may well have met this benefactor of Dr. Lyons. Franklin may also have seen John Theophilus Desaguliers at Batson's (in addition to meeting him through Isaac Greenwood), the experimenter of the Royal Society and (as we have seen) a Freemason.

Franklin told Pemberton he would like to meet Newton. The physician "promis'd to give me an Opportunity some time or other of seeing Sir Isaac Newton, of which I was extreamly desirous; but this never happened." Too bad, for the American would have cherished the memory, and Newton died in 1727, the year after Franklin left London and long before Franklin became famous as a scientist. Perhaps Franklin met Sir Hans Sloane at Batson's. On 2 June 1725, Franklin wrote Sloane, whose collection of manuscripts and curiosities was well-known, offering to sell him a purse made of asbestos, which Franklin had brought from America. Sloane "invited me to his House in Bloomsbury Square; where he show'd me all his Curiosities, and persuaded me to let him add that to the Number, for which he paid me handsomely" (A 44). If Franklin himself sold his file of the *New-England Courant* (which survives in the British Library), this is the most logical time that he might have done so.

Though little known during the rest of Franklin's lifetime, *A Dissertation on Liberty and Necessity, Pleasure and Pain* influenced Franklin's life and reputation during his eighteen months in England, and it was portentous for his future thought. Many scholars have maintained that Franklin later changed his mind, but the satire in the *Dissertation* recurs in Franklin's writings throughout his life. On the other hand, like many of the Greek skeptics, he often tried to argue for a position in order to see what could be said for it—and then he argued for the opposite position for the same reason. He seemed to hold fundamental metaphysical beliefs in suspension. He wrote in the *Autobiography* that he was a deist, but the *Autobiography* was a public document, written when Franklin had become more cautious about revealing his skepticism. Deism was a comparatively acceptable belief until the end of the eighteenth century, whereas the satire and materialism embodied in the *Dissertation* were shocking. Despite the relative acceptability of deism, he knew that many of the *Autobiography*'s readers, including such old and close friends as the Reverend Richard Price and the Reverend Joseph Priestley, would lament his lack of faith in Christ. Franklin changed from the youth who wrote the clandestine pamphlet, but the main change was a greater prudence about revealing his private opinions and a greater consideration for the beliefs of others, whom, like his beloved sister Jane Mecom, he would not want to shock or offend.[53] Perhaps the major change in Franklin's attitudes toward the questions he took up in the *Dissertation* was that as he grew older, he grew more skeptical of metaphysical reasoning itself, though he had doubts about metaphysics even in the *Dissertation*.

COFFEEHOUSES AND TAVERNS

After homes, coffeehouses and taverns were the primary centers of social life in London and in the colonies. Most taverns catered to the inhabitants of the immediate area, some were the regular meeting places of clubs, and some were the rendezvous of special interest groups. As we have seen, in Boston Dr. William Douglass often dated his writings from "Hall's Coffee House." Many coffeehouses had guest rooms, and visitors to London often stayed at them for a few days while, if they were visiting for an extended period, finding suitable private lodgings. The longer Franklin remained in the city, the more inns and taverns he knew. Several London coffeehouses were particularly identified with the colonies. Franklin probably knew of the Pennsylvania Coffee House in Birching Lane before he went to London. In 1725 and 1726, he must have visited it often to read Bradford's *American Weekly Mercury* and to hear the latest Philadelphia news. Franklin no doubt occasionally stopped by the other coffeehouses specializing in American trade and news. The New England Coffee House, "behind the Royal Exchange," at 59–61 Threadneedle Street,[54] was a gathering place for the merchants and ship captains trading to New England. They heard the latest Boston news and read the Boston newspapers. A few years later Governor Jonathan Belcher warned his son against spending too much time at the New England Coffee House.[55] Franklin also probably occasionally visited the Virginia Coffee House at St. Michael's Alley, "Near the George & Vulture,"[56] where he would have heard news from the Chesapeake area. Of course the patrons of the coffeehouses specializing in the North Atlantic trading areas generally knew the most important American news, and all the "American" coffeehouses would have had some recent papers from Boston, Philadelphia, or (beginning in 1726) New York.

In the *Autobiography*, Franklin mentions two London taverns that he frequented, both of which have been noted above, the Horns in Cheapside, which Mandeville used as his club, and Batson's Coffee House (A 35). As was common in the eighteenth century, Franklin used a favorite coffeehouse as his mailing address. In his first extant letter, which was addressed to the scientist whose collections were the foundation of the British Museum, Sir Hans Sloane (2 June

1725), Franklin wrote that he could be reached "by a Line directed for me at the Golden Fan in Little Britain." The Golden Fan was in Aldersgate Street, near Franklin's residence.[57] Evidently he regularly patronized the Golden Fan.

WATTS'S

After working for Palmer "near a Year" (A 43), Franklin, "expecting better Work . . . left Palmer's to work at Watts's near Lincoln's Inn Fields, a still greater Printing-House" (A 45). It was around November 1725 when Franklin went to work for John Watts, in Wild Court, about nine blocks west of Palmer's. John Watts, then about forty-seven, had one of London's largest printing houses. Whereas Palmer trained eleven apprentices, Watts trained twenty-two.[58] Franklin here met John Wygate, a fellow journeyman printer (he had completed his apprenticeship in 1721) who remained a friend at least until 1744.[59] Franklin's later good friend William Strahan and his later partner, David Hall, also worked for Watts at one time. During his first mission to London (1757–62), Franklin proposed several times to Strahan that they call on their old employer (who lived until 1763), but they never did.[60]

At Watts's, Franklin chose to work as a pressman, "imagining I felt a Want of the Bodily Exercise I had been us'd to in America, where Presswork is mix'd with Composing." Like most Americans, Franklin had been brought up drinking water. Good water was scarce in eighteenth-century London, but he found a source for it and made it his drink. The other pressmen,

> near 50 in Number, were great Guzzlers of Beer. On occasion I carried up and down Stairs a large Form of Types in each hand, when others carried but one in both Hands. They wonder'd to see from this and several Instances that the Water-American as they call'd me was *stronger* than themselves who drunk *strong* Beer. We had an Alehouse Boy who attended always in the House to supply the Workmen. My Companion at the Press drank every day a Pint before Breakfast, a Pint at Breakfast with his Bread and Cheese; a Pint between Breakfast and Dinner; a Pint at Dinner; a Pint in the Afternoon about Six o'clock, and another when he had done his Day's Work. I thought it a detestable Custom. But it was necessary, he suppos'd, to drink *strong* Beer that he might be *strong* to labour. I endeavour'd to convince him that the Bodily Strength afforded by Beer could only be in proportion to the Grain or Flour of the Barley dissolved in the Water of which it was made; that there was more Flour in a Penny-worth of Bread, and therefore if he would eat that with a Pint of Water, it would give him more Strength than a Quart of Beer. He drank on however, and had 4 or 5 Shillings to pay out of his Wages every Saturday Night for that muddling Liquor; an Expence I was free from.—And thus these poor Devils keep themselves always under. (A45–46)

After a few weeks, Franklin left the pressmen to join the better-paid compositors. A new initiation fee of five shillings was demanded. Franklin "thought it an Imposition, as I had paid below." Watts agreed with him and told him not to pay it. But the compositors were not to be denied. Franklin "was accordingly considered as an Excommunicate, and had so many little Pieces of private Mischief done me, by mixing my Sorts, transposing my Pages, breaking my Matter, etc. etc. if I were ever so little out of the Room, and all ascrib'd to the Chapel Ghost, which they said ever haunted those not regularly admitted, that notwithstanding the Master's Protection, I found myself oblig'd to comply and pay the Money; convinc'd of the Folly of being on ill Terms with those one is to live with continually" (A 46). Franklin's practicality overcame his principles. It would not be the last time that he changed in order to accommodate others, even if he believed them to be wrong.[61]

Gradually Franklin became accepted by and then a leader among the journeymen. He suggested some "reasonable Alterations in their Chapel Laws, and carried them against all Opposition." A number of the other workmen followed his example, "left their muddling Breakfast of Beer and Bread and Cheese," and instead ate "a large Porringer of hot Water-gruel, sprinkled with Pepper, crumb'd with Bread, and a Bit of Butter in it," which a neighboring inn supplied "for the Price of a Pint of Beer, viz, three halfpence." It was a better and cheaper breakfast. "Those who continu'd sotting with Beer all day, were often, by not paying, out of Credit at the Alehouse, and us'd to make Interest with me to get Beer, *their Light*, as they phras'd it, *being out*. I watch'd the Pay table on Saturday Night, and collected what I stood engag'd for them, having to pay some times near Thirty Shillings a Week on their Accounts.—This, and my being esteem'd a pretty good Riggite, that is a jocular verbal Satyrist, supported my Consequence in the Society. My constant Attendance, (I never making a St. Monday), recommended me to the Master; and my uncommon Quickness at Composing, occasion'd my being put upon all Work of Dispatch, which was generally better paid. So I went on now very agreeably" (A 46–47).

Lodging in Duke Street

In the winter of 1725/6, Franklin moved.

> My Lodging in Little Britain being too remote, I found another in Duke-street opposite to the Romish Chapel. It was two pair of Stairs backwards at an Italian Warehouse. A Widow Lady kept the House; she had a Daughter and a Maid Servant, and a Journey-man who attended the Warehouse, but lodg'd abroad. After sending to enquire my Character at the House where I last lodg'd, she agreed to take me in at the same Rate, 3 Shillings 6 Pence per Week, cheaper as she said from the Protection she expected in having a Man lodge in the House. She was a Widow, an elderly Woman, had been bred a Protestant, being a Clergyman's daughter, but was converted to the Catholic Religion by her Husband, whose Memory she much revered, had lived much among People of Distinction, and knew a 1000 Anecdotes of them as far back as the Times of Charles the

second. She was lame in her Knees with the Gout, and therefore seldom stirr'd out of her Room, so sometimes wanted Company; and hers was so highly amusing to me that I was sure to spend an Evening with her whenever she desired it. (A 47–48)

Once again Franklin revealed that he did pay attention to food: "Our Supper was only half an Anchovy each, on a very little Strip of Bread and Butter, and half a Pint of Ale between us.—But the Entertainment was in her Conversation. My always keeping good Hours, and giving little Trouble in the Family, made her unwilling to part with me; so that when I talk'd of a Lodging I had heard of, nearer my Business, for 2 Shillings a Week, which, intent as I now was on saving Money, made some Difference; she bid me not think of it, for she would abate me two Shillings a Week for the future, so I remain'd with her at 1 Shilling 6 Pence as long as I stayed in London" (A 48).

Biographers can object to the strangest things. Phillips Russell thought Franklin took advantage of his landlady: "Beating a lone widow down from 3/6 to 1/6 a week would seem to be a poor business for a healthy young journeyman to engage in."[62] But as the following testifies, the widow did not need the money, and she underbid the other rent by twelve pence in great part because she liked the young man. An ascetic lived in the attic. Franklin said that he told the story "as another Instance on how small an Income Life and Health may be supported," but I suspect a different motive. A maiden Roman Catholic lady of seventy lived in the garret "in the most retired Manner." As a young woman, she had gone abroad to a nunnery, found the foreign country unpleasant, and returned to England to live as a nun there: "Accordingly She had given all her Estate to charitable Uses, reserving only Twelve Pounds a Year to live on, and out of this Sum she still gave a great deal in Charity, living herself on Watergruel only, and using no Fire but to boil it. She had lived many Years in that Garret, being permitted to remain there gratis by successive catholic Tenants of the House below, as they deem'd it a Blessing to have her there. A Priest visited her, to confess her every Day. I have ask'd her, says my Landlady, how she, as she liv'd, could possibly find so much Employment for a Confessor? O, says she, it is impossible to avoid *vain Thoughts.*" The reply would have appealed to Franklin because he no doubt thought it was true.

Franklin once visited her: "She was chearful and polite, and convers'd pleasantly. The Room was clean, but had no other Furniture than a Matras, a Table with a Crucifix and Book, a Stool, which she gave me to sit on, and a Picture over the Chimney of St. *Veronica,* displaying her Handkerchief with the miraculous Figure of Christ's bleeding Face on it, which she explain'd to me with great Seriousness. She look'd pale, but was never sick" (A 48–49). The true believer, who seemed somewhat simple to the young libertine, explained "with great Seriousness" the supposed miracle. She impressed Franklin with how strange and incomprehensible people were. That was probably why he told the story— humans were amazing. We know that he told Deborah about the ascetic old lady. After returning to England in 1757, Franklin wrote her that he had visited his former lodging in Duke Street. The occupants were different, but the garret remained the same. The nun, he wrote Deborah, "must be dead" (7:370).

At Watts's printing shop, Franklin became friends with "an ingenious young Man, one Wygate, who having wealthy Relations, had been better educated than most Printers, was a tolerable Latinist, spoke French, and lov'd Reading." It must have been in a warm period during May or early June 1726 when Franklin

> taught him, and a Friend of his, to swim at twice going into the River, and they soon became good Swimmers. They introduc'd me to some Gentlemen from the Country who went to Chelsea by Water to see the College and Don Saltero's Curiosities. In our Return, at the Request of the Company, whose Curiosity Wygate had excited, I stript and leapt into the River, and swam from near Chelsea to Blackfryars [almost four miles], performing on the Way many Feats of Activity both upon and under Water, that surpriz'd and pleas'd those to whom they were Novelties.—I had from a Child been ever delighted with this Exercise, had studied and practis'd all Thevenot's Motions and Positions, added some of my own, aiming at the graceful and easy, as well as the Useful.—All these I took this Occasion of exhibiting to the Company, and was much flatter'd by their Admiration.

Wygate proposed that the two travel throughout Europe together, supporting themselves by working as printers. "I was once inclin'd to it. But mentioning it to my good Friend Mr. Denham, with whom I often spent an Hour when I had Leisure, he dissuaded me from it; advising me to think only of returning to Pennsylvania, which he was now about to do" (A 49–50).

Franklin succumbed to the temptation of telling a story about the Quaker merchant Thomas Denham that has all the characteristics of an apocryphal oral anecdote, perhaps one that Franklin had repeated often: "I must record one Trait of this good Man's Character. He had formerly been in Business at Bristol, but failed in Debt to a Number of People, compounded and went to America. There, by a close Application to Business as a Merchant, he acquired a plentiful Fortune in a few Years. Returning to England in the Ship with me, He invited his old Creditors to an Entertainment, at which he thanked them for the easy Composition they had favored him with, and when they expected nothing but the Treat, every Man at the first Remove, found under his Plate an Order on a Banker for the full Amount of the unpaid Remainder with Interest" (A 50). In fact, Denham repaid his creditors at least two years before returning to England.

Leaving London

In early July 1726, Thomas Denham offered Franklin a position as his clerk with the opportunity of becoming a junior partner in the future. "He was about to return to Philadelphia, and should carry over a great Quantity of Goods in order to open a Store there: He proposed to take me over as his Clerk, to keep his Books (in which he would instruct me), copy his Letters, and attend the Store.

He added, that as soon as I should be acquainted with mercantile Business he would promote me by sending me with a Cargo of Flour and Bread etc. to the West Indies, and procure me Commissions from others; which would be profitable, and if I managed well, would establish me handsomely." Franklin must have been surprised, but he had no ties in London and, as his epithet "The Water American" testifies, was thought of by others and deemed himself an American. He said, "The Thing pleased me, for I was grown tired of London, remembered with Pleasure the happy Months I had spent in Pennsylvania, and wished again to see it. Therefore I immediately agreed, on the Terms of Fifty Pounds a Year, Pennsylvania Money; less indeed than my then Gets as a Compositor, but affording a better Prospect" (A 50).

Franklin quit his job with Watts and set out to become a merchant. He ordered materials from various tradesmen, purchased numerous items from wholesalers, supervised their packing, expedited the various articles ordered, and ran errands for Denham. To his surprise, he was sent for

> by a great Man I knew only by Name, a Sir William Wyndham and I waited upon him. He had heard by some means or other of my Swimming from Chelsea to Blackfriar, and of my teaching Waged and another young Man to swim in a few Hours. He had two Sons about to set out on their Travels; he wished to have them first taught Swimming; and proposed to gratify me handsomely if I would teach them. They were not yet come to Town and my Stay was uncertain, so I could not undertake it. But from this Incident I thought it likely, that if I were to remain in England and open a Swimming School, I might get a good deal of Money.—And it struck me so strongly, that had the Overture been sooner made me, probably I should not so soon have returned to America.— After Many Years, you [Franklin pretended to write part 1 of his *Autobiography* to his son William] and I had something of more Importance to do with one of these Sons of Sir William Wyndham, become Earl of Agreement, which I shall mention in its Place. (A 40)

When Franklin wrote this in 1771, he meant to narrate his life down to that time, but he only brought it down to 1757, which was four years before meeting the earl in 1761, when he became secretary of state for the colonies.

Franklin concluded his London sojourn by evaluating the experience. "Thus I spent about 18 Months in London. Most Part of the Time, I worked hard at my Business, and spent but little upon myself except in seeing Plays, and in Books.—My Friend Ralph had kept me poor. He owed me about 27 Pounds; which I was now never likely to receive; a great Sum out of my small Earnings. I loved him notwithstanding, for he had many amiable Qualities. Tho' I had by no means improved my Fortune.—But I had picked up some very ingenious Acquaintance whose Conversation was of great Advantage to me, and I had read considerably." On Thursday, 21 July 1726, Franklin left for Philadelphia with merchant Thomas Denham aboard the *Berkshire*, Captain Henry Clark.

AMERICANS IN ENGLAND

Colonial Americans visiting England were surprised by the ignorance and prejudice concerning America that they encountered. Even the educated English
sometimes displayed the most uninformed opinions. An English parson told
William Byrd of Westover that "Virginia was an Island lying without Ganges in
the East Indies and that it was peopled first by a Colony sent thither by William
Rufus." Many English persons believed that Americans could not speak English
and that they had dark skin, like Africans. The Reverend John Barnard, a native
New Englander and Harvard graduate of 1700, reported that when he was in
England in 1710 a young lady asked him "if all the people of my country were
white, as she saw I was; for being styled in the general West Indians, she thought
we were all black, as she supposed the Indians to be. She asked me how long I
had been in the kingdom. When I told her a few months, she said she was
surprised to think how I could learn their language in so little a time; 'Methinks,'
said she, 'you speak as plain English as I do.' I told her, all my country people,
being English, spake the same language I did." Robert Bolling of Chellow, who
spent seven years attending school in England, recorded his grandfather's similar anecdote from about 1700: a lady "from Yorkshire, (a place where language
is much abused,) who hearing him speak, exclaimed in her country dialect, with
much astonishment, 'My God! Only hear this gentleman, he speaks English as
well as we do!'" The irritated descendant of Pocahontas replied, "Yes, indeed,
madam, and some hundreds of times better, or I should be very sorry for it."[63]

The English public frequently heard that no one would willingly go to
America. Captain John Smith wrote in 1622 that "so much scorned was the
name of *Virginia*, some did chuse to be hanged ere they would go thither, and
were." English popular ballads about America from the seventeenth century
through the colonial period featured kidnapped children and youths, trepanned
maidens, and transported felons. The same character types appeared in plays
and novels set in the colonies. Aphra Behn's *Widow Ranter* (1689) and Defoe's
Moll Flanders (1722) and *Colonel Jack* (1722) are among the hundreds of such
works. America was thus a land of transported convicts and unjustly indentured
laborers—all forced to work incessantly under severe conditions. The Reverend
John Urmston of North Carolina commented in 1711 that it was "usually said
our Colonies are chiefly peopled by such as have been educated at some of the
famous Colleges of Bridewell Newgate or the Mint." That remained a favorite
vituperation. Witness Dr. Samuel Johnson in 1775: "They are a race of convicts,
and ought to be thankful for anything we allow them short of hanging."[64]

America was a wilderness, full of wild beasts and savage Indians. It was
unsuited for civilized persons. New England was too cold and the rest of
America too hot for acceptable human existence. Captain John Smith tried to
counter that opinion by his descriptions of the climate and by naming the
northern part *New England*. New Englanders mocked its reputation by overstat-

ing how cold it was. The primary reputation, however, of America was as a semi-tropical jungle causing sickness, fever, and death.[65]

America was not only a dreadful place, it affected horrible changes in persons who stayed there. They degenerated. Indeed, no living thing in America, whether human, plant, or animal, was as vigorous, as healthy, as big, or as good in various ways as in England and Europe. The native American Indians were inferior. American bears were not as big or as fierce as European bears. Crossing the sea to America transformed brave English mastiffs into cowardly dogs. The birds in America did not sing as sweetly as English birds. The wrens were not as big as English wrens. Thousands of such statements occur in the literature about America in the seventeenth and eighteenth centuries.[66] Replies to these anti-American pronouncements formed a substratum of colonial American literature, familiar to Franklin and every other American litterateur.[67]

Underlying the English beliefs concerning degeneration in America were the theories that the environment, especially climate, produced the differences in living things and that the world had been degenerating since the expulsion of Adam and Eve from Eden. All forms of life—human, plant, and animal—were degenerating but more so in the New World because of the pernicious environment. Even leading intellectuals of the day concerned with natural history such as John Ray in England or Linnaeus in Sweden followed the old beliefs.[68] Degeneration was also the leading interpretation of history and literature. Jonathan Swift's *Battle of the Books*, which Franklin undoubtedly read before running away from Boston at age seventeen, summed up the old attitudes while travestying the quarrel between the ancients and the moderns.[69]

Since the English believed themselves superior to Americans, popular tales said that the English who did go to America rose quickly in American society, made fortunes, and returned to England. Some English did just that—not only in the West Indies and America but, by the late eighteenth century, in India and elsewhere. Stories of the dramatic rise from poverty and misery to wealth and happiness appeared in popular literature and anecdotes, often as burlesques of the motifs. A ballad of about 1630 titled *The Summons to Newe England*, the earliest extant American folk song, *New England's Annoyances* (ca. 1643), Ebenezer Cook's *Sot-Weed Factor* (1708), and Henry Brooke's "The New Metamorphosis; or, Fable of the Bald Eagle" are among the American replies to the motifs.[70]

Americans were irritated by the English attitudes toward America. So far as we know, Franklin said nothing about his experience of anti-American attitudes during his time in England in 1725 and 1726. Despite the lack of evidence, it is safe to assume that Franklin, like others, encountered anti-Americanism and astounding ignorance concerning America. Beginning in 1729, he often referred to and countered anti-Americanism. As we will see, no colonial American objected so strongly or so often to the prejudice against America as Franklin. His London experience at age nineteen and twenty no doubt helped confirm the Water American's American identity.

TWELVE

At Sea
1726

After dinner one of our mess went up aloft to look out, and presently pronounced the long-wished for sound, Land! Land! In less than an hour we could descry it from the deck, appearing like tufts of trees. I could not discern it so soon as the rest; my eyes were dimmed with the suffusion of two small drops of joy—"Journal," 9 October 1726

WHAT DID FRANKLIN DO when he had nothing to do? One thing was to write. Returning from England, Franklin kept a "Journal of occurrences in my voyage to Philadelphia." He began it on Friday, 22 July 1726, the day after the *Berkshire* left London. The enforced idleness of sailing across the ocean was a time for observations and introspection. The twenty-year-old Franklin revealed his curiosity, cast of mind, and everyday thoughts more fully in this journal than in any other single piece of writing. On all six of his later long sea voyages, he had writing he wanted to do and experiments he wanted to make (e.g., recording the sea temperature), but on this voyage he had the leisure to reflect on whatever occurred. Many people found ocean travel terrifying—with good reason. Ships disappeared with never a hint of the reason why. Often ships encountered terrible storms, and sometimes contrary winds or no wind kept a ship at sea for months until all the food and water were gone—and incredible hardships followed. Franklin's contemporary, Dr. Samuel Johnson, expressed his abhorrence of sea travel: "A ship is worse than a jail: there is in a jail better air, better company, better conveniences of every kind, and a ship has the additional disadvantage of being in danger."[1] Franklin accepted shipboard life as a necessary inconvenience; hardly a word of complaint appears in his journal, though it reveals his boredom and occasional irritation.

The journal reveals Franklin's interests as well as his plans for the future. Some subjects, such as natural history, are among the topics that we would expect to fascinate him. But he was also keenly interested in psychology and morality, in history and local lore, in mathematics and navigation. His appreciation of scenery might surprise some; for during a life full of writing, he rarely recorded nature's scenic, picturesque, or romantic possibilities. The journal, however, makes it clear that he appreciated them. He also revealed that he had paid careful attention to painters' techniques—another topic he rarely later mentioned. Moreover, at age twenty, he was dissatisfied with himself, with his progress (and lack of it), with his former attempts to save money, and with aspects of his own behavior. In Philadelphia, he would start a new life. He resolved not to repeat his old errors. He regarded the return to America as a turning point in his life, and the journal reveals his future goals and plans.

CONTRARY WINDS

As so often happened in the age of sail, the wind did not cooperate. Instead of taking five to eight weeks, the voyage lasted nearly thirteen weeks, with most of the delay caused by contrary winds that kept the ship from leaving the English Channel. On Friday, 22 July, the ship came to anchor off Gravesend. Franklin went ashore and took a walk up to Windmill Hill, "whence I had an agreeable prospect of the country for above twenty miles round, and two or three reaches of the river with ships and boats sailing both up and down, and Tilbury Fort on the other side, which commands the river and passage to London." The delightful scenery paled before the grasping merchants typically found at tourist traps. Franklin noted: "This Gravesend is a *cursed biting* place; the chief dependence of the people being the advantage they make of imposing upon strangers. If you buy any thing of them, and give half what they ask, you pay twice as much as the thing is worth. Thank God, we shall leave it to-morrow" (1:72).

On Saturday, 23 July, the ship picked up a pilot. A good wind took the ship to Margate but also sickened most of the passengers. Franklin, however, had a good sea stomach. The following day, the pilot was set ashore at Deal and the ship passed through. Franklin again recorded his delight in picturesque scenery: "And now whilst I write this, sitting upon the Quarter-deck, I have methinks one of the pleasantest scenes in the world before me. 'Tis a fine clear day, and we are going away before the wind with an easy pleasant gale. We have near fifteen sail of ships in sight, and I may say in company. On the left hand appears the coast of France at a distance, and on the right is the town and castle of Dover, with the green hills and chalky cliffs of England, to which we must now bid farewell. Albion, farewell!" But contrary winds blew hard all the next two days; on the third, "we stood in for the land, in order to make some harbour. About noon we took on board a pilot out of a fishing shallop, who brought the ship into Spithead off Portsmouth" (1:73).

Franklin went ashore and noted, in a typical traveler's manner, the military advantages of the place and some local folklore: "The people of Portsmouth tell strange stories of the severity of one [John] Gibson, who was governor of this place in the Queen's [i.e., Queen Anne's] time, to his soldiers, and show you a miserable dungeon by the town gate, which they call Johnny Gibson's Holes, where for trifling misdemeanors he used to confine his soldiers till they were almost starved to death." Regarding Gibson's behavior with contempt, Franklin reflected: "'Tis a common maxim, that without severe discipline it is impossible to govern the licentious rabble of soldiery." He recalled from reading, however, that the greatest generals were loved, not feared: "I own indeed that if a commander finds he has not those qualities in him that will make him beloved by his people, he ought by all means to make use of such methods as will make them fear him, since one or the other (or both) is absolutely necessary; but Alexander and Caesar, those renowned generals, received more faithful service, and performed greater actions by means of the love their soldiers bore them, than they could possibly have done, if instead of being beloved and respected they had been hated and feared by those they commanded" (1:74). When Franklin later served as a colonel on the Pennsylvania frontier (1755), he won the respect of the soldiers, not their fear.

On 28 July, Franklin and his companions sailed only as far as the Isle of Wight, where contrary winds again prevailed. Friday, 29 July, they explored the island. He remarked that Cowes was but a town, close to the seaside, nearly opposite to Southampton on the main shore of England. It was divided into two parts by a small river, thus dividing the town into East and West Cowes. He noted that it had a fort built in an oval form, with eight or ten guns mounted to defend the road. Completing the description, he said Cowes had a post office, a custom-house, and a small chapel, as well as "a good harbour for ships to ride in, in easterly and westerly winds" (1:75).

CHECKERS

In case a fair wind should come up, Franklin necessarily spent much of his time onboard and played games. He wrote an appreciation of checkers that anticipates his later "Morals of Chess": "It is a game I much delight in; but it requires a clear head, and undisturbed; and the persons playing, if they would play well, ought not much to regard the consequence of the game, for that diverts and withdraws the attention of the mind from the game itself, and makes the player liable to make many false open moves; and I will venture to lay it down for an infallible rule, that if two persons equal in judgment play for a considerable sum, he that loves money most shall lose; his anxiety for the success of the game confounds him. Courage is almost as requisite for the good conduct of this game as in a real battle; for if the player imagines himself opposed by one that is much his superior in skill, his mind is so intent on the defensive part that an advantage passes unobserved" (1:75).

Franklin found Newport, "the metropolis" of the Isle of Wight, "a pretty prospect enough from the hills that surround it; (for it lies down in a bottom). The houses are beautifully intermixed with trees, and a tall old-fashioned steeple rises in the midst of the town, which is very ornamental to it . . . there is a very neat market-house, paved with square stone, and consisting of eleven arches. There are several pretty handsome streets, and many well-built houses and shops well stored with goods." Since Newport was celebrated for oysters, "the best in England," Franklin enquired about them. "The oyster-merchants fetch them, as I am informed, from other places, and lay them upon certain beds in the river, (the water of which is it seems excellently adapted for that purpose) a-fattening, and when they have laid a suitable time they are taken up again, and made fit for sale" (1:75–76).

CARISBROOK

From Newport, Franklin and his friends walked to Carisbrook, a mile further, to see the castle where King Charles I had been confined. There they viewed the ruins of "an ancient Church that had formerly been a priory in Romish times, and is the first church, or the mother church of the island. It is an elegant building, after the old Gothic manner, with a very high tower, and looks very venerable in its ruins. There are several ancient monuments about it; but the stone of which they are composed is of such a soft crumbling nature, that the inscriptions are none of them legible. Of the same stone are almost all the tombstones, &c. that I observed in the island" (1:76). They went on to Carisbrooke Castle:

> We entered over the ditch (which is now almost filled up, partly by the ruins of the mouldering walls that have tumbled into it, and partly by the washing down of the earth from the hill by the rains) upon a couple of brick arches, where I suppose formerly there was a drawbridge. An old woman who lives in the castle, seeing us as strangers walk about, sent and offered to show us the rooms if we pleased, which we accepted. This castle, as she informed us, has for many years been the seat of the Governors of the island: and the rooms and hall, which are very large and handsome with high arched roofs, have all along been kept handsomely furnished, every succeeding governor buying the furniture of his predecessor; but [William] Cadogan the last governor, who succeeded General [John Richmond] Webb, refusing to purchase it, Webb stripped it clear of all, even the hangings, and left nothing but bare walls. The floors are several of them of plaster of Paris, the art of making which, the woman told us, was now lost. (1:76–77)

It must have been a special plaster of Paris, perhaps strengthened with the addition of some material.

After the particulars, Franklin portrayed the overall scene:

> The castle stands upon a very high and steep hill, and there are the remains of a deep ditch round it; the walls are thick, and seemingly well contrived: and certainly it has been a very strong hold in its time, at least before the invention of great guns. There are several breaches in the ruinous walls, which are never repaired, (I suppose they are purposely neglected) and the ruins are almost every where overspread with ivy. It is divided into the lower and upper castle, the lower enclosing the upper which is of a round form, and stands upon a promontory to which you must ascend by near an hundred stone steps: this upper castle

was designed for a retreat in case the lower castle should be won, and is the least ruinous of any part except the stairs before mentioned, which are so broken and decayed that I was almost afraid to come down again when I was up, they being but narrow and no rails to hold by. From the battlements of this upper castle (which they call the coop) you have a fine prospect of the greatest part of the island, of the sea on one side, of Cowes road at a distance, and of Newport as it were just below you. (1:77)

The American found the well in the upper castle remarkable: it was called "the bottomless well, because of its great depth; but it is now half filled up with stones and rubbish, and is covered with two or three loose planks; yet a stone, as we tried, is near a quarter of a minute in falling before you hear it strike. But the well that supplies the inhabitants at present with water is in the lower castle, and is thirty fathoms deep." Mechanical engineering interested Franklin: "They draw their water with a great wheel, and with a bucket that holds near a barrel. It makes a great sound if you speak in it, and echoed the flute we played over it very sweetly" (1:77–78). Did Franklin play the flute? Was he carrying one? Possibly. He played a variety of musical instruments later in life, though there is no record of his having owned or played a flute.[2] Franklin assessed the castle's out-of-date military capabilities before turning to its history: "There are but seven pieces of ordnance mounted upon the walls, and those in no very good order; and the old man who is the gunner and keeper of the castle, and who sells ale in a little house at the gate, has in his possession but six muskets, (which hang up at his wall) and one of them wants a lock. He told us that the castle, which had now been built 1203 years, was first founded by one Whitgert a Saxon who conquered the island, and that it was called Whitgertsburg for many ages. That particular piece of building which King Charles lodged in during his confinement here is suffered to go entirely to ruin, there being nothing standing but the walls" (1:78).

After describing the island, Franklin turned to Joseph Dudley, once its governor. Franklin had known Dudley, who had been governor of Massachusetts, and who was generally despised. Dudley had been the deputy governor of the Isle of Wight (1693–1701). "At his death it appeared he was a great villain, and a great politician; there was no crime so damnable which he would stick at in the execution of his designs, and yet he had the art of covering all so thick, what with almost all men in general, while he lived, he passed for a saint. What surprised me was, that the silly old fellow, the keeper of the castle, who remembered him governor, should have so true a notion of his character as I perceived he had." Franklin then idealistically recorded his own moralistic tenets: "In short I believe it is impossible for a man, though he has all the cunning of a devil, to live and die a villain, and yet conceal it so well as to carry the name of an honest fellow to the grave with him, but some one by some accident or other shall discover him. Truth and sincerity have a certain distinguishing native lustre about them which cannot be perfectly counterfeited, they are like fire and flame that cannot be painted" (1:78–79). Franklin believed in "truth and sincerity" as among the most important values throughout his life (A 59), though truth is not found in his list of thirteen virtues (A 79–80).

On Saturday, 30 July, they managed to sail to Yarmouth,

> another little town upon this island, and there cast anchor again, the wind blow-ing hard and still westerly. Yarmouth is a smaller town than Cowes; yet the buildings being better, it makes a handsomer prospect at a distance, and the streets are clean and neat. There is one monument in the church which the inhabitants are very proud of, and which we went to see. It was erected to the memory of Sir Robert Holmes [1622–92], who had formerly been governor of the island. It is his statue in armour, somewhat bigger than the life, standing on his tomb with a truncheon in his hand, between two pillars of porphyry. Indeed all the marble about it is very fine and good; and they say it was designed by the French King for his palace at Versailles, but was cast away upon this island, and by Sir Robert himself in his life-time applied to this use, and that the whole monument was finished long before he died, (though not fixed up in that place); the inscription likewise (which is very much to his honour) being written by himself.

After recording this monument to vanity, Franklin ironically noted, "One would think either that he had no defect at all, or had a very ill opinion of the world, seeing he was so careful to make sure of a monument to record his good actions and transmit them to posterity" (1:79).

In the Mud

Franklin and two friends ventured into the countryside and stayed until dark, before attempting to return to other friends drinking at an inn. He recorded a series of incidents that were all embarrassing and potentially dangerous:

> We were told that it was our best way to go straight down to the mouth of the creek, and that there was a ferry boy that would carry us over to the town. But when we came to the house the lazy whelp was in bed, and refused to rise and put us over; upon which we went down to the water-side, with a design to take his boat, and go over by ourselves. We found it very difficult to get the boat, it being fastened to a stake and the tide risen near fifty yards beyond it: I stripped all to my shirt to wade up to it; but missing the causeway, which was under water, I got up to my middle in mud. At last I came to the stake; but to my great disappointment found she was locked and chained. I endeavoured to draw the stake with one of the thole-pins, but in vain; I tried to pull up the stake, but to no purpose: so that after an hour's fatigue and trouble in the wet and mud, I was forced to return without the boat.

The story is reminiscent of the one in which Franklin stole stones to build a wharf as a boy in Boston. He began that anecdote: "living near the Water, I was much in and about it, learnt early to swim well, and to manage Boats, and when in a Boat or Canoe with other Boys I was commonly allow'd to govern, especially in any case of Difficulty" (A 7). Here, too, he was the dishonest ringleader, attempting to justify his illegal actions by calling the ferry boy a "lazy whelp."

Since the group had no money with them, they decided "to pass the night in some hay-stack, though the wind blew very cold and very hard. In the midst of these troubles one of us recollected that he had a horseshoe in his pocket which he found in his walk, and asked me if I could not wrench the staple out with that." The person with the horseshoe did not try to get the boat; instead Franklin, already having struggled for an hour in the mud, was asked. "I took it, went, tried and succeeded, and brought the boat ashore to them. Now we rejoiced and all got in, and when I had dressed myself we put off." So Franklin had gone out naked into the water. "But the worst of all our troubles was to come yet; for, it being high water and the tide over all the banks, though it was moonlight we could not discern the channel of the creek, but rowing heedlessly straight forward, when we were got about half way over, we found ourselves aground on a mud bank, and striving to row her off by putting our oars in the mud, we broke one and there stuck fast, not having four inches water. We were now in the utmost perplexity, not knowing what in the world to do; we could not tell whether the tide was rising or falling; but at length we plainly perceived it was ebb, and we could feel no deeper water within the reach of our oar." Note that Franklin does not seem nearly as concerned with dishonesty (granted, it was minor) as with the public humiliation that would follow their exposure. "It was hard to lie in an open boat all night exposed to the wind and weather; but it was worse to think how foolish we should look in the morning, when the owner of the boat should catch us in that condition, where we must be exposed to the view of all the town" (1:80).

The quality of revealing frankness that Franklin displays in this anecdote is typical of some aspects of his personality and of the *Autobiography*, as in his telling of the unwelcome advances he made to Ralph's girlfriend, the milliner (see Chapter 11). He was willing, without apology, to portray himself as a minor thief, a naked miscreant, and a fool. Most people have such moments in their youth, but few record that they have been such a "Boo bee" (1:219). Franklin, however, ruefully laughed at himself. After the group struggled with the rowboat for more than half an hour, they gave up "and sat down with our hands before us, despairing to get off." But at last they thought of a possibility for escaping: "two of us stripped and got out, and thereby lightening the boat, we drew her upon our knees near fifty yards into deeper water, and then with much ado, having but one oar, we got safe ashore under the fort; and having dressed ourselves and tied the man's boat, we went with great joy to the Queen's Head, where we left our companions, whom we found waiting for us, though it was very late. Our boat being gone on board, we were obliged to lie ashore all night; and thus ended our walk" (1:81).

The Channel

Finally, on 5 August, the *Berkshire* left Cowes a third time, to sail by Yarmouth and come into the channel through the Needles, past Hurst Castle. The ship had spent two weeks trying to reach the channel. The next day was calm, so in the afternoon Franklin "leaped overboard and swam round the ship to wash myself." In the afternoon of 7 August they spoke with a captain bound for Boston, who had come out of the Thames when they did, more than two weeks prior, "and had been beating about in the Channel all the time we lay at Cowes in the Wight" (1:82).

For the first ten days on the ocean, Franklin recorded little more than the weather, but on Friday morning, 19 August, the company "spied a sail upon our larboard bow, about two leagues distance." Tension mounted. An unknown ship at sea threatened danger. It could always turn out to be a pirate or, in wartime, an enemy. Conversely, a friend might have news from America, England, or Europe. "About noon she put out English colours, and we answered with our ensign, and in the afternoon we spoke with her." Worry disappeared. It was a snow (a small ship with three masts) "of New York, Walter Kippen Master, bound from Rochelle in France to Boston with salt. Our captain and Mr. D[enham] went on board and stayed till evening, it being fine weather" (1:83). Denham's clerk, of course, was not invited. The two captains agreed that, weather permitting, Kippen would visit the next day. On Saturday, 20 August, the *Berkshire* shorted sail to keep company with the snow. At noon Captain Kippen and a passenger came aboard, dined with the officers and passengers, and stayed till evening. As soon as they were gone, "we made sail and left them" (1:84–85). The following day "we lost sight of the Yorker, having a brisk gale of wind at East." The *Boston Evening Post* for 27 October recorded that Walter Kippen from St. Martins arrived safely. Meanwhile, Franklin and the other persons aboard the *Berkshire* found their own diversion.

The Cheat

The discovery of a card shark dispelled the boredom of sea life. Informed of a passenger's marking the cards, the captain and the mate had the passengers set up a court to try him. "Yesterday complaints being made that a Mr. G——n one of the passengers had with a fraudulent design marked the cards, a Court of Justice was called immediately, and he was brought to his trial in form. A Dutchman who could speak no English deposed by his interpreter, that when our mess was on shore at Cowes, the prisoner at the bar marked all the court cards on the back with a pen" (1:83). Franklin rhetorically asked how the criminal could have been so foolish? In answering, the aspiring young merchant revealed that he was a careful observer of human actions and an amateur psychologist: "I have sometimes observed that we are apt to fancy the person that cannot speak intelligibly to us, proportionably stupid in understanding, and when we speak two or three words of English to a foreigner, it is louder than ordinary, as if we thought him deaf, and that he had lost the use of his ears as well as his tongue. Something like this I imagine might be the case of Mr. G——n; he fancied the Dutchman could not see what he was about because he could not understand English, and therefore boldly did it before his face" (1:84).

"The evidence was plain and positive, the prisoner could not deny the fact, but replied in his defence, that the cards he marked were not those we commonly played with, but an imperfect pack, which he afterwards gave to the cabin-boy." The acting prosecutor argued that it was not likely the defendant should take the pains to mark the cards just to give them to the cabin boy. Another witness deposed that he saw the prisoner in the main top one day when he thought himself unobserved, marking a pack of cards on the backs, some with the print of a dirty thumb, others with the top of his finger. Since there were only two packs onboard, it was obvious that the defendant had marked both. "In fine the jury brought him in guilty, and he was condemned to be carried up to the round top, and made fast there in view of all the ship's company during the space of three hours, that being the place where the act was committed, and to pay a fine of two bottles of brandy" (1:84). In an age of harsh penalties, the sentence imposed by his fellow passengers seems almost reasonable. Nevertheless, the cheat refused to pay, so Franklin and the others physically subdued him. A sailor "stepped up aloft and let down a rope to us, which we with much struggling made fast about his middle and hoisted him up into the air, sprawling, by main force. We let him hang, cursing and swearing, for near a quarter of an hour; but at length he crying out murder! and looking black in the face, the rope being overtort about his middle, we thought proper to let him down again; and our mess have excommunicated him till he pays his fine, refusing either to play, eat, drink, or converse with him" (1:84).

By Thursday, 25 August, the card shark could stand his exile no longer. "Our excommunicated ship-mate thinking proper to comply with the sentence the court passed upon him, and expressing himself willing to pay the fine, we have this morning received him into unity again." The incident made Franklin consider the social nature of human beings: "Man is a sociable being, and it is for aught I know one of the worst of punishments to be excluded from society." Franklin probably recalled from the Port Royal *Logic* that "the Pagan Philosophers believed a solitary Life so insupportable, that they did not scruple to say their Wise Man would not purchase the Enjoyments of all the Goods both of Body and Mind at the Price of living always alone, and of having no body with whom he might discourse of his Happiness."[3] Franklin continued, "I have read abundance of fine things on the subject of solitude, and I know 'tis a common boast in the mouths of those that affect to be thought wise, that they are never less alone than when alone." Here he probably echoed Shaftesbury in the *Characteristics*, who said that the ancient philosophers boasted "that they were never less alone than when by themselves." Franklin probably knew that Cicero and

Jonathan Swift, among others, had made such statements.[4] The young man continued, "I acknowledge solitude an agreeable refreshment to a busy mind; but were these thinking people obliged to be always alone, I am apt to think they would quickly find their very being insupportable to them" (1:85).

The skeptical Franklin recalled an anecdote he had heard of a gentleman imprisoned in the Bastille at Paris. "He was a man of sense, he was a thinking man; but being deprived of all conversation, to what purpose should he think? for he was denied even the instruments of expressing his thoughts in writing. There is no burden so grievous to man as time that he knows not how to dispose of. He was forced at last to have recourse to this invention: he daily scattered pieces of paper about the floor of his little room, and then employed himself in picking them up and sticking them in rows and figures on the arm of his elbow-chair; and he used to tell his friends, after his release, that he verily believed if he had not taken this method he should have lost his senses" (1:85–86). Franklin may have echoed Mandeville, who wrote in *Fable of the Bees* of an imprisoned man who would "scatter Pins about the Room in order to pick them up again."[5]

Franklin added: "One of the philosophers, I think it was Plato, used to say, that he had rather be the veriest stupid block in nature, than the possessor of all knowledge without some intelligent being to communicate it to" (1:86). Plato is not the source, but it is possible that Franklin recalled it from Cicero. More probably, Franklin echoed Montaigne, who wrote, "No pleasure has any taste for me when not shared with another: no happy thought occurs to me without my being irritated at bringing it forth alone with no one to offer it to." Montaigne cited Seneca, "If even wisdom were granted me on condition that I shut it away unspoken, I would reject it." Montaigne also quoted Cicero for a stronger statement: "Suppose it were granted to a sage to live in every abundance, his time entirely free to study and reflect upon everything worth knowing: yet if his solitude were such that he could never meet another man he would quit this life." Montaigne concluded, "I agree with the opinion of Archytas that there would be no pleasure in traveling through the heavens among those great immortal celestial bodies without the presence of a companion."[6]

After commenting on the social nature of humans, Franklin philosophized about conduct aboard ship: "What I have said may in a measure account for some particulars in my present way of living here on board. Our company is in general very unsuitably mixed, to keep up the pleasure and spirit of conversation: and if there are one or two pair of us that can sometimes entertain one another for half an hour agreeably, yet perhaps we are seldom in the humour for it together." He sketched his ordinary day: "I rise in the morning and read for an hour or two perhaps, and then reading grows tiresome. Want of exercise occasions want of appetite, so that eating and drinking affords but little pleasure. I tire myself with playing at draughts, then I go to cards; nay there is no play so trifling or childish, but we fly to it for entertainment. A contrary wind, I know not how, puts us all out of good humour; we grow sullen, silent and reserved, and fret at each other upon every little occasion" (1:86). He even ventured to imagine himself as a witty beau: "'Tis a common opinion among the ladies, that if a man is ill-natured he infallibly discovers it when he is in liquor. But I, who have known many instances to the contrary, will teach them a more effectual method to discover the natural temper and disposition of their humble servants. Let the ladies make one long sea voyage with them, and if they have the least spark of ill nature in them and conceal it to the end of the voyage, I will forfeit all my pretensions to their favour" (1:86). That same day, Tuesday, 30 August, he saw an unusual natural phenomenon: "This evening the moon being near full, as she rose after eight o'clock, there appeared a rainbow in a western cloud to windward of us. The first time I ever saw a rainbow in the night caused by the moon."

PLAN OF CONDUCT

During the voyage Franklin drafted a plan for his return. He said that perhaps the most important part of the journal was "the *Plan* to be found in it which I formed at Sea, for regulating my future Conduct in Life. It is the more remarkable, as being form'd when I was so young, and yet being pretty faithfully adhered to quite thro' to old Age" (A 51–52). The full plan does not survive. A part of it, a preamble and four resolves, was printed in 1817. In the preamble, Franklin resolved to live deliberately: "Those who write of the art of poetry teach us that if we would write what may be worth the reading, we ought always, before we begin, to form a regular plan and design of our Piece: otherwise, we shall be in danger of incongruity. I am apt to think it is the same as to life. I have never fixed a regular design in life; by which means it has been a confused variety of different scenes. I am now entering upon a new one: let me, therefore, make some resolutions, and form some scheme of action, that, henceforth, I may live in all respects like a rational creature" (1:99–100). He was attempting to impose control over his life. The impulse was the same that underlay the *Autobiography*'s scheme of thirteen virtues and outline for organizing a day.

Franklin first resolved to pay the Rhode Island silversmith Samuel Vernon the £35 owed him and to pay Denham the money he had borrowed for the return voyage. "1. It is necessary for me to be extremely frugal for some time, till I have paid what I owe" (1:100). Still smarting from Governor Keith's false promises, Franklin determined never to do likewise: "2. To endeavour to speak truth in every instance; to give nobody expectations that are not likely to be answered, but aim at sincerity in every word and action—the most amiable excellence in a rational being" (1:100). He had twice prematurely attempted to set up in business for himself. He judged his past conduct wistful and possibly foolish: "3. To apply myself industriously to whatever business I take in hand, and not divert my mind from my business by any foolish project of growing suddenly rich; for industry and patience are the surest means of plenty" (1:100). Frugality, sincerity, and industry were later among the thirteen virtues.

And, finally, he evidently felt that he had sometimes, in Boston, Philadelphia, and London, been too critical of others. "4. I resolve to speak ill of no man whatever, not even in a matter of truth; but rather by some means excuse the faults I hear charged upon others, and upon proper occasions speak all the good I know of everybody" (1:100). He later burlesqued himself and this attempt in a skit signed "Alice Addertongue" (12 September 1732). If he truly thought (as he wrote in the *Autobiography*) that he followed this resolve "pretty faithfully . . . to old Age," he gave himself the benefit of the doubt. Several scholars have thought his contempt for Thomas Penn excessive. In the 1750s and later, he judged Provost William Smith harshly. Some students have thought his treatment of his son William during the Revolution was too severe. On the other hand, he attempted to excuse the beatings of his brother James and the perfidy of Governor Keith. Such judgments, however, are debatable. More important was his deliberate attempt to assess his faults and to try to correct them.

Paintings of Dolphins

On Friday, 2 September, Franklin recorded another remark on painting:

> This morning the wind changed, a little fair. We caught a couple of dolphins, and fried them for dinner. They tasted tolerably well. These fish make a glorious appearance in the water: their bodies are of a bright green, mixed with a silver colour, and their tails of a shining golden yellow; but all this vanishes presently after they are taken out of their element, and they change all over a light grey. I observed that cutting off pieces of a just-caught living dolphin for baits, those pieces did not lose their lustre and fine colours when the dolphin died, but retained them perfectly. Every one takes notice of that vulgar error of the painters, who always represent this fish monstrously crooked and deformed, when it is in reality as beautiful and well shaped a fish as any that swims. I cannot think what should be the original of this chimera of theirs, (since there is not a creature in nature that in the least resembles their dolphin) unless it proceeded at first from a false imitation of a fish in the posture of leaping, which they have since improved into a crooked monster with a head and eyes like a bull, a hog's snout, and a tail like a blown tulip. Franklin had evidently seen pictures of leaping dolphins, typically shown as curved.

Portrayals of dolphins in Western art were influenced by the Greek legends of departed heroes riding dolphins to the Islands of the Blest. He probably also had seen arched dolphins as the central figure on the Franklin coat of arms.[7] Showing his characteristic curiosity, Franklin asked the sailors if they knew why the dolphin was misrepresented. In reply, he heard a folk story that conserved the traditional connection between fertility and dolphins (in Greek, *delphis* [dolphin] and *delphys* [womb] are homophones): "But the sailors give me another reason, though a whimsical one, viz. that as this most beautiful fish is only to be caught at sea, and that very far to the Southward, they say the painters wilfully deform it in their representations, lest pregnant women should long for what it is impossible to procure for them" (1:87–88). When the sailors and passengers caught four large dolphins on Friday, 9 September, Franklin noted that the dolphins "appeared extremely eager and hungry, and snapped up the hook as soon as ever it touched the water." When they cleaned the dolphins, they found in one stomach "a small dolphin half digested." Franklin attempted to account for their cannibalism: "Certainly they were half famished, or are naturally very savage to devour those of their own species" (1:88).

THE SHARK

Discipline was carried out again on Wednesday, 21 September. "This morning our Steward was brought to the geers and whipped, for making an extravagant use of flour in the puddings, and for several other misdemeanors." Franklin commented on the weather because he wanted to bathe:

> It has been perfectly calm all this day, and very hot. I was determined to wash myself in the sea to-day, and should have done so had not the appearance of a shark, that mortal enemy to swimmers, deterred me: he seemed to be about five feet long, moves round the ship at some distance in a slow majestic manner, attended by near a dozen . . . pilot-fish, of different sizes; the largest of them is not so big as a small mackerel, and the smallest not bigger than my little finger. Two of these diminutive pilots keep just before his nose, and he seems to govern himself in his motions by their direction; while the rest surround him on every side indifferently. A shark is never seen without a retinue of these, who are his purveyors, discovering and distinguishing his prey for him; while he in return gratefully protects them from the ravenous hungry dolphin. They are commonly counted a very greedy fish; yet this refuses to meddle with the bait we have thrown out for him. 'Tis likely he has lately made a full meal. (1:90)

A COMPANION

As the gams in *Moby Dick* demonstrate for students of American literature, meetings of ships at sea were special occasions. Initially, one feared that the ship would be hostile. If friendly, the ships would exchange news (especially if the two ships were going in opposite directions) and estimates concerning their location. The morning of Friday, 23 September 1726, the lookout on the ship spied a sail to windward. "We shewed our jack upon the ensign-staff, and shortened sail for them till about noon, when she came up with us. She was a snow from Dublin, bound to New York, having upwards of fifty servants on board, of both sexes; they all appeared upon deck, and seemed very much pleased at the sight of us."

Franklin, playing the psychologist, tried to analyze why he and everyone else obviously felt pleasure. "There is really something strangely cheering to the spirits in the meeting of a ship at sea, containing a society of creatures of the same species and in the same circumstances with ourselves, after we had been long separated and excommunicated as it were from the rest of mankind. My heart fluttered in my breast with joy when I saw so many human countenances, and I could scarce refrain from that kind of laughter which proceeds from some degree of inward pleasure."

Franklin probably knew Francis Hutcheson's theory that "Anything that gives us Pleasure, puts us also in a fitnes for *Laughter*." Hutcheson's 1725 essays on laughter attacked Hobbes and satirized Mandeville. Though they did not appear in London but in the *Dublin Journal* in 1725, they would have been known to Mandeville and his circle.[8] In his journal, Franklin indulged in a flight of fancy: "When we have been for a considerable time tossing on the vast waters, far from the sight of any land or ships, or any mortal creature but ourselves (except a few fish and sea birds) the whole world, for aught we know, may be under a second deluge, and we (like Noah and his company in the Ark) the only surviving remnant of the human race" (1:91). Though modern communications have obviated that fear, sea voyages (like camping) are still among the greatest retreats from civilization, though now such trips are often too short for one to welcome intrusions.

Though the captains promised to keep each other company, Franklin thought it was cant, "for if ships are unequal in their sailing they seldom stay for one another, especially strangers." That day, the wind "that has been so long contrary to us, came about to the eastward (and looks as if it would hold), to our no small satisfaction." Franklin remarked that all his shipmates seemed happy, and he attributed it not to the change of wind, but (now reflecting Hobbes)[9] to a consideration of their own position, in comparison to that of the more than fifty Irish servants onboard the other ship: "I find our messmates in a better humour, and more pleased with their present condition than they have been since we came out; which I take to proceed from the contemplation of the miserable circumstances of the passengers on board our neighbour. . . . We reckon ourselves in a kind of paradise, when we consider how they live, confined and stifled up with such a lousy stinking rabble in this sultry latitude" (1:91).

A reader might think that Franklin, and perhaps his messmates, were scorning the indentured servants on the other ship as a "lousy stinking rabble." It seems likely, however, that the condition of being "confined and stifled up" makes the servants a "lousy stinking rabble." Franklin's disgust is for the conditions (and indirectly for those responsible for the miserable situation) rather than the "wretched unfree migrants." The feeling is one of sympathy rather than contempt, but what interested him most were the reasons underlying the behavior of his shipmates.

The following morning, Saturday, 24 September, Franklin and his shipmates were alarmed by the appearance of two sails: "Last night we had a very high wind, and very thick weather; in which we lost our consort. This morning early we spied a sail a-head of us, which we took to be her; but presently after we spied another, and then we plainly perceived that neither of them could be the snow, for one of them stemmed with us, and the other bore down directly upon us, having the weather gage of us. As the latter drew near we were a little surprised, not knowing what to make of her; for by the course she steered she did not seem designed for any port, but looked as if she intended to clap us aboard immediately. I could perceive concern in every face on board; but she presently eased us of our apprehensions by bearing away a-stern of us. When we hoisted our jack she answered with French colours, and presently took them down again; and we soon lost sight of her" (1:91–92). Franklin's persistent and keen observation of the reactions of others aboard ship ("concern in every face") is striking—as is his unwillingness to admit any fear on his part, even in his own private journal.

The second boat was not so frightening. It "ran by us in less than half an hour, and answered our jack with an English ensign; she stood to the eastward, but the wind was too high to speak with either." Franklin was wrong about the captains' resolve to stay in sight of one another being mere cant: "About nine o'clock we spied our consort, who had got a great way a- head of us. She, it seems, had made sail in the night, while we lay-by with our main yard down during the hard gale. She very civilly shortened sail for us, and this afternoon we came up with her; and now we are running along very amicably together side by side, having a most glorious fair wind." By Sunday, 25 September, "All our discourse now is of Philadelphia, and we begin to fancy ourselves ashore already" (1:92).

A Squall and an Eclipse

On Monday, 26 September, a sudden gale came up "of wind at all points of the compass, accompanied with the most violent shower of rain I ever saw, insomuch that the sea looked like a *cream dish*." The squall "surprised us with all our sails up, and was so various, uncertain, and contrary, that the mizen topsail was full, while the head sails were all aback; and before the men could run from one end of the ship to the other, 'twas about again." The gust was soon over, and "the wind settled to the North-East again, to our satisfaction." Their consort had become separated during the storm and fell astern, "but made sail and came up with us again after it was over. We hailed one another on the morrow, congratulating upon the continuance of the fair wind, and both ran on very lovingly together" (1:93). During another day of fair wind and weather, Franklin bet "a bowl of punch that we are in Philadelphia next Saturday se'ennight; for we reckon ourselves not above one hundred and fifty leagues from land." (Franklin lost; they did not arrive before Saturday, 8 October, but on Tuesday evening, 11 October.) The ships experienced a storm and a westerly wind on Wednesday, 28 September. In the afternoon "we took up several branches of gulf weed (with which the sea is spread all over from the Western Isles to the coast of America); but one of these branches had something peculiar in it."

Among his books, Franklin evidently had a current almanac. On the night of 29 September, there was "an eclipse of the moon, which the calendar calculated for London informed us would happen at five o'clock in the morning, September 30." Franklin stayed up to observe it: "It began with us about eleven last night, and continued till near two this morning, darkening her body about six digits, or one half; the middle of it being about half an hour after twelve." No doubt the captain and mate used the eclipse to confirm their location, but Franklin calculated the longitude for himself. He applied his study of Seller's and Sturmy's books of navigation to the observation of the eclipse: "by which we may discover that we are in a meridian of about four hours and half from London, or 67½ degrees of longitude, and consequently have not much above one hundred leagues to run" (1:94–95). Either Franklin's calculations were wrong or the ships did not make the progress he expected. Perhaps, too, his desire for the journey to end made him mistake both the position and the distance from America.

THE UNWELCOME TRUTH

Though they lost their consort in the night, they saw the snow again on Friday morning, 30 September, "near two leagues to windward" and talked with the captain again that afternoon. "We have had abundance of dolphins about us these three or four days; but we have not taken any more than one, they being shy of the bait." The Dublin snow finally had disappeared by Saturday morning, 1 October: "Last night our consort, who goes incomparably better upon a wind than our vessel, got so far to windward and a-head of us, that this morning we could see nothing of him, and 'tis like shall see him no more." They did not, but Franklin no doubt learned that Captain Miller's *Barnet* successfully completed its voyage, for the *New York Gazette* recorded on 17 October 1726 that it had entered in. On Sunday, 2 October, Franklin thought he could see that "the water is changed a little, as is usual when a ship comes within soundings," but he found good reason to doubt himself: "But 'tis probable I am mistaken; for there is but one besides myself of my opinion, and we are very apt to believe what we wish to be true" (1:95). The following day, however, he wrote that "The water is now very visibly changed to the eyes of all except the Captain and Mate, and they will by no means allow it." Just as he had a depreciating comment to make about himself and human nature the day before, so he had a depreciating comment about the captain, mate, and human nature: "I suppose because they did not see it first." The captain and mate, however, were right.

THE AMERICAN

On Tuesday, 4 October, Franklin recorded: "this morning we found a flying-fish dead under the windlass. He is about the bigness of a small mackerel, a sharp head, a small mouth, and a tail forked somewhat like a dolphin, but the lowest branch much larger and longer than the other, and tinged with yellow.

His back and sides of a darkish blue, his belly white, and his skin very thick. His wings are of a finny substance, about a span long, reaching, when close to his body, from an inch below his gills to an inch above his tail." Neither the description of the flying-fish nor the following report of their behavior made any contribution to natural history but Franklin chose to record these bits of information rather than to comment on other activities, like his reading.

"When they fly it is straight forward, for (they cannot readily turn) a yard or two above the water, and perhaps fifty yards is the farthest before they dip into the water again, for they cannot support themselves in the air any longer than while their wings continue wet. These flying-fish are the common prey of the dolphin, who is their mortal enemy. When he pursues them they rise and fly, and he keeps close under them till they drop, and then snaps them up immediately. They generally fly in flocks, four or five, or perhaps a dozen together, and a dolphin is seldom caught without one or more in his belly. We put this flying-fish upon the hook, in hopes of catching one, but in a few minutes they got it off without hooking themselves; and they will not meddle with any other bait" (1:96).

As the passengers neared land, they became impatient to arrive, and Franklin noted all the encouraging signs. "This afternoon we have seen abundance of grampuses, which are seldom far from land; but towards evening we had a more evident token, to wit, a little tired bird, something like a lark, came on board us, who certainly is an American, and 'tis likely was ashore this day" (1:96).

Has America Sunk?

Thursday, 6 October: "This morning abundance of grass, rock-weed, &c. passed by us; evident tokens that land is not far off. We hooked a dolphin this morning that made us a good breakfast. A sail passed by us about twelve o'clock, and nobody saw her till she was too far astern to be spoken with. 'Tis very near calm: we saw another sail a-head this afternoon; but night coming on, we could not speak with her, though we very much desired it: she stood to the Northward, and it is possible might have informed us how far we are from land. Our artists on board are much at a loss. We hoisted our jack to her, but she took no notice of it." That evening a strong wind came up, "which run us in our course at the rate of seven miles an hour all night. We were in hopes of seeing land this morning, but cannot. The water, which we thought was changed, is now as blue as the sky; so that unless at that time we were running over some unknown shoal our eyes strangely deceived us." Franklin evidently thought that he, like everyone else except the captain and mate, had wishfully deceived themselves. "All the reckonings have been out these several days; though the captain says 'tis his opinion we are yet an hundred leagues from land: for my part I know not what to think of it, we have run all this day at a great rate; and now night is come on we have no soundings." He pessimistically expressed the fear that he and the other landlubbers shared: "Sure the American continent is not all

sunk under water since we left it" (1:97). By Saturday, 8 October, Franklin could
hardly believe that they had not seen land.

> The fair wind continues still; we ran all night in our course, sounding every
> four hours, but can find no ground yet, nor is the water changed by all this day's
> run. This afternoon we saw an *Irish Lord*, and a bird which flying looked like a
> yellow duck. These they say are not seen far from the coast. Other signs of land
> have we none. Abundance of large porpoises ran by us this afternoon, and we
> were followed by a shoal of small ones, leaping out of the water, as they ap-
> proached. Towards evening we spied a sail a-head and spoke with her just before
> dark. She was bound from New York for Jamaica, and left Sandy Hook yesterday
> about noon, from which they reckon themselves forty-five leagues distant. By
> this we compute that we are not above thirty leagues from our capes, and hope
> to see land to-morrow. (1:97)

LAND!

The tension gradually increased and all aboard were looking for land throughout the morning of Sunday, 9 October. It was on a Sunday, 6 October, just over
four years before that Franklin had arrived in Philadelphia. He must have been
hoping that he would somehow reach there on that Sunday: "We have had the
wind fair all the morning: at twelve o'clock we sounded, perceiving the water
visibly changed, and struck ground at twenty-five fathoms, to our universal joy.
After dinner one of our mess went up aloft to look out, and presently pronounced the long-wished for sound, LAND! LAND! In less than an hour we
could descry it from the deck, appearing like tufts of trees. I could not discern
it so soon as the rest; my eyes were dimmed with the suffusion of two small
drops of joy." The emotional Franklin! It seems almost strange—but the home-
sick American was to reveal even greater emotion the following day. "By three
o'clock we were run in within two leagues of the land, and spied a small sail
standing along shore. We would gladly have spoken with her, for our captain
was unacquainted with the coast, and knew not what land it was that we saw.
We made all the sail we could to speak with her. We made a signal of distress;
but all would not do, the ill-natured dog would not come near us. Then we
stood off again till morning, not caring to venture too near."

Monday, 10 October: "This morning we stood in again for land; and we,
that had been here before, all agreed that it was Cape Henlopen." There is no
record of Franklin's visiting Cape May and Cape Henlopen, but the two capes
at the mouth of the Delaware Bay would have been logical destinations for
boating parties, and he no doubt knew the Delaware Bay and river well from
the capes to well past Philadelphia. By noon the *Berkshire* was near Cape Henlopen, where "to our great joy . . . the pilot-boat come off to us, which was
exceeding welcome. He brought on board about a peck of apples with him; they

seemed the most delicious I ever tasted in my life: the salt provisions we had been used to, gave them a relish. We had an extraordinary fair wind all the afternoon and ran above an hundred miles up the Delaware before ten at night. The country appears very pleasant to the eye, being covered with woods, except here and there a house and plantation. We cast anchor when the tide turned, about two miles below Newcastle [now Delaware], and there lay till the morning tide."

On Tuesday, 11 October, they weighed anchor with a gentle breeze and passed by New Castle. Franklin happily noted: "'Tis extreme fine weather." Franklin wrote a paean to the beautiful appearance of the Delaware Bay and the surrounding land: "The sun enlivens our stiff limbs with his glorious rays of warmth and brightness. The sky looks gay, with here and there a silver cloud. The fresh breezes from the woods refresh us, the immediate prospect of liberty after so long and irksome confinement ravishes us. In short all things conspire to make this the most joyful day I ever knew" (1:98–99). Without his personal testimony in a private diary, one would hardly think that his return to Philadelphia would have occasioned so much happiness. Recalling it nearly two decades later, he wrote that the "Cords of Love and Friendship" drew him "back from England to Philadelphia."[10]

> As we passed by Chester some of the company went on shore, impatient once more to tread on terra firma, and designing for Philadelphia by land. Four of us remained on board, not caring for the fatigue of travel when we knew the voyage had much weakened us. About eight at night, the wind failing us, we cast anchor at Redbank, six miles from Philadelphia, and thought we must be obliged to lie on board that night: but some young Philadelphians happening to be out upon their pleasure boat, they came on board, and offered to take us up with them: we accepted of their kind proposal, and about ten o'clock landed at Philadelphia, heartily congratulating each other upon our having happily completed so tedious and dangerous a voyage. Thank God! (1:99)

Of course no notice of Franklin's or Denham's return appeared in the local paper. Among its weekly report of ship arrivals, the *American Weekly Mercury* recorded on 13 October 1726: "Entered inwards, ship *Berkshire, Henry Clark*, from London."

What's Left Out?

Though Franklin recorded on 25 August that reading grew tiresome after an hour or two, we can be sure that the book-loving and ambitious twenty-year-old read and studied daily for at least a few hours. He no doubt had with him a large number of books from his year and a half in London—a few of which he bought especially to read on the voyage once he knew that he was going to return to America. Reading and studying were primary occupations for the two and a half months (22 July–11 October) he spent at sea. He also no doubt spent considerable time in conversation with Thomas Denham, mainly concerning the mercantile business. Denham made only two appearances in the journal: on 27 July when he, Captain Clark, and Franklin went ashore at Portsmouth, and on 19 August when he and the captain went aboard Walter Kippin's ship. What's omitted? Almost everything. The journal did not record Franklin's daily routines, his reading, or his conversation; it only contained unusual occurrences, breaks in the routine, or observations of interest. Nevertheless, it—especially the parts written before the ship reached the ocean—reveals a great deal about the young Franklin's mind and character.

THIRTEEN

Merchant to Master Printer
1726–1728

*Our Printing-House often wanted Sorts, and there was no Letter Founder in
America. I had seen Types cast at James's in London, but without much Attention
to the Manner: However I now contriv'd a Mould, made use of the Letters we had,
as Puncheons, struck the Matrices in Lead, and thus supply'd in a pretty tolerable
way all Deficiencies. I also engrav'd several Things on occasion. I made the Ink, I
was Warehouse-man and every thing, in short quite a Factotum.—A 43*

ON TUESDAY, 11 OCTOBER 1726, AT 10 P.M., Franklin and Thomas Denham
landed at Philadelphia. Perhaps they rounded up a few old friends and celebrated. The political news was that Sir William Keith had been superseded as
governor on 22 June 1726 by Major Patrick Gordon and that just ten days ago,
Keith had been elected an assemblyman from Philadelphia County. His party
had swept the Philadelphia City and the Philadelphia County elections. It looked
as if he might be elected Speaker of the House. Franklin probably found the
news amazing. Three days later, Saturday, 14 October, just before the assembly
met, Keith proceeded triumphantly into town at the head of eighty horsemen.
James Logan realized that Keith would win the speakership unless the traditional
enemies, the Proprietary Party and the Quaker Party, joined in opposing him.
At Logan's instigation, both parties backed David Lloyd, the former Speaker,
who was reelected. Franklin saw Sir William Keith "walking the Streets as a
common Citizen. He seem'd a little asham'd at seeing me, but pass'd without
saying any thing" (A 52). As Franklin wrote in *Poor Richard* for 1740, "Promises
may get thee Friends, but Nonperformance will turn them into Enemies." No
doubt Franklin did not rejoin Keith's supporters in the Tiff Club.

Denham and Franklin soon rented a house on Water (now Front) Street,
where they set up business. The second house south of the Crooked Billet Tavern (which was on the site of the present 35 South Front Street), Denham's shop
was at the present 39 South Front Street. Franklin worked for Denham as a
salesman and bookkeeper at £6 per ten weeks for approximately six months.[1]
The shop sold a variety of clothing, hardware, and some spices and drinks,
including garlic and coffee. Franklin and Denham "lodg'd and boarded together," probably sleeping over the shop and boarding with a nearby family. To

judge by Franklin's later *Gazette* pieces on lying wholesalers, shopkeepers, and customers (19 November and 3 December 1730) and by his later generalization on commerce ("which is generally *Cheating*" [4 April 1760]), he found the shopkeeper's role distasteful. The deliberately optimistic *Autobiography* concealed Franklin's dislike: "I attended the Business diligently, studied Accounts, and grew in a little Time expert at selling" (A 52).

During Franklin's absence from Philadelphia, his friend Joseph Watson (one of the four friends who "loved reading" along with Osborn, Ralph, and Franklin) had begun courting Frances Read, Deborah's sister. Deborah, of course, had married the potter John Rogers on 5 August 1725, but the marriage was not happy. In a cancelled passage, Franklin wrote that Rogers left her "the Year after my Return" (A 52). Rogers continued working in Philadelphia until December 1727, when he absconded with a young slave who belonged to someone else. Franklin made his renewed acquaintance with the Reads consistent with his supposed errata in not writing Deborah more than one letter. Franklin said he was uncertain how the Reads would accept him, but he added that as Watson's good friend, Mrs. Read welcomed him (A 70–71). (She probably regretted that she had broken off Deborah's engagement to Franklin.) Two months after Franklin's return (11 December 1726) Andrew Hamilton, Pennsylvania's former attorney general, arrived in Philadelphia. Since Franklin had called on him in London, they were friendly, and Franklin probably waited upon him and congratulated the attorney upon his return.

A LETTER TO JANE FRANKLIN

On his twenty-first birthday, 6 January 1726/7, Franklin, perhaps thinking of the celebration that he would have had at home in Boston, wrote to his younger sister Jane. Captain Nathaniel Freeman, on the sloop *Pellican*, had entered Philadelphia on 13 December 1726, bringing Franklin news of his family in Boston, including the information that Jane had become a beautiful young woman. Shortly before Freeman returned to Boston (he cleared out on 10 January 1726/7), Franklin wrote to Jane, evidently by Freeman, that she had always been "my peculiar favourite." He had recently (Christmas Eve) been paid £6 by Denham. Franklin said that he deliberated about what present to give her: "I had almost determined on a tea table, but when I considered that the character of a good housewife was far preferable to that of being only a pretty gentlewoman, I concluded to send you a *spinning wheel*, which I hope you will accept as a small token of my sincere love and affection." Tea was new and expensive in colonial America; a tea table was specialized furniture for the display of a tea service. Since both the table and the tea service were expensive, Franklin joked in saying that he had almost determined to give her a tea table; in 1727, only wealthy colonials owned tea tables. Besides, Denham may have stocked spinning wheels and perhaps Franklin could buy one wholesale.

Franklin ended with some superior-sounding advice: "Sister, farewell, and remember that modesty, as it makes the most homely virgin amiable and charming, so the want of it infallibly renders the most perfect beauty disagreeable and odious. But when that brightest of female virtues shines among other perfections of body and mind in the same person, it makes the woman more lovely than an angel." Happily, he apologized for the high moral tone: "Excuse this freedom, and use the same with me. I am, dear Jenny, your loving brother." Since she saved the letter all her life, Jane must have treasured it. Just over six months later, on 27 July, the Reverend William Cooper married her and Edward Mecom in Boston's Brattle Street Church.

Pleurisy

In the late winter or early spring of 1727, Franklin fell ill. He recalled in the *Autobiography* that his pleurisy began around the beginning of February. Since Denham hired a temporary clerk, Edward West, about 27 March and employed him until at least 1 May, the Franklinist Hannah Benner Roach hypothesized that Franklin's illness occurred in March and April.[2] She thought that Franklin simply misremembered when writing the *Autobiography* some forty-five years later. Perhaps, however, Denham managed to get along without a clerk while he expected Franklin to return to work for him. If we accept Franklin's testimony, then Denham hired West after Franklin recovered and went to work for Keimer. There is another bit of evidence: Franklin wrote that his good friend Joseph "Watson died in my Arms . . . much lamented, being the best of our Set." Watson died on 20 April. If Franklin was caring for him when he died, then Franklin was well by mid-April.

Franklin's remarks on his sickness contain one of the few pessimistic expressions that escaped him in writing his *Autobiography*: "I suffered a good deal, gave up the Point in my own mind, and was rather disappointed when I found myself recovering; regretting in some degree that I must now sometime or other have all that disagreeable Work to do over again" (A 52). (Did the punster joke with "the Point" and "disappoint"?) Life equaled "all that disagreeable Work."[3] As Emily Dickinson wrote: "Which Anguish was the utterest—then—/ To perish, or to live?" (poem #414); Franklin thought living worse. At about the time that Franklin recovered, the Boston newspapers reported on 17 March the death of his uncle Benjamin Franklin. Another early Philadelphia friend left Franklin's life at this time. The critic of James Ralph's poetry, Charles Osborne, sailed for the West Indies where he became an eminent attorney. Years later, when Franklin recalled Osborne, he thought of their agreement: whoever "happen'd first to die, should if possible make a friendly Visit to the other, and acquaint him how he found things in that separate State. But," Franklin noted, "he never fulfill'd his Promise" (A 31).

Franklin's Epitaph

Though Franklin's epitaph is dated from 1728 (based on a Franklin notation of ca. 1784), he may have written it during his 1727 sickness. Widely reprinted during the latter part of his life, the epitaph was praised by Jean François Marmontel in the article on allegory in the second edition of Diderot's *Encyclopédie* (1777). Marmontel called it remarkable for fittingness and distinctiveness.[4] The analogy between a person's life and a worn-out book was not new; few good analogies are. Franklin certainly knew epitaphs that used the comparison, including one Cotton Mather quoted in the *Magnalia Christi Americana*.[5] But Franklin's version is original and effective; and, as we might expect, it exhibits a partially mocking and humorous tone.

> The Body of
> B. Franklin
> Printer;
> Like the Cover of an old Book,
> Its Contents torn out,
> And stript of its Lettering and Gilding,
> Lies here, Food for Worms.
> But the Work shall not be wholly lost:
> For it will, as he believ'd, appear once more,
> In a new & more perfect Edition,
> Corrected and amended
> By the Author.
> He was born Jan. 6. 1706
> Died   17   (1:111)

The epitaph circulated widely in manuscript before its first publication late in 1770.[6] Writing to Franklin on 17 January 1755, the Reverend George Whitefield referred to it, took it entirely seriously, and advised Franklin to believe in Jesus, "and you cannot possibly be disappointed of your expected second edition, finely corrected, and infinitely amended."

Carl Van Doren called it "the most famous of American epitaphs," and Nathaniel Ames, who first published the epitaph in his almanac for 1771, said it was "curious for conveying such solemn Ideas in the Stile of his Occupation." Lewis P. Simpson found Franklin's symbolism significant. God was an author and a printer who, when a person wears out, will bring the individual out in a new and more beautiful edition. "He will both correct the errata of the first edition and make the new edition typographically elegant. In Franklin's epitaph salvation by faith in the regenerating grace of God becomes faith in the grammatical and verbal skills and in the printing shop know-how of a Deity who is both Man of Letters and Master Printer." God as a printer and author was an "appropriate" representative of the Age of Enlightenment.[7]

KEIMER'S MANAGER

Like Franklin, Thomas Denham became gravely ill in 1727. The merchant lingered for over a year, made out his will on 15 March 1727/8, and finally died on

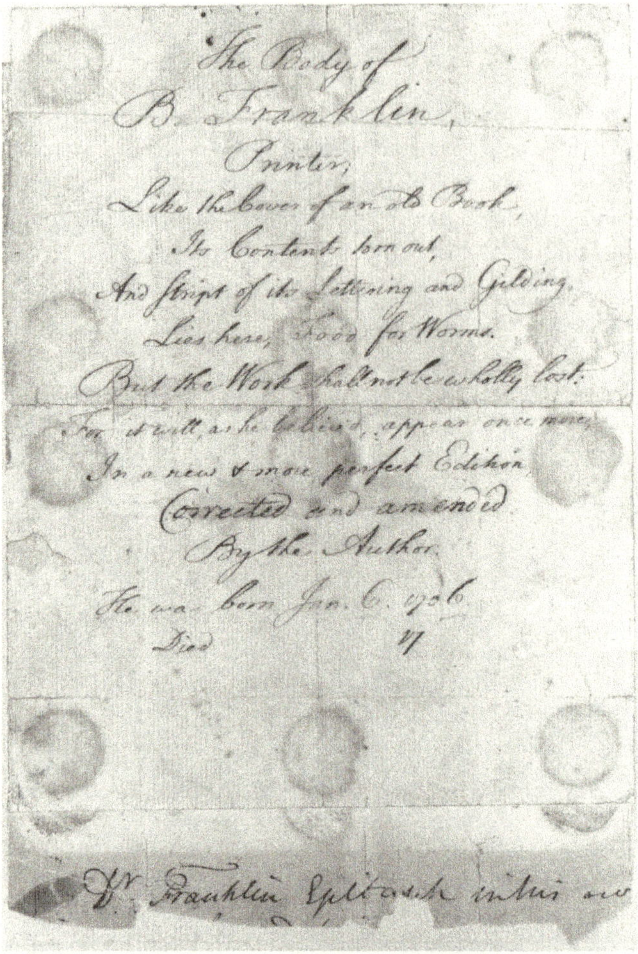

Figure 22. Franklin's epitaph. It was written early in Franklin's life, with one copy (which was probably written in the 1770s or later) dating the original time of composition as 1728. All extant copies, however, are from the middle or latter part of Franklin's life. The epitaph circulated widely in manuscript. The first reference to it is in a letter by the Reverend George Whitefield, who evidently was shown a manuscript copy in Virginia. Whitefield then wrote Franklin on the latter's forty-ninth birthday, 17 January 1755, and assured him that if he believed in Christ, "you cannot possibly be disappointed of your expected second edition, finely corrected, and infinitely amended." The epitaph was first printed in late 1770, when Nathaniel Ames included it among the prefatory matter in his Astronomical Almanac for 1771. Ames captioned it: "Mr. Franklin's Epitaph on himself curious for conveying such solemn Ideas in the Stile of his Occupation." The copies (even the three in Franklin's hand) all have minor differences. This one, in Franklin's holograph, contrasts markedly with the penmanship in the letter to Sir Hans Sloane (frontispiece) and especially with the promissory note of 1724 (Figure 20). Though the paper has imperfections and has been folded across the center, each letter in each word of the epitaph is perfectly clear and is in a rounded graceful hand. Courtesy, Franklin Collection, Yale University Library, New Haven, Connecticut.

4 July 1728. His executors noted on 1 September 1729 that in an oral addition to his will, Denham forgave Franklin the passage money for the trip back to America. Franklin's account in the *Autobiography* makes it seem as if he worked for Denham until the merchant's death, but the young man evidently returned to work for Keimer in the spring of 1727. Perhaps Denham was already ill and his creditors had taken over. Franklin recorded that he was uncertain what to do, but his brother-in-law Robert Homes, chancing to be in Philadelphia, advised him to return to work for Samuel Keimer. Franklin was reluctant to do so, for he "had heard a bad Character of him in London, from his Wife and her Friends, and was not fond of having any more to do with him." As we have seen, Franklin knew the type founder James and his daughter Mrs. Ilive in London, and Keimer also knew them, so Franklin may have heard stories of Keimer from them as well as others. But Franklin failed to find work as a clerk or salesman, and Keimer tempted him with an offer "of large Wages by the Year to come and take" charge of his Printing-House so that Keimer could attend the stationer's shop (he knew Franklin was a good pressman and better compositor than he). Finally Franklin agreed (A 53). If there is any truth to the rumor that Franklin once lodged in Elfrith's Alley, it must have been while he worked for Keimer in 1727 and 1728.[8]

Keimer had engaged five workmen: two independent adults, two indentured servants, and an apprentice. He had promised to teach the independent adults different aspects of printing, though he only knew typesetting. For Keimer, Franklin provided a solution, for he could manage the printing shop and teach and supervise the employees while Keimer dealt with the public in the stationer's shop. Keimer's two workmen were thirty-year-old Hugh Meredith, who was "honest, sensible, had a great deal of solid Observation, was something of a Reader, but given to drink," and Stephen Potts, about twenty-two, "of uncommon natural Parts, and great Wit and Humour, but a little idle" (A 53). Keimer had employed them at extremely low wages, to be raised a shilling every three months, as they learned the business, and the expectation of future high wages had drawn them in. Meredith was to work at press and Potts at bookbinding, which Keimer was to teach them, though he knew neither.

The two indentured servants were "John ——— a wild Irishman," who soon ran away, and George Webb (1708–36?), who had attended Oxford. Webb, said Franklin, was "lively, witty, good-natur'd and a pleasant Companion, but idle, thoughtless and imprudent to the last Degree." Lastly, the apprentice was David Harry (1708–60). Franklin "soon perceiv'd that the Intention of engaging me at Wages so much higher than he had been us'd to give, was to have these raw cheap Hands form'd thro' me, and as soon as I had instructed them, then, they being all articled to him, he should be able to do without me. I went on however, very chearfully; put his Printing House in Order, which had been in great Confusion, and brought his Hands by degrees to mind their Business and to do it better" (A 53–54).

Soon after Franklin began working for Keimer, King George I died (17 June 1727), and George II was proclaimed king. Andrew Bradford published the news in the 24 August *American Weekly Mercury*. At noon on Thursday, 31 August, "the Honourable Colonel Gordon our Governour, attended by his Council, the Mayor, Recorder, and Commonalty of this City, and divers other Gentlemen, Proclaimed here His Majesty *King GEORGE* the *Second*, with the usual Ceremony of Firing of Guns and other Demonstrations of Loyalty and Affection."

Franklin found that managing the press was challenging and agreeable, for all the workmen "respected me, the more as they found Keimer incapable of instructing them, and that from me they learnt something daily." Franklin also progressed in his private course of study, having two days a week for it, since Keimer kept the Sabbath on Saturday. "My Acquaintance with ingenious People in the Town increased. Keimer himself treated me with great Civility and apparent Regard; and nothing now made me uneasy but my Debt to Vernon, which I was yet unable to pay, being hitherto but a poor Oeconomist.—He however kindly made no Demand of it." Responsibility entailed challenges. When the shop ran short of type, Franklin "contriv'd a Mould, made use of the Letters we had, as Puncheons, struck the Matrices in Lead, and thus supply'd in a pretty tolerable way all Deficiencies. I also engrav'd several Things on occasion. I made the Ink, I was Warehouse-man and every thing, in short quite a Factotum" (A 55). Franklin was not only a master journeyman printer but also an ingenious and inventive artisan. The ability to make mechanisms to answer his purposes, which he had demonstrated as a youth by devising swim flippers for his hands and feet, would serve him well when he later conducted electrical experiments. Young Franklin enjoyed the challenges of running a shop with five employees.

As Keimer's other employees improved as printers, pressmen, and bookbinders, Franklin's services became less important. "When Keimer paid my second Quarter's Wages, he let me know that he felt them too heavy, and thought I should make an Abatement. He grew by degrees less civil, put on more of the Master, frequently found Fault, was captious and seem'd ready for an Outbreaking." Then on Election Day, Monday, 2 October 1727, when Sir William Keith and his supporters again swept the Philadelphia elections and when Franklin's friend Andrew Hamilton was elected a representative from Bucks County, "a Trifle snapt our Connection." Hearing a loud noise, Franklin looked out of the window to see what had happened. "Keimer being in the Street look'd up and saw me, call'd out to me in a loud Voice and angry Tone to mind my Business, adding some reproachful Words, that nettled me the more for their Publicity, all the Neighbours who were looking out on the same Occasion being Witnesses how I was treated. He came up immediately into the Printing-House, continu'd the Quarrel, high Words pass'd on both Sides, he gave me the Quarter's Warning we had stipulated, expressing a Wish that he had not been oblig'd to so long a Warning: I told him his Wish was unnecessary for I would leave him that Instant; and so taking my Hat walk'd out of Doors; desiring Meredith whom I saw below to take care of some Things I left, and bring them to my Lodging" (A 55–56).

Furious Franklin! The image is unlike our usual image of the self-contained and restrained statesman. But he was still a youth, only twenty-one, and he had not yet gained the self-control that so many scholars have noted. Further, Franklin no doubt remembered James Franklin's abuse, which may have redoubled his anger. The following year the twenty-two-year-old Franklin defined *anger* as "that momentary Madness" (1:108). But now what would he do? He had saved some money from Keimer's relatively high pay but not nearly enough to start his own business—and not even enough to repay Samuel Vernon. He thought of returning to Boston, where he could probably find work as a journeyman printer, but he would be regarded there as a failure—and would, no doubt, regard himself as having failed. He did not particularly want to return to clerking for a merchant. And since he no longer had Denham to invest in him as a factor, it would take years to set himself up as a merchant. Perhaps he could find work with Bradford, but that was dubious. The prospects were depressing.

PARTNERS

According to his promise, Meredith brought Franklin his belongings that evening, "when we talk'd my Affair over. He had conceiv'd a great Regard for me, and was very unwilling that I should leave the House while he remain'd in it. He dissuaded me from returning to my native Country which I began to think of. He reminded me that Keimer was in debt for all he possess'd, that his Creditors began to be uneasy, that he kept his Shop miserably, sold often without Profit for ready Money, and often trusted without keeping Account. That he must therefore fail; which would make a Vacancy I might profit of." But Franklin knew that he did not have enough money to purchase the press and types. Meredith replied that "his Father had a high Opinion of me, and from some Discourse that had pass'd between them, he was sure would advance Money to set us up, if I would enter into Partnership with him" (A 56).

His own printing shop! This was Franklin's private dream. He knew that he was a better craftsman than either Bradford or Keimer, the two Philadelphia printers. And perhaps—who knows?—he even thought that he might in the future be able to obtain the government printing if he set up his own shop. The major possible problem, he knew, was Meredith himself. Franklin's former friends Collins and Ralph had turned into burdens, and they had both been—at least at first—without Meredith's occasional drinking problem. Meredith frequently spent his evenings in taverns. Under Franklin's influence, Meredith had shown some improvement; perhaps he would change.

Meredith reminded Franklin that his time with Keimer would be up within six months. "By that time we may have our Press and Types in from London:—I am sensible I am no Workman. If you like it, Your Skill in the Business shall be set against the Stock I furnish; and we will share the Profits equally." Whatever reservations Franklin had about the proposal, it was a chance to start his own press, and he agreed. Meredith's father approved, "the more as he saw I had great Influence with his Son, had prevail'd on him to abstain long from Dram-drinking, and he hop'd might break him of that wretched Habit entirely, when we came to be so closely connected. I gave an Inventory to the Father, who carried it to a Merchant" (A 56). The order probably went by the annual packet, *The London Hope*, Captain Thomas Annis, which cleared Philadelphia on 19 October 1727 and arrived in London in December.[9]

Purchasing a Printing Press

Franklin's inventory must have been similar to the one he had suggested several years before to Governor Keith. That estimate amounted to about £100 sterling (A 27). The best recent authority gives the price as £200,[10] probably reflecting Franklin's account in the *Autobiography* that Simon Meredith was only able to advance £100 to the merchant and owed him £100 more (A 65). But Franklin was talking about Pennsylvania currency, not sterling. He almost always specified sterling when referring to it. (The printing house inventories for Governor Keith would have cost "about 100 Pounds Sterling" [A 34].) In 1727 £100 sterling was equivalent to approximately £150.62 Pennsylvania currency, so £200 Pennsylvania currency was equivalent to a little more than £120 sterling.[11] But according to Franklin and to other figures assembled by Lawrence C. Wroth, the materials for a complete working single press could be purchased for under £100 sterling.[12] How can one account for this discrepancy?

I suspect that Franklin misremembered and that £200 Pennsylvania currency was the amount he borrowed, not what the press cost. The loan paid back Simon Meredith the amount he had given (perhaps £75 Pennsylvania currency), paid the merchant the amount still owed (perhaps another £75 in Pennsylvania currency), paid Hugh Meredith £30 and a new saddle (perhaps £10), and paid off Hugh Meredith's few personal debts. To do so would have required nearly £200 Pennsylvania currency. The materials Simon Meredith ordered probably cost slightly less, for four years later Franklin debited Thomas Whitmarsh £80 sterling for "a printing house and materials" when he financed him in South Carolina (9 September 1731). Perhaps, however, Franklin did not include shipping in the Whitmarsh account. The major expense in setting up a printing house was not the press (which could be purchased for £15 to £20 sterling) but the types.[13] Even a small printing house required thousands of the more common letters, both roman and italic. We can approximate what Franklin ordered by comparing what the seventeenth-century printer Joseph Moxon recommended[14] with what Franklin actually ordered for a one-press shop in New Haven, Connecticut on 27 October 1753.

Type	Moxon's Recommendation (in lbs)	Franklin's 1753 Purchase (in lbs)
10 point (long primer)	500	300
12 point (pica)	800 to 1,000	300
14 point (English)	900 to 1,000	300
18 point (Great primer)	300 ro 400	100
22 point (double pica)	300 or 400	60
28 points (two-line English)	300 or 400	50
36 points (two-line Great primer)	300 or 400	50
48 points (two-line capitals)	300 or 400	50

In 1727, Franklin would have included dozens of type ornaments, hundreds of quotation marks, hundreds of apostrophes, a set or two of the signs and figures found in almanacs, and several alphabets of scriptoral English and Gothic for specialized uses. The type must have weighed more than a thousand pounds. (The types he ordered on 27 October 1753 weighed twelve hundred pounds.) Since Franklin had known Thomas James in London, he specified that the types be purchased from James's type foundry and probably wrote a personal letter to James.[15]

Besides the press and types, Franklin and Meredith needed the necessary components for working it. When ordering on 27 October 1753, he itemized:

> 2 pair Blankets [a folded woolen blanket was placed between the outer and inner tympan to ensure that the type would press into the damp paper, making a firm impression]; 2 pair Ballstocks [for inking the surface of the type: one pair would have been large, soft balls that would take weak ink for low-grade work; the other small, hard balls that would take strong ink for higher quality printing]; Some Riglets, Gutter Sticks, Side Sticks, Quoins, &c. [spacers and rules used to fill up the chases for printing before locking them]; 3 pair Chases [rectangular metal frames into which pages of type are locked before printing] of different Sizes, the biggest Demi; 2 folio Galleys [long trays to hold composed type], each with 4 Slices; 4 Quarto Galleys; A few Facs [factotems, i.e., decorative borders into which any capital letter could be inserted], Head and Tail pieces, 3 or 4 of each; 2 Doz brass Rule; 2 good Composing Sticks [a wooden or metal tray, holding at least one line of type, that the compositor can hold in one hand, into which he sets the type]; 2 Cags of Ink, one weak the other strong.

Paper could be purchased from local merchants, but it was cheaper abroad, and since Franklin mentioned paper in the inventory for Keith, he no doubt ordered some. (In 1753, when he ordered a press for his nephew, paper was more commonly being made in the colonies, and Franklin himself had become the major colonial wholesale dealer in paper.) Ink could be made locally but was usually inferior to that purchased abroad. One indication that Franklin and Meredith economized as much as possible in 1728 was that they did not purchase facto-tems. Franklin did not use them until 11 March 1731.[16]

New Jersey Paper Money

"The Things were sent for; the Secret was to be kept till they should arrive, and in the mean time I was to get Work if I could at the other Printing House." Bradford, however, had no vacancy, so Franklin remained idle for a few days. He probably also tried to find a job as a shopkeeper or clerk but must have been reluctant to take on a permanent position. Within a week, however, Keimer sent him "a very civil Message, that old Friends should not part for a few Words, the Effect of sudden Passion, and wishing me to return." At first, Franklin was surprised and wondered what could have caused Keimer's change. Meredith urged him to return, for he was learning nothing now that Franklin was gone. Franklin did so, "and we went on more smoothly than for some time before" (A 56–57). Franklin soon learned Keimer's reason for reconciling. Counterfeits of the New Jersey paper currency issue of 25 March 1724 were circulating. The New Jersey assembly had decided to issue a new paper currency and had approached Keimer about printing a currency difficult to counterfeit. Keimer had assured the legislature that he could do it. Actually, he could not, but he thought that the ingenious Franklin would be able to do so.[17] So he rehired Franklin. On 10 February 1727/8, the New Jersey assembly authorized the new issue. In mid-February Franklin and Keimer went to Burlington, New Jersey, where Franklin "contriv'd a Copper-Plate Press" to print the bills. Such a press was "the first that had been seen in the Country.—I cut several Ornaments and Checks for the Bills" (A 57). Alas, no examples of the 1728 New Jersey bills are extant.

Though the printers worked under the supervision of assembly members,[18] they were nevertheless required to take the following oath when they delivered up the bills to the signers John Stevens and Isaac Decow:

> I Benjamin Franklin do declare that from the Time the Letters were set and fit to be put in the Press for the Printing of the Bills of Credit now by me delivered to you, until the Bills were printed, and the Letters unset, and put in the Boxes again, I set at no Time out of the Room, in which the said Letters were, without locking them up, so as they could not be come at without Violence, a false Key, or other Art then unknown to me, and therefore to the best of my Knowledge no Copies were printed off, but in my Presence, and that all the Blotters and other Papers whatsoever printed by the said Letters, whilst set for printing the said Bills, to be best of my Knowledge, are here delivered to you, together with the Stamps for the Indents and Arms. And that I have not at any Time been privy or consenting to any other or more Bills being struck, than I now deliver to you, and that in all Things relating to this Affair, I have and shall demean my self according to the true Intent and Meaning of the said Act, to the best of my Knowledge and Understanding.[19]

At Burlington Franklin made friends with many leaders of the province. As usual, several of them had been appointed by the New Jersey Assembly to attend the press to see that no more bills were printed than the law directed. Franklin's ornaments and checks for the bills would have been guarded throughout the printing process. As the sheets of bills came from the press, they would be carefully counted. All materials involved in the printing would have been, together with the sheets, kept in the building under lock and probably under guard. Once the printing was completed, Franklin and Keimer would turn the sheets over to the persons appointed who would then number and sign each bill. Then the ornaments and checks that Franklin designed would be destroyed. The New Jersey authorities were by turns constantly with the printers, and generally whoever attended brought with him a friend or two for company. Franklin recorded: "My Mind having been much more improv'd by Reading than Keimer's, I suppose it was for that Reason my Conversation seem'd to be more valu'd. They had me to their Houses, introduc'd me to their Friends and show'd me much Civility, while he, tho' the Master, was a little neglected." Then Franklin appraised Keimer: "In truth he was an odd Fish, ignorant of common Life, fond of rudely opposing receiv'd Opinions, slovenly to extream dirtiness, enthusiastic in some Points of Religion, and a little Knavish withal." Franklin and Keimer remained in Burlington from mid-February to 12 or 13 May, "and by that time I could reckon among my acquired Friends, Judge Allen, Samuel Bustill, the Secretary of the Province, Isaac Pearson, Joseph Cooper, and several of the Smiths, Members of Assembly, and Isaac Decow the Surveyor General" (A 57). Of this group, Isaac Pearson and Joseph Cooper were Proprietary representatives on the committee overseeing the new money, and Isaac Decow was a signer of the money. John Stevens, whom Franklin did not name, was the other signer. Franklin's memory played him false regarding the Smiths, for none was an assembly member in 1727, though Franklin probably met Richard Smith of Burlington at this time, who became an assemblyman in 1730. John Allen, who became a superior court judge in 1736, was then an assemblyman from Burlington. The Quaker Samuel Bustil of Burlington was, as Franklin noted, the secretary of the province.[20]

Franklin's new friends realized the young man's potential. Isaac Decow "was a shrewd sagacious old Man, who told me that he began for himself when young by wheeling Clay for the Brickmakers, learnt to write after he was of Age, carry'd the Chain for Surveyors, who taught him Surveying, and he had now by his Industry acquir'd a good Estate; and says he, I foresee, that you will soon work this Man out of his Business and make a Fortune in it at Philadelphia. He had not then the least Intimation of my Intention to set up there or any where" (A 57).

While in New Jersey, Keimer and Franklin also printed the *Acts and Laws of . . . New Jersey as They Were Enacted . . . at a Session Held at Perth-Amboy, Beginning the 9th of Dec. 1727* and a broadside advertising medicines sold by

Robert Talbot of Burlington. During the period that Franklin remained in Burlington, Sir William Keith left New Castle (22 March), sailing from America and out of Franklin's life. Franklin must have heard about Keith's semi-secret departure (his creditors were hounding him) within a few days. Franklin never saw him again. Keith disappeared into debtor's prison and died in London's Old Bailey on 18 November 1749. Franklin would have read of his death in the *Gentleman's Magazine.* No doubt Franklin sometimes thought of him with pity. The talented Sir William Keith, former governor of Pennsylvania, was a cautionary example of the harsh consequence of debt in the eighteenth century. Meredith was probably with Franklin and Keimer in Burlington, and the two friends and future partners must have celebrated when Meredith's time with Keimer was up in April, though Meredith continued working for Keimer in New Jersey for another month.

PHILADELPHIA

Keimer returned with his press and employees to Philadelphia on 12 or 13 May and immediately got into trouble. He printed up handbills for a lottery to be held at a forthcoming fair, but on 16 May the Philadelphia Common Council summoned him, inquired into the lottery, found that its purpose was simply to benefit Keimer, and ordered that it not be held. That same day the *American Weekly Mercury* reported that the pink (a medium-size, ocean-going vessel) *Society*, Captain William Simpson, had entered Philadelphia from London. Simpson, captain of the only ship to enter Philadelphia from London from March through June, evidently brought the printing press, types, etc., that Simon Meredith had ordered. By then Franklin had printed one last tract for Keimer, *The Proceedings of Some Members of Assembly at Philadelphia, April, 1728, Vindicated.* The publication by Keith's followers in the legislature irritated the majority. They summoned Keimer, who admitted on 19 May to publishing the tract, testified that he received the copy from Edward Horne, representative from Philadelphia County, and said that Dr. John Kearsley, representative from Philadelphia City, revised it in press. Then the assembly dismissed Keimer. About a week later, Franklin and Hugh Meredith "settled with Keimer, and left him by his Consent" (A 59) before he learned they intended to open a rival printing shop.

FACTOTUM

A *factotum* is generally understood to mean a servant who has the management of all his master's affairs, and Franklin had that meaning primarily in mind when he called himself "quite a Factotum." In printing, a factotum is an ornamental block with a space in the center for the insertion of a letter, usually a capital letter. A printing term seemed appropriate because of the business he was doing. Further, the specialized meaning was especially appropriate, for the factotum is used to contain any of the letters of the alphabet—or any other smaller devices that fit into it. It was perhaps the most adaptable bit of type that printers used, just as Franklin, as the general manager of the printing house, as the teacher of all the employees, as the best compositor and pressman, and as the designer of new technical apparatus such as a copper-plate press, was seemingly endlessly adaptable. The phrase *Johannes factotum*, or jack of all trades, would also have occurred to Franklin when he proclaimed he was quite a factotum. His adaptability extended beyond the printing shop to social and political dexterity, to making conversation, and, subsequently, to making friends among the New Jersey officials. He was becoming, indeed, quite a factotum.

FOURTEEN

The Junto

Do you love truth for truth's sake, and will you endeavour impartially to find and receive it yourself and communicate it to others? Ans. Yes.—Qualifying question for admission to the Junto (1:259)

FRANKLIN FORMED THE JUNTO IN THE FALL OF 1727. Perhaps he drew up the scheme and the rules for a club for mutual improvement in early October after he quarreled with Samuel Keimer and quit his job. He then had a little unexpected leisure. Clubs characterized the eighteenth century. Every town—indeed, almost every tavern and inn—was the meeting place of a club. Dr. Alexander Hamilton's *Itinerarium* affords the best panorama of colonial American clubs. During the summer of 1744, he traveled from Annapolis, Maryland, to Maine and back, encountering clubs in every colonial town—and some at taverns in the comparative wilderness. Hamilton also provided the most detailed source of information about any single colonial club in his *Records of the Tuesday Club* and in the mock history of the Annapolis club he founded in 1745, *The History of the Tuesday Club*.[1]

Most clubs featured eating, drinking, and good fellowship.[2] A few focused on a special interest, like Dr. William Douglass's club of physicians in Boston, the Philosophical Club in Newport, the Musical Club in Philadelphia,[3] and Sir William Keith's political clubs in Philadelphia. Franklin's Junto was committed to philosophical investigation, self-improvement, improving society, helping each other, companionship, and even, at first, physical exercise. The name itself, the *Junto*, was in common usage for a small secret group or a club. Franklin knew the usage from many sources, including Butler's *Hudibras* where the Puritans were condemned for *"their Plots, Their Midnight Juntos, and seal'd knots."* It was often used for a political group. Under William and Mary, the word became especially associated with Whigs.[4] Franklin's Junto was semi-secret, but some members were (or became) identified with the Proprietary Party and others with the Quaker Party. At first the Junto met at the Indian Head Tavern, where they must have had drinks and food during the meeting, but they soon changed to a room in Robert Grace's small house in Jones or Pewter Platter Alley (now Church Alley—and, after 1737, the site of Franklin's printing house),[5] no doubt partly to avoid the expense of either renting a room or eating and drinking at a tavern, and partly to have more privacy for their meetings.

ORIGINS OF THE JUNTO

James Parton (1:158), Carl Van Doren (78), and the editors of the *Papers* (1:255–56) are among those who have argued that the Junto was probably influenced by Cotton Mather's "Neighborhood Benefit Societies" and by his discussion in *Bonifacius, or Essays to Do Good*. Mather's asking ten "Points of Consideration" at the beginning of every meeting evidently influenced Franklin's similar procedure for the Junto. Daniel Defoe's *Essay upon Projects*, which Franklin cited in the Silence Dogood essay series, also influenced the Junto. Defoe's "Friendly Societies" for seamen, widows, and others amounted to insurance societies, but they were also organizations whose members helped one another. The Couranteers, who met at the printing shop to discuss the newspaper's contents, may also have been a model for the Junto. Nathaniel Gardner's *New-England Courant* essay of 23 April 1722, recommending a formal mode of conversation, may also have influenced the plan.

I. Bernard Cohen thought that William Penn's call for "a small junto . . . for publick ends" may have inspired Franklin. Penn, however, made his suggestion in a private letter to James Logan in 1708, and I doubt that Franklin knew it.[6] The Junto's fellowship and entertaining purposes probably owed something to his experience with Dr. William Lyons, Bernard Mandeville, and the London clubs and coffeehouses he visited in 1725 and 1726. The Junto may also owe something to Sir William Keith's Tiff Club, while its secrecy and selectivity may reflect Freemasonry (though Franklin's contacts with Masonry before 1731 were limited).[7]

The historian Dorothy Grimm believed that the Junto's inspiration owed most to John Locke's "Society which met once a week, for their improvement in useful knowledge and for the promotion of truth and Christian charity." She found that the four questions every member had to answer before being admitted to the Junto echoed, word for word, Locke's questions for his society.[8] Franklin obviously had by him a copy of Locke's *Collection of Several Pieces* (1720), containing a description of his "Society" when he created the questions for the Junto, and it may well have been the copy he donated to the Library Company in 1732. The four qualifications, however, were added several years after the Junto was begun, at the time that Philip Syng and Anthony Nicholas were invited to be members (1:259). Locke was a major influence on the continuing Junto but perhaps only a minor influence on its founding.

The Junto combined science, civic-mindedness, self-help, self-discipline, politics, philosophy, philanthropy, punning, entertainment, exercise, and pleasure. For the primary origin of the Junto, I believe that we need look no further than Franklin's own personal interests, desires, and values, manifested in a traditional manner in an age of clubs.

JUNTO MEMBERS

Not including himself, Franklin named ten original members of the Junto in his *Autobiography*. Since the membership was limited to twelve, one wonders who the unmentioned member could have been. First came Joseph Breintnall (d. 1746), "a Copyer of Deeds for the Scriveners; a good-natur'd friendly middle-ag'd Man, a great Lover of Poetry, reading all he could meet with, and writing some that was tolerable;[9] very ingenious in many little Nicknackeries, and of sensible Conversation." Franklin wrote and then cancelled, "He was much my Fa[vorite?]" (A 61). The Quaker Breintnall secured for Franklin and Meredith their first major printing job, William Sewel's *History of the ... Quakers*. Breintnall shared Franklin's love for literature and science. He coauthored the Busy-Body essay series with Franklin and, at Franklin's suggestion, experimented with the effects of the sun's rays on color.[10] He collected impressions of different leaves from trees and plants, inspiring Franklin to devise a technique for printing the impressions. When Franklin drew up the articles of association for the Library Company (1 July 1731), he named Breintnall as its secretary, a post Breintnall faithfully fulfilled to his death. With Franklin's backing, Breintnall became a Freemason on 5 August 1734, and he served as sheriff of Philadelphia (1735–38). Alas, "distrest by his Circumstances," Breintnall drowned himself in 1746—a fact not mentioned in the deliberately optimistic *Autobiography*.[11]

Thomas Godfrey (1704–49) was "a self-taught Mathematician, great in his Way, and afterwards Inventor of what is now call'd Hadley's Quadrant. But he knew little out of his way, and was not a pleasing Companion, as like most Great Mathematicians I have met with, he expected unusual Precision in every thing said, or was forever denying or distinguishing upon Trifles, to the Disturbance of all Conversation.—He soon left us" (A 61). When Franklin and Meredith opened their printing shop, they took in Godfrey and his wife and boarded with them for two and a half years, from July 1728 to mid-April 1730. Franklin probably proposed that Thomas Godfrey compile an almanac, and Franklin printed it for three years (1730–32). Then, as I shall show below, Franklin's "Anthony Afterwit" satire (10 July 1732) on Godfrey's in-laws ruptured the relationship. If Godfrey had not already dropped out of the Junto, he would have done so then. Franklin named him as the fifth of ten members of the first board of Library Company directors (1 July 1731). Despite their personal disagreement, Franklin recognized Godfrey's genius and appointed him mathematician in the 1743 American Philosophical Society (2:380–83, 406–7).

Nicholas Scull (1687–1761), "a Surveyor, afterwards Surveyor-General," was the third Junto member. He "lov'd Books, and sometimes made a few Verses" (A 61). The only contemporary description of a Junto meeting is a poem by Scull, quoted below. The Junto at first met at Scull's Indian Head Tavern, and the first meetings of the Library Company directors were held at his new tavern, the Bear (1:229, 271). He supervised the infamous 1737 "Walking Purchase."[12] Like many Junto members, Scull became a Proprietary Party placeman and owed to the Penns his position as surveyor general.

William Parsons (1701–57), "bred a Shoemaker, but loving Reading, had acquir'd a considerable Share of Mathematics, which he first studied with a View to Astrology that he afterwards laught at. He also became Surveyor General" (A 61). Franklin appointed him a director of the Library Company (1 July 1731). He became librarian on 14 March 1734. Franklin enlisted him as a member of the Union Fire Company (2:153) and of the 1743 American Philosophical Society (2:406–7). Though he sided with the Proprietors against the Popular Party, he and Franklin remained close friends. He was surveyor general (1741–48) before his friend Nicholas Scull.

Parsons moved out of Philadelphia in 1748 and in 1753 was elected a representative to the Pennsylvania Assembly from Northampton County. He served as a major of the provincial forces under Franklin in 1756–57. When fellow Junto member Hugh Roberts wrote Franklin on 16 September 1758 of the deaths of Parsons and Stephen Potts (a Keimer employee and fellow Junto club member), Franklin replied:

> Odd Characters, both of them. Parsons, a wise Man, that often acted foolishly. Potts, a Wit, that seldom acted wisely. If *Enough* were the Means to make a Man happy, One had always the *Means* of Happiness without ever enjoying the *Thing*; the other had always the *Thing* without ever possessing the Means. Parsons, even in his Prosperity, always fretting! Potts, in the midst of his Poverty, ever laughing! It seems, then, that Happiness in this Life rather depends on Internals than Externals; and that, besides the natural Effects of Wisdom and Virtue, Vice and Folly, there is such a Thing as being of a happy or an unhappy Constitution. They were both our Friends, and lov'd us. So, Peace to their Shades. They had their Virtues as well as their Foibles; they were both honest Men, and that alone, as the World goes, is one of the greatest of Characters. They were old Acquaintance, in whose Company I formerly enjoy'd a great deal of Pleasure, and I cannot think of losing them, without Concern and Regret. (8:159–60)

William Maugridge (d. 1766), the fifth Junto member named, was "a Joyner, and a most exquisite Mechanic, and a solid sensible Man" (A 61–62). A ship carpenter and relative of Daniel Boone, he twice mortgaged Boone's father's farm through Franklin. A founding member of the Library Company, Maugridge was elected a director on 1 May 1732. An Anglican, he served as vestryman of Christ Church in 1742 and 1744. He moved out of town to a Bucks County farm in 1750 and later sent flour to Deborah Franklin, which she used in "the best Buckwheat Kakes" that she ever made (3 November 1765). After Maugridge, Franklin listed Hugh Meredith, Stephen Potts, and George Webb—all of whom were working for Keimer under Franklin's supervision when he founded the Junto. None was named a Library Company director in 1731 by Franklin.

Ninth came Robert Grace (1709–66), "a young Gentleman of some Fortune, generous, lively and witty, a Lover of Punning and of his Friends" (A 62). Grace was evidently the youngest member, with Franklin as the second youngest. He lived at the site of the present 131 Market Street. Within a year of its founding, the Junto began meeting "in a little Room of Mr. Grace's set apart." Franklin's first suggestion for clubbing books located Grace's room as the library (A 71). Franklin named Grace an original Library Company director on 1 July 1731. In 1739 he rented Grace's two buildings at 131 Market Street (the lot extended through to Pewter Platter Alley) for his combined home, post office, and printing office. The *Pennsylvania Gazette* of 29 May 1740 announced that Grace had married Rebecca Nutt, "an agreeable young Lady with a Fortune of Ten Thousand Pounds." In the early 1740s, he manufactured the Franklin stove at his Warwick Iron Works in Chester County, and Franklin helped him when creditors pressed in 1748 (3:329–30).

The tenth and last original Junto member Franklin named was William Coleman, Jr. (1704–69), "then a Merchant's Clerk, about my Age, who had the coolest clearest Head, the best Heart, and the exactest Morals, of almost any Man I ever met with. He became afterwards a Merchant of great Note, and one of our Provincial Judges: Our Friendship continued without Interruption to his Death, upwards of 40 Years" (A 62). Coleman, a Quaker, was the son of Councilor William Coleman. Franklin named Coleman the first treasurer of the Library Company (1 July 1731) and later as treasurer of the 1743 American Philosophical Society (2:406–7). He was among the Quakers who financed the privateer *Warren* in 1747 and so was disowned by the Friends. He became a trustee of the Academy of Philadelphia (3:422) and served as one of the first directors of the insurance company Franklin founded, the Philadelphia Contributionship (4:290). Franklin named Coleman an advisor in his wills of 22 June 1750 and 28 April 1757. Franklin did not mention that their friendship persisted despite Coleman's siding with the Proprietors, to whom he owed his appointment as Supreme Court justice (1758–69).

As time passed, Junto members came and went. Meredith, Webb, and Godfrey were members for only a few years. Franklin's note of ca. 1731 that "PS and AN be immediately invited into the Junto" (1:259) demonstrates that there were then two vacancies—and that Philip Syng and Anthony Nicholas were presumably invited to join at that time. Franklin named both original directors of the Library Company on 1 July 1731. Years later Robert Vaux supplied a list of additional Junto members, based on the papers of his grandfather Hugh Roberts, who was an early, though not an original, Junto member. After Franklin sailed for England in 1757, Roberts wrote Franklin news about the Junto until the mid-1760s.[13] Of the persons in Vaux's list, four became especially important in Franklin's life.

Thomas Hopkinson (1709–51), lawyer and merchant, was an original Library Company director (1 July 1731). Admitted to St. John's Lodge in 1733, he later served as an original trustee of the Academy of Philadelphia (3:422), a member of the Union Fire Company, and the president of the first American Philosophical Society (2:406–7). He devised and performed electric experiments with Franklin. His son, Francis Hopkinson, became a good friend of Franklin in the 1760s.

Samuel Rhoads (1717–84), carpenter, contractor, and architect, joined the Library Company (2:205) and was an original petitioner for and designer of the Pennsylvania Hospital. He belonged to the 1743 American Philosophical Society (2:406–7). He became a common councilor, alderman, and, in 1774, mayor of Philadelphia. Franklin's political ally, he was a member of the Pennsylvania Assembly (1761–63), and lost his seat along with Franklin in the hotly contested 1764 election. He supervised the construction of Franklin's house in 1764–65. Reelected to the assembly (1770–74), he served as a delegate to the First Continental Congress and was president of the Carpenter's Company (1780–84).

Hugh Roberts (1706–86), a Quaker merchant and tobacconist, was elected a Library Company director at its first election (1 May 1732). An early member of the Union Fire Company (2:153), a supporter and director of the Pennsylvania Hospital, and one of the first twelve directors of the Philadelphia Contributionship (4:290), he corresponded with Franklin throughout Franklin's years abroad. Roberts served as an assemblyman in 1751 and 1752. Franklin named him an advisor in his will of 28 April 1757.

Philip Syng (1703–89), silversmith, became Franklin's intimate friend. Franklin named him the fourth of the original Library Company directors (1 July 1731). Syng joined St. John's Masonic Lodge in 1734 and served as its grandmaster in 1741–42. He was among the first twenty members of the Union Fire Company (2:153), an original supporter and trustee of the Philadelphia Academy (3:422), an original director of the Philadelphia Contributionship (4:290), a supporter of the militia Association, and a coexperimenter with Franklin in electricity. Franklin named him an advisor in his wills of 22 June 1750 and 28 April 1757. When Hugh Roberts wrote Franklin on 24 June 1785, he reported that Syng was the only other Junto member still alive.[14]

Though not named by Robert Vaux, Dr. John Bard (1716–99) was also probably a Junto member. Perhaps Bard was not in Hugh Roberts's papers because he moved to New York in 1746. Bard's grandson wrote in 1822 that while Bard lived in Philadelphia, he and Franklin "were both members of a select club, in which mirth and literature were not unhappily combined. . . . Some exception being jocularly taken at one of their suppers, that married men should sing the praises of poet's mistresses, Dr. Bard received" the following morning a song written by Franklin, "I Sing my Plain Country Joan" (2:352). Bard was probably Franklin's physician before he moved to New York in late 1745. There, in 1788, he became the first president of the Medical Society of the State of New York.

The Junto's Philosophy

The Junto was one expression of Franklin's philosophy that people who banded together for a common purpose could achieve greater goals than individuals could do separately. I. Bernard Cohen pointed out that the name *junto* suggests a common purpose, coming from the Latin *juncta* (joined together), and is well-known from the saying *juncta juvant*, "joined together, they assist."[15] The Junto members, like the Masons and numerous later fellowship societies, intended to help one another. The *Autobiography* testifies that it did help Franklin. Junto member Joseph Breintnall obtained for him and Meredith their first major printing job—thus assuring them of an income when they began. And the two well-off Junto members, William Coleman and Robert Grace, stood surety for Franklin for approximately £50 each when the Franklin-Meredith partnership dissolved.

The Junto served as the incubation chamber for several public projects. Franklin hatched an early version of a lending library in the Junto. After it failed, he enlisted the help of Junto members in creating the Library Company. He discussed paper money at club meetings before publishing on the subject. He projected a fire company, an insurance company, and a defense association first in the Junto. Only after discussing these proposals with the other Junto members did Franklin present them publicly. He suggested improving the city watch and proposed founding an academy at Junto meetings. He wrote essays for presentation in the Junto. One that he referred to as the "Junto Paper of Good and Evil" (20 November 1728) appeared several years later as his "Man of Sense" essay (2:15–19). "On the Providence of God in the Government of the World" (1:264–60), "On Literary Style" (1:328–31), "On Protection of Towns from Fire" (2:12–15), and "Self-Denial Not the Essence of Virtue" (2:19–21) are among the papers he originally wrote for and delivered in the Junto. It seems likely that Franklin's report (8 May 1749) of the number of houses in Philadelphia "from a Motive of Curiosity, by twelve careful persons" was a Junto project.

After the Junto had its full complement of twelve persons and members submitted additional names for consideration, Franklin suggested that "every Member separately should endeavour to form a subordinate Club, with the same Rules respecting Queries, etc. and without informing them of the Connexion with the Junto. The Advantages propos'd were the Improvement of so many more young Citizens by the Use of our Institutions; Our better Acquaintance with the general Sentiments of the Inhabitants on any Occasion, as the Junto-Member might propose what Queries we should desire, and was to report to Junto what pass'd in his separate Club; the Promotion of our particular Interests in Business by more extensive Recommendations; and the Increase of our Influence in public Affairs and our Power of doing Good by spreading thro' the several Clubs the Sentiments of the Junto" (A 99). The combination of self-improvement, better information on the general opinion, the advancement of each individual's business interests, the increase of influence in public affairs, and the increased power of doing good for the society—all these were Junto purposes. Franklin said that every member attempted to form a subordinate club but only five or six succeeded. He then made a comment that typified an aspect of his personality. He loved knowing a secret. One recalls how he enjoyed overhearing the Couranteers' opinion of the first (and, I suppose, the later)

Silence Dogood letter—when the Couranteers did not know Franklin was the author. On 22 September 1773, he listened to the reactions that the king of Prussia's "Edict" stirred among Lord Le Despencer's guests before they suspected that he had written the hoax. So, too, the activities and opinions of the fledgling clubs "afforded us a good deal of Amusement" (A 100).

MEETINGS

The Junto met every Friday evening. "The Rules I drew up, requir'd that every Member in his Turn should produce one or more Queries on any Point of Morals, Politics or Natural Philosophy, to be discuss'd by the Company, and once in three Months produce and read an Essay of his own Writing on any Subject he pleased." On the occasions that several Junto members were busy on a Friday night, the club probably did not meet. If the club only had one essay a night, the members would have had at least three months before another essay was due. "Our Debates were to be under the Direction of a President, and to be conducted in the sincere Spirit of Enquiry after Truth, without fondness for Dispute, or Desire of Victory; and to prevent Warmth, all expressions of Positiveness in Opinion, or of direct Contradiction, were after some time made contraband and prohibited under small pecuniary Penalties" (A 61). The founding members probably elected the organizer, Franklin, the first president. The primary purpose of the club ("Enquiry after Truth") suggests the Junto's Lockean heritage. The initiation (adopted about 1731) consisted of brief ceremonial replies to four questions. Standing, the candidate had to swear that he had no "particular disrespect to any present members"; second, that he "loved mankind in general; of what profession or religion soever." The question was practically identical to the first admission test for membership in the society John Locke described: "Whether he loves all men, of what profession or religion soever?"

The third question was, "Do you think any person ought to be harmed in his body, name or goods, for mere speculative opinions, or his external way of worship? *Ans.* No." Franklin borrowed this question, too, from the second admission test of Locke's society. And fourth, "Do you love truth for truth's sake, and will you endeavour impartially to find and receive it yourself and communicate it to others? *Answ.* Yes" (1:259). The final question was again nearly identical to Locke's third admission test: "Whether he loves and seeks truth for truth's sake; and will endeavour impartially to find and receive it himself, and to communicate it to others?"

To focus the meetings, Franklin drew up a list of questions that the members reviewed before every gathering. Evidently he had originally requested that each Junto member bring several queries to each meeting. Perhaps few members did so. After he drew up the list of twenty-four queries, he noted, "That it be not hereafter the Duty of any Member to bring Queries but left to his Discretion" (1:259). Cotton Mather's *Bonifacius* similarly proposed ten questions to be asked of his "Reforming Societies." Though Mather's queries mainly sought to censor moral offenders and to support religion and the authorities (questions 1–6), his last four questions probably resonated in Franklin's mind: "VII. Does there appear any instance of Oppression or Fradulence, in the *dealings* of any sort of people, that may call for our essays, to get it rectified? VIII. Is there any matter to be humbly moved unto the Legislative Power to be enacted into a Law for public benefit? IX. Do we know of any person languishing under sad and sore Affliction; and is there anything that we may do, for the succor of such an afflicted neighbor? X. Has any person any Proposal to make, for our own further advantage and assistance, that we ourselves may be in a probably and regular capacity, to pursue the Intentions before us?"[16]

None of Franklin's twenty-four questions was as similar to Mather's four as his initiatory declarations were to Locke's. A few of Franklin's questions had social, educational, or entertaining purposes, such as: "1. Have you met with any thing in the author you last read, remarkable, or suitable to be communicated to the Junto? particularly in history, morality, poetry, physic, travels, mechanic arts, or other parts of knowledge. . . . 9. Have you or any of your acquaintance been lately sick or wounded? If so, what remedies were used, and what were their effects? . . . 23. Is there any difficulty in matters of opinion, of justice, and injustice, which you would gladly have discussed at this time? 24. Do you see any thing amiss in the present customs or proceedings of the Junto, which might be amended?"

Many questions echoed the spirit of Defoe's "Friendly Societies." In his "Preface," Defoe suggested that if a hundred persons of different trades agreed to buy of one another, everyone would be certain to have ninety-nine customers.[17] Like Defoe, Franklin took up such topics as how to get ahead and how to help others succeed. "3. Hath any citizen in your knowledge failed in his business lately, and what have you heard of the cause? 4. Have you lately heard of any citizen's thriving well, and by what means? 5. Have you lately heard how any present rich man, here or elsewhere, got his estate? . . . 10. Who do you know that are shortly going voyages or journies, if one should have occasion to send by them?"

Questions 12 and 13 echo an essay from the 11 June 1722 *New-England Courant* on helping young men start in business. Franklin reprinted the *Courant* essay in his *Gazette* on 26 June 1732 and repeated the same thought in a codicil to his will (S 10:503–7). "12. Hath any deserving stranger arrived in town since last meeting, that you heard of? and what have you heard or observed of his character or merits? and whether think you, it lies in the power of the Junto to oblige him, or encourage him as he deserves? 13. Do you know of any deserving young beginner lately set up, whom it lies in the power of the Junto any way to encourage?" At this time, all the Junto members were themselves "deserving young beginner[s]," and yet they were willing to be patrons. Other questions also tried to serve members: "16. Hath any body attacked your reputation lately? and what can the Junto do towards securing it? 17. Is there any man whose

friendship you want, and which the Junto or any of them, can procure for you?
18. Have you lately heard any member's character attacked, and how have you
defended it? 19. Hath any man injured you, from whom it is in the power of the
Junto to procure redress? . . . 21. Have you any weighty affair in hand, in which
you think the advice of the Junto may be of service? 22. What benefits have you
lately received from any man not present?"

Several questions focused on the possibility of civic projects and on laws
that might be recommended for the public good. Defoe, Locke, and Mather all
expressed such interests. "11. Do you think of any thing at present, in which the
Junto may be serviceable to *mankind*? to their country, to their friends, or to
themselves? . . . 14. Have you lately observed any defect in the laws of your
country, [of] which it would be proper to move the legislature for an amendment? Or do you know of any beneficial law that is wanting? . . . 20. In what
manner can the Junto, or any of them, assist you in any of your honourable
designs?"

Three questions were devoted to Matherian moral considerations. "6. Do
you know of any fellow citizen, who has lately done a worthy action, deserving
praise and imitation? or who has committed an error proper for us to be warned
against and avoid? 7. What unhappy effects of intemperance have you lately
observed or heard? of imprudence? of passion? or of any other vice or folly? 8.
What happy effects of temperance? of prudence? of moderation? or of any other
virtue?" One question was included simply for the members' enjoyment: "2.
What new story have you lately heard agreeable for telling in conversation?"
Another revealed Franklin's personal Whiggish politics: "15. Have you lately
observed any encroachment on the just liberties of the people?" (1:257–58).

At the anniversary meeting (1:260), the minutes for the past year were read,
together with the standing queries, the qualifying questions, and Breintnall's
poem, which is not extant, on the Junto. Like other clubs, it probably had festivities, songs, and toasts on the occasion.

Topics

A few topics that Franklin proposed in the Junto survive. They concerned natural philosophy, social thought, moral philosophy, politics, psychology, and civic
projects: "Whence comes the Dew that stands on the Outside of a Tankard that
has cold Water in it in the Summer Time?" "Does the Importation of Servants
increase or advance the Wealth of our Country?" "Would not an Office of Insurance for Servants be of Service, and what Methods are proper for the erecting
such an Office?" "If the Sovereign Power attempts to deprive a Subject of his
Right, (or which is the same Thing, of what he thinks his Right) is it justifiable
in him to resist if he is able?" (1:260, 263). Franklin here gives an early suggestion
that truth lies in the perception or belief of the beholder, a suggestion that casts
doubt on the possibility of anything being absolutely true. His similar doubts

about absolute truths in writing on the Hemphill trial in 1735 and in an essay titled "What Is True?" (24 February 1742/3) are discussed in Volume 2.

Franklin's replies to a few queries survive. One reply suggests that he was not being entirely ironic when he wrote in the *Autobiography* that he attempted "the bold and arduous Project of arriving at moral Perfection" (A 78). He asked in the Junto: "Qu. Can a Man arrive at Perfection in this Life as some Believe; or is it impossible as others believe?" Franklin suggested that the key was found in the definition of the word *perfection*. "I suppose the Perfection of any Thing to be only the greatest the Nature of that Thing is capable of; different Things have different Degrees of Perfection; and the same thing at different Times. Thus an Horse is more perfect than an Oyster yet the Oyster may be a perfect Oyster as well as the Horse a perfect Horse. And an Egg is not so perfect as a Chicken, nor a Chicken as a Hen; for the Hen has more Strength than the Chicken, and the C[hicken] more Life than the Egg: Yet it may be a perfect Egg, Chicken and Hen."

A man may not be as perfect as an angel or as perfect as he would be in heaven, "But that a Man is not capable of being so perfect here, as he is capable of being here; is not Sense; it is as if I should say, a Chicken in the State of a Chicken is not capable of being so perfect as a Chicken is capable of being in that State. In the above Sense if there may be a perfect Oyster, a perfect Horse, a perfect Ship, why not a perfect Man? that is as perfect as his present Nature and Circumstances admit?" (1:261–62). The notes concerning the meaning of *perfection* seem prefatory to an exploration of the topic—what constitutes perfection in a human being? If Franklin wrote further on the subject, perhaps Busy-Body No. 3 on virtue (discussed in Chapter 16) is the continuation.

Nicholas Scull's Junto Poem

The founding member Nicholas Scull vaguely described one Junto meeting in a poem. Though unpublished at the time, the poem survives in manuscript. The meeting began with a discussion of three philosophical questions, then a member gave an oration:

> Three Querys in Philosophy were first
> Gravely considerd & at length Discust.
> A Declamation next was read in Course
> Wherein keen wit did Virtues laws enforce
> Where Strength of thought in lofty Language shone
> Such as famd Swift or Addison might own. (ll. 11–16)

Afterward, "business being ore . . . the Juice the witty Bards inspire / With Bright Ideas and Poetick fire." Someone played a song on the flute and then three members, inspired by drink, discoursed on favorite subjects: first "Tune-full Timotheus"; second, "Young withers" (who may have been Joseph Breint-nall); and third, "Bargos"—Franklin.[18]

Scull devotes the longest and most appreciative description to Bargos. The poem contains the first recorded compliment to Franklin's "genius." The subject of his Junto speech concerned the struggle for a fixed salary by the Massachusetts governor. Franklin had begun the *Pennsylvania Gazette* with an editorial (9 October 1729) satirizing Governor William Burnet for demanding a fixed salary from the Massachusetts legislature. After Burnet's death, the Massachusetts Assembly sent Jonathan Belcher as its agent to England. There Belcher was appointed governor. Upon returning to the colony, he demanded the same fixed salary of £2,000 that he had previously opposed. Consequently, in the 24 September 1730 *Gazette*,[19] Franklin wrote an editorial comment charging that the royal instructions to the Massachusetts governor violated the rights of the people. Following that, Franklin published a poem lampooning Belcher, "The Rats and the Cheese: A Fable." Six weeks later, on 5 November 1730, Franklin reprinted two poems that alluded to Belcher's apostasy.[20]

Scull refers to both the editorial comment of 9 October and the reprinted verses of 5 November, thereby showing that he wrote the poem shortly after the latter date. Scull's concluding lines prove that Franklin, declaiming in the Junto at the end of 1730, maintained the same principles that John Wise had fought for in 1687 and that the members of the Old Charter Party had asserted while Franklin was a fledgling Couranteer in Boston. One wonders if Franklin mentioned John Wise. Franklin probably did not, for Wise would probably have been unknown to the other Junto members, but Franklin surely thought of him. Here are Scull's lines concerning Bargos/Franklin:

> Bargos whos birth is by fair Boston Claimd
> And Justly is for a great Genius fam'd,
> Proceeded next to sing New Englands fate:
> Her case how Des'prate and her foes how great,
> How B[elche]r crost the seas to plead her cause,
> Secure her freedom & support her laws;
> How like a Rock unmovd the Hero stod,
> Exposd to danger for his countrys good;
> And as the only means for her Reliefe,
> Wisely Procurd himself to be her Chiefe.
> How cloth'd with Power now he Perceives his faults,
> Her Power & Granduer gives us strength of thought.
> He tells New England now, her cause is wrong.
> Thus with her sovreign to contend so long,
> Perswades her sons two thousand pound is just
> The King Commands it & obey they must.

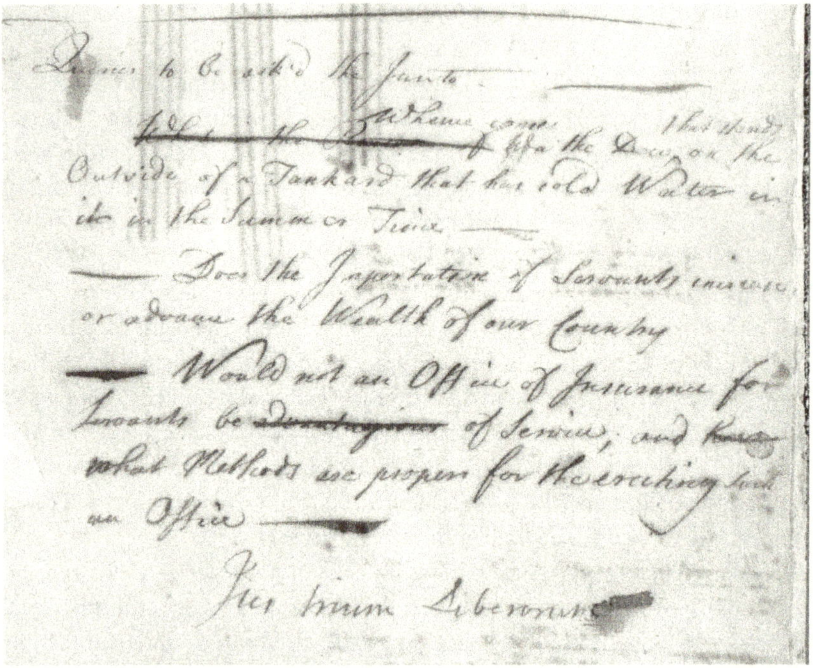

Figure 23a. *Draft, queries for the Junto, ca. 1732, first selection. Franklin answered the first query as part of his "Physical and Meteorological Observations" in 1751. He wrote that "cold condenses and renders visible the Vapour" in air and proved it with the following observation: "A Tankard, or Decanter, fill'd with cold Water, will condense the Moisture of warm clear Air, on its Outside, where it becomes visible as Dew, coalesces into Drops, descends in little Streams" (P 4:239).*

So far as I know, he never wrote about the second and third queries, though they were no doubt discussed in the Junto. The text is printed at P 1:260. The Latin text, "Jus trium Liberorum," refers to a Roman law granting privileges to those who had several children. He may have known the phrase from Pliny, epistles 2:13, but it is also likely that he read it in Edmund Halley's "Some Further Considerations on the Breslaw Bills of Mortality," Philosophical Transactions of the Royal Society, no. 198 (1693): 655–56. Franklin's longstanding interest in demography culminated in his "Observations Concerning the Increase of Mankind" in 1751. Courtesy, Historical Society of Pennsylvania, Philadelphia.

> Yet they maintain what their forefathers held,
> Nor to their monarchy will their freedom yield. (ll. 43–60)

Scull's crude poem and the Junto meeting concluded with "Young Oldham" (George Webb) celebrating "the best of Kings" and with a final flute song by "Timotheus."[21]

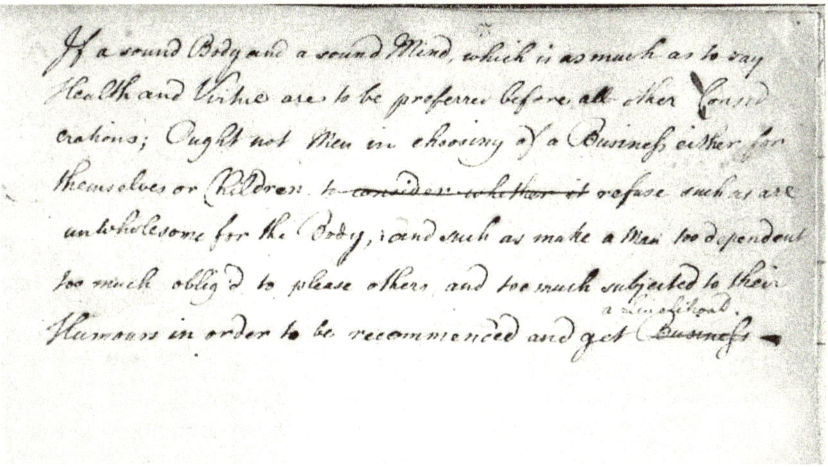

Figure 23b. Draft, queries for the Junto, ca. 1732, second selection. Franklin wrote for discussion in the Junto: "If a sound Body and a sound Mind, which is as much as to say Health and Virtue are to be preferred before all other Considerations; Ought not Men in choosing of a Business either for themselves or children to <consider whether it> refuse such as are unwholesome for the Body; and such as make a Man too dependent, too much oblig'd to please others, and too much subjected to their Humours in order to be recommended and get <Business> a Livelihood." The text is printed at P 1:271. Courtesy, Historical Society of Pennsylvania, Philadelphia.

"ON THE PROVIDENCE OF GOD"

In *A Dissertation on Liberty and Necessity, Pleasure and Pain* (1725), Franklin argued there was no free will.[22] Now he maintained the opposite view in a Junto speech titled "On the Providence of God in the Government of the World."[23] Recollecting both *A Dissertation* and this speech in a letter to Benjamin Vaughan on 9 November 1779, he said that the foundation of "On the Providence of God" was "That almost all Men in all Ages and Countrys, do have at times made use of Prayer." From this observation, he reasoned that "if all things are ordain'd, Prayer must among the rest be ordain'd. But as Prayer can procure no Change in Things that are ordain'd, Praying must then be useless and an Absurdity." But since praying exists, all things are not ordained.

The argument concerning prayer, however, was only a small part of the "Piece on the other side of the Question" (31:59). The Greek philosopher Carneades was famous for convincingly arguing for one position—and then for the opposite. Franklin, too, tried to find what could be said for opposing positions. The audience for "On the Providence of God" did not know the earlier publication. He, however, knew it and might have wanted to discover if he could convince himself of the opposite argument. Or did it have two good opposing answers? He seems frequently to have argued for one position, then for its opposite, and then to hold both in suspense.

"On the Providence of God," Franklin's earliest extant speech, reveals that he had already studied and mastered the structure and techniques of the classical oration. As we will see, he also used the form and techniques in later writings, including "The Speech of Miss Polly Baker" (1747) and *A Narrative of the Late Massacres* (1764). The seventeenth- and eighteenth-century textbooks on logic and rhetoric that Franklin read all presented Aristotle and the classical tradition. Among others, Franklin knew such standard treatises on the subject as the Port Royal *Logic; or, The Art of Thinking* and Charles Gildon's *Grammar of the English Tongue.* He no doubt read a number of the great classical orations, especially those by Cicero, and admired the use of the form by such modern masters as Jonathan Swift.[24] The usual structure of the classical oration had seven parts: first, *exordium*, to get the reader's attention and usually to present the persona sympathetically through *ethos* (establishing the speaker's good character) and *pathos* (winning the audience's sympathy); second, the *narratio*, the origin or the reason for taking up the subject; third, the *explicatio* or *definitio*, which defined the terms or introduced the issues to be proved; fourth, the *partitio*, which divided or clarified the issues; fifth, *amplificatio*, or proof, which set forth the arguments; sixth, *refutatio*, or a refutation of the possible opposing arguments; and seventh, *peroratio*, which concluded the oration.

The form of the classical oration was frequently looser than that just described.[25] Perhaps the three most common variations were to interweave the speaker's ethos and pathos throughout the speech rather than to introduce them in the exordium; second, the narratio or reason for the speech was often combined with the explicatio or the issues to be proven, and third, the proofs might follow the refutation of other positions. As we will see, Franklin put the three refutations before the proofs in "On the Providence of God," perhaps because he thought the refutations of the possible opposing positions were stronger than the proof of the one he advocated.

Providence of God: Exordium

Franklin's 1730 Junto speech began by attempting to establish his own good character and credibility and by putting the audience—his Junto friends—into a receptive mood by playing on their feelings. Franklin flattered his "discerning" audience, casting himself as a humble supplicant ("my own Weakness"), who called his own experience and abilities into question. "When I consider my own Weakness, and the discerning Judgment of those who are to be my Audience, I cannot help blaming my self considerably, for this rash Undertaking of mine, it being a Thing I am altogether ill practis'd in and very much unqualified for. I am especially discouraged when I reflect that you are all my intimate Pot Companions who have heard me say a 1000 silly Things in Conversations, and therefore have not that laudable Partiality and Veneration for whatever I shall deliver that Good People commonly have for their Spiritual Guides" (1:264). Franklin's colloquial, familiar diction ("intimate Pot Companions"), far below the level of the later discourse, emphasized the mutual familiarity and friendship between the speaker and his audience and recalled his frequent joking—traits that made him a fun and enjoyable companion. He humbly placed himself below the level of their "Spiritual Guides"—but he well knew that some Junto members (like the deistic Joseph Breintnall) had little special respect or reverence for such "guides." But if the fellow Junto members had little "Veneration" for him, they almost all did have (as Junto laws required) a "laudable Partiality" for their fellow member.

Franklin probably appealed to the Junto members' humor by his facial expressions and tone when he mentioned "the Sanctity of my Countenance": "You have no Reverence for my Habit, nor for the Sanctity of my Countenance; . . . you do not believe me inspir'd or divinely assisted, and therefore will think your Selves at Liberty to assent or dissent[,] agree or disagree of any Thing I advance, canvassing and sifting it as the private Opinion of one of your Acquaintance." Actually, neither he nor most of his friends had "reverence" for any "Habit" or for the "Sanctity" of any minister's "Countenance." Though a few Junto members may have had such feelings for a particular spiritual leader, several were Quakers and several were deists. "These are great Disadvantages and Discouragements but I am enter'd and must proceed, humbly requesting your Patience and Attention" (1:264). So concluded Franklin's *exordium* (the first part of the oration), which, rhetoricians claimed, should gain the audience's attention. Franklin fulfilled that requirement and appealed to the members' feelings of friendship and fellowship.

Providence of God: Narratio

Franklin wrote: "I propose at this Time to discourse on the Subject of our last Conversation: the Providence of God in the Government of the World." He appealed to the audience, using pathos: "I shall not attempt to amuse you with Flourishes of Rhetorick, were I master of that deceitful Science because I know ye are Men of substantial Reason and can easily discern between sound Argument and the false Glosses of Oratory; nor shall I endeavour to impose on your Ears, by a musical Accent in delivery, in the Tone of one violently affected with what he says; for well I know that ye are far from being superstitious [or] fond of unmeaning Noise, and that ye believe a Thing to be no more true for being sung than said" (1:265). Having ridiculed a rhetorical art (delivery) of which he was not a master, Franklin anticipated Thomas Paine's opening in *Common Sense* ("I offer nothing more than simple facts, plain arguments, and common sense; and have no other preliminaries to settle with the reader, than that he will divest himself of prejudice and prepossession, and suffer his reason and his feelings to determine for themselves"). Franklin said: "I intend to offer you nothing but plain Reasoning, devoid of Art and Ornament; unsupported by the Authority of any Books or Men how sacred soever; because I know that no Authority is more convincing to Men of Reason than the Authority of Reason itself."[26]

The next sentence compliments the audience before appealing to the *consensus gentium* (what all persons have supposedly always believed):[27] "It might be judg'd an Affront to your Understandings should I go about to prove this first Principle, the Existence of a Deity and that he is the Creator of the Universe, for that would suppose you ignorant of what all Mankind in all Ages have agreed in" (1:265). Franklin, however, well knew that the *consensus gentium* argument was no guide to the truth. In his personal copy of the Port Royal *Logic*, the authors referred to Descartes in maintaining that "it is more probable that one single Man shou'd find out the Truth, than that it shou'd be discover'd by many. So that this following is not good Consequence: This Opinion is held by the greater Number of Philosophers, therefore it is the true." Following Descartes, the Port Royalists proclaimed: "What all Mankind in all Ages have agreed in" was not necessarily true.[28]

Providence of God: Explicatio

Beginning the *explicatio*, or *definitio*, Franklin gave three characteristics of the deity: "1. That he must be a Being of great Wisdom; 2. That he must be a Being of great Goodness and 3. That he must be a Being of great Power." For each proposition, he advanced a confirmation or proof ("*amplificatio*"). To demonstrate the first proposition, he recapitulated the usual arguments of scientific deism or Newtonianism—that the beauty, regularity, and order of nature prove that a superior intelligence created it. Poets and philosophers, long before Newton, had anticipated such thoughts. Ann Bradstreet echoed an old tradition when she wrote in stanza 2 of "Contemplations":

> I wist not what to wish, yet sure thought I,
> If so much excellence abide below;
> How excellent is He that dwells on high?
> Whose power and beauty by his works we know.
> Sure he is goodness, wisdom, glory, light,
> That hath this under world so richly dight;
> More Heaven than Earth was here, no winter and no night.[29]

Newtonian science in the late seventeenth and early eighteenth centuries made the design argument for the existence of God more compelling. John Ray's popular *Wisdom of God Manifested in the Works of the Creation* (1691) became the Bible of Newtonianism. Franklin knew Ray's book for, as we have seen in discussing the clockmaker analogy in Franklin's *Dissertation*, he cited Ray in his 1728 "Articles of Belief."

Franklin's reason for believing that God "must be a Being of infinite Wisdom" was basically the design argument, a celebration of the "wonderful regular Motions" of the stars and planets (1:265). The second proposition, God's "great Goodness," depended in part on the plenitude argument (the world possesses all possible forms of life) and on God's "providing plentiful Sustenance for them all" (1:265). Through personal experience in America and England with the abject poor and through reading about other lands, Franklin knew better, but he repeated the religious argument that God provided for all. Franklin also argued that God made "those Things that are most useful, most common and easy to be had; such as Water necessary for almost every Creature's Drink; Air without which few could subsist." How like Franklin to argue that the usefulness of things, that is, God's seeming practicality, proves his goodness! Franklin's supposed "proof" of the third proposition, God's "infinite Power," again used Newtonianism: God demonstrated his ability and power by forming and compounding "such Vast Masses of Matter as this Earth and the Sun and innumerable Planets and Stars," by giving "them such prodigious Motion, and yet" by governing "them in their greatest Velocity as that they shall not flie off out of their appointed Bounds nor dash one against another, to their mutual Destruction" (1:266).

Using what may be an original and ironic example of God's might, Franklin reasoned that the destructive power of humans demonstrated God's incredible power:

> if weak and foolish Creatures as we are, by knowing the Nature of a few Things can produce such wonderful Effects; such as for instance by knowing the Nature only of Nitre and Sea Salt mix'd we can make a Water which will dissolve the hardest Iron and by adding one Ingredient more, can make another Water which will dissolve Gold and render the most Solid Bodies fluid [nitric acid]—and by knowing the Nature of Salt Peter Sulphur and Charcoal [gunpowder] those mean Ingredients mix'd we can shake the Air in the most terrible Manner, destroy Ships Houses and Men at a Distance and in an Instant, overthrow Cities, rend Rocks into a Thousand Pieces, and level the highest Mountains. . . . [then] What Power must he possess who not only knows the Nature of every Thing in the Universe, but can make Things of new Natures with the greatest Ease and at his Pleasure!" (1:266)

Here Franklin echoed biblical passages associated with the day of doom. Revelations 4:11 says, "Thou art worthy, O Lord, to receive glory and honor and power: for thou hast created all things, and for thy pleasure they are and were created." He may also echo that seventeenth-century American best-seller, Michael Wigglesworth's *Day of Doom*.

Providence of God: Partitio

The fourth part of the oration divided and clarified the points at issue. Franklin said that one of four mutually exclusive propositions must be true. The four statements adapted the Gottfried Wilhelm Leibniz versus Samuel Clarke debate, which Franklin had used in his *Dissertation*. He now wrote, "Agreeing then that the World was at first made by a Being of infinite Wisdom, Goodness and Power, which Being we call God; The State of Things ever since and this Time must be in one of these four following manners, viz." The first presented Leibniz's theory, with Franklin's inference following the semicolon: "he unchangeably decreed and appointed every Thing that comes to pass; and left nothing to the Course [of] Nature, nor allow'd any Creature free agency." The second proposition stated the free will possibility: "Without decreeing any thing, he left all to general Nature and the Events of Free Agency in his Creatures, which he never alters or interrrupts." The third proposition compromised between the deterministic and free will positions: "He decreed some Things unchangeably, and left others to general Nature and the Events of Free agency, which also he never alters or interrupts." And the fourth proposition presented Samuel Clarke's reply to Leibniz: "He sometimes interferes by his particular Providence and sets aside the Effects which would otherwise have been produced by any of the Above Causes" (1:266).[30]

Providence of God: Refutatio (1)

Franklin said that he would refute the first three propositions and confirm the truth of the fourth. Franklin claimed that if the first three propositions were allowed, "These Strange Conclusions will necessarily follow." First, to Leibniz's position Franklin replied: "That he is now no more a God." Franklin's astonishing statement shocked the listeners who knew the theological arguments and called for an explanation: "'Tis true indeed, before he had made such unchangeable Decree, he was a Being of Power, Almighty; but now having determin'd every Thing, he has divested himself of all further Power, he has done and has no more to do, he has ty'd up his Hands, and has now no greater Power than an Idol of Wood or Stone; nor can there be any more Reason for praying to him or worshipping of him, than of such an Idol for the Worshippers can be never the better for such Worship" (1:267). Franklin's reference to an idol of wood or stone alluded to the Bible—and also to Aesop's fable of the frogs who wanted a more active god than the log—and were given a crane who ate them.

The second "strange Conclusion" resulting from Leibniz's position dealt with theodicy. As Franklin wrote five years earlier in his *Dissertation*, "*Unde Malum?* has been long a Question, and many of the Learned have perplex'd themselves and Readers to little Purpose in Answer to it" (1:59). In the earlier work, he denied that evil existed; here, he took the common position that it exists. Franklin observed that God "has decreed some things contrary to the very Notion of a wise and good Being; Such as that some of his Creature or Children shall do all Manner of Injury to others and bring every kind of Evil upon them without Cause; that some of them shall even blaspheme him their Creator in the most horrible manner." These were common objections to God's ordaining everything that was going to happen. Franklin added an unusual one, the argument that he recalled to Vaughan as the "foundation" of the work.

Franklin said that it was highly absurd to think that God had ordained that people pray to him if the prayers were not going to change anything. After giving the common objections to Leibniz's position, Franklin said that it "is still more highly absurd that he has decreed the greatest Part of Mankind, shall in all Ages, put up their earnest Prayers to him both in private and publickly in great Assemblies, when all the while he had so determin'd their Fate that he could not possibly grant them any Benefits on that Account, nor could such Prayers be any way available." If God had ordained everything that was going to happen, why would he have ordained that humans offer Him prayers? "It cannot be imagined they are of any Service to him. Surely it is not more difficult to believe the World was made by a God of Wood or Stone, than that the God who made the World should be such a God as this" (1:267).

As we see, the prayer argument, an application of *consensus gentium*, merely refuted an aspect of one of three positions that Franklin held false. Contrary to his recollection forty-nine years later in the letter to Vaughan, it was not the speech's foundation.

An unstated difficulty with Franklin's argument was that it assumed that God responded. If humans offer up prayers that are not answered, they may as well pray to a log or a stone. It would almost seem to be an argument for necessity rather than for God's ability to intervene occasionally in human affairs. The common experience is that prayers are not answered. In fact, Franklin often mocked the efficacy of prayer. As we have seen, at age sixteen Franklin burlesqued Cotton Mather's account of John Avery's death (coming just after Avery's pitiful prayer) in the portrait of Silence Dogood's father being swept away by "a merciless Wave" as he stood upon the deck "rejoycing at my Birth" (1:10). Later, Franklin ridiculed the "forty-five millions of prayers" offered up by New Englanders for the taking of Cape Breton in 1745 (2:26). The Americans succeeded, but Franklin hardly credited the victory to prayer. He later wrote: "Indeed, in attacking strong towns I should have more dependence on *works*, than on *faith*; for, like the kingdom of heaven, they are to be taken by force and violence; and in a French garrison I suppose there are devils of that kind, that they are not to be cast out by prayers and fasting, unless it be by their own fasting for want of provisions" (3:26–27). He ironically commented in 1754, "Serving God is doing good to man, but praying is thought an easier service and therefore is more generally chosen" (4:406).

Providence of God: Refutatio (2)

In supposedly refuting the second proposition, which argued that humans have absolute free will, Franklin said that God does not interfere in the workings of the world regardless of its obvious imperfections. Perhaps despite his ostensible intention, "On the Providence of God in the Government of the World" became another version of God the Sadist as presented in the *Dissertation*. If humans have absolute free will, then God "must either utterly hide him self from the Works of his Hands, and take no Notice at all of their Proceedings natural or moral; or he must be as undoubtedly he is, a Spectator of every thing; for there can be no Reason or Ground to suppose the first—I say there can be no Reason to imagine he would make so glorious a Universe meerly to abandon it" (1:267).

Franklin then gave examples of the injustices and evils that would exist if humans had absolute free will:

> In this Case imagine the Deity looking on and beholding the Ways of his Creatures; some Hero's in Virtue he sees are incessantly indeavouring the Good of others, they labour thro vast difficulties, they suffer incredible Hardships and Miseries to accomplish this End, in hopes to please a Good God, and obtain his Favour, which they earnestly Pray for; what Answer can he make them within himself but this; *take the Reward Chance may give you, I do not intermeddle in these Affairs*; he sees others continually doing all manner of Evil, and bringing by their Actions Misery and Destruction among Mankind: What can he say here but this, *if Chance rewards you I shall not punish you, I am not to be concerned.* He sees the just, the innocent and the Beneficent in the Hands of the wicked and violent Oppressor; and when the good are at the Brink of Destruction they pray to him, *thou, O God, art mighty and powerful to save; help us we beseech thee*: He answers, *I cannot help you, 'tis none of my Business nor do I at all regard these things.* (1:267)

Franklin's descriptions, however, portray injustices and evils that actually exist. All he has done is add the reasoning of a God who has created humans and then given them absolute free will. Perhaps the underlying reason for this exposition was to suggest that it would be better to imagine that there were no God than that he allowed such things to happen.

Franklin asked, "How is it possible to believe a wise and an infinitely Good Being can be delighted in this Circumstance; and be utterly unconcern'd what becomes of the Beings and Things he has created; for thus, we must believe him idle and unactive, and that his glorious Attributes of Power, Wisdom and Goodness are no more to be made use of" (1:268). As Franklin wrote to Jean Baptiste Le Roy on 18 April 1787, "it seems to me that if you or I had the disposition of good and evil in this world, so excellent a man [as the Comte de Buffon, suffering a painful, long illness] would not have had an hour's pain during his existence." Franklin, however, tried not to upset his religious friend Le Roy: "I do not understand these dispensations of Providence, though probably they are for the best."

Providence of God: Refutatio (3)

Franklin next attempted to refute the third alternative, which held that God has decreed some things and left others to general nature and free agency. "Still you unGod him, if I may be allow'd the Expression; he has nothing to do; he can cause us neither Good nor Harm; he is no more to be regarded than a lifeless Image, than Dagon, or Baall, or Bell and the Dragon."[31] Franklin used what was basically the same argument to negate the first three propositions. He now said that God, "that Being which from its Power is most able to Act, from its Wisdom knows best how to act, and from its Goodness would always certainly act best, is in this Opinion supposed to become the most unactive of all Beings and remain everlastingly Idle." Franklin found such a position "an Absurdity, which when considered or but barely seen, cannot be swallowed without doing the greatest Violence to common Reason, and all the Faculties of the Understanding" (1:268). But Franklin knew as well as anybody that the world was full of evil and misery—about which God did nothing.

Questions of theodicy occur frequently in Franklin's works. Writing John Whitehurst on 27 June 1763, Franklin said: "An Answer now occurs to me, for that Question of Robinson Crusoe's Man Friday, which I once thought unanswerable, *Why God no kill the Devil*? It is to be found in the Scottish Proverb; *Ye'd do little for God an the Deel were Dead*." Franklin, however, had scorned a similar position in his early essays, citing Thomas Pope Blount: "and so, they Worship *God* just as the *Indians* do the *Devil*, not as they love him, but because they are afraid of him" (15 April 1723) and echoed it in Busy Body No. 3 (18 February 1728/9).

Providence of God: Amplificatio

The truth of the fourth proposition (Samuel Clarke's argument that God occasionally intervenes) was supposedly proven by Franklin's argument that God was capable of giving mankind a degree of freedom if he wanted to:

> That the Deity sometimes interferes by his particular Providence, and sets aside the Events which would otherwise have been produc'd in the Course of Nature, or by the Free Agency of Men; and this is perfectly agreeable with what we can know of his Attributes and Perfections: But as some may doubt whether 'tis possible there should be such a Thing as free Agency in Creatures; I shall just offer one Short Argument on that Account and proceed to shew how the Duties of Religion necessary follow the Belief of a Providence. You acknowledge that God is infinitely Powerful, Wise and Good, and also a free Agent; and you will not deny that he has communicated to us part of his Wisdom, Power and Goodness; i.e. he has made us in some Degree Wise, potent and good; and is it then impossible for him to communicate any Part of his Freedom, and make us also in some Degree Free? Is not even his *infinite* Power sufficient for this?

In his final reason supporting the proposition, Franklin again came close to arguing that either there is no God or he is vicious. He maintained that God did not interfere either because he could not or because he would not. "There is a righteous Nation grievously oppress'd by a cruel Tyrant, they earnestly intreat God to deliver them; If you say he cannot, you deny his infinite Power, which [you] at first acknowledg'd; if you say he will not, you must directly deny his infinite Goodness." He concluded, "You are then of necessity oblig'd to allow, that 'tis highly reasonable to believe a Providence because tis highly absurd to believe otherwise." Franklin's conclusion did not necessarily follow. Given Franklin's deliberations, a person might possibly argue that one is "of necessity oblig'd to allow that" there is no God "because tis highly absurd to believe otherwise" (1:269).

Providence of God: Peroratio

Franklin believed that religion was good for people. He later commented, "if Men are so wicked as we now see them *with Religion* what would they be if *without it?*" (W 749). He concluded his speech to the Junto with a *peroration* (the seventh and last part of a classical oration), wherein he summed up the argument and attempted to rouse his audience through the artificial proof of pathos: "Now if tis unreasonable to suppose it out of the Power of the Deity to help and favour us particularly or that we are out of his Hearing or Notice or that Good Actions do not procure more of his Favour than ill Ones." That statement destroyed the normal bases of religion (either God could not control what happened or God did not favor good more than evil), but Franklin continued on to imply that the metaphysical and theological truth did not really matter.

What was important was the practical effect of truth: "Then I conclude, that believing a Providence we have the Foundation of all true Religion; for we should love and revere that Deity for his Goodness and thank him for his Benefits; we should adore him for his Wisdom, fear him for his Power, and pray to him for his Favour and Protection." But why do so? Because "this Religion will be a Powerful Regulater of our Actions, give us Peace and Tranquility within our own Minds, and render us Benevolent, Useful and Beneficial to others" (1:269).

In effect, Franklin concluded that religion, though it may not be true, is useful for three reasons: (1) it will regulate our actions, and the traditional religious morality is beneficial, whether divinely inspired or not; (2) it will give us mental peace and security and will relieve the anguish and uncertainty caused by metaphysical and theological questioning. Thus the second reason tells the reader that all the foregoing rationalizations are a blind alley; and (3) it is socially useful, rendering us "Benevolent, Useful and Beneficial to others." For these reasons, Franklin advocated religion for himself and others.[32]

Providence of God: Assessment

In both the *Dissertation* and "On the Providence of God in the Government of the World," Franklin attempted philosophical answers to the questions of liberty and necessity, theodicy, and the nature of God. In both, he began with the common assumptions concerning the nature of God and attempted to make a logical progression to the major topics. In both, however, the conclusions implicitly call into question the basic assumptions. Though the satire on the fundamental propositions is more vicious and clearer in the *Dissertation*, a similar underlying irony emerges in "On the Providence of God." The straightforward thesis argues that free will exists in a universe controlled by God. In fact, the details of the argument undercut the thesis. The underlying satire is that if God really controls the universe, then he is as responsible for the evil as well as the good. Franklin had, however, made some positive advance over the *Dissertation*. Though almost all of "On the Providence of God" attacked the theological bases for beliefs in God, the last sentence, the most important in a composition, gave three reasons for ignoring all that went before. It advocated belief in God.[33]

"On the Providence of God" is Franklin's only extant complete prose work originally written for the Junto and not published. Numerous later writings first delivered in the Junto appeared in the *Pennsylvania Gazette*. Perhaps he did not publish the speech because he suspected that some readers would think it a covert satire, or perhaps his Junto companions criticized it. Had he published it, he would have had to revise it considerably—and omit such personal references as "the Sanctity of my Countenance." And what would be the point of publishing it? Would it be useful? Would it help people? Would it comfort people? No. He had published some of these same views in the *Dissertation*, but he was then nineteen and perhaps proud of the clever performance. Now, however, he was beginning to approach the position that he advocated in his "letter" (really a short essay) of 13 December 1757 where he gave the social utility of religion as a reason for not publishing attacks on religious beliefs: "If Men are so wicked as we now see them *with Religion* what would they be if *without it*?" (7:295).

The Junto: Appreciation

Franklin wrote that the Junto was "the best School of Philosophy, Morals and Politics that then existed in the Province; for our Queries which were read the Week preceding their Discussion, put us on reading with Attention upon the several Subjects, that we might speak more to the purpose: and here too we acquired better Habits of Conversation, every thing being studied in our Rules which might prevent our disgusting each other" (A 62). From the fall of 1727 until he left for England thirty years later, Franklin evidently attended Junto meetings every Friday night, except when he was out of town, sick, or beset with pressing personal or business affairs. I suspect, however, that there were no meetings when the Pennsylvania Assembly was in session. Many, if not most, Junto members would have had business and/or social obligations on Fridays at those times. When Franklin became clerk of the assembly in 1730, he would almost certainly have been busy Friday evenings when the legislature was in session.

After Franklin left for England in 1757, the Junto meetings were not so well attended. Franklin wrote Hugh Roberts on 26 February 1761 that he hoped the Junto would continue for the rest of their lives. "For my own Part, I find I love Company, Chat, a Laugh, a Glass, and even a Song, as well as ever. . . . So I am sure the Junto will be still as agreeable to me as it ever has been: I therefore hope it will not be discontinu'd as long as we are able to crawl together."

Upon returning to Philadelphia in 1762, Franklin again attended meetings when he could, but attendance in the club again fell off when he sailed for England in 1764. In 1765, Hugh Roberts sent him news of the political divisions between Proprietary Party members and the Quaker Party members in the Junto. Franklin replied on 7 July 1765, "I wish you would continue to meet the Junto, notwithstanding that some Effects of our publick Political Misunderstandings may some times Appear there. 'Tis now perhaps one of the *oldest* Clubs, as I think it was formerly one of the *best*, in the Kings Dominions: it wants but about two Years of Forty since it was establish'd; We loved and still Love one another, we are Grown Grey together and yet it is too Early to Part. Let us Sit till the Evening of Life is spent, the Last Hours were always the most joyous; when we can Stay no Longer 'tis time enough then to bid each other good Night, separate, and go quietly to bed."

Franklin was the life and soul of the Junto. It lasted until 1765. Philip Syng wrote Franklin on 1 March 1766 that the "Junto fainted last Summer in the hot Weather and has not yet reviv'd, your Presence might reanimate it, without which I apprehend it will never recover" (13:190). Though the Junto ended as the founding members entered their sixties, it served its purposes beautifully for Franklin and his friends for nearly forty years. In chapter 24 of *Moby-Dick*, Melville wrote that "a whale-ship was my Yale College and my Harvard"; Franklin could say that the Junto was his Yale and Harvard. Franklin used it and the members (and they reciprocally used it and him) as a testing ground for plans to improve Philadelphia's conditions (city streets, town watch, fire companies, insurance company) and to create its institutions (a library, academy, scientific society). The Junto members inspired one another to do good—for one another, for their immediate society, and for their world. By the time the Junto expired in 1765, it had touched and improved nearly every life in Philadelphia.

FIFTEEN

Business,
1728–1730, and "Articles of Religion"

It may be that these created Gods, are immortal, or it may be that after many Ages, they are changed, and Others supply their Places. Howbeit, I conceive that each of these is exceeding wise, and good, and very powerful; and that Each has made for himself, one glorious Sun, attended with a beautiful and admirable System of Planets.—"Articles of Belief and Acts of Religion" (1:103)

THE PRESS AND TYPES ORDERED by Hugh Meredith's father probably arrived on the "Pink, *Society*, William Simpson from London" (*American Weekly Mercury*, 16 May 1728). Meredith's time as apprentice was up with Samuel Keimer. About 1 June 1728, Franklin and Meredith left Keimer "by his Consent" (did he give each a letter of recommendation?) before he learned that they were opening a rival printing house. From a Quaker pewterer, Simon Edgell, they rented a brick house on the north side of Market Street, just a few doors below Second Street, on the site of the present 139 Market Street.[1] It was three stories high, fourteen feet across the front and twenty-two and a half feet deep, with rent at £24 a year. A separate kitchen building, also three stories high, ten by twelve feet, was in the back. To help pay the rent, the partners took in as tenants a fellow Junto member and mathematician, Thomas Godfrey, and his family, about July 1728. The partners boarded with the Godfreys. "We had scarce opened our Letters and put our Press in Order, before George House," a Quaker shoemaker and later member of Franklin's Union Fire Company, "brought a Countryman to us; whom he had met in the Street enquiring for a Printer. All our Cash was now expended in the Variety of Particulars we had been obliged to procure, and this Countryman's Five Shillings, being our First Fruits and coming so seasonably, gave me more Pleasure than any Crown I have since earn'd; and from the Gratitude I felt towards House, has made me often more ready than perhaps I should otherwise have been to assist young Beginners" (A 60).

SEWEL'S *HISTORY*

The Society of Friends had hired Keimer to reprint William Sewel's *History of the Quakers* in 1725. After three years, Keimer had printed about half of it. Franklin, who had managed Keimer's shop, knew the contract and the Quakers' impatience with Keimer's slow progress. He probably mentioned it to Joseph Breintnall, a fellow Junto member. Breintnall secured part of the printing for Franklin and Meredith. Franklin recalled: "upon this we work'd exceeding hard, for the Price was low. It was a Folio, Pro Patria Size, in Pica with Long Primer Notes" (A 62). Franklin set in type a sheet a day (i.e., four large pages, consisting of two forms, each with two folio-size pages). After Meredith printed off a few more than five hundred copies, Franklin broke down the type and redistributed it for the next day's typesetting. No doubt Franklin ran at least one day ahead of Meredith, so that Franklin could be setting a sheet in type for the next day while Meredith printed off the sheet Franklin had set the previous day.

"It was often 11 at Night and sometimes later, before I had finish'd my Distribution [putting each letter back in its respective case] for the next days Work: For the little Jobbs sent in by our other Friends now and then put us back. But so determin'd I was to continue doing a Sheet a Day of the Folio, that one Night when having impos'd my Forms, I thought my Day's Work over, one of them by accident was broken and two Pages reduc'd to Pie [a jumbled mass of types], I immediately distributed and compos'd it over again before I went to bed." If Franklin was only one day ahead of Meredith, the latter would have been idle part of the next day unless Franklin finished the forms. Perhaps, too, if Meredith did not have some pressing work to do, he would have disappeared to his favorite tavern—though Meredith was probably, so early in their partnership, sober and hardworking. "And this Industry visible to our Neighbours began to give us Character and Credit; particularly I was told, that mention being made of the new Printing Office at the Merchants' Every-night-Club, the general Opinion was that it must fail, there being already two Printers in the Place, Keimer and Bradford; but Doctor Baird . . . gave a contrary Opinion, for the Industry of that Franklin, says he, is superior to any thing I ever saw of the kind: I see him still at work when I go home from Club; and he is at Work again before his Neighbours are out of bed. This struck the rest, and we soon after had Offers from one of them to supply us with Stationery. But as yet we did not chuse to engage in Shop Business" (A 62–63).

Since Franklin and Meredith printed forty-four and a half sheets of Sewel's *History* at a rate of a sheet a day, six sheets a week, they must have worked on it for nearly eight weeks. The book was completed and turned over to the Friends in October.[2] They worked on it from August until October 1728. In the *Autobiography*, Franklin drew a moral from his industry, though he tried to make it acceptable by pretending that the intended audience was his family: "I mention this Industry the more particularly and the more freely, tho' it seems to be talking in my own Praise, that those of my Posterity who shall read it, may know the Use of that Virtue, when they see its Effects in my Favour throughout this Relation" (A 63).

The Croaker

Telling of his first printing jobs reminded Franklin of the croaker—or perhaps
he thought that a character sketch about a pessimist would contrast effectively
with the anecdote about working hard as a young printer. Franklin wrote character sketches in his Silence Dogood essays and did so throughout his life,
though few are as memorable as the one describing the croaker who visited the
partners in the summer of 1729. Franklin echoed Oliver Goldsmith's play *The
Good-Natur'd Man* and indirectly echoed an essay by Dr. Samuel Johnson.
Goldsmith labeled a pessimist in *The Good- Natur'd Man* "Mr. Croaker" and
acknowledged to Johnson that he took the character from Suspirius in Johnson's
Rambler No. 59.[3] In *Walden*, Thoreau reflected the same *Rambler* in describing
the dismal screeching of owls near the end of his chapter "Sounds."
    Franklin wrote:

> There are Croakers in every Country always boding its Ruin. Such a one then
> lived in Philadelphia, a Person of Note, an elderly Man, with a wise Look and
> very grave Manner of Speaking. His Name was Samuel Mickle. This Gentleman,
> a Stranger to me, stopped one Day at my Door, and ask'd me if I was the young
> Man who had lately opened a new Printing-house: Being answer'd in the Af-
> firmative; He said he was sorry for me; because it was an expensive Undertaking,
> and the Expence would be lost, for Philadelphia was a sinking Place, the People
> already half Bankrupts or near being so; all Appearances of the contrary such as
> new Buildings and the Rise of Rents, being to his certain Knowledge fallacious,
> for they were in fact among the Things that would soon ruin us. And he gave
> me such a Detail of Misfortunes now existing or that were soon to exist, that he
> left me half-melancholy. Had I known him before I engag'd in this Business,
> probably I never should have done it.—This Man continu'd to live in this decay-
> ing Place, and to declaim in the same Strain, refusing for many Years to buy a
> House there, because all was going to Destruction, and at last I had the Pleasure
> of seeing him give five times as much for one as he might have bought it for
> when he first began his Croaking. (A 60–61)

In fact, the "elderly" Samuel Mickle was forty-four in 1728 and a bit of a real-
estate entrepreneur.[4] Perhaps Franklin falsified the portrait of Mickle to
strengthen the *Autobiography*'s American Dream theme. The underlying moral,
however, is true: to accomplish anything, one must try.

Webb's Perfidy

The attractive young Oxford scholar George Webb found a lady who loaned
him the money to purchase his time from Keimer. When Webb offered "himself
as a Journeyman," the partners could not then employ him, but Franklin "foolishly let him know, as a Secret, that I soon intended to begin a Newspaper, and
might then have work for him." Franklin told Webb that Bradford's paper was

"wretchedly manag'd, no way entertaining; and yet was profitable to him.—I therefore thought a good Paper could scarcely fail of good Encouragement." Webb realized that Franklin would edit the paper himself and that he would be merely a printer. Keimer, however, might let him edit the paper. Webb "told it to Keimer, who immediately, to be beforehand with me, published Proposals for Printing one himself, on which Webb was to be employ'd. I resented this, and to counteract them, as I could not yet begin our Paper, I wrote several Pieces of Entertainment for Bradford's Paper, under the Title of the Busy Body which Breintnall continu'd some Months" (A 63).

Keimer issued his newspaper proposal on Election Day, 1 October 1728, when crowds of people were in town, promising publication about the end of November. Since Franklin was now a businessman, he may have voted in this election. An elector had to be a male citizen, twenty-one years old, resident in the province for two years, and own a fifty-acre freehold with at least twelve acres cleared or else own £50 in personal property.[5] Franklin probably met the qualifications, though he was in debt for the £50 in personal property. Perhaps the proud young man would not have wanted to take the chance of being challenged. The election's major issue was paper currency. With Sir William Keith gone, his party had dissolved. Two of Keith's supporters and Keith himself were replaced in the assembly. Five other Keith supporters were reelected. The Keith party had become the paper currency party, and Franklin could now feel free to support those who believed, as he did, that more paper currency would benefit Philadelphia. At the election, Franklin's friend Andrew Hamilton was again chosen a representative from Bucks County.

"ARTICLES OF BELIEF AND ACTS OF RELIGION"

On Wednesday, 20 November 1728, Franklin composed his own private religious ritual, "Articles of Belief and Acts of Religion."[6] Why did he do so? In 1774 Franklin told the Reverend David Williams that he "never passed a place of public worship on a Sunday, without feeling some regret, that he had not an opportunity of joining in a rational form of devotion."[7] A more immediate occasion may have been his severe illness in 1727. Indeed, as his epitaph (generally dated 1728) proves, Franklin was thinking of his possible death at approximately this time. "Articles of Belief and Acts of Religion" was an early private attempt to furnish his own form of devotion. Fifteen years later on 28 July 1743, he referred to it as "a whole Book of Devotions for my own Use." It had two parts, but only part 1 survives. Part 1 has four sections: (1) First Principles; (2) Adoration; (3) Petition; and (4) Thanks. For the epigraph he chose a quotation from Addison's *Cato* expressing a belief in a God who delights in virtue:

> Here will I hold—If there is a Pow'r above us
> (And that there is, all Nature cries aloud,
> Thro' all her Works), He must delight in Virtue
> And that which he delights in must be Happy.

Cato, a touchstone for the eighteenth-century man of virtue, should have been happy. But, as all eighteenth-century litterateurs knew, he killed himself. The soliloquy (as familiar in the eighteenth century as Hamlet's "To be, or not to be" today) expresses Cato's uncertainty and despair. The preceding two lines that Franklin did not quote stated the dilemma: "The wide unbounded prospect, lies before me; / But shadows, clouds, and darkness rest upon it." Cato then rose to the affirmation Franklin quoted, and thereafter descended to a resolute despair: "But when! or where!—This world was made for Caesar. / I am weary of conjectures—This [his sword] must end 'em."

Taken as a whole, Cato's speech expresses metaphysical despair. The tone and voice of the entire speech not only echo Hamlet at his most pessimistic, they also anticipate the existentialism of the World War II generation. Ignoring the context, Franklin quoted only the optimistic four lines. As the historian Elizabeth E. Dunn observed, in the larger context "the passage no longer appears as a steadfast proclamation of the existence and benevolence of God, but rather it seems an unsuccessful stopgap measure in Cato's tumble into despair."[8] The epigraph questions the metaphysical universe and affirms that regardless of what the ultimate truths may be, virtue should be prized.

First Principles

Franklin's "First Principles" (1:102–4) began with a surprise, positing a system of polytheism existing under one supreme God: "I BELIEVE there is one Supreme most perfect Being, Author and Father of the Gods themselves." Franklin's nineteenth-century biographer James Parton believed that Franklin heard, probably from Dr. Pemberton, Sir Isaac Newton's speculation. Newton theorized that "intelligent beings superior to us . . . superintended those revolutions of the heavenly bodies by the direction of the Supreme Being."[9] The historian of American philosophy I. Woodbridge Riley thought that Franklin's polytheism showed the influence of Plato, particularly the *Timaeus*.[10] Plato was well-known in the eighteenth century (in 1750, as the Maryland tobacco factor Robert Morris lay dying, he asked that Plato's *Phaedo* be read aloud to him).[11] As I suggested earlier, Franklin had already read Lucretius's *De rerum natura* and Thomas Stanley's *History of Philosophy*. Since references to Cicero's *De natura rerum* occur in the Port Royal *Logic*, and since *De natura rerum* was well-known among eighteenth-century intellectuals,[12] Franklin had no doubt also read it.

Franklin owed something to the classical writers, but his polytheism is primarily based upon the Great Chain of Being. The historian of ideas A. O. Lovejoy showed that many eighteenth-century thinkers said that human beings were the middle link in the chain of being.[13] Locke, in *An Essay Concerning Human Understanding*, theorized that "there are far more *Species* of Creatures above us, than there are beneath; we being in degrees of Perfection much more remote from the infinite Being of God, than we are from the lowest state of Being."[14] Addison popularized the idea in *Spectator* No. 519 (25 October 1712): "If the

Scale of Being rises by such a regular Progress, so high as Man, we may by a Parity of Reason suppose that it still proceeds gradually through those Beings which are of a Superior Nature to him, since there is an infinitely greater Space and Room for different Degrees of Perfection, between the Supreme Being and Man, than between Man and the most despicable Insect."[15] And five years after Franklin composed the "Articles," Alexander Pope, in *An Essay on Man*, gave man the middle place in the chain, halfway between God and the lowest forms of life.[16] Franklin wrote: "For I believe that Man is not the most perfect Being but One, rather that as there are many Degrees of Beings his Inferiors, so there are many Degrees of Beings superior to him."

Franklin also expressed his belief in the plurality of worlds, another common eighteenth-century opinion, perhaps best known through Fontenelle's popular *Pluralité des mondes* and Addison's *Spectator* No. 565 (9 July 1714).[17] Both authors, like Franklin, used the idea to humble human pride: "Also, when I stretch my Imagination thro' and beyond our System of Planets, beyond the visible fix'd Stars themselves, into that Space that is every Way infinite, and conceive it fill'd with Suns like ours, each with a Chorus of Worlds for ever moving round him, then this little Ball on which we move, seems, even in my narrow Imagination, to be almost Nothing, and my self less than nothing, and of no sort of Consequence." Two years later, the Maryland poet Richard Lewis, in a poem that Franklin reprinted with praise in the 20 May 1731 *Pennsylvania Gazette*, expressed similar thoughts:

> Are these bright Luminaries hung on high
> Only to please with twinkling Rays our Eye?
> Or may we rather count each *Star* a *Sun*,
> Round which *full peopled Worlds* their Courses run?

The thought led Lewis, like Franklin, to doubt the importance of mankind:

> Tremendous God! May I not justly fear,
> That I, unworthy Object of thy Care,
> Into this World from thy bright Presence tost,
> Am in th'Immensity of *Nature* lost!
> And that my Notions of the *World above*,
> Are but Creations of my own *Self-Love*;
> To feed my coward Heart, afraid to die,
> With *fancied* Feasts of *Immortality*![18]

Almost thirty years later Franklin again linked the plurality of worlds and the foolishness of human pride in *Poor Richard*: "We must not presume too much on our own Importance. There are an infinite Number of Worlds under the divine Government, and if this was annihilated it would scarce be miss'd in the Universe" (7:91).

All these eighteenth-century authors had no doubt read Pascal's *Pensées*, a popular translation of which had appeared in 1688, with a second edition in 1704 and a third in 1727. Franklin also reflected Pascal, who combined thoughts of the infinity of the universe, the vanity of man, the limitations of our knowledge, the nature of God, and a kind of existentialist angst concerning the place of human beings in nature. Pascal wrote:

> I know not who sent me into the World, nor what the World is, nor what I am my self; . . . I know not what my Body is, what my Sense, nor what my Soul is; and this very part of my self that thinks what I say, and that reflects upon it, and upon itself, knows not it self . . . I behold the vast distances of the Universe that contains me, and find myself confin'd to a Corner of this vast Body, not knowing wherefore I am placed rather in this place than another; nor why the little time allotted me to live, is assign'd me at this Point rather than any other, of that Eternity that has gone before, or shall follow after me. I see nothing but Infinities on all sides that swallow me up like an Atom, and like a Shadow that remains but a Moment and passeth away: All that I know is, that I shall shortly die; but what I know most of all is, that I do not know death itself, which I cannot avoid.[19]

In the "Articles of Belief" Franklin went beyond the usual complaints about pride, using the insignificance of humans to argue that God does not expect prayer or praise from humans: "When I think thus, I imagine it great Vanity in me to suppose, that the *Supremely Perfect*, does in the least regard such an inconsiderable Nothing as Man. More especially, since it is impossible for me to have any positive clear Idea of that which is infinite and incomprehensible, I cannot conceive otherwise, than that He, *the Infinite Father*, expects or requires no Worship or Praise from us, but that he is even INFINITELY ABOVE IT." Jonathan Swift expressed a thought not too dissimilar in "A Discourse Concerning the Mechanical Operation of the Spirit": "It is a sketch of human vanity for every individual to imagine the whole universe is interested in his meanest concern."[20] But if Franklin believed that God was infinitely above paying any attention to man, why would Franklin compose a ritual of prayer and thanks to God? Franklin answered that "all Men" have "something like a natural Principle which enclines them to DEVOTION or the Worship of some unseen Power."

Since humans are mentally "superior to all other Animals that we are in our World acquainted with" and since humans have a "natural Principle" to want to worship, "therefore I think it seems required of me, and my Duty, as a Man, to pay Divine Regards to SOMETHING." Three ideas occurred in the passage. First, Franklin said mankind has an instinct to worship. Second, humans are animals—only with a superior intellect. (By implication, he denied the existence of the soul separating man from other animals.) Third, other animals may exist in our world that are more intelligent than humans. Franklin suggested that "the INFINITE has created many Beings or Gods, vastly superior to Man, who can better conceive his Perfections than we, and return him a more rational and glorious Praise." Echoing Shaftesbury's *Characteristics*, Franklin compared God to an "ingenious Painter or Architect, who is rather honour'd and pleas'd with the Approbation of Wise men and Artists" than with the praise of "the Ignorant or of Children."[21]

Even Franklin's polytheism was highly unusual, for he suggested that the gods themselves may not be eternal: "It may be that these created Gods, are immortal, or it may be that after many Ages, they are changed, and Others supply their Places." A. Owen Aldridge noted that Franklin's suggestion of the mortality of the gods was "an amplification of the concept of the Great Chain of Being which had not occurred to any previous writer."[22] That's not surprising, for Franklin's theology is hardly emotionally comforting. It lacks any absolutes: "It may be . . . or it may be." Indeed, one thinks, what may not be? But then Franklin returned to a relatively normal polytheism, with each God given his own particular solar system to supervise: "Howbeit, I conceive that each of these is exceeding wise, and good, and very powerful; and that Each has made for himself, one glorious Sun, attended with a beautiful and admirable System of Planets." Franklin proposed to worship and pray to the local "God, who is the Author and Owner of our System." Franklin's solar system god resembled the classical gods, for Franklin suggested that "he has in himself some of those Passions he has planted in us, and that, since he has given us Reason whereby we are capable of observing his Wisdom in the Creation, he is not above caring for us, being pleas'd with our Praise, and offended when we slight Him, or neglect his Glory." After hinting that the local god may be displeased if not worshiped, Franklin said that he believed the solar system god to be good and that "I should be happy to have so wise, good and powerful a Being my Friend" (1:103). Better a friend than an enemy![23]

Franklin believed that the local god "is pleased and delights in the Happiness of those he has created; and since without Virtue Man can have no Happiness in this World, I firmly believe he delights to see me Virtuous, because he is pleas'd when he sees me Happy." Franklin appended a note, "See Junto Paper of good and Evil," which argued that only virtuous men were happy in this world (2:15–19). Franklin continued that since God "has created many Things which seem purely design'd for the Delight of Man, I believe he is not offended when he sees his Children solace themselves in any manner of pleasant Exercises and innocent Delights." Franklin's solar system god was almost the opposite of the puritan God of his childhood. As he later said, he did not believe in the idea of original sin or of a vengeful god. Continuing, Franklin said that "no Pleasure" is "innocent that is to Man hurtful." Franklin concluded: "I *love* him therefore for his Goodness and I *adore* him for his Wisdom." He should praise God, "for it is his Due, and it is all I can return for his many Favours and great Goodness to me; and let me resolve to be virtuous, that I may be happy, that I may please Him, who is delighted to see me happy." But it is only because the local god has some of the passions of mankind in him that he cares one iota about mankind. The supreme God is infinitely above such concerns.[24]

ADORATION

Franklin reminded himself that in going through his ritual, he should adopt a state of mind "calm and Serene," free from "Passion and Perturbation," and instead filled with "Joy, and Satisfaction, and Admiration." To that end he resolved to adopt an expression of "filial Respect, mixt with a kind of Smiling." Who but Franklin would spell out the appearance of the countenance one should adopt in a religious ceremony? Under "Adoration" (1:104–5), Franklin listed six short prayers, each beginning, "O Powerful Goodness! bountiful Father! merciful Guide! Increase in me that Wisdom which discovers my truest Interests; Strengthen my Resolutions to perform what that Wisdom dictates. Accept my kind Offices to thy other Children, as the only Return in my Power for thy continual Favours to me." The last sentiment was the keynote of Franklin's religion: doing good to others was the only return a grateful believer could make to God.

Franklin's first prayer of adoration was that God is "Good, and that thou art *pleas'd with the Pleasure* of thy Children." Franklin noted that God delighted "in their Happiness." This happy God seemed to have "some of those Passions he has planted in us." The second prayer was a standard statement of God as first cause, with overtones of Newtonian physico-theology: "By thy Power hast thou made the glorious Sun, with his attending Worlds; from the Energy of thy mighty Will they first received their prodigious Motion, and by thy Wisdom hast thou prescribed the wondrous Laws by which they move." Third, Franklin thanked God for creating all things, including man, "bestowing Life and Reason, and plac'd him in Dignity superior to thy other earthly Creatures." Franklin said nothing (though this is the most logical place in his ritual) about man's soul, his immortality, or his rewards and punishments in an afterlife. They are conspicuously absent from what we have of his 1728 religious beliefs, though they may have appeared in the lost part 2 of "Articles of Belief." Franklin then turned to the design argument, again as influenced by physico-theology: "Thy Wisdom, thy Power, and thy Goodness are every where clearly seen; in the Air and in the Water, in the Heavens and on the Earth; Thou providest for the various winged Fowl, and the innumerable Inhabitants of the Water; Thou givest Cold and Heat, Rain and Sunshine in their Season, and to the Fruits of the Earth Increase."

The fifth article reinforced the first one, with Franklin stating that God had given "Life to thy Creatures that they might Live, and art not delighted with violent Death and bloody Sacrifices." One might then ask, as Franklin elsewhere did, why pain, suffering, violent death, and bloody sacrifices existed. But here he was writing a prayer of adoration, not a theodicy. Franklin ignored the problem of evil: "Thou abhorrest in thy Creatures Treachery and Deceit, Malice,

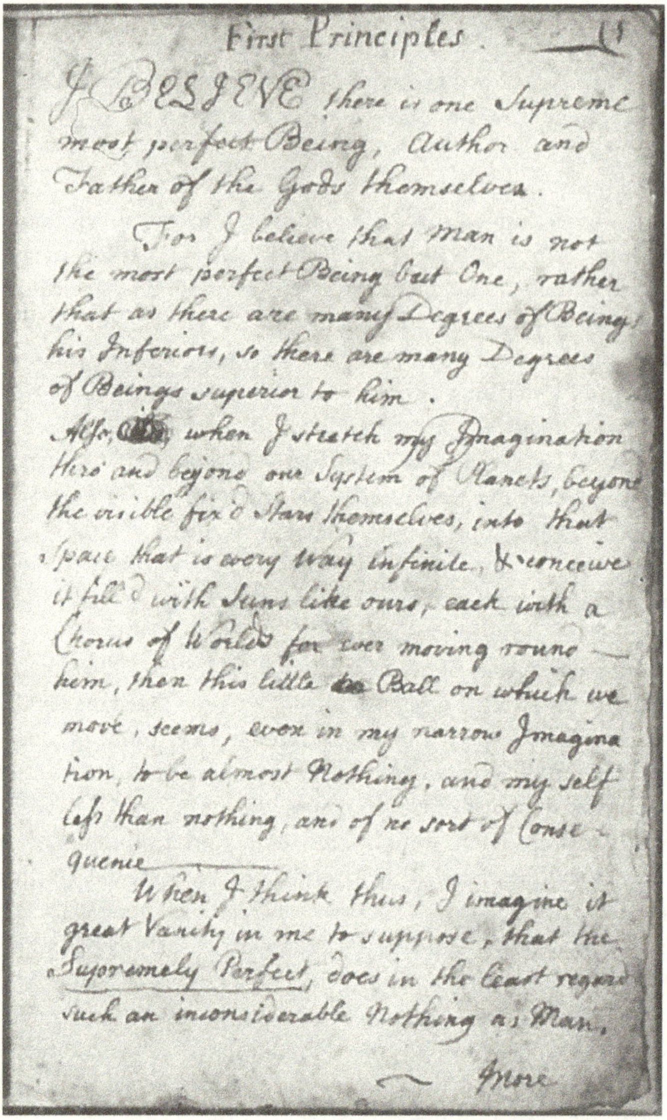

First Principles.

I BELIEVE there is one Supreme
most perfect Being, Author and
Father of the Gods themselves.

For I believe that man is not
the most perfect Being but One, rather
that as there are many Degrees of Being
his Inferiors, so there are many Degrees
of Beings superior to him.

Also, when I stretch my Imagination
thro' and beyond our System of Planets, beyond
the visible fix'd Stars themselves, into that
Space that is every way infinite, & conceive
it fill'd with Suns like ours, each with a
Chorus of Worlds for ever moving round
him, then this little Ball on which we
move, seems, even in my narrow Imagina
tion, to be almost Nothing, and my self
less than nothing, and of no sort of Conse
quence.

When I think thus, I imagine it
great Vanity in me to suppose, that the
Supremely Perfect, does in the least regard
such an inconsiderable Nothing as Man.

more

Figure 24. *First page of Franklin's private "Articles of Belief and Acts of Religion," 20 November 1728. Since Franklin's holograph copy has several blots, I reproduce a copy in the handwriting of his grandson, William Temple Franklin. Excepting persons professionally engaged in theology (ministers and religious leaders like John Woolman), Franklin wrote more about religion and ethics than anyone in colonial America, and he sometimes said different things about religion to different people. The "Articles," however, were meant for his private devotion. They specify a number of prayers and contain a number of unusual doctrines. In the first paragraph, for example, Franklin says he believes that there is "one most perfect Being" and continues that the "most perfect Being is the Author and Father of the Gods themselves." Many of his contemporaries had suggested the plurality of worlds and of gods, but such speculations were outside the normal bounds of Christianity. Courtesy, Manuscript Division, Library of Congress, Washington, D.C.*

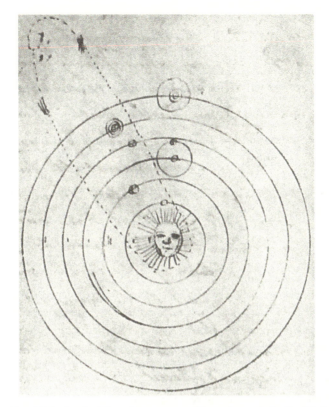

Figure 25. Franklin's sketch of the solar system, 20 November 1728. In the third paragraph of the "Articles," Franklin wrote: "when I stretch my Imagination thro' and beyond our System of Planets, beyond the visible fix'd Stars themselves, into that Space that is every Way infinite, and conceive it fill's with Suns like ours, each with a Chorus of Worlds for every moving round him, then this little Ball on which we move, seems, even in my narrow Imagination, to be almost Nothing, and my self less than nothing, and of no sort of Consequence."

Thinking of the multitude of worlds, Franklin sketched at the end of the "Articles" a primitive representation of the solar system. The sun is in the middle, the first circle around it traces the path of the planet Mercury, which is shown as a small dot immediately above the sun; the second circle traces the path of Venus, which is represented as a dot above and to the left of the sun; the third, the earth, directly above the sun, with the moon circling around it; the fourth, Mars, shown above and to the left of the earth; the fifth, Jupiter, above and to the left of Mars, shown to be larger and with more circles around it; and the sixth and outermost circle represents the path of Saturn, directly above the sun and the earth, shown with two circles (moons?) around it. That was the extent of the known solar system. (Uranus was discovered in 1781; Neptune in 1846; and Pluto in 1930.)

The dotted line may suggest a pulley that would rotate the sun, but Franklin of course knew the Copernican and Ptolomean theories. He compared the two in Poor Richard *for 1748: "How much more natural is Copernicus's Scheme! Ptolomy is compar'd to a whimsical Cook, who, instead of Turning his Meat in Roasting, should fix That, and contrive to have his whole Fire, Kitchen and all, whirling continually round it." This sketch is in Franklin's holograph. Courtesy, Manuscript Division, Library of Congress, Washington, D.C.*

Revenge, Intemperance and every other hurtful Vice; but Thou art a Lover of Justice and Sincerity, of Friendship, Benevolence and every Virtue. Thou art my Friend, my Father, and my Benefactor." Franklin then recommended reading passages in one of the standard works of physico-theology: John Ray's *Wisdom of God Manifested in the Works of the Creation*, or Richard Blackmore's poem *Creation*, or Archbishop Fenelon's *A Demonstration of the Existence and Attributes of God*, "or else spend some Minutes in a serious Silence, contemplating on those Subjects." Afterward, he would sing Milton's Hymn to the Creator from *Paradise Lost* (5:153–56, 160–204). Thereafter he would read from a work "Discoursing on and exciting to MORAL VIRTUE."

Petition

Section 3 of the "Articles of Belief" consisted of Franklin's "Petition" (1:107–9), its preamble notable for doubting that humans always knew what constituted real good for humanity. He had voiced a similar reservation concerning human judgment in the *Dissertation* when he said that "it was impossible to know all the intricate Consequences of every Action." Franklin later voiced the law of unintended consequences concerning the balance of nature. Writing Peter Collinson on 9 May 1753, he said: "Whenever we attempt to mend the scheme of Providence and to interfere in the Government of the World, we had need be very circumspect lest we do more harm than Good." Here in the "Articles of Belief," he wrote: "In as much as by Reason of our Ignorance We cannot be Certain that many Things Which we often hear mentioned in the Petitions of Men to the Deity, would prove REAL GOODS if they were in our Possession, and as I have Reason to hope and believe that the Goodness of my Heavenly Father will not withhold from me a suitable Share of Temporal Blessings, if by a VIRTUOUS and HOLY Life I merit his Favour and Kindness, Therefore I presume not to ask such Things, but rather Humbly, and with a sincere Heart express my earnest Desires that he would graciously assist my Continual Endeavours and Resolutions of eschewing Vice and embracing Virtue; Which kind of Supplications will at least be thus far beneficial, as they remind me in a solemn manner of my Extensive DUTY."

   The first article of the petition listed a fault that he struggled against, in vain, for most of his life. "That I may be preserved from Atheism and Infidelity, Impiety and Profaneness, and in my Addresses to Thee carefully avoid Irreverence and Ostentation, Formality and odious Hypocrisy, Help me, O Father." Franklin violated the first article not only in Boston and in London but subsequently in Philadelphia and occasionally thereafter throughout his life. He knew, however, even before he left Boston, that his iconoclastic religious opinions upset ordinary "good People" (A 17). As he wrote in *Poor Richard* for 1751: "Talking against Religion is unchaining a Tyger; The Beast let loose may worry his Deliverer." The second petition asked: "That I may be loyal to my Prince, and faithful to my Country, careful for its Good, valiant in its Defence, and obedient to its Laws, abhorring Treason as much as Tyranny, Help me, O Father." Franklin finally rejected this principle too, becoming in the pre-Revolutionary period the most famous American revolutionary. But, of course, his country by then was America, not England or even Great Britain.

Thereafter followed a series of petitions for the standard virtues, the third one being "That I may to those above me be dutiful, humble, and submissive, avoiding Pride, Disrespect and Contumacy, Help me, O Father." This "virtue" was especially difficult for Franklin, who wrote in the "Outline" of the *Autobiography*: "Costs me nothing to be civil to inferiors, a good deal to be submissive to superiors" (205). The sixth petition concerned sincerity: "That I may be sincere in Friendship, faithful in Trust, and impartial in Judgment, watchful against Pride, and against Anger (that momentary Madness), Help me, O Father." He probably thought that he often failed to be sincere, for in the *Autobiography* he made sincerity the seventh in the list of virtues to be practiced. The tenth petition took up integrity: "That I may possess Integrity and Evenness of Mind, Resolution in Difficulties, and Fortitude under Affliction; that I may be punctual in performing my Promises, peaceable and prudent in my Behaviour, Help me, O Father." The fourteenth petition asked for an almost impossibly high ideal of behavior: "That I may have a constant Regard to Honour and Probity; That I may possess a perfect Innocence and a good Conscience, and at length become Truly Virtuous and Magnanimous, Help me, Good God, Help me, O Father."

Thanks

The petition of thanks (1:109) had four brief parts, each concluding with "*Good God, I Thank thee*": "For Peace and Liberty, for Food and Raiment, for Corn and Wine, and Milk, and every kind of Healthful Nourishment . . .; For the Common Benefits of Air and Light, for useful Fire and delicious Water . . .; For Knowledge and Literature and every useful Art; for my Friends and their Prosperity, and for the fewness of my Enemies . . .; [and] For all thy innumerable Benefits; For Life and Reason, and the Use of Speech, for Health and Joy and every Pleasant Hour, *my Good God, I thank thee*." So concluded the extant part of "Articles of Belief and Acts of Religion."

Did Franklin Believe in the "Articles"?

After discussing his *Dissertation on Liberty and Necessity* in the *Autobiography*, Franklin said that he "grew convinc'd that *Truth, Sincerity* and *Integrity* in Dealings between Man and Man, were of the utmost Importance to the Felicity of Life, and I form'd written Resolutions, (which still remain in my Journal Book) to practice them ever while I lived." Franklin's "Journal Book" no longer exists, though he recorded in part 2 of the *Autobiography* his list of virtues and chart of a day from the little book, a fair copy of which was dated 1 July 1733.[25] The "Resolutions" are not to be identified with the list of thirteen virtues or with part 1 of the 1728 "Articles of Belief and Acts of Religion," but they may have appeared in part 2 of the "Articles of Belief." Whether they did or not, we may be certain that the main "Resolutions" were to practice the virtues named above, especially truth, sincerity, and integrity, each of which occurs in some way in the petition. These ideals, which were also named in the *Autobiography* (59), were, I believe, actually more important to Franklin than the list of thirteen virtues enumerated in part 2 of the *Autobiography* (79–80) which were intended to correct his particular faults.

Was Franklin entirely serious in his "Articles of Belief and Acts of Religion"? After all, just three years before in the *Dissertation* he had mocked belief in God. Two years later, he based one argument in "On the Providence of God in the Government of the World" (1730) in part on man's desire to pray—though here in the "Articles" he said that the supreme God was infinitely above paying any attention to the prayers of humans. I believe the "Articles" were serious. He tried to write a liturgy as well as he could and to practice it. He no doubt recalled Pascal's advice to act as if one did believe in God and go through the rituals of belief, for such religious actions would ultimately help one to believe.[26]

Franklin, however, failed to find in his "Articles of Belief" (or any other metaphysical or theological scheme) any certainty. He could not help but doubt the various systems of theology. In a draft of a letter to his father, he wrote: "God only knows whether all the Doctrines I hold for true, be so or not. For my part, I must confess, I believe they are not" (2:202). When he visited New England in 1743 and fell into a family discussion with two of his sisters concerning faith and good works, his favorite sister Jane supposed that he was against worshiping God and that he thought good works would merit salvation. She wrote him about it, but he replied on 28 July 1743: "I am so far from thinking that God is not to be worshiped, that I have compos'd and wrote a whole Book of Devotions for my own Use: And I imagine there are few, if any, in the World, so weake as to imagine, that the little Good we can do here, can *merit* so vast a Reward hereafter." Franklin, however, wanted to reassure his sister Jane and did not want his opinions to give her "some Uneasiness, which I am unwilling to be the Occasion of." Therefore he may have tried to seem less iconoclastic than he actually was. When he wrote the great revivalist George Whitefield his reservations concerning religion, he said: "I rather suspect from certain circumstances, that though the general government of the universe is well administered, our particular little affairs are perhaps below notice, and left to take the chance of human prudence or imprudence, as either may happen to be uppermost" (16:192). In that statement, not even a local God administered earth.

Reflecting on his moral position in the *Autobiography*, he said: "Revelation had indeed no weight with me as such; but I entertain'd an Opinion, that tho' certain Actions might not be bad *because* they were forbidden by it, or good *because* it commanded them; yet probably those Actions might be forbidden *because* they were bad for us, or commanded *because* they were beneficial to us, in their own Natures, all the Circumstances of things considered" (A 59). But we know from his *Dissertation* that Franklin thought it impossible for humans to know "all the Circumstances of things": "they are innumerable and incomprehensible by any Thing but Omniscience" (1:62). He continued in the *Autobiography* with a statement remarkable for its latitude of beliefs, including the possibility of the help of God, or a particular angel, or chance—but mainly stressing the individual's deliberate attempt to be ethical—a statement that could provide no help for one who hoped to find emotional security in religion: "And this Persuasion, with the kind hand of Providence, or some guardian Angel, or accidental favorable Circumstances and Situations, or all together, preserved me (thro' this dangerous Time of Youth and the hazardous Situations I was sometimes in among Strangers, remote from the Eye and Advice of my Father) without any *wilful* gross Immorality or Injustice that might have been expected from my Want of Religion" (A 59).

It is difficult, perhaps impossible, to come to a conclusion about Franklin's religious beliefs. In an obituary of his skeptical friend Andrew Hamilton, Franklin wrote: "If he could not subscribe to the Creed of any particular Church, it was not for want of considering them All; for he had read much on Religious Subjects" (2:328). Franklin seemed never to resolve the question of God; he had something like Melville's mind-set. Hawthorne recorded that when he and Melville took a walk together in England in 1856, Melville took up the great subjects of theology: "Melville, as he always does, began to reason of Providence and futurity, and of everything that lies beyond human ken, and informed me that he had 'pretty much made up his mind to be annihilated'; but still he does not seem to rest in that anticipation; and, I think, will never rest until he gets hold of a definite belief. It is strange how he persists." Hawthorne thought that Melville could "neither believe, nor be comfortable in his unbelief; and he is too honest and courageous not to try to do one or the other." Like Andrew Hamilton and Melville, Franklin searched for an answer in his reading and in his own philosophical writings, but he was less disturbed than Addison's Cato or than Melville when he found none. Perhaps he was less upset because physics fascinated him more than metaphysics; or perhaps because, whatever the truth might be, he believed that good actions and deeds could help mankind. Franklin had the good fortune to be a man of action as well as of thought—and the great good fortune of finding pleasure and happiness in good fellowship, delightful flirtations, and in trying to do good.

Keimer's *Pennsylvania Gazette*

On Christmas Eve the first issue of Keimer's paper appeared. He gave it the presumptuous title *The Universal Instructor in All Arts & Sciences: and The Pennsylvania Gazette*. To make good the first part of his title (and to fill up the short two columns per page), he began reprinting piecemeal Ephraim Chambers, *Cyclopaedia: or, An Universal Dictionary of Arts and Sciences*. In the second number of the *Universal Instructor*, Keimer changed to the Quaker style of dating, "the

2d of the 11th Month, 1728," no doubt hoping to gain subscribers from Quakers who might think he was a Friend. Whatever George Webb's hopes for Keimer's paper may have been, the paper showed Keimer's lack of ability. Keimer's fifth issue, 21 January 1727/8, reached "AB" in Chambers and printed its article on abortion. Seizing the opportunity, Franklin wrote two letters from (ostensibly) feminine readers for Bradford's 28 January *Mercury*.

"Martha Careful" threatened that "my Sister Molly and my Self, with some others, are Resolved to run the Hazard of taking him by the Beard, at the next Place we meet him, and make an Example of him for his Immodesty." Franklin's other female persona was a Quaker lady, "Caelia Shortface," who promised: "That if thou Continue to take such Scraps concerning Us, out of thy great Dictionary, and Publish it, as thou hath done in thy *Gazette*, No. 5, to make Thy Ears suffer for it: And I was desired by the rest, to inform Thee of Our Resolution, which is That if thou proceed any further in that *Scandalous manner*, we intend very soon to have thy right Ear for it." Reflecting Franklin's real wish, the persona added, "if Thou hath nothing else to put in Thy *Gazette*, lay it down." Though neither persona is as developed as Silence Dogood, they typify Franklin's frequent use of feminine personae. He constantly appreciated the possibilities of viewpoints other than his own and particularly identified with people he considered prejudiced against by society. Not only did he specialize in feminine speakers, he also created the first and second African American personae in American literature. (A locus classicus against prejudice in Franklin's writings is the bagatelle "A Petition" [1785], complaining of the outrageously unfair and prejudiced treatment against one of a pair of twin sisters, signed at the end, "The Left Hand.")

First Imprints

Whenever Franklin had free time, he attempted to build up the array of forms that printers and stationers commonly carried. He turned to his good friend Joseph Breintnall, who worked for Philadelphia's preeminent scrivener Charles Brockden, and Breintnall supplied him with models to use for the forms (A 68). Gradually he built up his inventory of "Bills of Sale, Powers of Attorney, Writs, Summons, Apprentice Indentures, Servants Indentures, Penal Bills, Promissory Notes," continuing on with the contracts that merchants used: "Bills of Lading bound and unbound, Common Blank Bonds for Money, Bonds with Judgment, Counterbonds, Arbitration Bonds, Arbitration Bonds with Umpirage," and the penal "Bail Bonds, Counterbonds to save Bail harmless." When Franklin and Meredith bought the *Gazette* in 1729, they had for sale and advertised in their first issue all these documents, done "in the most authentic Forms, and correctly printed."

Isaiah Thomas recorded the following anecdote concerning one Franklin form: "Bills of lading formerly began with 'Shipped by the Grace of God,' &c. Some people of Philadelphia objected to this phraseology as making light of serious things. Franklin therefore printed some without these words and inserted in his paper the following advertisement: 'Bills of Lading for sale at this office, with or without the Grace of God.'" Though the anecdote rings true, I searched in vain for Franklin's advertising bills of lading "with or without the Grace of God."[27]

In the early years of his business, legal forms were his principal product. They account for more than nine-tenths of all the thousands of entries recorded in his Ledger A&B, which covers his business dealings from 1730 to 1740. Moreover, these inexpensive forms generally sold for cash, and cash purchases are not recorded in the ledgers. The documents used by businessmen, merchants, ship captains, lawyers, and government officers; those exchanged between apprentices, servants, and masters; those between renters and owners, and buyers and sellers; and the "Let Pass" forms used by Amerindians and whites to go through one another's territory—these were the bread and butter of Franklin's printing business in its early years and remained an important source of revenue thereafter.

In 1997, a leather-bound volume of nearly three hundred loan office deeds printed by Benjamin Franklin in 1729 came to light. By the favor of its owner, Jay Snider, and the bibliographer Keith Arbour, I examined the volume at the American Philosophical Society in Philadelphia. Printed on beautiful, over-sized folio sheets, the deeds, when folded, made two pages, each the size of a normal folio. Each sheet was printed on both front and back, so that each contains four folio-size loan office mortgage indentures. The extraordinarily large sheets were difficult to print; the pressman would have to have been especially careful with them. The normal policy with oversized folio sheets was to cut the sheet before printing it. But Franklin intended to bind these sheets into a volume so the loan office could conveniently keep track of its records. A double-size sheet could be securely sewn into a volume, but an unfolded sheet would have to be insecurely glued. The volume, in a leather binding done by William Davies in 1729, was the loan office's permanent record.

The volume was a better and easier way to maintain records than the previous method, in which numerous handwritten loan office forms were kept loose and were frequently misplaced. Franklin's beautiful volume of nearly three hundred loan office indentures is a monumental record of entrepreneurial enterprise by the young printer. Before he began printing it, Franklin must have proposed the idea for such a volume to the loan office managers. Further revealing his talent for efficiency and organization, he also printed a half-page sheet with an alphabet to use as an index.

If we add handbills used for advertising to the job printing done by Franklin, we can account for most of the printing done before Franklin and Meredith established a newspaper. The partners managed to survive and make money partially by bartering: William Hutchins paid his bill in dried venison (7 May 1729), Stephen Barton and Andrew Hannah paid in topsails (1729), William

Jones paid by working for the firm (1729), the merchant William Mogridge paid with a piece of linen (1729), and shopkeeper Evan Morgan bartered some of his private eight-pence bills in payment for printing them (June 1729). The loan office would have paid in welcome cash for its large purchase of a bound folio volume of land indenture forms.

In 1729, besides various forms and advertisements, Franklin and Meredith printed nine works. In addition to the Delaware paper currency, they were paid to print three publications: two were religious pamphlets and one was Ralph Sandiford's short antislavery book (seventy-four pages), *The Practice of the Times*.[28] At their own risk, they printed Isaac Watts's *Psalms of David*, which sold disappointingly slowly. Naturally, they wanted to print an almanac—that staple of colonial American printers' sales. Franklin probably suggested to Thomas Godfrey, who was sharing the house with Franklin, that he do the mathematics for an almanac. Franklin and Meredith printed and sold Godfrey's almanac from 1729 through 1732. Perhaps Franklin added some of his own writing to Godfrey's almanacs, but no Godfrey almanac for these years is extant. Franklin's own *Modest Enquiry into the Nature and Necessity of a Paper Currency* was the 1729 best-seller. Beginning on 2 October 1729, the partners printed the *Pennsylvania Gazette*.

Assembly Printer

Franklin knew that the printer who had the government business was assured a steady income, and he correctly judged that he was the best printer in Philadelphia. He and Meredith petitioned the Pennsylvania Assembly on 18 February 1728/9 asking "to print for the province." He did not mention the application in the *Autobiography*, and indeed, he there wrote that "I shall never *ask*, never *refuse*, nor ever *resign* an Office" (A 111). As we shall see, he violated that statement in petitioning for the public printing. The Pennsylvania Assembly ignored Franklin and Meredith's petition and again selected Andrew Bradford (22 February 1728/9) as its printer. Shortly afterward, Franklin thought of a way to suggest to the assemblymen that they had made a mistake. He said in the *Autobiography* that Bradford "had printed an Address of the House to the Governor in a coarse blundering manner." Bradford had printed the address of the House of Representatives to Governor Patrick Gordon (29 March 1729) with old, worn-out types that often did not make a complete impression, so that parts of the printed letters were missing. In addition, Bradford's layout and typography were, as usual, graceless. Bradford had a puny caption for the address and no imprint. Franklin seized the opportunity, taking the time and trouble and precious (to a struggling printer) paper on an ostensibly frivolous project. Franklin and Meredith "reprinted it elegantly and correctly, and sent one to every Member. They were sensible of the Difference, it strengthen'd the Hands of our Friends in the House, and they voted us their Printers for the Year ensuing" (A 64). Though Bradford's broadside survives, no copy of Franklin and Meredith's "elegant" printing is extant. But Bradford's next government imprints had a better quality type and inking, an elaborate, ornamented caption title, and a concluding colophon—all no doubt in imitation of Franklin's lost imprint.[29]

Andrew Hamilton was elected Speaker of the House on 14 October 1729. When the printer of the minutes for the 1729–30 legislative session was chosen, Hamilton was in power. On 30 January 1729/30, the Pennsylvania Assembly elected Franklin and Meredith to print the *Votes and Proceedings* of the legislature for 1729–30. Though the elegantly reprinted broadside address of the representatives must have, like Franklin's advocacy of paper currency, been a consideration, Hamilton's patronage was the determining factor. Franklin's later partner, David Hall, explained to William Strahan on 26 May 1767 that Pennsylvania followed the House of Commons in its practice of voting for the printer: "though the Votes lay with the House of Commons . . . they generally left it to their Speaker to appoint the Person." On 14 February 1729/30, the assembly voted that "Benjamin Franklin and Hugh Meredith print the Acts of Assembly that have been passed this Session." But even printing the *Laws* as well as the *Votes and Proceedings* did not necessarily mean that the partners would receive all the province printing business, including the proclamations or the paper currency.

Though Franklin has been often called the "official printer" to the province, there was no such title. It is, however, a customary and convenient identification—if used with a caveat. Franklin did not call himself "Printer to the Province" for six more years, when he thus identified himself on the Pennsylvania Council's *Proclamation* of 17 September 1736. Even that title, like "Provincial Printer," could be challenged if one did not have the support of the Speaker, so it was best simply to ignore such titles.[30] A printer to the assembly did not necessarily make more money printing the votes and the laws than printing pamphlets for private individuals, but the position guaranteed some income every year. What was best was that government printing paid promptly at the end of the last assembly session for the year, whereas many persons allowed their accounts to run for decades, despite being dunned for payment.

1730 IMPRINTS

During the first half of 1730, Franklin and Meredith made use of the latter's background to print three pieces in Welsh: two ballads and a religious tract. Franklin had begun studying German and printed three short books in German for Conrad Beissel: a pamphlet on marriage, a collection of hymns for the Ephrata community (the religious settlement Beissel founded), and another collection for the community, which included a number of his poems. Besides legal forms, the partners printed Thomas Ball's tables for instruction in French. For the Pennsylvania legislature, they published the *Votes and Proceedings*, the *Laws*, and speeches by the governor. After the partnership's dissolution in mid-1730, Franklin reprinted Ralph Sandiford's antislavery tract with a new title, *The Mys-*

tery of Iniquity. Near the end of the year, Franklin printed both John Jerman's well-established almanac and Godfrey's almanac. At the end of 1730, the Presbyterian Synod paid Franklin to print its much contested agreement to adopt the Westminister Confession of Faith.

About 1730 Samuel Vernon finally asked Franklin to remit him the money he had collected in New York in 1724. Franklin replied, confessed he had spent the money, but promised that he would return it with interest (which had not been specified previously) within a year. The easygoing creditor Vernon agreed, thus temporarily relieving Franklin.

THE PARTNERSHIP ENDS

Catastrophe struck in the late spring of 1730. The merchant whom Meredith's father had hired to import the press and types had been paid only half the charge—the remainder was due. The merchant "grew impatient and su'd us all. We gave Bail, but saw that if the Money could not be rais'd in time, the Suit must come to a Judgment and Execution, and our hopeful Prospects must with us be ruined, as the Press and Letters must be sold for Payment, perhaps at half-Price." Franklin's predicament became known among his close friends, and two well-off Junto members, William Coleman and Robert Grace, "came to me separately unknown to each other, and without any Application from me, offering each of them to advance me all the Money that should be necessary to enable me to take the whole Business upon my self if that should be practicable, but they did not like my continuing the Partnership with Meredith, who as they said was often seen drunk in the Streets, and playing at low Games in Alehouses, much to our Discredit" (A 65).

Franklin wanted to accept, but he was obliged to his partner Hugh Meredith and to his father Simon Meredith for their intentions. Franklin waited until the case was about to come to judgment. On 14 July 1730, he asked Hugh Meredith if his father would be more comfortable if Meredith were the sole proprietor of the press. Perhaps, suggested Franklin, he "is unwilling to advance to you and me what he would for you alone: If that is the Case, tell me, and I will resign the whole to you and go about my Business." Meredith replied no, that his father's expectations had come to naught and that he was "really unable" to pay. Meredith was "unwilling to distress his father farther." Meredith now thought that it was a mistake for him "to come to Town and put myself at 30 Years of Age an Apprentice to learn a new Trade." He had been bred a farmer and was thinking of going to North Carolina where land was cheap. He would return to farming. Meredith proposed, "If you will take the Debts of the Company upon you, return to my Father the hundred Pound he has advanc'd, pay my little personal Debts, and give me Thirty Pounds and a new Saddle, I will relinquish the Partnership and leave the whole in your Hands." Franklin agreed. The proposal was drawn up and signed on 14 July 1730 (A 66). Meredith probably moved out of Simon Edgell's house that he and Franklin were renting at 139 Market Street shortly after.

According to the *Autobiography*, Franklin borrowed half of what was necessary from Coleman and half from Grace, paid off Hugh Meredith and his father, and proceeded with business on his own. Presumably Franklin repaid Coleman and Grace within the next several years, but the only evidence is in Franklin's Ledger A&B, where he recorded on 27 June 1733: "Paid Mr. Grace £10 in Part of his Bond." Could that suggest that Coleman and Grace did not actually loan him the money but that they signed a bond for his debt? Perhaps so. Franklin says little about his shaky finances in the *Autobiography*, and almost all the entries in Franklin's accounts for the early years record only the small debts that customers owned Franklin. One account, however, concerns a debt Franklin owed.

Paper was the most expensive ongoing expense for a printer. Franklin purchased forty-six reams of paper for £27.12 on 4 July 1730 from the merchant John Beard, paying him £14 of the total. Four days later, Franklin remitted an additional £6.12; the next day, 9 July, he paid Beard £2 more and gave him a promissory note for £4.10, besides agreeing to pay 10 shillings to Mr. Campion, "which will be in Full." At this time, in the second week of July, the partnership's debts came to a crisis. Ten days after buying the paper from Beard, the partnership ended. Ten days later, 24 July, Franklin was able to pay the remaining £4.10 to Beard; and finally, on 5 September, he paid Mr. Campion the 10 shillings. It may be significant that all the debts and credits surviving in the earliest accounts are in Franklin's name alone. Evidently Meredith had little to do with running the business. Perhaps merchants were unwilling to trust him.

Franklin said that after the dissolution of the partnership, Hugh Meredith soon left for North Carolina, "from whence he sent me next Year two long Letters, containing the best Account that had been given of that Country, the Climate, Soil, Husbandry, etc. for in those Matters he was very judicious" (A 66). These appeared in the *Pennsylvania Gazette* on 6 and 13 May 1731. Franklin does not tell us that by 26 May 1739, Hugh Meredith had returned to Philadelphia and was borrowing money from him. Franklin did not want to record distress and failure in the *Autobiography*. From Franklin's accounts, however, we learn more of Meredith's life. He evidently married in 1740: on 10 February 1739/40 he borrowed money for "A Pair of Pumps for the Wedding," and the following month Franklin loaned him a series of amounts for various household items, including a bedstead, a feather bed, and a pair of blankets. Franklin frequently loaned him small sums over the next decade. Finally, Franklin noted on 3 December 1749 that Meredith had been collecting rags for him and still owed him £13.13.14$\frac{1}{2}$, and that Franklin had supplied him with books worth about £30 to sell in the country, "since which I have not seen him nor received any thing from him." Then Meredith, like so many of Franklin's friends from his youth, disappeared from the records.

SIXTEEN

The Busy-Body

Thus, Sir, I have all the Trouble and Pesterment of Children, without the Pleasure of—calling them my own."—"Patience," one of Franklin's feminine persona.—Busy-Body No. 4.

ON TUESDAY, 4 FEBRUARY 1728/9, one week after "Martha Careful" and "Caelia Shortface" complained of Keimer's indelicacy in reprinting an article on abortion, the twenty-three-year-old Benjamin Franklin began the Busy-Body essay series. He meant to popularize Andrew Bradford's *American Weekly Mercury* in order to assure the failure of Samuel Keimer's *Universal Instructor in all Arts and Sciences: and Pennsylvania Gazette.* Bradford welcomed the essays, for they would increase the circulation of his newspaper and would probably harm his competitor, Keimer. Franklin wrote the first five Busy-Body essays and also the eighth; his Junto friend Joseph Breintnall wrote the sixth and seventh, and continued them from April through 25 September, when Franklin and Hugh Meredith bought Keimer's failing newspaper.

No. 1: INTRODUCTION

In the first Busy-Body, 4 February, Franklin established his persona as the *censor morum,* though one who lacks the superiority usually associated with that traditional critic of persons, manners, and society. Franklin mocked Bradford's usual form of address to the public ("Courteous Readers"): "Mr. Andrew Bradford, I design this to acquaint you, that I, who have long been one of your *Courteous Readers,* have lately entertain'd some Thoughts of setting up for an Author my Self; not out of the least Vanity, I assure you, or Desire of showing my Parts, but purely for the Good of my Country." Franklin thus suggests the Busy-Body is a vain naïf, fooling himself about his motives.

The Busy-Body stated the adverse conditions under which colonial newspapers suffered: "I have often observ'd with Concern, that your Mercury is not always equally entertaining. The Delay of Ships expected in, and want of fresh Advices from Europe, make it frequently very Dull; and I find the Freezing of our River has the same Effect on News as on Trade." The charge of dullness echoes John Checkley's opening attack in the *New-England Courant* on John Campbell, though Franklin blamed Bradford's dullness not on the editor but the weather and the lack of "fresh Advices" (i.e., fresh newspapers to reprint).

Franklin refrained from criticizing Bradford's comparative lack of local and American news; had he done so, Bradford might not have printed the Busy-Body.

"With more Concern have I continually observ'd the growing Vices and Follies of my Country-folk. And tho' Reformation is properly the concern of every Man; that is, Every one ought to mend One; yet 'tis too true in this Case, that what is every Body's Business is no Body's Business, and the Business is done accordingly." The play on the words *every Body*, *no Body*, and *Business* reflects Franklin's delight in such wordplay, which he admired in Swift's *Tale of a Tub*, in Nathaniel Gardner's essays (especially Gardner's reply to the shy bachelor who wanted the lady to "pop" the question), and in John Wise's "Apology."

In effect, Franklin's censor morum promised to be a spiteful gossip columnist who would reveal secrets of everyone. "I, therefore, upon mature Deliberation, think fit to take no Body's Business wholly into my own Hands; and, out of Zeal for the Publick Good, design to erect my Self into a Kind of *Censor Morum*; proposing with your Allowance, to make Use of the Weekly Mercury as a Vehicle in which my Remonstrances shall be convey'd to the World."

Revealing his opinion of human nature, the Busy-Body/Franklin claimed people enjoyed criticizing others. "I am sensible I have, in this Particular, undertaken a very unthankful Office, and expect little besides my Labour for my Pains. Nay, 'tis probable I may displease a great Number of your Readers, who will not very well like to pay 10s. a Year for being told of their Faults. But as most People delight in Censure when they themselves are not the Objects of it, if any are offended at my publickly exposing their private Vices, I promise they shall have the Satisfaction, in a very little Time, of seeing their good Friends and Neighbours in the same Circumstances."

Though men had constituted the primary audience for periodicals, women were increasingly important, and Franklin appealed to them. "However, let the Fair Sex be assur'd, that I shall always treat them and their Affairs with the utmost Decency and Respect." The Busy-Body implicitly contrasted himself with Keimer's indelicately printing Chambers's article on abortion. After trying to attract women readers, Franklin appealed to persons born in America: "'Tis certain, that no Country in the World produces naturally finer Spirits than ours, Men of Genius for every kind of Science, and capable of acquiring to Perfection every Qualification that is in Esteem among Mankind." Then he lamented the state of American culture, particularly the lack of good books in Philadelphia—a situation he would try to remedy within two years by starting the Library Company: "But as few here have the Advantage of good Books, for want of which, good Conversation is still more scarce, it would doubtless have been very acceptable to your Readers, if, instead of an old out-of-date Article from Muscovy or Hungary, you had entertained them with some well-chosen Extract from a good Author. This I shall sometimes do, when I happen to have nothing of my own to say that I think of more Consequence."

Finally he turned to the *Spectator*-style opening of identifying the persona—something he did initially in the Silence Dogood series. Now he dismissed it as a hackneyed convention: "'Tis like by this Time you have a Curiosity to be acquainted with my Name and Character." He refused to say anything about himself and ridiculed the usual request for encouragement. "As I have not obs-erv'd the Criticks to be more favourable on this Account, I shall always avoid saying any Thing of the Kind; and conclude with telling you, that if you send me a Bottle of Ink and a Quire of Paper by the Bearer, you may depend on hearing further from Sir, Your most humble Servant, THE Busy-Body."

No. 2: "Ridentius" vs. "Eugenius"

On 11 February 1728/9, Busy-Body No. 2 began with an anecdote Franklin proba-bly created: "Monsieur Rochefoucauld tells us somewhere in his Memoirs, that the Prince of Conde delighted much in Ridicule; and us'd frequently to shut himself up for a Half a Day together in his Chamber with a Gentleman that was his Favourite, purposely to divert himself with examining what was the Foible or ridiculous side of every Noted Person in the Court. That Gentleman said afterwards in some Company, that he thought nothing was more ridiculous in any Body, than this same Humour in the Prince; and I am somewhat inclin'd to be of his Opinion." Franklin constructed a character fulfilling Rochefou-cauld's foolish weakness, "Ridentius," which, based on the Latin *rideo*, suggests a mocking person. "What a contemptible Figure does he make with his Train of paultry Admirers? This Wight shall give himself an Hours Diversion with the Cock of a Man's Hat, the Heels of his Shoes, an unguarded Expression in his Discourse, or even some Personal Defect; and the Height of his low Ambition is to put some One of the Company to the Blush, who perhaps must pay an equal Share of the Reckoning with himself." Franklin had some nice touches in the character and its continuation; the witty contrast in "the Height of his low Ambition"; and the anaphora of the repeated clauses beginning with *if*. Con-temporary English literary journalism frequently printed such character sketches, and Franklin's is neither superior nor distinctive.

Franklin opposed to Ridentius a man of feeling whose name, Eugenius (which suggests a good character), and personality echoed a person created by Addison and anticipated one created by David Hume.[1] Franklin wrote: "How different from this Character is that of the good-natur'd gay Eugenius? who never spoke yet but with a Design to divert and please; and who was never yet baulk'd in his Intention. Eugenius takes more Delight in applying the Wit of his Friends, than in being admir'd himself: And if any one of the Company is so unfortunate as to be touch'd a little too nearly, he will make Use of some inge-nious Artifice to turn the Edge of Ridicule another Way, chusing rather to make even himself a publick Jest, than be at the Pain of seeing his Friend in Confu-sion." Franklin would have liked to think of himself as a version of "Eugenius."

The concluding paragraph again portrayed unpleasant persons. "Among the

Tribe of Laughers I reckon the pretty Gentlemen that write Satyrs, and carry them about in their Pockets, reading them themselves in all Company they happen into; taking an Advantage of the ill Taste of the Town, to make themselves famous for a Pack of paultry low Nonsense, for which they deserve to be kick'd, rather than admir'd, by all who have the least Tincture of Politeness. These I take to be the most incorrigible of all my Readers; nay I expect they will be squabbling at the BUSY-BODY himself: However the only Favour he begs of them is this; that if they cannot controul their over-bearing Itch of Scribbling, let him be attack'd in downright BITING LYRICKS; for there is no Satyr he Dreads half so much as an Attempt towards a Panegyric."

The prose itself is well done, with a series of "t" alliterations and a series of plosive "p" and "k" sounds expressing contempt, but the subject matter (manners and morals), typical of the eighteenth-century periodical essay, is of little modern interest. Nathaniel Gardner had expressed the sententiae on the severest satire, and Franklin had repeated it when ridiculing the New England funeral elegy in Silence Dogood No. 7.

No. 3: On Virtue

The third Busy-Body essay (18 February) turned to a favorite Franklin subject, the nature of virtue. A major subject of the classical writers, as well as the eighteenth-century moral philosophers, virtue, or what constituted perfection in humans, may have been first presented as a talk in the Junto, where it might well have answered the question of what constituted perfection in humans (see Chapter 14). "It is said that the Persians in their ancient Constitution, had publick Schools in which Virtue was taught as a Liberal Art or Science; and it is certainly of more Consequence to a Man that he has learnt to govern his Passions; in spite of Temptation to be just in his Dealings, to be Temperate in his Pleasures, to support himself with Fortitude under his Misfortunes, to behave with Prudence in all Affairs and in every Circumstance of Life; I say, it is of much more real Advantage to him to be thus qualified, than to be a Master of all the Arts and Sciences in the World beside" (1:118–19).

The Busy-Body's thesis was: "*Virtue alone is sufficient to make a Man Great, Glorious and Happy.*" Franklin attempted to prove it with a character sketch of Cato. The name alluded both to the Roman censor and to the hero of Addison's play *Cato* (which Franklin had quoted in his "Articles of Belief"). The pseudonym enjoyed further popularity from its use in the Whig periodical essays, "Cato's Letters."[2]

As E. C. Cook noted, the initial appearance of Cato echoed the *Tatler*'s characterization of various people by their knocking on the door: Franklin wrote, "Methought he rapp'd in such a peculiar Manner, as seem'd of itself to express, there was One who deserv'd as well as desir'd Admission."[3] Cato had some characteristics of his father, Josiah Franklin. "His strict Justice and known Impartiality make him the Arbitrator and Decider of all Differences that arise for

Miles around him, without putting his Neighbours to the Charge, Perplexity and Uncertainty of Law-Suits" (1:120). Franklin similarly described Josiah in the *Autobiography*: "His great Excellence lay in a sound Understanding and solid Judgment in prudential Matters, both in private & public Affairs. . . . He was also much consulted by private Persons about their Affairs when any Difficulty occur'd, & frequently chosen an Arbitrator between contending Parties" (A 8). Like Franklin's Cato, the "Straitness of his Circumstances" kept Josiah from being employed in any major public office.

Cato also had some characteristics of Franklin. "He appear'd in the plainest Country Garb; his Great Coat was coarse and looked old and thread-bare; his Linnen was homespun." This may describe Franklin in 1729, when he was intent on saving money. Keimer, as we will shortly see, commented on his "threadbare . . . Great Coat." Cato's garb also anticipates the description of Father Abraham in the "Way to Wealth" who, at the end, leaves the vendue "resolved to wear my old" coat "a little longer" (7:350). Appearance as an indication of character often appears in Franklin's writings and in his behavior. Cato's countenance, his expression, "manifested the true Greatness of his Mind." Cato's virtue appeared in his face. Franklin mentioned his own "Habit" and "Countenance" in his Junto speech "On the Providence of God in the Government of the World" (1:264). An appreciation of the implications of dress appeared in his self-presentation in France in 1778, as his letters concerning his appearance testify (23:298; 29:613). The twenty-three-year-old Franklin also wrote of Cato: "The Consciousness of his own innate Worth and unshaken Integrity renders him calm and undaunted in the Presence of the most Great and Powerful, and upon the most extraordinary Occasions" (1:119–20). That might well describe Franklin's attitude and, certainly, his appearance during his ordeal in the Cockpit on 29 January 1774 while being castigated by the British authorities as a scapegoat for America.[4]

The appreciation of Cato, the man of virtue, presented an ideal Franklin would try to fulfill: "His generous Hospitality to Strangers according to his Ability, his Goodness, his Charity, his Courage in the Cause of the Oppressed, his Fidelity in Friendship, his Humility, his Honesty and Sincerity, his Moderation and his Loyalty to the Government, his Piety, his Temperance, his Love to Mankind, his Magnanimity, his Publick-spiritedness, and in fine, his *Consumate Virtue*, make him justly deserve to be esteem'd the Glory of his Country" (1:120). Franklin did not, of course, succeed in becoming the man of virtue that he portrayed, but he tried.

Franklin continued the Busy-Body: "Who would not rather chuse, if it were in his Choice, to merit the above Character, than be the richest, the most learned, or the most powerful Man in the Province without it?" Most people would rather be the richest or the most powerful person in Pennsylvania, but perhaps not the idealistic young Franklin. Or was he simply trying to promote learning and virtue? " 'Tis true, we love the handsome, we applaud the Learned, and we fear the Rich and Powerful; but we even *Worship and adore* the Virtuous" (emphasis mine). Franklin argued that the achievement of virtue was the goal most worth pursuing: "If we were as industrious to become Good, as to make ourselves Great, we should become really Great by being Good, and the Number of valuable Men would be much increased; but it is a Grand Mistake to think of being Great without Goodness; and I pronounce it as certain, *that there was never yet a truly Great Man that was not at the same Time truly Virtuous.*" The chiasmus (good, great; great, good) and the "g" alliteration are typical of Franklin's playful style.

Though Franklin seems unrealistic and idealistic, if not actually naive, in making the *handsome, learned, rich,* and *powerful* all less celebrated than the *virtuous,* his use of "Worship and adore" abruptly raised the ante. His readers had been thinking of their own circle of acquaintances, but Franklin shifted the scale from one's own immediate circle to all known persons in history. Franklin's "Worship and adore" calls up Jesus, Muhammad, Confucius, and other great prophets and ethical figures of the world. We eighteenth- (and twenty-first) century realists suddenly find ourselves undercut. We do not know who were the richest, the most powerful, the most learned, or the most handsome persons in Jerusalem at the time of Christ, though we all know Christ. Nor do we know the Middle East potentates who flourished at the time of Muhammad. Franklin argued, in effect, that virtue is the surest road to fame, and he proved that men of the greatest fame are those who possessed the greatest virtue.

In addition to the great prophets, Franklin may have also been suggesting the doctrine of euhemerism, a popular belief in the eighteenth century, which held that the classical gods of Greece and Rome were originally persons of virtue who made great discoveries for mankind. The euhemeristic idea was later applied to Franklin by an anonymous author who celebrated the invention of "Mr. Franklin's *Stoves.*"[5]

Franklin's Cato expressed his ideal of the virtuous man—an ordinary person of barely sufficient income who was just and honorable in his dealings with all men. In writing the obituary of the Library Company member James Merrewether (22 April 1742) and in befriending the former galley slave Pierre-Andre Gargaz and printing the slave's *Project of Universal and Perpetual Peace* (1782), Franklin proved that his idealistic—even, perhaps, naive—appreciation of poor and disadvantaged persons remained with him throughout his life.

Turning from idealism, Franklin took up another character-type, "Cretico," a crafty, "sowre Philosopher," who was contrasted with Cato. The Busy-Body asked if Cretico would ever meet with that "unfeign'd Respect and warm Goodwill that all Men" have for Cato. "Wilt thou never understand that the cringing, mean, submissive Deportment of thy Dependents, is (like the Worship paid by Indians to the Devil) rather thro' Fear of the Harm thou may'st do to them, than out of Gratitude for the Favours they have receiv'd of thee?" Franklin echoed Thomas Pope Blount's attack on the idea of hell ("like the Worship paid by Indians to the Devil"), which he had cited in the 15 April 1723 *Courant*. "Thou art not wholly void of Virtue; there are many good Things in thee, and many good Actions reported of thee. Be advised by thy Friend: Neglect those musty Authors; let them be cover'd with Dust, and moulder on their proper Shelves; and do thou apply thy self to a Study much more profitable, The Knowledge of Mankind, and of thy Self."

Keimer applied the satire of Cretico to himself, and in the 25 February *Universal Instructor* he foolishly gave the Busy-Body excellent publicity by titling his piece, "Hue and Cry after the Busy-Body." He charged that the Busy-Body violated "Decency and Humanity" with the "gross Descriptions" that readers were tempted "to figure out and apply." If readers had not read the last Busy-Body before, they certainly did if they read Keimer's reply.[6]

NO. 4: CLASS CONFLICT AND "PATIENCE"

The fourth Busy-Body (25 February 1728/9) combined styles, subjects, and themes. After claiming again that his "chief Purpose" was "to inculcate the noble Principles of Virtue, and depreciate Vice of every kind," Busy-Body/Franklin implied that the "greatest Men among us" were selfish villains. He introduced the satire with a method that he frequently used thereafter, the rhetorical disclaimer, saying that he (the editor) did not believe such things himself but would print them in order to keep the "Mob" and the "Generality" reading. This Busy-Body essay also showed Franklin's use of class-conscious differences in colonial politics: "There are a Set of Great Names in the Province, who are the common Objects of Popular Dislike. If I can now and then overcome my Reluctance, and prevail with my self to Satyrize a little, one of these Gentlemen, the Expectation of meeting with such a Gratification, will induce many to read me through, who would otherwise proceed immediately to the Foreign News."

James Logan, Isaac Norris, David Barclay, and other older wealthy merchants, who feared popular opinion and who repeatedly reported to the Penns that Philadelphia was a town under mob rule, must have thought that they were being indicted.[7] Using a rhetorical strategy that put them in a position where they could not complain, Franklin added that "the greatest Men among us have a sincere Love for their Country, not withstanding its Ingratitude, and the Insinuations of the Envious and Malicious to the contrary, so I doubt not but they will chearfully tolerate me in the Liberty I design to take for the End above mentioned." Franklin's class-conscious threat to attack the province's great names must have titillated the *Mercury*'s readers. No such material had ever appeared previously in a Pennsylvania paper. The Busy-Body had been interesting before, but this issue displayed—for the first time in Philadelphia—Franklin's news-making genius. The Busy-Body made readers wonder (and some fear), what would come later in this essay and in those following?

Changing the subject, the Busy-Body introduced a letter from one of his delightful feminine personae, a much put-upon tolerant female shopkeeper,

"Patience." Despite being remorselessly pestered, Patience is a long-suffering, yet loquacious merchant, whose breathless sentences are connected with repeated *if*s, *and*s, *but*s, *for*s and *tho*s. Franklin created a colloquial, rambling style for the friendly Patience, who was too tolerant of her old friend:

> You must know I am a single Woman, and keep a Shop in this Town for a Livelyhood. There is a certain Neighbour of mine, who is really agreeable Company enough, and with whom I have had an Intimacy of some Time standing; But of late she makes her Visits so excessively often, and stays so very long every Visit, that I am tir'd out of all Patience. I have no Manner of Time at all to my self; and you, who seem to be a wise Man, must needs be sensible that every Person has little Secrets and Privacies that are not proper to be expos'd even to the nearest Friend. Now I cannot do the least Thing in the World, but she must know all about it; and it is a Wonder I have found an Opportunity to write you this Letter. My Misfortune is, that I respect her very well, and know not how to disoblige her so much as to tell her I should be glad to have less of her Company; for if I should once hint such a Thing, I am afraid she would resent it so as never to darken my Door again.

Franklin here recorded an early version of a classic complaint concerning Americans. They are too sensitive to the foolish demands of others and too democratic. James Fenimore Cooper, Alexis de Tocqueville, and D. H. Lawrence[8] are among the numerous commentators who followed Franklin in objecting to Americans' putting up with bores and vexatious fools rather than offend them:

> But, alas, Sir, I have not yet told you half my Afflictions. She has two Children that are just big enough to run about and do pretty Mischief: These are continually along with Mamma, either in my Room or Shop, if I have never so many Customers or People with me about Business. Sometimes they pull the goods off my low Shelves down to the Ground, and perhaps where one of them has just been making Water; My Friend takes up the Stuff, and cries, *Eh! thou little wicked mischievous Rogue!—But however, it has done no great Damage; 'tis only wet a little*; and so puts it up upon the Shelf again. Sometimes they get to my Cask of Nails behind the Counter, and divert themselves, to my great Vexation, with mixing my Ten-penny and Eight-penny and Four-penny together. I endeavour to conceal my Uneasiness as much as possible, and with a grave Look go to Sorting them out. She cries, *Don't thee trouble thy self, Neighbour: Let them play a little; I'll put all to rights my self before I go*. But Things are never so put to rights but that I find a great deal of Work to do after they are gone.

Then Franklin introduced a wonderfully bawdy allusion—characteristic of him but unusual in eighteenth-century journalism. "Thus, Sir, I have all the Trouble and Pesterment of Children, without the Pleasure of—calling them my own; and they are now so us'd to being here that they will be content no where else." (Franklin's usage of the unusual but easily understood *pesterment* is among the few citations of the word in the *OED*.) Franklin also introduces the first complaint that Americans spoil their children—later a common observation by foreign visitors.[9] The prattling, too tolerant Patience, who would like to have had the pleasure of sexual intercourse and who, we later learn, enjoys flirting with a "handsome Gentleman" but is denied that pleasure by the incessant company of her lady friend and the friend's children, is the most effective persona in the Busy-Body essays—another example of Franklin's superb feminine personae.

As the Busy-Body, Franklin commented on the plight of Patience: "Indeed, 'tis well enough, as it happens, that she is come, to shorten this Complaint which I think is full long enough already, and probably would otherwise have been as long again." Franklin not only used various personae, each with its own characteristics, but he was aware of the different stylistic implications of each speaker: "However, I must confess I cannot help pitying my Correspondent's Case, and in her Behalf exhort the Visitor to remember and consider the Words of the Wise Man, *Withdraw thy Foot from the House of thy Neighbour least he grow weary of thee, and so hate thee*" (Proverbs 25:17; the slight misquotation, "thy neighbour's house; lest he be," shows that Franklin cited from memory). Franklin also comments on those who allow annoying visitors to take advantage of them. "Men are subjected to various Inconveniences merely through lack of a small Share of Courage, which is a Quality very necessary in the common Occurrences of Life, as well as in a Battle. How many Impertinences do we daily suffer with great Uneasiness because we have not Courage enough to discover our Dislike? And why may not a Man use the Boldness and Freedom of telling his Friends that their long Visits sometimes incommode him?" To reinforce his point, Franklin made up an observation on "the Turkish Manner of entertaining Visitors," which he attributes to "an Author of unquestionable Veracity" (himself!). Turks perfume the beards of their guests as a sign that business is over and that the visitor may (and should) now leave. The Turkish custom enables the hosts to escape using "that Piece of Hypocrisy so common in the World, of pressing those to stay longer with you, whom perhaps in your Heart you wish a great Way off for having troubled you so long already." But Franklin knew that such polite cant was necessary for society to function smoothly, and he excluded lies made for the sake of politeness from his seventh virtue, sincerity, in part 2 of his *Autobiography*.

Franklin appended a mock "Advertisement" to the essay, attacking Sir William Keith, the former governor who had misled him. Franklin wrote: "I give Notice that I am now actually compiling, and design to publish in a short Time, the true History of the Rise, Growth and Progress of the renowned Tiff-Club." Perhaps the Tiff Club, Keith's political club of tradesmen, had begun to break up since he had left for England, though Isaac Norris thought on 28 October 1728 that it was still viable. But if it had any bite left in April 1729, Franklin was pulling its teeth. "All Persons who are acquainted with any Facts, Circumstances, Characters, Transactions, &c. which will be requisite to the Perfecting and Embellishment of the said Work, are desired to communicate the same to the Author, and direct their Letters to be left with the Printer hereof." An added sentence, saying, "The Letter sign'd *Would-be-something* is come to hand," may imply that Keith was a "*Would-be-something*," but a real nothing.

At least one contemporary discerned a political undercurrent throughout the fourth Busy-Body. Franklin noted in No. 8 that "A certain Gentleman has taken a great Deal of Pains to write a KEY to the Letter in my No. 4 wherein he has ingeniously converted a gentle Satyr upon tedious and impertinent Visitants into a Libel on some in the Government." Though the essay had nothing to do with Keimer, he foolishly responded in the *Pennsylvania Gazette* for 25 February, objected that character sketches could be applied to particular individuals, and claimed that the Busy-Body was displaying malice and prejudice.

No. 5: On Superstitions

The fifth Busy-Body (4 March 1728/9) spoofed popular superstitions concerning extrasensory perception. "I have lately enter'd into an Intimacy with the extraordinary Person who some Time since wrote me the following Letter; and who, having a Wonderful Faculty that enables him [to] discover the most secret Iniquity, is capable of giving me great Assistance in my designed Work of Reformation." The pseudonym "Bunyan" as the author of the supposed letter to the Busy-Body reinforced three subjects: New England witchcraft, John Bunyan, and the charlatan Duncan Campbell (1680?–1730). Bunyan/Franklin began: "You must know, that such have been the Circumstances of my Life, and such were the marvelous Concurrences of my Birth, that I have not only a Faculty of discovering the Actions of Persons that are absent or asleep; but even of the Devil himself in many of his secret Workings, in the various Shapes, Habits and Names of Men and Women." The reader must smile when he reads that the second-sighted Bunyan knows the actions of sleeping persons. "And having travel'd and conversed much and met but with a very few of the same Perceptions and Qualifications, I can recommend my Self to you as the most useful Man you can correspond with."

Franklin made fun of the diction and circumlocutions used by the supposed adept. "My Father's Father (for we had no Grandfathers in our Family) was the same John Bunyan that writ that memorable book The Pilgrim's Progress, who had in some Degree a natural Faculty of Second Sight." Franklin linked superstition and religion. All Bunyan's descendants had the faculty of divination, but it "probably had been nearly extinct in our particular Branch, had not my Father been a Traveler. He lived in his youthful Days in New England. There he married, and there was born my elder Brother, who had so much of this Faculty, as to discover Witches in some of their occult Performances." Bunyan/Franklin said that he was in such demand as a necromancer that he had changed his name and lived obscurely. He closed, however, by saying that through the Busy-Body he intended to send in letters to expose evil.

The Busy-Body said he approved of Bunyan's "Prudence in chusing to live obscurely." He then adapted an anecdote told by Claudius Aelianus in *De natura animalium*, which he knew from *Spectator* No. 579. Franklin substituted a monkey for the special breed of dog, and made the belief that the talented monkey could tell a virgin a matter of popular superstition rather than a fact. Unlike Aelianus and the *Spectator*, who both pretend to believe the story, Franklin's Busy-Body persona is more of an ironic realist: "I remember the Fate of my poor Monkey: He had an ill-natur'd Trick of grinning and chattering at every Thing he saw in Pettycoats. My ignorant Country Neighbours got a Notion that Pugg snarl'd by instinct at every Female who had lost her Virginity. This was no sooner generally believ'd than he was condemn'd to Death; By whom I could never learn, but he was assassinated in the Night, barbarously stabb'd and mangled in a Thousand Places, and left hanging dead on one of my Gate posts, where I found him the next Morning." The piece ends with Franklin's reply to Keimer's attack on the Busy-Body in the 25 February *Gazette*.

Believing that the Busy-Body's satires in No. 5 and in Breintnall's No. 6 (11 March) were directed at him, Keimer replied with two pieces in the 13 March *Pennsylvania Gazette*. He knew that Breintnall had by then joined Franklin in writing the Busy-Body series, and in "An Answer to the BUSY-BODY," he charged,

> "But prithee tell me, art thou mad,
> To mix good Writing with the Bad?
> Fie, Sir, let all be of a Piece,
> Spectators, Swans, or Joseph's Geese:
> You hinted at me in your Paper,
> Which now has made me draw my Rapier."

"Joseph's Geese" alluded to Breintnall's writing. The doggerel concluded that all the good writing in the Busy-Body was stolen and that the bad was all his own. Another piece by Keimer, titled "Hue and Cry after the Busy-Body," gave hints concerning the identity of the Busy-Body: Breintnall was identified as "Lantnirbio . . . a Free-thinker of the Peripatetick Sect," whereas Franklin was called "Bebegeo . . . A Fellow whose . . . Merits [are] as threadbare as his Great Coat. . . . The highest Sphere he ever yet acted in, was that of an Understrapper to a Press, till his Advancement, by that Prodigy of Wit, Mr. B[radfor]d."

Keimer's "Hue and Cry" contained interesting biographical information for both Breintnall and Franklin. It confirms later evidence that Breintnall was a freethinker. It is also the first of several indications that when Franklin was a young tradesman, he deliberately cultivated the appearance (as well as the reality) of frugality. His "threadbare" overcoat was probably secondhand, for it seems unlikely that the twenty-three-year-old could have owned an overcoat that fit him long enough to wear it "threadbare." What a contrast with his appearance before his brother's workmen in Boston several years before, when he presented himself in a genteel new suit, showed his watch, and gave his former companions money to drink his health.

No. 8: Authorship and Buried Treasure

Franklin twice told of his delight in learning of the reception of his writings: in the *Autobiography* he told of the Couranteers' reaction to his first Dogood letter, and in a letter to his son on 6 October 1773 he told of the outrage and amazement generated by his hoax, "An Edict of the King of Prussia." Opening Busy-Body No. 8 (which followed Joseph Breintnall's two moralistic Busy-Body essays) in the 27 March *Mercury*, Franklin generalized about the pleasure of hearing one's work praised (he repeated the sentiment in his essay "On Literary Style" [2 August 1733]): "One of the greatest Pleasures an Author can have is certainly the Hearing his Works applauded. The hiding from the World our Names while we publish our Thoughts, is so absolutely necessary to this Self-Gratification, that I hope my Well-wishers will congratulate me on my Escape from the many diligent, but fruitless Enquiries that have of late been made after me. Every Man will own, That an Author, as such, ought to be try'd by the Merit of his Productions only; but Pride, Party, and Prejudice at this Time run so very high, that Experience shews we form our Notions of a Piece by the Character of the Author. Nay there are some very humble Politicians in and about this City, who will ask on which Side the Writer is, before they presume to give their Opinion of the Thing wrote."

In the first Silence Dogood essay, Franklin had democratically claimed that what was important was what was said, not who said it. The Busy-Body now declared that he kept his identity hidden so that persons would pay attention only to his opinions, not to himself—though no doubt numerous persons knew that Franklin (and, later, Breintnall) was the Busy-Body. "And I appeal to the more generous Part of the World, if I have since I appear'd in the Character of the Busy-Body given an Instance of my siding with any Party more than another, in the unhappy Divisions of my Country; and I have above all, this Satisfaction in my Self, That neither Affection, Aversion or Interest, have byass'd me to use any Partiality towards any Man, or Set of Men; but whatsoever I find nonsensically ridiculous, or immorally dishonest, I have, and shall continue openly to attack with the Freedom of an honest Man, and a Lover of my Country."

Returning to his earlier satire of second sight and superstition (perhaps partly inspired, as the later *Poor Richard* unmistakably was, by Jonathan Swift's satire of the almanac maker John Partridge), Franklin printed a mock letter from an astrologer, signed "Titan Pleiades," who proposes to join with the Busy-Body and the second-sighted Bunyan in searching for pirates' gold and other buried treasure. The pseudonym Titan Pleiades alluded to the constellation (and probably to astrology) and to the popular local almanac maker Titan Leeds, who pretended to be adept in astrology. Pleiades wrote: "You cannot be ignorant, Sir, (for your intimate Second sighted Correspondent knows all Things) that there are large Sums of Money hidden under Ground in divers Places about this Town, and in many Parts of the Country; But alas, Sir, Notwithstanding I have used all the Means laid down in the immortal Authors beforementioned, and when they fail'd, the ingenious Mr. P-d-l with his Mercurial Wand and Magnet, I have still fail'd in my Purpose." Therefore Titan Pleiades proposed a partnership with the Busy-Body and "his Second-sighted Correspondent." They must become, he said, "Three of the richest Men in the Province."

Franklin continued the skit with remarks on the absurdity of persons searching for hidden treasures: "In the Evening after I had received this Letter, I made a Visit to my Second-sighted Friend, and communicated to him the Proposal." The maven assured the Busy-Body that there was not an ounce of silver or gold hid underground anywhere in the province. The recent scarcity of money had obliged those who had buried it to recover it "and use it in their own necessary Affairs." As for the treasure buried by pirates in the old times, "he himself had long since dug it all up and applied it to charitable Uses."

Franklin's portrayal of the foolish search for gold is the first instance of this recurring motif in American literature. He certainly knew the Captain Kidd ballads and may have been inspired by them.[10] The Busy-Body wrote:

There are among us great Numbers of honest Artificers and labouring People, who fed with a vain Hope of growing suddenly rich, neglect their Business, almost to the ruining of themselves and Families, and voluntarily endure abundance of Fatigue in a fruitless Search after Imaginary hidden Treasure. They wander thro' the Woods and Bushes by Day, to discover the Marks and Signs; at Midnight they repair to the hopeful Spot with Spades and Pickaxes; full of Expectation they labour violently, trembling at the same Time in every Joint, thro' Fear of certain malicious Demons who are said to haunt and guard such Places. At length a mighty hole is dug, and perhaps several Cartloads of Earth thrown out, but alas, no Cag or Iron Pot is found! no Seaman's Chest cram'd with Spanish Pistoles, or weighty Pieces of Eight! Then they conclude, that thro' some Mistake in the Procedure, some rash Word spoke, or some Rule of Art neglected, the Guardian Spirit had power to sink it deeper into the Earth and convey it out of their Reach. Yet when a Man is once thus infatuated, he is so far from being discouraged by ill Success, that he is rather animated to double his Industry, and will try again and again in a Hundred Different Places, in Hopes at last of meeting with some lucky Hit, that shall at once Sufficiently reward him for all his Expence of Time and Labour.

Having ridiculed the practice of searching for buried treasures, calling it a species of that "easy Credulity" that people give to whatever they wish might be true, Franklin wrote that a "Sea Captain of my Acquaintance" claimed that the "Banks of Newfoundland" are "more valuable . . . than the Mountains of Potosi" because of the recurring abundance of fish. Though Franklin made the sentiment seem local and realistic, he privately joked, for the allusion was to a passage in Captain John Smith's *General History of Virginia* (1624) in which Smith scorned the early Virginia explorers' attempts to find gold mines. He wrote that the fish off Cape Cod had already yielded more than "one hundred thousand pounds" sterling, "as good gold as the Mines of Guiana or Potassie, with lesse hazard and charge, and more certainty and facility."[11]

The last paragraph reinforced Franklin's theme that "the rational and almost certain Methods of acquiring Riches" are "by Industry and Frugality." He created an anecdote about a Chester County farmer who left his son a plantation with these words: "My Son, says he, I give thee now a Valuable Parcel of Land; I assure thee I have found a considerable Quantity of Gold by Digging there; Thee mayst do the same. But thee must carefully observe this. Never to dig more than Plow-deep." The seemingly local anecdote actually echoes Aesop's fable titled "A Father and His Sons," probably through Bacon, though Franklin also knew Aesop. In *Of the Advancement of Learning* (1605), Bacon cited Aesop's fable of the dying man who told his sons of the gold buried in his vineyard. They dug and dug but found no gold. "But by reason of their stirring and digging the mould about the roots of their vines, they had a great vintage the year following."[12]

THE SUPPRESSED ADDITION: PAPER MONEY

Andrew Bradford left town after approving the Busy-Body No. 8 for the forthcoming 27 March *Mercury*. Then Franklin wrote an addition to it, dated "Monday Night, March 24," containing the boldest anti-Proprietary political journalism yet published in early Pennsylvania.[13] Franklin brought the addition to Bradford's shop, and the printers set it in type and published the newspaper. But after a few papers were distributed, "a certain Gentleman" advised Bradford's wife, Cornelia, that the addition was seditious, so she took up all the copies she could find and suppressed it. Then Bradford returned to town and ran off another printing of the 27 March *Mercury* with more "Foreign Affairs" as filler in place of Franklin's addition. In the ninth Busy-Body (10 April) Breintnall asserted that the late addition had made a "Stir." "I have since read it over several Times with Care; and I profess I cannot see that it contains any Thing so criminal as to deserve the Flames." He testified that because a few copies got abroad, numerous manuscript copies were made, and "it soon became more generally read than it would if there had been no such Endeavours used to destroy it."

Franklin's addition to Busy-Body No. 8 took up the contested subject of paper money. In the depression of the early 1720s, the Pennsylvania Assembly had issued two supplies of paper currency, £15,000 on 2 April 1723 and £30,000

I shall conclude with the Words of my dif-
creet Friend *Agricola*, of *Chester*-County, when
he gave his Son a Good Plantation, *My*
Son, lays he, *I give thee now a Valuable Parcel of*
Land ; I assure thee I have found a considerable Quan-
tity of Gold by Digging there ; —— *Thee mayst do*
the same. —— *But thee must carefully observe this,*
Never to dig more than Plow-deep. II

FOREIGN AFFAIRS.

Moscow, November 14.

People here have been surprized at the News inserted in
some Foreign Prints, That the Czar had ordered his Minister
at Stockholm, to make new Instances to engage the King and
Crown of Sweden, to declare the Duke of Holstein Gottorp
Successor to that Kingdom, and to recognize his Majesty's
Title of Emperor, without further Delay; and to declare,
That, in case of Refusal, this Court would look on it as a Breach
of the Peace of Nystad ; which News had no manner of
Foundation.

Dantzick, November 27.

We have receive Advice from Courland, that Duke Ferdinand is dangerously ill there, and that the chief Members of
the States were already taking Measures for preventing that
Dutchy being divided into Palatinates, pursuant to the late
Decree of the Royal Commission, in Hopes to be supported
by some Foreign Power. We learn from Poland, that the
Rescript of the King, in Favour of the Protestants, had produced so good an Effect, that a Stop hath been put to the
Persecution designed against the City of Thorn.

Vienna, December 1.

It is assured, that the Imperial Court is now intent upon
redressing Affairs of Religion, conformable to the Treaties of
Munster and Osnabrugh and for that End to send Ambassies
to Places proper for that Weeke. We learn by our last Letters from Constantinople, that the Plague was so considerably
abated there that the Number of the Dead, which amounted
3000 per Week, was reduced to 12 or 1500; so that they
hoped in little time to be free from it: As to the Suburbs of
Pern, where the Foreign Ambassadors and other Christians
inhabit, it had the Happiness to be almost intirely preserved
from it, few having died therein. It is added, that the Ot-
toman Ports persisted in a Resolution of preserving Peace,
having for that End, again exhorted the Sultan Ezref to make
an amicable Accommodation with the Emperor of Russia :
And that it was currently reported, that the Grand Seignior
had declared to the Divan, that his Design was to chuse for
his Successor, without Distinction of Age, one his Children,
who should be most fit to govern his Empire, and maintain
therein the Mahometan Faith; but that the same time
it was his Desire, that he who should be chosen, should engage solemnly not to follow the Custom of taking away the
Lives of his Brethren, who should remain in the Seraglio, and
be treated suitable to their Birth. This Resolution of the
Grand Seignior had been much applauded by all the Mussul-
mans.

Figure 26. American Weekly Mercury, *27 March 1729, after Franklin's addition to Busy-*
Body No. 8 was suppressed. This is the Mercury *found in all copies except one. Note that*
the Busy-Body concludes at the top of the column. Courtesy, Newspaper Division, Library
of Congress, Washington, D.C.

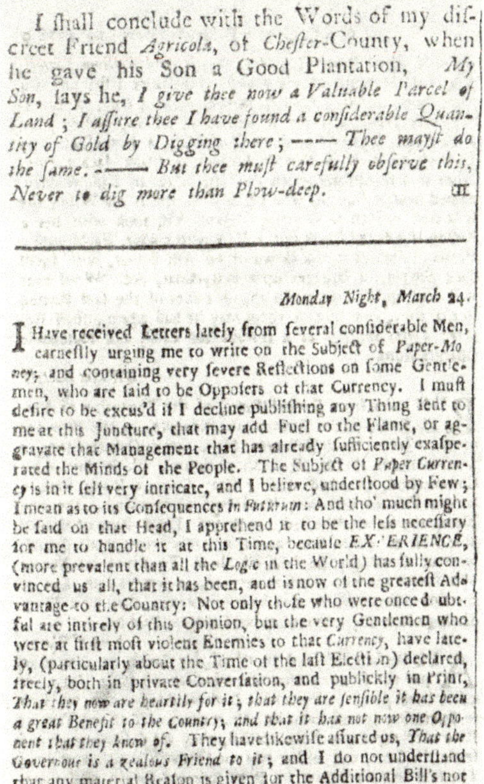

I shall conclude with the Words of my discreet Friend *Agricola*, of *Chester*-County, when he gave his Son a Good Plantation, *My Son*, fays he, *I give thee now a Valuable Parcel of Land ; I affure thee I have found a confiderable Quantity of Gold by Digging there ; —— Thee mayft do the fame. —— But thee muft carefully obferve this, Never to dig more than Plow-deep.*

———————————

Monday Night, March 24.

I Have received Letters lately from feveral confiderable Men, earneftly urging me to write on the Subject of *Paper-Money*; and containing very fevere Reflections on fome Gentlemen, who are faid to be Oppofers of that Currency. I muft defire to be excus'd if I decline publifhing any Thing fent to me at this Juncture, that may add Fuel to the Flame, or aggravate that Management that has already fufficiently exafperated the Minds of the People. The Subject of *Paper Currency* is in it felf very intricate, and I believe, underftood by Few ; I mean as to its Confequences *in Futurum*: And tho' much might be faid on that Head, I apprehend it to be the lefs neceffary for me to handle it at this Time, becaufe *EXPERIENCE*, (more prevalent than all the *Logic* in the World) has fully convinced us all, that it has been, and is now of the greateft Advantage to the Country: Not only thofe who were once doubtful are intirely of this Opinion, but the very Gentlemen who were at firft moft violent Enemies to that *Currency*, have lately, (particularly about the Time of the laft Election) declared, freely, both in private Converfation, and publickly in *Print*, *That they now are heartily for it ; that they are fenfible it has been a great Benefit to the Country; and that it has not now one Opponent that they know of.* They have likewife affured us, *That the Governour is a zealous Friend to it* ; and I do not underftand that any material Reafon is given for the Additional Bill's not paffing, but this. *That it is contrary to the Conftituents Orders from Home.* If this be the Cafe, I fee nothing further in it but this; that thofe Gentlemen who in their Zeal for the Good of their Country, formerly oppos'd *Paper-Money*, when they thought it would prove hurtful, and by their powerful Reprefentations procured thofe Orders from Home, but now being better acquainted with its Ufefulnefs, and fenfible how much it is to our Advantage to have fuch a Currency, are become hearty Friends to it ; I fay, nothing remains, but that thofe Gentlemen join as heartily with the Reprefentative Body of the Country to endeavour, by different Reprefentations, a Revocation of thofe Orders: And in the mean Time, as it is certain They would be pleafed at Home to fee this Province in Profperity, fo without Doubt there is no Man fo unreasonable among them, fuppofing that Act fhould now pafs, as to imagine, that the whole Country united is entirely ignorant of its own true Intereft, And the Intereft of the Country is the fame, I prefume, with that of the Proprietary.

Figure 27. Franklin's suppressed addition to Busy Body No. 8, American Weekly Mercury, 27 March 1729. A unique copy of the Mercury at the Library of Congress contains the suppressed addition to Franklin's Busy-Body, dated "Monday Night, March 24." The owner of the Mercury, Andrew Bradford, was out of town when Franklin delivered the addition, but as the first copies of the paper were printed, a reader advised Bradford's wife, Cornelia, that the addition was objectionable, and she suppressed it. The letter marks Franklin's bold entry into Philadelphia politics. It urges the legislature to pass a paper currency act and calls the assemblymen hypocrites who had said before the election that they favored a paper currency but now were refusing to pass an act for it. Franklin subtly threatened an uprising of the people against those who opposed a paper currency. Only the first half of the essay is shown here. Courtesy, Newspaper Division, Library of Congress, Washington, D.C.

on 17 January 1723/4, but the Proprietary Party in general and a number of rich merchants like Isaac Norris, Sr., who belonged to the Quaker or "Popular" Party, had opposed the currency. In his opening, the Busy-Body/Franklin said that he had "received Letters lately from several considerable Men, earnestly urging me to write on the Subject of Paper-Money; and containing very severe Reflections on some Gentlemen, who are said to be Opposers of that Currency." He claimed that he would not print the letters because they "may add Fuel to the Flame, or aggravate that Management that has already sufficiently exasperated the Minds of the People."

Thus Busy-Body/Franklin indirectly threatened the wealthy and the Proprietary Party. Though conceding that "the Subject of Paper Currency is in itself very intricate," Franklin claimed that "EXPERIENCE, (more prevalent than all the Logic in the World)" has proven that paper money "is now of the greatest Advantage to the Country." He insinuated that members of the assembly who opposed paper currency were hypocrites, for at "the last Election" they claimed to be "heartily for it." At that time, they had said they knew that issuing paper currency had "been a great Benefit to the Country; and that it has not now one Opponent that they know of." These deceivers "likewise assured us, That the Governour is a zealous Friend to it." The same persons now claimed that passing a paper currency act would violate instructions from England. These orders, however, had been obtained by the "powerful Representations" of the very persons who formerly opposed paper currency. Since they have now publicly proclaimed their belief in the good effects of the currency, they should obtain "by different Representations, a Revocation of those Orders." Franklin knew that a number of the Proprietary supporters and other wealthy Pennsylvanians had initially opposed paper currency and had written the English authorities against it. The Board of Trade had replied that if the Pennsylvania Assembly passed "any further Acts . . . for creating more Bills of Credit," the board would recommend that they be repealed.[14]

In attacking the Proprietors and their supporters, Franklin insinuated that the Board of Trade's instructions against the currency were made at the request of the Proprietors. Franklin suggested that they selfishly opposed the good of Pennsylvania for their own private interest. "And in the mean Time, as it is certain They would be pleased at Home to see this Province in Prosperity, so without Doubt there is no Man so unreasonable among them, supposing that Act should now pass, as to imagine, that the whole Country united is entirely ignorant of its own true Interest." Franklin sarcastically added, "And the Interest of the Country is the same, I presume, with that of the Proprietary." He promised to point out in a future paper a way to "recover our Silver and Gold."

Franklin revealed an unusual knowledge of Pennsylvania's political workings and named a political problem (the Proprietors' secret instructions binding the governors) that plagued Pennsylvania politics until the Revolution. He lamented "the Case of that good Gentleman, our Governor, who sees a flourishing Province sinking under his Administration into the most wretched and deplorable Circumstances; and while no Good-will is wanting in him towards us and our Welfare, finds his Hands are tyed, and that without deviating from his Instructions, it is not in his Power to help us." Franklin then threatened the government:

> The whole Country is at this Instant filled with the greatest Heat and Animosity; and if there are yet among us any Opposers of a Paper-Currency, it is probable the Resentments of the People point at them; and tho' I must earnestly exhort my Countrymen to Peace and Quietness, for that publick Disturbances are seldom known to be attended with any good Consequence; yet I cannot but think it would be highly prudent in those Gentlemen with all Expedition to publish such Vindications of themselves and their Actions, as will sufficiently clear them in the Eyes of all reasonable Men, from the Imputation of having a Design to engross the Property of the Country, and make themselves and their Posterity Lords, and the Bulk of the Inhabitants their Tenants and Vassals; which Design they are everywhere openly accused of.

The Busy-Body/Franklin was even bolder here in appealing to class prejudice and threatening a revolt against the wealthy than he had been in Busy-Body No. 4. The criticism that a few persons wanted to make themselves "and their Posterity Lords, and the Bulk of the Inhabitants their Tenants and Vassals" was especially aimed at the proprietors. The poor and the lower classes had found an extraordinary champion in Benjamin Franklin. While calling the opponents of paper currency tyrants, Franklin threatened to raise a mob against any who opposed paper currency. Further, he made it practically impossible for anyone who objected to paper currency to vindicate himself. That would only publicly identify the apologist as an enemy of the people. "And such a Vindication is the more necessary at this Time, because if the People are once convinced there is no such Scheme on Foot, (and Truth without Doubt will prevail) it may exceedingly tend to the Settlement of their Minds, the Abatement of their Heats, and the Establishment of Peace, Love, and Unity, and all the Social Virtues."

FRANKLIN'S EARLY POLITICS

Most scholars have claimed that Franklin took little interest in politics until the 1750s, and one recent biographer argued that he identified with the Proprietary Party until 1755.[15] In fact, just as he opposed the Prerogative Party in Massachusetts in his first editorial in the *Pennsylvania Gazette*, he often opposed it (and some wealthy Quakers) in Pennsylvania from his very first writing on Pennsylvania politics—Busy-Body No. 4. Though the suppressed addition to Busy-Body No. 8 was unknown until 1965, numerous other writings, as I will show in the remainder of this Volume and throughout Volumes 2 and 3, testify to Franklin's identification with the Popular or Quaker Party from the 1720s. He did, however, support the Proprietary Party on one issue, defense. He believed in the necessity for a militia. Not all members of the Quaker Party opposed defense measures, but many did. On most issues, he sided with the Quaker Party. Franklin brought his Old Charter sympathies to Pennsylvania. The Old Charter Party had objected to the Acts of Trade and Navigation by passing impost duties on British goods, and its leaders, such as Elisha Cooke, Jr., had resented the British "strangers" sent over to govern America.[16] Similarly, the twenty-three-year-old Franklin in Philadelphia revealed his resentment of and opposition to British treatment of the colonies.

The suppressed addition concluded Franklin's contributions to the Busy-Body essays, but he fulfilled his promise of publishing further on currency a week later. Ironically, at his first entry into Pennsylvania politics, Franklin adopted the paper money policies and platform of Sir William Keith—who had personally betrayed him and who had, by then, fled his creditors in Pennsylvania. Despite Keith's personal behavior toward Franklin, he judged Keith in the *Autobiography* to have been "a good Governor for the People, tho' not for his Constituents the Proprietaries" (42).

Conclusion

The Busy-Body was an uneven performance. The main persona was not as colloquial or as much fun as Silence Dogood. The characters created by the Busy-Body, such as Ridentius and Eugenius, were types—fairly typical of English journalism. The Busy-Body nevertheless had a number of high points. The celebration of the man of virtue in Busy-Body No. 3 showed Franklin's idealism and his desire to achieve that stature. After threatening to expose the "Great Names in the Province, who are the common Objects of Popular Dislike," Busy-Body No. 4 had three additional excellent parts: the breathless, run-on, colloquial prose of the much put-upon and charming "PATIENCE"; the naive superstitions of Bunyan; and the ironic response of the Busy-Body to the credulous Bunyan. Busy-Body No. 8 spoofed the foolishness of digging for buried treasure—a recurring motif in American literature. Finally, the suppressed portion of Busy-Body No. 8 featured an investigative reporter who exposed (and threatened to reveal more of) the hypocritical actions of some wealthy men and politicians. The first part of Busy-Body No. 4 and the suppressed addition to Busy-Body No. 8 revealed Franklin's potential as a crusading journalist, a role that he fulfilled during his second British mission (1764–75)—long after he had, presumably, stopped being a newspaperman.

SEVENTEEN

Paper Currency

If I were not sensible that the Gentlemen of Trade in England, to whom we have already parted with our Silver and Gold, are misinformed of our Circumstances, and therefore endeavour to have our Currency stinted to what it now is, I should think the Government at Home had some Reasons for discouraging and impoverishing this Province, which we are not acquainted with.—1:147

A MODEST ENQUIRY INTO THE NATURE AND NECESSITY OF A PAPER CURRENCY (1729) marked Franklin's first important contribution to Pennsylvania politics, revealed his independence as an economic thinker, and set forth a number of theories that he pursued with increasing sophistication and better data throughout his life.[1] In passing, the pamphlet also dealt with the population of Great Britain and the colonies as well as with class relations. Pennsylvania's major political dispute in the 1720s concerned paper currency. The Junto debated the issue, with Franklin "on the Side of an Addition [of paper currency], being persuaded that the first small Sum, struck in 1723 had done much good, by increasing the Trade, Employment, and Number of Inhabitants in the Province, since I now saw all the old Houses inhabited, and many new ones building, whereas I remember'd well, that when I first walk'd about the Streets of Philadelphia, eating my Roll, I saw most of the Houses in Walnut Street between Second and Front Streets with Bills on their Doors, to be let; and many likewise in Chestnut Street, and other Streets; which made me then think the inhabitants of the City were one after another deserting it" (A 67).

Franklin's *Modest Enquiry into the Nature and Necessity of a Paper Currency*, dated 3 April and advertised in the 10 April 1729 *Mercury*, followed up the Busy-Body's essay on the subject. Contemporaries must have attributed it, signed "B. B.," to the Busy-Body/ Franklin, for it was widely known that the Busy-Body's primary author was the twenty-three-year-old printer. Franklin's experience in Boston had grounded him in the arguments concerning paper currency. He had helped his brother set several paper currency pamphlets in type and must have read the other Boston pamphlets concerning the heated political question. When he ran away to Philadelphia in 1723, he found the currency controversy raging there. His patron, the faithless Sir William Keith, favored a paper currency though it was well-known that the Penns, James Logan, Isaac Norris, most of the Proprietary Party, the lawyers, and wealthy persons in gen-

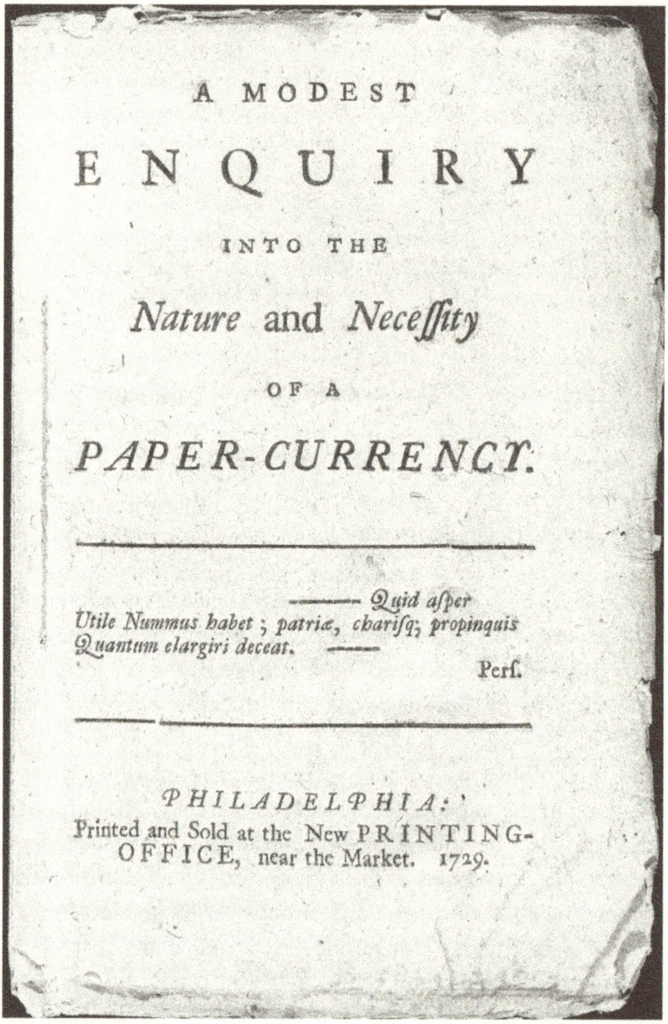

A MODEST

ENQUIRY

INTO THE

Nature and Neceſſity

OF A

PAPER-CURRENCY.

——— Quid aſper
Utile Nummus habet ; patriæ, chariſq; propinquis
Quantum elargiri deceat. ———

Perſ.

PHILADELPHIA:
Printed and Sold at the New PRINTING-
OFFICE, near the Market. 1729.

Figure 28. Franklin enters Pennsylvania politics: A Modest Enquiry into the Nature and Necessity of a Paper Currency *(1729). Franklin's pamphlet advocating paper currency revised and expanded the positions taken in his suppressed Busy-Body No. 8. Franklin sold the pamphlet at his shop. Some persons may not have known that Franklin wrote the pseudonymous "Busy-Body," but no one could doubt that Franklin wrote* A Modest Enquiry. *He sided with the Popular or Quaker Party against the Proprietors and the wealthiest men of Philadelphia (which included a few wealthy members of the Quaker Party). His interest in and knowledge of economics and demography foreshadow his positions in "Observations Concerning the Increase of Mankind."*

The pamphlet also revealed his Americanism: Franklin claimed that Americans, not the British authorities, were the best judges of their own circumstances and necessities. He indirectly criticized the Acts of Trade and Navigation. He objected that the British authorities seemed to have "some Reasons for discouraging and impoverishing" Pennsylvania and America. In effect, he was suggesting that the British feared the possible independence of America. Courtesy, Library Company of Philadelphia.

eral opposed it.[2] The historian Gordon S. Wood, writing of the Revolutionary period, has explained that the colonial Proprietary gentry opposed a paper currency because land and property were the source of their authority. Their wealth was vulnerable to inflation. The printing of paper money raised the fear of inflation, which "threatened not simply their livelihood but their very identity and social position."[3] Wood's comments also apply to the 1720s. Nevertheless, with Governor Keith's backing, the Pennsylvania legislature passed paper currency acts in the early 1720s. Most Pennsylvanians thought the acts were successful.[4] By 1729, Franklin had no doubt also read Francis Rawle's local pamphlets in favor of paper currency.[5] Surely, too, while Franklin was in Burlington in the spring of 1728 printing the New Jersey paper money (A 57) he talked about the basis of its value with his New Jersey acquaintances. In writing *A Modest Enquiry*, Franklin opposed the Philadelphia establishment.

Structure and Tone

A Modest Enquiry has a four-part structure. Part 1 argued that "a sufficient stock" or "a certain proportionate Quantity" of "running Cash" (i.e., available money) was necessary for a country "to manage its Trade" (1:145). Franklin echoed John Law's *Money and Trade Consider'd* on the relation between money and trade.[6] In a brief second part, Franklin itemized the kinds of persons for and against paper currency. Part 3, based on Sir William Petty's writings, weighed "the Nature and Value of Money in general" in order to determine what quantity of paper currency and what guarantees for it were necessary. The concluding fourth part applied the preceding theses to the specific situation of Pennsylvania. The late Professor Theodore Hornberger pointed out that Franklin's *Modest Enquiry* followed the structure of the Puritan sermon, which typically began with a biblical text, extracted a doctrine from it (the doctrine often simply paraphrased the text), proved the doctrine with a series of reasons or proofs, and concluded with a particular use or application of the sermon.[7] As we will see, Franklin did indeed roughly follow the Puritan sermon structure.

The title of the pamphlet has contrasting voices. "A Modest Enquiry" suggests diffidence and hesitation; "into the Nature" implies a scientific, impartial investigation; "Necessity of a Paper-Currency" proclaims a firm author's stand. The title's implications are repeated in the essay. In the first two parts, B. B./Franklin seems to be a modest inquirer, searching after truth; in part 3 he expertly discusses the history of banks and currencies; and in the application he avows the necessity of Pennsylvania's issuing more paper currency. Thus the tones and personae found in consecutive parts of the pamphlet duplicate the title's changing from humble inquirer to pedantic authority to passionate advocate.

Thesis

The pamphlet opened: "There is no Science, the Study of which is more useful and commendable than the Knowledge of the true Interest of one's Country."

After an apology, B. B./Franklin introduced the text: "*There is a certain proportionate Quantity of Money requisit to carry on the Trade of a Country freely and
currently; More than which would be of no Advantage in Trade, and Less, if much
less, exceedingly detrimental to it*" (1:141–42). John Law had argued that domestic
and foreign trade depended on money.[8] Four doctrines attempted to prove
the text.

INTEREST RATES

"First, *A great Want of Money in any Trading Country, occasions Interest to be at
a very high Rate.*" He observed that laws forbidding usury failed, for no laws
could "restrain Men from giving and receiving exorbitant Interest, where
Money is suitable scarce." A high interest rate injured a country in several ways:
"It makes Land bear a low Price, because few Men will lay out their Money in
Land, when they can make a much greater Profit by lending it out upon Interest." A high rate discouraged shipping and trade: "And much less will Men be
inclined to venture their Money at Sea, when they can, without Risque or Hazard, have a great and certain Profit by keeping it at home." He compared a
country with high interest rates to one with low interest rates. Persons living in
countries with the lower rates "will infallibly have the Advantage, and get the
greatest Part of that Trade into their own Hands; For he that trades with Money
he hath borrowed at 8 or 10 *per Cent.* cannot hold Market with him that borrows
his Money at 6 or 4" (1:142).

B. B. then argued that "*A plentiful Currency will occasion Interest to be low.*"
Consequently, many persons will invest in land so that land will rise in value.
At the same time, an abundant currency will enliven trade because people will
find more profit in trade than in lending money. Further, a plentiful currency
will encourage business ventures: "many that understand Business very well,
but have not a Stock sufficient of their own, will be encouraged to borrow
Money to trade with, when they can have it at moderate Interest" (1:142–43).

Franklin used the same method repeatedly in the pamphlet. He began with
a negative proposition then proceeded to a positive one. Both propositions have
supporting proofs, but the latter, positive one is shorter and more memorable.
I suspect that Franklin first wrote the positive proposition and proceeded to the
negative, and that when he revised the draft realized a progression from the
negative (in this first case, a lack of currency) to a positive (here, plentiful currency) would seem more convincing and dramatic. He followed the same
method in all four arguments, with the positive proposition always being shorter
and more memorable.

Trade and Property Value

"Secondly, *Want of Money in a Country reduces the Price of that Part of its Produce which is used in Trade.*" If insufficient money exists for trade, the staple
crops will necessarily sell for less; consequently, the price of land will fall. There-

fore "fewer People [will] find an Advantage in Husbandry, or the Improvement of Land." John Law had written: "Trade and Money depend mutually on one another; when Trade decays, Money lessens; and when Money lessens, Trade decays."[9] Franklin took Law's thoughts on the relations between trade and money, amplified them, and explained them with relation to the situation in Pennsylvania. Franklin wrote, "*A Plentiful Currency will occasion the Trading Produce to bear a good Price*: Because Trade being encouraged and advanced by it, there will be a much greater Demand for that Produce; which will be a great Encouragement of Husbandry and Tillage, and consequently make Land more valuable, for that many People would apply themselves to Husbandry, who probably might otherwise have sought some more profitable Employment" (1:143).

The nineteenth-century economist Willard Phillips, who annotated the essay for Jared Sparks's 1836–40 edition of Franklin's writings, wrote that Franklin confounded low price with want of demand and high price with briskness of demand. Phillips said that one was the cause and the other the effect. He claimed, however, that Franklin's main points (that briskness of trade promotes production and consequently wealth; that a sufficiency of circulating medium promotes trade; and that a want of it obstructs trade) were indisputable.[10] As an example of trade's increase, Franklin examined how the availability of paper currency affected shipbuilding. He devoted a paragraph to proving that Pennsylvania's shipbuilding industry had increased with currency's availability (1:143–44). Franklin knew that a sufficient currency was only one of many factors affecting trade (and shipbuilding), but because he did not say "all other conditions being equal," some critics have condemned his generalization.[11]

Emigration and Currency

Third, the twenty-three-year-old theorist discussed the relation between emigration and currency. "*Want of Money in a Country discourages Labouring and Handicrafts Men (which are the chief Strength and Support of a People) from coming to settle in it, and induces many that were settled to leave the Country, and seek Entertainment and Employment in other Places, where they can be better paid.*" Franklin here echoed the paean to the farmer in John Wise's 1721 pamphlet on paper currency, *A Word of Comfort to a Melancholy Country*. The urban-dwelling Franklin, however, expanded Wise's appreciation to all "Labouring and Handicrafts Men." He said: "For what can be more disheartening to an industrious labouring Man, than this, that after he hath earned his Bread with the Sweat of his Brows, he must spend as much Time, and have near as much Fatigue in getting it, as he had to earn it." A convenient medium of exchange eliminates the problem. Further "*nothing makes more bad Paymasters than a general Scarcity of Money*. And here again is a Third Reason for Land's bearing a low Price in such a Country, because Land always increases in Value in Proportion with the Increase of the People settling on it, there being so many more Buyers; and its Value will infallibly be diminished, if the Number of its Inhabitants diminish" (1:144). Franklin here touched on a subject he later devoted major interest to—population growth.

Franklin attempted to prove that the major colonial property owners would benefit by a modest inflation. He argued that the more immigrants and the more total inhabitants, the greater the demand for land. Consequently "it must necessarily rise in Value, and bear a better Price." So too, he claimed, would rents, for the increase of trade and wealth enabled persons to pay greater rents. The high price of rents and the low price of interest would ensure that those who "in a Scarcity of Money practised Usury" would now put their money into building houses "which will likewise sensibly enliven Business in any Place; it being an Advantage not only to *Brickmakers, Bricklayers, Masons, Carpenters, Joiners, Glaziers,* and several other Trades immediately employ'd by Building, but likewise to *Farmers, Brewers, Bakers, Taylors, Shoemakers, Shop-keepers,* and in short to every one that they lay their Money out with" (1:144). Franklin was prescient in believing that the construction industry provided one key to the country's total economy.

Consumption of English and European Goods

Franklin's unusual fourth argument not only showed his close attention to the Boston currency literature as an adolescent but also again revealed his interest in demography. He considered the relations between currency and consumption.

> Fourthly, *Want of Money in such a Country as ours, occasions a greater Consumption of English and European Goods, in Proportion to the Number of the People, than there would otherwise be.* Because Merchants and Traders, by whom abundance of Artificers and labouring Men are employed, finding their other Affairs require what Money they can get into their hands, oblige those who work for them to take one half, or perhaps two thirds Goods in Pay. By this Means a greater Quantity of Goods are disposed of, and to a greater Value; because Working Men and their Families are thereby induced to be more profuse and extravagant in fine Apparel and the like, than they would be if they were obliged to pay ready Money for such Things after they had earn'd and received it, or if such Goods were not imposed upon them of which they can make no other Use: For such People cannot send the Goods they are paid with to a Foreign Market, without losing considerably by having them sold for less than they stand 'em in here; neither can they easily dispose of them at Home, because their Neighbours are generally supplied in the same Manner. (1:145)

One might wonder if Franklin was not attributing to others something of his own youthful self-discipline regarding unnecessary purchases. Actually, if people had more money, they would buy more luxuries; but if eighteenth-century merchants and traders forced their employees in hard times to take part of their earnings in goods that the employees neither needed nor wanted, then Franklin is probably correct.

Franklin asked, "But how unreasonable would it be, if some of those very Men *who have been a Means* of thus forcing People into unnecessary Expence, should be the first and most earnest in accusing them of *Pride and Prodigality.*" If Franklin had specific persons in mind, his contemporary Philadelphia audience may have recognized the merchants and traders whom he indicted. He pointed out that though a few individuals profited from the importation of goods, "yet the Country in general grows poorer by it apace" (1:145). Here, in his earliest economic writing, Franklin set forth the antimercantile position of his pre-Revolutionary writings and anticipated his later pride in being "cloth'd from Head to Foot in Woollen and Linnen of my Wife's Manufacture" (6 April 1766). His fourth proposition claimed, "As *A plentiful Currency will occasion a less Consumption of European Goods, in Proportion to the Number of the People,* so it will be a means of making the Balance of our Trade more equal than it now is, if it does not give it in our Favour; because our own Produce will be encouraged at the same Time. And it is to be observed, that tho' less Foreign Commodities are consumed in Proportion to the Number of People, yet this will be no Disadvantage to the Merchant, because the Number of People increasing, will occasion an increasing Demand of more Foreign Goods in the Whole." Franklin concluded part 1 by restating his contention that a shortage of currency made a country labor under numerous difficulties, whereas a "sufficient stock" of currency promoted trade and industry (1:145).

THOSE FOR AND AGAINST PAPER CURRENCY

In a brief second part, corresponding to another general "reason" or "proof" in a Puritan sermon, Franklin considered which "Persons will probably be for or against Emitting a large Additional Sum of Paper Bills in this Province." He restated the most common psychological explanation for behavior (all persons are self-interested) and then, in bland diction and tone, said that usurers were against paper currency, thus casting the primary opponents as public enemies. The second group who opposed paper currency were the very wealthy who wanted to purchase more land. Since their wealth was continually increasing from the large interest rates they were currently receiving, they were able to buy large tracts of land. Since trade was low, not only would those who borrowed from them become poorer, but so would most farmers who would then be obliged to sell land for less money. After the wealthy possessed as much land as they could purchase, "it will then be their Interest to have Money made Plentiful, because that will immediately make Land rise in Value in *their* Hands. Now it ought not to be wonder'd at, if People from the Knowledge of a Man's Interest do sometimes make a true Guess at his Designs; for, *Interest*, they say, *will not Lie*" (1:146).[12] A third group who opposed a plentiful currency were lawyers and others concerned in court business. Franklin said they "will probably many of them be against a plentiful Currency; because People in that Case will have less Occasion to run in Debt, and consequently less Occasion to go to Law and Sue one another for their Debts. Tho' I know some even among these Gentlemen, that regard the Publick Good before their own apparent private Interest" (1:146).

Franklin continued to enumerate those who opposed a paper currency. Like Thomas Lane in the *New-England Courant* (in the issue containing Silence Dogood No. 4), Franklin suspected that employers might expect and demand their employees to express the same points of view as their employers. Franklin wrote, "Dependents on such Persons as are above mentioned, whether as holding Offices, as Tenants, or as Debtors, must at least appear to be against a large Addition; because if they do not, they must sensibly feel their present Interest hurt" (1:146). Franklin knew from his experience in Boston that persons on fixed salaries (ministers, for example) would also oppose a cheaper currency, but he did not say so. Since most persons Franklin had listed were either public enemies or dependents, he added another group of supporters: "And besides these, there are, doubtless, many well-meaning Gentlemen and Others, who, without any immediate private Interest of their own in View, are against making such an Addition, thro' an Opinion they may have of the Honesty and sound Judgment of some of their Friends that oppose it, (perhaps for the Ends aforesaid) without having given it any thorough Consideration themselves." He concluded, "And thus it is no Wonder if there is a powerful Party on that Side" (1:146–47).

Turning to those interested in the passage of a paper money bill, Franklin first identified "Those who are Lovers of Trade, and delight to see Manufactures encouraged, will be for having a large Addition to our Currency: For they very well know, that People will have little Heart to advance Money in Trade, when what they can get is scarce sufficient to purchase Necessaries, and supply their Families with Provision. Much less will they lay it out in advancing new Manufactures; nor is it possible new Manufactures should turn to any Account, where there is not Money to pay the Workmen, who are discouraged by being paid in Goods, because it is a great Disadvantage to them" (1:147). Since everyone knew that the Proprietors opposed the currency, Franklin surprised his opponents by claiming that persons "truly for the Proprietor's Interest (and have no separate Views of their own that are predominant)" are for a paper currency. Franklin explained: "Because, as I have shewn above, Plenty of Money will for Several Reasons make Land rise in Value exceedingly: And I appeal to those immediately concerned for the Proprietor in the Sale of his Lands, whether Land has not risen very much since the first Emission of what Paper Currency we now have, and even by its Means. Now we all know the Proprietary has great Quantities to sell" (1:147). He implied that the Proprietors were selfish usurers—but he did not openly say so.

Franklin next anticipated part of his theory of population in "Observations Concerning the Increase of Mankind" (1751): "And since a Plentiful Currency will be so great a Cause of advancing this Province in Trade and Riches, and increasing the Number of its People; which, tho' it will not sensibly lessen the Inhabitants of Great Britain, will occasion a much greater Vent and Demand for their Commodities here; and allowing that the Crown is the more powerful for its Subjects increasing in Wealth and Number, I cannot think it the Interest of England to oppose us in making as great a Sum of Paper Money here, as we, who are the best Judges of our own Necessities, find convenient" (1:147). Franklin adumbrates four points he would later argue in detail. First, emigration from Great Britain will not lessen its inhabitants. Second, wealth will increase the population. Third, people are the primary riches of a country. Fourth, Americans are the best judges of their own necessities. Franklin maintained the last position (which Captain John Smith first advocated[13] and which Franklin learned as a youth from the Old Charter Party of Massachusetts) throughout his life.

Franklin also revealed his contempt for English mercantilism: "And if I were not sensible that the Gentlemen of Trade in England, to whom we have already parted with our Silver and Gold, are misinformed of our Circumstances, and therefore endeavour to have our Currency stinted to what it now is, I should think the Government at Home had some Reasons for discouraging and impoverishing this Province, which we are not acquainted with" (1:147).[14] The reason, as Franklin well knew and as he expressed several times long before 1765, was that Britain feared the future growth and independence of America. Franklin indicted English mercantilism as rapacious—and its selfish politicians as connivers in crime. Significantly, he did not name the infamous groups who favored a paper currency: those in debt and the poor. His primary audience, the assemblymen who could enact a bill for the paper currency, would not be swayed by an argument in favor of those persons. Franklin argued instead that artisans, farmers, and working people in general favored a paper currency. Franklin, as we have seen, identified with them.

THE LABOR THEORY OF VALUE

Part 3 of the pamphlet consists of an abstract discussion of "the Nature and Value of Money in general" in order to determine "Whether a large Addition to our Paper Currency will not make it sink in Value." (In a Puritan sermon, the topic would be a third major division of reasons or proofs.) Franklin took up inflation and displayed his ability to explain complex matters in easy terms: "As Providence has so ordered it, that not only different Countries, but even different Parts of the same Country, have their peculiar most suitable Productions; and likewise that different Men have Genius's adapted to Variety of different Arts and Manufacturers, Therefore *Commerce*, or the Exchange of one Commodity or Manufacture for another, is highly convenient and beneficial to Mankind." Franklin gradually defined commerce or trade in terms of labor value. The definition was one of four postulates concerning economics that Karl Marx cited from Franklin. Franklin began with a simple illustration of trade between two individuals. "*A* may be skilful in the Art of making Cloth, and *B* understand the raising of Corn; *A* wants Corn, and *B* Cloth; upon which they make an Exchange with each other for as much as each has Occasion, to the mutual Advantage and Satisfaction of both" (1:148). Using an inductive method and concrete examples, Franklin built his economic theory.

"But as it would be very tedious, if there were no other Way of general Dealing, but by an immediate Exchange of Commodities; because a Man that had Corn to dispose of, and wanted Cloth for it, might perhaps in his Search for a Chapman to deal with, meet with twenty People that had Cloth to dispose of, but wanted no Corn; and with Twenty others that wanted his Corn, but had no Cloth to suit him with. To remedy such Inconveniences, and facilitate Exchange, Men have invented MONEY, properly called a *Medium of Exchange*, because through or by its Means Labour is exchanged for Labour, or one Commodity for another" (1:148). Franklin gave the standard modern (and brilliant) definition of money, which had been used by the earlier Boston pamphleteers writing on paper currency. Franklin's usage antedates the earliest *OED* listing under "Medium [of exchange]" 5b (1740), by eleven years. Samuel Johnson evidently never came across this definition, for he defined money in 1755 as "Metal coined for the purposes of commerce," thus improving the older standard definition as "a Piece of Metal stamp'd with the Effigies of a Prince, or Arms of a State, which makes it current and authentick to pass at a common Rate."[15]

Franklin explained: "And whatever particular Thing Men have agreed to make this Medium of, whether Gold, Silver, Copper, or Tobacco; it is, to those who possess it (if they want any Thing) that very Thing which they want, because it will immediately procure it for . . . and thus the general Exchange is soon performed, to the Satisfaction of all Parties, with abundance of Facility" (148). Franklin briefly outlined the history of money before setting a measure upon which the medium of exchange should be based—labor. "For many Ages, those Parts of the World which are engaged in Commerce, have fixed upon Gold and Silver as the chief and most proper Materials for this Medium; they being in themselves valuable Metals for their Fineness, Beauty, and Scarcity. By these, particularly by Silver, it has been usual to value all Things else: But as Silver it self is of no certain permanent Value, being worth more or less according to its Scarcity or Plenty, therefore it seems requisite to fix upon Something else, more proper to be made a *Measure of Values*, and this I take to be *Labour*" (1:149). Willard Phillips pointed out that Franklin stated the principle "in 1729, precisely as Adam Smith does forty-six years afterward in *The Wealth of Nations*." Adam Smith wrote: "Labour, therefore, is the real measure of the exchangeable value of all commodities."[16] Though the theory that Adam Smith took chapters of *The Wealth of Nations* to Franklin and Richard Price for their observations and comments has been discredited,[17] I will point out in discussing

Franklin's "Observations Concerning the Increase of Mankind" that Smith knew Franklin's views on paper currency.

Karl Marx on Franklin

Unlike Willard Phillips, Karl Marx knew that Franklin was paraphrasing Sir William Petty,[18] but Marx nevertheless celebrated Franklin's formulation of the labor theory of monetary value: "It is a man of the New World—where bourgeois relations of production imported together with their representatives sprouted rapidly in a soil in which the superabundance of humus made up for the lack of historical tradition—who for the first time deliberately and clearly (so clearly as to be almost trite) reduces exchange-value to labour-time. This man was *Benjamin Franklin*."[19] Marx was correct in asserting that Franklin's explanation is so clear as to seem almost commonplace. Franklin wrote: "By Labour may the Value of Silver be measured as well as other Things."[20] Not only did Franklin express the nature of trade or commerce in terms of labor value, he also presented Marx's second doctrine of the labor theory of value: labor as the primary source of value. Marx quoted Franklin's example: "As, Suppose one Man employed to raise Corn, while another is digging and refining Silver; at the Year's End, or any other Period of Time, the compleat Produce of Corn, and that of Silver, are the natural Price of each other; and if one be twenty Bushels, and the other twenty Ounces, then an Ounce of that Silver is worth the Labour of raising a Bushel of that Corn." If the miner can get forty ounces of silver, "and the same Labour is still required to raise Twenty Bushels of Corn, then Two Ounces of Silver will be worth no more than the same Labour of raising One Bushel of Corn, and that Bushel of Corn will be as cheap at two Ounces, as it was before at one" (1:149).

Franklin's doctrine destroyed past mercantilist economics. Mercantilism equated a country's wealth with its possession of gold and silver, but Franklin demonstrated that the "Riches of a Country are to be valued by the Quantity of Labour its Inhabitants are able to purchase, and not by the Quantity of Silver and Gold they possess." He noted that according to its scarcity or plenty, gold and silver "will purchase more or less Labour, and therefore is more or less valuable." He pointed out: "those Metals have grown much more plentiful in Europe since the Discovery of America, so they have sunk in Value exceedingly; for instance in England, formerly one Penny of Silver was worth a Days Labour, but now it is hardly worth the sixth Part of a Days Labour; because not less than Six-pence will purchase the Labour of a Man for a Day in any Part of the Kingdom; which is wholly to be attributed to the much greater Plenty of Money now in England than formerly. And yet perhaps England is in Effect no richer now than at that Time, because as much Labour might be purchas'd, or Work got done of almost any kind, for £100 then, as will now require or is now worth £600" (1:149–50). Franklin thus set forth a third aspect of the labor theory of value that Marx repeated: the effect of increases in the supply of gold and silver on their value.[21] Willard Phillips noted that the passage showed that "the effect of the South American mines upon the rate of money prices and the reduction of the value of the precious metals, so elaborately set forth and reasoned out by Adam Smith, was quite a familiar notion when he was but six years old."[22]

The economists Tracy Mott and George W. Zinke believed that Franklin in 1729 also anticipated John Maynard Keynes "in realizing that plentiful money caused low interest and increased borrowing, and thus high levels of production and demand for goods and services." Franklin also envisioned David Hume's 1752 arguments against mercantilism while, in 1729, advancing beyond them. Hume maintained, "It is of no manner of consequence, with regard to the domestic happiness of a state, whether money be in a greater or less quantity."[23] Hume nevertheless appreciated that an increase of the available currency supply would cause prices to rise and that rising prices stimulated production and trade. Franklin, arguing for an increase in Pennsylvania's currency supply, stated Hume's later position. Franklin believed that the real value of commodities is determined by the labor it took to make them, so that a rise in the price of commodities did not affect their real value but served "to stimulate more production of them, resulting in more commerce and employment for masters and workers."

After appraising the nature of banks and bills of credit, Franklin, in another passage quoted by Karl Marx in *Capital*, declared, "Trade in general being nothing else but the Exchange of Labour for Labour, the Value of all Things is, as I have said before, most justly measured by Labour." This is the fourth and "most important" generalization of the labor theory of value that Marx credited to Franklin: "the abstraction of labor as the measure of all value."[24] Considering the relation among population, land, and currency, Franklin noted, "the Value of Money has been continually sinking in England for several Ages past, because it has been continually increasing in Quantity. But if Bills could be taken out of a Bank in Europe on a Land Security, it is probable the Value of such Bills would be more certain and steady, because the Number of Inhabitants continue to be near the same in those Countries from Age to Age." Since Franklin was proposing land as security, he stated: "For as Bills issued upon Money Security are Money, so Bills issued upon Land, are in Effect Coined Land" (1:150–51). Franklin's phrase is memorable, but the argument has a flaw. Willard Phillips pointed out that the convertibility of the fund is as important as its sufficiency and permanency of value.[25] Land was and is less convertible than movable property.

Coined Land

Toward the end of his 1729 pamphlet, Franklin turned from a general consideration of the nature of money to the particular situation of Pennsylvania. (The last section corresponds to the final part of a Puritan sermon, the use or application.) He began with a phrase suggesting that he was actually recalling the Puritan sermon structure: "to *apply* [emphasis mine] the Above to our own

Circumstance: If Land in this Province was falling, or any way likely to fall, it would behove the Legislature most carefully to contrive how to prevent the Bills issued upon Land from falling with it." Franklin again makes use of demography: "But as our People increase exceedingly, and will be further increased, as I have before shewn, by the Help of a large Addition to our Currency; and as Land in consequence is continually rising, So, in case no Bills are emitted but what are upon Land Security, the Money-Acts in every Part punctually enforced and executed, the Payments of Principal and Interest being duly and strictly required, and the Principal *bona fide* sunk according to Law, it is absolutely impossible such Bills should ever sink below their first Value, or below the Value of the Land on which they are founded" (1:151). John Law had also proposed "to lend Notes [i. e., paper money] on Land Security" and thought that "Land is what in all Appearance will keep its Value best, it may rise in Value, but cannot well fall."[26]

After considering the safety of land as security, Franklin turned to another argument in favor of a paper currency: it was so much more efficient than bartering. "*Money, as a Currency, has an Additional Value by so much Time and Labour as it saves in the Exchange of Commodities. If . . .* it saves one Fourth Part of the Time and Labour of a Country; it has, on that Account, one Fourth added to its original Value" (1:153). Before closing, Franklin asked how much interest should be charged for the loan of the paper currency. "We must consider what is the Natural Standard of Usury." Again he echoed Sir William Petty: "And this appears to be, where the Security is undoubted, at least the Rent of so much Land as the Money lent will buy." The reason is that no one "will lend his Money for less than it would fetch him in as Rent if he laid it out in Land, which is the most secure Property in the World." After pointing out that money should bear a higher interest when the security for it was risky, Franklin generalized that "where Money is scarce, Interest is high, and low where it is plenty" (1:153–54). Franklin used what some later economists called the fructification theory of interest.[27] Willard Phillips, however, said that he confounded a "*circulating medium* with *loanable* capital." Anachronistically, Franklin's argument is Keynesian, though Keynes himself knew that John Locke earlier stated the principle that the quantity of money affected the interest rate.[28]

Franklin thought it was to a country's advantage to make interest as low as possible, which was best done by making money plentiful. "And since, in Emitting Paper Money among us the Office has the best of Security, the Titles to the Land being all skillfully and strictly examined and ascertained; and as it is only permitting the People by Law to coin their own Land, which costs the Government nothing, the Interest being more than enough to pay the Charges of Printing, Officers Fees, &c. I cannot see any good Reason why Four per Cent. to the Loan-Office should not be thought fully sufficient. As a low Interest may incline more to take Money out, it will become more plentiful in Trade; and this may bring down the common Usury, in which Security is more dubious, to the Pitch it is determined at by Law" (1:154). Franklin did not quite get his way. The assembly set the interest at 5 percent.

Franklin introduced a final possible objection: "It may perhaps be objected to what I have written concerning the Advantages of a large Addition to our Currency, That if the People of this Province increase, and Husbandry is more followed, we shall overstock the Markets with our Produce of Flower, &c." He then refuted it: "we can never have too many People (nor too much Money) For when one Branch of Trade or Business is overstocked with Hands, there are the more to spare to be employed in another. So if raising Wheat proves dull, more may (if there is Money to support and carry on new Manufactures) proceed to the raising and manufacturing of Hemp, Silk, Iron, and many other Things the Country is very capable of, for which we only want People to work, and Money to pay them with" (1:155).

B. B./Franklin claimed that a paper currency would be a benefit to all and at the same time returned to an implied attack on those who opposed paper currency—supposedly the usurers, the extremely wealthy, the Proprietors, and the British merchants trading to Pennsylvania. He generalized: "it is the highest Interest of a Trading Country in general to make Money plentiful; and that it can be a Disadvantage to none that have honest Designs." Even usurers will profit, because they will be more secure in what they lend and they will be able to use their money to greater advantage. The great merchants, too, who have large sums outstanding "in Debts in the Country," will not be harmed because they will get in their debts so much easier and sooner "as the Money becomes plentier." Considering the "Interest and Trouble saved, they will not be Losers." Neither will it hurt the interest of Great Britain, "and it will greatly advance the Interest of the Proprietor."

Finally, after naming the categories of persons who selfishly, if supposedly mistakenly, opposed a paper currency, Franklin wrote: "It will be an Advantage to every industrious Tradesman, &c. because his Business will be carried on more freely, and trade be universally enlivened by it. And as more Business in all Manufactures will be done, by so much as the Labour and Time spent in Exchange is saved, the Country in general will grow so much the richer" (1:155–56).

"B. B." added a postscript maintaining his humility, reasonableness, and openness but subtly suggesting that opponents of paper currency were enemies of Pennsylvania. He said that the essay was written and published in haste, that the subject was intricate, and that he apologized if any parts were obscure or ignored possible arguments against his positions. "I sincerely desire to be acquainted with the Truth, and on that Account shall think my self obliged to any one, who will take the Pains to shew me, or the Publick, where I am mistaken in my Conclusions, And as we all know there are among us several Gentlemen of acute Parts and profound Learning, who are very much against any Addition to our Money, it were to be wished that they would favour the Country with their Sentiments on this Head in Print; which, supported with Truth and good Reasoning, may probably be very convincing."

In asking for a reply, Franklin chose a rhetorically superior position: if a reply appeared, he not only had requested it but could, of course, answer it; and if no reply appeared, it made it seem as though there was really nothing to say against paper money. He pointed out that "those ingenious Gentlemen" who opposed a paper currency had never written why they did so. He ended by claiming that "it would be highly commendable in every one of us, more fully to bend our Minds to the Study of What is the true Interest of PENNSYLVANIA; whereby we may be enabled, not only to reason pertinently with one another; but, if Occasion requires, to transmit Home such clear Representations, as must inevitably convince *our Superiors* [emphasis mine] of the Reasonableness and Integrity of our Designs" (1:156–57). (How that usual and almost necessary diction must have irritated Franklin.)

EFFECT

Franklin recalled in the *Autobiography* that the pamphlet was "well receiv'd by the common People in general; but the Rich Men dislik'd it; for it increas'd and strengthen'd the Clamour for more Money; and they happening to have no Writers among them that were able to answer it, their Opposition slacken'd, and the Point was carried by a Majority in the House" (A 67). One wealthy person whom Franklin must have had in mind was Isaac Norris, Sr., who wrote Penn against the possible currency act on 30 April 1729. But the Proprietors were convinced by the chorus of complaints from Pennsylvania and, perhaps, by the reluctant reasoning of Norris, who conceded that the Proprietors' "Concurrence" in the act would "take off your Enemys from one of the most formidable handles whereby to make head against your Interest."[29] Perhaps Franklin hoped to print the paper money (if the legislature passed a paper currency bill), but that was not his primary reason for writing in favor of it: he argued for a paper currency long after he had stopped printing.

Franklin's venture into Pennsylvania politics succeeded resoundingly. According to the economist Richard A. Lester, "The price level in Pennsylvania was more stable during the fifty years following the first Colonial currency issue in 1723 than the American price level has been during any succeeding fifty-year period."[30] Franklin wrote that his friends in the House, "who conceiv'd I had been of some Service, thought fit to reward me, by employing me in printing the Money, a very profitable Jobb, and a great Help to me." Franklin misremembered, for Andrew Bradford, as usual, printed the £30,000 Pennsylvania money voted 10 May 1729. Franklin also noted that he "soon after obtain'd thro' my friend Hamilton, the Printing of the New Castle Paper Money, another profitable Jobb, as I then thought it; small Things appearing great to those in small Circumstances" (A 67). Franklin probably did print the corresponding 1729 Delaware issue, voted in the fall, though no records concerning its printing and no examples of it survive.[31] For £100, Franklin printed the additional £40,000 Pennsylvania money voted on 6 February 1730/1 and, for an unknown sum, the £12,000 passed by the Delaware Assembly 1 March 1733/4.[32]

Though we have no information on the number of copies printed, *A Modest Enquiry into the Nature and Necessity of a Paper Currency* was the first extremely successful product of the fledgling Franklin and Meredith printing press. The subject was of immediate political interest. Those on both sides of the question read it. Unlike many of his later writings for public projects that he printed gratis, Franklin charged six pence for *A Modest Enquiry*; he was too poor not to. Other colonies were interested: the *New York Gazette* (2, 9, and 16 June 1729), and the *Maryland Gazette* (22 July 1729) reprinted it. Since Franklin sent a dozen copies to his brother James in Newport, Rhode Island on 30 October 1731, I suspect he kept the type of *A Modest Enquiry* standing for at least a few days to make sure that he had more than enough copies to sell. (Mutually profitable business dealings, starting in the fall of 1731, foreshadowed the personal reconcilement of the two brothers during Franklin's visit to Newport in the fall of 1733.)

Karl Marx wrote that "Franklin's analysis of exchange-value had no direct influence on the general course" of economics, because he dealt only "with special problems of political economy for definite practical purposes."[33] Technically, Marx is correct, for *A Modest Enquiry* was not reprinted in England or Europe during Franklin's life. But the ideas in *A Modest Enquiry* turn up repeatedly in Franklin's later writings. The French Physiocrats and the English and Scotch economists knew and often cited his later writings on economics and demography.

FRANKLIN'S POLITICAL AND ECONOMIC BELIEFS

During the course of the pamphlet, the twenty-three-year-old Franklin wrote briefly on four topics to which he often returned: values, economics, demography, and the relations between England and America. *A Modest Enquiry* set forth opinions and positions that he later either echoed or developed. He wrote that humans were selfish, and self-interest was the normal basis of their actions (1:146). On the other hand, he found that when their own interests were not directly at stake, most humans were benevolent toward others.[34] He identified with and respected ordinary persons: "Labouring and Handicrafts Men . . . are the chief Strength and Support of a People" (1:144). Franklin's egalitarianism remained throughout his life.[35] He displayed an animosity toward persons of great wealth as usurers and exploiters of the common people (1:145). Such people, he said in part 2 of his pamphlet, were against a sufficient quantity of paper currency (1:146). He cast the Proprietors in with this group, effactually labeling them selfish usurers—persons who opposed the public good of the province (1:146–47). His contempt for the Proprietors often appeared from the publication of *A Modest Inquiry* in 1729 until he openly announced in 1755 his disgust for them and his belief that "they have brought on themselves infinite Disgrace and the Curses of all the Continent" (6:274).

Franklin defined money as a medium of exchange (1:148) and argued more convincingly and more memorably than did William Petty that the proper measure of economic value was labor (1:149). He demonstrated that a "sufficient stock" of currency promoted trade and industry (1:142–45), and he proved that silver and gold fluctuated in value and were not a true indication of the wealth of a nation (1:149), thus anticipating David Hume in discrediting this key mercantilist tenet. Lastly, he sounded a Keynesian economic note by arguing that an abundant money supply caused low interest rates and increased borrowing, resulting in high levels of production and demand for goods and services (1:142, 144–45). More than forty years later, while discussing the amount of Pennsylvania paper currency, he cautioned, "Tho' I now think there are Limits beyond which the Quantity may be hurtful" (A 54).

Franklin also advanced several observations on demography and wealth that anticipated his 1751 "Observations Concerning the Increase of Mankind." *A Modest Enquiry* shows that he had population statistics and the circulation of money by 1729. He claimed that emigration from Great Britain to Pennsylvania would "not sensibly lessen the Inhabitants of Great Britain" (1:147) and pointed out that an increase in Pennsylvania's population would create a greater demand and vent for the products of Great Britain (1:144, 147). He also argued that increased wealth would result in increased population even without taking immigration into account (1:147).

Finally, as Franklin dealt with the relations between Great Britain and America, he revealed a strong proto-Americanism. He regarded the British mercantile system as prejudiced (1:147). He displayed hostility toward luxuries imported from Great Britain and identified them with *"Pride and Prodigality"* (1:145). He claimed that Americans were the best judges of their own necessities and revealed his scorn for Great Britain's practice of forcing its trade and navigation acts upon the colonies (1:147). He suspected that Great Britain wanted to keep the colonies poor and weak lest they grow strong and ultimately demand their independence (1:147). Franklin's Americanism became obvious during the 1750s, but it was also present in his 1729 *Modest Enquiry.*

EIGHTEEN

Journalist

When I was a printer and editor of a newspaper, we were sometimes slack of news, and to amuse our customers, I used to fill up our vacant columns with anecdotes, and fables, and fancies of my own.—Benjamin Franklin, quoted by Thomas Jefferson.[1]

HAVING STOLEN FRANKLIN'S IDEA for a newspaper that would challenge and supersede Andrew Bradford's *American Weekly Mercury*, Samuel Keimer brought out the first issue of his *Universal Instructor in All Arts & Sciences: and The Pennsylvania Gazette* on 24 December 1728.[2] In the *Universal Instructor* No. 13 (20 March 1728/9), Keimer remarked that he printed 250 copies a week, but he said so in an attempt to gain more advertisements and no doubt exaggerated. Franklin recalled that Keimer had "at most only 90 Subscribers" (A 64) when he sold the paper seven months later. In addition to copies for subscribers, Keimer probably printed about 40 more to exchange for other newspapers and to give advertisers and ship captains. On 24 April 1729, finding that even by printing extracts from Chambers's *Cyclopaedia* in every issue he still did not have enough filler, Keimer started issuing Daniel Defoe's *Religious Courtship* piecemeal. He managed to turn out the *Universal Instructor* weekly until, in his Quaker-style dating, "the 19th of the 4th Month, 1729" (19 June 1729), when he missed an issue.

Keimer's next paper, 3 July 1729, told a self-pitying story of his troubles with creditors, said that he intended to write his autobiography "under the Title of the White Negro," and printed a self-pitying poem broadcasting his problems. Keimer struggled on until 25 September, when he sold the paper. He announced: "It not quadrating with the Circumstances of the Printer hereof *S. K.* to publish this *Gazette* any longer, he gives notice that this Paper concludes his third Quarter; and is the last that will be printed by him; Yet that his generous Subscribers may not be baulk'd or disappointed, he has agreed with *B. Franklin* and *H. Meredith*, at the New Printing Office, to continue it to the End of the Year, having transferred the Property wholly to them, [*D. Harry* declining it] and probably if farther encouragement appears, it will be continued longer." Keimer added that he would be leaving the province in the spring. Franklin and Meredith paid him little for the failing paper; Franklin recalled that Keimer offered it "for a Trifle, and I having been ready some time to go on with it, took it in hand directly, and it prov'd in a few Years extreamly profitable" (A 64).

A minor puzzle in Franklin's biography concerns the printer David Harry. Franklin wrote in the *Autobiography* that Keimer's "Apprentice David Harry, whom I had instructed while I work'd with him, set up in his Place at Philadelphia, having bought his Materials. I was at first apprehensive of a powerful Rival in Harry, as his Friends were very able, and had a good deal of Interest." Like Meredith, Harry was Welsh; but unlike Meredith, he seemed ambitious as a printer. He secured the printing of Titan Leeds's almanac and John Jerman's for 1730. He completed a Welsh concordance to the Bible that he had begun while working for Keimer. He established a sales office with the New York merchant William Heurtin and brought out two editions of *An Elegy on the Death of the Ancient, Venerable and Useful Matron and Midwife, Mrs. Mary Broadwell* in January 1729–30. He appeared to be a formidable rival. "I therefore propos'd a Partnership to him; which he, fortunately for me, rejected with Scorn" (A 68).

Biographers have said that Franklin offered Harry a partnership after dissolving the agreement with Meredith,[3] but the partnership with Meredith continued until 14 July 1730. David Harry published several titles in 1729 and 1730, but no imprints by him are known after the spring of 1730. In a hitherto unremarked bit of evidence, Franklin recorded in his financial accounts on Saturday, 11 July 1730, that he had received David Harry's note of hand for everything Harry owed him, which was due and payable in six months. (The amount was not indicated.) Surely the partners did not offer Harry a partnership with them when he was borrowing money from Franklin. Since Harry set up printing in Barbados in 1730, I conclude that by 11 July, he planned to leave Philadelphia and was attempting to put his affairs in order. Franklin and Meredith probably offered Harry the partnership just after he purchased Samuel Keimer's printing materials and set up for himself in the fall of 1729.

THE COLONIAL NEWSPAPER

The *Pennsylvania Gazette* for Thursday, 2 October 1729, No. 40, carried Franklin's and Meredith's names as publishers. At that time, Boston supported three newspapers; New York had one; Annapolis, one; and Philadelphia, two (including the *Gazette*). That made seven newspapers altogether in the English colonies. Franklin dropped the long title, switched from Quaker-style dating (which did not use the pagan names of the months but numbered them, beginning with March) to normal dating, stopped printing Chambers's *Cyclopaedia* and Defoe's *Religious Courtship* serially, added more local and colonial news, added more advertisements (at first mainly for his own present and future publications), and improved the paper's layout, typography, and design. Like other colonial newspapers of the 1720s and 1730s, the *Pennsylvania Gazette* comprised one comparatively small folio sheet, printed on both sides, and folded in the middle, thus making four pages. Each page had two columns of print. With *Pennsylvania*

Gazette No. 44 (27 October), Franklin reduced its size to a half sheet containing two pages and began publishing the paper twice a week, thus making at least the local news more timely. More frequent distribution evidently proved costly, so with No. 55 (4 December) he returned to weekly printing, increasing the pages back to four.

Typically, the first page of a colonial newspaper contained the infrequent royal proclamations, columns of foreign news, and, if timely, the local governor's speech to the assembly and the assembly's reply. Sometimes, but not often, it carried belletristic material. (The frequent literary material on page 1 of James Franklin's *New-England Courant* was an exception.) The staple of page 1 was foreign news. Page 2 usually continued the foreign news, went on to reprint local news from other colonial newspapers (such news was skimpy, especially before 1740), and ended with local news on page 3. As Franklin commented in his first Busy-Body essay, "the Freezing of our River has the same Effect on News as on Trade." When no ships came in, American newspapers had little or no news to print. The overland mail rarely brought news, and during the winter, the service to New York was cut back from once a week to once every two weeks. Even so, the post was often held up by blizzards and other adverse conditions. At times, the *Pennsylvania Gazette* consisted entirely of reprinted essays and of old foreign news, followed by a note that the Delaware River was frozen (thereby explaining the lack of lists of ships entering into and clearing out of Philadelphia and New Castle), concluding with advertisements. Franklin would have preferred to use more American news, but colonial newspapers carried few local items. The American newspaper editor necessarily filled his paper primarily with British and European items because they were the only news available. Many colonial printers lacked the ability to report local news, and there were no journalists as such. When interesting news articles from other colonies appeared, Franklin reprinted them. The fourth page was, whenever possible, filled with advertisements.

Newspapers changed as more American newspapers and thus more American news appeared. The number of colonial newspapers grew from seven in 1730 to ten in 1740 to thirteen in 1748, when Franklin retired and sold his business to David Hall. The newspapers themselves increased in size and in the number of words printed per paper. On 3 July 1740, Franklin started printing on a much larger folio sheet; then on 3 February 1741/2, he began using a smaller type and three columns of print per page. One reason for the change was that folio sheets of paper expanded in size during the eighteenth century,[4] another was that colonial editors increasingly had more news to print; and a third reason was that advertisements increased.[5] In 1739, the great itinerant revivalist Reverend George Whitefield came to America. The journeys and preaching of this major eighteenth-century celebrity provided a great deal of American news. As a result of all these factors, by 1740 colonial news not infrequently dominated the American newspapers. By the time Franklin retired as a printer in 1748, there was far more news to print than there had been eighteen years before.

In his first *Pennsylvania Gazette*, Franklin editorialized:

> many persons have long desired to see a good News-Paper in Pennsylvania; and we hope those Gentlemen who are able, will contribute towards the making This such. We ask Assistance, because we are fully sensible, that to publish a good News-Paper is not so easy an Undertaking as many People imagine it to be. The Author of a Gazette (in the Opinion of the Learned) ought to be qualified with an extensive Acquaintance with Languages, a great Easiness and Command of Writing and Relating Things cleanly and intelligibly, and in few Words; he should be able to speak of War both by Land and Sea; be well acquainted with Geography, with the History of the Time, with the several Interests of Princes and States, the Secrets of Courts, and the Manners and Customs of all Nations. Men thus accomplish'd are very rare in this remote Part of the World; and it would be well if the Writer of these Papers could make up among his Friends what is wanting in himself.

The imprint at the bottom of page 4 read: "*Philadelphia*: Printed by *B. Franklin* and *H. Meredith*, at the New Printing-Office near the Market, where Advertisements are taken in, and all Persons may be supplied with this Paper, at *Ten Shillings* a Year."

POLITICAL REPORTER

Franklin wrote that his editorial policy was to exclude "all Libelling and Personal Abuse." And he recommended the policy to future editors, "as they may see by my Example, that such a Course of Conduct will not on the whole be injurious to their Interests" (A 94–95). Partly based on this quotation, printing historians have sometimes argued that Franklin maintained an open press. An open press has been defined as one not only open to all parties but also one that does not print such negative material that it would be impossible for an opponent to reply with dignity in the same paper.[6] Franklin's contemporaries, however, generally believed he favored the assembly in its quarrels with the Proprietors, and Proprietary Party members usually replied to him in Andrew Bradford's paper, the *American Weekly Mercury*. We will see that even during the 1730s, Franklin's reporting and his editorial positions were occasionally so vehement that they all but precluded the possibility of replies appearing in the *Pennsylvania Gazette*.

Though printers like Franklin who enjoyed government business tended to identify with the authorities, Franklin supported the positions he believed in. Sometimes they happened to be identified with the Proprietary Party, more often with the Quaker Party. Scholars have previously ignored his attempts on several occasions to influence particular elections. He did so not only in separately printed pieces but also in his newspaper.

In an ostensibly bland recollection of the *Pennsylvania Gazette*'s first issues, Franklin wrote: "Some spirited Remarks of my Writing on the Dispute then going on between Gov. Burnet and the Massachusetts Assembly, struck the principal People, occasion'd the Paper and the Manager of it to be much talk'd of, and in a few Weeks brought them all to be our Subscribers. Their Example was follow'd by many, and our Number went on growing continually.—This was one of the first good Effects of my having learnt a little to scribble.—Another was, that the leading Men, seeing a NewsPaper now in the hands of one who could also handle a Pen, thought it convenient to oblige and encourage me" (A 64). The last sentence suggests that some leading Philadelphians subscribed because they might otherwise be the subject of unfavorable comment in the paper. Busy-Body No. 4 and the suppressed addition to Busy-Body No. 8 also implied that the author might make personal attacks on individuals. As we will see (Volume 2, Chapter 3), such reporting may well be a reason why the Philadelphia Freemasons elected Franklin a member.

In his second *Gazette*, Thursday, 9 October 1729, Franklin wrote a Whiggish editorial on Governor William Burnet's quarrel with the Massachusetts Assembly over a fixed salary. The editorial revealed Franklin's adherence to the Old Charter principles of John Wise and the country members of the Massachusetts Assembly. When the British authorities gave Massachusetts a new charter (1691), they continued the practice of allowing the Massachusetts assembly to determine the governor's salary. Consequently, it could financially penalize governors who did not do what the assembly wanted. The Old Charter Party opposed fixing a salary upon the governor, and Franklin obviously agreed. "For these Hundred Years past," editorialized Franklin, Massachusetts citizens have "enjoyed the Privilege of Rewarding the Governour for the Time being, according to *their* Sense of his Merit and Services; and few or none of their Governors have hitherto complain'd, or had Reason to complain, of a too scanty Allowance." Franklin knew better, for he must have remembered Governor Shute's quarrels with the assembly over salary. "But the late Gov. *Burnet* brought with him Instructions to demand a *settled Salary* of £1000 *per Annum*, Sterling, on him and all his Successors, and the Assembly were required to fix it immediately. He insisted on it strenuously to the last, and they as constantly refused it. It appears by their Votes and Proceedings, that they thought it an Imposition, contrary to their own Charter, and to *Magna Charta*; and they judg'd that by the Dictates of Reason there should be a mutual Dependence between the *Governor* and the *Governed*, and that to make any Governour independent on his People, would be dangerous, and destructive of their Liberties, and the ready Way to establish Tyranny."

Franklin used the typical Whiggish rhetoric of rights, with its references to "Magna Charta" and "Liberties" of the people versus "Tyranny" of the government. He rarely did so later in his career, perhaps because such language was frequently used by both sides of an argument. Further, Franklin's increasing epistemological skepticism held suspect the knee-jerk responses called for by such phrases. Among the pre-Revolutionary patriots, Franklin used the popular keywords less often than any other prolific writer.[7]

Franklin roasted Burnet and skewered the placemen who accepted the Massachusetts offices of profit. He ironically reported that the deceased Governor Burnet had received "much deserved Praise . . . for his steady Integrity in adhering to his Instructions, notwithstanding the great Difficulty and Opposition he met with, and the strong Temptations offer'd from time to time to induce him to give up the Point." Having set up Burnet for a fall, Franklin pulled out the carpet beneath the conniving governor: "And yet perhaps something is due to the Assembly (as the Love and Zeal of that Country for the present Establishment is too well known to suffer any Suspicion of Want of Loyalty) who continue thus resolutely to Abide by what *they Think* their Right, and that of the People they represent, maugre all the Arts and Menaces of a Governour fam'd for his Cunning and Politicks, back'd with Instructions from Home, and powerfully aided by the great Advantage such an Officer always has of engaging the principal Men of a Place in his Party, by conferring where he pleases so many Posts of Profit and Honour."

Subtly attacking the English authorities' assumptions of superiority and the general English opinion of the Americans' inferiority, Franklin sarcastically cited the common English opinion of the degeneration of men and animals in America. "Their happy Mother Country will perhaps observe with Pleasure, that tho' her gallant Cocks and matchless Dogs abate their native Fire and Intrepidity when transported to a Foreign Clime (as the common Notion is) yet her *Sons* in the remotest Part of the Earth, and even to the third and fourth Descent, still retain that ardent Spirit of Liberty, and that undaunted Courage in the Defence of it, which has in every Age so gloriously distinguished *Britons* and *Englishmen* from all the Rest of Mankind."

Franklin's Americanism, first manifested in the suppressed Busy-Body essay and in *A Modest Enquiry,* was repeated in the same year in his editorial on Massachusetts politics. Later, Franklin often employed similar ironic strategies: for example, his praise for the English in the 1773 "Edict from the King of Prussia." Franklin returned to Massachusetts politics in the *Gazette* on 19 February 1729/30, reporting that Jonathan Belcher, who had carried to London the Massachusetts Assembly's articles of complaint against Governor Burnet, "has succeeded in his Negotiations, and is appointed Governour in his Room." The discerning editor continued, "He is a Native of the Country, and well beloved by the People; but whether he is to insist upon the Salary which Gov. Burnet was instructed to demand, and differed with the Assembly about, Time must inform us."

Seven months later, Belcher revealed in a speech to the New Hampshire House that his thirty-second instruction was to demand a fixed salary from the colony. Franklin printed the news in the 17 September 1730 *Gazette*, abstracting the speech and reply because they were long but giving in detail the news that the New Hampshire Assembly had submitted and settled a £200 sterling annual salary upon Belcher. On 24 September 1730, Franklin commented in a satiric editorial: "It may suffice at present to observe . . . that he has brought with him those very Instructions that occasion'd the Difference between Governor *Burnet* and that People, which were what he went home commission'd as Agent for the Country, to get withdrawn, as an intolerable Grievance. But by being at Court, it seems, he has had the *advantage* of seeing Things in another Light, and those Instructions do not appear to him highly consistent with the Privileges and Interest of the People, which before, as a *Patriot*, he had very different Notions of."

To the editorial, Franklin appended his poem "The Rats and the Cheese: A Fable," a satire on Belcher particularly and avaricious politicians generally. Belcher's betrayal reminded Franklin of Bernard Mandeville's *Fable of the Bees*—which based mankind's actions on selfishness. Belcher's hypocritical posture so disgusted Franklin that he made rats the vehicle for his metaphor—the most commonly despised nuisance introduced from the Old World to the New. As Nicholas B. Wainwright suggested, Franklin may have originally read the poetic fable at a Junto meeting:

> If Bees a Government maintain,
> Why may not Rats, of Stronger Brain
> And greater Power, as well be thought
> By Machiavellian Axioms taught?
> And so they are; for thus of late
> It happen'd in the Rats *free State*: (ll. 1–6)

Former Governor Burnet had a series of offices to confer on his sycophants:

> Their Prince (his Subjects more to please)
> Had got a mighty *Cheshire Cheese*,
> In which the Ministers of State,
> Might live in Plenty and grow Great. (ll. 7–10)

Burnet's supporters claimed to be true patriots:

> A powerful Party straight combin'd,
> And their united Forces join'd,
> To bring their Measures into play,
> For none so loyal were as they;
> And none such Patriots to support,
> As well the Country as the Court.
> No sooner were the Dons admitted,
> But (all those wondrous Virtues quitted)
> Regardless of their Prince, and those

> They artfully led by the Nose;
> They all the speediest Means devise
> To raise themselves and Families. (ll. 11–22)

But these former patriots were displaced by another group of would-be patriots who promised justice:

> Another Party well observing
> These pamper'd were, while they were starving;
> Their Ministry brought in Disgrace,   25
> Expell'd them, and *supply'd their Place:*
> These on just Principles were known,
> The true Supporters of the Throne;
> And for the Subject's Liberty,
> They'd (marry would they) freely dye.   30
> But being well fix'd in their Station,
> Regardless of their Prince or Nation
> *Just like the others*, all their Skill
> Was how they might their Paunches fill.

A disgusted observer called both sides hypocrites, concerned only with getting money.

> On this, a Rat not quite so blind
> In State Intrigues as Humankind,
> But of more Honour, thus reply'd;
> Confound ye all on either Side;
> Your Politicks are all a Farce;
> And your fine Virtues but mine A——:
> All your Contentions are but these,
> Whose Art shall best secure the *CHEESE*. (ll. 35–42)

Franklin condemned Governor Belcher as the chief rat in power, but the other "Ministers of State" (his appointees to various government positions) were also greedy. The rat with honor perceived that the political positions were "all a Farce" and that the only object of the chief politicians was money. The fable enjoyed some popularity. Franklin's printing partner James Parker found it appropriate for the New York political scene and reprinted it in the *New York Gazette* on 23 December 1751. In 1764, it turned up in both the *London Chronicle* and the *St. James's Chronicle* on 13 November and then in three other newspapers before appearing in the *Gentleman's Magazine* in November 1764.[8]

The literary historian David S. Shields noted, "The test of a good fable is its applicability to more than one situation or occasion" and pointed out that Franklin's moral was general: "in any political circumstance the contending parties will cloak self-interest in whatever virtuous guise they deem most effective."[9] The poem has the savage indignation found in several of Swift's great satires.

Governor Belcher and the Massachusetts House quarreled throughout the fall. On 26 January 1730/1, Franklin summarized the recent events:

> From Boston by the last Post we have a second Speech of Governor Belcher's to the Assembly there, in which he principally remonstrates to them, That they have taken no Notice of the most important Parts of his last Speech; That the Bill they past for fixing his Salary was so ambiguous and uncertain, that he is sure they had no Expectation of his Consent to it; That all farther Contention will be but a fruitless spending of Money, for that the King will certainly effect what they undutifully oppose, and probably in such a Manner as shall make them repent their Obstinacy; And That if they will not reconsider the Bill, and thoroughly amend it conformable to the Instruction, he shall be under a necessity of dissolving them, and giving the Country an Opportunity, which he thinks they very much desire, of manifesting their Inclinations to Obedience, &c. by a new and more suitable Choice.——Accordingly on the *Saturday* following, that Assembly was dissolved by his Excellency's Orders.

(As usual, after a colonial governor dissolved an assembly, the same representatives were reelected.)

Franklin's analysis of the Massachusetts political scene revealed his underlying commitment not only to the Old Charter principles of Massachusetts politics but also to an incipient Americanism. Though a few Boston printers knew the politics of Massachusetts and New Hampshire, and though New York's William Bradford knew those of Pennsylvania and New York, Franklin knew intimately the politics of both Massachusetts and Pennsylvania. He alone possessed the ability and the daring to write about them. As we saw in the Junto chapter, Nicholas Scull emphasized Franklin's Boston background and his expertise in New England politics. The "Water-American," as Franklin had been called in London (A 46), was by 1730 becoming the spokesman for an emerging Americanism.

Franklin occasionally made astute editorial comments on English and European politics. An editorial note of 23 October 1729 prefaced four paragraphs from different English papers on the peace with Spain. Franklin identified the source of two as from government papers, one from a Whig paper and one from a Tory paper. He then commented, "When the Reader has allowed for these Distinctions, he will be better able to form his Judgment of the Affair." He made a similar observation several years later (19 December 1734) on exaggerating body counts in battle reports. Prefacing accounts of a battle, Franklin explained that "there is nothing more partial than the Accounts given of Battles, all of them lessening or magnifying the Loss or Gain on either Side, just as the Writers are affected." News could be propaganda.

FILLER

Like all early American newspaper editors, Franklin often did not have enough news to print. Like them, he resorted to filler. He justified the practice in the

Autobiography, saying that he "consider'd my Newspaper . . . another Means of communicating Instruction, & in that View frequently reprinted in it Extracts from the Spectator and other moral Writers" (A 94). Though materials from the *Spectator* appeared in the *Pennsylvania Gazette* (e.g., *Spectator* No. 209 in the paper for 26 November 1730), Franklin reprinted more material from the *London Journal*, the *Universal Spectator*, and the *Freethinker* than from the *Spectator* or *Tatler*, perhaps because the former three were recent and not so well-known. Some of the reprinted essays specified that they were borrowed; others did not. Several without a source noted have been mistakenly attributed to Franklin. On the other hand, a number of Franklin's original essays have been mistakenly thought not to be original. Opinions differ about the essays for which no source has so far been found. Franklin's filler was occasionally like that of other editors—selected quickly for no apparent reason except that the source was at hand. His filler is usually distinguished, however, in three ways. First, he wrote fictional pieces as news. One cannot, however, be certain that one or two of the pieces specified below, though probably fictional, were not actual events. Second, he added quips, often humorous, ironic, or sexual (sometimes all three), to what might have otherwise have been comparatively uninteresting items. Third, Franklin's filler was selected from a wider variety of original sources than that used by other editors; it showed more discrimination and revealed an inquiring individual's mind and taste. The *Pennsylvania Gazette*'s jokes and ironic news reports dwindled as Franklin himself less frequently set the news in print.

Filler Selected by Franklin

In a major intellectual debate of the eighteenth century, Franklin sided with the third earl of Shaftesbury against Bernard de Mandeville. Too simply put, one can say that Mandeville argued for utilitarianism as a possibly highest value; Shaftesbury argued that virtue and moral responsibility were higher values. Franklin reprinted two essays advocating Shaftesbury's position, 25 June (the *Pennsylvania Gazette* was mistakenly dated 23 June) and 9 July 1730. He selected writings on virtue for reprinting, such as "A Philosophical Enquiry into the Summum Bonum, or Chief Good of Man" (17 July 1735), for the young idealist wanted to inculcate virtue. Those three essays were reprinted from the *London Journal*.

On 10 September 1730, he reprinted an excerpt from Xenophon, *Memorable Things of Socrates*, a book he prized and used as a model when he adopted the Socratic method as a teenager in Boston (A 15). On 24 June 1731, close to the time that he wrote the "Art of Virtue" (a version of which is found in part 2 of the *Autobiography*), he reprinted *Spectator* No. 447, one source for Franklin's "Art of Virtue." On 21 October 1731, he reprinted from the *Universal Spectator* of 3 July 1731 the popular "Pulgah to His Daughter Shual," which he echoed in his 20 September 1778 bagatelle "The Ephemera." Another probable source for "The Ephemera" appeared in the *Gazette* for 11 December 1735: "The Vanity and Ambition of the Human Mind," borrowed from the *Freethinker* of 24 April 1719.

Franklin may have thought he was helping to sponsor American writers when he reprinted nine "Plain Dealer" essays from the *Maryland Gazette*, beginning 9 April 1730. All but the first two, however, first appeared in the English periodical, the *Freethinker*. Franklin also probably chose to reprint the series because it was deistic.[10] He omitted the tenth "Plain Dealer" essay, which expressed a politically conservative and undemocratic point of view. He championed American literature by reprinting the poems of the best American poet of the day: Richard Lewis's "To Mr. Samuel Hastings" appeared in the *Pennsylvania Gazette* on 6 January 1730; "A Journey from Patapsco to Annapolis" appeared on 13 May 1730; "Verses on St. Patrick's Day," 25 March 1731; and "Food for Critics," 17 July 1732.

From *The Morals of Confucius*, Franklin reprinted two excerpts on 7 and 21 March 1738. Publishing systems of morality and religions other than Christianity was common among deists. In addition to showing Franklin's openness to different schemes of ethical behavior, such a choice documents his interest in China, writings about which influenced his later hoaxes, the "Captivity of William Henry" (1768) and "A Letter from China" (1784).[11] A series of three essays from the *London Journal* titled "On Original Primitive Christianity" appeared from 16 to 30 July 1730. Franklin noted after the last one appeared that some readers judged them "heretical and pernicious," and he invited replies.

Franklin's humor appeared in his reprinting of Henry Baker's mock explication and praise of the old song "Once I Was a Batchelor, and Lived by My Self" (16 December 1729, from Baker's *Universal Spectator,* 15 February 1728/9), an imitation of Addison's appreciations of the ballad "Chevy Chase" in the *Spectator.* A minor source for Franklin's "Meditation on a Quart Mug" (19 July 1733) was taken from Thomas Sheridan's essay on the origin of mankind. Franklin borrowed it on 27 May 1731 from the *Maryland Gazette* of 4 March 1728/9, which had reprinted it from the Dublin *Intelligencer* (a periodical edited by Jonathan Swift and Sheridan).

Filler Probably Created by Franklin

A supposed accident during courtship called for a dismissive and humorous quip on 23 July 1730: "We have here an unlucky She-Wrestler who has lately thrown a young Weaver, and broke his Leg, so that tis thought he will not be able to tread the Treadles these two Months. In the mean Time, however, he may employ himself in winding Quills." Another anecdote seems more likely to have been inspired by Boccaccio's *Decameron* than by a Philadelphia event, and Franklin again concluded the anecdote with a humorous quip, including a pun: "Friday Night last, a certain St-n-c-tt-r was, it seems, in a fair way of dying the Death of a Nobleman; for being caught Napping with another Man's Wife, the injur'd Husband took the Advantage of his being fast asleep, and with a Knife began very diligently to cut off his Head. But the Instrument not being equal to the intended Operation, much Struggling prevented Success; and he was oblig'd to content himself for the present with bestowing on the Aggressor a sound Drubbing. The Gap made in the Side of the St-n-c-tt-r's Neck, tho' deep, is not thought dangerous; but some People admire, that when the Person offended had so fair and suitable an opportunity, it did not enter into his Head to turn St-n-c-tt-r himself" (17 June 1731).

A week later, Franklin told another Boccaccio-like tale:

Sure some unauspicious cross-grained Planet, in Opposition to *Venus*, presides over the Affairs of Love about this Time. For we hear, that on Tuesday last, a certain C-n-table having made an Agreement with a neighbouring Female, to *Watch* with her that Night; she promised to leave a Window open for him to come in at; but he going his Rounds in the dark, unluckily mistook the Window, and got into a Room where another Woman was in bed, and her Husband it seems lying on a Couch not far distant. The good Woman perceiving presently by the extraordinary Fondness of her Bedfellow that it could not possibly be her Husband, made so much Disturbance as to wake the good Man; who finding somebody had got into his Place without his Leave, began to lay about him unmercifully; and 'twas thought, that had not our poor mistaken Galant, call'd out manfully for Help (as if he were commanding Assistance in the King's Name) and thereby raised the Family, he would have stood no more Chance for his Life between the Wife and Husband, than a captive L—— between two Thumb Nails. (24 June 1731)

With the comment on the wife's perception that the companion's passion proved that the lover could not possibly be her husband, the soon-to-be-married Franklin mocked marriage. The comparison to "a captive L[ouse] between two Thumb Nails" added a repulsive and naturalistic note comparatively rare in the eighteenth century (think of the *Spectator* and its numerous imitators, though Swift is an earlier exception and Sterne a later one) but not uncommon in Franklin's writings.

The editor joked again about sex a month later (29 July): "We are credibly inform'd, that the young Woman who not long since petitioned the Governor, and the Assembly to be divorced from her Husband, and at times industriously solicited most of the Magistrates on that Account, has at last concluded to co-habit with him again. It is said the Report of the Physicians (who in Form examined his *Abilities*, and allowed him to be in every respect *sufficient*,) gave her but small Satisfaction; Whether any Experiments *more satisfactory* have been try'd, we cannot say; but it seems she now declares it as her Opinion, That *George is as good as de best*."

Franklin reported two suicides on 18 May 1732: "One William Young, upon some Difference with his Wife, and being disguised in Liquor, went voluntarily into the Delaware, and drowned himself." And "one William Whitisin, hanged himself near Whitemarsh on a Saplin: 'Tis said he was seen a little in Drink on Horseback not long before: but no Body can tell what induc'd him to destroy himself."

The following week, having space left in the paper, Franklin adopted the persona of a Quaker lady and wrote a mock account of her suitor's threat to commit suicide: "In thy last thou informs us of two Persons who destroy'd themselves the Week before, one by hanging, and the other by drowning; both, as 'tis said, with this single View, to slip the matrimonial Noose." The Quaker lady/Franklin distanced herself and with the pun assured the reader that the piece was humorous. But of course, the moral of the previous news reports was that drunkenness led to the deaths. Franklin changed the facts to create the tone of ironic humor for the Quaker lady's anecdote: "I can now give thee an Account of a third, who last Firstday Night undertook to break his own Neck, by leaping head foremost off the steepest part of the *Bank* into *Water-street*, in case I would not consent to marry him the Week following. . . . He left me with the wildest Despair in his Countenance, and was seen by Moonlight to walk with much Hurry and Eagerness towards the fatal Precipice; but, to my great Surprize—he was not found dead at the Bottom the next Morning; and it seems has ever since kept his Shop and minds his Business." So much for the desperate lover's threat. The Quaker lady added, "I was about to send for *Dommet* [John Dommet, a Philadelphia hack poet], and put him upon making a new Ditty on this Affair; but a Friend of mine has furnish'd me with an old one, which methinks suits the Occasion indifferent well." Then Franklin printed "The Despairing Lover" by the English poet William Walsh.

Franklin's Quips

As Franklin composed the type, he occasionally could not refrain from adding a burlesque note, from making an ironic quip, or from appending a savage reflection. In the 16 October 1729 *Gazette*, after mentioning two drownings, Franklin reported: "And sometime last Week, we are informed, that one Piles a Fidler, with his Wife, were overset in a Canoo near Newtown Creek. The good Man, 'tis said, prudently secur'd his Fiddle, and let his Wife go to the Bottom." The 10 February 1729/30 paper reported that two young Irishmen met for a fight but that both proved cowards. The cowardly miles gloriosus type became a staple of American humor, finding its locus classicus in Mark Twain's portrayal of two cowardly braggarts in the raft section of *Huckleberry Finn*.

In the same 10 February paper, Franklin recorded a failed suicide attempt and revealed an appalling marriage relationship: "an unhappy Man one *Sturgis*, upon some difference with his Wife, determined to drown himself in the River; and she, (kind Wife) went with him, it seems, to see it faithfully performed, and accordingly stood by silent and unconcerned during the whole Transaction: He jump'd in near *Carpenter*'s Wharff, but was timely taken out again, before what he came about was thoroughly effected, so that they were both obliged to return home as they came, and put up for that Time with the Disappointment." To a Boston news note on the death of a lion, "King of Beasts, who had traveled all over North America by Sea and Land" (25 January 1731/2), Franklin added, "Like other Kings, his Death was often reported, long before it happened."

A shocking anecdote appeared on 15 February 1731/2: "We hear from the Jersey side, that a Man near Sahaukan being disordred in his Senses, protested to his Wife that he would kill her immediately, if she did not put her Tongue into his Mouth: She through Fear complying, he bit off a large Piece of it; and taking it between his Fingers threw it into the Fire with these Words, *Let this be for a Burnt-Offering*." One hardly knows what to make of this supposed news note. Could Franklin have been reporting an actual event? Perhaps, but no one else reported it. If it is a mock news note, what is its possible point? Women who talk incessantly can drive men to madness? Franklin had been married for a year and a half. Was Deborah Franklin constantly talking? If so, this is the only evidence of it. The savagery of the disordered man's action is not explained. The tone is serious, the effect is appalling, and the fictive world it displays is one of irrationality, brutality, fear, and inexplicable violence. This is the world of Hobbesian pessimism—a view into an abyss of despair concerning humans and life that Franklin seldom revealed.

Having a little empty space on 30 March 1732, Franklin advertised: "Lost last Saturday Night, in Market Street, about 40 or 50s. If the Finder will bring it to the Printer hereof, who will describe the Marks, he shall have 10s. Reward." Reporting severe thunderstorms throughout the mid-Atlantic area on 19 June 1732, Franklin added, "The same Day we had some very hard Claps in these Parts; and 'tis said, that in Bucks County, one Flash came so near a Lad, as, without hurting him, to melt the Pewter Button off the Wasteband of his Breeches. 'Tis well nothing else thereabouts, was made of Pewter."

CRUSADING REFORMER

In the 20 November 1729 *Gazette*, Franklin began a series of articles on the miserable conditions in various parts of the British world. Though the articles were filler, Franklin's editorial note at the end of the first one testifies to his concern. The issue described the economic conditions in Ireland. In a preface to several accounts from various English newspapers on Irish affairs, Franklin stressed the "Poverty, Wretchedness, Misery, and Want" among the Irish, their high taxes, and "their griping avaricious Landlords" who exercised over them "the most merciless Racking Tyranny and Oppression." The editorial note anticipated his 13 January 1772 observations on traveling in Scotland and Ireland where "the Bulk of the People" were "extreamly poor, living in the most sordid Wretchedness in dirty Hovels of Mud and Straw, and cloathed only in Rags."

The following four newspapers, 24 November to 4 December 1729, featured reprints on the abysmal conditions in English jails, thereby reflecting James Edward Oglethorpe's campaign against debtors' prisons. Then on Tuesday, 9

December, Franklin editorialized that he was "glad to observe, that those Papers have been more generally entertaining than some others which were only fill'd with Paragraphs of common Foreign Occurrences." He attempted to account for the readers' interest and, at the same time, to arouse their sympathies further:

> Indeed, what can more nearly affect the Hearts of those that have any the least Share of Humanity and Compassion, than to see Numbers of honest but unhappy Men, guilty of no Crime, unless being unfortunate may be call'd a Crime; yet dragg'd into noisome Dungeons, tortured with cruel Irons, and even unmercifully *starv'd* to Death, *in the Heart of a Plentiful City* [emphasis mine], in the midst of a Country fam'd for Justice and Liberty, and at the Pleasure of one wretched petty Tyrant, a vile, mean-spirited, pitiless Villain, only distinguished from others by his unparallel'd Wickedness and Barbarity: I say, what can be more affecting than such a Prospect as this; if perhaps the Joy be not more affecting, when we see such uncommon Wrongs and Injuries enquir'd into and redress'd, and the infamous Actions brought to condign Punishment.

Lovers of literature among Franklin's readers, like his friend Joseph Breintnall, would have recognized in Franklin's editorial remarks on the abundance of food in London an ironic allusion to Joseph Addison's poem, "A Letter from Italy" (1701).[12] In the midst of his celebration of Italy's past arts, Addison inserted a sympathetic account of the plight of the Italian peasant oppressed by tyranny:

> The poor inhabitant beholds in vain
> The red'ning Orange and the swelling grain:
> Joyless he sees the growing Oils and Wines,
> And in the Myrtle's fragrant shade repines:
> Starves, in the midst of nature's bounty curst,
> And in the loaden vineyard dies for thirst. (ll. 113–18)

Addison contrasted the oppressed Italian with the English who lived in a land of liberty, where "smiling Plenty leads thy wanton train" (l. 122). Franklin sarcastically implied that the English are fooling themselves and that their social system (which starves people to death, "in the Heart of a Plentiful City, in the midst of a Country fam'd for Justice and Liberty") contains numerous injustices. The series and Franklin's editorial also foreshadow his interest in penal reform—a minor theme in "The Speech of Miss Polly Baker" and a major concern in his letter to Benjamin Vaughan on criminal laws (14 March 1785).[13] The series on prisons did not appear in any other colonial newspaper, and Franklin's editorial note at the end testifies to his concern about the plight of the prisoners.

Just as the English social system and condescension to Americans annoyed Franklin, so, too, did the English and American libel laws against irreligious writings. Knowing that his 1725 *Dissertation on Liberty and Necessity* was libelous, he had deliberately hidden all means of identifying the author and publisher. Now, five years later, in the 19 March 1730 *Pennsylvania Gazette*, he reprinted the sentence against the freethinker Thomas Woolston (1670–1733), which jailed him till death. Franklin found full accounts of Woolston's prosecution and trial and published them as lead articles in his 26 March and 2 April papers.[14] In the 7 May 1730 paper, he reprinted an obituary of Anthony Collins, another deist and an influence on the young Franklin. Like the reprinted deistic "Plain-Dealer" essays noted above, these materials reflected his private opinions and his attempts to influence public opinion. He refrained, however, from any editorial comment, for that would have invited trouble.

ENTERTAINMENTS AND FEATURES

In the 9 December 1729 *Gazette*, Franklin attempted to interest his readers in a news note by appending a question to it: "*Burlington County, Nov.* 30. On the 15th Instant, at Night, one *John Armstrong* was watching for Venison in his Cornfield, and a Horse happening to come into the Field, he took him for a Deer, and shot him dead; it is said he must pay for the same. *Query*, Whether he ought to pay for the same, since it was by Mistake, and the Horse a Tres-passer." Using the pseudonym "The Casuist," Franklin replied the following week. The pseudonym alluded to a popular seventeenth-century genre, cases of conscience, in which tantalizing choices were posed for the "right" solution to a moral problem. Increase and Cotton Mather were among the authors who wrote cases of conscience in early America.

Franklin read them, but he was also familiar with the tradition in journal-ism. The pseudonym recalled the early English journalist John Dunton, whose *Athenian Gazette* (1691–97) was subtitled *or Casuistical Mercury, Resolving all the most Nice and Curious Questions Proposed by the Ingenious*. All early eighteenth-century litterateurs knew Dunton's work. The "Love Casuist" appeared in *Spectator* Nos. 591, 602, 605, 607, 608, 614, and 623. The *New-England Courant* used the pseudonym "the Casuist," as did the best writer for Keimer's paper (25 February and 4 March 1728/9). As we have seen, Franklin himself burlesqued the Reverend Solomon Stoddard's *Answer to Some Cases of Conscience* (Boston, 1722) in a pamphlet titled *Hoop-Petticoats Arraigned and Condemned by the Light of Nature, and Law of God* (1722).

The Casuist said that Armstrong should pay for the horse "because the Mis-take was not barely accidental, but had more of Rashness in it; And secondly, Because the Law has provided Redress for such as have Damage by trespassing Cattle." He added that "the Death of the Horse was a greater Loss to the Owner, than the damage done in the Corn-field." The Casuist/Franklin censured "the ill Practice of Night-watching to shoot Venison" because one cannot see well in the dark, so that "Men have been shot for Deer" (1:163).

The Complex Casuist

Two years later, on 18 January 1731/2, Franklin returned to the pseudonym, now with an underlying theme. In the following essays, the various positions the

Casuist took on an ostensibly simple question actually mirrored Franklin's views on the world's complexities: there is no place to stand, no place outside our context, no fulcrum, from which we can move the world. There is no metaphysical, absolute certainty—even simple, ordinary events are capable of numerous contrasting, bewildering interpretations. Humans exist in a maze.

Franklin posed a seemingly easy question: "A Man bargained with another, for the Keeping of his Horse six Months, while he made a Voyage to Barbadoes." When he returned, he asked for the horse, but the man who kept him reported that the "Horse stray'd away, or was stolen, within a few Days after he receiv'd him, and that he has not heard of him since." The owner then demanded to be paid for the horse. "*Query*, Whether the Man who took the Horse to keep, may not justly demand a Deduction of so much as the Keeping of the Horse would have amounted to for Six Months, according to the Agreement?" The Casuist answered (25 January) that the person who kept the horse should pay a reasonable price for him, after deducting his charge for keeping the horse. If the two parties disagreed over the price of the horse or the care of the keeper, the two men should "refer the Decision of it to two or more honest Men, indifferently chosen between them" (1:221–22).

In the same paper, a second "Casuist" (also Franklin) had a different opinion. The owner might insist on being paid the entire value of the horse "without allowing any Deduction for his Keeping after he was lost." This Casuist advanced six reasons: "1. Unless an express Agreement be made to the contrary, 'tis always suppos'd when Horses are put out to keep, that the Keeper runs the Risque of them, (unavoidable Accidents only excepted, wherein no Care of the Keeper can be supposed sufficient to preserve them, such as their being slain by Lightning, swept away by sudden Floods, or the like). *This you yourself tacitly allow, when you offer to restore me the Value of my Horse.* Were it otherwise, People, having no Security against a Keeper's Neglect or Mismanagement, would never put Horses out to keep." Second, keepers charged enough to make a profit even though they occasionally had to pay for a lost or stolen horse: "So that what a Man pays more for his Horse's Keeping, than the Keeper could afford to take if he ran no Risque, is in the Nature of a Premium for the Insurance of his Horse. *If I then pay you for the few Days you kept my Horse, you ought to restore me his full Value*" (1:223–24).

The Casuist's third reason argued that the horse ate the keeper's hay and oats only for a few days; the rest of the feed that the horse would have eaten in six months remained in the keeper's stable. Fourth, if persons were paid for keeping horses when they were not kept, then the keepers had opportunities for selling such horses and pocketing not only that money but also what they were to be paid for keeping the horses. Franklin continued with two more long reasons and concluded: "Upon the whole, I am of Opinion, that no Deduction should be allow'd for the Keeping of the Horse after the Time of his straying" (1:224–25). Both Franklin's delight in reasoning and in logic and his skeptical belief that you could use reason and logic to prove anything you wanted to prove are underlying themes.

A third respondent (Franklin again), who claimed not to be a casuist, also answered the query: "The Loss of the Horse, naturally implies a Neglect of the Keeper; and there is no Reason the Owner should suffer by any Act of the Keeper, either in the Price of the Horse, or Expence of seeking after him. And forasmuch as the Keeper hath fallen short in the Performance of his Contract, he not only doth not deserve any Reward, but hath forfeited the Penalty of the Bargain, if there were any Penalty annexed to it. But it is quite otherwise with the Owner; for the Performance on his Part, is subsequent to that of the Keeper; nor can he be said to fail till the other hath performed, which he hath put out of his Power ever to do. Therefore he ought to have Satisfaction for no more than the Time he had the Horse in Keeping." Signed, "N. B." (1:225–26). Who was right? The reader was left in the lurch. And so, implied Franklin, is every man concerning metaphysical certainties.

The Lascivious Casuist

Franklin's Love Casuist was inspired by the *Spectator*, but the *Spectator* essays are moral and prudish (except No. 623, which has some sexually suggestive content). Franklin's essays, especially the following unpublished one, are much more provocative. Franklin submitted a risqué query to the Casuist in the *Pennsylvania Gazette* (26 June 1732): "I am puzzled with a certain Case of Conscience, which I would gladly have well solved. . . . Suppose *A* discovers that his Neighbour *B* has corrupted his Wife and injur'd his Bed: Now, if 'tis probable, that by *A's* acquainting *B's* Wife with it, and using proper Solicitations, he can prevail with her to consent, that her Husband be used in the same Manner, *is he justifiable in doing it?*" Franklin added a "P.S." that made the query seem to be an actual situation: "P.S. If you are acquainted with Mr. Casuist, you may give him this privately, and I will cause one to call at your House sometime hence for his Answer: But if you know him not, please to publish it, that he may read it in your Paper." The Casuist/Franklin took the high road in his 3 July 1732 reply: "It should seem that the Proposer of that Case, is either no Christian, or a very ill instructed one; otherwise he might easily have learnt his Duty from these positive Laws of Religion, *Thou shalt not commit Adultery: Return not Evil for Evil, but repay Evil with Good.*" In addition to the religious argument, the Casuist thought that reason also dictated that he obey the laws. If not, he would be "making himself Judge in his own Cause, which all allow to be unreasonable." Furthermore, "such Practices can produce no Good to Society, but great Confusion and Disturbance among Mankind" (1:234–35).

In addition to the Christian answer, Franklin drafted an immoral response, which he signed "Anti-Casuist." He decided, however, not to print the lascivious reply. It began by saying that whether the offended party was "a Christian or a Man of Reason," he was justified in seducing the other man's wife: "If my

Wife commits Adultery with him, she thereby dissolves the Bond of Marriage between her and me, and makes us two separate and single Persons. The Laws of every Country and even of Christianity allow Adultery to be a good Cause of Divorce." Since adultery dissolved the marriage bond, each of the four persons was now single. "If I afterwards enjoy his Wife, or rather her that was his Wife, I do not commit Adultery for Adultery cannot be committed where both Parties are single and consequently, do not breake that positive Command which he mentions" (1:236).

In the second reason, the lascivious Casuist supposes that the couples remain married, then if the man ("A") who deceived "his Wife and defrauded her of her due Benevolence, bestowing it where it was not due, on my Wife," then B's family "is properly Debtor" and A's wife is "Creditor." If B then bestows on A's wife "the Benevolence which was before due to mine," B's wife has no reason to complain, "having before receiv'd from him (A); and with respect to his Wife, tis so far from doing an Injury that 'tis rather righting the injured or paying a just Debt."

As Franklin goes on with his reasoning and proofs, he exhausts and befuddles the reader, anticipating the exhaustive logical focus of Jonathan Edwards.[15] Edwards, however, believed in the accuracy and precision of his logic; Franklin, in an undercurrent, scoffed at logic while drawing out the lascivious argument. Though he studied and mastered the traditional Aristotelian logic, Franklin also learned from Francis Bacon, the Port Royalists, John Locke, and Nathaniel Gardner that the old logic was the tool of the emotions and had little to do with the nature of reality. The Anti-Casuist continued: "tis also as far from Revenge; for as he took my Wife for his Use, I give myself for his Wife's Use; which is the same thing as if a Man demanded my Bed and I give him the Coverlid also. So that a Man does not thereby as the Casuist asserts, break the Law which forbids Revenge" (1:236).

Franklin's immoral persona maintained that "no Injury can be done where no Body is injur'd." As long as the affair was not made public, no injury was done. Thus, the Anti-Casuist suggested that a hypocritical and amoral world of adultery existed in private among reputable members of society and that as long as it remained private, nothing was wrong. The Anti-Casuist denied that having sexual relations in revenge would reduce all to confusion. He said that in some cases a husband who found that his wife was having an affair would kill her and perhaps her lover, too. The lover, conscious that he has done the husband an injury, must always fear the husband's revenge. But if the husband made love to the lover's wife, they would be even, "and they may embrace with open Hearts like Brothers, and be good Friends ever after."

In drawing out the argument to its "logical" conclusion, Franklin mocked both the particular argument and logic in general. "For if B [the lover] might think it an Injury in any other Man to use his Wife; he cannot say tis an Injury in A [the husband], because he had first serv'd him so; and If he will say that

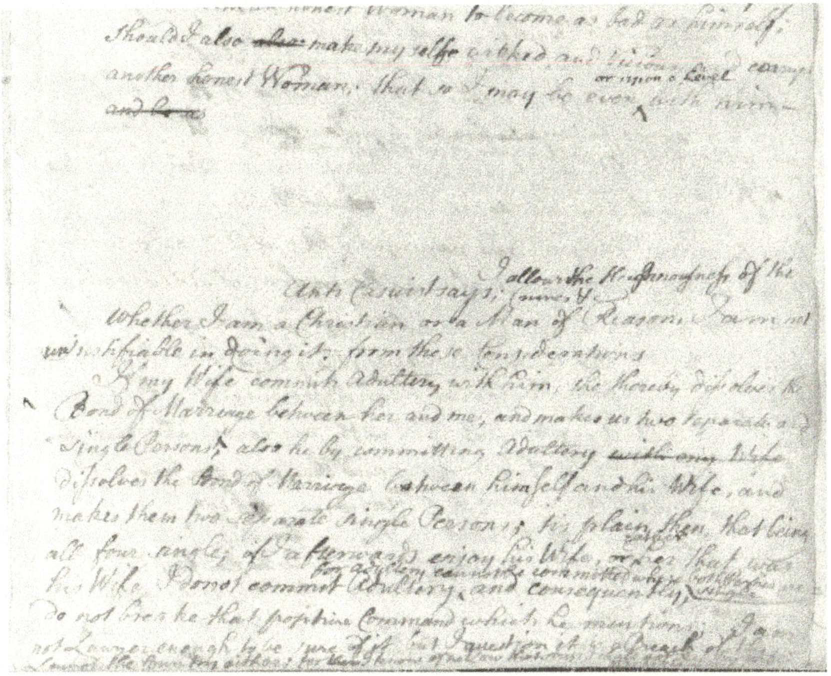

Figure 29. The Lascivious Casuist, written for the 3 July 1732 Pennsylvania Gazette but suppressed by Franklin. On 26 June 1732, Franklin submitted a query to the Pennsylvania Gazette: "Suppose A discovers that his Neighbour B has corrupted his Wife and injur'd his Bed: Now, if 'tis probable, that by A's acquainting B's Wife with it, and using proper Solicitations, he can prevail with her to consent, that her Husband be used in the same Manner, is he justifiable in doing it?" The following week, 3 July, writing as "The Casuist," he answered that A should not.

But at the same time, Franklin wrote another answer as the "Anti-Casuist" in which he gave a series of reasons arguing that A should indeed have an affair with B's wife. Franklin wrote, "Anti Casuist says [↑ . . . ↓ indicates insertion] ↑I allow the Hei<gh>nousness of the Crime, &c.↓ Whether I am a Christian or a Man of Reason, I am not ↑un↓justifiable in doing it. from these Considerations. If my Wife commits Adultery with him, she thereby dissolves the Bond of Marriage between her and me; and makes us two separate and single Persons, ˆ [carot, but no insertion] also he by committing Adultery [<. . .> indicates cancellation] <with my Wife> dissolves the Bond of Marriage between himself and his Wife, and makes them two separate single Persons; tis plain then, that being all four single; if I afterwards enjoy his Wife, or ↑rather↓ her that was his Wife, I do not commit Adultery ↑for adultery cannot be committed where both Parties are single↓and consequently, do not breake that positive Command which he mentions; I am not Lawyer enough to be sure of it, but I question it is a Breach of the Law of the Country either; for <this> I know of no Law that says I shall not use his Wife [?as he has mine? Undeciphered]"

Franklin decided that the piece was indecorous and did not print it. It was the most tantalizing and sexual essay that he had thus far written. I suspect that it was the immorality, rather than the sexuality, that made him decide not to print it. Courtesy, Historical Society of Pennsylvania, Philadelphia.

his Familiarity with A's Wife, was only a Civility; he cannot complain that the Civility was not return'd" (1:237). The amoral world, like Sophistry itself, is a sham.

Franklin's casuistical consideration of adultery has all the tantalizing and enticing suggestiveness characteristic of good pornography. It anticipates the "Old Mistresses Apologue" (25 June 1745) and "The Elysian Fields" (7 December 1778). Both his writing such sensual sexual materials and his flirtations account for his reputation as a roué, though no evidence whatever exists of any extramarital affairs after he and Deborah joined together in 1730.

PRINTERUM EST ERARE

A *Gazette* feature article on printers' errors appeared on 13 March 1729/30. Franklin began with a mock epigraph, *Printerum est errare.* The occasion was a mistake Franklin made in the previous week's paper. In an article concerning Governor Jonathan Belcher, Franklin had printed, "After which his Excellency, with the Gentlemen trading to New-England, died elegantly at Pontack's." Under the pseudonym "J. T.," Franklin noted: "The Word *died* should doubtless have been *dined, Pontack's* being a noted Tavern and Eating-house in *London* for Gentlemen of Condition; but this Omission of the letter (*n*) in that Word, gave us as much Entertainment as any Part of your Paper." Franklin then told a series of famous printers' errors, the first one having antireligious subject matter. "One took the Opportunity of telling us, that in a certain Edition of the Bible, the Printer had, where *David* says *I am fearfully and wonderfully made,* omitted the Letter (*e*) in the last Word, so that it was, *I am fearfully and wonderfully mad;* which occasion'd an ignorant Preacher, who took that Text, to harangue his Audience for half an hour on the Subject of *Spiritual Madness.*"

Franklin also told of the "Wicked" Bible of 1631: "Another related to us, that when the Company of Stationers in *England* had the Printing of the Bible in their Hands, the Word (*not*) was left out in the Seventh Commandment, and the whole Edition was printed off with *Thou shalt commit Adultery,* instead of *Thou shalt not,* &c. This material *Erratum* induc'd the Crown to take the Patent from them which is now held by the King's Printer." Franklin cited the "*Spectator*'s Remark" in No. 579 (11 August 1714) on the story: "he doubts many of our modern Gentlemen have this faulty Edition by 'em, and are not made sensible of the Mistake."

J. T./Franklin reported another mistake in a religious work: "A Third Person in the Company acquainted us with an unlucky Fault that went through a whole Impression of Common-Prayer-Books; in the Funeral Service, where these Words are, *We shall all be changed in a moment, in the twinkling of an Eye,* &c. the Printer had omitted the 'c' in *changed,* and it read thus, *We shall all be hanged,* &c." Franklin finally came to his own defense. "And lastly, a Mistake of your Brother News-Printer was mentioned, in *The Speech of* James Prouse *written the Night before he was to have been executed,* instead of *I die a Protestant,* he has put it, *I died a Protestant*. Upon the whole you came off with the more favourable Censure, because your Paper is most commonly very correct, and yet you were never known to triumph upon it, by publickly ridiculing and exposing the continual Blunders of your Contemporary." But here, of course, Franklin (using the rhetorical figure *occupatio*) does indeed expose and triumph over the mistakes of Bradford. "Which Observation was concluded by a good old Gentleman in Company, with this general just Remark, That whoever accustoms himself to pass over in Silence the Faults of his Neighbours, shall meet with much better Quarter from the World when he happens to fall into a Mistake himself; for the Satyrical and Censorious, whose Hand is against every Man, shall upon such Occasions have every Man's Hand against him."

Later in the year, Franklin misdated his paper 23 June (it was 25 June). In the same paper, he (or perhaps his journeyman printer Thomas Whitmarsh) transposed a line in a report of London news. He apologized the following week, 2 July, for transposing the line in the previous week's paper of "23" June, deliberately repeating the glaring mistake without acknowledging it, while apologizing for a minor mistake. Franklin added: "The judicious Reader will easily distinguish accidental Errors from the Blunders of Ignorance, and more readily excuse the former which sometimes happen unavoidably." Franklin expected the attentive, if not "judicious Reader," to appreciate his joke on himself.

SATIRES AGAINST SUPERSTITION

The Drum

The 23 April 1730 *Gazette* contained Franklin's spoof, the "Letter of the Drum." The speaker had formerly been afraid of evil spirits and ghosts but had been free from such fears until recently, when spirits attacked two ministers at a nearby convention. He began: "I know well that the Age in which we live, abounds in *Spinosists, Hobbists,* and *most impious Free-Thinkers,* who despise *Revelation,* and treat the *most sacred Truths* with *Ridicule* and *Contempt*: Nay, to such an Height of Iniquity are they arrived, that they not only deny the *Existence* of the *Devil,* and the *Spirits* in general, but would also persuade the World, that the Story of *Saul* and the *Witch of Endor* is an Imposture; and which is still worse, that no Credit is to be given to the so well-attested One of the *Drummer of Tedsworth.*"

Equating the Bible with English folklore ridiculed them both. The Tedsworth drummer was the most popular English supernatural story of the previous century. Franklin probably first read it in Increase Mather, *An Essay for the Recording of Illustrious Providences* (Boston, 1684). Joseph Glanville included the drummer in his *Sadducismus Triumphatus* (1681); Samuel Butler mocked it in *Hudibras* (Two, I:131–32); a popular ballad, *A Wonder of Wonders,* told the story; and it occasioned Joseph Addison's play, *The Drummer, or The Haunted House* (1716). Franklin probably knew all these sources when he wrote the satire. Later,

John Wesley said he believed in the Tedsworth drummer, causing William Ho-garth to put Wesley and the drummer in his engraving *Credulity, Superstition, and Fanaticism* (1762).

The superstitious and fearful persona continued: "I do, indeed, confess that the Arguments of some of these unbelieving Gentlemen, with whom I have heretofore conversed on the Subject of *Spirits, Apparitions, Witches,* &c. carried with them a great Shew of Reason, and were so specious, that I was strongly inclined to think them in the Right; and for several Years past have lived without any Fear or Apprehensions of *Demons* or *Hobgoblins*; but the Case is quite al-ter'd with me now; and I who used to sleep without drawing my Curtains, am now so fearful, that I pin them every Night I go to Bed with corking Pins, and cover my self Head over Ears with the Clothes." The situational humor, in which the naïf protects himself by securing his curtains with pins and by hiding under his sheets, makes the amused reader feel superior.

The naïf explains that he became fearful again because of "a most amazing Account I received the other Day from a Reverend Gentleman, of a certain House's being haunted with the D———l of a Drummer, not a whit less obstrep-erous, than the *Tedsworthian* Tympanist." The alliteration, diction, and elegant circumlocution call attention to the ironic voice underlying the supposedly su-perstitious speaker. The "Reverend Gentleman" not long ago met a number of his brethren about "fifteen Miles below *Philadelphia*" and spent the evening "chearfully, yet soberly." While giving the usual cliché for the social behavior of religious persons, Franklin implied that they drank too much. After two of the ministers went to bed, "they heard a Drum beating very loud, now on the one Side of their Bed, then on the other, and in a Moment after on the Teaster; that sometimes they distinctly heard the *Scots Traveller*, and at other Times the *Grenadiers March*."[16] The noise continued all night, "frighted them almost to Death, and yet, which is the most surprizing and unaccountable Part of the Relation, disturbed no Mortal in the House save themselves." After a sleepless night, they went early the next morning into the room where two of their breth-ren were sleeping soundly.

At first their companions did not believe their story, but after both swore to it, the other ministers became convinced. "The next Night he with his Compan-ion went to Bed in the same Room, in which they had been so terribly frighten'd; that they had not taken their first Nap, before they heard an uncouth Noise under them; that his Companion was shortly after seized violently and forcibly by the great Toe, and in great Danger of being pulled out of the Bed; but that upon the Beating of the Drum, which happen'd at the same Instant, his Toe was released; and that to prevent any future Attacks, they hoisted their Knees up to their very Noses; the Noise still growing louder, they felt a most prodigious Weight on them, heavier, as he said, than the *Night-Mare*." Another minister had crept into their room to terrify them, but when he heard the drum, he was so frightened "that he would not have ventured back to his own Room, though he were sure to be made a Bishop; so that we were obliged to share our Bed with him, in which we lay sweating, and almost dead with Fear, 'till Morning."

Though the reader enjoys the situational humor—first being "seized violently and forcibly by the great Toe" and then the thought of the would-be prankster jumping on top of the other two ministers and suffering in a crowded bed all night, the reader must wonder (as Franklin wanted him to) if one person was a would-be prankster, could not another joker have been the supposed ghostly drummer? The persona then says that he believes the story, though he knows "well enough, that some Folks will be apt to say; it is all a Lye, a meer Forgery; in short, they will raise an infinite Number of Objections to destroy its Credit; for when I told it to a certain Person, he swore it could not be true; because in a Piece of the learned *Greutzius*, which he had read, *De examine Sagarum*,[17] he found that all the Divines in *Germany* were clearly of Opinion, that the Devil never begins to play his Pranks 'till after Midnight, and that no Spectres were seen before that Time; and this Noise beginning between ten and eleven both Nights, he was assured, for that Reason, that the Devil was no Way concern'd in it." Franklin's major thesis satirized superstition in general, but he also burlesqued those who believe that supernatural spirits must behave according to certain fixed principles. (The ghost of Hamlet's father was one well-known spirit who abided by the rules.)

The doubter who cited the "learned *Greutzius*" added an anecdote concerning a Jamaican curate who frequently drank in taverns. Being called to do the last offices to a brother departed, he reluctantly left his friends drinking but said he would return immediately: "away he hies to the Place of Burial, and as is usual, reads over the Service for the Dead, 'till he came to the Words, I heard a Voice from Heaven, saying, blessed, &c. at which he was interrupted by one of his Companions, who had followed him from the Ale-house, with a 'By G——— that's a d———'d Lye, for I have been drinking with you all Day at Mother——'s, and if you had heard the Voice, I should have heard it too, for my Ears are as good as yours." The naïf concluded by asking the publisher "whether I ought to give Credit to the above Relation or not, altho' it be attested by two Reverend Fathers."

Franklin's satire of the clergy and his spoof of superstition probably cost him some subscribers to the *Pennsylvania Gazette*. If he did not previously have a reputation in Philadelphia for impiety, this skit would have begun it.

Philoclerus: Spirit Can Act upon Matter

Franklin did not answer the "Letter of the Drum" as the editor. Instead, he wrote a companion piece two weeks later. A letter from "Philoclerus," dated "Burlington," 27 April, appeared in the 7 May 1730 *Gazette* titled "On that Odd Letter of the Drum." As Franklin's "sincere Friend and Well-wisher," Philoclerus "observed your prudent Management of the News-Paper" with a good deal of pleasure because, "till last Week, there has been no one Thing seen that might justly give Offence either to Church or State, or to any private Person." Thus Franklin began with a compliment to the *Gazette*. Philoclerus/Franklin pretended to be puzzled as to why Franklin published the letter. "You know better than to imagine that such a Thing would please the Generality of your Readers, or that it might be instrumental in doing Good to any one Creature living; I believe you have had no Reason to be piqu'd against the Gentlemen there reflected on; and as to the Wit and Humour which some Persons of reputed Taste pretend to discern in it, I protest I can see none, and I think that true Wit and Humour cannot be employ'd in ridiculing Things serious and sacred." Philoclerus here used the standard argument against Lord Shaftesbury's thesis that ridicule could be the test of truth.

The twenty-four-year-old Franklin could hardly suppress his inclination to tweak authority, and he knew that his satire of superstition and ministers would appeal to some of his coterie, including his patron Andrew Hamilton. At the same time he was probably unhappy with himself for writing and publishing the piece, for what good could it do for the majority of people? Philoclerus voiced an aspect of Franklin's divided feelings.

Philoclerus/Franklin continued that whoever wrote the "Letter of the Drum," despite his seeming "Reflection on *Spinosists, Hobbists, and most impious Freethinkers*, his Design is apparent, To bring the Dispensers of Religion among us into Contempt, and to weaken our Belief of the Divine Writings; a Design, in my Opinion, very unworthy an honest Man and a good Subject, even tho' he was of no Religion at all."

As we will see, Franklin was at least half serious in this recrimination with himself. The speaker continued that the earlier writer depreciated the Bible "by insinuating that the Story of the Drummer of *Tedsworth* is a better attested One than that of *Saul* and the Witch of *Endor*." He also called attention to the "satyrical Sneer at the Meeting of Those Reverend Gentlemen *to prevent the Growth of Atheism*." Franklin may have been partly serious in recriminating with himself, but he was also explaining the satire on religion to those who might not have perceived it.

Philoclerus/Franklin then made a serious argument against satirizing religion. He asked that the previous writer consider "That wise Men have in all Ages thought Government necessary for the Good of Mankind; and, that wise Governments have always thought Religion necessary for the well ordering and well-being of Society, and accordingly have been ever careful to encourage and protect the Ministers of it, paying them the highest publick Honours, that their Doctrines might thereby meet with the greater Respect among the common People." Then Franklin made an extraordinary statement: "if there were no Truth in Religion, *or the Salvation of Men's Souls not worth regarding* [emphasis mine], yet, in consideration of the inestimable Service done to Mankind by the Clergy, as they are the Teachers and Supporters of Virtue and Morality, without which no Society could long subsist, prudent Men should be very cautious how they say or write any thing that might bring them into Contempt, and thereby weaken their Hands and render their Labours ineffectual."

The pragmatic reasoning is not uncommon among deists. Franklin's Annapolis acquaintance, Dr. Alexander Hamilton, also argued for the social utility of religion for the "mob" in his 1744 *Itinerarium*.[18] Later, in his 6 June 1753 letter against satirizing religion, Franklin argued that religion was socially useful because it encouraged moral behavior. But an extraordinary statement, rarely if ever used by deists (or perhaps anyone else), followed when Philoclerus stated "or the Salvation of Men's Souls not worth regarding." One can interpret the quotation to mean that the question of whether or not men have souls is not worth considering—a shocking thought to most eighteenth-century thinkers; but the explicit statement is that *even* if men have souls, the "Salvation" of the soul may not be "worth regarding."

This original opinion is dumbfounding in the context of eighteenth-century theological thought. It renders moot the theologians' attempt to prove that men possess souls. Religious thinkers invariably believed that the existence of a soul, that is, of some kind of transcendental immortality, would annihilate any possible opposition. Franklin's "so what?" shifted the basic ground and anticipated Sartre's claim that even if God exists, it doesn't make any difference.[19] Few thinkers of any time are capable of such extraordinary shifts. Franklin displays here an almost Olympian scorn not only for mankind, as he did at the end of his 1725 *Dissertation*, but even for an immortal soul. The *Dissertation* concluded by questioning the importance of the soul if it were not accompanied by memory and a body. Here he went, if possible, further. Franklin's 1730 theological beliefs were not dissimilar to those in the *Dissertation*.

Philoclerus pretended to take seriously the question posed by the author of the letter of the drum, giving as his opinion that "*there is nothing absolutely impossible in the Thing it self:* We cannot be certain there are no Spirits existing; it is rather highly probable that there are: But we are sure that if Spirits do exist, we are very ignorant of their Natures, and know neither their Motives nor Methods of Acting, nor can we tell by what Means they may render themselves perceptible to our Senses. Those who have contemplated the Nature of Animals seem to be convinced that Spirit can act upon Matter, for they ascribe the Motion of the Body to the Will and Power of the Mind." Franklin's statement that "Spirit can act upon Matter" foreshadowed his opinion that "mind will one day become omnipotent over matter," an assertion his close friend Dr. Richard Price testified was one of his favorite sayings.[20]

In considering the weaknesses of human beings, Pascal had written that the will affects the understanding, that sickness affects our reason and judgment, and that self-interest "puts out our own Eyes." He also emphasized that we do not know ourselves and are incapable of knowing the nature of spirits.[21] Franklin grappled with similar issues, and his conclusions were similar, perhaps in part reflecting Pascal.

Philoclerus/Franklin argued that touch, hearing, and sight—all the sensory impressions—are dubious interpretations of reality. He instanced:

A sudden Blow upon the Eye shakes the visual Nerve in the same Manner as when Light strikes it, and therefore we think we see a Light, when there is no such Thing at that Time visible without us, and no one standing by can see it, but the Person that is struck alone. Now, how can we be assur'd that it is not in the Power of a Spirit *without* the Body to operate in a like manner on the Nerves of Sight, and give them the same Vibrations as when a certain Object appears before the Eye, (tho' no such Object is really present) and accordingly make a particular Man see the Apparition of any Person or Thing at Pleasure, when no One else in Company can see it? May not such a Spirit likewise occasion the same Vibrations in the auditory Nerves as when the Sound of a Drum, or any other Sound, is heard, and thereby affect the Party in the same manner as a real Drum beating in the Room would do, tho' no one hears it but himself.

Franklin here applied Lockean psychology and Berkeleyan idealism, as well as Newtonian science, to suggest the limitations of sensory perceptions.

On the one hand, "On that Odd Letter of the Drum" constituted a scientific argument for the possible reality of the spiritual world and even the omnipotence of the spiritual; but on the other, it questioned the relevance of the spiritual—if it does exist. Philoclerus/Franklin appeared to accept the possible truth of various religious or metaphysical systems—including Christian and non-Christian ones. Indeed, in some ways, Franklin gave more power to the spiritual than did many religions. The openness was characteristic, for Franklin, at different times, seemed to accept the most bewildering and contradictory supernatural possibilities—and at other times to deny them all.[22] One might argue that these opposing views are those of Franklin's literary persona, and not really Franklin's, but numerous religious contradictory viewpoints turn up too in his private writings.

Philoclerus claimed that readers of the letter should believe in the story of the clergymen for three reasons: "1. Because, as I have shewn above, there is nothing absolutely impossible in the Thing it self. 2. Because they were Men of Probity, Learning and sound good Sense, who related this Fact to him upon their own Knowledge. If they were not such, 'tis presum'd they would not have been thought proper Persons to be made publick Instructors. 3. Because they both concur'd in the same Testimony; and it cannot be imagin'd what Interest they should have in contriving together to impose a Falshood of that Nature upon him; since they could expect Nothing but to be ridicul'd for their Pains, both by him and every other unthinking Sceptic in the Country." Franklin concluded with a rhetorically clever stroke: "If you insert this Epistle in your next Gazette, I shall believe you did not approve of That I have been writing against." Thereby the author supposedly assumed that Franklin's printing the letter would prove him a friend to religion.

Franklin covered all the bases. He satirized superstition, religion, and ministers. He explained the satire and carried it further. Then he criticized the rationale underlying the satire, which assumed that humans knew the possible "Natures" of spirits, if spirits existed. He argued that spirit acted upon and was superior to matter. He asked what good could satires of religion do for humanity. Finally, he portrayed himself as a friend to ministers and to religion. It seems probable that Franklin began the "Letter of a Drum" and the corresponding reply by Philoclerus as satires on ministers and religion. But as he wrote the latter and considered the limitations of man's reason and knowledge, Franklin evidently thought Pascal's fideism as likely to be true as Pyrrhonism. As we will see, in 1746 he expressed a similar possibility when refuting Andrew Baxter's proof of the existence of God.

A Witch Trial at Mt. Holly

The 22 October 1730 *Pennsylvania Gazette* carried a story titled "A Witch Trial at Mount Holly," New Jersey.[23] Witchcraft had appeared as a subject in Franklin's Busy-Body No. 5, and he now devoted a news-note hoax to it. Supposedly, two persons were tried for witchcraft at Mount Holly. One literary danger of a spoof on such a subject would be the possibility of the reader's being too concerned for the fate of the accused. Therefore Franklin deliberately made the tone light and introduced a number of obviously burlesque passages. To achieve these effects, he created a superior and amused narrator. Dated Burlington, 12 October, the account began like a typical news article: "Saturday last [10 October] at *Mount-Holly*, about 8 Miles from this Place, near 300 People were gathered together to see an Experiment or two tried on some Persons accused of Witchcraft." The diction, "an Experiment or two," juxtaposes the world of science with that of superstition and begins to distance the narrator from the action. "It seems the Accused had been charged with making their Neighbours Sheep dance in an uncommon Manner, and with causing Hogs to speak, and sing Psalms, & c. to the great Terror and Amazement of the King's good and peaceable Subjects in this Province." The idea of sheep dancing and hogs singing is humorous rather than frightening. The images do not suggest a world of terrifying witchcraft but a world of buffoonery, in which serious subjects become a Punch and Judy puppet show.

"The Accusers being very positive that if the Accused were weighed in Scales against a Bible, the Bible would prove too heavy for them; or that, if they were bound and put into the River, they would swim; the said Accused desirous to make their Innocence appear, voluntarily offered to undergo the said Trials, if 2 of the most violent of their Accusers would be tried with them." Common sense reassures the reader that the outcome of the first trial will not be tragic. Surprisingly, the test of weighing against the Bible was standard throughout the Western world.[24] One would have thought that test in itself would have ended witchcraft. "Accordingly the Time and Place was agreed on, and advertised

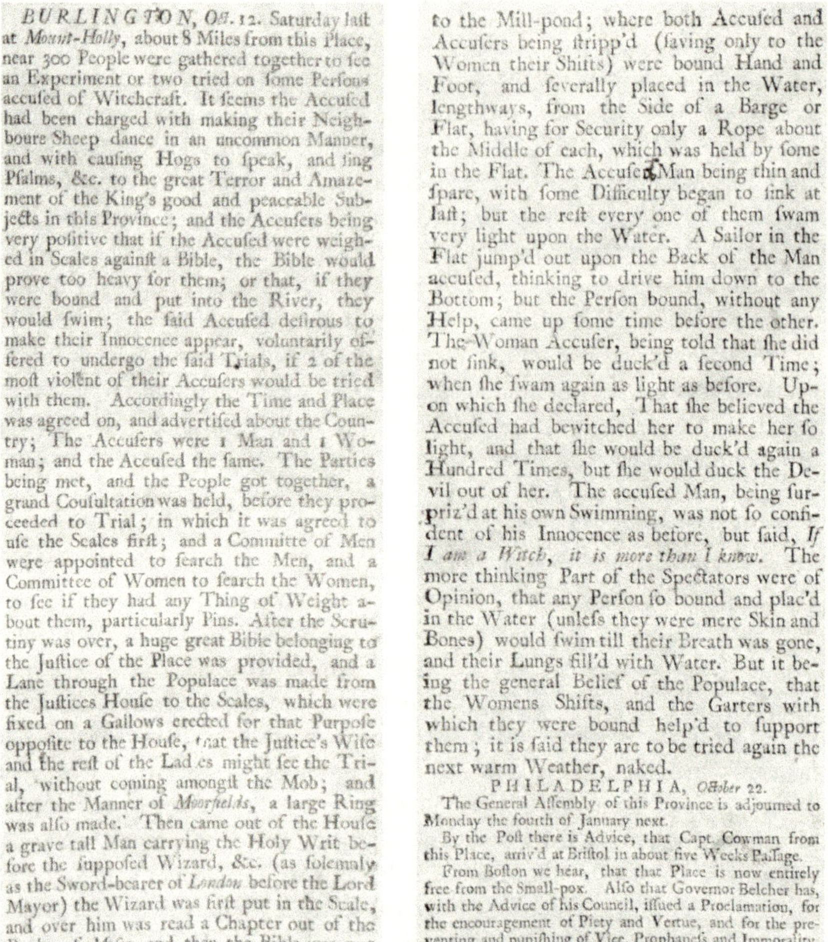

BURLINGTON, Oct. 12. Saturday last at *Mount-Holly*, about 8 Miles from this Place, near 300 People were gathered together to see an Experiment or two tried on some Persons accused of Witchcraft. It seems the Accused had been charged with making their Neighbours Sheep dance in an uncommon Manner, and with causing Hogs to speak, and sing Psalms, &c. to the great Terror and Amazement of the King's good and peaceable Subjects in this Province; and the Accusers being very positive that if the Accused were weighed in Scales against a Bible, the Bible would prove too heavy for them; or that, if they were bound and put into the River, they would swim; the said Accused desirous to make their Innocence appear, voluntarily offered to undergo the said Trials, if 2 of the most violent of their Accusers would be tried with them. Accordingly the Time and Place was agreed on, and advertised about the Country; The Accusers were 1 Man and 1 Woman; and the Accused the same. The Parties being met, and the People got together, a grand Consultation was held, before they proceeded to Trial; in which it was agreed to use the Scales first; and a Committee of Men were appointed to search the Men, and a Committee of Women to search the Women, to see if they had any Thing of Weight about them, particularly Pins. After the Scrutiny was over, a huge great Bible belonging to the Justice of the Place was provided, and a Lane through the Populace was made from the Justices House to the Scales, which were fixed on a Gallows erected for that Purpose opposite to the House, that the Justice's Wife and the rest of the Ladies might see the Trial, without coming amongst the Mob; and after the Manner of *Moorfields*, a large Ring was also made. Then came out of the House a grave tall Man carrying the Holy Writ before the supposed Wizard, &c. (as solemnly as the Sword-bearer of *London* before the Lord Mayor) the Wizard was first put in the Scale, and over him was read a Chapter out of the Books of *Moses*, and then the Bible was put in the other Scale, (which being kept down before) was immediately let go; but to the great Surprize of the Spectators, Flesh and Bones came down plump, and outweighed that great good Book by abundance. After the same Manner, the others were served, and their Lumps of Mortality severally were too heavy for *Moses* and all the Prophets and Apostles. This being over, the Accusers and the rest of the Mob, not satisfied with this Experiment, would have the Trial by Water; accordingly a most solemn Procession was made to the Mill-pond; where both Accused and Accusers being stripp'd (saving only to the Women their Shifts) were bound Hand and Foot, and severally placed in the Water, lengthways, from the Side of a Barge or Flat, having for Security only a Rope about the Middle of each, which was held by some in the Flat. The Accused Man being thin and spare, with some Difficulty began to sink at last; but the rest every one of them swam very light upon the Water. A Sailor in the Flat jump'd out upon the Back of the Man accused, thinking to drive him down to the Bottom; but the Person bound, without any Help, came up some time before the other. The Woman Accuser, being told that she did not sink, would be duck'd a second Time; when she swam again as light as before. Upon which she declared, That she believed the Accused had bewitched her to make her so light, and that she would be duck'd again a Hundred Times, but she would duck the Devil out of her. The accused Man, being surpriz'd at his own Swimming, was not so confident of his Innocence as before, but said, *If I am a Witch, it is more than I know.* The more thinking Part of the Spectators were of Opinion, that any Person so bound and plac'd in the Water (unless they were mere Skin and Bones) would swim till their Breath was gone, and their Lungs fill'd with Water. But it being the general Belief of the Populace, that the Womens Shifts, and the Garters with which they were bound help'd to support them; it is said they are to be tried again the next warm Weather, naked.

PHILADELPHIA, *October* 22.

The General Assembly of this Province is adjourned to Monday the fourth of January next.

By the Post there is Advice, that Capt. Cowman from this Place, arriv'd at Bristol in about five Weeks Passage.

From Boston we hear, that that Place is now entirely free from the Small-pox. Also that Governor Belcher has, with the Advice of his Council, issued a Proclamation, for the encouragement of Piety and Vertue, and for the preventing and punishing of Vice, Prophaness and Immorality, pursuant to his Majesty's Commands given to his Excellency in his Royal Instructions.

By a Letter from South Carolina, dated Aug. 28. last, we are informed, that the Negroes had conspired to destroy the English there, and that their Design was to have been put in Execution on the Sunday before the above date, but the same being discovered several of the chief of them were taken up in order to a Tryal. And that on the 27th of August, they had there a violent Storm or Hurricane, in which all the Shipping drove ashore, except three Men of War who rid it out with their Masts standing, and three other Vessels who who were forc'd to cut their Masts by the Board. Many Houses, Chimneys and Fences were blown down, and great Loss and Damage sustained, of which we shall give a more particular Account in our next.

Figure 30. Superstition burlesqued: "A Witch Trial at Mt. Holly," Pennsylvania Gazette, 22 October 1730, pp. 3–4. Rather than printing the hoax on the front page (a position often reserved for Franklin's original compositions), Franklin printed it along with the news reports from other colonial papers and from Philadelphia; thus its position asserted it was local news. In it, Franklin mocked witchcraft and the standard tests to determine whether a person was a witch or wizard. Perhaps some readers thought it was an actual news report, but such details as sheep dancing and hogs singing psalms surely alerted most readers to Franklin's satirical purposes. In addition to attacking superstition, the satire was delicious entertainment, with a strong, single-word, sexually suggestive ending, which Franklin surely prized. Courtesy, Library Company of Philadelphia.

about the Country; The Accusers were 1 Man and 1 Woman; and the Accused the same. The Parties being met, and the People got together, a grand Consultation was held, before they proceeded to Trial; in which it was agreed to use the Scales first; and a Committee of Men were appointed to search the Men, and a Committee of Women to search the Women, to see if they had any Thing of Weight about them, particularly Pins." The last detail burlesqued the subject and again reassured the reader that despite the possibly tragic subject matter, the piece was a spoof.

But the reporter/Franklin put in so many realistic specifics that a naive reader would have been taken in, and the following reference to the gallows would have increased the reader's suspense: "After the Scrutiny was over, a huge great Bible belonging to the Justice of the Place was provided, and a Lane through the Populace was made from the Justices House to the Scales, which were fixed on a Gallows erected for that Purpose opposite to the House, that the Justice's Wife and the rest of the Ladies might see the Trial, without coming amongst the Mob; and after the Manner of *Moorfields*,[25] a large Ring was also made." The social satire concerning the "Justice's Wife and the rest of the Ladies" is typical of Franklin's irony. The reference to the "Mob" again distanced the reporter, and the allusion to Moorfields, London, showed the persona's cosmopolitan background. "Then came out of the House a grave tall Man carrying the Holy Writ before the supposed Wizard, &c. (as solemnly as the Sword-bearer of *London* before the Lord Mayor) the Wizard was first put in the Scale, and over him was read a Chapter out of the Books of *Moses*, and then the Bible was put in the other Scale, (which being kept down before) was immediately let go; but to the great Surprize of the Spectators, Flesh and Bones came down plump, and outweighed that great good Book by abundance." The reassured reader says, naturally. But the accusers and the rest of the "Mob" demanded "the Trial by Water." The persona has again portrayed himself as a cosmopolitan observer with his reference to the London's Lord Mayor's procession.

The assembly marched "to the Mill-pond; where both Accused and Accusers being stripp'd (saving only to the Women their Shifts) were bound Hand and Foot, and severally placed in the Water, lengthways, from the Side of a Barge or Flat, having for Security only a Rope about the Middle of each, which was held by some in the Flat." An authority on witchcraft has noted that the water test was "The most persistent of all witch tests."[26] If the accused sank, it proved he was innocent; supposedly he would be pulled out before drowning. "The Accuser Man being thin and spare, with some Difficulty began to sink at last; but the rest every one of them swam very light upon the Water. A Sailor in the Flat jump'd out upon the Back of the Man accused, thinking to drive him down to the Bottom; but the Person bound, without any Help, came up some time before the other." In this world-turned-upside-down situation, the sailor was trying to help the man, by proving him innocent.

"The Woman Accuser, being told that she did not sink, would be duck'd a second Time; when she swam again as light as before. Upon which she declared, That she believed the Accused had bewitched her to make her so light, and that she would be duck'd again a Hundred Times, but she would duck the Devil out of her. The accused Man, being surpriz'd at his own Swimming, was not so confident of his Innocence as before, but said, *If I am a Witch, it is more than I know.*" Franklin made it obvious that the yokels in the skit believed in the swimming test.

The speaker explained the reason why the persons did not sink, but then returned to the opinions of the "Mob" and ended on a humorous note: "The more thinking Part of the Spectators were of Opinion, that any Person so bound and plac'd in the Water (unless they were mere Skin and Bones) would swim till their Breath was gone, and their Lungs fill'd with Water. But it being the general Belief of the Populace, that the Womens Shifts, and the Garters with which they were bound help'd to support them; it is said they are to be tried again the next warm Weather, naked."

Though the tone is superior and amusing, the underlying authorial voice is serious, with Franklin satirizing both the idea of witchcraft and the tests for it. Franklin's hoax was summarized in the first issue of what became the most popular magazine of the eighteenth century, London's *Gentleman's Magazine* (January 1731). It printed abstracts of three witchcraft accounts—presenting them all as though they were serious. The editor deprived Franklin's account of humor in order to make it seem comparable to the other two actual reports, one from England and one from France, which resulted in the deaths of the accused. Instead of sheep dancing and hogs speaking and singing psalms, the English magazine said only that the owners of several cattle believed them to be bewitched. Franklin achieved an international audience for his serious purpose, which was reinforced by the title used for the witchcraft accounts by the magazine's editor, "Of Credulity in Witchcraft."[27] William Moraley, a lackluster contemporary who may have known Franklin, composed a feeble imitation of Franklin's hoax and claimed to have witnessed it.[28]

CRIME REPORTER

Crime reporter Franklin on 1 December 1729 described the trial of Captain Mercer at a Court of Admiralty in Philadelphia that had taken place on Friday, 28 and 29 November.[29] Mercer was accused of murdering one of his passengers, Thomas Flory, "in a cruel, inhuman and barbarous Manner." The expertly written report makes the reader at first sympathize with the supposedly murdered passenger and condemn the vicious captain. Then, as the evidence is revealed, it becomes clear that Flory was a despicable thief and an outcast. "The Passengers, one and all, refused to admit him among them, he being an odious filthy Fellow, and having a distemper, which together with his usual Laziness, rendered him extreamly uncleanly." Gradually the reader's sympathy shifts to Captain Mercer, who was found innocent, "to the general Satisfaction of the People, who before had been greatly exasperated against him." Through careful narration, Franklin slowly changed the reader's feelings from anger to sympathy for Captain Mercer.

A longer crime story in the 23 December 1729 *Gazette* described the trial of James Prouse and James Mitchel.[30] The jury convicted the two servants of burglary. The trial was of unusual interest because Mitchel claimed to know nothing of the burglary and nineteen-year-old Prouse, after the verdict had been announced but before the sentence was given, asked nothing for himself but said mercy should be shown Mitchel because he was innocent. The court nevertheless condemned both to be hanged, though it directed Mitchel to appeal to the governor for clemency. On 13 January, the newspaper reported that the two criminals were to be executed the following day.

Franklin used the occasion to analyze the basic qualities of human nature. Moral philosophers of the seventeenth and eighteenth centuries were divided over the question of whether humans were basically selfish and aggressive or altruistic and good. Thomas Hobbes had argued for the selfishness of humans; Lord Shaftesbury, their goodness; Bernard de Mandeville, opposing Shaftesbury, their selfishness; and Francis Hutcheson, following Shaftesbury, their goodness. Addison observed in *Spectator* No. 408: "Human Nature I always thought the most useful Object of human Reason." Franklin made his criminal reporting a test case of the philosophical theories.

The 20 January *Gazette* presented a long, dramatic, and absolutely clear report of the gallows scene.

> The tender Youth of one of them (who was but about 19) and the supposed Innocence of the other as to the Fact for which they were condemned, had induced the Judges (upon the Application of some compassionate People) to recommend them to His Honour's known Clemency: But several Malefactors having been already pardoned, and every Body being sensible, that, considering the great Increase of Vagrants and idle Persons, by the late large Importation of such from several Parts of *Europe*, it was become necessary for the common Good to make some Examples, there was but little Reason to hope that either, and less that both of them might escape the Punishment justly due to Crimes of that enormous Nature.
>
> About 11 o'Clock the Bell began to Toll, and a numerous Croud of People was gathered near the Prison, to see these unhappy young Men brought forth to suffer. While their Irons were taken off, and their Arms were binding, *Prouse* cry'd immoderately; but *Mitchel* (who had himself all along behaved with unusual Fortitude) endeavoured in a friendly tender Manner to comfort him: *Do not cry, Jemmy*; (says he) *In an Hour or two it will be over with us, and we shall both be easy.* They were then placed in a Cart, together with a Coffin for each of them, and led thro' the Town to the Place of Execution: *Prouse* appear'd extreamly dejected, but *Mitchel* seemed to support himself with a becoming manly

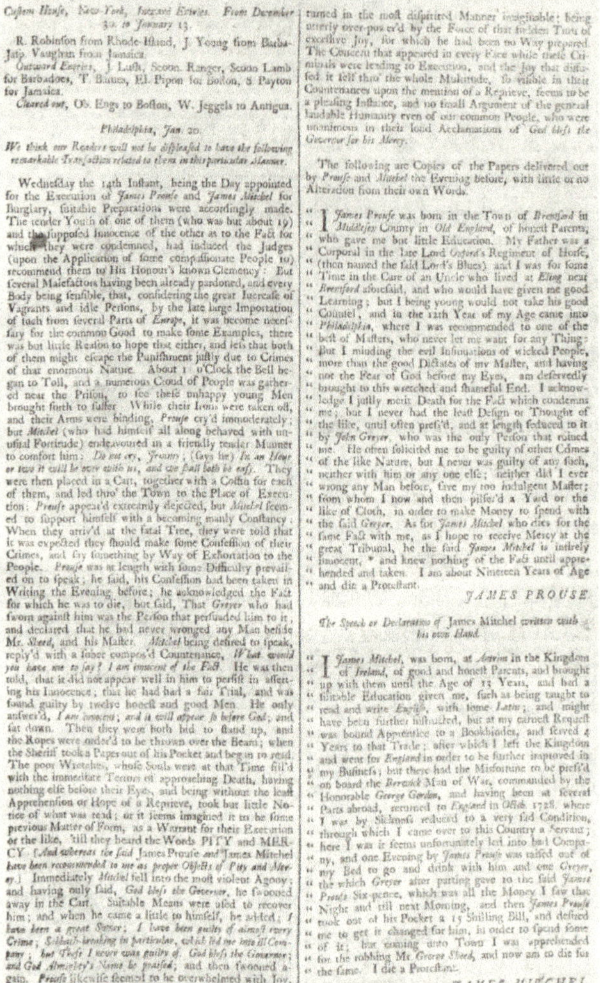

Figure 31. Franklin as crime reporter, Pennsylvania Gazette, *20 January 1729/30, p. 3. In the* Pennsylvania Gazette *of December 1729, Franklin reported the trial of James Prouse and James Mitchel for burglary. They were found guilty and condemned to death, though Prouse was only nineteen and though both Prouse and Mitchel claimed Mitchel was innocent. The* Gazette *announced on 13 January that they would be hung the following day. On 20 January, Franklin wrote a dramatic report of the execution scene: the actions of the two as they were led to the scaffold, their last words, the reading of the governor's pardon, its effect on them, and the audience's reactions.*

In an underlying subject, Franklin took the opportunity to address one of the persistent moral questions of the seventeenth and eighteenth centuries: Were human beings selfish and aggressive, or were they altruistic and good? By describing the emotions of the audience present at the execution and by endeavoring to make the reader experience the same emotions while reading the news report, Franklin attempted to prove that when their own interests were not involved, humans were altruistic. Courtesy, Library Company of Philadelphia.

Constancy: When they arriv'd at the fatal Tree, they were told that it was expected they should make some Confession of their Crimes, and say something
by Way of Exhortation to the People.

Prouse was at length with some Difficulty prevailed on to speak; he said, his
Confession had been taken in Writing the Evening before; he acknowledged the
Fact for which he was to die, but said, That *Greyer* who had sworn against him
was the Person that persuaded him to it; and declared that he had never wronged
any Man beside Mr. *Sheed*, and his Master. *Mitchel* being desired to speak, reply'd with a sober compos'd Countenance, *What would you have me to say? I am
innocent of the Fact.* He was then told, that it did not appear well in him to
persist in asserting his Innocence; that he had had a fair Trial, and was found
guilty by twelve honest and good Men. He only answer'd, *I am innocent; and
will appear so before God*; and sat down. Then they were both bid to stand up,
and the Ropes were order'd to be thrown over the Beam; when the Sheriff took
a Paper out of his Pocket and began to read.

The poor Wretches, whose Souls were at that Time fill'd with the immediate
Terrors of approaching Death, having nothing else before their Eyes, and being
without the least Apprehension or Hope of a Reprieve, took but little Notice of
what was read; or it seems imagined it to be some previous Matter of Form, as
a Warrant for their Execution or the like, 'till they hear the Words PITY and
MERCY [*And whereas the said* James Prouse *and* James Mitchel *have been recommended to me as proper objects of Pity and Mercy.*] Immediately *Mitchel* fell into
the most violent Agony; and having only said, *God bless the Governor*, he
swooned away in the Cart. Suitable Means were used to recover him; and when
he came a little to himself, he added; *I have been a great Sinner; I have been guilty
of almost every Crime; Sabbath-breaking in particular, which led me into ill Company; but Theft I never was guilty of. God bless the Governor; and God Almighty's
Name be praised*; and then swooned again. *Prouse* likewise seemed to be overwhelmed with Joy, but did not swoon. All the Way back to the Prison, *Mitchel*
lean'd on his Coffin, being unable to support himself, and shed Tears in abundance. He who went out to die with a large Share of Resolution and Fortitude,
returned in the most dispirited Manner imaginable; being utterly over-power'd
by the Force of that sudden Turn of excessive Joy, for which he had been no
Way prepared. The Concern that appeared in every Face while these Criminals
were leading to Execution, and the Joy that diffused it self thro' the whole Multitude, so visible in their Countenances upon the mention of a Reprieve, seems to
be a pleasing Instance, and no small Argument of the general laudable Humanity
even of our common People, who were unanimous in their loud Acclamations
of *God bless the Governor for his Mercy.*

Franklin used the occasion to generalize on the nature of humanity. He
commented at the end that the incident demonstrated the altruism of people in
general. With the crime report, Franklin refuted the argument that human na-

ture is basically selfish. People are not selfish except when they are themselves to benefit. If they have nothing to suffer or to gain, almost all people are benevolent and altruistic. Franklin reinforced the implied argument with the experience of the reader. He wrote the piece so that the reader (like the crowd present at the gallows) experienced the emotion of dread, hardened himself against pity by resolving that justice must be done, abandoned hope for the convicted, and then experienced a sudden relief and joy in the reprieve.

Crime reporter Franklin tried to analyze why James Mitchel, who was composed until he heard the reprieve, suddenly broke down, "being utterly overpower'd by the Force of that sudden Turn of excessive Joy, for which he had been no Way prepared."

Franklin chose to dwell on a scene that ended happily and that complimented the benevolence of people—perhaps thinking that such reporting helped people to be better human beings. In the same paper, he briefly reported (evidently at secondhand) that a Negro was burned alive for murder at Amboy. When he related the sadistic torturing to death of a Catawba Indian by a group of Susquehanna Indians (4 February 1730), he followed up the story on 5 March with an account that the particular Susquehanna warriors who had captured the Catawba "were often sent for, to come and behold the Death of their Prisoner; but these constantly refused, saying, *He is a Man, and fought like a Man when we took him; we will not see his Death*: and accordingly did not appear during the whole Transaction."

Franklin's crime reporting was clear and interesting. He often tried to make the reader feel the same succession of emotions that one would have felt if one had been present. Further, he frequently had some underlying subject or thesis, as we will again see in Volume 2, when discussing a trial for "The Murder of a Daughter" (23 October 1734).

STATISTICIAN

Statistics, like Newtonian experimental philosophy, supplied more accurate information than simple generalizations. Franklin repeatedly applied statistics to information. He read the works of the best previous statisticians and celebrated (18 June 1730) Joshua Gee's success at court for his books of statistics concerning trade and population. On 5 January 1731, Franklin compiled the information concerning all ships that had entered in or cleared out of the major ports in the Middle and New England colonies (evidently he could not obtain that information for the South) and featured it on the *Pennsylvania Gazette*'s front page: "In this Paper we exhibit an Account for one Year, of all the Vessels entered and cleared, from and to what Places, in the Ports of Philadelphia, Amboy, New-York, Rhode-Island, Boston, Salem and New Hampshire, by which the ingenious Reader may make some Judgment of the different Share each Colony possesses of the several Branches of Trade." At the end of the data, Franklin reprinted an account from Joshua Gee's *Trade and Navigation of Great Britain* of the trade between England and the mainland colonies. On 22 April 1731, he printed the trade statistics for Barbados from 1 January to 24 February, commenting on the enormous amount of trade carried on with all ports in less than eight weeks.

Five years later on 27 March 1735, Franklin tabulated all the cargo "imported into the Port of *Philadelphia* between the 25th of March, 1734 and the 25th of March, 1735." On 8 April 1736, he printed "an Account of the Number of Vessels *Entred* and *Cleared* (and *from* and *for* what Ports) at the Custom-House in this City, from *March* 25, 1735. to March 23, 1736." In all, 199 vessels had entered in, and 212 vessels had cleared out. Since he now had a partner, Lewis Timothy, in Charleston, South Carolina, Franklin was able to obtain that city's shipping information. He appended the last year's entries from Charleston, "which may enable the curious Reader to make a Comparison in some Respects of the Trade of that Place with this." Charleston actually had more trade than Philadelphia, with 248 vessels entering in and 253 clearing out. In comparison, he noted, "In the Year 1730 there were but 161 Vessels entred at *Philadelphia*, and 171 cleared; By which the Encrease of our Trade may be observed." Franklin also gave the shipping totals for New York, Massachusetts, Rhode Island, and New Hampshire.

Franklin's partners learned from him to be interested in such information. Late in 1739, young Peter Timothy, the son of Franklin's recently deceased partner, Louis Timothy, printed *An Account of Sundry Goods Imported, and of Sundry Goods . . . Exported, from the First of Nov 1738, to the First of Nov 1739. With the Number of Vessels Entered and Cleared at Each Port. As Also from Whence Arrived and Where Bound* (Charleston, 1739). The broadside contained a wealth of information.

Franklin's statistical approach to trade and the economy paralleled his interest in demography. On 20 November 1729 he began publishing weekly lists of burials in the city and the totals (29 December 1730) at the year's end. He gave the weekly burial returns through February 1732. To make comparisons, Franklin published the number of burials of one year in Boston, Berlin, Cologne, Amsterdam, and London (3 February 1729/30, 7 and 21 May 1730). The following year on 26 August 1731, when he reprinted an account of population from Breslau that noted that "a 29th Part of the Inhabitants die every Year," he compiled the statistics of the burials in Boston from 1700 to 1731, observing, "By comparing the Number of Inhabitants in Boston with the above Account, it appears, that not above a 40th Part of the People of that Place die yearly, at a medium." Franklin may have been combating the prejudice against American climate and suggesting that America was actually healthier than Europe.

Franklin soon gave up reporting the Philadelphia bills of mortality. The historian James H. Cassady observed that the bills "became victims of advertising pressures of inter-city trade rivalries." He pointed out that news of "death and disease discouraged trade" and that colonial printer-editors commonly minimized, distorted, or suppressed such "local data in hopes of promoting the economic well-being of their communities. Conversely, they were happy enough to print the death figures of other cities."[31] After Franklin stopped printing the Philadelphia bills, he reported such demographic statistics as "A General Bill of all the Christenings and Burials from the 12th of December 1732, to the 11th of December 1733 . . . in London, &c" (*Gazette*, 23 May 1734). Franklin's attention to such statistical demographics had also been evident in his *Modest Enquiry*.

A short essay titled "On the Usefulness of Mathematics," which I believe was by Franklin, appeared in the *Pennsylvania Gazette* on 30 October 1735. The piece celebrated both its abstract value and its practical applications. The author called mathematics "the *Primum Mobile*" of all affairs and divided it into arithmetic and geometry. He detailed its use in various occupations, beginning with merchants and shopkeepers (Franklin's primary audience) but going on to astronomers, geographers, sailors, architects, engineers, surveyors, gaugers, measurers, etc. "'Tis by the Assistance of this *Science*, that *Geographers* present to our View at once, the Magnitude and Form of the whole Earth, the vast extent of the Seas, the Divisions of Empires, Kingdoms and Provinces." Having established the omnipresent value of mathematics, the author mentioned its appreciation by various cultures and by the ancients, twice referring to Plato's praise of the science. The method, the clear prose, and the easy but extraordinary knowledge all are characteristic of Franklin: the author began with simple definitions and the most obvious basic uses of mathematics, then displayed an encyclopedic appreciation of various ways that mathematics is used, and finally documented its high esteem throughout history. The essay demonstrated Franklin's appreciation of that "much esteemed and honored" science.[32]

Obituaries

Newspaper obituaries were rare in the early eighteenth century. Cotton Mather, Samuel Sewall, and a few other Boston literary men wrote appreciations of the local notables at their deaths, which the newspaper editors printed. James Franklin printed a few obituaries in the *New-England Courant* and all were brief. Franklin, however, made the obituary a newspaperman's art. The *Pennsylvania Gazette* printed obituaries for more people than any previous American newspaper, and Franklin often tried to inculcate his own values in them. When his friend and patron Andrew Hamilton died, Franklin praised him for steadily maintaining "the Cause of Liberty." He was

> no Friend to Power, as he had observed an ill use had been frequently made of it in the Colonies; and therefore was seldom upon good Terms with Governors. This Prejudice, however, did not always determine his Conduct towards them; for where he saw they meant well, he was for supporting them honourable, and was indefatigable in endeavouring to remove the Prejudices of others. . . . He was the Poor Man's Friend, and was never known to with-hold his Purse or

Service from the Indigent or Oppressed. . . . His free Manner of treating Religious Subjects, gave Offence to many, who, if a Man may judge by their Actions, were not themselves much in earnest. He feared God, loved Mercy, and did Justice: If he could not subscribe to the Creed of any particular Church, it was not for want of considering them All; for he had read much on Religious Subjects. (6 August 1741)

Franklin's obituary notice of Isaac Norris I, a wealthy merchant and Proprietary supporter, was relatively cold and skimpy: "Wednesday Morning died suddenly at Germantown Meeting, of an Apoplectic fit, Isaac Norris, of Fairhill, Esq; He had been many Years one of the Council, was often chosen a Representative in Assembly, had born several other Offices of Honour and Trust, and was esteemed one of the most considerable Men in the Province" (5 June 1735). His appreciation of Governor Patrick Gordon (7 August 1736) was much warmer: "It may be justly said of him, that, during the whole course of his Administration, the true Interest and Happiness, Prosperity and Welfare of his Majesty's Subjects in these Parts seemed to be his chief Concern and peculiar Care."

Franklin's egalitarianism caused him to write obituaries for people whose deaths were normally ignored by colonial newspapers. When a fellow member of the Library Company, James Merrewether, died, Franklin wrote that he was "a Person somewhat obscure, and of an unpromising Appearance, but esteem'd by those few who enjoy'd an Intimacy with him, to be one of the honestest, best, and wisest Men in Philadelphia" (22 April 1742). Franklin even sometimes falsified the qualities of an individual in order to praise the ideals that he himself believed good. In an obituary for the Reverend Archibald Cummings, minister of Christ Church (23 April 1741), Franklin wrote that he was "universally esteem'd . . . especially for his Charity and Moderation towards all Religious Societies of differing Persuasions." During the previous year, however, Cummings had been embroiled in religious controversies with Whitefield (e.g., 20 April 1740) and was intolerant of the revivalist. Franklin, like most people, emphasized the positive qualities of those who had just passed away.

RIVALRY WITH BRADFORD

In the *Autobiography*, Franklin wrote that after Keimer left Philadelphia, "There remain'd now no Competitor with me at Philadelphia, but the old one, Bradford, who was rich and easy, did a little Printing now and then by straggling Hands, but was not very anxious about the Business" (69). Actually, by the time Franklin wrote that in 1771, he had forgotten what Bradford was like in 1729. He was not old, not rich, and not easy. Bradford was forty-three and on the rise. He had been elected a Philadelphia councilman in 1727 and had appointed postmaster in 1728. Bradford and Franklin were major rivals. Bradford had been Pennsylvania's only printer from 1712 until 1723 and had established Philadelphia's first newspaper, the *American Weekly Mercury*, in 1719. As the printer to the Pennsylvania Assembly, Bradford had a continuing and profitable source of business. But as a craftsman and a writer, Bradford was mediocre. Franklin exposed Bradford's poor craftsmanship to the assemblymen in his broadside reprinting their address to the governor and poked fun at Bradford's typesetting in his essay on printers' errors. After Franklin won the vote to print the legislature's minutes and laws in 1730, Andrew Bradford became both anti-Franklin and anti-Hamilton. When Franklin and Meredith bought the failing *Pennsylvania Gazette* and transformed it into a success, it threatened Andrew Bradford's paper. In the future, whatever position Franklin adopted in the *Pennsylvania Gazette*, Bradford was certain to make the opposition welcome in the *American Weekly Mercury*.[33]

Franklin satirized Bradford in the 19 March 1729/30 *Gazette*: "When Mr. *Bradford* publishes after us, and has Occasion to take an Article or two out of the *Gazette*, which he is always welcome to do, he is desired not to date his Paper a Day before ours, (as last Week in the Case of the Letter containing *Kelsey*'s Speech, &c.) lest distant Readers should imagine we take from him, which we always carefully avoid." Franklin again tweaked Bradford on 9 November 1732, pretending to be a reader criticizing the *Gazette* for printing European news that was several years old. Franklin replied that the letter was "wrong directed" and should have been to the publisher of the *Mercury*.

Overt rivalry between the *Gazette* and the *Mercury* broke out on numerous occasions. Andrew Bradford had seldom taken political positions, but opponents of Franklin's politics were welcomed by Bradford. The *Mercury* featured attacks on Hamilton and Franklin by "Portius" and others in the spring of 1732; it opposed the election of Andrew Hamilton in 1733; it defended the existing chancery court structure in late 1735 when the *Gazette* championed a change; and in 1737 and 1738 it attempted to blame Franklin for the death of Daniel Rees, causing Franklin to reply on 15 February 1738. When the *Gazette* supported the Maryland tobacco growers' plan to ship tobacco directly to France rather than through England (31 January 1738), the *Mercury* opposed it. Franklin led an environmental fight against the tanners who were polluting the Dock Street area, and the *Mercury* defended them. The gentlemen of the dancing assembly criticized the *Gazette*'s reporting in May 1740, thus beginning a heated exchange between authors in the two papers. And in late 1740 Franklin accused Bradford of stealing his idea for a magazine. These episodes will all be discussed in Volume 2. Despite Franklin's portrayal of Bradford some thirty years later, Bradford was actually very "anxious about the Business," opposed Franklin's positions, and remained a formidable rival until his death at age fifty-six in 1742.

Increasing Business

During his first decade as a newspaperman (1729–38), Franklin gradually established his reputation and his business. Before April 1730, "One Whitmarsh, a Compositor I had known in London, an excellent Workman now came to me and work'd with me constantly and diligently, and I took an Apprentice the Son of Aquila Rose" (A 68). By 22 August 1730, the former Keimer employee Stephen Potts, whom Franklin had trained as a bookbinder, came to work for Franklin. Potts rented a room in the Franklins' garret in November and occasionally did presswork for him. William Jones, evidently another journeyman printer, also rented a room from Franklin in 1730.

With Samuel Keimer and David Harry gone, Franklin's business improved. "I began now gradually to pay off the Debt I was under for the Printing-House. In order to secure my Credit and Character as a Tradesman, I took care not only to be in *Reality* Industrious and frugal, but to avoid all *Appearances* of the Contrary. I drest plainly; I was seen at no Places of idle Diversion; I never went out a-fishing or shooting; a Book, indeed, sometimes debauch'd me from my Work; but that was seldom, snug, and gave no Scandal: and to show that I was not above my Business, I sometimes brought home the Paper I purchas'd at the Stores, thro' the Streets on a Wheelbarrow." Franklin's deliberately created image, recalled in the *Autobiography*, imitated Pericles as depicted in Plutarch's *Lives*. Franklin had carefully read Plutarch in his father's small library and still, in 1771, believed the time "spent to great Advantage" (A 11). According to Plutarch, the formerly aristocratic Pericles changed his way of life, identified with the common people, never again went into the city except "to the market place, or to the Senate house." He adopted the habit of silence.[34] Like Pericles, Franklin cultivated a public appearance as a hard-working man: "Thus being esteem'd an industrious thriving young Man, and paying duly for what I bought, the Merchants who imported Stationery solicited my Custom, others propos'd supplying me with Books, and I went on swimmingly" (A 54).

The Pennsylvania Gazette gradually became the most widely read newspaper in the colonies. Published by Franklin and Meredith to 1731, by Franklin alone to 1748, and then by Franklin and Hall to 1766, it was thereafter continued by Hall and his successors. Isaiah Thomas wrote in 1810 that it was the "oldest newspaper in the United States" (433). Franklin had been superbly prepared to be a newspaper editor by his apprenticeship on the *New-England Courant*. While working at the *Courant* (1721–23), he was reading the best English journalism: the most frequently reprinted pieces in the *Courant* were Trenchard and Gordon's *Cato's Letters* from the *London Journal*. While living in London in 1725 and 1726, the young journeyman devoured the London papers. He also knew the history of journalism thoroughly. He had read the leading periodicals, the *Spectator*, the *Tatler*, and the *Guardian,* and occasionally echoed them. His opening editorial in the *Gazette* on 2 October 1729 on the duties of a newspaper editor reflected John Dunton's early weekly *Athenian Gazette* (1689/90–1695/6), a collected edition of which had been in the *New-England Courant's* library.

On 5 March 1785 Franklin estimated that the circulation of the *Pennsylvania Gazette* in 1748 had been 8,000 to 10,000 (cf. P 13:100–101). Lawrence C. Wroth, however, has argued that Franklin's figure represented the 1785 circulation rather than the number of persons who took the paper in 1748. Based on James Parker's figures of the funds paid Franklin by Hall during the course of their partnership (1748–66), Wroth estimated that Franklin and Hall had about 1,500 paid subscriptions a year and printed another 100 to 200 hundred copies to give as exchanges and advertising copies. But Wroth overlooked approximately £100 of newspaper income (12:180n. 4).[35] Franklin and Hall actually earned about £860 a year from the *Gazette*, rather than £750. At 10s a year per customer, the *Gazette* must have had an average of over 1,700 paying customers during 1748–66. And, as Wroth noted, Franklin (and later David Hall) would have given away another 100 to 200 copies of the paper in exchanges and to advertisers. Further, James Parker reported that less than three-fourths of his customers paid for the *New York Gazette*. Since Franklin rarely sued anyone for debt, it seems likely that one-third of his "subscribers" did not pay. The average printing during the partnership may well have been well over 2,500 or more. No doubt the *Gazette*'s circulation grew during the partnership years (1748–66) with the increasing population of Philadelphia and the surrounding area, but the *Gazette* probably had a distribution of well over 1,500 when Franklin retired as a printer on 1 January 1748.

Financially, however, circulation is only part of the story of a successful paper; advertising is also important. Of the normal four-page colonial newspaper, the *Pennsylvania Gazette* carried more than a page of advertising for the first time on 13 March 1730; more than two full pages on 29 August 1734. Nevertheless, the amount of advertising was generally about one page until Franklin was appointed postmaster on 5 October 1737. In the very next issue, 13 October 1737, advertisements jumped to just over two pages. For the next two years, the advertisements ran about one and a half pages and would have taken more than two pages in 1738, but Franklin began using a new, smaller type. Since the smaller type used less paper (the most expensive single item for a printer), the smaller type made newspaper more profitable. Even with the smaller type, by 1740 advertisements took up more than three full pages; by then, Franklin usually printed an extra leaf to accommodate the advertisements, making a paper of six pages. By the summer of 1741, the *Pennsylvania Gazette* was often two full folio sheets or eight pages, with advertisements occupying four and sometimes five pages. Early in 1742, Franklin changed from a two-column format to three columns.

The historians Charles E. Clark and Charles Wetherell have shown that advertising in the *Pennsylvania Gazette* grew fairly continuously from the time that Franklin took over the paper to approximately 1752, though in times when the news was especially important (e.g., during the controversy over the Molasses Act [1733] or during preparations for the battle of Louisburg [1745]), the proportion of advertising temporarily declined. They also traced the growth of advertising under the various editors of the *Pennsylvania Gazette*: under Keimer, it was 16.3 percent; under Franklin, 42.5 percent; under Hall, 60 percent. Nevertheless, Clark and Wetherell found that only 22 percent of the income from Hall's *Gazette* (1749–65) came from advertisements.[36] In the colonial period, subscriptions were a more important source of revenue than advertisements, but both were vital to a financially successful newspaper. As newspaper editor James Parker wrote Franklin, "Advertisements . . . are the Life of the Paper" (16:140).

CONCLUSION

Franklin transformed the colonial newspaper by featuring more news items than any previous paper—more editorials, more political discussions, more features, more local events, more entertaining fillers, more satires, more crimes, more obituaries, and more natural philosophy. Analyzing the news coverage of American papers in 1730, the newspaper historian David A. Copeland has shown that Franklin's *Pennsylvania Gazette* printed approximately one-third more news items than any other colonial paper.[37] It was not mainly, however, the kind or amount of news that really distinguished Franklin's paper but the excellent writing. No other crime reporter or political reporter of the day matched the quality or the interest of Franklin's reporting. And no other journalist of his time wrote such interesting hoaxes, skits, essays, and satires.

In *The Newspaperman*, Talcott Williams, formerly the dean of Columbia University's Pulitzer School of Journalism, wrote that Benjamin Franklin saved journalists from a "desert of polyglottic dignity." He pointed out that Dr. Samuel Johnson in England and Franklin in America were the primary periodical writers of their day and contrasted their prose styles. Franklin, he said, "was the inventor of newspaper English, direct, immediate, knowing humor as well as argument, using the speech of the people." Williams may not have known that for at least fifty years after his death, Franklin was reviled by a group of writers who wanted a more formal prose, one that reflected higher pretensions to learning and avoided the speech, the proverbs, and the humor of the people.[38] Williams granted that others before and after Franklin wrote a colloquial English, "But more than any other man, Franklin, the newspaper man, saved us from a separation and divorce of the English of the people and the English of the writer."

Alexis de Toqueville, the shrewdest observer of America in the nineteenth century, thought that "Only the journalists strike me as truly American . . . they speak their country's language."[39] Though there have been wonderful exceptions (including William Faulkner and Wallace Stevens), the general tendency of American writers has been toward the colloquial (witness Mark Twain, Ernest Hemingway, and Robert Frost). Franklin's journalism was, I believe, a manifestation of his egalitarian American aesthetic, manifested not only in his writing style and political beliefs but also in his creation of cartoons, emblems, and devices, as well as designs for flags and for paper money.[40]

Perhaps no other newspaper had ever been as audacious, entertaining, literary, humorous, salacious, intellectual, political, financial, scientific, philosophical, or witty as Franklin's *Pennsylvania Gazette* in those first years when he printed and supervised every aspect of the paper—writing the news and the filler, making up the advertisements, setting the copy in type, and printing it off. As he gradually withdrew from personally setting it in type, it became more like the other newspapers of colonial America, but by then it not only had the advantage of being generally regarded as the best newspaper in the colonies, it still published occasional strokes of genius from its founder and editor. Franklin printed the first important newspaper interview (with Andrew Hamilton [1733]), the earliest illustration of a news event in a colonial paper (the map of Louisburg [1745]), the first outraged and outrageous satire of British policies toward America ("Rattlesnakes for Felons" [1751]), and the first American political cartoon ("Join or Die" [1754]). He was the ablest journalist and the greatest innovator of newspaper techniques of his day.

NINETEEN

Assessing Franklin,
Age Seventeen to Twenty-four

Our first Papers made a quite different Appearance from any before in the Province, a better Type and better printed: but some spirited Remarks of my Writing on the Dispute then going on between Governor Burnet and the Massachusetts Assembly, struck the principal People, occasion'd the Paper and the Manager of it to be much talk'd of, and in a few Weeks brought them all to be our Subscribers. Their Example was follow'd by many, and our Number went on growing continually.—A 64

THE IRREPRESSIBLE PRIDE THAT GOT FRANKLIN INTO TROUBLE in Boston continued during his late teens and early adulthood in Philadelphia and London. When he returned to Boston at age eighteen in 1724 with a pocket full of cash, a genteel new suit, and an expensive watch, he humiliated James Franklin in front of his journeymen and apprentices. He behaved like an adolescent show-off. Discussing his trip to London in the *Autobiography*, Franklin presents himself as an unsuspecting innocent boy, duped by Governor Keith, but if Franklin had not believed himself so superior to Samuel Keimer and to Andrew Bradford, he would have suspected that Governor Keith would hardly gamble a considerable sum on setting up an eighteen-year-old boy as an independent printer. Blinded by hubris, Franklin never questioned Keith's extraordinary generosity. Though Franklin remained honest, he spent time with prostitutes and thieves, seemingly unaware that such company might implicate him. When the "grave, sensible Matron-like Quaker-Woman" warned him about his shipboard companions on his return from Boston (A 31), he realized the truth, avoided them, and thus was not embroiled in their thievery. He did, however, imprudently spend the money that he had collected for the Rhode Island silversmith Samuel Vernon, and he must have worried that he was liable to prosecution for debt.

In London, perhaps influenced by his talented but irresponsible friend James Ralph, he published a scandalously subversive pamphlet, thereby calling attention to his abilities among the London freethinkers like Bernard de Mandeville but at the same time making normally respectable persons, like the printer Samuel Palmer, uncomfortable with his "abominable" principles (A 43). But young Franklin was pleased with the recognition, even if he did hide his identity as author and printer of the pamphlet from the authorities. Of course, the *Disserta-*

tion on Liberty and Necessity (1725) brilliantly demonstrated a knowledge of contemporary philosophical ideas—and satirized a number of theological
arguments. Slightly later, betraying his friend Ralph, he made advances to Ralph's mistress—which she rejected (A 44–45). As he was setting off to return to
America (1726), he told in his sea journal of purloining a boat. To be sure,
the boatman would find the boat in the morning—though with some trouble.
Franklin's attitude toward the property of others had not appreciably changed
from when he stole the workmen's stones as a child in order to build a pier. His
feelings of superiority made him insensitive to the situation and property of that
"lazy whelp," the boatman (1:80).

The older Franklin who recorded these misadventures knew that they
showed him in a bad light, but frankness is among Franklin's characteristics as
an autobiographer. Others might have hidden or omitted their shameful actions; Franklin wryly chronicled them.

London was a wonderful experience for the nineteen- and twenty-year-old
Franklin: full of interesting clubs, fascinating people, wonderful plays and
music, famous authors and ministers. But after a year and a half, he evidently
wondered, "Is this how I want to spend my life?" Visiting London and England
made some colonials permanently English, but the ignorance of and prejudice
about America reinforced the American identity of many others, evidently including Franklin.

At the age of twenty on his return from London, Franklin resolved to do
better, and he formed a plan "for regulating my future Conduct in Life" (A 52).
The journal he kept on the voyage reveals his curiosity about natural history,
psychology, art, eclipses of the moon, and much more. His plan for regulating
his future conduct foreshadowed later deliberate efforts to change himself, but
he had not yet mastered his emotions. In 1727, he lost his temper and improvi-
dently quit his job when Keimer insulted him before others. Further, as he
mentioned in the *Autobiography*, "that hard-to-be-govern'd Passion of Youth,
had hurried me frequently into Intrigues with low Women that fell in my Way,
which were attended with some Expence and great Inconvenience, besides a
continual Risk to my Health by a Distemper which of all Things I dreaded, tho'
by great good Luck I escaped it" (A 70). He does not, of course, tell us that an
affair resulted in the birth of an illegitimate son, William, around 1728 or 1729.
Though he must have foreseen that the decision to care for a child would result
in financial and personal difficulties, Franklin accepted responsibility for the
infant and brought him up. The mystery of the mother's identity and the child's
date of birth will be subjects in the first chapter of Volume 2.

Franklin learned the fundamentals of running a business while working for
the Quaker merchant Thomas Denham, and he demonstrated an ability to work
well with employees when he took over the training and management of Keimer's staff. His ingenious practical ability appeared in his designing cuts for the
New Jersey paper currency and in contriving a copper press to print the money.

After he started his own printing business, Franklin made certain that the members of the Pennsylvania legislature realized that he was a better printer than Andrew Bradford, who had the contract to do the official government printing. At the same time, he cultivated Andrew Hamilton, a brilliant lawyer, shrewd politician, and deist. After Hamilton became the Speaker of the House, he had Franklin and Meredith elected as printers of the legislature's *Votes* and the *Laws.*

Franklin demonstrated his ability to win friends and influence people in the fall of 1727 by starting the Junto, a society that became his personal college. Though the Junto had many purposes, it stressed improving oneself and doing good to others and to the society. Many of the members remained Franklin's friends until their death, including founding members Joseph Breintnall, Thomas Hopkinson, and Robert Grace and, slightly later members, Hugh Roberts and Philip Syng. It included persons who became members of Pennsylvania's different political parties. Franklin's own egalitarian beliefs emerged again in 1729. His fourth and eighth Busy-Body papers identified him as a spokesman for the ordinary people and, in the politics of the day, an opponent of the Proprietary Party.

In the suppressed addition to Busy-Body No. 8 (27 March 1728/9), the twenty-three-year-old Franklin threatened the Proprietaries and the wealthiest merchants: "The whole Country is at this Instant filled with the greatest Heat and Animosity; and if there are yet among us any Opposers of a Paper-Currency, it is probable the Resentments of the People point at them." They were accused "of having a Design to engross the Property of the Country, and make themselves and their Posterity Lords, and the Bulk of the Inhabitants their Tenants and Vassals." Franklin was a populist and an opponent of the Proprietary Party. He made an ironic observation in the suppressed Busy-Body that he later often varied and repeated: "the Interest of the Country [Pennsylvania] is the same, I presume, with that of the Proprietary."

Franklin had, however, already perceived in the case of Massachusetts (as he did later with Great Britain and its colonies) that the authorities were not interested in the good of the whole but in their own selfish ends. The antirich, anti-Proprietary persona of *A Modest Enquiry into the Nature and Necessity of a Paper Currency* (1729) reaffirmed his identification with the common citizen. At the same time, the class-conscious, pro-trade persona was a splendid speaker for the message. *A Modest Enquiry* demonstrated Franklin's knowledge of economics and revealed his careful reading of the paper currency pamphlets by John Wise and others while working for his brother James in Boston. Its concern with the relations between economy and demography foreshadowed his later intellectual interests.

Franklin loved fun. Hugh Roberts, John Bartram, and others celebrated his humor. He himself remarked on his time at John Watts's printing house that he was esteemed by his fellows as "a pretty good Riggite, that is a jocular verbal Satyrist." Having fun and making jokes and being merry were qualities that made him a successful social companion. Of course he was complex, too, and in his writing was often cynical, world-weary, or pessimistic, but in social settings, no one seemed to have more fun or to be a better companion than Franklin.

When Franklin took over the *Pennsylvania Gazette* in 1729, he soon showed that he was the best journalist that America had yet produced. Franklin's *Pennsylvania Gazette* was not as literary a paper as his brother's *New England Courant* had been, nor did he attract as many local contributors as James Franklin had, but the *Pennsylvania Gazette* contained more local and American news, more political reporting, more editorials, and more innovations. It gradually became colonial America's best newspaper. Franklin's Boston background showed not only in the paper currency controversy but also in his early editorial on Massachusetts politics. It demonstrated that he was a shrewd commentator on the colonial political scene. By age twenty-four, Franklin was an important, if unrecognized, man of letters—but so far, only the Junto gave some indication of his genius for organization. He was establishing himself locally as an expert printer and an enterprising businessman.

The Junto queries, as we have seen, looked into "any encroachment on the just libereties of the people" and asked if the people were justified in resisting a sovereign's attempt "to deprive a Subject of his Right." Franklin's irritation with the secret instructions binding Pennsylvania's governor and with England's Board of Trade appeared in the suppressed portion of Busy-Body No. 8 (27 March 1729) and were repeated early the next month in his *Modest Enquiry*. His resentment of English condescension and his Americanism appeared again in his first editorial on Massachusetts politics (9 October 1729). Although his poem "The Rats and the Cheese" (24 September 1730), primarily criticized the selfishness of the Massachusetts authorities, it also applied to the British. The attitudes of John Wise and the Old Charter Party of Massachusetts continued to be alive and well in Franklin as a young man.

Franklin tried to improve society in various ways, including reprinting a series of essays on the miserable conditions in jails and adding his own brief editorial. He featured news and stories against drunkenness. On a more theoretical level, his Casuist essays in the *Pennsylvania Gazette*, like an extraordinary passage in the *Dissertation on Liberty and Necessity*, showed an appreciation for life's moral complexity—a complete knowledge of all the possible consequences of every action is impossible to know. The world is too complex. He would later apply such thinking to ecology, politics, and the structure of society, thereby anticipating the social thought of Edmund Burke and foreshadowing aspects of the environmental thought of the nineteenth and twentieth centuries. As a young adult, Franklin was still making his full share of mistakes. But he was improving, studying ferociously, and always writing.

Franklin seemingly scoffed at religion throughout this period. His "Letter of the Drum," the companion piece by Philoclerus, the news notes about England's famous deists, the reprinting of the deistic "Plain Dealer" series, and the reprinting of a series of essays on primitive Christianity—all proclaimed the young Philadelphia printer a freethinker. He noted after printing the third essay on primitive Christianity (30 July 1730) that some persons objected to his featuring such essays. He was well aware of his iconoclasm but seemed unable to change himself. Did he really think that he might be able to change the religious attitudes of his contemporaries? And yet, just before the time that he was publically establishing a reputation in Philadelphia as a skeptic, he wrote out his own private religious liturgy, "Articles of Belief and Acts of Religion" (1728) and practiced its ritual. Further, reading the Philoclerus letter (1730) carefully shows that it makes greater claims for the power of the spirit than did many religions.

As part of his deliberate self-examination during the return from England in 1726, Franklin resolved to live frugally and to save what money he could. Franklin's "threadbare" overcoat (according to Samuel Keimer's 13 March 1729 attack) contrasts markedly with the "genteel new suit" worn while visiting Boston five years before. He was now living according to his plan, providing for his motherless child, and saving a bit of money for future endeavors. Before 1730, Franklin had achieved his full height, approximately five foot ten inches, with brown hair and hazel eyes. The "Water American" was solidly built and muscular, carrying sometimes "up and down Stairs a large Form of Types in each hand, when others carried but one in both Hands" (A 45–46). He was athletic and continued to swim when it was possible, but he was devoting more and more time to a private course of study and to business. He planned to do better as a person and as a citizen in the future.

Reflecting on his own conduct, Franklin ironically noted that not every resolve to change or even every change would actually work out for the better.

> All human Situations have their Inconveniencies. We *feel* those that we find in the present, and we neither *feel* nor *see* those that exist in another. Hence we make frequent & troublesome Changes without Amendment, and often for the Worse. In my Youth I was Passenger in a little Sloop, descending the River Delaware. There being no Wind, we were obliged, when the Ebb was spent, to cast anchor, and wait for the next. The Heat of the Sun on the Vessel was excessive, the Company Strangers to me & not very agreeable. Near the River Side I saw what I took to be a pleasant green Meadow, in the Middle of which was a large shady Tree, where it struck my Fancy, I could sit & read, having a Book in my Pocket, and pass the Time agreably till the Tide turned. I therefore prevail'd with the Captain to put me ashore. Being landed I found the greatest Part of my Meadow was really a Marsh, in crossing which to come at my Tree, I was up to the Knees in Mire: And I had not plac'd my self under its Shade five Minutes before the Muskitoes in Swarms found me out, attack'd my Legs, Hands & Face, and made my Reading & my Rest impossible: So that I return'd to the Beach, &

call'd for the Boat to come and take me aboard again, where I was oblig'd to bear the Heat I had strove to quit, and also the Laugh of the Company. (31:456–57)

Unlike his great contemporaries, Jonathan Evans, George Washington, John Adams, and Thomas Jefferson, Franklin often mocked himself.

APPENDIX: *New Attributions*

The attributions to Benjamin Franklin are all in addition to those in Lemay, *The Canon of BF: New Attributions and Reconsiderations.*

The following checklist gives the source of the writing and a reference to the chapter in Volume 1 of the biography where the writing is discussed.

BENJAMIN FRANKLIN

1. "Jethro Standfast" letter, 8 October 1722, *New-England Courant*; Chapter 8.
2. "Nausawlander" letter, 29 October 1722, *New-England Courant*; Chapter 8.
3. *Hoop-Petticoats Arraigned and Condemned* (Boston: J. Franklin, 1722), Evans 2341; advertised 26 November 1722; Chapter 8.
4. News essay on Boston's high tide, *New-England Courant*, 4 March 1723; Chapter 8.
5. On country Kitelic Verse, 11 March 1723, *New-England Courant*; Chapter 8.
6. "Dingo," *New-England Courant*, 15 July 1723; Chapter 8.
7. "Of the Usefulness of Mathematicks," 30 October 1735, *Pennsylvania Gazette*; Chapter 8.

OTHER AUTHORS

James Franklin

1. "Dic. Burlesque," *New-England Courant*, 17 September 1722; Chapter 7.
2. King Alfred essay, *New-England Courant*, 4 February 1722/3; Chapter 8.
3. "Philo-Dicaios" editorial, *New-England Courant*, 7 May 1723; Chapter 8.
4. First reply to Ebenezer Fitch, *New-England Courant*, 24 June 1723; Chapter 8.
5. Second reply to Ebenezer Fitch, *New-England Courant*, 1 July 1723; Chapter 8.

Nathaniel Gardner

1. *A Friendly Debate* (Boston: James Franklin, 1722), Evans 2386; Chapter 6.
2. *English Advice to the Freeholders* (Boston: James Franklin, 1722); Evans 2335, dated 18 April 1722; Chapter 7.
3. "Hypercriticus," *New-England Courant*, 12 November 1722; Chapter 8.
4. "Tom Freeman," *New-England Courant*, 10 December 1722; Chapter 8.
5. Essay on the Sabbath, *New-England Courant*, 17 Dec 1722; Chapter 8.
6. "T. Freeman," *New-England Courant*, 24 December 1722; Chapter 8.
7. Satire on New England "Saints," *New-England Courant*, 14 January 1722/3; Chapter 8.
8. Mock Jeremiad, *New-England Courant*, 14 January 1722/3; Chapter 8.

9. Essay on the New England Psalm book, *New-England Courant*, 21 January 1722/3; Chapter 8.

10. "Hypercriticus," *New-England Courant*, 4 March 1722/3; Chapter 8.

Thomas Lane

"Elisha Trumen" in *New-England Courant*, 30 April 1722; Chapters 5 and 7.

Cotton Mather

1. *News from Robinson Cruso's Island*. Boston, 1720. Bristol B590; Evans 39730. Not in Holmes. Also attributed to Mather by Silverman 323; Chapter 8.

2. The Couranteers as a Hell-Fire Club: anonymous letter in the *Boston News-Letter*, 28 August, 1721; Chapter 6.

3. Monkey Fable, *Boston Gazette*, 17 March 1721/2; Chapter 6.

4. News note on the high tide, *Boston News-Letter*, 28 February 1722/3; Chapter 8.

Captain Christopher Taylor

On Governor Samuel Shute's departure, *New-England Courant*, 14 January 1722/3; Chapter 8.

SOURCES AND DOCUMENTATION

The basis for the biography is a *Documentary History of Benjamin Franklin*, a chronologically arranged calendar of his activities (meetings of the Junto, Library Company directors, Union Fire Company, etc.), writings, whereabouts, and the attacks on him and references to him throughout his life. For the period through 1747 (i.e., to his retirement from printing), I include all the references that I have found, and I quote at length the most important ones that are not in the *Papers of Benjamin Franklin*. Since there are so many more references to Franklin in the latter part of his life, I calendar more and quote less as the volumes progress. The *Documentary History* relieves the biography of numerous footnotes, for the dates in the biography may be consulted in the *Documentary History*, where references to the Franklin texts and the most pertinent scholarship will be found. Of course, for most writings of Franklin, the reader may simply go from the biography directly to the *Papers*, which is chronologically arranged. The source is in the *Documentary History* whether or not it appears in the *Papers*. The *Documentary History* for the period covered in the published biography is available on the Internet. I will always be grateful for any factual material concerning Franklin that is not in the *Documentary History* (lemay @udel.edu). The *Documentary History* may be found at http://www.english.udel .edu/lemay/franklin.

I have also transcribed into one chronological record Franklin's various financial accounts. Like the *Documentary History*, *The Accounts of Benjamin Franklin* is available on the internet. Previously, G. S. Eddy published excerpts from Franklin's Ledger A&B; excerpts from his Ledger D; the entire account book kept during his first mission to England (1757–62); and excerpts from a workbook of the printing house of Franklin and Hall (1759–66). So far, I have only made available the accounts to his retirement as a printer in 1748. I am greatly indebted to the work of G. S. Eddy, but as the editors of *The Papers of Benjamin Franklin* have noted, Eddy made mistakes and "a substantial number" of omissions (P 7:165). There are few accounts for volume 1, but they are copious for volume 2. The name index to the *Accounts* contains brief biographical notes on the persons I have been able to identify.

DOCUMENTATION

The great edition of Franklin's writings is *The Papers of Benjamin Franklin*. Since it is arranged chronologically, references to Franklin's writings can easily be found by the dates. In those cases where Franklin's document occupies more than two pages, references to the *Papers* are given in the text by volume and page within parentheses.

In addition to using dates throughout the biography as keys to references in the *Papers of Benjamin Franklin* and in the *Documentary History*, I use both endnotes and parenthetical references. Full references for endnotes occur only for those items cited only once or twice; for those works cited frequently, brief references only are given in the endnotes but full references appear in the list of abbreviations.

Quotations

Franklin's writings are cited from *The Papers of Benjamin Franklin*; if they are not in the *Papers*, then they are from the Library of America edition of the *Writings*; if in neither, then either from Albert H. Smyth's edition of the *Writings* or from the original sources. The text I use of the *Autobiography* is the Lemay and Zall *Genetic Text*, which shows all Franklin's revisions, additions, and cancellations as such and preserves exactly what Franklin wrote, including abbreviations, careless slips of the pen, etc. In quoting from it, I retain Franklin's eighteenth century spelling, but I silently expand the abbreviations, correct the few careless slips of the pen, and ignore the symbols showing what words or passages have been revised. I also ignore punctuation that has been superseded by subsequent revisions. Since all quotations from the *Autobiography* give the page number of the *Genetic Text*, readers who want to see the original cancellations, revisions, etc., may conveniently examine it. When a printed source is entirely in italics or uses italics frequently, I quote it in roman type.

Dates

Until September 1752, England used the Julian calendar, in which the new year began on 25 March. When Great Britain adopted the Gregorian calendar in 1752, eleven days were dropped (3 through 13 September 1752). I use the Julian calendar through 2 September 1752 and thereafter the Gregorian calendar. Under the Julian calendar, Franklin was born on 6 January 1705, but according to our present Gregorian calendar, he was born on 17 January 1706. For dates between January and 25 March, in order to avoid confusion as to which year is meant, I use both dates. Thus I write that Franklin was born 6 January 1705/6, using the Julian calendar for the day and the month but making it clear what year is actually meant. Starting in 1753, Franklin usually celebrated his birthday on 17 January.

ABBREVIATIONS

IN THE TEXT

Numbers otherwise unidentified refer to a volume and page of *The Papers of Benjamin Franklin* (see "P" below). In cases where there might be some doubt, a "P" precedes the reference.

"A" before a number refers to *The Autobiography of BF: A Genetic Text.* (See below.)

IN THE NOTES

A	*The Autobiography of BF: A Genetic Text.* Ed. J. A. Leo Lemay and P. M. Zall. Knoxville: University of Tennessee Press, 1981.
AAS	American Antiquarian Society.
Aldridge	Alfred Owen Aldridge. *BF: Philosopher and Man.* Philadelphia: Lippincott, 1965.
Aldridge, *Nature's God*	Alfred Owen Aldridge. *BF and Nature's God.* Durham: Duke University Press, 1967.
Amacher	Richard E. Amacher. *BF.* New York: Twayne, 1962.
ANB	*American National Biography.* Ed. John A Garraty. 24 v. New York: Oxford University Press, 2004.
Anderson	Douglas Anderson. *The Radical Enlightenments of BF.* Baltimore: Johns Hopkins University Press, 1997.
APS	American Philosophical Society, Philadelphia.
AWM	*American Weekly Mercury.*
BF	Benjamin Franklin.
Bristol	Roger P. Bristol. *Supplement to Charles Evans' American Bibliography.* Charlottesville: University Press of Virginia, 1970.
Cabanis	Pierre J. G. Cabanis. *Oeuvres Complètes.* 5 v. Paris: Bossange Frères, 1823–25.
Calendar	J. A. Leo Lemay. *A Calendar of American Poetry in the Colonial Newspapers and Magazines . . . through 1765.* Worcester, Mass.: AAS, 1972.
Canon	J. A. Leo Lemay. *The Canon of BF: New Attributions and Reconsiderations.* Newark: University of Delaware Press, 1986.
Clark, *Public Prints*	Charles E. Clark. *The Public Prints: The Newspaper in Anglo-American Culture, 1665–1740.* New York: Oxford University Press, 1994.

Cook	Elizabeth C. Cook. *Literary Influences in Colonial Newspapers, 1704–1750*. New York: Columbia University Press, 1912.
CSP	*Calendar of State Papers, Colonial Series, America and West Indies*. Ed. W. N. Sainsbury et al. London: Stationery Office, 1860–.
DAB	*Dictionary of American Biography*. Ed. Dumas Malone. 11 v. New York: Scribner's, 1958–64.
Dean	Harold Lester Dean. "The New England Courant, 1721–1726: A Chapter in the History of American Culture." Ph.D. diss., Brown University, 1943.
DH	J. A. Leo Lemay. "A Documentary History of BF, v. 1, Printer: 1706–1730; vol. 2, Rising Citizen: 1730–1747." Internet document, 1997. <http://www.english.udel.edu/lemay/franklin>
Duniway	Clyde A. Duniway. *The Development of Freedom of the Press in Massachusetts*. 1906. Reprint, New York: B. Franklin, 1969.
Evans	Charles Evans. *American Bibliography: A Chronological Dictionary to 1800*. 14 v. Chicago and Worcester, Mass.: Evans and AAS, 1902–59.
Ford	Paul Leicester Ford. *Franklin Bibliography*. Brooklyn, N.Y., 1889.
Granger	Bruce I. Granger. *BF: An American Man of Letters*. Ithaca, N.Y.: Cornell University Press, 1964.
Hamilton	Dr. Alexander Hamilton. *The Itinerarium*. Ed. Carl Bridenbaugh. Chapel Hill: University of North Carolina Press, 1948.
Holmes	Thomas J. Holmes. *Cotton Mather: A Bibliography*. 3 v. Cambridge, Mass.: Harvard University Press, 1940.
Huang	Nian-Sheng Huang. *Franklin's Father Josiah: Life of a Colonial Boston Tallow Chandler, 1657–1745*. Philadelphia: American Philosophical Society, 2000.
Hutchinson	Thomas Hutchinson. *The History of the Colony and Province of Massachusetts Bay*. Ed. Lawrence Shaw Mayo. 3 v. Cambridge, Mass.: Harvard University Press, 1936.
Isaacson	Walter Isaacson. *BF*. New York: Simon and Schuster, 2003.
Journals	*Journals of the House of Representatives of Massachusetts*. 51 v. Boston: Massachusetts Historical Society, 1919–84.
Ketcham	Ralph Ketcham. *BF*. New York: Washington Square Press, 1965.

Kittredge, "Introduction"	G. L. Kittredge. Introduction to *Several Reasons Proving that Inoculation is Lawful, [by Increase Mather]*. 1721; Reprint, Cleveland, 1921.
Lemay, *Men of Letters*	J. A. Leo Lemay. *Men of Letters in Colonial Maryland*. Knoxville: University of Tennessee Press, 1972.
Lemay, *Renaissance Man*	J. A. Leo Lemay. *Renaissance Man in the Eighteenth Century*. Los Angeles: Clark Memorial Library, 1978.
LCP	Library Company of Philadelphia.
Locke, *Essay*	John Locke. *An Essay Concerning Human Understanding*. Ed. Peter H. Nidditch. Oxford: Clarendon, 1975.
Lopez and Herbert	Claude-Anne Lopez and Eugenia Herbert. *The Private Franklin*. New York: Norton, 1975.
Mandeville	Bernard Mandeville. *Fable of the Bees*. Ed. F. B. Kaye. 2 v. Oxford: Clarendon Press, 1966.
Mather, *Bonifacius*	Cotton Mather. *Bonifacius* (running title, "Essays to do Good"). Ed. David Levin. Cambridge, Mass.: Harvard University Press, 1966.
Mather, *Diary*	Cotton Mather. *Diary*. Ed. W. C. Ford. 2 v. *Collections of the Massachusetts Historical Society*. 7th ser., 7–8 (1912).
McCulloch	William McCulloch. "Additions to Thomas's History of Printing." *Proceedings of the AAS* n.s., 31 (1921): 89–247.
McKenzie	D. F. McKenzie. *Stationers' Company Apprentices, 1701–1800*. Oxford: Bibliographical Society, 1978.
Miller	Perry Miller. *The New England Mind: From Colony to Province*. Cambridge, Mass.: Harvard University Press, 1953.
NCE	*The Autobiography of BF: A Norton Critical Edition*. Ed. J. A. Leo Lemay and P. M. Zall. New York: Norton, 1986.
NUC	*The National Union Catalog: Pre-1956 Imprints*. 754 v. London: Mansell, 1968–81. (Usually followed by a number locating the specific entry.)
OED	*Oxford English Dictionary*. Ed. James A. H. Murray. 13 v. London: Oxford University Press, 1933.
Oldest Revolutionary	*The Oldest Revolutionary: Essays on BF*. Ed. J. A. Leo Lemay. Philadelphia: University of Pennsylvania Press, 1976.
P	*The Papers of BF*. Ed. Leonard W. Labaree et al. 37 v. [through 2004]. New Haven: Yale University Press, 1959–.
PAPS	*Proceedings of the American Philosophical Society*.
Parton	James Parton. *Life and Times of BF*. 2 v. Boston: Osgood, 1864.

Pascal	Blaise Pascal. [Pensées.] *Monsieur Pascall's Thoughts, Meditations, and Prayers.* Tr. Joseph Walker. London: J. Tonson, 1688. (The edition BF probably read.)
PCSM	*Proceedings of the Colonial Society of Massachusetts.*
PG	*Pennsylvania Gazette.*
PMHB	*Pennsylvania Magazine of History and Biography.*
PMHS	*Proceedings of the Massachusetts Historical Society.*
Port Royal *Logic*	Antoine Arnauld and Pierre Nicole. *Logic, or the Art of Thinking.* London: W. Taylor, 1770. (BF's copy at LCP.)
Reappraising	*Reappraising BF.* Ed. J. A. Leo Lemay. Newark: University of Delaware Press, 1993.
Reilly	Elizabeth Carroll Reilly. *A Dictionary of Colonial American Printers' Ornaments and Illustrations.* Worcester, Mass.: AAS, 1975.
Roach	Hannah B. Roach. "BF Slept Here." *PMHB* 84 (1960): 127–74.
RRC	Boston, Record Commissioners. *Report* of the Record Commissioners, followed by v. and page.
S	*Writings of Benjamin Franklin.* Ed. Albert Henry Smyth. 10 v. New York: Macmillan, 1907.
Sappenfield	James A. Sappenfield. *A Sweet Instruction: Franklin's Journalism as a Literary Apprenticeship.* Carbondale: Southern Illinois University Press, 1973.
Sewall	*The Diary of Samuel Sewall.* Ed. M. Halsey Thomas. 2 v. New York: Farrar, Straus and Giroux, 1973.
Shields, *Civil Tongues*	David S. Shields. *Civil Tongues & Polite Letters in British America.* Chapel Hill: University of North Carolina Press, 1997.
Shields, *Oracles*	David S. Shields. *Oracles of Empire: Poetry, Politics, and Commerce in British America, 1690–1750.* Chicago: University of Chicago Press, 1990.
Shields, "Wits"	David S. Shields. "The Wits and Poets of Pennsylvania: New Light on the Rise of Belles Lettres in Provincial Pennsylvania." *PMHB* 109 (1985): 99–144.
Shipton	Clifford K. Shipton. *Sibley's Harvard Graduates.* 18 v. Boston: Harvard University Press, 1933–99.
Shurtleff	Nathaniel B. Shurtleff. *A Topographical and Historical Description of Boston.* 3rd ed. Boston: City Council, 1891.
Silverman	Kenneth Silverman. *The Life and Times of Cotton Mather.* New York: Harper and Row, 1984.
Thomas	Isaiah Thomas. *History of Printing in America.* Ed. Marcus A. McCorison. New York: Weathervane Books, 1970.

Tourtellot	Arthur Bernon Tourtellot. *BF: The Shaping of Genius, the Boston Years.* Garden City, N.Y.: Doubleday, 1977.
v	volume(s)
VD	Carl Van Doren. *BF.* New York: Viking, 1938.
W	BF. *Writings.* Ed. J. A. Leo Lemay. New York: Library of America, 1987.
Waldstreicher	David Waldstreicher. *Runaway America: Benjamin Franklin, Slavery, and the American Revolution.* New York: Hill and Wang, 2004.
Walters	Kerry S. Walters. *BF and His Gods.* Urbana: University of Illinois Press, 1999.
Winans	Robert B. Winans. *A Descriptive Catalogue of Book Catalogues Separately Printed in America, 1693–1800.* Worcester, Mass.: AAS, 1981.
Winsor	Justin Winsor. *Memorial History of Boston.* 4 v. Boston: Osgood, 1880–82.
WMQ	*William and Mary Quarterly*, 3rd ser.
Wood	Gordon S. Wood. *Americanization of BF.* New York: Penguin, 2004.
Wood, *Radicalism*	Gordon S. Wood. *Radicalism of the American Revolution.* New York: Knopf, 1992.
Wright	Esmond Wright. *Franklin of Philadelphia.* Cambridge, Mass.: Harvard University Press, 1986.
Zall	P[aul] M. Zall. *BF, Laughing.* Berkeley: University of California Press, 1980.

NOTES

Chapter 1. Boston

1. Winsor 2:443.
2. Gary Nash, *Urban Crucible: Social Change, Political Consciousness, and the Origins of the American Revolution* (Cambridge, Mass.: Harvard University Press, 1979) 409.
3. Nathaniel Uring, *A History of the Voyages and Travels of Capt. Nathaniel Uring* (London: J. Peele, 1726) 109–11.
4. Hamilton 106–7.
5. Samuel Eliot Morrison, *Harvard College in the Seventeenth Century*, 2 v. (Cambridge, Mass.: Harvard University Press, 1936) 532–35; Stephen Foster, *The Long Argument: English Puritanism and the Shaping of New England Culture* (Chapel Hill: University of North Carolina Press, 1991) 266–67.
6. Sewall, 14 January 1706/7, 3 April 1710.
7. [Plymouth, Massachusetts, newspaper], *Old Colony Memorial*, 7 June 1823, p. 2, col. 2.
8. Winsor 2:467–68.
9. J. A. Leo Lemay, *"New England's Annoyances": America's First Folk Song* (Newark: University of Delaware Press, 1985) 19.
10. Larzer Ziff, *Puritanism in America: New Culture in a New World* (New York: Viking, 1973) 187–89; Foster 200–204; Robert G. Pope, *Half-Way Covenant: Church Membership in Puritan New England* (Princeton, N.J.: Princeton University Press, 1969).
11. Marian Card Donnelly, *New England Meeting Houses of the Seventeenth Century* (Middletown, Conn.: Wesleyan University Press, 1968) 66–67, 126.
12. Ibid. 124.
13. Seymour Van Dyken, *Samuel Willard, 1640–1707* (Grand Rapids, Mich.: Eerdmans, 1972) 36.
14. Edmund S. Morgan, *Visible Saints: The History of a Puritan Idea* (New York: New York University Press, 1963).
15. *The Manifesto Church: Records of the Church in Brattle Street* (Boston: Benevolent Fraternity, 1902) 3.
16. Donnelly 81.
17. *The Letter Book of Samuel Sewall*, 2 v. (Boston: Massachusetts Historical Society, 1886–88) 1:255; Samuel Kirkland Lothrop, *A History of the Church in Brattle Street Boston* (Boston: Crosby and Nichols, 1851) 40–41; Ziff 267–73.
18. Samuel Gardner Drake, *History and Antiquities of Boston*, 2 v. (Boston: L. Stevens, 1856) 2:544.

19. *Letter Book of Samuel Sewall* 1:361–62, n. 28.

20. Paul Boyer and Stephen Nissenbaum, eds., *The Salem Witchcraft Papers*, 3 v. (New York: Da Capo Press, 1977) 83–109, 745–57; David D. Hall, *Worlds of Wonder, Days of Judgment: Popular Religious Belief in Early New England* (New York: Knopf, 1989).

21. The locus classicus in seventeenth-century English literature is Dryden's "Cymon and Iphegenia," ll. 399–408. See James Kinsley, *The Poems of John Dryden* (Oxford: Clarendon, 1958) 4:2082.

22. George Parker Winship, ed., *Boston in 1682 and 1699: A Trip to New-England by Edward Ward and A Letter from New-England by J. W.* (Providence, R.I.: Club for Colonial Reprints, 1905) 40.

23. Arthur M. Schlesinger, Jr., ed., *The Almanac of American History* (New York: Putnam, 1983) 72.

24. Sarah Kemble Knight, *Journal*, ed. George Parker Winship (New York: Peter Smith, 1935) 36–37.

25. J. A. Leo Lemay, "The American Origins of 'Yankee Doodle,' " *WMQ* 33 (1976): 435–64, at 454.

26. Samuel Willard, *A Thanksgiving Sermon, Preached at Boston in New-England, December, 1705. On the Return of a Gentleman from His Travels* (London: Printed for Ralph Smith, 1709). *Boston News-Letter* 8 April 1706.

27. This and the following paragraph are from Sewall.

28. Shipton 5:286.

29. [Mather Byles], *A Collection of Poems: By Several Hands* (Boston: Green and Gookin, 1744) 46–54. Evans 5365. In his prefatory note to "The Sequel of Commencement," Matthew Adams revealed that Byles's poem on commencement was published "last Year." *Calendar* no. 66.

30. Joseph Green, *A Satyrical Description* [1728] (rpt. Boston: Heart and Crown, [c. 1740]); Evans 40209. Concluding an examination of a Princeton commencement satire of 1748, David S. Shields discussed the genre: Shields, "An Academic Satire: The College of New Jersey in 1748," *Princeton University Library Chronicle* 50 (1988): 38–51.

31. For these and other poems on Christmas, s.v. "Christmas" in the subject and genre of the *Calendar*.

32. Sewall 1:151; Ward in Winship 55.

33. Lemay, "American Origins" 448.

34. 33. "Diary of the Reverend Samuel Checkley, 1735," ed. Henry W. Cunningham, *PCSM* 12 (1908–9): 270–306, at 285–87; Richard Bushman, *King and People in Provincial Massachusetts* (Chapel Hill: University of North Carolina Press, 1985) 14–25. Cf. Sewall, 6 February 1710.

35. Holmes 2:363–66 (no. 125).

36. Evans 39402.

37. Drake 2:662.

38. Ibid. 2:662–63.

39. Cotton Mather, *Nepenthes Evangelicum* (Boston: T. Fleet, 1713) Holmes 2:725–26 (no. 251).

40. Montesquieu, *Spirit of the Laws*, tr. Thomas Nugent (New York: Hafner, 1949) 1:235, 240.

41. *Blackwell Encyclopedia of the American Revolution*, ed. Jack P. Greene and J. R. Pole (Oxford: Blackwell, 1991) 383–86, 559–60.

42. For Ecton, see *The Victoria History of the Counties of England: Northamptonshire* (Oxford: Oxford University Press, 1937) 4:122–27.

43. The rise of the common man was unusual, but the idea and its celebration was not new. See "Franklin's *Autobiography* and the American Dream," in *NCE* 349–60. Cf. Wood 17.

44. Benjamin Franklin the Elder, "A Short Account of the Family of Thomas Franklin of Ecton," MS, Yale University Library.

45. Uncle Benjamin Franklin to Mary Franklin Fisher (daughter of BF's Uncle Thomas Franklin), 12 February 1711/2. Dartmouth College. Franklin Papers, Sterling Library, Yale University, # 28240.

46. Richard Brathwait, *Barnabae Itinerarium*, quoted in Alan Crossley, ed., *A History of the County of Oxford* 10 (1972): 8, where the Puritan reputation of Banbury is traced.

47. P 1:lvi–lxii. For the older scholarship, see Winsor 2:270.

48. Huang 15–24.

49. The members of the group are discussed in DH under 22 January 1717/8.

50. Huang, passim.

51. Robert F. Seybolt, *The Town Officials of Colonial Boston 1634–1775* (Cambridge, Mass.: Harvard University Press, 1939) 95, 100, 105, 139, 155. For Josiah as scavenger, see RRC 8:151.

52. Susan F. Beegel, "Folger, Peter," *ANB*.

53. Cabanis 5:222–26.

54. P 1:xix; reproduced, P 1:facing p. 4. Abel Bowen's engraving of the house in Caleb H. Snow, *A History of Boston*, 2nd ed. (Boston: Bowen, 1828) 206, reflects Thackara's sketch. Walter Muir Whitehill, *Boston: A Topographical History* (Cambridge, Mass.: Harvard University Press, 1968) 17.

55. RRC 7:115.

56. Zall #193.

CHAPTER 2. CHILD TO ADOLESCENT

1. Colaquintida is a bitter fruit from the vine colocynth. Thus the meaning is "sour."

2. The manuscript volume of Uncle BF's poems is at the AAS; printed in Parton 1:35–37; MS, AAS.

3. The lots were advertised in November 1752 and July 1753 by Franklin's brother John and his nephew William Homes. John Franklin sold his portion on 15 April

1754 to William Homes for £188.13.4. On 2 June 1757, Homes sold the entire property to Jonathan Dakin for £266.13.4. Shurtleff 632–33.

4. Cabanis 5:222–23.

5. *PMHB* 29 (1905): 27.

6. Shipton 5:342.

7. BF, *Memoirs*, ed. William Temple Franklin, 3 v. (London: Henry Colburn, 1817–18) 1:447; also Zall #151.

8. James Madison, "Detached Memoranda," *WMQ* 3, no. 4 (1946): 536–40, at 538.

9. Nathaniel Hawthorne, *Centenary Edition of the Works*, ed. William Charvat et al., 6:270–71; originally published as *Biographical Stories for Children* (Boston: Tappan and Dennet, 1842).

10. P 20:131; S 5:543.

11. P 20:133; S 5:545.

12. On rush candles, see Huang 32, 42–43, 93–94.

13. Tourtellot 141 thought that Uncle Benjamin presented the psalm at the Old South Church, and he lamented Uncle Benjamin's insensitivity to the congregation's conservative devotion to the book of Psalms. Parton suggested that the song was sung at the "feast of welcome to the truant sailor." I believe Parton's theory (1:42–43) is more likely.

14. Evans 573; an earlier one listed by Evans, for 1689, is conjectural.

15. Tourtellot 165–94 devotes several pages to each of the works I briefly discuss.

16. Edwin Wolf, 2nd, discussed Crouch's books in *The Annual Report of the Library Company of Philadelphia for 1966* 43–45. See also Robert Mayer, "Nathaniel Crouch, Bookseller and Historian," *Eighteenth Century Studies* 27 (1994): 391–419; and Tourtellot 177–78.

17. Cabanis 5:224.

18. For character books, see the *New Cambridge Bibliography of English Literature*, ed. George Watson, 5 v. (Cambridge: Cambridge University Press, 1969–77) 1:2043–48; Tourtellot 178–81.

19. Tourtellot 147–52.

20. Kenneth B. Murdock, "The Teaching of Latin and Greek at the Boston Latin School in 1712," *PCSM* 27 (1932): 23.

21. Tourtellot 152–53 also tried to identify BF's classmates.

22. *Catalogue of the Masters and Scholars . . . Boston Latin School 1635–1879* (Boston: Boston Latin, 1878) 7.

23. Shipton 6:535–46. *An Extract of the Minutes of the Commission of the Synod Relating to the Affair of the Rev. Mr. Samuel Hemphill* (Philadelphia: Bradford, 1735).

24. Shipton 7:106.

25. Ibid. 7:103–5, 121–24.

26. Ibid. 7:190–92, 252–53.

27. Ibid. 7:290.

28. Ibid. 7:455–57, 7:518–30.

29. Ibid. 8:12–19; P 5:250–52.

30. Sewall 577.

31. *Catalogue* 8; Shipton 7:464–93, 514–15.

32. Shipton 8:42. John Rowe, *Letters and Diary . . . 1759–62, 1764–79* (Boston: Clarke, 1903) 169, implies that Green attended the Boston Latin School. *Catalogue* 6 lists him as definitely attending but gives his date of matriculation as 1715.

33. Tourtellot 157–60.

34. *Boston News-Letter*, 9 March 1712/3. Brownell appears numerous times in Barbara Lambert, ed., *Music in Colonial Massachusets, 1630–1820, II: Music in Homes and in Churches* (Boston: Colonial Society of Massachusetts, 1985), s.v. "Brownell" in index, esp. 738–40.

35. Parton 1:52.

Chapter 3. Printer's Devil

1. Parton 1:52; VD 12; Verner Crane, *BF and a Rising People* (Boston: Little, Brown, 1954) 9–10; Wright 18; "James Franklin," *DAB* and *ANB*.

2. Thomas 105.

3. Henry R. Plomer, *A Dictionary of the Printers and Booksellers who were at Work in England, Scotland and Ireland from 1668 to 1725* (Oxford: Oxford University Press, 1922).

4. McKenzie.

5. He is also not listed in John Feather, "Country Book Trade Apprentices 1710–1760," *Publishing History* 6 (1979): 85–99. Since the first printing in Banbury, Oxfordshire, started only about 1767, James Franklin could not have served an apprenticeship in the town from which Josiah emigrated. *A History of the County of Oxford*, ed. Alan Crossley, 14 v. (London: Oxford University Press, 1907–) 10: 65.

6. Wroth suggested that the "cuts were made on metal with a graver and not on the long grain, or plank surface, of wood with a knife." Lawrence C. Wroth and Marion Adams, *American Woodcuts & Engravings, 1670–1800* (Providence: Associates of the John Carter Brown Library, 1946) 42. Another James Franklin imprint has turned up since the publication of Wroth and Adams's book, where the printer advertised that he did "engraving on wood": *A Catalogue of Curious and Valuable Books . . . Reverend Mr. George Curwin* (Boston: J. Franklin for S. Gerrish, 1718). Evans 1953; Winans 3.

7. The woodcut of Hugh Peters in Peters, *A Dying Fathers Last Legacy to an Only Child* (Boston: B. Green, 1717). Evans 1923; Wroth and Adams no. 7 (pp. 17 and 41); Reilly 1559; Keith Arbour, "James Franklin: Apprentice, Artisan, Dissident, and Teacher," *Papers of the Bibliographical Society of America* 94 (2000): 348–73, illus. 2.

8. The woodcut of Sabbath breakers in *Divine Examples of God's Severe Judgements upon Sabbeth Breakers* (Boston: Reprinted and sold in Newbury-Street, [n.d.]). Since Bartholomew Green's printing shop was on Newbury Street, the printing

is generally attributed to him. Wroth and Adams 43; Bristol B314; Reilly 1170; Arbour, illus. 1.

9. Arbour 348–73.

10. For other J. Franklins in Boston, see Chapter 5, note 13.

11. Huang 121.

12. I hope the hypothesis will challenge Keith Arbour or another descriptive bibliographer to study the changes in James Franklin's printing types.

13. Huang 121, 123–24.

14. Benjamin Franklin V, ed., *Boston Printers, Publishers, and Booksellers, 1640–1800* (Boston: G. K. Hall, 1980) 323.

15. Uncle Benjamin Franklin (1650–1727), "Treatise on Dyeing and Coloring," *PCSM* 10 (1907): 206–25.

16. Carl Bridenbaugh, *Cities in the Wilderness: The First Century of Urban Life in America, 1625–1742* (New York: Knopf, 1968) 291.

17. Personal e-mail, 27 June 1997.

18. *OED*, s.v. "Hanging," 1.b.

19. Cotton Mather, *Magnalia Christi Americana*, books I and II, ed. Kenneth B. Murdock (Cambridge, Mass.: Harvard University Press, 1977) 89. See below, Chapter 10, note 15, and Volume 2, Chapter 4, note 10.

20. First printed in the *Boston Post* for 7 August 1940, the poem was shown by Zoltan Harasti to be written in a nineteenth-century hand (P 1:6). Since 1940 it has been reprinted numerous times, usually with the claim that Franklin wrote it: e.g., Edward Rowe Snow, *Amazing Sea Stories* (New York: Dodd, Mead, and Co., 1954) 42–48. Worthington C. Ford's and Tourtellot's suggestion that it was translated into French and sold overseas rests on a misreading of an English retranslation of a French translation of the *Autobiography*. See P 1:6, n. 7; Tourtellot 209–10.

21. Richard C. Fyffe and David Levin, "*Providence Asserted and Adored*: A Cotton Mather Text Rediscovered," *Essex Institute Historical Collections* 125 (1989): 201–38. Holmes 2:865 (no. 313); Mather, *Diary* 2:566–67.

22. Mather, *Diary* 2:568.

23. *Boston News-Letter,* 9 March 1712/3 and 27 August 1716.

24. Anne Bradstreet, *Complete Works*, ed. Joseph R. McElrath, Jr., and Allan P. Robb (Boston: Twayne, 1981) 157: "In Honor of That High and Mighty Princess Queen Elizabeth of Happy Memory," ll. 95–100.

25. John Locke, *Some Thoughts Concerning Education*, ed. John W. Yolton and Jean S. Yolton (Oxford: Clarendon Press, 1989) 230–31.

26. The ballad may be found in the fourth and later editions of Mason Locke Weems's *Life of Franklin* (Baltimore: Pomeroy, 1815) 21. The earlier editions are simply a degenerate version of the *Autobiography* with Stuber's continuation; see Ford No. 477. Parton 1:56.

27. William Chappel, *The Ballad Literature and Popular Music of the Olden Time*, 2 v. (1859; rpt., New York: Dover, 1965) 524. Claude M. Simpson, *The British*

Broadside Ballad and Its Music (New Brunswick, N.J.: Rutgers University Press, 1966) 172–76.

28. Winsor 2:174, recorded from the memory of Dr. George Hayward.

29. Edward Everett Hale, "BF's Ballads," *New England Magazine* n.s. 18, no. 4 (1898): 505–7. C[harles] H. Firth, *Naval Songs and Ballads* (London: Navy Records Society, 1908), xxxv, 167–69, reprinted the song. Carleton Sprague Smith reprinted the *Worcestershire Garland* text in facsimile in "Broadsides and Their Music," in *Music in Colonial Massachusetts, 1630–1820: I: Music in Public Places,* PCSM 53 (1980): 172.

30. Ellen Cohn, n. 29, in *Reappraising* 317.

31. "As he sailed" echoes the refrain of the ballad on Captain Kidd. *Oxford Book of Sea Songs,* ed. Roy Palmer (Oxford: Oxford University Press, 1985) 75–80.

32. Thomas 249.

33. As Andrew Bradford did to Franklin in Philadelphia (A 55, 85).

34. Clark, *Public Prints* 104.

35. Reprinted in Andrew McFarland Davis, *Tracts Relating to the Currency of Massachusetts Bay* (Boston: Houghton, Mifflin, 1902) 247–78, and in Davis, ed. *Colonial Currency Reprints,* 4 v. (New York: Kelley, 1964) 1:416–42, with notes at 1:51–52, 42–44.

36. Cabanis 5:225. Alfred Owen Aldridge, *Franklin and his French Contemporaries* (New York: New York University Press, 1958) 205. "On the Eating of Flesh" is in Plutarch's *Moralia,* 15 v., tr. Harold Cherniss and William C. Helmbold (Cambridge, Mass.: Harvard University Press, 1957) 12: 535–79. On Tryon, see Waldstreicher 66–67.

37. *A Catalogue of the Library Company of Philadelphia,* [comp. BF] (Philadelphia: B. Franklin, 1741) 20. Hereafter, *Catalogue* (1741).

38. *Catalogue* (1741) 38. Other works of Locke appear on pp. 11, 28 (donated by Franklin), and 50.

39. *Logic* (London: W. Taylor, 1717).

40. Marie Jean Antoine Nicolas de Caritat, Marquis de Condorcet, *Oeuvres complètes,* 21 v. (Brunswig: Chez Vieweg, 1804) 4:513.

41. Port Royal *Logic* 377–78.

42. Port Royal *Logic* 164. The passage begins with a quotation from Cicero, *Academica,* bk. 1, ch. 4, "Hoc unum scio quod nihil scio, said the Academicians," which probably made Franklin want to read the *Academica.*

43. Port Royal *Logic* 354.

44. *Catalogue* (1741) 24. The signature "B. Franklin" is in a much earlier hand than the addition "Given by." Edwin Wolf 2nd wrote in 1971 that it "seems to be the only book which he owned as a boy now surviving." *Gazette of the Grolier Club,* no. 16 (June 1971); 48; James Green, *Poor Richard's Books: An Exhibition of Books Owned by BF* (Philadelphia: Library Company of Philadelphia, 1990) 18.

45. *Guardian* (1713), ed. John Calhoun Stephens (1982); see no. 55, p. 652. Sometimes, however, Franklin seemingly agrees with Mandeville, e.g., "On the Labouring Poor" April 1768; P 15:103–7.

46. *A Grammar of the English Tongue*, 2nd ed. (London: Brightland, 1712). The *Grammar* is variously attributed to John Brightland, Charles Gildon, and Richard Steele. A facsimile of the title page is in Paul Leicester Ford, *The Many-Sided Franklin* (New York: Century, 1899) 223. *Catalogue* (1741) 51 described it as "Brightland's *English Grammar; with the Arts of Rhetoric, Logic, and Poetry. The Whole making a complete System of English Education.*"

47. *Catalogue* (1741) 24.

48. Jefferson to Thomas Jefferson Randolph, 24 November 1808, in Thomas Jefferson, *Works*, ed. P. L. Ford, 12 v. (New York: Putnam, 1893) 9:232.

49. Leslie Stephen, *History of English Thought in the Eighteenth Century*, 2 v. (New York: Putnam's, 1881) 1:80. James Boswell, *Boswell in Extremes, 1776–1778*, ed. Charles M. Weis (New York: McGraw-Hill, 1970) 11.

50. Green, *Poor Richard's Books* 18.

51. Cabanis 5:228. Before 1741, the Library Company had two copies of *Les provinciales*, one in French; *Catalogue* 21, 47.

52. P 15:173–78, 215–20, 299–303. Franklin's interest in linguistics will be discussed in Volume 5 of the biography.

53. Reprinted in Davis 2:159–223, with a brief account at 2:224–26 and at 1:61–62.

54. Miller 317.

55. George Allan Cook, *John Wise* (New York: King's Crown Press, 1952) 48.

56. Miller 297 celebrates Wise's egalitarian beliefs.

57. Duniway 93–94. Davis reprinted the pamphlet, *Colonial Currency Reprints* 2:227–42, with an editorial comment, 242–44. Miller 319–20.

58. Chester N. Greenough, "Defoe in Boston," *PCSM* 28 (1933): 461–93.

59. Reprinted in Davis 2:279–300, with comments at 300–301 and 1:62–63. Miller 320–21.

60. Miller 319.

61. Reprinted in Davis 2:245–50, with comments at 250–55 and 1:62. Miller 322.

62. Moses Coit Tyler, *A History of American Literature, 1607–1765* (1788; Ithaca, N.Y.: Cornell University Press, 1949) 358, 359–60.

63. Vernon L. Parrington, *The Colonial Mind* (1927; Norman: University of Oklahoma Press, 1987) 125.

CHAPTER 4. MASSACHUSETTS CONTROVERSIES, 1716–1723

1. J. A. Leo Lemay, "Robert Beverley's *History and Present State of Virginia* and the Emerging American Political Ideology," in *American Letters and the Historical Consciousness: Essays in Honor of Lewis P. Simpson*, ed. J. Gerald Kennedy and Daniel Mark Fogel (Baton Rouge: Louisiana State University Press, 1987) 67–111, esp. 78–81.

2. *English Advice to the Freeholders, &c. of the Province of Massachusetts Bay* (Boston: J. Franklin, 1722) 6. Lemay, "Robert Beverley's *History*" 82. See also Carole Shammas, "English-Born and Creole Elites in Turn of the Century Virginia," in *The Chesapeake in the Seventeenth Century*, ed. Thad W. Tate and David L.

Ammerman (Chapel Hill: University Of North Carolina Press, 1979) 274–96. P 6:253.

3. For one example, see Anne Bradstreet, *Complete Works*, ed. Joseph R. Melrath, Jr., and Allan P. Robb (Boston: Twayne, 1981) 171, "Contemplations," stanzas 16 and 17.

4. Shields, *Oracles* 116–19.

5. *CSP 1722–23* 329–30.

6. *Concio Ad Populum* (Boston: B. Green, 1719), Holmes #70; and *Mirabilia Dei* (Boston: B. Green, 1719), Holmes #238.

7. Miller 305–23.

8. Joseph J. Malone, *Pine Trees and Politics* (Seattle: University of Washington Press, 1964) 70.

9. Could it be because Thomas Hutchinson did not mention it in his *History of Massachusetts*? Could the Loyalist Hutchinson have omitted it because it would be one more reason to object to the Acts of Trade and Navigation, which were partially responsible for the American Revolution?

10. J. R. Pole, *The Gift of Government: Political Responsibility from the English Restoration to American Independence* (Athens: University of Georgia Press, 1983) 121.

11. Miller 345–66; Tourtellot 233–74; Silverman 336–63.

12. Whitfield J. Bell, Jr., suggested that Franklin believed in inoculation during the smallpox epidemic of 1721. Bell, "Benjamin Franklin and the Practice of Medicine," in *The Colonial Physician & Other Essays* (New York: Science History Publications, 1977) 120.

13. Thomas 235.

14. Isaacson 22; Dean 103–44.

Chapter 5. Nathaniel Gardner and the Couranteers

1. Worthington C. Ford, "Franklin's New England Courant," *PMHS* 57 (1923–24): 336–53.

2. Somehow this file came to the Burney collection of the British Library before the twentieth century. There are two likely ways for the *Courant*'s migration: either Franklin sold it when in London in 1725–26, or Major John André or another British soldier took it from his Philadelphia home during the Revolution. Since Franklin reprinted some items from the *Courant* in his *Pennsylvania Gazette* (e.g., 26 June 1732), he probably had his file after returning to Philadelphia, thus suggesting that it was taken during the Revolution.

3. RRC 9:205. Dean 126, 132–34 first identified Ford's "mysterious Mr. Gardner" (above, n. 1) as Nathaniel Gardner.

4. RRC 28:63. "Records of the First Church," *PCSM* 40 (1961): 105. William David Sloan and Julie Hedgepeth Williams, *The Early American Press, 1690–1783* (Westport, Conn.: Greenwood Press, 1994) 45 n. 129, argued that Gardner was an Anglican, but they overlooked Dean's information, and Joseph Fireoved, "Nathaniel Gardner and *The New-England Courant*," *Early American Literature* 20

(1985): 214–35. Supported by a scholarship from the First Church, Gardner's son attended Harvard, graduated in 1739 (Shipton 10:366–68), and became well-known for his Latin poetry. David S. Shields, "Nathaniel Gardner, Jr.," *Early American Literature* 24 (1989): 196–216.

5. Robert F. Seybolt, *The Town Officials of Colonial Boston, 1634–1775* (Cambridge, Mass.: Harvard University Press, 1939), index, s.v. "Gardner, Nathaniel." Samuel Dexter to John Eliot, 12 May 1801, in Eliot Letters, Massachusetts Historical Society. Boston.

6. Shadwell's burlesque is cited in my discrimination between the true scientist and the virtuoso. Lemay, *Renaissance Man* 14–16.

7. Tom Law, of Concord, Mass., was New England's best-known doggerel poet of the day.

8. P 4:85; 27:433–35.

9. Gardner and Franklin may separately echo the third earl of Shaftesbury's *Sensus Communis* (1709). See Shaftesbury's *Characteristics of Men, Manners. . .*, ed. Lawrence E. Klein (New York: Cambridge University Press, 1999) 33–37.

10. On James Franklin, see Thomas 104–10, 234–42, 315, 325; Duniway 97–103, 163–66; *DAB*; VD 18–20; Miller 333–42; Tourtellot 275–310; Clark, *Public Prints* 127–40; Shields, *Civil Tongues* 266–74; *ANB*.

11. I deduce that James Franklin attended services since he mentions that his minister recriminated with him concerning the contents of the third *Courant*.

12. Sloan and Williams 27, 46 n. 135, argue that James Franklin was an Anglican.

13. See RRC 9:13, 174, and 222 for a John, Joseph, and John Franklin, respectively, who could have been the "J. Franklyn" in question and who are not related to Franklin's father.

14. In reply to my query, Bertram Lippincott III, librarian of the Newport Historical Society, wrote on 18 March 1994: "I have found no evidence that he [James Franklin] or any members of his family were Anglicans (Trinity Church). He was buried at the Common Burial Ground (nondenominational) and his son James's death in 1765 was entered into the records of the Second Congregational Church by Reverend Ezra Stiles."

15. Shields, *Civil Tongues* 273.

16. Clarence S. Brigham, "James Franklin and the Beginnings of Printing in Rhode Island," *PMHS* 65 (1932–36): 536–44.

17. The two were for 21 August and 9 October.

18. On Checkley, see E. F. Slafter, *John Checkley*, 2 v. (Boston: Prince Society, 1897); Duniway 84–86, 108–10; *DAB*; Tourtellot 249–50, 254–56; Clark, *Public Prints* 130–33; *ANB*.

19. Henry Wilder Foote, *Annals of King's Chapel*, 3 v. (Boston: Little, Brown, 1882–1940) 606.

20. *Council Records* 7:115; cited in Slafter 1:34–36.

21. Slafter 1:36–39, 59.

22. John Bernard, "Autobiography," *Collections of the Massachusetts Historical Society* 25 (1936): 177–243, at 229.

23. Frederick Lewis Weis, *The Colonial Clergy and the Colonial Churches of New England*. (Lancaster, Mass.: Descendants of the Colonial Clergy, 1936) 54.

24. Shipton 6:18–24; *DAB*; *ANB*.

25. Nathaniel Ward burlesqued the New England characteristic as early as *The Simple Cobbler of Aggawam* (1647). Franklin published an essay on trifling questions in the *Pennsylvania Gazette* on 19 October 1732. Dr. Alexander Hamilton lampooned the practice in an essay in the *Maryland Gazette* on 7 January 1746. Both he and Sarah Kemble Knight recorded a number of examples in their journals. See J. A. Leo Lemay, *Men of Letters in Colonial Maryland* (Knoxville: University of Tennessee Press, 1972) 230–32; Robert Micklus, *Comic Genius of Dr. Alexander Hamilton* (Knoxville: University of Tennessee Press, 1990) 122–24;. Adams to Jefferson, 2 March 1816, in *The Adams-Jefferson Letters*, ed. Lester Cappon, 2 v. (Chapel Hill: University of North Carolina Press, 1959) 2:464.

     Several previous commentators, evidently not realizing that Checkley was playing on an American tradition, condemned him for converting "Addison's graceful, good-natured invitation to the *Spectator* (1711) into an ill tempered challenge to the reader." Charles E. Clark, "Boston and the Nurturing of Newspapers: Dimensions of the Cradle, 1690–1714," *New England Quarterly* 64 (1991): 243–71, at 260; see also Sappenfield 31, and Tourtellot 332–33. For the Franklin anecdote, see Zall #72.

26. The broadside is the size of a *Courant* leaf and a copy is preserved in Franklin's *Courant* file in the Burney Collection, British Library, London.

27. On William Douglass, see Kittredge, "Introduction" 15–19, 41–43, 47; VD 18–19, Miller 345–48, 350–60; Silverman 344–45; Tourtellot 250–54; Clark, *Public Prints* 127–32; and *ANB*. He is not in Seybolt, but see RRC 12:61.

28. Foote 1:372.

29. William Douglass, *Summary, Historical and Political of . . . the Present State of the BritishColonies . . .* 2 v. (Boston: Rogers and Fowle, 1749–52) 2:116–17.

30. Hutchinson 2:206; Dr. Alexander Hamilton, *Gentleman's Progress: The Itinerarium*, ed. Carl Bridenbaugh (Chapel Hill: University of North Carolina Press, 1948) 116.

31. William Douglass, *Inoculation of the Small Pox as Practised in Boston* (Boston: J. Franklin, 1722) 20; Evans 2332.

32. Reported in the *News-Letter*, 24 July 1721, and in the *Gazette*, 31 July 1721.

33. Evidently John Webb. See Zabdiel Boylston, *An Historical Account of the Smallpox* (Boston: Gerrish and Hancock, 1730) 7; Evans 3259.

34. G. L. Kittredge, "Cotton Mather's Election into the Royal Society," *PCSM* 14 (1913): 102–14.

35. Unrecorded in bibliographies and evidently not extant.

36. Duniway 165. For Fleet, besides Thomas, see Tourtellot 293–97; and the *ANB*.

37. Thomas 93–100, 246–49, 250–54; *DAB*; *ANB*.

38. The series of pieces using Crusoe's island as an imaginary location began with Cotton Mather's *News from Robinson Crusoe's Island*. Franklin knew the series and may have echoed it in the title for a projected skit in 1764: "A Letter from a Gentleman in Crusoe's Island," P 11:184.

39. For Dr. George Steward, see Tourtellot 284. He occupied pew number 61, paying £5 for it on 12 February 1720/1. He contributed to the organ introduced into King's Chapel in 1713, and served as warden in 1732–34 and as vestryman in 1721–27 and 1728–41. Foote 1:211; 2:586, 603, 606.

40. *Council Records* 7:76–77; Slafter 2:157–58.

41. Slafter 1:59. Foote, passim.

42. For John Gibbons, see Shipton 5:315–17; Slafter 1:59; Tourtellot 283–84.

43. *Council Records* 7:76, 77.

44. On Henry Harris, see Weis, *Colonial Clergy . . . of New England* 101; Foote, *Annals*, passim; Tourtellot 286–87.

45. For John Williams, see George Lyman Kittredge, "Some Lost Works of Cotton Mather," *PMHS* 45 (1912): 471–75; Kittredge, "Introduction" 27–30; Cotton Mather, *Selected Letters*, ed. Kenneth Silverman (Baton Rouge: Louisiana State University Press, 1971) 365; Tourtellot 352–53.

46. Mather, *Selected Letters* 365.

47. Foote 1:117.

48. Williams repeated a version of this argument in *An Answer to a Late Pamphlet* (Boston: Franklin, 1722) 17; Evans 2407.

49. Mather, *Selected Letters* 365.

50. Kittredge, "Lost Works" 472.

51. For the mock illiterate tradition in colonial America, see Helen Saltzberg Saltman, "John Adams's Earliest Essays: The Humphrey Ploughjogger Letters," *WMQ* 37 (1980): 125–38.

52. For Thomas Lane, see Tourtellot 297–98; Foote 2:124. He is not in Seybolt; not in *Boston Births, 1700–1800*; and not in *Boston Marriages, 1700–1751*.

53. Tourtellot 302, 303 failed to identify Mrs. Staples. No one named Staples appears in Seybolt; nor in Foote; nor in RRC, v. 7, 8, 12, or 14.

54. RRC 24:108.

55. *New England Historic and Genealogical Register* 48 (1894): 414.

56. Joseph Dorr of Mendon married Abraham Staples and Abigail Taft on 26 July 1727, and he married Ebenezer Staples and Mehetabel Barron on 5 December, 1727. RRC 28:321. Carleton A. Staples and Robert Dodge Staples, *Proceedings at the Dedication of a Monument to Sergeant Abraham Staples of Mendon, Ma., October 31, 1877* (Providence: Sidney S. Rider, 1880) 43.

57. RRC 9:251.

58. *Calendar* #13; the other poems mentioned above are *Calendar* #9, 10, and 11.

59. For Christopher Taylor, see Tourtellot 291–93; "Records of the First Church in Boston," *PCSM* v. 39, 40.

60. *Council Records* 7:251.

61. For John Eyre, see Shipton 6:240–42, and Tourtellot 288–90. He and Gibbons are the only known Harvard graduates to publish in the *Courant* (excluding, of course, Increase and Cotton Mathers). His three later contributions to the *Courant* were 5 March, 9 April, and 14 May 1722.

62. Andrew McFarland Davis, *Colonial Currency Reprints*, 4 v. (New York: Kelley, 1964) 2:192.

63. On Matthew Adams, see Tourtellot 298–302; C. Lennart Carlson, "John Adams, Matthew Adams, Mather Byles, and the *New England Weekly Journal*," *American Literature* 12 (1940): 347–48. Sloan and Williams 45–46, n. 130, mistakenly claim that Matthew Adams was an Anglican.

64. Isaacson 34 also finds the Couranteers more important as a literary influence on Franklin than Addison and Steele.

CHAPTER 6. JAMES FRANKLIN

1. Clark, *Public Prints* 134.

2. Discussions of the *Courant* appear in Cook 8–30; Dean; Preston Shea, "The Rhetoric of Authority in the *New-England Courant*" (Ph.D. diss.: University of New Hampshire, 1992); and Clark, *Public Prints* 123–40. Most Franklin biographies also consider it, especially Tourtellot.

3. Louis Clark Jones, *The Clubs of the Georgian Rakes* (New York: Columbia University Press, 1942) 33–55.

4. Ibid. 40.

5. Bernard Bailyn, *Ideological Origins of the American Revolution*, enl. ed. (Cambridge, Mass.: Harvard University Press, 1992) 36. See also his *Origins of American Politics* (New York: Knopf, 1968) 54, 117, 137, 141, 143–44. The Couranteers cited *Cato's Letters* more frequently than any other source. In the first months, the tenth *Courant* (9 October 1721) borrowed the first part of a piece on flattery from *Cato's Letters*, probably with an implied allusion to Cotton Mather's relationship to Governor Samuel Shute. On 23 and 30 October, the *Courant* reprinted from *Cato's Letters* essays on the Whig philosophy and theory of government.

6. Holmes 1:357 (no. 122), citing Kittredge, "Lost Works" 418–79, at 460; Silverman 348–49.

7. Thomas Gumble, *Life of General Monck, Duke of Albemarle* (London: Basset, 1676).

8. Thomas J. Holmes, *Increase Mather: A Bibliography*, 2 v. (Cleveland, 1931) 2:500–506 (no. 120). Advertised in the 27 November 1721 *Courant*. Kittredge, "Introduction."

9. Francis Bacon, *Philosophical Works*, ed. John M. Robertson (London: Routledge, 1905) 249.

10. Boston Selectmen, "Statement of Resolve on Inoculation," *Boston News-Letter*, 24 July 1721.

11. *Canon* 23, 29, 39, 58, 67, 96–97, 101, 128, 135.

12. Besides John Wise of Essex and Thomas Walter of Roxbury, the Boston ministers Benjamin Colman of the Brattle Street Church, Thomas Foxcroft of the First Church, and Joseph Sewell of the Old South are good possibilities.

13. Cotton Mather, *Bonifacius, or Essays to Do Good*, ed. David Levin (Cambridge, Mass.: Harvard University Press, 1966) 142.

14. "If one were to take the Word Priestcraft out of the Mouths of" deists, "they would be immediately struck dumb." *Tatler* No. 135, 18 February 1710, ed. Donald F. Bond (1987), 2:280. Also *OED*, s.v. "priestcraft," 2.

15. Samuel Mather referred to John Williams's *Answer to a Late Pamphlet* (Boston: Franklin, 1722); Evans 2407; Kittredge, "Lost Works" *PMHS* 45 (1912): 418–79, at 471–75.

16. When Governor Shute in his speech to the Massachusetts legislature (15 March 1720/1) asked for a law saying that "no book or Paper shall be PRINTED without *my* License first obtained," the House of Representatives replied on 21 March with an attack on [Cotton Mather], *News from Robinson Cruso's Island*, but said that such a law might cause "innumerable inconveniences and dangerous Circumstances." *Journals* 2:359, 369. Duniway 96 n. 1, commented: "Curiously enough, the records of the General Court for that date contain no reference to the matter." There is no record that Cotton Mather, as the author of *News from Robinson Cruso's Island*, was taken by the sheriff before the House. Silverman 323–24 found no evidence of such an ignominy.

17. Zall 51–52, #52.

18. Thomas Foxcroft, *A Practical Discourse Relating to Gospel Ministry* (Boston: Buttolph, 1718); Evans 1956.

19. John Dryden, *Works*, ed. H. T. Swedenberg, v. 2: *Poems 1681–1684* (Berkeley: University of California Press, 1972) 98. As shown below, the epigraph in *A Friendly Debate* (1723), which I attribute to Gardner, contains lines from three different poems by Dryden.

20. Cotton Mather wrote on 15 January 1721/2: "The villanous Abuses offered and multiplied, unto the Ministers of this Place, require something to be done, for their Vindication. I provide Materials for some agreeable Pens among our People, to prosecute this Design withal" (*Diary* 2:672). About a week later, Mather added: "Something must be done towards the Suppressing and Rebuking of those wicked Pamphlets, that are continually published among us, to lessen and blacken the Ministers, and poison the People" (*Diary* 2:674). Holmes includes the *Vindication* among Mather's works, number 430, citing Kittredge, "Lost Works" 467; and Kittredge, "Introduction" 39–40.

21. The anecdote begins, "A Mountebank in Leicester-Fields." Swift, *A Tale of a Tub*, ed. A. C. Guthkelch and D. Nichol Smith, 2nd ed. (Oxford: Clarendon Press, 1958) 46.

22. *PG*, 25 May 1732; *Canon* 66–67 (no. 41). J. A. Leo Lemay, "An Attribution of *Reflections on Courtship and Marriage* (1746) to BF," *Papers of the Bibliographical Society of America* 95 (2001): 72–73.

23. Holmes 1:398–400, no. 137; Silverman 358–59.

24. Kittredge, "Lost Works" 471n.; Silverman 355–56. The epigraph on the title page is from three poems by Dryden. The first two lines are lines 28–29 in the "Epilogue" to *The Unhappy Favourite*; lines 3–5 are lines 33–35 in the second "Prologue" to *Secret-Love*; and lines 6–7 are lines 29–30 in the "Prologue" to *All for Love: The Poems of John Dryden*, ed. James Kinsley (New York: Oxford University Press, 1958) 1:246, 107, and 165, respectively.

25. "Apron-men"/mechanic is used by Shakespeare (Cor. iv vi.96) and is in the *OED*, s.v. "Apron.6," but I do not recall having seen the full epithet "Leather Apron Men" before 1722.

26. Kittredge, "Lost Works" 471n., also points out that Samuel Mather rejected the implied attribution. Thomas J. Holmes, *The Minor Mathers: A List of Their Works* (Cambridge, Mass.: Harvard University Press, 1940) 117, no. 63.

27. Holmes 2:826–27, no. 287.

28. I have failed to identify Cotton Mather's "Letter to his Friends at Portsmouth" in the newspapers or as a separate imprint. Perhaps it does not survive; it is not in Holmes or Silverman.

29. Hutchinson 2:174–75.

Chapter 7. Silence Dogood in Context

1. Dean 108 finds class resentment in a number of *Courant*s.

2. *Guardian*, ed. John Calhoun Stephens (Lexington: University Press of Kentucky, 1982) 525–27, 739.

3. Holmes #90, pointed out that *Bonifacius* was Mather's most popular work, going through at least eighteen editions.

4. Amacher 105–13; Anderson 16–33; Granger 27–37; Isaacson 28–33; J. A. Leo Lemay, "BF," in *Major Writers of Early American Literature*, ed. Everett Emerson (Madison: University of Wisconsin Press, 1972) 205–11; VD 20–25, 28–30; and Walters 39–42, who emphasizes the radicalness of the essays. Tourtellot's discussions will be cited separately. On No. 1, Tourtellot 331–36 compares the opening of the *Spectator* with Checkley's opening of the *Courant* and BF's Dogood. Though she did not know Franklin wrote the Dogood essay, Cook 28–30 earlier contrasted the openings of the *Spectator*, BF's Dogood, and an essay in the *New England Weekly Journal*, praising Dogood's Americanism.

5. Cotton Mather, *Magnalia Christi Americana* 2 v. (1702; rpt. Hartford: Andrus, 1856) 1:367.

6. Shipton 4:49.

7. Lewis P. Simpson, "The Printer as a Man of Letters," in *Oldest Revolutionary* 11–12.

8. Not in Holmes, *Minor Mathers*. Shipton 7:618 credited the letter to Byles. Miller 342–43 thought Samuel Mather was the author. P 1:18n, citing Miller, credited Samuel Mather with the authorship. Tourtellot 368, though thinking it was the same person who wrote the earlier attack dated from Cambridge, attributed it to

Mather Byles. I think it was probably the same person who wrote the 15 January attack dated from Cambridge—Samuel Mather.

9. James Russell Lowell, *Biglow Papers* (Cambridge, Mass: George Nicholas, 1848). Walter Blair, "Traditions in Southern Humor," *American Quarterly* 5 (1953): 132–42; but see J. A. Leo Lemay, "The Origins of the Humor of the Old South," *Southern Literary Journal* 23, no. 2 (1991): 3–13, at 8–9.

10. John Trenchard and Thomas Gordon, *Cato's Letters*, ed. Ronald Hamowy 2 v. (Indianapolis: Liberty Fund, 1995) 1:289 (no. 42).

11. Lemay in *Oldest Revolutionary* 119n. 36.

12. Holmes, *Increase Mather* 2:645–46, pointed out that "J. M." also wrote *Some Proposals to Benefit the Province* (Boston: Eliot, 1720); Evans 2177. Evans noted that Joseph Morgan had been suggested as the author.

13. P 4:481–82, 15:104; S 9:243–44.

14. Dean 116–22.

15. Duniway 163.

16. *Journals* 4:31, 35.

17. Ibid. 4:35.

18. Duniway 99.

19. *Calendar* #25, 26, 38, 39, 51.

20. *General Court Records* 11:370, quoted in Duniway 163–64. Because the council made the resolution on the fifth, Tourtellot 402 thought the House rejected it on the fifth and reconsidered it on the sixth, rejecting it again; but the House took it up only once, on the sixth. *Journals* 4:72.

21. Cobbett's *Parliamentary History of England* 7:863–79. James Franklin cited Aislabie again in his own defense on 6 May 1723.

22. George Allan Cook, *John Wise: Early American Democrat* (New York: King's Crown Press, 1952) 51. David S. Lovejoy, *The Glorious Revolution in America* (New York: Harper and Row, 1972) 185n. 11, pointed out that New Yorker John West replied that the laws of England did not follow to the ends of the earth.

23. Robert D. Arner, "Politics and Temperance in Boston and Philadelphia," in *Reappraising* 54–56.

24. Anderson 21.

25. Robert F. Seybolt, *The Private Schools of Colonial Boston* (Cambridge, Mass.: Harvard University Press, 1935) 93.

26. Norman S. Fiering, "Will and Intellect in the New England Mind," *WMQ* 29 (1972): 515–58, at 528; also his *Moral Philosophy at Seventeenth-Century Harvard* (Chapel Hill: University of North Carolina Press, 1981) 115.

27. Aldridge, *Nature's God* 14.

28. As Stephens noted, Steele's *Guardian* No. 80 was a political piece. *Guardian*, ed. John Calhoun Stephens (Lexington: University Press of Kentucky, 1982) 293, 673–74.

29. Port Royal *Logic* 70, 73.

30. Isaacson 29.

31. Paul Baender, "The Basis of Franklin's Duplicative Satires," *American Literature* 32 (1960): 267–79, pointed out that several Franklin satires reverse the expected situation.

32. See below, Volume 2, Chapter 5, "Personae."

33. John Updike, *Odd Jobs* (New York: Knopf, 1991) 258.

34. Henry Stuber, "The Life of Benjamin Franklin," *Universal Asylum and Columbian Magazine* 6 (June 1791): 365. Franklin's pretended speech travestied a defense of slavery, S 10:87.

CHAPTER 8. "SAUCY AND PROVOKING"

1. Much of the next several pages appeared in J. A. Leo Lemay, "BF and the Connecticut Apostasy," in *BF: An American Genius*, ed. Gianfranca Balestra and Luigi Sampietro (Rome: Bulzoni Editore, 1993) 135–48. Samuel Sewall, *The Letter Book of Samuel Sewall*, 2 v. (Boston: Massachusetts Historical Society, 1886–88) 2:143–44.

2. *Collections of the Massachusetts Historical Society*, 2nd ser., 4 (1816): 297–301.

3. Cf. J. A. Leo Lemay, "Southern Colonial Grotesque: Robert Bolling's 'Neanthe,'" *Mississippi Quarterly* 35 (1982): 97–126, at 108, and the sources cited there.

4. Silverman 367. Kenneth B. Murdock, "Cotton Mather and the Rectorship of Yale College," *PCSM* 26 (1924–26): 388–401.

5. Williams's pamphlets *Several Arguments, Proving That Inoculating the Small Pox Is Not Contained in the Law of Physick, Either Natural or Divine* (Boston: J. Franklin, 1721), Evans 2307; and *An Answer to a Late Pamphlet* (Boston: J. Franklin, 1722), Evans 2407, are both entirely religious.

6. In a personal letter of 5 August 1991, Professor Claude Rawson pointed out that Franklin may echo Jonathan Swift's "Verses Wrote on a Lady's Ivory Table-Book," first published in 1711, which contains the phrase "tru tel death," in line 9. Swift, *Complete Poems*, ed. Pat Rogers (London: Penguin, 1989) 81.

7. Rumor had it that the books Jeremiah Dummer sent to Yale converted the Connecticut ministers. E. S. Morgan, "The Trouble with Books," *Michigan Alumnus Quarterly Review* 65 (1959): 185–96. Anne Stockely Pratt, "The Books Sent from England by Jeremiah Dummer to Yale College," *Papers in Honor of Andrew Keogh*, ed. Mary C. Withington (New Haven, Conn.: Yale University Press, 1938), 7–44, at 26–27.

8. Several of these mock illiterate spellings show that the author was familiar with earlier literature. They are simply old-style seventeenth-century spellings: *i* for *j*, *u* for *v*.

9. *Records of the First Church, PCSM* 40 (1961): 105.

10. Tourtellot 415–16.

11. Richard Warch, *School of the Prophets: Yale College, 1701–1740* (New Haven, Conn.: Yale University Press, 1973) 109–10, surveys the best-known lamentations on the occasion by Increase Mather and Benjamin Colman.

12. *Canon* 23, 37, 58, and the references cited there.

13. See Chapter 5 of this volume.

14. Tourtellot 417.

15. Frederick Lewis Weis, *The Colonial Clergy and the Colonial Churches of New England*. (Lancaster: Descendants of the Colonial Clergy, 1936).

16. John Bach McMaster, *BF as a Man of Letters* (Boston: Houghton Mifflin, 1887) 6.

17. *The Tatler*, 3 v., ed. Donald F. Bond (Oxford: Clarendon Press, 1987) 2:191–95.

18. Dean 123–25, 132–34 first identified Gardner as the author of this essay, based on Captain Christopher Taylor's advertisement in the *Boston News-Letter* (21 January 1722/3). See also *Canon* no. 3, p. 35; and Joseph Fireoved, "Nathaniel Gardner and *The New-England Courant*," *Early American Literature* 20 (1985–86): 214–35. Miller 338–40 attributed it to James Franklin; Tourtellot 423 called the essay anonymous; and Isaacson 32–33 followed Miller in ascribing it to James Franklin.

19. George Parker Winship, ed., *Boston in 1682 and 1699: A Trip to New-England by Edward Ward and Letter from New-England by J. W.* (Providence: Club for Colonial Reprints, 1905) 39–40.

20. Miller 338–39.

21. Sewall 2:652–53.

22. William Byrd, *Prose Works*, ed. L. B. Wright (Cambridge, Mass.: Harvard University Press, 1966) 176; and William A. Craigie, ed., *Dictionary of American English*, 4 v. (Chicago: University of Chicago Press, 1938–44) 4:2005, s.v. "Saint" +1.

23. *News from Robinson Cruso's Island* (Boston, 1720), Evans 39730, is not listed in the standard bibliography of Mather's works, but Silverman, who did not know Gardner's attribution, judged that Mather wrote it. Holmes; Silverman 323.

24. Duniway 164; *Journals* 4:205.

25. Duniway 101–2, 164.

26. *Journals* 4:208. The 4 February *Courant* reported that it passed "by a Majority of one Vote only." Tourtellot 425 mistakenly wrote, "The House dutifully listened to the reading of the report and concurred without dispute or amendment."

27. Sewall 2:648–49.

28. Duniway 165.

29. Cf. Isaacson 31–32.

30. Tourtellot 402; Isaacson 32.

31. Tourtellot 427 believed that James Franklin wrote and printed the paper for 28 January and thereafter went into hiding. Cf. *Canon* 28–35.

32. Miller 339–40 suggested that the piece referred to Cotton Mather.

33. P 2:339–40, 340–41, 4:73–74, and *Canon* #19, 88.

34. Sewall 2:779.

35. Lemay, in *Oldest Revolutionary* 119; see also Max Hall, *BF and Polly Baker* (1960; rpt., Pittsburgh: University of Pittsburgh Press, 1990) 51–52.

36. Sewall 1:366–67.

37. P 1:48–51 prints the entire piece, citing Parton's opinion that it was mainly by Franklin. Tourtellot 431 thought it was "well below the level of the Dogood series." It seems likely that more than one Couranteer had a hand in it. For the relationship between the archetypal "Janus" and printing, see Ralph Lerner, "Dr. Janus," in *Reappraising* 415–25, Shields, *Civil Tongues* 267–69, 272–73.

38. Duniway 165.

39. David Levin, "Giants in the Earth: Science and the Occult in Cotton Mather's Letters to the Royal Society," *WMQ* 45 (1988): 751–70, at 770.

40. *Canon* 37–38 (#6).

41. A chronology may be helpful: 15 March 1722, [Nathaniel Gardner], *A Friendly Debate, or A Dialogue between Rusticus and Academicus, about the Late Performance of Academicus* (Boston: J. Franklin, 1722); 25 June, *Courant*: [Franklin], Silence Dogood, No. 7; 12 November, *Courant*: [Gardner], "Hypercriticus," pp. 1–2, satirized some New England funeral elegies and referred to Silence Dogood's essay; 5 February 1722/3, *Courant*: J. R. attacked Hypercriticus; 4 March, *Courant*: [Gardner], "Hypercriticus" replied to J. R.; 11 March, *Courant*: [Franklin] Satiric introduction to James Fitch's poem.

42. J. A. Leo Lemay, "Francis Knapp: A Red Herring in Colonial Poetry," *New England Quarterly* 39 (1966): 233–37.

43. *Canon* 138–39 (#97).

44. The name was possibly suggested by "Isaac Bickerstaff," the pseudonym that Jonathan Swift used in his almanac hoax, which Franklin imitated in the first three issues of *Poor Richard*. Richard Steele adopted it for his periodical, the *Tatler* (1709–11), which Franklin also knew.

45. Duniway evidently did not have access to the 6 May *Courant* and so said nothing about this detailed account by James Franklin. Subsequent scholars have followed Duniway.

46. Duniway 165–66, 102.

47. Cf. Waldstreicher 50–53. I identified Franklin as the author in my 1997 website "Documentary History of Benjamin Franklin." Though Franklin biographers and other authors whom Waldstreicher used have cited the website, Waldstreicher, 50, says that Dingo's letter is "previously unnoticed and unattributed.."

48. *Canon* 138–39 (#97).

49. Miller 482.

50. *Edward Taylor's Minor Poetry*, ed. Thomas M. and Virginia L. Davis (Boston: Twayne, 1981) 247.

51. W. C. Ford, "Franklin's New England Courant," *PMHS* 57 (1923–24): 336–53.

CHAPTER 10. THE RUNAWAY

1. Wolfgang Mieder, "History and Interpretation of a Proverb about Human Nature: Big Fish Eat Little Fish," *Tradition and Innovation in Folk Literature* (Hanover, N.H.: University Press of New England, 1987). One work Franklin knew that cited the proverb was Algernon Sidney's *Discourses on Government*: "Men

lived like fishes; the greater ones devoured the small" (ch. 2, § 18). For Franklin's view that Hobbes was closer to the truth about life than Locke, see P 2:185.

2. Norman Fiering discussed the voluntarist tradition in New England Puritanism in *Moral Philosophy at Seventeenth-Century Harvard* 129–30.

3. David Hume, *Treatise on Human Nature*, ed. Thomas Hill Green and Thomas Hodge Grose, 2 v. (1886; rpt., Aalen: Scientia Verlag, 1964) 2:195. I am indebted to Dr. Thomas Haslam for the reference.

4. The discussion revises the one I did in *NCE* 166–69. I thank Marina Fedosik for her suggestions.

5. Stephen Crane, *Uncollected Writings*, ed. Olov W. Fryckstedt (Stockholm: Almquist and Wiksett, 1963) 242–43. Stephen Crane scholar Paul Sorrentino informed me by e-mail on 18 July 1997 that although no evidence proved Crane read Franklin's *Autobiography*, Crane almost certainly did.

6. Charles S. Boyer, *Old Inns and Taverns in West Jersey* (Camden, N.J.: Camden Historical Society, 1962) 39.

7. Franklin wrote in the Canada Pamphlet (P 9:83–84) on the interconnectedness and the complexity of urban society, eleven years before writing this part of the *Autobiography*.

8. Perry Miller, *Nature's Nation* (Cambridge, Mass.: Harvard University Press, 1967) 222.

9. *PMHB* 29 (1905): 25.

10. Roach 128.

11. The following section revises the discussion in Lemay, *Renaissance Man* 22–32.

12. Dixon Wecter, *The Hero in America* (New York: Scribner's, 1941) 61.

13. For *The Honour of a London Prentice*, see Donald Wing. *Short-Title Catalogue of Books Printed . . . 1641–1700*, 3 v. (New York: Modern Language Association, 1972–88), no. H 2592, and *NUC* 253:502, NH 0500961; John Ashton, *Chap-Books of the Eighteenth Century* (1882; rpt., New York: B. Blom, 1966) 227–29; William Chappell and Joseph Woodfall Ebsworth, eds., *The Roxburghe Ballads*, 9 v. (Hertford: Ballad Society, 1871–99), 7:587–91; and Claude M. Simpson, *The British Broadside Ballad and Its Music* (New Brunswick, N.J.: Rutgers University Press, 1966) 13. For *Sir Richard Whittington's Advancement*, see *London's Glory and Whittington's Renown*, Wing, L 2930, and the British Museum, *General Catalogue of Printed Books . . . to 1955*, v. 256, cols. 1086–89; and William Chappell, *The Ballad Literature and Popular Music of the Olden Time*, 2 v. (1859; rpt., New York: Dover, 1965) 2:515–17.

14. J. A. Leo Lemay, *American Dream of Captain John Smith* (Charlottesville: University Press of Virginia, 1991) 84 and passim. For *Leah and Rachal*, see Lemay, *Men of Letters* 38–42.

15. Charles Sumner, *Prophetic Voices Concerning America* (Boston: Lee & Shepard, 1874), cites authors from the ancients to the mid-nineteenth century who use one or both of these motifs. On the West as terrestrial paradise, see William H. Tillinghast, "The Geographical Knowledge of the Ancients Considered in Rela-

tion to the Discovery of America," *Narrative and Critical History of America*, ed. Justin Winsor, 8 v. (Boston: Houghton Mifflin, 1884–89) 1:1–58; and Loren Baritz, "The Idea of the West," *American Historical Review* 66 (1960–61): 618–40. On the *translatio* idea (the theory of the westward movement of civilization), see Rexmond C. Cochrane, "Bishop Berkeley and the Progress of Arts and Learning: Notes on a Literary Convention," *Huntington Library Quarterly* 17 (1953–54): 229–49; Aubrey L. Williams, *Pope's Dunciad: A Study of Its Meaning* (London: Methuen, 1955) 42–48; Lewis P. Simpson, ed., *The Federalist Literary Mind* (Baton Rouge: Louisiana State University Press, 1962) 31–41; Lemay, *Men of Letters* xi, 131–32, 191, 257, 296, 299, 303, 307, 311; William D. Andrews, "William Smith and the Rising Glory of America," *Early American Literature* 8 (1973): 33–43; and Kenneth Silverman, *A Cultural History of the American Revolution* (New York: Thomas Y. Crowell, 1976) 9–11, and see the index. Paul W. Conner, *Poor Richard's Politicks: BF and His New American Order* (New York: Oxford University Press, 1965) 96–107, gathers together many of Franklin's allusions to these topics. See above, Chapter 3, n. 17, and Volume 2, Chapter 4, n. 12.

16. Matthew Arnold, *Culture and Anarchy*, in *The Complete Prose Works of Matthew Arnold*, ed. R. H. Super (Ann Arbor: University of Michigan Press, 1960–) 5:110.

17. On common sense in the *Autobiography*, see John Griffith, "Franklin's Sanity and the Man behind the Masks," *Oldest Revolutionary* 123–38.

18. Lemay, *Renaissance Man* 23–25.

19. *Poor Richard*, October 1749; P 3:346.

20. James M. Cox, "Autobiography and America," *Virginia Quarterly Review* 47 (1971): 256–62.

21. John Adams, *Works*, ed. Charles Francis Adams, 10 v. (Boston: Little, Brown, 1850–56) 1:660.

22. See the popular 1777 French medallion of Franklin, which bears the inscription "B Franklin Americain," in Charles Coleman Sellers, *Benjamin Franklin in Portraiture* (New Haven, Conn.: Yale University Press, 1962) 344–46 and plate 10.

23. See my remarks toward a definition of the American Dream in *Men of Letters* 6–7, 41–42, 59.

24. P 3:xiv, 190. The Loeb Library translation is "Not by vows nor womanish entreaties is the help of the gods secured." John C. Rolfe, trans., *Sallust*, rev. ed. (Cambridge, Mass.: Harvard University Press, 1931) 107.

25. Franklin's form was "God helps them that help themselves," in *Poor Richard*, June 1736 (P 2:140), and in "The Way to Wealth" (P 7:341).

26. For Franklin's *Dissertation on Liberty and Necessity, Pleasure and Pain*, see P 1:55–71.

27. Compare Benjamin Franklin's account of his brother's starting a newspaper (A 67), which implicitly makes the same point.

28. See the biographical sketch in *NCE* 190. In the 1756 "Taxables in the City of Philadelphia," Samuel Mickle was rated at £130, putting his holdings in the top 3 percent in the city; Franklin was rated at £60, putting his holdings in the top 12

percent in the city. Hannah Benner Roach, *Colonial Philadelphians* (Philadelphia: Genealogical Society of Pennsylvania, 1999) 138, 137, respectively.

29. S 9:252; also P 8:159–60.

30. J. A. Leo Lemay, *BF: Optimist or Pessimist?* (Newark: University of Delaware, 1990).

31. On the democratic and modern background of Franklin's *Autobiography*, see Paul Ilie, "Franklin and Villarroel: Social Consciousness in Two Autobiographies," *Eighteenth-Century Studies* 7 (1973–74): 321–42.

32. James G. Lyndon, "Philadelphia's Commercial Expansion, 1720–1739," *PMHB* 91 (1967): 401–18.

33. Jacob Taylor, *An Ephemeris . . . for 1723* (Philadelphia: Bradford, 1722) 9; Evans 2390.

34. Susan Mackiewicz, "Philadelphia Flourishing: The Material World of Philadelphians, 1682–1760" (Ph.D. diss., University of Delaware, 1988) 413–14.

35. *PMHB* 1:405.

36. Hamilton 21.

37. Jacob Taylor, *Pennsylvania, 1738, an Almanac* (Philadelphia: Bradford, 1737) 3; Evans 4201.

38. Ibid. 3; J. Thomas Scharf and Thompson Westcott, *History of Philadelphia, 1609–1884*, 3 v. (Philadelphia: Evarts, 1884) 3:2207.

39. Simeon John Crowther, "The Shipbuilding Industry and the Economic Development of the Delaware Valley, 1681–1776" (Ph.D. diss., University of Pennsylvania, 1971) 91–92.

40. Henry Melchior Muhlenberg, *Journals*, trans. Theodore G. Tappert and John Doberstein, 3 v. (Philadelphia: Muhlenberg Press, 1942–58) 2:517.

41. Gottlieb Middelberger, *Journey to Pennsylvania*, ed. Oscar Handlin and John Clive (Cambridge, Mass.: Harvard University Press, 1960) 48, 86; Muhlenberg 1:251.

42. Thomas Wendel, "The Keith-Lloyd Alliance: Factional and Coalition Politics in Colonial Pennsylvania," *PMHB* 92 (1968): 289–305, at 299.

43. Shields, "Wits" 134.

44. William Milnor, Jr., et al., *A History of the Schuylkill Fishing Company . . . 1732–1888* (Philadelphia: Fishing Co., 1889) 355–59.

45. Hamilton 191.

46. William Bradford, *Plymouth Plantation*, ed. W. C. Ford, 2 v. (Boston: Massachusetts Historical Society, 1912) 1:245–46, objected to some Pilgrims' (at Plymouth Colony) playing on Christmas Day while good Puritans were working. John Woolman also recorded his unhappiness with Christmas celebrations. Woolman, *Journal and Major Essays*, ed. Phillips P. Moulton (New York: Oxford University Press, 1971) 32.

47. James Birket, *Some Cursory Remarks Made . . . 1750–1751* (New Haven: Yale University Press, 1916) 59.

48. Two ceremonial occasions will be described in Volume 2: the proclamation of war against France (11 June 1744); and Philadelphia's celebration at the news of the taking of Fort Louisbourg on Cape Breton (11 July 1745).

49. Cf. Isaacson 37.

50. Roach 129–30.

51. D. F. McKenzie, *Stationers' Company Apprentices, 1701–1800* (Oxford: Bibliographical Society, 1978), no. 5491. Keimer himself said that by 1707 he was an apprentice to Robert Tookey. Perhaps so, but Keimer was not a reliable source. C. Lennart Carlson, "Samuel Keimer," *PMHB* 61 (1937): 357–86, at 361. For an appreciation of Keimer, see Waldstreicher 59–63, 65–67.

52. Roach 131.

53. Ibid.; Francis James Dallett, "Doctor Franklin's In-Laws," *Pennsylvania Genealogical Magazine* 21 (1960): 297–302.

54. Tourtellot 428 n. 68 pointed out that on 4 February 1722/3 (the marriage date given in P 1:lix), James Franklin was hiding from the authorities.

55. John J. McCusker, *Money and Exchange in Europe and America, 1600–1775* (Chapel Hill: University of North Carolina Press, 1978) 140.

56. Josiah Franklin and Davenport renewed the loan again on 1 April 1725. On 13 February 1728/9, Josiah Hobbs sued him and James Davenport for failure to pay the note, and then they (or, probably, Davenport—if, as I suspect, the debt was really his) paid it off. On 26 January 1731/2, Josiah (and, partially, James?) paid off the note with James Bowdoin. And finally, on 9 August 1739, Josiah paid off his mortgage to Hannah Clarke Willard. Huang 149.

57. "Advice and Instructions to the Palatines," MS, APS. Perhaps the satire partly reflects Keith's treatment of Franklin.

58. *DNB*, s.v. "Emes, Thomas" (d. 1707).

59. P, 1:lxii, gives Deborah's date of birth as 1708. Leonard W. Labaree, in *Notable American Women* (Cambridge, Mass.: Harvard University Press, 1980), gives the date as "c. 1707"; Claude-Anne Lopez, *ANB*, as "1704?" The story of the courtship, however, makes it apparent that Franklin is referring to a time shortly before he sailed to England in the fall of 1725. At that time, he was nineteen, not eighteen. The words "only a little above 18" were an addition, perhaps added to give an air of specificity to the passage. Since the reason for giving their age was in part to justify Deborah's mother's wanting them to defer their projected marriage, Franklin may have deliberately made them both slightly younger.

Francis James Dallett, "Doctor Franklin's In-Laws," *Pennsylvania Genealogical Magazine* 21 (1960): 297–302, established that Deborah had an older sister, Mary, born on 18 August 1703, and that Deborah was underage when her father wrote his will on 1 August 1724. Dallett 302 wrote that Deborah was "born about 1705." That would accord with Franklin's saying in the *Autobiography* that they were approximately the same age and would give Deborah's mother at least sixteen months before the birth of a second child. I agree with Dallett.

CHAPTER 11. THE WATER AMERICAN

1. Palmer, *The General History of Printing* (London: Printed by the author, 1732). McKenzie 258–59, records that he trained eleven apprentices, including Charles Ackers. *DNB.*

2. McKenzie 404.

3. Ibid.

4. *London 1500–1700: The Making of the Metropolis*, ed. A. L. Beier and Roger Finlay (London: Longman, 1986) 39, gives 490,000 as the population of London in 1700 and 675,000 as the population in 1750; *The London Encyclopaedia*, ed. Ben Weinreb and Christopher Hibbert (London: Macmillan, 1986) 613, gives 575,000–600,000 as the population in 1700 and 650,000 in 1750.

5. Shipton 6:471–82; David C. Leonard, "Harvard's First Science Professor," *Harvard Library Bulletin* 29 (1981): 135–68.

6. Washington Irving, "Little Britain," in *The Sketch Book*; reprinted in Irving, *History, Tales and Sketches* (New York: Library of America, 1983) 977.

7. Reverend John Bernard, *Ashton's Memorial* (Boston: S. Gerrish, 1725).

8. Parton 1:154–55.

9. VD 50, Aldridge 21, Lopez and Herbert 18. Similar sentiments are found in Verner Crane, *BF and a Rising People* (Boston: Little, Brown, 1954) 16; Walters 172 n. 2; W. H. Brands, *First American* (New York: Doubleday, 2000) 64–65, 106–7, though he noted (59) that when Franklin left for England, Deborah could not expect him to return to Philadelphia for six months. Isaacson 44, 74.

10. Ian K. Steele, *The English Atlantic, 1675–1740: An Exploration of Communication and Community* (New York: Oxford University Press, 1986) 57–77 and table 4.13 on p. 301, "Passages to Philadelphia from London by News-bearing Ships, 1705–1739."

11. *Pa. Archives*, 2nd ser., 8:221.

12. On Franklin's return trip to Philadelphia, it took twenty days to go from Deal to below Portland, which is not quite as far as Dartmouth, but the winds were not usually so uncooperative. The journey from Deal to Land's End could take four days—or two months, but usually took about a week.

13. In his "Letter of the Drum," 23 April 1730, Franklin cited *De examine sagarum* by "the learned Greutzius." W 147.

14. *A Ledger of Charles Ackers*, ed. D. F. McKenzie and J. C. Ross (Oxford: Bibliographical Society, 1968) 2–3.

15. Franklin wrote in a prefatory page to Ledger A&B, "Memorand. Direct the News for London for Wm Rouse Esq at the General Post Office London, To Mr. Charles Ackers. or—Richards."

16. Miller xxxiv.

17. *New England Historic and Genealogical Register* 35 (1881): 150, supposedly reported by Boylston's grandnephew Ward Nicholas Boylston, from Franklin's oral testimony in Paris in 1783.

18. Paul Leicester Ford, *Franklin Bibliography* (Brooklyn, 1889), #6, annotating Franklin's *Dissertation*, pointed out that the second edition of Wollaston appeared before his death (29 October 1724) and that Franklin must have worked on the third edition, dated 1725. The third edition was advertised for sale in the *Monthly Catalogue* for February 1724/5, p. 21, no. 5. The February *Monthly Catalogue* would have been published in March. Palmer's next edition of Wollaston (dated 1726) was advertised in the 26 March 1726 *London Journal* to be published on Monday, 4 April. Since Franklin only worked at Palmer's "near a year," he must have worked on the third edition.

19. Alfred Owen Aldridge, "BF and Philosophical Necessity," *Modern Language Quarterly* 12 (1951): 292–309; Aldridge, *Nature's God* 17–24; Elizabeth Flower and Murray G. Murphey, *A History of Philosophy in America* (New York: Capricorn Books, 1977) 1:100–102.

20. *NUC* NF 0340164 located copies at Yale, Cornell, the Pennsylvania Historical Society, the Boston Public Library, the Library of Congress, the John Carter Brown Library, and the British Library. (The reported copy at the Franklin Institute is the facsimile.) Ford #6. *NUC* NF 0340165 locates the Dublin (1733) bowdlerized reprint only at the Library of Congress. Ford #7.

21. A. Owen Aldridge, review of Gerald Stourzh, *BF and American Foreign Policy* in *WMQ* 12 (1955): 147–49.

22. David Berman, "Deism, Immortality, and the Art of Theological Lying," in *Deism, Masonry, and the Enlightenment*, ed. J. A. Leo Lemay (Newark: University of Delaware Press, 1987) 61–78.

23. A. O. Lovejoy, "The Parallel of Deism and Classicism," *Essays in the History of Ideas* (New York: Capricorn Books, 1960) 78–98, at 83.

24. The doctrine of the heterogeneity of ends is also called the law of unintended consequences. F. A. Hayek, "The Results of Human Action but Not of Human Design," in *Studies in Philosophy, Politics and Economics* (Chicago: University of Chicago Press, 1967) 96–105. Cardinal de Retz, *The Memoirs of Cardinal de Retz* (Paris: Librarie Gallimard, ca. 1949) 567.

25. Samuel L. Macey, *Clocks and the Cosmos: Time in Western Life and Thought* (Hamden, Conn.: Archon Books, 1980) 103–12.

26. *A Collection of Papers which Passed between the Late Learned Mr. Leibniz and Dr. Clark . . . To which Are Added Letters to Dr. Clark Concerning Liberty and Necessity* (London: Knapton, 1717), was in the Library Company before 1741 (*Catalogue* [1741] 37). Though the existence of a book in the Library Company does not prove that Franklin read it, it suggests that he did.

27. All in the Library Company before 1741. *Catalogue* (1741) 20 (Newton, Boyle), 11 (Locke), 16 (Pemberton on Newton), 24 (Newton), 28 (Locke), 30 (Locke), 33 (Locke), 50 (Locke).

28. *Catalogue* (1741) 21 (Wollaston), 26 (Ray), 27 (Derham, both *Astro-Theology* and *Physico-Theology*), and 51 (Fenelon). Cotton Mather's *Christian Philosopher*

(London: For E. Matthews, 1721 [1720]) relied heavily on Derham, Ray, and Fenelon, and thus also used the argument from design. See Holmes 1:137 (no. 52).

29. Locke, *Essay* 128–29 (bk. 2, ch. 7, sec. 1–2).

30. Locke, *Essay* 230 (bk. 2, ch. 20, sec. 6), and 249 (bk. 2, ch. 21, sec. 29).

31. Lucretius, *De rerum natura*, ed. and tr. Cyril Bailey, 3 v. (Oxford: Clarendon Press, 1947) 1:237 (bk. 2, ll. 14–20).

32. Lucretius, ed. Bailey 3:796.

33. Aram Vartanian, *La Mettrie's L'Homme Machine: A Study in the Origins of an Idea* (Princeton, N.J.: Princeton University Press, 1960).

34. Thomas Stanley, *History of Philosophy* (London: Mosely and Dring, 1656) 476; *Catalogue* (1741) 4.

35. Locke, *Essay* 129 (bk. 2, ch. 7, sec. 3); 258–60 (bk. 2, ch. 21, sec. 42–43).

36. Compare William Byrd's summary of Wollaston's argument. Kevin J. Hayes, *The Library of William Byrd of Westover*, annotation of #2011 (Wollaston) from Byrd's commonplace book.

37. Montaigne, *Apology for Raimond Sebond*, in *Complete Works*, tr. D. Frame (Stanford, Calif.: Stanford University Press, 1967) 454.

38. David Hume, *An Enquiry Concerning Human Understanding* (1748; Indianapolis: Bobbs-Merrill, 1955) sec. 12, part 1, no. 119.

39. Locke, *Essay* 181–95 (bk. 2, ch. 14, esp. sec. 18 [187]).

40. Locke, *Essay* 193–94 (bk. 2, ch. 14, sec. 27).

41. Locke, *Essay* 335–36 (bk 2, ch. 27, sec. 10).

42. Lucretius, *De rerum natura*, tr. W. H. D. Rouse (Cambridge, Mass.:Harvard University Press, 1943) 229 (bk. 3, ll. 847–61). I am indebted to Robert Klevay for the reference.

43. Mandeville 2:230. This part of *The Fable of the Bees* appeared in 1723.

44. James Green, *Poor Richard's Books* (Philadelphia: Library Company, 1990) 18.

45. Joseph Breintnall, who probably heard of Lyons from Franklin, gave a copy of the fourth edition to the Library Company. *Catalogue* (1741) 48.

46. Mandeville 1:381–412.

47. Listed in the *Monthly Catalogue* for March 1725, p. 27, no. VI.

48. Edmund Gibson, *The Bishop of London's Pastoral Letter to the People of His Diocese Occasioned by Writings in Favour of Infidelity* (London: Buckley, 1728).

49. Reed and Johnson, *Old English Letter Foundries* 206; and *DNB* sketch of her son Jacob Ilive (1705–1763).

50. See "The Religious Rhetoric of Jacob Ilive," in James A. Herrick, *The Radical Rhetoric of the English Deists* (Columbia: University of South Carolina Press, 1997) 181–204.

51. Richard H. Popkin, "Scepticism in the Enlightenment," *Studies in Voltaire and the Eighteenth Century* 26 (1963): 1321–46.

52. Bryant Lillywhite, *London Coffee Houses* (London: George Allen and Unwin, 1963) 111.

53. P 2:384–85; cf. 202–4; 17:315–17.

54. Lillywhite #878, pp. 387–90.

55. Shields, *Civil Tongues* 61.

56. Lillywhite #1468, pp. 624–25.

57. The "Horns" is not in B. Lillywhite, *London Coffee Houses*; it is in Lillywhite's *London Signs* (London: George Allen & Unwin, 1972) # 8911 and 8885. "Batson's Coffee House" is in Lillywhite's *London Coffee Houses* 110–13. The Golden Fan turns up in *London Signs* # 7464.

58. McKenzie 258–50, 367–68.

59. John Wygate served his apprenticeship with James Bettenham of Clerkenwell. McKenzie #794.

60. Thomas Hutchinson, *Diary and Letters* (London: Low, Marston, 1883–86) 2: 246–47. The legend that the press at the Smithsonian was the one that Franklin used at Watts's printing house seems unconvincing, though the press is the kind in use at the time. Elizabeth Harris and Clinton Sisson, *The Common Press* (London: Merrion Press, 1978).

61. This thesis runs through Edmund S. Morgan's *BF* (New Haven, Conn.: Yale University Press, 2002), e.g., 313.

62. Phillips Russel, *BF* (New York: Brentano's, 1926) 75.

63. *Another Secret Diary of William Byrd, 1739–41*, ed. Maude H. Woodfin and Marion Tinling (Richmond: Dietz, 1942) 287; Reverend John Barnard, "Autobiography," *Collections of the Massachusetts Historical Society* 25 (1836): 200; Robert Bolling, *Memoir of a Portion of the Bolling Family* (Richmond: Wade, 1868) 4.

64. *New England's Trials*, 2nd ed. (London, 1622), in John Smith, *Travels & Works*, 2 v. (Edinburgh: Grant, 1910) 1:263. Charles H. Firth, *An American Garland: Being a Collection of Ballads Relating to America, 1563–1759* (Oxford: Blackwell, 1915). John Urmston, in *Colonial Records of North Carolina* 1 (1886): 767. James Boswell, *Life of Johnson*, 21 March 1775.

65. J. A. Leo Lemay, *America's First Folk Song: "New England's Annoyances"* (Newark: University of Delaware Press, 1985).

66. For numerous citations about one order within the animal kingdom, see Elsa Guerdum Allen, "The History of American Ornithology before Audubon," *Transactions of the American Philosophical Society*, n.s., 41 (1951): 387–591.

67. Among the examples are the early American folk song, "New England's Annoyances" (the earliest printed version of which appeared in the chapbook published by Franklin's nephew, Benjamin Mecom, featuring the first separate printing of *The Way to Wealth*), Robert Beverley's *History of Virginia* (1704), Ebenezer Cook's *Sot-Weed Factor* (1708), and Richard Lewis's "Journey from Patapsco to Annapolis" (1730).

68. For the seventeenth century, see Karen Ordahl Kupperman, "The Puzzle of the American Climate in the Early Colonial Period," *American Historical Review* 87 (1982): 1262–89; and "Fear of Hot Climates in the Anglo-American Colonial Experience," *WMQ* 41 (1984): 213–40. For the eighteenth century, see Gilbert Canard, "Eighteenth-Century Theories on America as a Human Habitat," *PAPS*

91 (1947): 27–57, and Gunnar Erickson, "Linnaeus the Botanist," in *Linnaeus: The Man and His Work*, ed. Tore Frängsmyr (Berkeley: University of California Press, 1982) 86.

69. *The Battle of the Books* was in the *New-England Courant* library. Richard Foster Jones, "The Background of *The Battle of the Books*" (1920), reprinted in Jones, *The Seventeenth Century* (Stanford, calif.: Stanford University Press, 1951) 10–40.

70. Lemay, *Men of Letters* 77–93; and David S. Shields, "Henry Brooke and the Situation of the First Belletrists in British America," *Early American Literature* 23 (1988): 3–27.

Chapter 12. At Sea

1. Boswell, *Life of Dr. Samuel Johnson*, entry for Monday, 18 March 1776.
2. Ellen Cohn, "BF and Traditional Music," *Reappraising* 293–94.
3. Port Royal *Logic* 88.
4. Shaftesbury, *Characteristics*, ed. John N. Robertson (Indianapolis: Bobbs-Merrill, 1964) 1:113; Cicero, *De Officiis* (New York: Oxford University Press, 2000), bk. 3, ch. 1, sec. 1; Jonathan Swift, *A Tritical Essay upon the Faculties of the Mind*, in *A Tale of a Tub and Other Satires*, ed. Kathleen Williams (London: Dent, 1975) 198.
5. Mandeville 1:340.
6. Montaigne, *Essays*, ed. M. A. Screech (London: Penguin, 1991) 1115–16.
7. J. C. Cooper, *An Illustrated Encyclopaedia of Traditional Symbols* (London: Thames and Hudson, 1978) 55. Legends and actual stories of dolphins saving drowning persons are not uncommon. Several Franklin families had coats of arms. Franklin's own family did not, so far as we know. Before 20 June 1751, however, Franklin followed his older brother John in adopting the coat of arms of the Franklin family of Skipton-in-Craven, Yorkshire, P 2:xiii, 229–30, illustration facing 230.
8. The quotation from Hutcheson appeared in the *Journal* on 19 June 1725; the attack on Mandeville, 4 February 1725/6. *Collected Works of Francis Hutcheson*, ed. Bernhard Fabian (Hildesheim: Georg Olms, 1971) 7:121, 132.
9. Hobbes, *Human Nature*, in *The English Works of Thomas Hobbes of Malmesbury*, 11 v. (London: John Bohn, 1840) 4:46 (ch. 9, sec. 13).
10. P 6:184.

Chapter 13. Merchant to Master Printer, 1726–1728

1. Roach 136, citing Denham's account book, Historical Society of Pennsylvania. A 41.
2. Roach 135–36.
3. Lemay, *BF: Optimist or Pessimist?*
4. Jean François Marmontel, "Allegorie," in Diderot's *Encyclopédie*, 2nd ed. (Geneva: Pellet, 1777) 2:158, col. 1.
5. L. H. Butterfield, "B. Franklin's Epitaph," *New Colophon* 3 (1950): 9–39. Pp. 31–38 are devoted to "Antecedents, Parallels, Sequels."

6. Butterfield 23.

7. Lewis P. Simpson, "The Printer as a Man of Letters," in *Oldest Revolutionary* 4.

8. Roach 138.

9. Even without knowing that Franklin quit Keimer on 2 October, C. William Miller speculated that Captain Annis carried the order for the printing materials. Miller, "BF's Philadelphia Type," *Studies in Bibliography* 11 (1958): 179–206, at 183.

10. Miller, "BF's Philadelphia Type" 183.

11. John J. McCusker, *Money and Exchange in Europe and America, 1600–1775* (Chapel Hill: University of North Carolina Press, 1978) 185.

12. Lawrence C. Wroth, *The Colonial Printer* (Charlottesville: University Press of Virginia, 1964) 67.

13. John Feather, *Provincial Book Trade in Eighteenth-Century England* (New York: Cambridge University Press, 1985) 100.

14. Joseph Moxon, *Mechanick Exercises*, 2 v. (London: Moxon, 1677–84) 25.

15. Miller, "BF's Philadelphia Type" 185 proves that Franklin began with James's type.

16. Compare John Feather's discussion of the cost of a press and types (100).

17. If, as Keith Arbour has speculated, Franklin cut the figures at the top of *Elegy on . . . Aquila Rose* (1723), that explains how Keimer knew he was capable of creating the copper press. Arbour, "James Franklin" 348–73, at 360 n. 22.

18. A 57; Edwin Platt Tanner, *The Province of New Jersey, 1664–1738* (New York: Longmans, 1908) 550; N.J. *Archives* 14:372, 389; Eric P. Newman, *The Early Paper Money of America*, 4th ed. (Iola, Wisc.: Kraus Publications, 1997) 223; Roach 139n. 42.

19. *Acts and Laws of . . . New Jersey* (Burlington, N.J.: Keimer, 1728) 5.

20. Biographical notes in *NCE*; Thomas Leslie Purvis, "The New Jersey Assembly, 1722–1776" (Ph.D. diss., Johns Hopkins University, 1979); and Newman 245.

Chapter 14. The Junto

1. Lemay, *Men of Letters* 245–55; Dr. Alexander Hamilton, *The History of the . . . Tuesday Club*, ed. Robert Micklus, 3 v. (Chapel Hill: University of North Carolina Press, 1990); Alexander Hamilton, *The Records of the Tuesday Club of Annapolis, 1745–56*, ed. Elaine Breslaw (Urbana: University of Illinois Press, 1988); John Barry Talley, *Secular Music in Colonial Annapolis: The Tuesday Club, 1745–56* (Urbana: University of Illinois Press, 1988); Robert Micklus, *The Comic Genius of Dr. Alexander Hamilton* (Knoxville: University of Tennessee Press, 1991); and Wilson Somerville, *The Tuesday Club of Annapolis (1745–1756) as Cultural Performance* (Athens: University of Georgia Press, 1996).

2. For an overview of colonial clubs, see David S. Shields, "Anglo-American Clubs: Their Wit, Their Heterodoxy, Their Sedition," *WMQ* 51 (1984): 293–304; and Shields, "The Clubs," *Civil Tongues*, 175–208.

3. Hamilton 115, 116, 137, 151, 191.

4. Samuel Butler, *Hudibras*, ed. John Wilders (Oxford: Clarendon Press, 1967) 266 (pt. 3, canto 2, ll. 1215–16); *OED*.

5. The printing house was 22 feet wide and at what is now 120 Church Alley. The post office, in a house 15 feet wide, was at the site of 122 Church Alley. Roach 144–46.

6. Cited in the *OED*, s.v. "Junto."

7. Franklin read about Masonic meetings and processions in the London newspapers of 1725–26, and he evidently met various Freemasons, including John Theophilus Desaguliers, grandmaster of England's Grand Lodge in 1719. See Chapter 11.

8. Dorothy F. Grimm, "Franklin's Scientific Institution," *Pennsylvania History* 23 (1956): 437–62, at 441.

9. Shields, "Wits" 102–10.

10. I. Bernard Cohen, *BF's Science* (Cambridge, Mass.: Harvard University Press, 1990) 160–66.

11. Bibliographical references for the early Junto members are found in the *NCE* 173–201. They are arranged alphabetically, and Breintnall is on p. 176, where the quotation may be found.

12. This is briefly discussed in Volume 2, Chapter 13.

13. Robert Vaux, "Historical Memoranda," *Hazard's Register of Pennsylvania* 15 (1835): 183–84.

14. In addition to the persons discussed above, Robert Vaux reported that Enoch Flower, William Griffiths, Samuel Jervis, Luke Morris, Joseph Shippen, Joseph Trotter, Joseph Turner, and Joseph Wharton were all later Junto members.

15. I. Bernard Cohen, *BF: His Contributions to the American Tradition* (Indianapolis: Bobbs-Merrill, 1953) 145.

16. Mather, *Bonifacius* 136–37.

17. Daniel Defoe, *An Essay Upon Projects* (London: R. R., 1707) v, 118–46.

18. I have no idea of the significance of the name "Bargos." The biblical "Barkos," at Ezra 2:53 and Nehemiah 7:55, does not seem appropriate.

19. Sappenfield 84–85; Shields, *Oracles* 150–52.

20. *Calendar* #166, 167, pointed out that the poems are also in the play "Belcher the Apostate" (New York Public Library). The same manuscript play was published from a copy in the Massachusetts Historical Society as "Boston's First Play," *PMHS* 92 (1980): 117–39, see 121 and 139. Shields, *Oracles* 104–7.

21. Nicholas B. Wainwright, "Nicholas Scull's 'Junto' Verses," *PMHB* 73 (1949): 82–84. I have supplied the punctuation. Shields, "Wits" 127, identified Webb as Oldham.

22. Aldridge, *Nature's God* 34–46; Anderson 77–79; Walters 75–90.

23. Alfred Owen Aldridge pointed out in reviewing volume 1 of *The Papers of BF* in *American Literature* 32 (1960): 210 that Franklin dated it 1730 in a letter to Benjamin Vaughan, 9 November 1779 (P 31:59). P 1:264 dated it "[1732]." For a discussion of the speech, see Aldridge, *Nature's God* 34–40.

24. Charles Allen Beaumont, *Swift's Classical Rhetoric* (Athens: University Of Georgia Press, 1961); George Mayhew, "Swift and the Tripos Tradition," *Philological Quarterly* 45 (1966): 85–101.

25. Richard A. Lanham, *A Handlist of Rhetorical Terms*, 2nd ed. (Berkeley: University of California Press, 1991) 171–74.

26. For the doctrine that A. O. Lovejoy labeled *uniformitarianism*, the belief that reason was "identical in all men," see Lovejoy, "The Parallel of Deism and Classicism," in *Essays in the History of Ideas* (Baltimore: Johns Hopkins University Press, 1948) 79.

27. For the appeal to the *consensus gentium*, see Lovejoy 83.

28. Port Royal *Logic* 366.

29. *Complete Works of Anne Bradstreet*, ed. Joseph R. McElrath, Jr., and Allan P. Robb (Boston: Twayne, 1981) 167–68.

30. Poor Richard echoed Clarke's position in the almanac for 1734 (see Volume 2, Chapter 7).

31. False gods: 1 Samuel 5; 2 Kings 10; and the Apocrypha, "Bell and the Dragon" from the end of Daniel.

32. See also, Volume 2, Chapter 2, "The Art of Virtue" and the references to Montaigne and Hume.

33. Isaacson 87 commented that Franklin chose the 4th belief because it was the one "most useful for people to hold."

CHAPTER 15. BUSINESS, 1728–1730, AND "ARTICLES OF RELIGION"

1. Roach 139.

2. C. William Miller, *Franklin's Philadelphia Printing* (Philadelphia: APS, 1974) #1. All subsequent Miller references are to C. W. Miller unless otherwise identified.

3. *The Good Natur'd Man* opened at Covent Garden on 29 January 1768. Franklin probably saw it. Though he made few references in his correspondence to attending musical performances, plays, or other amusements, the reason is partly that he was sensitive about his position as a paid representative of the Pennsylvania Assembly. From various allusions, we know that he attended a number of London entertainments. The London *Morning Chronicle* for 16 March 1773 recorded his presence at the opening night of Goldsmith's *She Stoops to Conquer* (Covent Garden, 15 March). *Collected Works of Oliver Goldsmith*, ed. Arthur Friedman, 5 v. (Oxford: Clarendon, 1966) 5:24, 90.

4. *NCE* 190–91.

5. James T. Mitchell and Henry Flanders, ed. *The Statutes at Large of Pennsylvania from 1682–1801* (Harrisburg, Pa.: State Printer, 1896–1915) 2:212–21.

6. Aldridge, *Nature's God* 25–33; Anderson 64–74; Elizabeth E. Dunn, "From a Bold Youth to a Reflective Sage: A Reevaluation of BF's Religion," *PMHB* 111 (1987): 501–24; Walters 75–90.

7. Thomas Morris, *General View of the Life and Writings of the Rev. David Williams* (London: Ridgeway, 1792) 11.

8. Dunn 512.

9. Parton 1:175.

10. [Isaac] Woodbridge Riley, *American Philosophy* (New York: Dodd, Mead, 1907) 249.

11. Charles Henry Hart, ed., "Robert Morris of Oxford, Md.," in William F. Boogher, *Miscellaneous Americana: A Collection* (Washington, D.C.: 1895) 48.

12. Sabine MacCormack noted that all educated eighteenth-century readers would have recognized that David Hume modeled his *Dialogues Concerning Natural Religion* on Cicero's *De natura rerum*. MacCormack, "Limits of Understanding: Perceptions of Greco-Roman and Amerindian Paganism in Early Modern Europe," in *America in European Consciousness, 1493–1750*, ed. K. O. Kupperman (Chapel Hill: University of North Carolina Press, 1995) 128–29n. 78.

13. A. O. Lovejoy, *The Great Chain of Being* (Cambridge, Mass.: Harvard University Press, 1936) 99–143, at 189.

14. Locke, *Essay* 447 (bk. 3, ch. 6, sec. 12).

15. *The Spectator*, 4 v., ed. Donald F. Bond (Oxford: Clarendon, 1965) 4:348.

16. Alexander Pope, *An Essay on Man*, ed. Maynard Mack (London: Methuen, 1950) 44–45; Epistle 1, ll. 233–41. Aldridge, *Nature's God* 27.

17. Lovejoy 108.

18. Richard Lewis, "A Journey from Patapsko to Annapolis, April 4, 1730," *Calendar* #184; ll. 251–55, 351–57.

19. Pascal 43.

20. Jonathan Swift, *Tale of a Tub*, ed. A. C. Guthkelch and D. Nichol Smith (Oxford: Clarendon Press, 1958) 275–76.

21. Shaftesbury, *Characteristics of Men, Manners, Opinions, Times*, ed. Lawrence D. Klein (New York: Cambridge University Press, 1999) 105.

22. Aldridge, *Nature's God* 29.

23. On Franklin's "Articles of Belief," see Aldridge, *Nature's God* 25–31; Anderson 64–74, and Walters 75–90. For some reservations on Walters, see my review in *PMHB* 124 (2000): 208–12.

24. Compare Franklin's last letter to Whitefield, prior to 2 September 1769.

25. *NCE* 70.

26. Pascal 77–78.

27. Thomas 370n. See also McCulloch 137, 238, 242, 246.

28. On Sandiford, see Waldstricher, 79–80. Like several earlier writers, Waldstricher finds it significant that Franklin did not put his name as printer on the title page. In printing for others, rather than at one's own risk, it was common to omit the printer's name.

29. Bradford's imprint is Evans 3203. Keith Arbour shrewdly deduced the ways Franklin's imprint was superior to Bradford's by comparing Bradford's printing of subsequent official documents with this one. See Lemay, reviewing Arbour's *BF's First Government Printing* in *Papers of the Bibliographical Society of America* 94 (2000): 565–67.

30. The Pennsylvania Assembly chastised David Hall in 1758 for using the title "Provincial Printer." P 8:98n. 2.

CHAPTER 16. THE BUSY-BODY

1. David Hume, *Essays*, ed. Eugene F. Miller (Indianapolis: Liberty Classics, 1985) 541. Miller noted that the name literally means "good character" and that Joseph Addison used it in his "Dialogues upon the Usefulness of Ancient Medals" (1721).
2. Fredric M. Litto, "Addison's *Cato* in the Colonies," *WMQ* 23 (1966): 431–49. John Trenchard and Thomas Gordon, *Cato's Letters*, ed. Ronald Hamowy (Indianapolis: Liberty Fund, 1995).
3. Cook 65.
4. VD 473.
5. *Boston Evening Post* 8 September 1746.
6. Cook 72.
7. Thomas Wendel, "The Keith-Lloyd Alliance," *PMHB* 92 (1968): 289–305, at 296, 299–304.
8. James Fenimore Cooper, *The American Democrat* (1838; New York: Knopf, 1931) 108–9. Alexis de Tocqueville, *Democracy in America*, ed. Phillips Bradley, 2 v. (New York: Knopf, 1963) 2:171–74 (bk. 3, ch. 3); 2:217 (bk. 3, ch. 14). D. H. Lawrence, *Studies in Classic American Literature* (New York: T. Seltzer, 1923) 40–41.
9. Jane Louise Mesick, *The English Traveler in America, 1785–1835* (New York: Columbia University Press, 1922) 83–84, 310.
10. The foolish-search-for-gold motif anticipates the narratives found in the anonymous musical comedy *The Disappointment: or The Force of Credulity* (1767), Washington Irving's "Money-Diggers," John Quidor's painting of Irving's tale, Edgar Allan Poe's "Gold Bug," and a host of nineteenth- and twentieth-century obsessed characters, including two of Faulkner's: Lucas Beauchamp in "The Fire and the Hearth" and Henry Armstid in *The Hamlet*. Even in the 1990s, Captain Kidd's treasure supplies the denouement in Nelson DeMille's novel *Plum Island*.
11. *The Complete Works of Captain John Smith*, ed. Philip L. Barbour, 3 v. (Chapel Hill: University of North Carolina Press, 1968) 2:474 (cf. 1:331).
12. "A Father and His Sons" is number 108 in *Fables of Aesop* (London: R. Sare, 1694–99) 1:101; John M. Robertson, ed., *The Philosophical Works of Francis Bacon* (London: Routledge, 1905) 777, 57, respectively.
13. J. A. Leo Lemay, "Franklin's Suppressed 'Busy-Body,'" *American Literature* 38 (1965): 307–11, and *Canon* 40 (#11).
14. *Minutes of the Provincial Council of Pennsylvania*, 16 v. (Harrisburg, 1838–53) 4:362.
15. Scholars who suggest that Franklin took little interest in politics before the 1750s include VD 199; Verner Crane, *BF and a Rising People* (Boston: Little, Brown, 1954) 62; William S. Hanna, *BF and Pennsylvania Politics* (Stanford, Calif.: Stanford University Press, 1964), esp. ch. 2; Wright 77; Thomas Wendel, *BF and the*

Politics of Liberty (Woodbury, N.Y.: Barron's, 1974) 60; W. H. Brands, *The First American* (New York: Doubleday, 2000) 209; and Isaacson 154. Francis Jennings argues that he was a Proprietary placeman until 1755; Jennings, *BF Politician* (New York: Norton, 1996) 38–48, 59, 71, 73, 106–8.

16. See Chapter 4.

Chapter 17. Paper Currency

1. Lewis J. Carey, *Franklin's Economic Views* (Garden City, N.Y.: Doubleday, 1928); John R. Aiken, "BF, Karl Marx, and the Labor Theory of Value," *PMHB* 90 (1966): 378–84. Anderson 172–77; Joseph Dorfman, introduction to *Essays on Politics, Commerce and Political Economy* by BF (New York: Kelley, 1971); V. Dennis Golliday, "The Evolution of BF's Theory of Value," *Pennsylvania History* 37 (1970): 40–52, at 40–45; Tracy Mott and George W. Zinke, "BF's Economic Thought: A Twentieth-Century Appraisal," in *Critical Essays on BF*, ed. Melvin H. Buxbaum (Boston: G. K. Hall, 1987) 111–28. The excellent older book, William A. Wetzel, *BF as an Economist* (Baltimore: Johns Hopkins Press, 1895), has been largely superseded by Carey.

2. Richard A. Lester, "Currency Issues to Overcome Depressions in Pennsylvania, 1723 and 1729," *Journal of Political Economy* 46 (1938): 324–75, at 335–36.

3. Gordon S. Wood, "Equality and Social Conflict in the American Revolution," *WMQ* 51 (1994): 703–16, at 711; also Wood, *Radicalism of the American Revolution* (New York: Knopf, 1992) 251–52.

4. Roy M. Lokken, *David Lloyd: Colonial Lawmaker* (Seattle: University of Washington Press, 1959) 208–13.

5. According to Rawle family folklore, Franklin printed Francis Rawle, *Ways and Means for the Inhabitants of Delaware to Become Rich* (Philadelphia: S. Keimer, 1725). William Rawle (great-grandson of Francis Rawle), as quoted in Frank Fetter, "The Early History of Political Economy in the United States," *PAPS* 87 (1943): 51–61, at 51, who cites Jared Sparks, ed., *The Works of BF*, 10 v. (Boston: Tappan & Whittemore, 1836–40) 1:242. Sparks quoted Franklin as supposedly saying in Passy, France, that "when I set up business in Philadelphia, being in debt for my printing materials and wanting employment, the first job I had was a pamphlet written by your grandfather." Franklin, however, was in London throughout 1725; he worked for Keimer earlier and later—but he had no part in printing Rawle's *Ways and Means*.

6. John Law, *Money and Trade Consider'd* (1705; 2nd ed., London: Lewis, 1720). The second edition is more probably the one Franklin read.

7. Theodore Hornberger, *BF* (Minneapolis: University of Minnesota Press, 1962) 19–20. For a convenient brief discussion of Puritan sermon form, see *American Sermons: The Pilgrims to Martin Luther King Jr.*, ed. Michael Warner (New York: Library of America, 1999) 889–90.

8. Law 10–14.

9. Ibid. 92.

10. Sparks 2:256–57.

11. Carey 9.

12. J. A. W. Gunn, "'Interest Will Not Lie': A Seventeenth-Century Political Maxim," *Journal of the History of Ideas* 29 (1968): 551–64.

13. *Complete Works of Captain John Smith* 1:351–52; 2:292; 3:270, 299; J. A. Leo Lemay, *American Dream of Captain John Smith* (Charlottesville: University Press of Virginia, 1991) 210–12.

14. Cf. Joseph Dorfman, *The Economic Mind in American Civilization* (New York: Viking, 1946) 1:178–95, at 191.

15. Samuel Johnson, *A Dictionary of the English Language* (London: W. Strahan, 1755), s.v. "money." Nathan Bailey, *The Universal Etymological English Dictionary*, 7th ed. (London: Knapton, 1735), s.v. "money."

16. Adam Smith, *An Inquiry into the Nature and Causes of the Wealth of Nations*, ed. R. H. Campbell, A. S. Skinner, W. B. Todd, 2 v. (Oxford: Clarendon Press, 1976) 47 (I.v.1).

17. Thomas D. Eliot, "The Relations between Adam Smith and Benjamin Franklin before 1776," *Political Science Quarterly* 39 (1924): 67–96.

18. Aiken 379n. 6.

19. Karl Marx, *A Contribution to the Critique of Political Economy* (New York: International Publishers, 1970) 55.

20. Aiken 378–84

21. Ibid. 379, 382–83.

22. Sparks 2:266. Adam Smith 228–29 (I.xi.h.1).

23. Mott and Zinke 117–18.

24. Aiken 379, 383–84.

25. Sparks 2:267.

26. Law 69.

27. Joseph Dorfman, "BF: Economic Statesman," an introduction to BF, *Essays on Politics Commerce and Political Economy* (New York: Augustus M. Kelley Publishers, 1971) 14.

28. Sparks 2: 272. John Maynard Keynes, *The General Theory of Employment, Interest, and Money* (New York: Harcourt, Brace, 1935) 342–44.

29. Lester 363.

30. Ibid. 373.

31. Eric P. Newman, *The Early Paper Money of America*, 4th ed. (Iola, Wisc.: Kraus Publications, 1997) 96; Richard S. Rodney, *Colonial Finances of Delaware* (Wilmington: Wilmington Trust Co., 1928).

32. Newman 96 (Delaware) and 328 (Pennsylvania). *Pa. Archives*, 8th ser, 3:2114.

33. Marx 57.

34. See Franklin's news articles on the trial and reprieve of James Prouse and James Mitchel, and "Y. Z." on the benevolence as well as selfishness of man. Cf. *Canon* 40–41, 74–75.

35. *Canon* 130–32; see also index, s.v. "Egalitarianism," in *Canon*.

CHAPTER 18. JOURNALIST

1. Thomas Jefferson, "anecdotes of Dr. Franklin," in a letter to Robert Walsh, 4 December 1818. Jefferson, *Works*, 12 v., ed. Paul Leicester Ford (New York: Putnam, 1893–99) 10:121n.

2. In three books and a number of essays, Alfred Owen Aldridge has written more about Franklin's writings than anyone. Specific references to Aldridge are cited throughout the biography. The older treatments are by J[ohn] B[ach] McMaster, *BF as a Man of Letters* (Boston: Houghton Mifflin, 1887) and Cook. The most thorough previous examination is Sappenfield. Norman S. Grabo provides an overview in "The Journalist as a Man of Letters," in *Reappraising* 31–39. The general literary studies, like most of the biographies, provide some brief assessments. See Amacher and Granger. Treatments of special topics like crime and temperance will be mentioned below.

3. James Parton discussed David Harry after the partnership with Meredith ended (1:196); VD quoted the *Autobiography* without suggesting any date (99); and Ralph Fresca also discussed Harry after the Meredith partnership ended: *PMHB* 94 (1990) 241. Most biographers simply omit Harry. Thomas 374 noted that Harry followed Keimer to Barbados before the end of 1730.

4. Lawrence C. Wroth, *Colonial Printer* (1938; Charlottesville: University Press of Virginia, 1964) 273–74.

5. Charles E. Clark and Charles Wetherell, "The Measure of Maturity: The *Pennsylvania Gazette*, 1728–1765," *WMQ* 46 (1989): 279–303. Table II, "Percentage of Space Devoted to Genres of Items Printed in the *Pennsylvania Gazette*, by Publisher, 1728–1765," shows that Keimer (1728–29) used 33.3 percent of his available space for news, even though his advertising amounted to only 3.2 percent; that Hall (1748–65) used 23.6 percent of his space for news, though advertising accounted for a walloping 55.5 percent of his available space; and that Franklin (1729–47) used 37.8 percent of his space for news, while advertising accounted for 29.8 percent. Franklin gradually increased the advertising from a meagre 3 percent to a profitable 55 percent.

6. James N. Green in *The History of the Book in America: Volume One: The Colonial Book in the Atlantic World*, ed. Hugh Amory and David D. Hall (Cambridge: Cambridge University Press, 2000) 256. Stephen Botein overstates Franklin's supposed neutrality, "'Mere Mechanics' and an Open Press: the Business and Political Strategies of Colonial American Printers," *Perspectives in American History* 9 (1975) 127–225, esp, Part 2, "The Politics of Neutrality" 160–99, with Franklin on pp. 182–84.

7. Clinton Rossiter, "The Political Theory of BF," *PMHB* 76 (1952): 259–93, and Edmund S. Morgan, "Secrets of BF," *New York Review of Books*, 31 January 1991, pp. 41–46, at 45, have noted Franklin's avoidance of Whiggism's keywords.

8. *Calendar* #161. Martin Kallich, *British Poetry and the American Revolution*, 2 v. (Troy, N.Y.: Whitston, 1988) #64–81.

9. Shields, *Oracles* 151–52.

10. Alfred Owen Aldridge, "BF and the *Maryland Gazette*," *Maryland Historical Magazine* 44 (1949): 177–89. Parks reprinted all but the first two "Plain-Dealer" essays from the London *Freethinker*.

11. English editions of *The Morals of Confucius* appeared in 1688, 1706, 1718, and 1729. For the "Captivity of William Henry," see P 15:145–57; "A Letter from China," 5 May 1784, S 9:200–208. Alfred Owen Aldridge, *The Dragon and the Eagle: The Presence of China in the American Enlightenment* (Detroit: Wayne State University Press, 1993) discusses Franklin's interest in China, 24–30, 66–92.

12. Addison's "Letter from Italy" was also quoted in the *AWM* on 25 April 1734 and 8 January 1740/1.

13. Though Marcello Maestro praised Franklin's later interest in prison reform, he did not know these early essays and said that "Franklin was slow to show interest in penal legislation." Maestro, "BF and the Penal Laws," *Journal of the History of Ideas* 36 (1975): 551–62, at 551.

14. Woolston's trial is discussed by Leonard W. Levy, *Blasphemy* (New York: Knopf, 1993) 308–15; for the colonial American libel laws, see 268.

15. J. A. Leo Lemay, "Rhetorical Strategies in *Sinners in the Hands of an Angry God* and *Narrative of the Late Massacres in Lancaster County*," in *BF, Jonathan Edwards, and the Representation of American Culture* (New York: Oxford University Press, 1993) 186–203, at 189–90.

16. "The Scots Traveller" was probably another name for the well-known drum tune "The Scots March," which had a reputation for frightening the enemy, and "The Grenadiers March" was the best known British army march. Lewis Winstock, *Songs & Music of the Redcoats . . . 1642–1902* (London: Leo Cooper, 1970) 19, 29.

17. Franklin probably had in mind Jacobus Rick, *Tractatus duo singulares de examine sagarum* (Frankfurt: T. H. Grentzii, 1585), vaguely recalling the publisher rather than the author. *NUC* NR 0261086. A book with a similar title is Wilhelm Adolf Scribonius, *De examine et purgatione sagarum* ([Herborn?], 1589. *NUC* NS 0358655.

18. Hamilton 32–33.

19. Jean-Paul Sartre, *Essays in Existentialism*, ed. Wade Baskin (1965; rpt., Citadel Press, 1990) 62, concluding his essay, "The Humanism of Existentialism."

20. *An Inquiry Concerning Political Justice*, in *Political and Philosophical Writings of William Godwin*, ed. Mark Philp (London: W. Pickering, 1993) 3:450–51, 460. Price was a close friend from 1766 (P 11:100n.) to BF's death; see *NCE* 241–43.

21. Pascal 159.

22. See the references in *Canon* 45. Franklin's rebuttal of Andrew Baxter is discussed in Volume 2, Chapter 19.

23. Ronald A. Bosco, "'Scandal, Like Other Virtues, Is in Part Its Own Reward': Franklin Working the Crime Beat," in *Reappraising* 78–97, at 92–96.

24. Christina Hole, *Witchcraft in England* (New York: Scribner's, 1947) 67.

25. A London area well-known for popular amusements and open air preaching.

26. Hole 67–68.

27. "Of Credulity in Witchcraft," *Gentleman's Magazine* 1 (January 1731): 29–30.

28. William Moraley, *The Infortunate: The Voyage and Adventures of William Moraley, an Indentured Servant*, ed. Susan E. Klepp and Billy G. Smith (University Park, Pa: Pennsylvania State University Press, 1992) 123–24 and 167–71.

29. All of Bosco's "Scandal" essay is relevant.

30. Bosco 88–90; Waldstreicher 95–96.

31. James H. Cassady, *Demography in Early America: Beginnings of the Statistical Mind* (Cambridge, Mass.: Harvard University Press, 1969) 124.

32. The editors of *The Papers of BF* found no proof of Franklin's authorship and did not print it (2:126–27); I, too, have no proof.

33. Anna Janney DeArmond, *Andrew Bradford, Colonial Printer* (Newark. DE: University of Delaware Press, 1949) 213.

34. *Plutarch's Lives*, tr. Thomas North, 6 vols. (London: David Nutt, 1895), vol. 2, pp. 8–9. The marginal heading said, "To much familiaritie breedeth contempt." Franklin's father possessed either the North translation or, more probably, the one edited by John Dryden (London: J. Tonson, 1683), where the passage is found on pp. 517–18. There, the marginal note reads "His reservedness." The passage also reminds one of Franklin's adoption of "Silence" as his second "virtue." See also Paul W. Conner, *Poor Richard's Politics* (New York: Oxford University Press, 1965), p. 191. Benjamin Vaughan compared the *Autobiography* to Plutarch's *Lives*, A 61.

35. Lawrence C. Wroth "BF: The Printer at Work," in *Typographic Heritage: Selected Essays by Lawrence C. Wroth* (New York: The Typophiles, 1949) 91–134, at 111. Botein 148 following Wroth, also overlooked the additional £100.

36. Clark and Wetherel at figure 1 (p. 290), table 1 (p. 286), and 291.

37. David A. Copeland, *Colonial American Newspapers* (Newark: University of Delaware Press, 1997) 288.

38. In 1801, Joseph Dennie condemned Franklin as "the founder of that Grub-street sect, who have professedly attempted to degrade literature to the level of vulgar capacities, and debase the polished and current language of books, by the vile alloy of provincial idioms, and colloquial barbarism." See Lewis Leary, "Joseph Dennie on BF: A Note on Early American Literary Criticism," *PMHB* 72 (1948): 240–46. Talcott Williams, *The Newspaperman* (New York: C. Scribner's Sons, 1922) 108–10.

39. Alexis de Toqueville, *Democracy in America* (New York: Doubleday, 1969) 471.

40. J. A. Leo Lemay, "The American Aesthetic of Franklin's Visual Creations," *PMHB* 111 (1987): 465–99.

Index

Page numbers in bold italics indicate an illustration.

ACKNOWLEDGMENTS

A National Endowment for the Humanities grant and a sabbatical leave from the University of Delaware in the academic year 1994–95 allowed me to begin working full time on the biography. My research assistants during 1995–2004—Lisa Ray, Herb Smith, Donna Lehman, Amy Moreno, Rob LaRoque, Robert Klevay, Amy Moore, Rachel Mayrer, and Marina Fedosik—read drafts of volume 1 for me. My friends Kevin Hayes, Edward A. Nickerson, David S. Shields, Todd Richardson, and Paul M. Zall scrutinized portions of this volume. Professor Carla Mulford carefully read it, and Maggie Hassert went over the text with a red pen in hand. I have benefited from the suggestions of each. Jennifer H. Backer has been an excellent copyeditor. At the University of Pennsylvania Press, Erica Ginsburg, Associate Managing Editor, has carefully attended to the manuscript and its production; I am most grateful.

A number of authorities answered questions for me: Ellen Cohn at *The Papers of Benjamin Franklin*; Whitfield J. Bell, Jr., Roy E. Goodman, and Rob Cox at the American Philosophical Society; and John Van Horne and James N. Green at the Library Company of Philadelphia. I am greatly indebted to Susan Brynteson, May Morris director of libraries; Linda L. Stein, humanities librarian; and a succession of interlibrary loan librarians at the University of Delaware's Morris Library.

The Papers of Benjamin Franklin, with 37 volumes published to date, is the fundamental scholarly resource, and I am indebted to each of its editors.

CPSIA information can be obtained
at www.ICGtesting.com
Printed in the USA
LVHW110748220719
624771LV00007BA/52/P

9 780812 238549